Coffins of the Brave

ED RACHAL FOUNDATION

NAUTICAL ARCHAEOLOGY SERIES

in association with the

Institute of Nautical Archaeology

and the Center for Maritime Archaeology

and Conservation

Coffins of the Brave
Lake Shipwrecks of the War of 1812

Edited by Kevin J. Crisman

With

Walter Rybka, Kenneth Cassavoy,

Christopher R. Sabick, LeeAnne Gordon,

Sara Hoskins, Erich Heinold,

Jonathan Moore, Christopher Amer,

Eric Emery, Erika Washburn, and

Arthur B. Cohn

TEXAS A&M UNIVERSITY PRESS

College Station

Copyright © 2014 by Kevin J. Crisman

Manufactured in the United States of America

First edition

This paper meets the requirements of
ANSI/NISO Z39.48-1992.
(Permanence of Paper)
Binding materials have been chosen for durability.

♾ ♻

Library of Congress Cataloging-in-Publication Data
Coffins of the brave : lake shipwrecks of the War of 1812 / edited
by Kevin J. Crisman ; with Walter Rybka, Kenneth Cassavoy,
Christopher R. Sabick, LeeAnne Gordon, Sara Hoskins, Erich
Heinold, Jonathan Moore, Christopher Amer, Eric Emery, Erika
Washburn, and Arthur B. Cohn.—First edition.

   pages cm — (Ed Rachal Foundation nautical archaeology series
in association with the Institute of Nautical Archaeology and the
Center for Maritime Archaeology and Conservation)
Includes bibliographical references and index.

   ISBN 978-1-62349-032-4 (hardcover, printed case : alk. paper)
   ISBN 978-1-62349-076-8 (e-book)
1. Naval architecture—Great Lakes (North America)—History—
19th century. 2. Shipwrecks—Great Lakes (North America)
3. Underwater archaeology—Great Lakes (North America) 4. Great
Lakes (North America)—Antiquities. 5. United States—History—
War of 1812—Naval operations. 6. United States. Navy—History—
War of 1812. 7. Great Britain. Royal Navy—History—War of 1812.
I. Crisman, Kevin James, 1959– editor of compilation. II. Series:
Ed Rachal Foundation nautical archaeology series.
VM23.7.C65 2014
973.5′25—dc23
2013039502

In memory of

J. RICHARD STEFFY

A quiet genius, a mentor, and

a pathfinder for all of us in the

field of nautical archaeology

Contents

Acknowledgments / ix

Introduction / 1
 Kevin J. Crisman

PART I: THE NAVAL WAR OF 1812 ON THE UPPER LAKES / 9
 Kevin J. Crisman

1. "We Have Met the Enemy and They Are Ours": The US Navy Brig *Niagara* / 19
 Walter Rybka

2. "Cast Away on the Canadian Shore": The British Brig *General Hunter* / 51
 Kenneth Cassavoy

3. "A Perfect Masterpiece of Workmanship": His Majesty's Hired Transport Schooner *Nancy* / 71
 Christopher R. Sabick

4. Echoes of a Naval Race: The Royal Navy Schooners *Tecumseth* and *Newash* / 86
 LeeAnne Gordon, Sara Hoskins, and Erich Heinold

PART II: THE NAVAL WAR OF 1812 ON LAKE ONTARIO / 109
 Kevin J. Crisman

5. Fore-and-Afters at Fifty Fathoms: The Wrecks of *Hamilton* and *Scourge* / 123
 Jonathan Moore

6. "Anticipated Laurels": The US Brig *Jefferson* / 153
 Kevin J. Crisman

7. Frontier Frigates and a Three-Decker: Wrecks of the Royal Navy's Lake Ontario Squadron / 187
 Jonathan Moore

8. "Smaller Vessels Are of No Less Consequence": The Browns Bay Vessel / 219
 Christopher Amer

PART III: THE NAVAL WAR OF 1812 ON LAKE CHAMPLAIN / 237
 Kevin J. Crisman

9. "Lt. Cassin Says There Is a New Boat Near Vergennes": The US Schooner *Ticonderoga* / 247
 Kevin J. Crisman

10. "A Perfect Willingness to See the Enemy on Fair Terms": The US Navy Row Galley *Allen* / 271
 Eric Emery

11. "A Remarkably Fine Looking Vessel": The Royal Navy Brig *Linnet* / 294
 Erika Washburn

12. "It Has Again Become Necessary to Add to Our Force on Lake Champlain":
    The US Navy Brig *Eagle* / 312
        Kevin J. Crisman

13. "I Never See Anything in This World Like It!": The Archaeological Legacy of a Naval Battle / 336
        Arthur B. Cohn and Kevin J. Crisman

14. Conclusions: "Coffins of the Brave"—Two Hundred Years Later / 354
        Kevin J. Crisman

APPENDIX A.
    Principal Dimensions, Armament, and Broadside Weight of the
    Ships Built at Kingston in 1814 / 371

APPENDIX B.
    Prince Regent (*Kingston*) Sailing Qualities Report, 1815 / 373

APPENDIX C.
    Principal Timber Scantlings (in Inches) and Wood Species of the
    Ships Built at Kingston in 1814 / 375

Glossary / 377
Bibliography and Sources / 385
General Index / 397
Index of Ships / 409

Acknowledgments

Any project that has been in the works as long as this book and that involves archaeological research on so many different shipwrecks is going to accumulate a long list of people and institutions that deserve acknowledgment for their contributions of time, money, and expertise. It is with great pleasure that the editor and authors recognize them in the following pages.

It seems appropriate to recognize the editor's home institutions and the press publishing this book first, since they have been there in so many ways from the start. The research on War of 1812 naval shipwrecks in general, and the preparation of this book in particular, have been tirelessly supported by the nonprofit Institute of Nautical Archaeology (INA) and its board of directors and by Texas A&M University (TAMU). Both have sponsored many of the excavation and recording projects described herein. The Nautical Archaeology Faculty Fellowship, a university research chair created by an INA benefactor and administered by TAMU, has contributed greatly to the completion of much field and laboratory work, as well as the preparation of this manuscript. The editor particularly wishes to thank INA founder George F. Bass and INA's current and former directors for their support over the years.

Texas A&M University Press and its staff warmly encouraged the editor's proposal to publish this book many years ago, and they have been unbelievably patient waiting for the final manuscript to arrive. In particular the editor would like to recognize former editor-in-chief Noel Parsons, current director Charles Backus, and the Press's own cheerleader and saint-in-residence, editor-in-chief Mary Lenn Dixon.

The editor also wishes to recognize faculty colleagues, staff members, and students in the TAMU Nautical Archaeology Graduate Program and the Department of Anthropology, many of whom have participated in 1812 ship projects, contributed expertise and resources, or have simply been encouraging over the years. A full list of these people is, alas, too long to include here, but special thanks must be tendered to Donny L. Hamilton, whose support and friendship for over thirty years have been consistent and greatly appreciated.

The list of federal, state, provincial, and private institutions managing 1812-era naval wrecks and sites and supporting research described in this book is extensive, and all deserve our thanks for the work they have done over the years to protect our heritage and promote the creation of new knowledge through archaeology. One organization has been extensively involved in this cause on Lake Champlain in particular but on other North American lakes as well: the Lake Champlain Maritime Museum (LCMM) at Basin Harbor, Vermont. The LCMM and its former director (and cofounder) Arthur B. Cohn have consistently taken the lead in promoting the responsible stewardship of our inland maritime heritage. It has been a pleasure to work with the LCMM and its staff over the years.

Other institutions involved in the management, study, or display of the wrecks and sites described in this book include the Pennsylvania Historical and Museum Commission; Erie Maritime Museum (home port of the flagship *Niagara*); Flagship *Niagara* League; Ontario Marine Heritage Committee; Southampton [Ontario] Marine Heritage Society; Nancy Island Historic Site, Wasaga Beach Provincial Park; Discovery Harbour, Huronia Historical Parks, Ontario Ministry of Tourism, Culture, and Sport; Royal Ontario Museum; Hamilton and Scourge Foundation, City of Hamilton, Ontario; National Geographic Society; Underwater Archaeology Service, Parks Canada; Sackets Harbor Battlefield State Historic Site, Bureau of Historic Sites, New York State Office of Parks, Recreation, and Historic Preservation; St. Lawrence Islands National Park and Fort Wellington National Historic Site, Parks Canada; Office of the State Archaeologist, New York State Museum, New York State Education Department; Skenesborough Museum and Historical Society of Whitehall, New York; Vermont Division for Historic Preservation; Underwater Archaeology Branch, Naval History and Heritage Command, United States Navy; and Clinton County [New York] Historical Association.

Contemporary plans, sketches, paintings, and prints of the 1812-era warships on the North American lakes are rare, and detailed, reliable illustrations are even harder to find. While this provides added incentive for archaeological studies, the lack of good images nevertheless often makes it difficult for professionals and the public to visualize the ships and battles. For these reasons we are lucky to have the talented, prolific marine artist Peter Rindlisbacher, formerly of Amherstburg, Ontario and currently residing in Texas, to bring the era alive for us. These days, few books on the 1812 inland naval war are published that do not include one or more of his superb paintings. Peter's generosity in providing images for this book is greatly appreciated.

The research for this book was assisted along the way by many fine scholars in the world of naval history and nautical archaeology. Long before many of the authors of this book were born, John R. Stevens of Greenlawn, New York, was investigating War of 1812 ships sunk in the lakes, preparing sketches and descriptions of their hulls, and advocating for their study and protection; his notes and recollections were most helpful to a number of us. Great Lakes naval history lost one of its finest scholars with the passing of Robert Malcomson of St. Catharines, Ontario, in 2009; the many citations of his publications in the chapters of this book are a testimony to the breadth and depth of his life's work. Other naval and War of 1812 historians contributed to our work over the years: the late W. M. P. Dunne of Hampton Bays, New York, was most generous with his extensive files; Dr. Christopher McKee of Grinnell College in Iowa shared archival materials he collected for his superb book *A Gentlemanly and Honorable Profession: The Creation of the U.S. Naval Officer Corps 1794–1815* (1991); Dana Ashdown of Etobicoke, Ontario, offered both his research and insights on Royal Navy gunboats on the lakes; and Gary M. Gibson of Sackets Harbor, New York, provided useful documents and observations on the Lake Ontario naval race. The editor is also grateful to Peter Barranco of Montpelier, Vermont, and Morris F. Glenn of Essex, New York, for all of the materials on Lake Champlain maritime history that they provided over our three decades of collaboration.

Glenn Gricco of the Center for Maritime Archaeology and Conservation at Texas A&M University has been enormously helpful as a resource and sounding board for ideas, and his model of *Jefferson* greatly advanced our understanding of Henry Eckford's approach to ship construction. As an MA student in the TAMU Nautical Archaeology Program, Daniel Walker of Vancouver carried out a detailed survey of the Royal Navy frigate *Princess Charlotte,* some of the results of which are cited in chapter 7. Bill Leege of Morrisville, New York, shared a trove of knowledge on the battle debris that he and his colleagues in the Lake Champlain Archaeological Association collected from the Battle of Plattsburgh Bay; Bill and TAMU Nautical Archaeology alumna Anne W. Lessmann contributed much research to chapter 13 in this book.

Finally, but not least, the editor owes a big thanks to all of the chapter contributors in this book (and their families). It has been a long, slow journey with frequent delays in harbor, but at last we can see some of our archaeological cargo delivered. Thank you for your dedication to the cause and for your patience. As a personal aside, I cannot thank Ginny and the girls enough for their love and encouragement over the years.

In completing these acknowledgments the editor sadly recognizes that in a book of this scope and with such a lengthy period of preparation, he has inevitably forgotten to mention people and institutions that made important contributions over the years. Forgive the oversight, and thank you all the same.

INTRODUCTION

KEVIN J. CRISMAN

Intro 1. *What Professor Silliman saw from the passing steamboat. A contemporary watercolor of the US Naval squadron in ordinary at Whitehall, New York. (Courtesy of the Shelburne Museum, Shelburne, VT.)*

On a brisk, sunny autumn afternoon in 1819, Yale College professor Benjamin Silliman embarked on the steamboat *Congress* at Whitehall, New York, beginning the final leg of a journey to Quebec. The cold weather perfectly matched the professor's internal state, for upon his arrival at Lake Champlain's southernmost port a few days earlier he contracted what he described as "a severe ague in my face and head." The illness curtailed sightseeing, but today, despite his continued feeling of malaise, Silliman remained on deck as the steamer pulled away from the dock. Just ahead, in the narrow channel that led north out of Whitehall, was a sight he was determined not to miss: five large wooden warships, veterans of a recent war that

had swept North America (intro. 1). Stripped of their topmasts and covered by rough board roofs, the ships were moored stem-to-stern in a line alongside a fetid swamp.

From his vantage point on *Congress,* Professor Silliman was deeply moved by what he saw. He wrote:

> As we passed rapidly by, a few seamen shewed their heads through the grim portholes, from which, five years ago, the cannon poured fire and death, and we caught a glimpse of the decks, that were then covered with the mutilated and slain, and deluged with their generous blood.
>
> Sparless, black and frowning, these now dis-

mantled ships look like the coffins of the brave, and will remain, as long as worms and rot will allow them, sad monuments of the bloody conflict.[1]

The empty hulks that so fascinated Professor Silliman in 1819 were not unique to Lake Champlain. Other naval squadrons, also boarded over and empty, quietly rotted at anchor in American and Canadian harbors on the Great Lakes. The war was over, but the ships lingered on, "coffins of the brave" that would prove to be surprisingly durable.

The conflict that created these lake warships, the War of 1812, is not well known to many present-day Americans, Canadians, or Britons (or, indeed, to the rest of the world). At best most of us recall only a montage of disparate events, images, and slogans: frigates battling on the high seas, soldiers marching and fighting along the US-Canadian border, Washington, DC, in flames, "the rockets' red glare" over Baltimore, and General Andrew Jackson's lopsided victory at New Orleans. The causes of the war seem both obscure and irrelevant to most of us today. "Free trade and sailors' rights"? What was that all that about? The War of 1812 has always defied simple explanations.

No single event led the United States to declare war on Britain in June 1812, but it was instead a steady accumulation of incidents and insults that brought matters to a head.[2] Under different circumstances these disagreements might have been smoothed over with diplomacy and a minor concession or two from each side, but the first decade of the nineteenth century was a tumultuous era with little time for polite or measured diplomacy. Britain, engaged in a two-decade-long, life-or-death struggle with France and its allies, used the "wooden walls" of its Royal Navy to isolate the European continent from the rest of the world. In time the blockade grew to exclude most neutral trade. US merchants found their ships shut out of formerly profitable markets, harassed, and in some cases seized. At the same time, the Royal Navy, straining to maintain a fleet of nearly one thousand vessels, acquired the habit of forcibly taking sailors from US merchantmen to fill out the complements of its chronically undermanned warships. Some of the sailors press-ganged in this manner were British nationals shirking duty to king and country, but others were US citizens, born and raised. Incidents of impressment led to overt clashes between British and US naval vessels in 1807 and 1811, further heightening public indignation on both sides of the Atlantic.[3]

The rallying cry of "Free Trade and Sailor's Rights" summed up two maritime points of friction, but another, more terrestrially located problem also plagued Anglo-American relations. In the years leading up to 1812, US western states and territories experienced episodes of organized resistance from native populations, most recently in 1811, when the Shawnee leader Tecumseh led a confederation of tribes into battle—unsuccessfully—against the US Army. The perception both on the frontier and in Washington was that the British were using their trade and alliances in the interior of North America to encourage these attacks and thereby thwart further expansion of the United States. Many Americans concluded that if the people of the west were to be safe in their homes and the country was to fulfill its transcontinental destiny, the Native Americans and their British supporters would have to be removed from the scene.[4]

For US War Hawks, there was a simple solution to all of these problems, one that had been attempted but not achieved during the Revolutionary War: conquer Canada. Seizure of Britain's North American territories was considered an appropriate response to the Royal Navy's transgressions on the high seas, and proponents of this measure were certain that British preoccupation with the war in Europe and pro–United States sympathies among Canadians would make the occupation effortless. Indeed, Congressman John C. Calhoun, a prominent War Hawk, predicted that only one month would be required to finish the job.[5] The issue of actually annexing Canada was not widely discussed, although a permanent end to British influence in North America and expansion of the United States far to the north and west was clearly a welcome possibility for many in the pro-war faction.[6]

The crisis simmered for over a decade, with incidents on land and sea, diplomatic protests, trade embargoes, and general bad feelings all around. The boiling point was reached during the winter of 1811–12, when the British government's reluctance to repeal certain trade restrictions—the Orders in Council—convinced the US Congress that more drastic action was necessary. After several months of debate, war was declared on June 18, 1812 (ironically, the Orders in Council had just been rescinded, but the news had

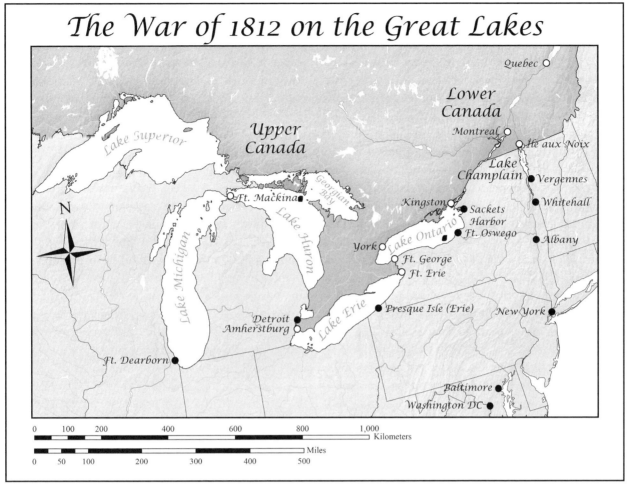

The War of 1812 on the Great Lakes

Intro 2. The US-Canadian border region during the War of 1812. (Map by Douglas Inglis.)

not yet crossed the Atlantic). The United States was far from prepared, for despite minor steps to put the country on a war footing, the army was still small, poorly trained, poorly led, and ill equipped, and the US Navy had fewer than twenty warships—none of them larger than a frigate—to pit against the might of the Royal Navy. Nor was there anything like unanimity in US public opinion. Support for the war in the expansionist western states was strong, but elsewhere, particularly in the northeastern states, many citizens felt they had little to gain and much to lose in a protracted war with Britain.[7]

Fighting quickly broke out in two theaters: on the oceans and along the US-Canadian border. On the oceans the US Navy caught the British unprepared and handily won a series of single-ship actions; these did nothing to change the unequal balance of naval power but did deflate the Royal Navy's pride and aura

of invincibility.[8] Along the US-Canadian border, on the other hand, events went very badly for the US Army. Repeated attempts to invade Canada fell apart and the small but professional British Army and its Native American allies consistently drubbed the invaders.[9] The US government's inadequate planning and preparations for war were amply evident throughout that first year.

A big part of the problem for the US Army was the lack of a freshwater navy. The lakes that straddle the US-Canadian border, the Great Lakes in the west and Lake Champlain in the east, were obvious pathways for a US invasion of Canada (intro. 2). Their utility for transporting armies, military equipment, and supplies was repeatedly demonstrated during the colonial wars of the eighteenth century, as was the need for naval flotillas to command the inland waterways.[10] These lessons were forgotten or ignored, however, for when war was declared in 1812, the US Navy had only three purpose-built warships on the lakes, a single brig on Lake Ontario and two gunboats on Lake Champlain. The British were rather more prepared thanks to the existence of an army-managed transportation service, the Provincial Marine, that kept frontier fortifications and outposts on the Great Lakes garrisoned and supplied. Altogether the Provincial Marine had six or seven ships employed on Lakes Ontario and Erie.

The need for more vessels was soon evident, but finding or building them met with problems. Both navies could purchase or capture merchant sloops and schooners to convert into warships, but they were poor substitutes for the real thing. Ships had to be built. Timber for construction of hulls grew in abundance around the lakes, and Lake Champlain had a modest ironworks at Vergennes, Vermont. Beyond these few resources, however, there was none of the extensive infrastructure upon which seagoing navies depended: established, well-stocked naval yards with building ways, graving or dry docks, rope walks, and sail lofts; foundries for the production of anchors, cannon, and shot; and victualing industries to supply ships with provisions. On the lakes, naval facilities had to be created from scratch, and nearly everything required to assemble and outfit warships had to come from somewhere else, even (for the British) from the far side of the Atlantic.

These unpromising circumstances gave rise to one of history's all-time great shipbuilding contests: the freshwater naval race of the War of 1812. Although brief, only two and a half years in duration, it was a struggle of epic proportions. Recognizing the stakes involved, each side invested heavily in the effort by spending enormous sums of money and diverting large quantities of equipment and shiploads of sailors to the lakes. In two of these contests the rival squadrons ultimately met in battle, with results that profoundly influenced the course of the war. On the third lake the naval race continued unchecked, resulting in the building of squadrons that, in terms of the numbers and the sizes of ships, far exceeded anything that could have been imagined at the start of the war (see plate 1a). A peace agreement in December 1814 ended the war, abruptly halting preparations for a titanic naval campaign on the lakes in 1815.

The decommissioning of the naval squadrons took place within a matter of months. Small sloops and schooners converted to warships were easily converted back to peacetime commerce, and so the US Navy sold off vessels of this type in 1815. Larger warships were placed in floating storage—"mothballed" is the modern term for it, although back then it was called "in ordinary"—and left in out-of-the-way harbors and anchorages. A naval disarmament agreement in 1817 restricted both sides to a few small vessels on the US-Canadian border lakes, and so, as Professor Silliman predicted in 1819, the frigates, corvettes, and sloops of war had short postwar careers as "sad monuments."

There are no wood-boring ship worms on North America's lakes, but wood-decaying rot was inevitable. In 1821, only two years after his first visit, Silliman again traveled down Lake Champlain and this time found the warships at Whitehall to be "mere wrecks, sunken, neglected and in ruins."[11] It was the same story elsewhere. By 1825 most of the large ships built during the war were rotted beyond repair and sinking at their moorings (if not already sunk). In that year the US Navy shut down its naval stations and sold its vessels to salvagers; one decade later the Royal Navy followed suit and disposed of its lake ships by public sales or abandonment.

The recorded history of the eighteen-twelvers, like the vessels themselves, becomes fragmentary in the post-navy era. With government bureaucracies no longer annually monitoring the ships, the available information sources are largely anecdotal and incidental: short newspaper stories, tourist travelogues, local histories, and old photographs. The ships met varying fates: some were entirely broken up for the iron fittings they contained, a few were raised and rebuilt for commercial service, but most were simply left where they lay. Hulls sunk on the bottom were to a certain extent protected by freshwater and by sediments that accumulated over the years, but the exposed topside frames, bulwarks, and decks continued to fall apart as rot and ice relentlessly eroded timbers.

For several decades after their abandonment, the vessels were considered—to the extent that anyone thought about them at all—quaint curiosities left over from an earlier era or troublesome obstructions to commercial navigation. By the later decades of the nineteenth century and the first half of the twentieth century, however, the perception of the old warships as symbols of past naval glory or as sources of interesting historical relics grew in the public's mind.[12]

Intro 3. *The US Navy brig* Niagara *is readied for launching in 1913. The Interstate Board of the Perry's Victory Centennial Commissioners celebrated the one-hundred-year anniversary of the War of 1812 by salvaging and rebuilding a decayed survivor of the 1813 battle. The warship was sunk in Misery Bay, a small inlet across the harbor from Erie, Pennsylvania. (From the* Journal of American History 8, no. 1 [1914], p. 32.)

This did not necessarily benefit the ships themselves. In 1876 a hull identified as the US brig *Lawrence* was raised from Lake Erie and cut into souvenir pieces for the US Centennial celebrations in Philadelphia.[13] Timbers salvaged from other wrecks were converted into desks, chairs, canes, and similar mementoes.[14] In 1913 another Erie wreck, identified as the US brig *Niagara,* was raised and extensively rebuilt as a floating display for the War of 1812 Centennial celebrations (intro. 3). More recoveries followed in the twentieth century: the Royal Navy schooner *Nancy* (1928), brig *Linnet* (1949), and schooner *Tecumseth* (1953) and the US Navy schooner *Ticonderoga* (1958). These salvage operations were undertaken to satisfy curiosity, recover relics, or create historical exhibits; most were well intentioned, but in each instance artifacts and archaeological data were lost and most resulted in substantial damage to the structure. None of the hulls received effective pres-

ervation treatments (which did not exist at the time), and all have deteriorated since their salvage.

By the 1960s a new ethic of heritage preservation and management began to take hold in North America, and local communities and archaeological societies, states, provinces, and national governments began to take active measures to protect historic wrecks from ill-conceived salvage projects. Around the same time, a new approach to studying the maritime past, nautical archaeology, emerged as a scientific discipline. By focusing on the material remains of seafaring, principally shipwrecks and the artifacts they contain, nautical archaeology provides us with new insights into the lives and work of shipwrights, merchants, and sailors, as well as the wider populations who supported the maritime trades. Its discoveries have both complemented and challenged the historical record, defining the physical parameters—the materials, structures,

Intro 4. *The mainmast step of Wreck Able. Diver William Dempsey of Kingston, Ontario, gives an indication of the size of the Royal Navy Frigate* Kingston *(ex–Prince Regent), a vessel built for service on Lake Ontario in 1814. The starboard floors, bilge ceiling, and mainmast step bolster are in the foreground. (Photo by Jonathan Moore.)*

and places—of maritime-oriented peoples and activities and forcing us to rethink earlier interpretations of past events. Archaeological inquiry is especially effective in providing us with an intimate look at the day-to-day lives, technology, and social and economic connections of our ancestors, at how they created, used, modified, exchanged, and disposed of everything from the smallest buttons and buckles, to buildings and ships, to local landscapes and wider regions.

The 1812-era lake ships offer a rich topic for archaeological investigation, for wartime records tell us only part of their stories. It is perhaps no surprise that so little was preserved on paper: the hectic pace of construction, outfitting, and campaigning during the war left little time for record keeping, and with the conclusion of fighting interest in the lake squadrons quickly waned among naval administrators in Washington and London. The Royal Navy measured and prepared plans for some of its vessels, but details of architecture and appearance were never preserved for the majority of

ships, especially the US Navy's ships. Similarly, the experiences of the thousands of men who served aboard these ships are largely unknown, for only a handful of officers and sailors kept journals or wrote memoirs. We know disappointingly little about the daily routines, living and working spaces, and tools and possessions of the freshwater "salts" who sailed to war in the wilderness.

In recent decades nautical archaeologists and naval historians have been seeking out the eighteen-twelvers in their final resting places (intro. 4). The locations of these ships vary widely: some still lie in the shallow anchorages where they were abandoned, one is buried beneath the beach where it wrecked, two are sunk in deep water, and four vessels salvaged in the twentieth century remain on display in museums. The extent of their hulls and related artifact collections also varies widely, from being nearly complete in every respect when found (with masts standing and cannon still mounted in the gunports) to a small, fragmentary portion of a very big ship, long since picked clean of artifacts by souvenir hunters. One is not even a wreck: the brig *Niagara* has undergone two more rebuildings since the 1913 salvage and reconstruction and serves as a living, sailing monument to the sailors and shipwrights who fought in the War of 1812.

Regardless of their condition or extent, all of these survivors have something to tell us about naval activity and construction during the War of 1812. By systematically measuring, sketching, and photographing the worn timbers and rusty spikes of wooden hulls, by studying artifacts large and small, by reexamining old letters and logbooks, and by experimenting with a replicated brig rig and a battery of muzzle-loading artillery, archaeological inquiries allow us to look back through time and get a glimpse, however distant and obscured, of ships on the stocks and under sail, of shipwrights toiling through bitterly cold winter afternoons, of sailors at work, at rest, or in battle.

This book presents the results of archaeological and historical studies of War of 1812 ships, shipwrecks, and artifacts found in North American lakes, written by the people who personally carried out the field research and data analysis. A total of sixteen vessels are examined, representing nearly every type of warship that served on the lakes. The wide range of ship and boat types may seem surprising at first glance, but it accurately represents the reality of the 1812–15 lake war. The naval squadrons were composed of vessels built for a variety of purposes, and on every lake the squadrons evolved rapidly, with a trend toward constructing ever-larger warships. The eighteen-twelvers featured here include prewar commercial schooners transformed into fighting ships or military transports (*Nancy, Hamilton,* and *Scourge*); a Provincial Marine armed transport brig launched in 1807 (*General Hunter*); US Navy 20-gun brigs built by the prolific New York City shipwrights Adam and Noah Brown and Henry Eckford (*Niagara, Jefferson,* and *Eagle*); Royal Navy warships ranging from a 104-gun ship of the line (*St. Lawrence*), to two large frigates (*Prince Regent* and *Princess Charlotte*), to a 16-gun brig (*Linnet*); a British and an American gunboat (the Brown's Bay Vessel and *Allen*); a steamboat converted mid-construction into a 17-gun schooner (*Ticonderoga*); and two sharp-built Royal Navy supply and patrol schooners assembled shortly after the end of the war (*Tecumseth* and *Newash*). The final chapter in this book differs from the others, for instead of examining a ship or a shipwreck it examines the material remains of a naval engagement: the ordnance, small arms, ship fittings, crew possessions, and particularly the anchors lost in Plattsburgh Bay during and immediately after the Battle of Lake Champlain.

The lake campaigns took place in three distinct theaters of operations, separated from one another by impassable barriers to navigation, defined by their own particular logistical, sailing, and fighting conditions, and subject to their own strategic imperatives. These theaters were, from west to east, the Upper Great Lakes (above Niagara Falls), with Lakes Erie and Huron being the focal point of the wartime activity; Lake Ontario and the Upper St. Lawrence River; and Lake Champlain and the Richelieu River. The book is therefore divided into three sections, with a short introduction for each section to provide the reader with a context for the archaeological and historical discoveries described in the individual chapters.

NOTES

1. Benjamin Silliman, *Remarks Made on a Short Tour Between Hartford and Quebec in 1819* (New Haven, CT: S. Converse, 1820), pp. 180–81.

2. The events leading to the War of 1812 have been examined by many scholars, notably Roger H. Brown, *The Republic in Peril: 1812* (1964; repr., New York: W. W. Norton, 1971), Bradford Perkins, *Prologue to War: England and the United States, 1805–1812* (Berkeley: University of California Press, 1968), and Chapters 1–3 in Donald R. Hickey, *The War of 1812: A Forgotten Conflict* (Urbana: University of Illinois Press, 1989) provide a concise summary of the prewar period and the debates leading to the declaration of war.

3. Spencer C. Tucker and Frank T. Reuter, *Injured Honor: The Chesapeake-Leopard Affair, June 22, 1807* (Annapolis: Naval Institute Press, 1996).

4. Hickey, *The War of 1812,* pp. 24–26.

5. Allen S. Everest, *The War of 1812 in the Champlain Valley* (Syracuse, NY: Syracuse University Press, 1981), p. 24.

6. Brown, *The Republic in Peril,* pp. 129–30.

7. Brown, *The Republic in Peril,* Chapters 7 and 8.

8. Robert Gardiner, ed., *The Naval War of 1812* (London: Caxton Editions, 2001), pp. 22–56.

9. George F. G. Stanley, *The War of 1812: Land Operations* (Toronto: Macmillan of Canada, 1983), Chapters 2–5. The US Army's disasters and the British Army's triumphs in the first year of the war are grippingly described in Pierre Berton, *The Invasion of Canada, 1812–1813* (Toronto: McClelland and Stewart, 1980).

10. Robert Malcomson, *Warships of the Great Lakes, 1754–1834* (London: Caxton Editions, 2003), Chapters 1 and 2.

11. Benjamin Silliman, *Remarks Made on a Short Tour Between*

Hartford and Quebec in 1819 (2nd ed. New Haven, CT: S. Converse, 1824); a visitor to Whitehall in 1820 reached the same conclusion as Silliman, writing "The Ships of War appear going to wreck," see William Dunlop, *Diary of William Dunlop (1766–1839),* vol. 2. (New York: The New York Historical Society, 1930), p. 544.

12. C. H. J. Snider, *In the Wake of the Eighteen-Twelvers: Fights and Flights of Frigates and Fore 'n' Afters in the War of 1812–1815 on the Great Lakes* (London: John Lane, 1913). Snider's book, which combined thrilling tales of naval battles with "where are they now" descriptions of shipwrecks, apparently did much to excite public interest in sunken 1812-era warships.

13. Allison Scarpitti, "Niagara/Lawrence," *The Journal of Erie Studies* 26, no. 1 (Spring 1997).

14. A good example of this kind of cottage industry can be seen in the August 29, 1873 edition of *Whitehall (NY) Times*: "Parties desirous of obtaining canes made from wood of Confiance should send $1.00 to the Times office. Mr. Lewis Waters has a limited supply." Great Lakes' historian C. H. J. Snider had an entire desk assembled from timbers scavenged from historic shipwrecks, including the 1812 lake warships *Lawrence, Niagara, Nancy, Jefferson, Newash,* and *St. Lawrence*; see Robert B. Townsend, ed., *Tales from the Great Lakes based on C.H.J. Snider's "Schooner Days"* (Toronto: Dundern Press, 1995), pp. 96–99. Courtesy of Peter Rindlisbacher, October 2010.

Part I

The Naval War of 1812 on the Upper Lakes

KEVIN J. CRISMAN

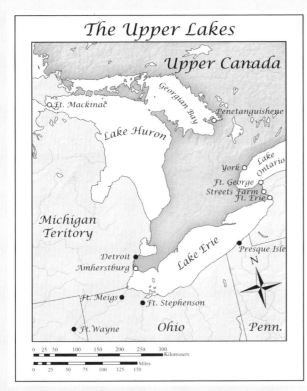

Figure I.1. *The Upper Lakes region in the War of 1812.*
(Map by Douglas Inglis.)

On June 18, 1812, the Congress of the United States declared war upon Great Britain. After years of unresolved friction over freedom of trade, impressments, and western expansion, the US government gave up on diplomatic protests and embargoes and instead unleashed its army and navy. A country declaring war might be expected to marshal overwhelming forces beforehand and then strike swiftly in order to achieve some level of surprise, but the United States in 1812 was a young and not very united republic. While there was a strategic goal for the war—to punish Britain by seizing Canada—the planning and the means assembled beforehand fell far short of what was required. Throughout the first year of this conflict US leaders would display a naive and disjointed approach to waging war, and as a result, every US offensive in 1812 failed miserably. Conquest of Canada proved to be more complicated than the "mere matter of marching" that Thomas Jefferson had predicted before the war.[1]

Nowhere was this military incompetence more manifest than along the western border between the two belligerents, the region surrounding Lakes Erie, Huron, Michigan, and Superior (fig. I.1). The four water bodies were known collectively as the *Upper Lakes* because they were above Niagara Falls and Lake Ontario. Here Britain's small but professionally led army took the initiative early and vigorously, seizing key US positions and repeatedly defeating its unprepared and ineptly led foe. In July the US fort at Mackinac Island, guardian of the straits between Lakes Huron and Michigan, fell before its commander even knew that war had been declared. In August the US Army that was supposed to invade Canada from the west instead surrendered at Detroit to a much smaller force of British and Native Americans. Other humiliating US defeats followed, until reversing the situation on the western frontier became something of an obsession for both the public and government.[2]

The US setbacks resulted from many errors in planning, leadership, and logistics, but the lack of a naval force on the Upper Lakes was an error of the highest order. At the start of the war the US Army had one armed transport in service, the brig *Adams* (14 guns), but this vessel was captured at Detroit in August. Thereafter, the British enjoyed a year of dominance on western waters; their communications, reinforcements, and supplies moved rapidly and safely from point to point, and British commanders could concentrate their troops to attack where and when they chose.

The Upper Lakes presented the most extensive and in many ways the most challenging arena for the inland navies of the War of 1812. Even discounting Lakes Michigan and Superior (which would remain on the periphery of the naval contest), the range of navigable waters far exceeded Lakes Ontario and Champlain to the east. Erie, the southernmost Great Lake, extends over a distance of 241 miles (388 km) with a maximum breadth of 57 miles (92 km), while Huron, to the north, the second largest Great Lake, is 206 miles (332 km) in length and up to 152 miles (245 km) in width. Together the two lakes offered countless natural hazards and difficult passages; the St. Clair and Detroit Rivers connecting Huron to Erie were particularly tricky for deep-drafted sailing ships. Fast-changing weather and harborless lee shores made navigation dangerous throughout the year. It was no place for faint-hearted mariners.

British naval forces on Lakes Erie and Huron at first consisted of only two modestly sized vessels, the recently completed ship *Queen Charlotte* (16 guns) and the small, older schooner *General Hunter* (6 guns). These were rapidly augmented by vessels built, captured, or hired into service, including the newly launched schooner *Lady Prevost* (10 guns), the brig *Detroit* (previously the US *Adams*), and eight or nine merchant vessels of varying rigs and tonnage (the largest was the 120-ton Northwest Company schooner *Nancy*). In 1812 the armed vessels carried fewer guns than they were capable of mounting since the absence of opposition made it unnecessary to crowd their decks with cannon (fig. I.2).[3]

All British government vessels on North American lakes operated under the purview of the Provincial Marine, a supply and transport service managed by the Quartermaster General's Department of the British Army. Charged with patrolling the lakes and provisioning frontier garrisons, this organization functioned adequately in peacetime, but the numbers and quality of its personnel were not up to the demands of wartime service. Alexander Grant, the "commodore" of the Provincial Marine on the Upper Lakes, was a seventy-eight-year-old veteran of the French and Indian War, while the army's proposed establishment of officers and seamen allocated just twenty-seven crewmen to *Queen Charlotte* and nineteen to *General Hunter*. Some of the Provincial Marine's defects were addressed in 1812 (Grant was retired and the crew numbers were slightly increased), but it was still something less than a professional force.[4]

If the war's planners in Washington underestimated the importance of commanding the lakes, the disasters in July and August provided a sharp correction to their thinking. The response of the US Navy was swift. On August 31, Secretary of the Navy Paul Hamilton ordered Capt. Isaac Chauncey, commander of the navy yard in New York City, to create two squadrons on the Great Lakes. "The President of the United States has determined to obtain command of the Lakes Ontario & Erie, with the least possible delay," Hamilton wrote, "and the execution of this highly important object is committed to you."[5] Chauncey was given free rein to hire or requisition the people and materials he needed to prepare the ships, defeat the British, and gain naval ascendancy.

Hamilton's orders stipulated that naval superiority be attained on both Lake Ontario and the Upper Lakes, an ambitious goal that appeared to run counter to the logic of regional geography and military strategy.[6] As the easternmost Great Lake, Lake Ontario was closest to Montreal and Quebec City, the sources of naval stores, munitions, and provisions required by Britain's inland warships. This lake was also the best route for transporting heavy or bulky supplies to the far west, and the United States had only to achieve naval supremacy on Ontario's waters to effectively starve the British Upper Lakes squadron out of existence. Hamilton's two-lake strategy diluted naval resources but was based on calculated political and military reasoning: the US defeats during the summer of 1812 exposed western states and territories to raids by the British and their Native American allies. With massacre and ruin looming, the government had to regain the initiative on the Upper Lakes if it was to protect US citizens and advance the war effort.

Figure I.2. Lake Erie Patrol 1812. *This conjectural painting by Peter Rindlisbacher shows the three warships that formed the core of the Provincial Marine squadron on the Upper Lakes at the start of the War of 1812. From left to right, they are the schooner* Lady Prevost, *brig* General Hunter, *and ship* Queen Charlotte. *(Courtesy of the artist.)*

Geography and strategy also figured prominently in another decision made that fall: where the US Navy was to build its new Upper Lakes squadron. Detroit had been lost to the enemy, and the US side of Lake Erie was nearly devoid of good natural harbors that could be defended against British raids. Black Rock, New York, was one early candidate. Located just inside the Niagara River outlet of Lake Erie, it was protected from storms and could be supplied via Lake Ontario, but the location was perilously close to the Canadian border. Two of Chauncey's subordinates, Lt. Jesse Elliot and Lt. Samuel Angus, attempted to establish a yard at Black Rock during the fall of 1812, but skirmishing in the vicinity frightened off the shipwrights and persuaded everyone that the better choice was 90 miles (145 km) west of the Niagara River, in the state of Pennsylvania.[7]

The harbor at Erie (referred to as Presque Isle in some documents) was first recommended to the navy secretary by an experienced lake mariner and shipwright, Daniel Dobbins.[8] Although farther from sources of supply, the place was sheltered by a curving sandspit arm, had a shallow bar across the mouth that kept large enemy ships from easily entering, and was in general more defensible than Black Rock. In September Dobbins offered to build warships at Erie, a proposal that met with the navy secretary's approval. Dobbins was issued a sailing master's warrant and a set of gunboat plans and told to contract for the timber and shipwrights he would need to build four vessels.[9]

The 1812 navigation season ended with the British squadron, however small and poorly manned, as the dominant force on the Upper Lakes. Nonetheless, there were glimmers of hope for the US Navy. Late one night in early October Lieutenant Elliot led a small-boat attack on the brigs *Detroit* and *Caledonia* while they were anchored at the entrance to the Niagara River; he and his sailors successfully brought away the latter, while *Detroit* was run aground and set afire.[10] Although hardly a grievous loss for the British, Elliot's attack did whittle down their squadron. With the addition of *Caledonia,* the US Navy had five small merchant vessels tucked away at Black Rock awaiting conversion to warships, and Dobbins was making progress on the four gunboats. Chauncey also authorized the building of a 360-ton brig at Erie to challenge the British in 1813.[11]

Most importantly for US efforts on the Upper Lakes, three men with unusual talents entered the scene: a government bureaucrat, a shipwright, and a naval officer. In Washington, William Jones replaced Paul Hamilton as secretary of the navy at the beginning of 1813 and brought a new standard of efficiency and purpose to the navy. A native of Philadelphia, Revolutionary War veteran, former congressman, and successful merchant, Jones's administrative skills surpassed those of his predecessor. He was also unwavering in his support of the lake squadrons in 1813. "It is impossible to attach too much importance to our naval operations on the Lakes," Jones wrote Chauncey in January, "the success of the ensuing campaign will depend absolutely upon our superiority on all the lakes & every effort, & resource must be directed to that object." As evidence of his determination to command the Upper Lakes, he recommended that Chauncey build a second large brig at Erie that winter.[12]

The construction at Erie was entrusted to Noah Brown of New York City, a ship carpenter of some renown, whose reputation—along with that of his brother Adam—would rise still further during the War of 1812. Innovative and fast working, the Brown brothers would produce a remarkable number of warships—from 2-gun gunboats to a 110-gun first rate—for service on the lakes and the seas. In mid-February Chauncey contracted with Brown for the Erie work; Brown then signed on fifteen New York carpenters, and more were hired by the navy from Philadelphia yards. By late spring the crew at the yard numbered two hundred shipwrights and laborers.[13]

The third man to contribute to the creation of the Upper Lakes squadron is the most celebrated: Oliver Hazard Perry (fig. I.3). This twenty-eight-year-old offi-

Figure I.3. *Oliver Hazard Perry, commodore of the US Navy squadron on the Upper Lakes. In this portrait he is shown in the midst of the Battle of Lake Erie, shifting his command from the battered* Lawrence *to the undamaged* Niagara. *The artist shows Perry as bold, serene, and remarkably free of gunpowder residue or other stains after enduring two and a half hours of intense fighting. (Painting by John Wesley Jarvis, Collection of the City of New York, Photograph by Glenn Castellano, Courtesy of the Design Commission.)*

cer had served in the navy for half of his life, rising from midshipman, to lieutenant, and finally to the rank of master commandant. The very model of an early-nineteenth-century US Navy officer, Perry was competent, a natural leader, and relentless in his pursuit of an objective, traits that would be vital in 1813. At the outbreak of the war he commanded the gunboat flotilla defending Newport, Rhode Island, but seeing scant prospect of action there, he requested transfer to the lakes in the fall of 1812. Chauncey enthusiastically seconded this request, telling Perry, "You are the very person I want for a particular service where you may gain honor for yourself & reputation for your country."[14]

The work of Brown and Perry during the late winter and spring at Erie has become one of the legends of the War of 1812: a small band of shipwrights and sailors battling cold and privations in a near-wilderness, scavenge for shipbuilding supplies to create two 20-gun warships from standing timber. The break up of the ice on the lake in mid-April brought the threat of a British raid on the harbor and the destruction of the nascent squadron. The situation remained highly precarious even after the launch of the brigs in late May: ordnance and ship stores were still in transit from Pittsburgh and Philadelphia, and Perry had only a fraction of the sailors he needed to man the squadron.[15] His brigs were afloat but hardly ready to fight.

Perry was not the only commander on Lake Erie experiencing setbacks: his British counterpart across the water was bedeviled by nearly identical problems at this time. The Provincial Marine's lackluster performance in 1812 persuaded the British government to turn the lake squadrons over to the Royal Navy in 1813, and in early March the Admiralty chose a commodore for all the Great Lakes, Capt. Sir James Lucas Yeo.[16] Like US Commodore Chauncey, Yeo considered Lake Ontario to be the critical theater of action, and he focused his efforts accordingly. Responsibility for the Upper Lakes fell to Cmdr. Robert Herriot Barclay, a veteran twenty-seven-year-old Scotsman who entered the navy as a midshipman at age eleven, fought at Trafalgar in 1805, and lost his left arm attacking a French convoy in 1809 (fig. I.4).[17]

Barclay was joined on this new assignment by a mere handful of officers and two dozen sailors, all that Yeo was willing to release from the Lake Ontario squadron. When Barclay arrived in early June at the Amherstburg naval yard on the Detroit River, he found a force sailing on the edge of disaster. The British squadron still commanded the lakes, but unless action was taken immediately, there was every possibility of the United States making a clean sweep of the Upper Lakes in 1813. The former Provincial Marine vessels *Queen Charlotte* (now 18 guns), *Lady Prevost* (12 guns), *General Hunter* (6 guns) and armed merchantmen *Little Belt, Erie,* and *Chippewa* (2 guns each) were short of stores and pitifully manned (their crews, Barclay noted, were "none of them seamen, and very few even in numbers").[18] Sol-

CAPT. ROBERT H. BARCLAY, 1814,
In Uniform of Period.

Figure I.4. *Robert H. Barclay, commodore of the Royal Navy squadron on the Upper Lakes in 1813. A capable sailor and seasoned veteran of Trafalgar and other battles, Barclay was ordered to maintain British naval superiority on Lakes Erie and Huron but never received the sailors or cannon he needed to accomplish this mission. (Courtesy of the Toronto Public Library, Canadian Historical Picture Collection, image JRR 1202.)*

diers had to be borrowed from Gen. Henry Proctor's western army to provide a bare minimum for the gun crews. A new 20-gun ship on the stocks at Amherstburg, *Detroit,* promised some level of parity with the Americans, but there were no guns, munitions, stores, or sailors to complete the vessel after it was launched in mid-July.[19]

Barclay's plan to attack Erie and destroy the unfinished US ships was thwarted by the condition of General Proctor's command: there were simply not enough troops to ensure success. Thus, throughout June and July, the Royal Navy could only cruise off the US shore and monitor Perry's progress. Barclay sent repeated requests for help to his superiors: he could meet the enemy on equal terms, he declared, but only if provided with guns and stores for *Detroit* and 250 to 300 sailors to serve as the backbone of his crews.[20]

The responses of Commodore Yeo and Governor General Sir George Prevost (the supreme commander of His Majesty's forces in Canada) indicated that the defense of Lake Ontario and Lower Canada had first priority in 1813. Prevost made this clear enough, for even as he exhorted Barclay and Proctor to "crush the Enemy's endeavors to obtain ascendancy on Lake Erie," he suggested that "the Ordnance & Naval Stores you require must be taken from the Enemy whose resources on Lake Erie must become yours."[21] How, exactly, Barclay was to capture these guns and stores was not explained by Prevost.

Events moved inexorably toward a showdown on Lake Erie. Despite Barclay's close watch, in early June Perry managed to extract the five renovated merchant vessels from Black Rock and sail them to Erie, where they joined the newly built vessels. This brought Perry's command up to eleven, including the Brown-built brigs *Lawrence* and *Niagara* (20 guns apiece); the Dobbins-and-Brown–built schooners *Porcupine* and *Tigress* (1 gun each), *Scorpion* (2 guns), and *Ariel* (3 guns); the brig *Caledonia* (3 guns); the schooners *Somers* (4 guns), *Ohio* (1 gun), and *Amelia* (1 gun); and the sloop *Trippe* (2 guns).[22] The tardy shipments of equipment finally arrived, enabling Perry to complete outfitting and, during a temporary absence of Barclay's squadron at the beginning of August, to float *Lawrence* and *Niagara* over the shallow bar at the harbor mouth. The US vessels were still undermanned: like Yeo, Chauncey was reluctant to release sailors from Lake Ontario, and like Barclay, Perry was forced to borrow troops from the army to serve as marines and gun crews. The British squadron, now outgunned, retired to Amherstburg to await completion of *Detroit*.[23]

The two squadrons on Lake Erie had very different imperatives in the late summer of 1813. The Royal Navy's were all defensive: survive the naval challenge, keep the meager supply of provisions and munitions flowing, and restrict the mobility of the US Army that was massing in the west. The US Navy's were to gain control of the Upper Lakes, cut off all British supplies, and assist the army under Gen. William Henry Harrison to invade Canada. Perry was under considerable pressure to act: the US government was deeply committed to regaining the initiative in the west and the season for campaigning was nearly over. The national mood after a year of bad news from the western front

may be gauged from an editorial comment in the July 31 edition of *Niles Weekly Register:* "We . . . are weary with looking to Erie for the sailing of the flotilla."[24]

The effects of the US Navy's presence on Lake Erie were soon evident to British forces in the far west: supplies were cut off, provisions ran out, and by the beginning of September the sailors, soldiers, and their native allies at Amherstburg were feeling the pinch of hunger. Barclay was in a predicament. He had completed *Detroit* by scavenging equipment from his other ships and borrowing guns from the defensive batteries of nearby Fort Malden; a contingent of forty officers and sailors had even been sent by Yeo to marginally bolster his crews. The squadron was still in no condition to fight, but the dwindling store of provisions left no choice. The Royal Navy's six ships sailed from Amherstburg on September 9 to challenge the US Navy to an all-or-nothing contest for control of the Upper Lakes.[25]

The two squadrons met at the western end of Lake Erie the next day (plate 1b). The events of the battle are described in the next chapter, but suffice it to say that it was a hard-fought match. Both sides suffered a fearsome rate of casualties that included all of the senior officers on five of the six British ships. Barclay was among the severely wounded, although he would eventually recover. Perry was extraordinarily lucky: untouched by the shot and splinters that cut down three-quarters of *Lawrence*'s crew, he took command of *Niagara* late in the action and went on to capture the entire Royal Navy squadron. His victory message to General Harrison—"We have met the enemy and they are ours"—became the rallying cry of a grateful nation.[26]

The battle on the lake turned the tide in the west. The US squadron required a short period for repairs, and then on September 27 it landed General Harrison's three thousand five hundred–man army near Amherstburg. The British base was overrun, and Detroit was retaken. The Americans met little resistance, for General Proctor had lost most of his guns and many troops with the capture of Barclay's squadron, and the remaining nine hundred or so regulars were worn out and hungry. On October 5 Harrison's force caught up with the retreating British near the Thames River and defeated them in a battle that ended large-scale campaigning in the west for the remainder of the war. Many of Britain's native allies, discouraged by the defeats on water and land and by the lack of material support, dispersed to their homelands. Some of the US objectives for the Upper Lakes region were thus achieved: the security of the western states and territories was no longer threatened and the ability of the Native American populations to resist expansion onto their lands was crippled. Harrison's army was too small to permanently occupy Canadian territory in the west, however, so this was in no sense a conquest of Canada.[27]

After the drama of 1813, the final year of the naval war on the Upper Lakes was mostly an anti-climax. Following Harrison's defeat of Proctor's army, the battered but much enlarged US Navy squadron settled into its winter quarters in Erie. Perry left the station to recover his health and enjoy the honors due a celebrated hero, and—the crisis now over—the ships and sailors languished in a state of disrepair and neglect.[28] In the spring of 1814 the squadron's serviceable vessels were overhauled by the new commodore, Capt. Arthur Sinclair, to transport a US Army force to recapture the fort at Mackinac Island.

The early-August amphibious landing on Mackinac was met by determined and skillful resistance from the fort's garrison and ended with the defeated US Army retreating back to the ships. The US squadron thereafter consoled itself by hunting down *Nancy,* the elderly supply schooner that was the last Royal Navy ship in service on the Upper Lakes. It found the vessel inside the mouth of the Nottawasaga River at the southern end of Lake Huron, and after a spirited, day-long defense, the schooner was burned by its crew.[29] In September Sinclair sailed to the eastern end of Lake Erie to support the US Army's campaign on the Niagara Peninsula; this location proved more hazardous than the enemy, for fall gales nearly piled the ships onto the lee shore. By late November the squadron was again laid up at Erie.[30]

The Battle of Lake Erie left the US Navy in control of the Upper Lakes, but a surprising number of its smaller vessels—nine in all—were lost over the course of the following year. The attrition began on December 30, 1813, when *Ariel, Trippe, Little Belt,* and *Chippewa,* trapped near Buffalo by the freezing of the lake, were burned during a British border raid.[31] On August 12, 1814, the schooners *Ohio* and *Somers* were taken by boarders while anchored at the Niagara River.[32] In early

September, the schooners *Scorpion* and *Tigress* were also boarded and seized while cruising Lake Huron.[33] At nearly the same time, the brig *Caledonia* was blown ashore at Erie and set afire by one or more crew members; the fire was extinguished, but not before the stern was burnt away.[34]

The British government decided to establish new shipyards, build more ships, and challenge its foe on the Upper Lakes in 1815. Under the circumstances this was ambitious, but with the war against Napoleon over in Europe, the Royal Navy had men and resources to spare. Building on the lakes forced the United States to divert its naval forces from the high seas, where they could do more damage to British interests. Amherstburg was no longer viable as a naval base and so two separate shipyards were planned, one at Turkey Point on Lake Erie and the other at Penetanguishene on Lake Huron. News of peace reached the lakes in February, however, and quickly brought this new campaign to a halt. Two armed transport schooners, *Newash* and *Tecumseth,* were completed by the Royal Navy that spring at a temporary shipyard along the Niagara River, but that was the end of it: the era of naval war on the Great Lakes was over.[35]

Despite the remoteness of the Upper Lakes and chronic supply problems that hobbled both adversaries, the naval activity on these waters proved decisive in the War of 1812. Britain's naval dominance in 1812 effectively foiled US plans to invade and occupy the western frontier of Canada. Perry's victory in 1813 ended a year of military failures, broke the back of the British–Native American alliance, and restored the confidence of the US government and public. Perry's terse announcement "We have met the enemy and they are ours" inspired then and still resonates to this day. The border between the two nations has remained peaceful since then, but the people, ships, events, and places of the war continue to loom large in regional and national histories.

The five ships and wrecks described in the following four chapters neatly illustrate the vessel types employed on the Upper Lakes, their varied service careers and fates, and their modern-day treatment by salvers and archaeologists. Two of them, the schooner *Nancy* and the brig *General Hunter,* were built before the war, the former as a commercial carrier for a fur trading company and the latter as a transport for the

British government. One of the five, the brig *Niagara*, was a product of wartime construction, while two others, the schooners *Newash* and *Tecumseth*, were built as part of the British effort to regain the lakes in 1815 and entered into service after the war was over.

Two of the ships described in this section, *Niagara* and *General Hunter*, played prominent roles in the Battle of Lake Erie, while another, *Nancy*, was lost during a fight the following year. The five vessels met their ends in different ways: *Nancy* was torched by its own crew to prevent capture, *General Hunter* was wrecked in one of Lake Huron's notorious gales, while *Niagara*, *Newash*, and *Tecumseth* succumbed to decay when they were laid up after the war. Finally, all five illustrate the shifting attitudes toward historical shipwrecks over the course of the twentieth and early twenty-first centuries: salvage and restoration (*Niagara*), salvage and display (*Nancy* and *Tecumseth*), and archaeological survey or full-scale excavation (*Newash* and *General Hunter*).

NOTES

1. Roger H. Brown, *The Republic in Peril: 1812* (New York: W. W. Norton, 1971), pp. 186–91; Donald R. Hickey, *The War of 1812: A Forgotten Conflict* (Urbana: University of Illinois Press, 1989), p. 73.

2. For background on the early weeks of the war in the far west, see Hickey, *War of 1812*, pp. 72–86; David Curtis Skaggs and Gerard T. Altoff, *A Signal Victory: The Lake Erie Campaign 1812–1813* (Annapolis: Naval Institute Press, 1997), pp. 6–32.

3. William S. Dudley, ed., *The Naval War of 1812: A Documentary History*, vol. 1 (Washington, DC: Naval Historical Center, 1985), p. 308.

4. William Wood, ed., *Select British Documents of the Canadian War of 1812*, vol. 1 (Toronto: The Champlain Society, 1920), pp. 240–44, 246–47, 557. Grant's first freshwater command was the 16-gun sloop *Boscawen* on Lake Champlain in 1759, the hull of which was excavated near Ticonderoga by Kevin Crisman and Arthur Cohn in 1984–1985; see Kevin J. Crisman, "Struggle for a Continent: Naval Battles of the French and Indian Wars," in *Ships and Shipwrecks of the Americas*, ed. George F. Bass (London: Thames and Hudson, 1988), pp. 142–47.

5. Dudley, ed., *Naval War of 1812*, vol. 1, p. 297.

6. Dudley, ed., *Naval War of 1812*, vol. 1, pp. 301–302.

7. Dudley, ed., *Naval War of 1812*, vol. 1, pp. 312–14, 320–22, 360–61.

8. Dudley, ed., *Naval War of 1812*, vol. 1, pp. 310, 321–22. For a detailed study of Dobbins's contributions, see Robert D. Ilisevich, *Daniel Dobbins Frontier Mariner* (Erie, PA: Erie County Historical Society, 1993).

9. Dobbins had to await final authorization for building from Chauncey and the work at Erie did not get fully underway until December. See Dudley, ed., *Naval War of 1812*, vol. 1, pp. 310–11, 360, 368–69.

10. Dudley, ed., *Naval War of 1812*, vol. 1, pp. 327–33.

11. William S. Dudley, ed., *The Naval War of 1812: A Documentary History*, vol. 2 (Washington, DC: Naval Historical Center, 1992), pp. 407–408, 425–26.

12. Edward K. Eckert, *The Navy Department in the War of 1812* (Gainesville, University of Florida Press, 1973); Hickey, *War of 1812*, p. 106; Dudley, ed., *Naval War of 1812*, vol. 2, pp. 419–20. In mid-September Lieutenant Elliot contracted for timber to plank two ships of 300 tons, suggesting that Chauncey was considering two large warships for the Upper Lakes before he left New York City for Lake Ontario; see Dudley, ed., *Naval War of 1812*, vol. 1, p. 312.

13. Noah Brown, "The Remarkable Statement of Noah Brown," *The Journal of American History* 8, no. 1 (January–March 1914), pp. 103–107; Dudley, ed., *Naval War of 1812*, vol. 2, pp. 426–27.

14. Gerard T. Altoff, *Oliver Hazard Perry and the Battle of Lake Erie* (Put-in-Bay, OH: The Perry Group, 1999), pp. 9–12; Dudley, ed., *Naval War of 1812*, vol. 1, p. 354; Dudley, ed., *Naval War of 1812*, vol. 2, pp. 422–23.

15. Brown, "Statement of Noah Brown," pp. 105–107; Dudley, ed., *Naval War of 1812*, vol. 2, pp. 422–23, 440–41, 480–82; Max Rosenberg, *The Building of Perry's Fleet on Lake Erie, 1812–1813* (Harrisburg, PA: Pennsylvania Historical and Museum Commission, 1968); David C. Skaggs and Gerard T. Altoff, *Signal Victory: The Lake Erie Campaign 1812–1813* (Annapolis: Naval Institute Press, 1997), pp. 58–88; Gerard T. Altoff, *Deep Water Sailors Shallow Water Soldiers: Manning the United States Fleet on Lake Erie—1813* (Put-in-Bay, OH: The Perry Group, 1993).

16. Dudley, ed., *Naval War of 1812*, vol. 2, pp. 435–37.

17. W. A. B. Douglas, "Barclay, Robert Heriot (Herriot)," *Dictionary of Canadian Biography Online* (Laval University, 2000, http://www.biographi.ca/009004-119.01-e.php?&id_nbr=3228, accessed July 2008).

18. William Wood, ed., *Select British Documents of the Canadian War of 1812*, vol. 2, pp. 248–49, 252. Another small vessel, the sloop *Erie* (2 guns), was part of the British squadron in 1813 but did not participate in the September battle; see Robert Malcomson, *Warships of the Great Lakes, 1754–1834* (London: Caxton Editions, 2003), p. 85.

19. Wood, ed., *Select British Documents*, vol. 2, pp. 250–51, 257–59. Attacks on York and the Niagara Peninsula by US military and naval forces resulted in the loss of equipment or disruption of shipments of stores and guns to the Upper Lakes; see Skaggs and Altoff, *Signal Victory*, p. 65.

20. Wood, ed., *Select British Documents*, vol. 2, pp. 245–46, 250–51.

21. Wood, ed., *Select British Documents*, vol. 2, pp. 247–48, 251–52.

22. Dudley, ed., *Naval War of 1812,* vol. 2, pp. 481–82, 549. Perry and his officers would continue to shift guns between the smaller vessels, and on the day of the battle one month later the numbers would vary slightly from this list. See Malcomson, *Warships of the Great Lakes,* p. 88.

23. Dudley, ed., *Naval War of 1812,* vol. 2, pp. 546–48.

24. *The Niles Weekly Register,* vol. 4, no. 22, July 31, 1813 (Baltimore), p. 354.

25. Wood, ed., *Select British Documents,* vol. 2, pp. 264–69.

26. Wood, ed., *Select British Documents,* vol. 2, pp. 272–77; Dudley, ed., *Naval War of 1812,* vol. 2, pp. 553–54, 557–59.

27. Skaggs and Altoff, *Signal Victory,* pp. 159–63; Michael J. Crawford, ed., *The Naval War of 1812: A Documentary History,* vol. 3 (Washington, DC: Naval Historical Center, 2002), p. 449.

28. Crawford, ed., *Naval War of 1812,* vol. 3, pp. 452–57.

29. Christopher R. Sabick, "His Majesty's Hired Transport Schooner *Nancy*" (Master's thesis, Texas A&M University, 2004), pp. 61–64; Barry Gough, *Through Water, Ice & Fire: Schooner Nancy of the War of 1812* (Toronto: The Dundurn Group, 2006), pp. 113–41.

30. Crawford, ed., *Naval War of 1812,* vol. 3, pp. 600–602; Malcomson, *Warships of the Great Lakes,* p. 98.

31. Wood, ed., *Select British Documents,* vol. 2, pp. 500–504, 511–12; Malcomson, *Warships of the Great Lakes,* p. 97.

32. Crawford, ed., *Naval War of 1812,* vol. 3, pp. 588–89.

33. Crawford, ed., *Naval War of 1812,* vol. 3, pp. 605–607.

34. Crawford, ed., *Naval War of 1812,* vol. 3, pp. 601–604.

35. LeeAnne Elizabeth Gordon, "*Newash* and *Tecumseth:* Analysis of Two Post-War of 1812 Vessels on the Great Lakes" (Master's thesis, Texas A&M University, 2009).

"WE HAVE MET THE ENEMY AND THEY ARE OURS"

The US Navy Brig *Niagara*

WALTER RYBKA

The Lake Erie Campaign of 1813

The surrender of Fort Mackinac, the capitulation of Detroit, and other defeats suffered by the US Army on the northwestern frontier in 1812 drove home the lesson that military success in this region depended upon naval control of Lakes Erie and Huron. Belatedly, the US Navy began building a squadron of warships at Erie, Pennsylvania. Four small gunboats were begun in November under the direction of a local shipmaster, Daniel Dobbins. On the last day of 1812, the commander of all US naval forces on the Great Lakes, Comm. Isaac Chauncey, inspected Dobbins' work and notified the Navy Department of his intent to augment the gunboats with a brig of "about 300 tons." Secretary of the Navy William Jones approved this vessel, and to assure ascendancy on the Upper Lakes, he also authorized the building of a second brig of the same size. The work did not begin until early March, when Noah Brown, an experienced New York shipbuilder, arrived at Erie to take charge of the building. He was accompanied by a handful of experienced carpenters from New York.[1]

Records of the time are typically vague about the navy's two brigs, and plans for them have never been found. Chauncey's orders to Brown stipulated that the brigs were to have a burthen of 360 tons, were to mount twenty guns (eighteen 32-pounder carronades and two long 12 pounders), and were to draw no more than 6½ to 7 feet (1.93 to 2.13 m) of water to allow them to pass over the sand bar at the entrance to the bay at Erie. Chauncey also requested that they be fast-sailing vessels, which, in combination with their shallow draft, was entirely at odds with his desire that the brigs "bear their guns with ease." The commodore instructed Noah Brown, "their frame &c. will be left to yourself," indicating that Brown was given a good deal of latitude in the design, materials, and assembly of the brigs. The overriding stipulation was that the new vessels were to be built in the shortest possible time.[2]

Late March saw the arrival of Master Commandant Oliver Hazard Perry, sent by Chauncey to command the squadron. Dobbins, Brown, and Perry made an effective team to deal with the daunting task of creating a naval force in a remote wilderness. The need for speed was uppermost in everyone's mind. Although unlimited quantities of timber were at hand, nothing else was readily available. Iron for fastenings, rope, sailcloth, anchors, ordnance, and ammunition all had to be freighted at great cost from Pittsburgh, Philadelphia, or other distant cities. The greatest shortage was labor, but as spring came more men arrived and Brown's shipyard eventually employed over two hundred craftsmen. The brigs, named *Lawrence* and *Niagara,* were finished and launched by early June, but the delays in the delivery of equipment dragged out the outfitting for two more months.[3]

In June the US Army's advance on the Niagara peninsula at Lake Erie's outlet allowed Perry to sail five armed merchant vessels from Buffalo to Erie to augment his squadron, bringing the total up to eleven ships. Nine of the eleven were quite small, mounting between one and four guns each. While Perry's force was small and his situation difficult, his foe's position on the lake was nearly impossible. Royal Navy Cmdr. Robert H. Barclay had the advantages of a base at Fort Malden on the Detroit River and his existing squadron of eight ships, but construction, supply, and manning proved even more difficult for the British. Despite Perry's fears, Barclay could neither attack Erie nor maintain an effective blockade in the spring and summer of 1813. When the British squadron left Erie uncovered for a few days at the end of July, Perry seized the opportunity to enter the lake.

Presque Isle peninsula encloses Erie harbor and guarded the entrance with a bar that had, at most, 6 feet (1.83 m) of water over it. *Lawrence* and *Niagara* reportedly drew 9 feet (2.74 m) and thus needed to be lifted over the bar with the aid of camels (barges that could be partially flooded, secured to the ship, and then pumped out to provide lift). It was a perilous undertaking: to reduce weight, all guns had to be lightered ashore, leaving the brigs as vulnerable as newly molted lobster. Fortune favored Perry, however, for it was only after his crews had nearly completed the laborious task of getting the brigs out and rearmed

that the Royal Navy's ships returned to blockade Erie. Barclay, finding the superior enemy squadron out and seemingly ready to sail, returned to Fort Malden to hasten completion of his new ship *Detroit.*

Although still shorthanded, Perry sailed to the western end of Lake Erie and established a forward base at Put-in-Bay, Ohio. From here Perry contacted Gen. William H. Harrison, augmented his crews with soldiers, and maintained a distant blockade of the Detroit River and Fort Malden. The US squadron's major problem now became disease: fever and dysentery put one-quarter of the ships' crews on the sick list at any given time.

The US counter blockade worked: Fort Malden became critically low on provisions by early September. Barclay's squadron went on half rations, Britain's Indian allies threatened to go home unless they were fed, and the British Army contemplated abandonment of its positions on the Upper Lakes. Although critically short of experienced sailors, outnumbered in vessels, and outgunned, Barclay felt compelled to seek battle as soon as *Detroit* was ready to sail. The Battle of Lake Erie was the day the hungry came out to fight the sick.

At dawn on September 10, 1813, Barclay's squadron was sighted northwest of Perry's anchorage at Put-in-Bay. Within minutes the US squadron was underway but had difficulty clearing the harbor (fig. 1.1). The light wind from the southwest forced Perry's ships to short tack in confined waters in an attempt to gain the weather gauge (that is, the advantageous position upwind of Barclay). Meanwhile the British drew steadily closer. By 10 a.m. Perry had given up hope of weathering his foes and was preparing to engage Barclay at a disadvantage, when the wind suddenly shifted nearly 90 degrees to the southeast, handing Perry the weather gauge. The tables were now turned. The British ships were stopped by a headwind and forced to tack; Barclay reformed his line and hove-to, slowly drifting to the west. Perry, leading a strung-out line of US ships, strove to overtake the Royal Navy squadron at a speed of three knots (5.56 kph).

In this battle the US squadron numbered nine vessels to the British six, but most of the firepower was concentrated on board the two largest vessels on each side. These were the US brigs *Lawrence* and *Niagara,* commanded by Perry and Master Commandant Jesse Duncan Elliott. Barclay's flagship was the 19-gun ship *Detroit,* supported by the 17-gun ship *Queen Charlotte.*

Figure 1.1. Prelude to Battle. *The American Lake Erie squadron on the morning of September 10, 1813. In this conjectural painting by Peter Rindlisbacher, the ships work their way out of the anchorage at Put-In Bay to meet the British squadron that has appeared to the northwest of the islands. (Courtesy of the artist.)*

Perry had a nearly two-to-one advantage in broadside weight due to the 32-pounder carronades his brigs mounted, yet he had to be in close range of his foe to use them (fig. 1.2a). *Detroit* was armed primarily with long guns and thus was better off engaging Perry at a distance (fig. 1.2b). Perry had an overall superiority in long gun weight as well, but here he had a distribution problem. The US squadron's heaviest long guns were on board the smaller gunboats, which in the very light air proved slow and lagged far astern of Perry as he closed with the British squadron.

Action commenced with British long gun fire at 11:45 a.m. and the flagship *Lawrence,* near the van of the US squadron, was soon taking casualties. Perry now had two choices. The safer option was to haul out of range and wait for his squadron to close up, achieving overwhelming superiority. There was some risk this would not happen in the dying breeze. Or perhaps Perry feared a wind shift would restore the weather gauge to the British.

Characteristically, Perry chose the audacious and risky option. He sailed directly at the British, enduring raking fire but closing as rapidly as possible to the range at which his carronades could be decisive. This was essentially Adm. Horatio Nelson's plan of action at Trafalgar, but Perry was already within British range without his force concentrated. If his ships were disabled on the way in, or if the light breeze died altogether and left him becalmed, he would have been in a disastrous and unrecoverable position.

Perry's pre-battle orders to his subordinate commanders were for each to engage his designated adversary, keep near *Lawrence,* and stay in line. At the time of ordering the run in, Perry felt he could count on support from the fast schooners *Scorpion* and *Ariel,* the small brig *Caledonia,* and, of course, *Niagara,* even if the rest of the gunboats were too far astern to join in the fight. Elliott in *Niagara* inexplicably decided that his priority was to keep station astern of *Caledonia,* a much slower vessel than either of the large brigs.

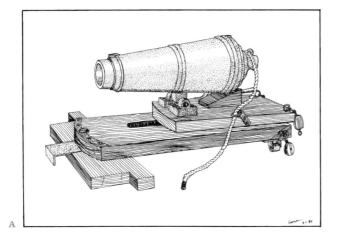

A

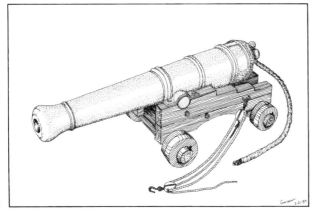

B

Figure 1.2. *Shipboard artillery of the War of the 1812 era: (a) the carronade; and (b) the long gun. The invention of the carronade in the late eighteenth century gave navies two principal choices of weapons and tactics: fight at short range with heavy-hitting carronades or engage at a greater distance with the relatively smaller shot of long guns. Many warships of the time carried a mix of both types. (Drawing by Kevin J. Crisman.)*

From the outset *Niagara* hovered on the outskirts of the battle, engaging only with its two 12-pounder long guns.

Elliott's actions infuriated the crew of *Lawrence* at the time and have baffled historians ever since. Why did he hold his brig back from the battle? Elliott had distinguished himself in earlier actions and was neither a coward nor a traitor. The most likely explanation is simply insubordination. Elliott could see Perry was taking an extreme risk, and he decided not to follow his commander in what he judged to be a foolish mistake. This decision nearly lost the battle.

Under a hot sun an intense drama unfolded. By 12:30 p.m. *Lawrence* was severely shot up aloft but

finally in position to use full broadsides against *Detroit. Queen Charlotte* could not reach Elliot's distant *Niagara* with carronades and so closed up with the British flagship and also began firing into *Lawrence.* The Royal Navy squadron achieved local superiority of firepower over the US flagship, and for the next two hours their battle positions remained static, implying that the breeze had gone flat calm, or very nearly so. *Lawrence* was slowly smashed to pieces under a steady hail of iron shot.

Perry somehow remained unscathed, while above and below deck his flagship became a slaughterhouse. Of the 103 men fit for duty that morning, 22 were killed and 61 were wounded, an astonishing 80 percent of the crew. About half of the wounded had only minor injuries, but the total number of casualties is nevertheless horrifying. A statistical overview of 1812-era naval engagements shows that the winning vessel usually suffered up to 15 percent casualties while the losing vessel typically surrendered when losses reached 30 percent.[4] Yet *Lawrence*'s crew suffered losses far beyond those of a typical engagement and still did not give up. History offers few examples of such single-minded dedication.

By 2:30 p.m. *Lawrence*'s last starboard gun was knocked out, but once again the wind came to Perry's aid. It freshened from the southeast and moved the action away from the helpless *Lawrence.* With the US flagship silenced and the two largest enemy ships greatly weakened, Elliott finally acted, steering *Niagara* past *Lawrence,* most likely to "cross the T" on the battered British line. Perry, however, had no intention of quitting the fight. In one of the most celebrated episodes of naval history, he hauled down his personal flag (which, ironically, read "Don't Give Up the Ship"), boarded a damaged but still useable cutter towing astern of *Lawrence,* and set off for *Niagara* (fig. 1.3). British gun crews perceived what was happening and shifted their fire, drenching Perry and the four sailors on board the cutter with the splashes of near misses, but the boat arrived alongside *Niagara* unharmed.

Understandably, accounts differ as to the words exchanged between Perry and Elliott, but the former took command of *Niagara* while the latter left in the cutter to rally the gunboats. From the quarterdeck of this fresh, nearly untouched brig, Perry ordered the crew to set the topgallants and foresail, square the yards, and

The launch of the Royal Navy line-of-battle ship St. Lawrence *at Kingston on Lake Ontario. This vessel, completed in September 1814, had 104 guns, the same number that Admiral Horatio Nelson's first-rate flagship* Victory *mounted at the Battle of Trafalgar in 1805. At the end of the war, four more ships of similar size were under construction at British and US shipyards on Lake Ontario. (Courtesy of the Royal Ontario Museum, Toronto, image 967.106.1.)*

The Battle of Lake Erie, an oil painting by Thomas Birch. During the final phase of the battle, Perry transferred his flag to the undamaged Niagara *and the shot-riddled US brig* Lawrence *(foreground) dropped out of the action. In this scene Perry has steered* Niagara *across the head of the British line to pound the entangled* Detroit *and* Queen Charlotte *at very close range. (Courtesy of the Pennsylvania Academy of Fine Arts, Philadelphia. Gift of Mrs. Charles H.A. Esling.)*

Niagara *breaks the British line. In this conjectural painting by Peter Rindlisbacher, the American flagship crosses the bows of the entangled* Detroit *and* Queen Charlotte. *The maneuver allowed* Niagara *to send shot raking down the lengths of their decks, while the British ships were unable to bring guns to bear in response. (Courtesy of the artist.)*

The aftermath of the Battle of Lake Erie. Provincial Marine Lt. Robert Irvine painted this watercolor, creating a unique contemporary record of the four principal warships on the Upper Lakes. Irvine was a survivor of the fight who ended up commanding Queen Charlotte *when the captain was killed and first lieutenant was wounded. His ship is on the left, with two of its three masts fallen, the dismasted* Detroit *is in the center, and the shot-pocked* Lawrence *is on the right. Only* Niagara *(behind the others) is relatively unscathed. (With permission of the Royal Ontario Museum, Toronto, 990.49.8.)*

Under way in a light breeze. Topsails and topgallant sails are sufficient to carry the brig over the placid waters of western Lake Erie on a clear summer morning. This photograph was taken at the same location where the American and British squadrons met in the Battle of Lake Erie on September 10, 1813. (Photo by Bradley Krueger.)

The Provincial Marine brig General Hunter *off Fort Malden in 1812. This conjectural painting by Peter Rindlisbacher shows the vessel sailing in a stiff breeze with most of its sails set. (Courtesy of the artist.)*

A view of Southampton Beach Wreck from the bow. During the excavation the public was invited inside the site fence each afternoon to hear about the ongoing work. Many of the families present had been sunbathing and swimming in the area for generations with no knowledge of the ship hull that lay buried just beneath the sand. (Photo by Larry LePage.)

A conjectural painting of General Hunter's *final hours. After the war* General Hunter *sailed the Upper Lakes as a US Army transport renamed* Hunter. *On a return voyage from Michilimackinac the brig was driven to the east side of Lake Huron by a violent gale. The crew saved their lives by intentionally beaching the vessel on a wilderness shore (now Southampton, Ontario) around midnight on August 19, 1816. (Courtesy of Peter Rindlisbacher.)*

Figure 1.3. *Comm. O. H. Perry transfers his flag during the Battle of Lake Erie. The decision to leave the shattered* Lawrence *and take command of* Niagara *was typical of the single-minded Perry. It also greatly enhanced his status as a US naval hero. This engraving, like most nineteenth-century depictions of the battle, takes liberties with the details (Perry was not wearing a full-dress uniform at the time), but it captures the drama of this pivotal moment in the War of 1812. (Courtesy of the Yale University Art Gallery.)*

put the helm up. *Niagara* ran before the wind to cross the bow of the badly damaged *Detroit.*

US gunnery had already taken a fearful toll on the Royal Navy squadron: many sailors and soldiers had fallen, and on five of the six British vessels the commanding officer and second in command were dead or seriously wounded. Barclay himself had suffered two wounds and was taken below, which may have spared his life. The junior officer commanding *Detroit* realized that his vessel was about to be raked and attempted to wear ship, but at the same time *Queen Charlotte,* with a rig too shot up to maneuver, came up from astern and rammed its headgear into the mizzen shrouds of *Detroit.* The two principal British vessels were thus

fatally locked together when *Niagara* crossed their bows. From a range of "half pistol shot," a double-shotted broadside scythed down the length of their decks.

It was over very quickly. *Niagara* rounded up under the lee of the British ships with backed yards and fired more broadsides into the helpless vessels (plate 2a). By this time the US gunboats had closed the range enough to switch to grapeshot, some of which carried over the Royal Navy ships to rattle in *Niagara*'s rigging. Hammered by intense fire from two directions, the British could no longer respond and surrendered at around 3:15 p.m.

All ships anchored to begin sorting out the wreckage (plate 2b). Three hours of battle left sailors on both sides exhausted, parched, and dazed, with their ears ringing (indeed, some were permanently deafened). The lucky ones were merely dazed and exhausted; the truly unlucky, approximately one of every four men who sailed into battle on that day, were dead (68) or seriously injured (189). Three of the four largest ships, *Lawrence, Detroit,* and *Queen Charlotte,* were shattered and splintered, their decks spattered with blood, tissue, and bone fragments.

From the deck of *Niagara,* Perry hastily scratched out his famous victory message to General Harrison: "We have met the enemy and they are ours."[5] The Battle of Lake Erie marked the first time the US Navy fought a decisive fleet action, and for the Royal Navy it resulted in the loss of an entire squadron, however small and outgunned. The action greatly boosted the morale of the US government and public, which had sagged under the many defeats its military forces had suffered along the US-Canadian border during the previous year.

Of more immediate consequence, the Royal Navy's defeat on the lake spelled disaster for the British Army and its native allies on the northwestern frontier. The path was now clear for the US Army to recapture Detroit and reverse the tide on the northwestern frontier. *Niagara* and the smaller vessels of the combined squadrons assisted Harrison with the offensive that culminated in US victory at the Battle of the Thames on October 5, 1813. With the onset of winter, the majority of the ships were moored in the harbor at Erie, where *Lawrence* was patched up for use the following year.

In 1814, *Niagara, Lawrence,* and the small warships sailed in support of various offensive operations against the British, but these accomplished little and four of the navy's small warships were lost to daring British boarding actions. At the conclusion of the war in 1815, the naval squadron of the Upper Lakes was laid up in Misery Bay, across Presque Isle Bay from Erie. The smaller vessels were subsequently sold into merchant service, but the larger ships and brigs, of limited commercial value, were left to decay.

When *Niagara* and *Lawrence* were under construction in 1813, Noah Brown cautioned an overmeticulous shipwright, "plain work is all that is required; they will only be wanted for one battle; if we win, that is all that is wanted of them; if the enemy are victorious, the work

Figure 1.4. *The salvaged lower hull of* Niagara *on the shore of Misery Bay in 1913. The photograph shows the sternpost and the lower frames and planking of the starboard side. Two of the rudder's gudgeons are still in place on the sternpost, and a mortise carved for the third gudgeon is visible near the top of the post. Also faintly visible atop the post's after face is the oval hollow where the brig's plug-stock rudder extended into the transom. (From the* Journal of American History 8, *no. 1 [1914], p. 25.)*

is good enough to be captured."[6] Brown plainly recognized the ephemeral nature of wartime-built ships. His brigs were not intended to last very long, but only to meet a crisis that loomed in the immediate future. In 1820, in an effort to preserve the wooden hulls just a little longer, the navy had them stripped and scuttled in the shallow waters of Misery Bay, but their services would never again be needed.

Niagara in the Twentieth Century

Time marches on. One hundred years after the War of 1812, the United States had grown hugely in area, population, and influence. Indeed, by 1912 the United States had become an ocean-spanning empire, and after a period of neglect the US Navy was building a battle fleet surpassed only by Great Britain and Germany. The coincidence of the War of 1812's centennial with this new naval mindedness led to a resurrection. In 1913, shortly before the one-hundredth anniversary of the Battle of Lake Erie, the remains of one of Noah Brown's brigs—identified as *Niagara*—were recovered from the bottom of Misery Bay (fig. 1.4).[7]

The intent of the salvagers was straightforward: rebuild the wreck into a floating exhibit in time for the "Perry Centennial" celebrations in the summer and fall of that year. The hull that surfaced in the ice-covered bay in late March 1913 was remarkably preserved, considering that it was a century old. It consisted of the bottom out to the turn of bilge, the lower stem and sternposts, and nearly 60 feet (18.29 m) of the port side that was intact amidships up through the bulwarks. Six gunports were wholly or partially preserved (fig. 1.5a, b). According to the salvers, the hull measured 118 feet (35.97 m) between the stem and sternpost, 30 feet (9.14 m) in beam, and had a draft of about 9 feet (2.74 m).[8]

The first *Niagara* restoration was not an archaeological preservation project as we would understand it today, for it was begun with the short-term goal of creating an exhibit for a commemorative event. Little effort was made to record what survived, nor were detailed plans prepared for the restoration work. The officer in charge of the work, US Navy Capt. William L. Morrison, reportedly took the lines off the salvaged hull, but his access to research material was limited, the need for haste was great, and it is obvious that his reconstruction depended heavily on unsupported conjecture. Many details of the new *Niagara* showed scant resemblance to early nineteenth-century design and building practices (fig. 1.6).[9] Reconstruction began on April 7, and the completed hull was launched just two months later, on June 7, 1913.

The original brig was abandoned due to rot, and after ninety-three years on the bottom the same rotten timbers could not have improved. Morrison nevertheless claimed that he was able to reuse many original components, including the entire keel, parts of the keelson, all of the lower frame timbers, the end posts, and "a large part" of the planking. This claim is open to question. Photographs of the hull taken before and after the restoration suggest that the planking, originally preserved up to the turn of the bilge, was replaced in its entirety. We do not have good photographs of the hull's interior after the rebuilding, but it appears that with the possible exception of the keel and a few frame floors, most of the ship's timbers were replacements.

The 1913 rebuilding obliterated much of *Niagara*'s original structure, but some details from the wreck were embodied in the 1913 vessel and in subsequent reconstructions. The length and dimensions of the keel, rake of stem and sternposts, degree of frame deadrise, depth of hold, spacing of deck beams, approxi-

A

B

Figure 1.5. *(a) Exterior and (b) interior views of a gunport and sweep port on Niagara. Taken during the salvage of the hull in 1913, these images reveal the existence of small ports in the bulwarks that allowed the crew to propel the brig with sweeps. Also evident in the interior view are two dagger knees that braced main deck beams; these may have been fitted after the war, since the commodore of the US squadron in 1814 complained that the brigs were built without knees. (From the* Journal of American History *8, no. 1 [1914], p. 17, and C. H. J. Snider,* In the Wake of the Eighteen-Twelvers, *p. 120.)*

mate dimensions of planking and frames, and fastening patterns seem to have been retained.[10] The remains of mast steps on the keelson showed the placement but not the rake of the masts (fig. 1.7). The size and spacing of gunports, the existence of sweep ports and

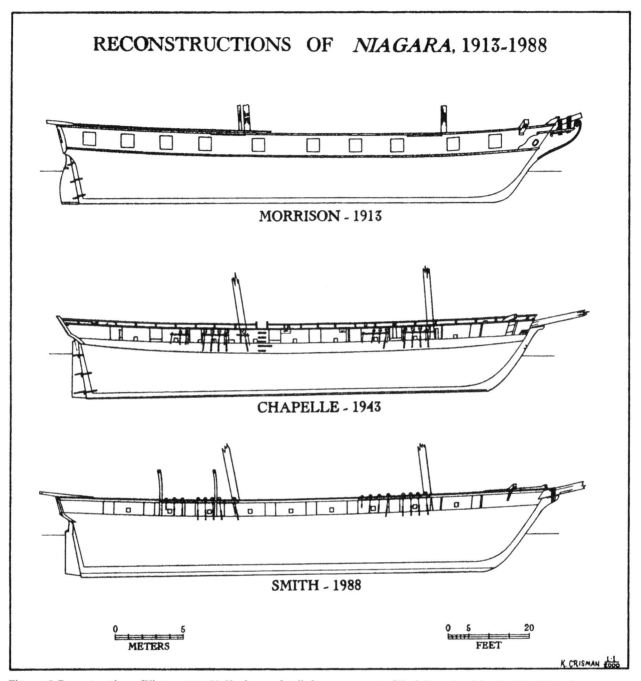

RECONSTRUCTIONS OF *NIAGARA*, 1913-1988

MORRISON - 1913

CHAPELLE - 1943

SMITH - 1988

0   5
METERS

0   5   20
FEET

K. CRISMAN 2000

Figure 1.6. *Reconstructions of* Niagara, *1913–88. No plans or detailed measurements of Noah Brown's original Lake Erie brigs have ever been found, and so the three twentieth-century reconstructions each reflected the current state of scholarly knowledge, budgetary and operational imperatives, and the preferences of the draftsmen who prepared the plans. Each differed in significant ways from the other two iterations. (Drawing by Kevin J. Crisman.)*

Figure 1.7. *An interior view of the salvaged* Niagara *taken in 1913. The photographer stood just forward of the foremast step (the four bolts show its location on the keelson). A similar pattern of bolts for the mainmast step can be seen toward the stern. Many of the notches on top of the keelson were for stanchions that supported deck beams. Nearly all of the ceiling has been taken up and workmen are cleaning sediment from between the frames (note the broom in the foreground). (From the* Journal of American History 8, no. 1 [1914], p. 26.)

Figure 1.8. *The reconstructed* Niagara *tours the Great Lakes in 1913. Salvaged and rebuilt at the last possible minute for the Perry Centennial celebrations, the brig was neither rigged nor manned for actual sailing. It was instead towed between Great Lakes ports by the Pennsylvania Naval Militia sidewheeler* Wolverine *(the former USS* Michigan, *launched in 1843). Here the two vessels pass a group of interested swimmers and excursionists in small boats. (Erie Maritime Museum Collection, courtesy of the Pennsylvania Historical and Museum Commission.)*

dagger knees, and the method of securing gun tackle bolts with forelock keys can all be approximately determined from photographs. The woods used in the original hull were identified during the 1913 rebuilding, giving us some idea of timber availability in 1813.[11]

Like the original, the second *Niagara* was built in a hurry, and probably with a great deal of green wood, to meet a short-term need. Rigged with an undersized set of masts and spars and armed with a battery of thin-walled replica carronades, the commemorative *Niagara* was towed around the Great Lakes on a tour by the US Navy sidewheel steamer *Wolverine* between July 6 and September 17, 1913 (fig. 1.8). During this time the brig was manned by a small navy crew and some sail was bent on, but only one photograph shows it sailing, and it may still have been under tow. After this tour, *Niagara* was berthed in Erie as a tourist attraction and proceeded to rot away over the next quarter century.

By the late 1920s *Niagara* was sinking at the pier with some regularity and becoming recognized as a public safety hazard. Sporadic efforts at organizing committees and raising funds for reconstruction were made over the next decade, but it was only in 1939 that the Federal government's Works Progress Administration funded a rebuilding of the hull. Naval Historian Howard I. Chapelle prepared a set of reconstruction plans for this effort.[12] The third incarnation of *Nia-*

gara was completed slowly because funds kept running out, and it was not until 1943 that the hull was finally launched. It was then towed to the Erie waterfront, hauled back out of the water, and dry berthed on a cradle. The ship, now the responsibility of the Pennsylvania Historical and Museum Commission (PHMC), remained on exhibit for over forty years. Masts and rigging had to wait until 1962, in time for the 150th anniversary of the Battle of Lake Erie.

By the late 1970s it was obvious that another major rebuilding (the third in the brig's history) was long overdue. Historian and naval architect William Avery Baker was hired to prepare plans but died before work was begun. The struggle to raise sufficient funds delayed the project for several years.

PHMC management decided that this time the ship should be rebuilt as a true sailing vessel that was to be maintained permanently afloat. This was in line with an interpretive philosophy requiring objects to be put in a proper context, but it was also a major commitment of resources, the extent of which was not fully realized at the time. The PHMC's desire to preserve the historic structure was also at cross-purposes with the stipulation of seaworthiness. Although the ship had continually maintained an identity since 1813, by this time it was very difficult to positively identify original fabric, if there was any, let alone retain it in a vessel intended to sail.

In 1986 the PHMC awarded a contract for design work to Melbourne Smith, a well-known designer and builder of historic reproduction ships. Smith conducted his own study, including surviving plans of other vessels built by Noah Brown, and produced a design that differed in many details from Chapelle's work. A building contract followed, and in 1988 Smith assembled a team of craftsmen in Erie and built the hull in only ninety days. This was not a plank-by-plank "restoration." Smith recognized that the existing ship was too rotten to be saved, let alone rendered seaworthy. The dismantling took little more than a day, and then the work of building a new ship from the keel up began. A number of frame timbers from the original were inserted between the frames of the new ship as a symbolic presence, but these pieces were not intended to perform any structural function.

The short construction schedule was aided by the use of laminated timbers preshaped at the factory. A crew of about twenty-five was employed at the construction site, and full advantage was taken of every modern power tool. Unlike the original, the present *Niagara* is almost entirely a softwood ship. Some tropical hardwoods were used for stem and sternposts, knightheads, stanchions, and pinrails, but the keel, frames, deck beams, waterways, and most spars are laminated from yellow pine. All planking is Douglas fir.

Once again, a commemorative event, this time the 175th anniversary of the battle, pushed the schedule for the rebuilding. A crane was used to launch the ship on September 10, 1988, with much ceremony and in view of a very large crowd (fig. 1.9). The bare hull then waited nearly a year and a half until funds could be allocated for rigging and interior joiner work. Finally, on July 18, 1990, the builder's crew, under command of Capt. Carl Bowman (USCG, ret.), sailed the new ship on a one-day sea trial before acceptance by the PHMC.

The restoration project was begun to preserve an historic property but now involved the maintenance and operation of a floating vessel. The PHMC was assisted by the local, nonprofit Flagship *Niagara* League, which provided hands-on volunteer support for shipkeeping chores and helped devise a sailing program. The PHMC's efforts to plan the brig's future were guided by a fourfold mission statement contained in a governor's executive order. First, *Niagara* was intended to commemorate and interpret the War of 1812, especially the Lake Erie campaign. Second, the brig was to provide public educational programs in both the history of the campaign and the sailing of square-rigged ships. Third, *Niagara* was to serve as the Flagship of the Commonwealth, promoting Pennsylvania tourism and commerce through visits to out-of-state ports. And, finally, the vessel was to be the focal point of Erie's bayfront revitalization.

In the late spring of 1991, I was contracted to serve as master of the vessel and directed to create a sailing program for the ship. That first summer everything had to happen at once, yesterday: a professional crew was hired, volunteers were recruited and trained, and contracts were issued for insurance, towage, port visits, and outfitting the ship. The ship lacked ground tackle, a stove, radar and navigational gear, lifesaving equipment, bedding and galley utensils, and sufficient ballast. It also lacked auxiliary propulsion, and a tug was therefore hired to accompany all operations. After lengthy preparations, a series of day sails were undertaken in 1991, followed by a short cruise to the battle site, to Put-in-Bay, Ohio, and finally to Cleveland.

The third rebuilding of *Niagara* was originally intended as a pristine museum exhibit that undertook occasional day sails, but the first summer's operation showed that the commitment to any kind of sailing was the most expensive part of the enterprise. Whether one intends to sail for only a few days or most of the summer, nearly the same preparation is required to do it responsibly and safely. A crew must be trained, and while volunteers contribute greatly to the effort, a ship of this size and complexity requires a professional core. After 1991, the PHMC committed to an ambitious sailing schedule and facilitated future voyaging by having twin diesel engines and propellers installed in the hull.[13]

By almost any standard, *Niagara* had an eventful career in the twentieth century. The ship started off the century as a rotted, sunken hulk and was then raised, hastily rebuilt, displayed for 25 years, allowed to rot, rebuilt, displayed for 40 years until it rotted again, and once more rebuilt, this time as a living, working memorial to a perilous hour in North American history. Now that we have caught up with *Niagara*'s history, let us take a closer look at the brig as it looks at the beginning of the twenty-first century.

Figure 1.9. *The launch of* Niagara *on September 10, 1988. The twentieth century's third iteration of the brig, the vessel entered the water with the aid of a crane on the 175th anniversary of the Battle of Lake Erie. Unlike the two previous reconstructions, this* Niagara *was designed and built from the keel up to be a fully functional sailing ship. (Photo by Barbara Klaproth, courtesy of the Erie Maritime Museum.)*

A Tour of the Brig

Today's *Niagara* captures well the overall appearance of an early-nineteenth-century brig of war (fig. 1.10). In some details it is faithful to the original, while in other areas anachronistic compromises have been made. Let us start our discussion of the reconstructed *Niagara* and its equipment with a tour, beginning with a pierside look at the vessel.

Masts and spars dominate the profile of *Niagara,* for the brig carries a very lofty rig by today's standards, although in its day the rig would not have been considered particularly tall. It was quite common in the War of 1812 era for the mainmast height to exceed the length of the vessel by 10 to 20 percent, yet *Niagara*'s mainmast is slightly shorter than the length of the hull. The shallowness of the hull forced the designer to be careful about overmasting. The spars that comprise

the headgear are quite long, nearly half the length of the vessel, but the bowsprit has little upward angle or "steeve." The low steeve is a liability in rough weather but was partially dictated by the hull's low freeboard. A high steeve on a shallow hull will not allow for adequate down angle on the bobstays; as it is, the staying angles relative to the length of headgear are the minimum acceptable.

Niagara's freeboard, the distance between the waterline and the main deck, is low at 3 feet 9 inches (2.06 m), although the 5-foot-high (1.52 m) bulwarks surmounted by hammock rails create the impression of a much higher vessel. Low freeboard was a characteristic of many nineteenth-century lake sailers, especially the lake warships, since it is vital to minimize topside weight in a shallow-draft hull. This does, however, place the gunports quite close to the water.

Figure 1.10. *The present-day* Niagara *fires a salute from its port-side carronade. Every effort has been made to re-create the appearance and spirit of the original vessel, although some compromises are necessary to assure safety, maintain efficiency of operations, and extend the life of the hull and rig. (Photo by John Baker, courtesy of the Erie Maritime Museum.)*

There is no definitive word on the colors of the original ship, just a small number of ambiguous clues. A contemporary watercolor of the Lake Erie warships painted by a British officer suggests that *Niagara*'s sister brig *Lawrence* had a uniformly dark hull (see plate 2b).[14] The easiest colors to produce were black and barn red, and it is possible the original ship used only these. It is also possible that due to the haste of construction, little paint was used anywhere. We just do not know. In the absence of definitive information, the present hull has been painted with colors typical of the period, with the exception of the buff used on rails, lower masts, and deck furniture. A light color was considered a practical necessity for the areas that would be most exposed to the sun.

On board *Niagara,* two striking features are the gun battery and the height of the bulwarks (fig. 1.11).

Today the brig carries only two guns, but the original ship carried eighteen 32-pounder carronades and two 12-pounder long guns. Nearly half the deck space was allocated to the "great guns" and their tackle, since floating this battery into action was the sole reason for the brig's existence. There were several reasons for limiting the number of guns on the present hull. Aside from financial considerations, carrying the authentic full armament would be a heavy burden on the structure of the brig. The original was a short-lived vessel, and this replica would be, too, if so loaded. The shallow-hulled lake warships were particularly prone to hogging, the drooping of the bow and stern due to too much weight on the deck and insufficient longitudinal strength.

Even more serious is the question of stability. The original vessel, with its internal ballast, massive arma-

Figure 1.11. *The deck of* Niagara *during a battle reenactment. In this photograph the gun crew surrounding Niagara's starboard carronade, the additional sailors and soldiers on the deck, and the high bulwarks with their hammock rails give the viewer a sense of the crowded, confined nature of the deck on the original vessel.* (Erie Maritime Museum Collection, courtesy of the Pennsylvania Historical and Museum Commission.)

Figure 1.12. *The expanded taffrail on* Niagara's *stern.* Niagara's *captain Wesley Heersen and third mate Chris Cusson rely on the high vantage point provided by this "bridge deck" to simultaneously oversee the operations of the crew and keep an eye out for navigational hazards on the lake.* (Photo by John Baker, courtesy of the Erie Maritime Museum.)

ment on deck, and main deck loaded with sailors, must have had frighteningly small stability margins. The only way to keep it right side up in a blow was to reduce sails and top hamper in a hurry as the wind rose. This started with reefing of the sails and often extended to sending down upper yards and topgallant masts, as well as rigging in the flying jibboom and even the jibboom. Carrying out such evolutions with alacrity required a very large crew, not to mention a high degree of discipline and training.

When the full naval complement of up to 155 crewmen was at general quarters, there were plenty of hands to carry out many tasks simultaneously and quickly. *Niagara* now sails with a crew of around forty, far fewer than the watch on deck in 1813. Today's crew, when further subdivided into watches, needs to be fast on its feet during sail evolutions; keeping the pinrails and deck space unencumbered by artillery is therefore important. Hosting large numbers of visitors would be difficult if the deck were crowded with guns, even though the appearance would be truer with a full battery. It was these practical considerations of longevity, stability, sail handling, and present usage that ruled out mounting the full battery.

The high bulwarks were meant to give the crew of the original brig protection against small-caliber ammunition. Cannonballs crashed right on through, but bulwarks stopped smaller grapeshot and canister shot.

Above the bulwarks are the hammock cloths, long canvas bags for stowing the crew's bedding, contained within iron brackets and wooden rails. Storing the hammocks on the rails by day got them out of the way and allowed for airing in good weather. During battle, the tightly packed mass of canvas and bedding gave a slight degree of added protection against musket balls and splinters.

The combined height over deck of bulwarks and hammock rails is just over 6 feet (1.83 m). Perhaps it was psychologically better for the original crew not to see the enemy about to loose a broadside at close range, but for today's crew it is a great inconvenience to have such a limited view out of the ship. The effect is to focus all attention on the deck area by screening out the outside world. In order to conn the ship, the officers must stand on a deck locker or similar elevated position. The taffrail across *Niagara*'s stern was therefore expanded into an anachronistic but extremely practical bridge deck to facilitate safe conning of the ship (fig. 1.12).

Another common feature of sailing warships was the covering of hatches by gratings. The mass of humans below deck required as much ventilation as possible, whereas a merchant ship with cargo to protect would have had hatches covered by canvas tarpaulins most of the time. *Niagara* today has several skylights and scuttles that are probably closer to a merchant vessel in appearance, and only the hatches in the forward half of the ship retain proper naval gratings. The reason for this compromise is again primarily one of manning. The original brig very likely had gratings in all its deck openings, yet today's brig has a small crew who cannot always be standing at the ready to open or close hatches in threatening weather.

The deck itself is also a compromise. The present ship has a deck of narrow planks sprung to follow the curve of the waterway, to keep the nibbing inboard as much as possible. This is a very good way to build a deck in terms of keeping it watertight. Narrow planks and many seams mean there is more caulking material to absorb the swelling and shrinking of the planks. The original ship would have had plank seams parallel to the centerline because it would have been far easier to lay a deck this way than to spring wide planks to a curve. The original planks would have been much wider because when hand-sawing every plank on a rush job, a few large planks can be cut from a log much faster than many small ones. In 1813, timber availability was not the problem; labor and time were.

Aside from the hurried construction using green wood (which would have shrunk mightily over the summer), there was a shortage of caulking material in 1813. Add in the tendency of wide planks to swell and shrink more than narrow planks, and we cannot escape the conclusion that the original deck leaked like a basket. A gruesome bit of corroborating evidence is found in one of Surgeon's Mate Usher Parson's accounts of the battle, wherein he mentions that the wounded on the berth deck had blood dripping on them through the seams of the deck above.[15]

At the forward end of the main deck, on the heel of the bowsprit, the ship's bell is mounted in a gallows. The present bell is a duplicate casting of an original now exhibited in the Erie Maritime Museum. The bell is considerably larger than normal for a ship of this size, for the good reason that it was not intended for a ship. The bell, dated 1799, was originally the town bell at Fort Erie, Ontario. In 1812, as the British naval squadron was being assembled, it was taken for use by *Queen Charlotte,* then flagship of the squadron. Upon its capture at the Battle of Lake Erie, the bell was transferred to *Niagara* and so came to the city of Erie.

Amidships, between the foremast and mainmast, are two sets of gallows, similar to heavy goal posts or the Greek letter Pi. The purpose of these was to allow for above-deck stowage of spare spars, sweeps, and probably the launch. The dimensions and location of these gallows are typical, but at 6 feet (1.83 m) the height is a modern compromise to avoid banging too many heads. The original height was probably 4 to 5 feet (1.22 to 1.52 m) in order to keep the weight of the boats and other items from getting too high off the deck.[16]

Proceeding down one of the hatches at either end of the gallows, we come to the berth deck, which runs the full length of the ship. This deck was home to the entire crew. The captain, two lieutenants, sailing master, purser, and surgeon had individual cabins around the wardroom, aft, which was their dining and meeting space. While cramped, the cabins did allow for some privacy and stowage of personal gear. The size and arrangement is typical of merchant vessels and warships throughout the age of sail. Even today the space allocation is not bad by sailing vessel standards. Amidships, in the vicinity of the mainmast, was the steerage, the much more cramped quarters where midshipmen and surgeon's mates hung their hammocks.[17]

It is when we go forward of the mainmast that the reality of a naval vessel is seen. Whereas a dozen or so commissioned and warrant officers occupied the area abaft the mainmast—about half of the living space in the ship—the rest of the crew, approximately 140 sailors, was crammed into the other half. If this sounds impossible on board a ship of this size, you guessed correctly. It was not possible to berth the entire crew at the same time. One watch, nearly half of the total company, had to be on deck at all times, if for no other reason than lack of room below.

Up near the bow are several small storerooms for the carpenter, gunner, armorer, steward, and sailmaker. These warrant officers or specialists also had small cabins, with perhaps two to four men per cabin, but they at least had a fixed bunk and a place for their sea chests. The galley is also up forward. Not much is known about its original arrangement. Perry's correspondence mentions the purchase of "iron cambooses" from Pittsburgh for the two large brigs.[18] The word *camboose* described a cast-iron galley stove, which on warships was typically placed beneath the weather deck and abaft the foremast, often beneath a hatch to permit the smoke and cooking smells to dissipate. The stove on the berth deck of the present *Niagara* is anachronistic, being of a late-nineteenth-century pattern, but it serves the same function well. *Niagara* underwent modifications to obtain a Certificate of Inspection from the US Coast Guard in 2005 for operation as a sailing school vessel. Watertight bulkheads were fitted and the galley became separated from the berthing area.

The remaining space on the berth deck is one undivided area, which was the sleeping and messing area for the enlisted crew. Marines berthed here at the after end, between the seamen and the wardroom. On board today's *Niagara,* up to twenty-four crew members can sling hammocks without jostling each other, if placed exactly according to allotted space. On some ships the spacing could not be varied because hammocks were slung from hooks driven into the deck beams. An alternate arrangement, a wooden jackstay batten fastened to the beams, allowed variation in lashing points. Today's *Niagara* loses some berthing space to the engine room, but even allowing for a more open berth deck and tighter hammock spacing, it would have been a sardine can of a squeeze for a watch of fifty to sixty in the original crew. The men did not "hot bunk," for each had his own hammock, but the space in which it was slung had to be shared.

Sleeping in a hammock, living out of a duffel bag, and extreme crowding were all part of naval life in this era. The coming and going of so many sailors and the working routines of the brig would have prevented any truly quiet time. The men probably were able to sleep only because the four-hours-on and four-hours-off watch schedule, with day work, drills, and all-hands evolutions in between, left everyone chronically fatigued. Given the least chance, sailors probably fell asleep on anything that did not have nails sticking out of it.

Today's ship has marine toilets below, in what would have been small storerooms in the original ship. The original crew had to answer nature's call by climbing out onto the headrig. There may have been a urinal trough, called a pissdale, on the inboard bulwarks forward, a practical arrangement that reduced the risk of falling overboard for the most frequent need. The officers may have had a small enclosed head in the stern quarters, but nothing definitive is known about these quite necessary practical details.

The headroom on the berth deck is only 5 feet (1.52 m) under the beams amidships, lessened by deck camber as one moves outboard. The single most common visitor comment is, "They must have been much shorter back then." True, but misleading. The average height at the time was less than today, but not under 5 feet; the original crew was obliged to duck as well. The height of the deck was set by the need to stow ballast and stores below the berth deck; the crew got what was left, and it was not much. On the few surviving inboard profiles of this period, it is not uncommon to find even less headroom on some vessels. Sailors went below to eat a meal or sleep and never had much time for either.

Below the berth deck lies the bilge. On board this brig the space is really too shallow to call a hold, being only 3 feet (0.91 m) from berth deck to ceiling along the keelson. Today's brig uses a large portion of the bilge space for storage tanks (diesel fuel, potable water, sewage holding) as well as engine beds and shaft alleys. None of this equipment would have existed in 1813. Then the space was used for a powder magazine, a shot locker, provisions in casks, various ship stores, and ballast.

It is here that the greatest difference between the original *Niagara* and her ocean-going contemporaries is apparent. Perry's brigs were built as shoal as possible to get over the bar in Erie Harbor. At the same time, they did not have to carry stores, especially fresh water, for a lengthy cruise. Sailors on Lake Erie drank right out of the lake. The original brig had a draft of 8 to 9 feet (2.44 to 2.74 m), while today's draws nearly 11 feet (3.35 m), the result of stern trim and an external ballast keel that doubles the depth of keel below the garboard. An ocean-going ship of this rate in 1813 would typically draw 15 to 19 feet (4.57 to 5.79 m) of water.[19]

A ship in saltwater service usually sailed on a cruise with food for six months and water for three. Water was relatively easy to obtain, usually by towing casks to a river with the boats, but large quantities of preserved food might not be available at any price in many foreign ports. The original *Niagara* was very similar in overall dimensions, armament, and rig to ocean-going sloops of war such as *Wasp, Frolic,* or *Peacock,* but those vessels had deeper holds for stores.

Below the stores lay the ballast. Stone had the advantage of being plentiful and free, but the Lake Erie brigs were too shoal to carry their armament and rigs if only stone was used. Among the squadron's correspondence is a letter from the secretary of the navy taking issue with Perry's "extravagance" in buying lead for ballast. Perry had little choice in the matter, for iron ballast was not available, and his brigs had not room enough below the berth deck to fit the quantity of stone ballast needed to keep them upright.[20]

Even on "authentic" museum ships, a great deal must be left to the imagination. No matter how correct the details and completeness of the outfit, the human presence of the crew is missing. During the months *Niagara* is in commission, it comes closer than most museum ships because a portion of the crew is always on duty during visiting hours. The wood-burning stove, painting or tarring work in progress, and operation of various hand tools all contribute authentic aroma and noise. *Niagara* would need a crew three times the present complement, living on board continuously to match the original vessel's pungent smells of many poorly washed men and boiling salt meat and the round-the-clock hubbub generated by 150 people living in cramped conditions.

In general, the level of effort required to do anything on board this brig is pretty daunting by modern standards. In the 1813 brig, there was always work for the many hands. Washing decks required drawing water by buckets. As stores were consumed, ballast needed to be shifted to maintain sailing trim. Bilges needed frequent pumping. The rig demanded constant adjustment and maintenance. The guns required frequent drill not only for crew proficiency but to keep the slides greased and the bores free of rust.

One of the more subtle differences between a sailing ship of the early nineteenth century and today's ships is the reliance on a human presence. Today's ships still require sailors, of course, but their numbers are much reduced. In the two hundred years since the War of 1812, vast design and engineering efforts have created machinery that eliminates the need for human muscle power. The square-rigged sailing ship is the product of another time, and as complicated as it may look, by today's standards it is a simple machine of wood and iron, sticks and string. Yet it only works with a large amount of effort. The complexity is not in the structure of the ship but is carried around in the heads of the crew. To get a feel for the technology of wooden warships, let us briefly examine some of the equipment and operations of *Niagara*.

Ground Tackle

Ground tackle, the seaman's collective term for anchors and cables, was among the heaviest and most vital gear on board a ship. In the age of sail, the greatest hazard ships faced was being driven ashore. This was particularly true on the confined waters of the Great Lakes, where one is never far from the hazard of a lee shore. Only the most developed ports of the early nineteenth century had wharves, and securing to a wharf was rarely an option on the undeveloped lakes.

A vessel of *Niagara*'s class ideally carried at least five anchors: two bowers, a sheet anchor, a stream anchor, and at least one kedge. The sailing of Perry's squadron in the summer of 1813 was delayed by a shortage of anchors when the Pittsburgh manufacturer was over a month late on a promised delivery. As a temporary measure, the ships were probably moored to pilings driven into the bottom.[21] The squadron may not have been fully equipped by the time it sailed, and it is possible some vessels had only one or two anchors each.

One of the most prominent pieces of deck equipment on board *Niagara* is the capstan, located abaft the mainmast (fig. 1.13). The capstan (or *capstern* in some contemporary sources) is a vertically mounted winch drum of heavy wooden construction. The lines or cables required to lift or pull heavy objects were led through blocks horizontally over the deck to be wound around the capstan. Motive power was provided by men pushing on long bars as they trudged in a circle around the device. The primary purpose of the capstan was to handle the ground tackle.

A frequently asked question on board *Niagara* is, "If the capstan is supposed to raise the anchors, why is it so far from the bow?" The answer to this lies in the method of handling anchor cables in the days before chain cable. The original anchor cables were of hemp, 4½ inches (11.5 cm) in diameter and quite stiff to handle. It was not feasible to wind this type of line directly around the capstan drum. Instead, the load was transferred to a smaller, more flexible cable called a messenger, which was set up as an endless loop around the perimeter of the deck. As the anchor cable came in at the bow, some room was needed for the crew to clean it of mud and sand. The cable was then attached to the messenger by a series of smaller lines called nippers. Ship's boys were responsible for binding with the nippers; they then walked aft with the moving cables, holding onto the nipper, not only

Figure 1.13. *Manning* Niagara's *capstan. This handy vertical winch allows the crew to efficiently carry out ponderous lifting and hauling jobs, chief among them the handling of the ground tackle (the anchors and their cables). When the capstan is not in use the long bars are removed and stowed to avoid encumbering the deck. (Photo by Sally Nuckles, courtesy of the Erie Maritime Museum.)*

to guard against slippage but to be ready to cast it off as the messenger neared the capstan. This had to be done before getting underfoot of the men walking the bars around. Passing a series of four to six nippers, and casting them off sequentially as the cables moved aft, demanded a long run of deck space.

The greatest strain on the cables and capstan is not in lifting the weight of the anchor but in breaking the anchor out of a firm bottom when a fluke is well set. Once the anchor is broken out and the crew is no longer struggling to haul the ship upwind or upstream, the bars can be hove round almost at a run to bring the anchor to the surface.

When the anchor is at the surface, the capstan is secured until a hand has gone over the bow to hook the catfalls onto the anchor ring. The catfalls are a sixfold purchase rove through the cat head, one of a pair of short timber davits projecting from either side of the bow. A hand-over-hand pull by a dozen hands gets the anchor catted, usually requiring some slack walked back on the anchor cable since the distance from anchor to cathead is greater than from hawse-pipe to surfaced anchor. To complete retrieving the anchor, it must be fished, meaning to get the flukes up and secured to the rail. On some ships this is done with a tackle from the topmast head, but on board *Niagara* and most sailing warships, an anchor davit is temporarily shipped and its tackle hooked to the flukes.

Ship's Boats

Boats were a vital part of working the ship. Because ships could rarely tie up to a wharf, instead having to anchor at some distance from land, communication with shore, communication with other ships, and the

Figure 1.14. *One of* Niagara's *small boats under sail. The logbook of Perry's brig* Lawrence *tells us that three boats were carried, the same number typically carried by the present-day* Niagara. *This boat proceeds under the sails of its two-masted sprit rig. (Courtesy of the US Brig* Niagara *Crew/Pennsylvania Historical and Museum Commission.)*

transfer of stores from shore to ship all required boats. A boat could be launched to rescue a man overboard or to ferry men ashore from a stranded vessel, but there was no thought of providing lifeboats for the ship's company in case of sinking. The various types of boats carried on a ship had specific functions depending on their size or design (fig. 1.14).

The only specific reference to the boats of the Lake Erie squadron is found in Sailing Master William Taylor's log of *Lawrence,* sister brig of *Niagara.* In his log, Taylor mentions a launch, a first cutter, and a second cutter but provides no dimensions or other details of these boats. As a whole, Perry's squadron seems to have been adequately (if minimally) equipped with small boats, for Noah Brown reported building fourteen of them and other boats were probably purchased

locally or came as existing outfit on the converted merchant vessels.[22]

The launch was a heavily built and capacious boat, intended for transporting anchors, provisions, guns, and other weighty cargoes. It was the single most important boat to be carried on a ship. A vessel of *Niagara*'s size required a launch between 20 feet and 26 feet (6.1 to 7.92 m), with the most likely length being around 24 feet (7.32 m). Most ships had only one launch, which was usually carried amidships on the gallows, the safest place at sea. The boat was launched by means of tackles from the stays and lower yards; this was not a quick procedure, but the launch was intended primarily for use in harbor. It was too heavy a boat to be carried in davits.

The cutter was a more lightly built yet still capacious

ship's boat, intended primarily for transporting men. Cutters were often fitted to sail as well as row. They could be either carvel or lapstrake built, but the latter was more likely in 1813. Warships usually carried two or more cutters, designated first, second, and so on. Cutters for a warship of *Niagara*'s class could be from 18 to 25 feet (5.49 to 7.62 m) in length, with most somewhere in the middle of this range. We know from Taylor that *Lawrence* carried a first and second cutter, and presumably *Niagara* had the same outfit. One cutter may have been nested in the launch, with the second hung from stern davits, or they both may have been carried in davits on the quarters. Since Taylor mentions no other boats, it is likely that each brig carried only a launch and two cutters, the two types most needed, although it was not uncommon for seagoing warships of this class to carry four or five boats.[23]

In 1813 the boats were not only a communication link between vessels or from ship to shore, they were also a means of moving the ship. This could be done by towing, but not very efficiently since it required tremendous effort from oarsmen in the boats in return for minimal progress. In shallow water, and much of Lake Erie qualifies as such, kedging was more practical. This meant employing the boats to carry a small kedge anchor some distance ahead of the ship. Once the anchor was dropped, the ship's company could haul the ship up to it using the windlass while the boat was moving forward to drop the next kedge.

"Out Sweeps!"

A third means of moving the ship in the absence of wind was to use sweeps. A sweep is a large oar worked by the crew standing between the guns and pushing or pulling. On a vessel of *Niagara*'s construction and size, this was not a practical way to travel any distance, yet for movements within harbor, to get the ship past a hazard she may have been drifting on, or perhaps to bring her broadsides to bear if becalmed in action, sweeps were invaluable.

Did *Niagara* have sweeps? The most direct evidence is in the photographs taken of the salvaged wreck in 1913, which clearly show small, square openings in the bulwarks between the gunports (see fig. 1.5). Many contemporary ship plans show sweep ports, including ships built by Noah Brown.[24] For a naval vessel with a large crew and the necessity of maneuver at all

times, sweeps made sense. Among the Daniel Dobbins Papers held at the Erie County Historical Society in Buffalo, New York, is a receipt from March 1813 for acceptance of sixty sweeps between 20 and 25 feet (6.09 and 7.62 m) long. Eighteen 25-foot-long sweeps would be a full outfit for the large brigs. Presuming thirty-six would be needed for both, that would leave six each for the smaller gunboats built in Erie.

Curiously, no account of the 1813 campaign mentions sweeps in use on board the large brigs. The absence of specific mention is puzzling, especially in Sailing Master Taylor's log of the *Lawrence*. This log, the only known surviving logbook of the squadron, records which sails were set and taken in, when boats were away, the routine work and drills on board, and the anchoring and weighing of *Lawrence*. It may be that use of sweeps was so common as not to be worthy of mention. This sounds unlikely, but then I have never found mention of sweeps in any contemporary seamanship treatise, perhaps because explanation was deemed unnecessary.

The question of whether *Niagara* had sweeps affects our interpretation of the great controversy of the Battle of Lake Erie, namely, Jesse Elliot's failure to close with the British early in the battle. Defenders of Elliot have claimed disparities in the sailing qualities of the two sister brigs or vagaries of the light breeze that day. Since we know Elliott was engaged at long gun range but not carronade range, the distance involved was only about two-thirds of a mile. If proof is ever found that sweeps were indeed part of *Niagara*'s outfit, there can be no doubt that deliberate intent rather than circumstance kept Elliot from closely supporting Perry.

Today's *Niagara* has eighteen sweeps, 30 feet (9.14 m) long, which are stowed on the gallows amidships. In 1995 an operational trial was carried out in Erie Harbor to assess the brig's maneuverability under oars (fig. 1.15). Several hours of pier-side drill preceded the event to practice getting the sweeps off the gallows and out the ports and to determine how best to work them. A volunteer crew of one hundred manned the sweeps, on the theory that a gun crew of six or seven would be available for each one.

It was quickly apparent that this many people could not be efficiently used simultaneously. The inboard portion of the sweep is about 8 feet (2.44 m), roughly the inboard-outboard ratio of a single banked pulling

Figure 1.15. *Propelling* Niagara *by sweeps. Operational trials showed that a two-person team was optimal for using the sweeps and that sweeps were only effective in calm or low-wind-and-wave conditions. (Photo by Linda Bolla, courtesy of the Erie Maritime Museum.)*

boat. Manning each sweep with six placed the outboard crew members in a position of insufficient leverage and too close to the deck to be effective. The most efficient method proved to be two people per sweep, facing each other while standing as far inboard as possible. The push-pull action could either be done for a long stroke, walking three paces for stroke and return, or standing in one place and limiting the stroke length to how far the rowers could lean without shifting footing. The short-stroke method proved least fatiguing and prevented the rowers on different sweeps from interfering with each other. This method also offered the least chance of tripping or barking shins on the gun carriages.

At the time of the sweep trials, the brig was rigged down to lower masts and housed topmasts, so the windage was greatly reduced. This was probably just enough of an advantage to offset the lack of experience on the part of the crew. The day began in nearly flat calm conditions, and it proved possible to get the ship up to two and a half knots for a distance of three-quarters of a mile before the crew needed a rest. Turning proved difficult. Giving way on one side while backwatering or holding water on the other was only feasible in flat calm. As a light breeze of three to five knots came up, it was only possible to turn with forward way on. Later in the day the breeze increased to eight knots or more, and it proved impossible to make any headway with the sweeps.

The conclusions were that the most efficient method

was to use only two people per sweep, working short strokes, but to relieve them every fifteen to twenty minutes. Even allowing for the lack of experience of our crew, I would venture to say that sweeps were only practical against winds of less than five knots for short periods. In a flat calm, however, a steady knot or knot and a half would be sustainable for quite awhile through frequent rotations. The sweeps are well counterweighted by the inboard loom, and the power required per stroke is minimal. Endurance would tell more than strength. The hardest part of the drill proved to be not the rowing but learning to shift the sweeps from gallows to ports without cracking heads or mashing knuckles.

Masts, Spars, Rigging, and Sails

Now that we have covered ground tackle, boats, and sweeps, we can get on to the subject of masts, spars, and rigging. But, first, another word about that vital factor in the design of all ships, and wooden sailing warships in particular: stability. Keeping the ship right side up is a prerequisite for arriving anywhere. For the crews of the 1812-era lakers, stability meant balancing the weight of the ballast and stores below the waterline against the weight of guns and wind heel on the sailing rig above. The center of gravity had to be within acceptable limits, neither too high nor too low.

Too much stability can be nearly as bad as not enough and was a common error. If the center of gravity was placed too low, the ship might whip like a metronome. The resultant hard rolling could exhaust and injure the crew and in some cases snap the masts out of the ship. While in theory the stiffer the better for windward performance and ultimate safety, a ship that was too stiff was simply unendurable on a passage.[25] A slow and easy roll was not only less wear on crew and rigging but was also a prerequisite for a steady gun platform.

Too much stability was a problem likely to plague a sailing merchant ship; warships of this era, and the shallow-hulled lake warships in particular, usually suffered from the opposite problem—too little stability. Warships carried a large sail area and were burdened with a great weight of armament carried on deck rather than low in the hold as a commercial cargo would be. As stores in the hold of a warship were consumed, the center of gravity proportionally rose, exacerbating stability problems.

Stability problems became particularly serious when

Figure 1.16. Niagara *with all sails set. The tall, high-performance sailing rig made* Niagara *fast and maneuverable, essential traits for a fighting vessel, but the rig also demanded a large, highly trained crew to be effective. (Photo by Robert Lowry, courtesy of the Erie Maritime Museum.)*

sailing in strong winds. In order to maintain stability as the wind force increased, it was a life or death matter to get sail off in time. Blustery weather with frequent squalls kept a crew constantly on the go. As mentioned previously, this shortening down included upper spars as well as sails. The log of *Lawrence* records several instances of sending down topgallant yards and masts as weather deteriorated.

One difference between *Niagara*'s rig and more modern square riggers is in the general proportion of spar weights (fig. 1.16). In the early nineteenth century, the lower masts of warships were often unusually heavy, on the expectation that they could not be replaced at sea and would be exposed to shot damage. Topmasts differed little over the course of the nineteenth century, but topgallant and royal masts were very light compared to later standards. Part of the reason for this was to provide ease of handling of a spar that would be sent up and down regularly. Just as important was the intent to provide a weak link. The upper sails were of

lighter cloth and the spars were also lighter, so that in the event the crew failed to anticipate the severity of a squall, the blowing out of sails or carrying away of spars might relieve the ship before it heeled beyond the point of no return. Later in the nineteenth century, as ships grew in size and steel spars became available, it became less practical to rig down spars for heavy weather but more realistic to expect them to survive if left aloft. Surviving a knockdown was then more dependent upon the sails blowing out and on the loading configuration and inherent stability of the hull.

Another feature of rigging in *Niagara*'s period is the absence of metal fittings. In the decades that followed the War of 1812, iron became increasingly available and affordable and was used more extensively for reinforcing bands, joints, and connections such as shackles. Yet on board *Niagara* there is not one shackle aloft; chainplates and lower deadeye straps are the only iron in the rig.

In the hemp and wood era, every item in the rigging, no matter how massive, was secured by binding it heavily with small cordage called *seizing.* Enough turns of small stuff added up to enough friction to hold. This meant that even on board a massive first rate such as HMS *Victory,* the entire rig could be assembled and dis-assembled with a sheath knife and a fid. The great advantage of this was that repair of storm or battle damage required no complicated tools, and even shot-up cordage could be respliced or recycled into small stuff for seizings. The crew could carry out rigging repairs independent of shipyard facilities. The disadvantage of a hemp-only rig is that it is much more subject to chafe and needs frequent adjustment. Clapping on several seizings takes much longer than replacing a shackle. A hemp-only rig has an insatiable appetite for hand labor. Keeping the rig set up tight enough, but not too tight, demanded constant vigilance from skilled mariners.

In fact, the seemingly primitive nature of the materials, the reliance on organic cordage rather than forged iron, can mask the true sophistication of the rig. It was critical for just the right knots, seizings, sennits, etc., to be employed both to minimize chafe and for workability. In short, such a rig was only viable with highly skilled labor available.

All large sailing craft contain two types of lines in their rigs: standing rigging and running rigging. Standing rigging consists of the shrouds and stays that support the masts and their weight of spars and sails. As the name suggests, these lines are more or less fixed in place and are often coated with tar for protection from the elements. Deadeyes and lanyards permitted the crew to loosen or tighten the tension in the rig as circumstances required. Standing rigging had to be substantial enough to hold the masts firmly against the strain of winds and the ship's motion, yet flexible enough to provide some give and take. It demanded a fine balance: not too tight, not too slack. Maintaining this balance with humidity- and temperature-sensitive hemp cordage was a constant struggle.

Modern yacht rigging works because of the vastly stronger materials that are available to us: fiberglass hulls, metal masts and spars, wire stays, and synthetic sails and cordage. A rig assembled from these materials needs few shrouds and stays, can withstand high tension, and does not have to be adjusted on a daily basis. The rig of the original *Niagara,* limited to traditional but much weaker organic materials, depended

instead upon multiple shrouds and stays to ease the load on individual lines and distribute the load over a larger area of the hull. The rig of *Niagara* was a complex instrument, however basic its component materials might seem to our modern sensibilities.

Today's *Niagara* compromises on the issue of authentic materials. Hemp cordage is hard to find, especially in the sizes required for this rig. Even if it were available and affordable, the authentic stuff would carry the authentic burden of high labor costs. Therefore, the standing rigging of the 1990-built brig initially consisted of wire rope for the lower shrouds, lower stays, topmast stays, topmast shrouds, and backstays. In 1993–94, standing rig above the lowers was replaced with a polyester material promisingly named "Ultra Strong," composed of four strands and with stretch characteristics similar to new hemp. The entire standing rigging was again renewed in 2007–2008 in four-strand Kevlar, which has proven very satisfactory while reducing the weight on each mast by about 1000 pounds (453 kg). "Shakedown," incidentally, is a truly accurate term. No matter how tautly set up the standing rig seems dockside, sailing for a few hours in winds over twenty knots and seas of 5 feet (1.52 m) will shift and loosen stays and shrouds. A second tuning of the rig will then last a long time.

Running rigging is the term used to describe the moving lines that work the spars and sails. The running rigging of the reconstructed *Niagara* is much closer to the original in that extensive use is made of organic fiber line, chiefly manila. This is a different material than hemp but is still subject to great changes due to moisture and requires care in use. Running rigging needs to be checked constantly for chafe and wear. A frequent job is end-for-ending, or reversing the lead of a line through the blocks to shift the wear points, or shifting the end splice or seizing enough to freshen the nip, the point of greatest strain where a line rides over a sheave.

There are about two hundred lines in *Niagara*'s running rigging (fig. 1.17). You might think the captain would know the exact number, but it changes from year to year as we experiment with slight alterations in the rig. In all, about four miles (6.4 km) of the stuff runs through nearly three hundred blocks. Maintaining this machine is a never-ending task, both then and now.

One of the major operational differences between a merchant ship and a warship was in how they set

Figure 1.17. *Some of the many lines in* Niagara's *rig. Looking aft at the mainmast from a vantage point at the foremast, this photograph shows the incredible profusion of standing and running rigging that supports the brig's masts and allows manipulation of the yards and sails. Two sailors pause on the topgallant mast shrouds, while a third climbs out on the topgallant yard. (Photo by John Baker, courtesy of the Erie Maritime Museum.)*

Prior to sailing *Niagara,* I sailed the *Elissa,* an iron barque built in 1877 and restored by the Galveston Historical Foundation. Both ships have nearly the same sail area, 12,000 square feet (3657.6 m), and many spar dimensions are similar, but *Niagara* has half the displacement and thus a proportionately larger rig. *Elissa* was designed to sail with ten overworked men, while *Niagara* was designed to sail with well over one hundred. Both ships sail today with crews of about forty. On board *Elissa* this is delightful; on board *Niagara* it is just enough. Coming to *Niagara* after *Elissa,* I expected the brig's rig to be more work, perhaps 30 percent more workload for the crew. It took no time at all to learn that I was dead wrong—the workload increase was more like 200 percent. For the mission of a warship, this was an acceptable price. Survival might hinge upon how quickly yards could be braced around to back or fill, pivoting the ship to keep her guns bearing or to prevent being raked.

The object of all this hauling of running rigging was control of the sails, the engine that runs on air to move the ship. Sails were a major investment, then and now. I have no data on their service life in naval ships, but research done for *Elissa* indicated that on board a merchant ship, about eighteen months of steady use was the average life. Sails had to be handled carefully and repaired frequently, and making new ones was a never-ending job.

The original brig's sails were most likely flax, as cotton did not come into general use on US ships until some years later. Flax or cotton, organic fiber sails were extremely vulnerable to mildew and rot and had to be loosed for drying after every spell of rainy weather. The reduced size of *Niagara*'s current crew makes such authenticity impractical. The present sails are Oceanus, a new synthetic, or Duradon, an earlier canvas substitute. These sails are inherently stronger than the originals, a plus in terms of replacement costs and freedom from incidents of blown-out sails. The downside is that since the sails are now unlikely to blow out, the weak link is only in the spars. The sails and standing rigging are stronger than the originals; the running rigging and spars are roughly the same.

The most oft heard myth about sailing is, "The wind is free!" So is oil as long as you leave it in the ground. Harnessing the energy for useful work is where the expense comes in. The fuel bill for sailing ships was expressed in men, wood, rope, and canvas.

up their running rigging. A merchant ship's operation was governed by economy, particularly the need to extract the maximum work from the minimum crew. To get by with fewer hands, merchant rigs typically used more multi-sheaved blocks (and more line) to gain a higher power of purchase in the tackles. The initial investment in blocks and line was a bit higher, but this would be offset in the long term by the ability of fewer people to sail the ship.

The running rigging of a merchant vessel was economical in terms of muscle power, but the penalty was slower performance as more line must be hauled through the blocks to accomplish a given task. In a warship the dominant need was for speed of maneuver, and the large crew needed to man the guns was more than enough to handle the ship under sail, so the availability of muscle power was not an issue. Warship rigs were characterized by low purchases on even the most heavily loaded rigging; this, combined with the larger sail areas typical of a warship, meant harder pulling. These rigs depended on a large number of strong young sailors.

Sailing Performance

What is my overall assessment of sailing *Niagara*? After many years of sailing the barque *Elissa*, the outstanding lesson for me is that while a naval and merchant ship might resemble each other as square riggers, they are two different animals. The naval rig being proportionately larger gives higher performance, but at the expense of much higher labor requirements.

Niagara is a relatively small vessel when measured by its hull dimensions, but it is a very large brig, about the upper limit for this type of sailing rig (plate 3a). Were the hull any larger, it would have been rigged as a three-masted ship. Early naval vessels were sometimes built as brigs and later re-rigged as ships to make them easier to handle. In a brig, the square sails are proportionately larger than in a ship rig of the same hull size, but the spanker is even more extreme. The large spanker gives speed, power, and the leverage to pivot the ship quickly for tacking. This is why the brig rig was so popular for vessels requiring quick and certain maneuver, such as collier brigs working up a river or naval brigs on inshore patrol.

The downside is that this sail can be a monster to get in, particularly if sailing closehauled with the yards braced up sharp. In this situation, the lee yardarm of the mainyard is near the gaff. If brailing in is not done properly, it is very easy to wrap the sail around the mainyard, which means the sail will not come in and the mainyards cannot be braced until the spanker is hauled taut again to clear it and the evolution started over. In certain circumstances, such as running off before a squall, this simple error could prevent a brig from falling off in time to avoid disaster. This is why most ocean-going vessels expecting to work in high latitudes opted for a three-mast rig. Both Cook's *Endeavour* and Darwin's *Beagle* were built as brigs but for voyages of exploration were converted to barques. Stepping a small mizzen mast retained a small spanker aft for leverage but got rid of the large spanker liability.

Niagara is very fast. How fast? I do not know and am not too anxious to find out. I get paid to bring it back in one piece, and lacking the incentive of shot splashing close astern, I will always be disinclined to push the limits of the performance envelope. For practical purposes, I consider it to be a good ten-knot ship, maybe eleven. Yes, the theoretical hull speed is at least 13.75 knots, and many smaller vessels have been driven faster. Speed records do not tell us, however, how fast a sailing vessel can be driven, only how fast anybody lived to boast about it.

What makes *Niagara* fast is not its top-end speed but how easily it gathers way in light air, how little wind it takes to get it moving at five to eight knots. Typically it will sail at half wind speed up to about twenty knots of wind. *Niagara* is comfortable sailing at speeds up to about ten and a half knots, by which time topsails are reefed and only about one-third of the total sail area is in use because by now it is blowing about twenty-five knots and the seas are lumping up. It is obviously capable of more speed, but creaking and groaning complaints from above make it equally obvious that masts are straining.

With its sharp hull, large rig, and low freeboard, *Niagara* is essentially a high-performance, light-air vessel, at its best in ten to fifteen knots of wind and seas under 3 feet (0.91 m). In these conditions it will outsail most vessels of this size. In winds of fifteen to twenty-five knots and seas up to 5 or 6 feet (1.52 to 1.83 m), it will sail well but require more extensive shortening down than your typical merchant square rigger or sail training ship. To date we have not sailed closehauled in winds over thirty knots and hope to continue to avoid this need. We have encountered several squalls in the forty-to-fifty-knot range but have always been able to get sail off and run off before the wind. The key to good passages in this ship is seeking shelter early and staying put until the right weather window comes along.

It was no different in 1813, just more difficult. With no weather warning systems, no exact charts, no auxiliary engine power, and weaker materials for sails, standing rigging, and ground tackle, sailing was an inherently dangerous business. Of course, compared to the hazards of combat, drowning was merely an incidental risk, albeit an ever-present one.

Guns and Round Shot: Fighting the Brig

This brings us to the last major element of this integrated machine, what in modern parlance is described as the weapons system. In War of 1812–era naval vessels, this was a battery of muzzle-loading cannon. The ultimate purpose of *Niagara,* of its hull, equipment, and rig, was to bring broadsides to bear upon the British foe, to defeat their ships, and to thereby achieve and maintain naval superiority on the Upper Lakes.

Niagara was designed around its battery. When Comm. Isaac Chauncey instructed Noah Brown to build *Lawrence* and *Niagara,* he specified that each was to carry twenty guns, which in contemporary naval classification defined the two brigs as "sloops of war" (vessels mounting eighteen to twenty-two guns). The original battery consisted of eighteen 32-pounder carronades and two 12-pounder long guns. The long guns were mounted on four-wheel carriages to permit shifting from bow to stern as chase guns, and the carronades were carried on pivoting mounts that consisted of a bed supporting a recoil-absorbing slide. The guns were mounted on 10-foot centers from stem to stern, a high concentration of hitting power in a small space.

By the War of 1812, most US Navy sloops of war were carrying 32-pounder carronades as principal armament (fig. 1.18). Carronades were short-range weapons. The tradeoff was that for the same weight of gun and carriage, roughly 3000 pounds (1360.8 kg), one could use a long gun to throw a 12-pound ball just over a mile (1.6 km) or use a carronade to project a 32-pound ball about one-third of a mile (.53 km). The opening of the Battle of Lake Erie showed the major disadvantage of carronades, for an opponent with long guns could inflict severe damage before the carronades were within range.

Why the reliance on carronades? The answer lies in the size of the ships. On a larger vessel such as a frigate, the displacement was sufficient to support a heavier battery of long guns, with carronades merely supplementing firepower at close range. The larger vessel was also the steadier gun platform, giving more chance of a hit at longer ranges. A frigate's armament was only about 5 percent of its total displacement, and thus the greater weight of long guns for a given size ball was less important. For a brig of *Niagara*'s rate, the armament was nearly 10 percent of total displacement and the weight of the battery was more critical.[26]

At the same time, the smaller ship was more subject to motion, thus decreasing the chances for accurate gunnery at long range. The accuracy of smooth bore guns was inherently poor, for besides the obvious lack of rifling, the windage of the bore (the degree to which the ball was undersized to facilitate loading) meant that the ball might leave the muzzle not exactly centered on the bore. Even more important on a moving vessel was the uncertainty of ignition relative to the roll of the vessel. A fraction of a second difference in the time it took for the priming to ignite the charge could be the difference between the shot splashing short of its target and flying high and over it. In any kind of shooting, the distribution of shot is in a cone of increasing diameter as the range opens, but smooth bore guns had a particularly short, wide cone of distribution.

The practical result was that most naval actions of this era were decided at short range. There was every incentive to open fire as soon as possible in the hope of getting lucky and bringing down a mast, smashing the tiller or wheel, or killing the enemy commander. Luck aside, the decisive factors were rate of fire and weight of fire once the range had been brought down to reduce the penalty of inaccuracy. If the battle was likely to end up at close quarters, and in most naval actions of the time it did, the carronade became very attractive. With a shorter barrel and sliding carriage, it was quicker to load than a long gun. Throwing heavier shot for a given weight of gun was of course the most desirable feature.

Capturing the enemy vessel was the object of sea battles during the era of sailing navies. Not only did capture allow the prize to be used by the victor, but on a practical level, sinking was hard to achieve and rarely a result. When balls hit the water, the tendency was either to skip or to sink rapidly. The only way a ship was likely to be hit below the waterline was when bottom planking was exposed during a roll or in the trough of a wave. Sometimes ships damaged in battle foundered in subsequent rough weather, but sinking during an action was a rare occurrence.

Inducing surrender meant killing and maiming the opposing crew until the remainder became discouraged enough to strike their colors. This was an elementary yet brutal exchange. Weight of shot was fixed by the gun, but rate of fire was dependent upon training, discipline, and courage. For obvious reasons, gunnery drill was a deadly serious business, being the key determinant between winning and losing. Naval battles in this era were mostly short-range artillery duels between closely packed masses of men in easily penetrated wooden structures, with predictably horrific results. A visitor to *Lawrence* the morning after the Battle of Lake Erie described a main deck "covered with blood, which was still adhering to the plank in clots— brains, hair and fragments of bones, were still sticking to the rigging and sides."[27] A review of all War of 1812 naval engagements in Theodore Roosevelt's *Naval War of 1812* reveals average losses of 12 to 15 percent for the

Figure 1.18. *One of* Niagara's *carronades. Known as "ship smashers," these handy, lightweight guns allowed small warships like* Niagara *to fire broadsides of very heavy shot. Fighting had to be done at very close range, which could be a problem if a foe was armed with long guns and kept beyond the reach of your carronades. Carronades were typically mounted on the special mount seen here, a combination bed and slide that pivoted on a bolt fastened to the gunport sill. (Courtesy of the US Brig* Niagara *Crew/ Pennsylvania Historical and Museum Commission.)*

winning crew and 30 percent on the losing vessel. Of these losses, typically 20 to 25 percent were fatalities.

Well-managed guns were a hazard to the enemy, but what is less obvious is how dangerous the guns were to their own crews. In rough sea conditions, guns might break free of their lashings and crush or maim crew members attempting to secure them before damage was done to the ship. The movement of the gun during drill or battle could crush feet or smash knees. In the heat of action, there were ample opportunities for accidents. A premature ignition of the powder while ramming home a charge would fire the ramrod out of the gun, usually with the hand and forearm of the loader as well. Cast-iron guns occasionally burst due to flaws in their manufacture, killing or injuring nearby gun crew.[28]

The literature of the time indicates that wooden splinters caused more casualties than shot. This makes perfect sense since the rate of fire was slow, at best one round a minute per gun, and the chances of being dismembered by a ball were slim. Yet the quantity of debris scattered about as a ball ripped through the wooden fabric of a ship made the chances of being speared by a jagged splinter very high.

The exact nature of 1812-era battle damage has never been fully documented. In the nature of an experiment, and to create an exhibit for the Erie Maritime Museum, a live fire exercise was conducted in early 1998 to replicate the effects of round shot fired into a ship's structure. Our specific intent was to reproduce the effect of British fire upon *Lawrence*. A 20-foot-long (6.1 m) section of hull was built to represent the brig from waterline up; it contained two gunports, two sweep ports, a length of channel with chainplates and deadeyes, and an 8-foot-wide (2.44 m) section of the deck. The plans of the present *Niagara* were used for the scantlings, but the species of wood were based on the original hull. The section was framed and planked with freshly cut red oak, and the decks and bulwark were planked with white pine. When completed, the section was mounted on a heavy timber cradle.

The replica guns on board *Niagara* were cast with this project in mind, and they were fully capable of live fire. *Niagara*'s carronades were 32 pounders, but the largest guns in the British squadron were 24 pounders, along with a variety of smaller sizes. The new guns were therefore cast as 32s, but only one was bored as such. Another was bored as a 24 pounder, and the others as 12 pounders.

This exercise was made possible by the assistance of the Pennsylvania National Guard and the US Army. The Guard made a logistics training exercise out of transporting both the guns and target section to and from the artillery training range at Fort Indiantown Gap in central Pennsylvania. Three carronades were transferred from the ship to a flatbed trailer and mounted as a broadside on timbers that secured the pivot bolts and ring bolts for breeching and tackles.

During the previous season, we had trained a gun crew on board *Niagara* and to get a feel for recoil had graduated from firing blanks to firing larger charges against heavier loads of sand in a bag. Recoil is simply the force of the gunpowder charge overcoming the inertia of whatever is in the bore. Sand allowed us to slowly work up to full charges against full weight of shot without wasting shot or needing a mile of empty lake downrange. A local foundry cast shot, and a few of these were fired into the lake as well. This careful program yielded a safe gun crew and functioning guns but no experience in actually hitting a target.

Firing at the ship section was done at ranges of 200 and 100 yards (182.88 and 91.44 m), typical of the Battle of Lake Erie.[29] Because we were intending to replicate British fire upon the *Lawrence,* only 12 and 24 pounders were used. The ground was level, and the trailer-mounted guns were at the same height they would have been on board the ship. The absence of motion helped accuracy, which offset our inexperience. Still, there were several misses, some of which may have been hits on a full-sized ship. After the first four rounds, hits were consistent except for the occasional shot that was on target but passed through a gunport.

Our procedure was to fire a round from both 12- and 24-pounder guns, then walk downrange to record damage while waiting for the guns to cool prior to reloading. Charges varied between one-eighth and one-sixth of the weight of the ball. This may have made a difference in accuracy with experienced gunners, but we could discern no difference in destructive effect. There was also no observable difference in damage between 200- and 100-yard ranges, although there might have been had we been able to fire at maximum range.

Ignition was by linstock and slow match. Perry's Lake Erie squadron may have had flint gunlocks, which were widely used by the US and Royal Navies at this time, but there is no definitive evidence of their availability on the US ships. Hearing protection was worn by all, and these guns were still extremely loud. Our earlier firing of reduced-charge blanks in no way compared with the noise of full charges fired against the resistance of a ball. In 1813, shattered eardrums must have been a common casualty.

Muzzle velocity was not accurately measured. Gunnery manuals of the time listed 750 feet (228.6 m) per second as typical, and a spherical projectile slows quickly due to aerodynamic drag.[30] The balls in flight could be clearly heard tearing the air with a "zzshh"

Figure 1.19. *The exterior of the deck-and-bulwark section after live-fire testing. Two strikes are visible in this photograph. One shot hit the edge of the channel supporting the deadeyes, tearing a gouge across the width of the timber. The second shot hit two planks beneath the channel and passed through the bulwark timbers, leaving a relatively small hole on the outside of the vessel. (Photo by Jeff Reidel/Flagship Media, courtesy of the Erie Maritime Museum.)*

sound. Impact on the ship section sounded like a sledge hammer striking on wood.

External damage was less than we expected (fig. 1.19). Every ball penetrated clean through the section, but the holes did not even admit daylight. The side of the section was composed of 3-inch (7.62 cm) oak planking, 10-inch (25.4 cm) oak frames, and 3-inch (7.62 cm) oak ceiling. Above deck, the bulwarks were planked with 2½-inch (6.35 cm) pine. The shot tore the surface grain of the outside planking, compressing the wood fibers, but the fibers had nowhere to go due to the density of the underlying wood. The result was that each time a ball passed through the plank, the torn and shredded wood sprung back into place. The exact size of the ball was evident in the broken paint line, but it was impossible to poke even a finger through the hole. Clearly, what often kept wooden ships afloat during and after battle was not only that the overwhelming majority of hits were above waterline, but that the filling in of the hole with wood fiber, almost a self-sealing phenomenon, limited ingress of water and made the holes easier to plug.

The interior was an entirely different story, offering a classic example of exit wounds in organic material (fig. 1.20). On the inside, each ball tore out large areas of ceiling and bulwark planking, spraying the debris

as far as 75 feet (22.86 m) away. Splinters varied from toothpick size to up to 4 feet (1.22 m) long and several inches thick. The ship section had been positioned in front of a small stand of dead locust trees, some of them 10 inches (25.4 cm) or more in diameter, and several of these were felled by balls that had already passed through the ship section. Based on this evidence, it seems that a large number of the shot a ship received in action would go right through both sides of a ship. The disengaged side might actually suffer worse damage because the planking torn out by the exiting shot would be on the exterior of the hull.

The deck in this exercise was populated with ten cutout figures representing the gun crew. These were plywood silhouettes with an inch of Styrofoam glued on. The intent was to get an idea of splinter distribution and the likelihood of getting hit. The figures were completely wiped out midway through the exercise, a demonstration that left us wondering how anyone was left fit for duty after a prolonged engagement.

One round of 24-pounder grapeshot was fired at 200 yards and two rounds at 100 yards. Two rounds of canister were also fired at the closer range. The grapeshot were 2-inch-diameter (5.08 cm) iron balls, fifteen to a round. At 200 yards, the scatter was so great that few hit the 10-foot-by-20-foot ship section. At 100 yards, grapeshot imbedded itself partway through the hull planking. Some bulwark planking was shot through where not backed up by a frame. The canister consisted of a tin of .75 caliber lead musket balls, 215 to a round. These imbedded beneath the surface of the planking. The pattern of hits on the planking gave a rough idea of how many of the grapeshot and canister balls would pass inboard through the large open gun-ports, and it proved to be quite enough to decimate a gun crew.

Twenty-five rounds in all were fired at the ship target, of which twenty-one were hits, including the grapeshot and canister. The target section represented about 10 percent of the total exposed hull area, while the two guns used were equal to the number that would be brought to bear on this much hull area in a close-range exchange of broadsides. In an actual engagement, the rate of fire would begin at perhaps one round per minute and deteriorate after the first half dozen broadsides as fatigue, casualties, and damage mounted. If we suppose twenty rounds per hour as an

Figure 1.20. *The interior of the deck-and-bulwark section after live-fire testing. Shot exiting the insides of the bulwarks tore splinters from the frame tops and interior planking, leaving this ragged damage and scattering pieces across the deck. The effect of such hits was devastating for gun crews on the tightly packed decks. (Erie Maritime Museum Collection, courtesy of the Pennsylvania Historical and Museum Commission.)*

average and no more than two-thirds hits, the damage inflicted in this exercise gives an idea of what *Lawrence* looked like midway through the battle.

Among the lessons learned was that even after victory, a secondary fight was just beginning to save the ship and as many of the wounded as possible, the human wreckage being the more daunting task by far. On board larger vessels, damage may not have been proportionately severe, for their heavier guns were still smaller relative to overall size and displacement. Smaller combatants such as *Lawrence* and *Niagara* were clearly "egg shells armed with hammers," and the only feasible defense in these warships was superior gunnery training: knock your foes to pieces before they could do the same to you.

Conclusions

The more one learns about the operation of sailing warships, the more respect one gains for the men who built them and served in them. When one understands the thought process behind the technology and how severely materials limited the options, one is struck by the efficiency of the solutions. These were intelligent people doing the best they could with what was available to them. It presumes a lot to hope the same will be said of us two centuries from now.

Sailing *Niagara* is not a reenactment. There is no "time out" or "cut" that permits you to take it again from the top of the script. It is a real-time activity with real wind, real waves, and real hazards. The dangers are only less in that we have more technology to limit them. The essence of seamanship is doing difficult tasks safely in a dangerous environment. In striving to best use our resources today to sail safely, we become all the more appreciative of how hard this was in previous centuries.

Knowledge is important, but it must be coupled with experience before it translates into ability. The lessons of traditional seamanship emerge only slowly, over time. On board *Niagara* we have been privileged to experiment for over two decades, and there is still no end of things to try and ways to improve. There are also limits to what we can extrapolate from *Niagara,* because the brig is not completely authentic: the hull is built in a different manner with different materials, it does not carry its full battery of guns, the rig is not all hemp, the sails are not organic, and so on. Such authenticity would carry authentic burdens of labor costs for construction, maintenance, and repair that are too expensive on this scale. There are nevertheless enough parallels to give valid insight into that distant time. Sailing *Niagara* and firing its carronades provides us with a three-dimensional understanding of the realities of naval life, an understanding that goes beyond what we can read in documents or infer from archaeological discoveries.

NOTES

1. William Dudley, ed., *The Naval War of 1812: A Documentary History,* vol. 2 (Washington, DC: Naval Historical Center, 1992), pp. 406–407, 426–27.

2. Dudley, ed., *Naval War of 1812,* vol. 2, pp. 426–27.

3. The extraordinary efforts of Brown, Perry, and Dobbins to build and outfit the US Navy's Lake Erie squadron have been described in a number of publications. These include Noah Brown, "The Remarkable Statement of Noah Brown," *Journal of American History* 8, no. 1 (January-March 1914), pp. 103–108; Max Rosenberg, *The Building of Perry's Fleet on Lake Erie, 1812–1813* (Harrisburg, PA: The Pennsylvania Historical and Museum Commission, 1987); David Curtis Skaggs and Gerard T. Altoff, *A Signal Victory: The Lake Erie Campaign of 1812–1813* (Annapolis: The Naval Institute Press, 1997).

4. *Lawrence*'s sick list numbered thirty-one or thirty-two on the day of battle. It is not clear if any of the sick were on board the brig on the day of the action and, if so, whether they were able to muster strength to fight. Dudley, ed., *Naval War of 1812,* vol. 2, pp. 561–63. The battle casualty percentages used for comparison were obtained by averaging the figures provided in Theodore Roosevelt's *The Naval War of 1812* (Annapolis: The Naval Institute Press, 1987).

5. W. W. Dobbins, *History of the Battle of Lake Erie* (Erie, PA: Ashby Printing, 1913), pp. 31–32.

6. The wreck raised in 1913 was identified as *Niagara* on the basis of written accounts and oral traditions postdating its abandonment in 1825. Some have argued that the wreck was probably *Lawrence* (see Allison Scarpitti, "Niagara/Lawrence," *The Journal of Erie Studies* 26, no. 1 [Spring 1997], pp. 68–95). Others have speculated that the wreck was actually one of the captured British ships (see Charles Alan Watkins and Mark Matusiak, "Is This the *Real* Niagara?" *Naval History* 15, no. 1 [February 2001], pp. 36–40). Photographs taken of the wreck in 1913 show a vessel nearly identical in its scantlings and construction to the Brown brothers–built *Eagle,* and there can be little question that it was either *Lawrence* or *Niagara.* The two Lake Erie brigs were built to the same plan, and since so little remains of the original fabric the question of *Lawrence* versus *Niagara* is of little consequence today.

7. Perry Memorial Commission, *Perry's Victory Memorial* (Washington, DC: Government Printing Office, 1921), p. 56.

8. Perry Memorial Commission, *Perry's Victory Memorial,* pp. 55–56. Problems with the 1913 restoration were recognized by contemporary experts on 1812-era naval vessels. Rear Admiral Charles H. Davis in Washington, DC, a naval historian, became involved with *Niagara*'s 1913 reconstruction when he perceived a general lack of knowledge on the part of Captain Morrison and the other individuals involved with the work. He wrote in 1917, "There were some mistakes made, and some omissions . . . I have hopes that, if money can be procured . . . these mistakes may be corrected and the ship be made more complete and realistic."

9. Photos of the wreck taken in 1913 show a pattern of corroded iron spikes in the planking, and the hull appears to be entirely iron fastened. Because iron was in short supply during the winter of 1812–1813, some writers have assumed that the squadron had to be fastened with wooden pegs known as "treenails," but there is no evidence for this. Iron may have been hard to come by, but time and labor were in even shorter supply. Cutting and shaping a treenail can take longer than forging a spike, and a much larger hole must be bored for a treenail, no small consideration when only muscle power was available to drill the hundreds of holes that would have been necessary. When all these factors are taken into account, it is no surprise that the most efficient way to get the ships built quickly was to find enough iron for fastenings.

10. Perry Memorial Commission, *Perry's Victory Memorial,* p. 56; Max Rosenberg, *The Building of Perry's Fleet,* p. 37. The keel was of black oak; frames were of oak, poplar, cucumber, and ash; top timbers were of red cedar and black walnut; the external planking was of oak; and bulwark planking was of white pine. An oakum shortage apparently led Noah Brown to substitute lead for caulking.

11. Howard I. Chapelle, *The History of the American Sailing Navy* (New York: Bonanza Books, 1949), pp. 270–71.

12. Since the first two seasons the sailing program has evolved

into a pattern of alternating home years with voyage years. Every year the ship is in sailing commission from early June through September, and every year she sails often. The year-round crew is seven: captain, chief mate, engineer, bosun, chief carpenter, and two able-bodied seamen/carpenters. In addition, from April through October up to a dozen seasonal crewmembers are hired as additional watch-standing mates, cook, sailmaker, and several able-bodied and ordinary seamen. This paid crew is supplemented by twenty to twenty-four volunteers. Some are from the Erie area, but others come from all parts of the country and outside the country to learn about sailing a square rig. New greenhands must sign on for at least three weeks, the minimum practical time for anyone to make sense out of the ship.

13. The watercolor painting of the American and captured British ships at Put-in-Bay was the work of Lt. Robert Irvine of the Royal Navy and is now part of the collections of the Royal Ontario Museum in Toronto.

14. Paul Cushman, "Usher Parsons, M.D.," *New York State Journal of Medicine* 71 (December 15, 1941), p. 2892; originally described in Usher Parsons, "Surgical Account of the Naval Battle of Lake Erie," *New England Journal of Medicine and Surgery* 7 (1818), p. 313; Seebert J. Goldowsky, *Yankee Surgeon: The Life and Times of Usher Parsons (1788–1868)* (Boston: The Francis A. Countway Library of Medicine in cooperation with the Rhode Island Publications Society, 1988).

15. The log of the *Lawrence* mentions taking aboard a spare topmast and topgallant mast prior to sailing from Erie in 1813, and it was typical practice to carry some spare timbers that could be fashioned into smaller spars.

16. The term "steerage" is derived from the practice of quartering midshipmen in the tiller compartment of larger warships; the name stuck, regardless of the size of the vessel and the location of the midshipmen's berths.

17. Dudley, ed., *Naval War of 1812,* vol. 2, p. 440.

18. Chapelle, *Sailing Navy,* pp. 256–65.

19. William Jones to Oliver H. Perry, August 18, 1813, William Jones Papers, Uselma Clark Smith Collection, Historical Society of Pennsylvania; Isaac Chauncey on Lake Ontario had the same difficulties finding enough iron ballast for his shallow warships, complaining, "stone fill up the vessels so completely," Chauncey to Jones, March 11 and 29, 1814, "Captains' Letters" microcopy 125, Naval Records Collection of the Office of Naval Records and Library, record group 45 (RG 45), National Archives and Records Administration (NARA).

20. Dudley, ed., *Naval War of 1812,* vol. 2, p. 481.

21. William V. Taylor Papers, "Sloop of War *Lawrence* Journal, 31 July-28 September, 1813," Newport Historical Society; Brown, "Statement of Noah Brown."

22. At present *Niagara* is equipped with three lapstrake boats. The first cutter is a 16-foot (4.87 m) heavy displacement, transom-sterned ship's boat carried in the starboard davits. It can pull six oars but typically relies on its 50-horsepower outboard; it serves as a rescue boat and also assists in docking ma-

neuvers. Our second cutter is a 22-foot (6.7 m) boat based on a US Navy design from the nineteenth century. This boat can pull eight oars or sail with a two-masted dipping lug rig and is usually carried in the port davits. The stern davits carry a 20-foot (6.09 m) boat that can pull six oars and sail with a two-masted sprit rig. This boat is rather narrow for a cutter and might better be termed a gig.

23. The Adam and Noah Brown–built privateer schooner *Prince de Neufchatel,* similar in dimensions and armament to *Niagara,* was provided with sweep ports in the bulwarks. Brown, "Statement of Noah Brown," p. 105; Robert Gardiner, *Warships of the Napoleonic Era* (London: Chatham Publishing, 1999), pp. 154–55.

24. An eight-second roll period is optimal for people living aboard a ship.

25. The percentage of displacement devoted to armament can be determined by approximate calculations. Weights of guns and their carriages varied, but were approximately as follows:

Cannon	Carriage	Total
32-pounder carronade 2000 lbs	500 lbs	2500 lbs
12-pounder long gun 3800 lbs	600 lbs	4400 lbs
24-pounder long gun 5800 lbs	800 lbs	6600 lbs

Displacement of 1812-era ships can only be approximated, even when we have lines drawings to work with, because we cannot be certain of the weight of consumable stores. With this caveat in mind, we can compare *Niagara,* which displaced about 296 long tons (@ 2240 lbs = 663,040 lbs) with *Constitution,* with an estimated mid-cruise displacement of about 2500 long tons (@ 2240 lbs = 5,600,000 lbs). *Niagara*'s eighteen 32-pounder carronades and two 12-pounder long guns, with an allowance of 1200 lbs for gun tools and tackle, added up to an armament weight of about 55,000 lbs, or 8.3% of the brig's total estimated displacement; *Constitution*'s twenty-four 32-pounder carronades and thirty 24-pounder long guns, with an allowance of gun tools and tackle, was probably in the range of 260,000 lbs, or 4.6% of the frigate's displacement. The true picture is complicated because larger vessels are inherently more stable than small ones: the area of sails and rigging subject to wind heel increases only arithmetically with vessel size, but displacement increases exponentially. Therefore the larger vessel can bear weights with greater ease, especially in rougher sea conditions. The important point here is that armament, a concentrated weight well above the waterline, is a much larger percentage of displacement on a smaller warship, which has inherently less stability than a large warship to begin with.

26. Samuel R. Brown, *An Authentic History of the Second War for Independence* (Auburn, NY: J. G. Hathaway, 1815), pp. 146–48.

27. US-made guns seemed particularly prone to bursting during this period, perhaps due to inexperience on the part of the nation's iron foundries. For examples of this problem, see "Extract from Commodore Rodgers' Journal, USS *President,* June 23, 1812," in *The Naval War of 1812, A Documentary History,* vol. 1,

ed. William S. Dudley (Washington, DC: Naval Historical Center, 1985), pp. 155–56, and Chauncey to Jones, October 1, 1813, in Dudley, ed., *Naval War of 1812,* vol. 2, p. 587. Ten of the twenty new 32-pounder carronades cast by John Dorsey of Baltimore in the summer of 1813 exploded into fragments during proving tests. See Kevin J. Crisman, "The *Jefferson*: The History and Archaeology of an American Brig from the War of 1812" (PhD diss., University of Pennsylvania, 1989), pp. 82–83.

28. To gain a better idea of accuracy, some target shooting was carried out prior to firing upon the hull section. Targets made from plywood squares measuring 8 feet (2.43 m) square were erected at a range of 100 yards (91.4 m), and three rounds of each size (12-, 24- and 32-pounder shot) were fired. The object was not so much to train our gunners as to establish the spread of fire from the guns. Each gun was carefully set to the same degree of train and elevation for each round. The 12 pounder put three rounds into a 2-foot-diameter (60 cm) circle. The 24 pounder had a wider spread, within a 5-foot (1.52 m) circle. The 32 pounder was a little wild: all three landed within the 8-foot (2.43 m) square target, but near the edges. The same pattern was repeated at 200 yards (183 m). The 12 pounder again had the tightest grouping, but at twice the spread. The same was true for the 24 pounder, while the 32 pounder had two hits and one near miss. We had planned on firing at 300 yards (274 m), but the increasing spread deterred us because the targets were too small at that distance. Ideally we should have been shooting at a drive-in movie screen marked with a grid, so even wide misses could have been recorded.

29. High-speed slow-motion cameras recorded shot penetration, and a film clip is now part of the exhibit at the Erie Maritime Museum.

30. Spencer Tucker, *Arming the Fleet: U.S. Navy Ordnance in the Muzzle-Loading Era* (Annapolis: Naval Institute Press, 1989), p. 124.

"CAST AWAY ON THE CANADIAN SHORE"

The British Brig *General Hunter*

KENNETH CASSAVOY

Introduction

As soon as I stepped onto the beach I could see the dark shapes a couple of hundred yards away, a dozen blackened timbers poking up through the sands of the Southampton shoreline. As I came closer, it was clear they were set at regular intervals in a slightly curving line (fig. 2.1). The wooden stubs were worn and rounded but strikingly robust. Protected only by a small section of hastily installed snow fence, they threw long, fascinating shadows in the afternoon sun. I wondered what shipwreck secret under the sand these timbers hinted at.

Two weeks earlier, on a late April morning in 2001, Duncan McCallum of Southampton, Ontario, was on his usual daily stroll along a section of the lake shore close to his home. The last of the winter ice had just been pushed off the beach by a brisk east wind, leaving a deep scour across the sand. As he walked, McCallum's foot struck the end of a timber, one of several in a row pushing up through the beach sand. Over the years, at least two dozen ships were known to have wrecked in the area, so McCallum was not surprised by what he had found: these timbers had to be part of a ship, probably an old one. He reported his find to colleagues in the Southampton Marine Heritage Society, and within a matter of days, I was contacted and agreed to take a look.

A fortnight later, here I was, with provincial archaeological license in hand, standing beside these tantalizing timbers and ready to start an initial investigation. My mind raced with thoughts of what we might find under this popular Lake Huron beach. It was obvious from the first view of the frame tips that a sizeable portion of a large vessel must lie beneath the sand.

With the help of colleagues from the Ontario Marine Heritage Committee, I quickly put together a plan for preliminary excavation of the site.[1] Work would start

Figure 2.1. *Southampton Marine Heritage Society members on the newly discovered wreck. Duncan McCallum, Ken Rothenberg, John Rigby, and Mike Sterling view shipwreck frame tips revealed on the Southampton beach by low Lake Huron water levels and a major ice scour in April 2001. The irregular, darker line on the beach behind the figures marks the approximate limit of the ice scour line. (Photo by John Weichel.)*

within two weeks, and I believed, with any kind of luck, we would soon know what ship McCallum had stumbled on. I could not know then, but it would take more than five years of excavation and research before we determined that our mystery shipwreck was, in fact, an amazing find—a British warship, His Majesty's brig *General Hunter.*

General Hunter's story began a couple of hundred years earlier, about 125 miles (200 km) south of present-day Southampton, where the new British vessel was laid down in 1806 at the Fort Malden naval yard on the Detroit River.[2] The handiwork of Master Shipwright William Bell, the schooner (later brig) was the latest addition to the small but vital Provincial Marine transport fleet on the Upper Great Lakes (plate 3b). *General Hunter*'s eventful career in peace and war ended a de-

cade later when the ship, now the aged and ailing US Army transport brig *Hunter,* struggled down a storm-swept Lake Huron to end its days wrecked, abandoned, burned, and buried on the beach at Southampton.

The fate of *General Hunter* remained a mystery for close to two centuries. With so many documented ship losses in the Southampton area, there was no particular reason to connect the newly exposed frame tips on the beach with the War of 1812–era *General Hunter.* That determination would come much later, after a series of archaeological excavations of the site, an intensive program of hull and artifact analyses, and considerable historical research.

2001 Test Excavations

In 2001, just a few weeks after the discovery of the frame tips, we began our initial investigation of the site. First we excavated a 39.4-inch-wide (1 m) trench that began at the exposed frame tips and extended across the apparent width of the wreck (fig. 2.2). In this excavation, designated Unit 1, we found interior (ceiling) and exterior planking below the frame tips. The ceiling exposed in our transverse trench followed a regular pattern down to the keelson, and a similar pattern of ceiling extended from the keelson to the frames tips on the other side. We now knew we had a reasonably intact hull under the sand, at least at this location.

Our next test trench, Unit 2, was excavated a short distance to the north, where local residents told us something substantial lay buried under the sand. One waterfront homeowner described hitting what he believed was an old dock while digging a pipeline trench from his cottage to the water. Separately, town work crews showed us an area they avoided when putting in winter snow fences on the beach because the posts would not penetrate whatever was under the beach. Both reports indicated the specific area in which we began excavation of Unit 2. What we found here only confused us: small boards nailed across some kind of substantial side or bottom timbers. The structure had no obvious relationship to the ship remains seen in Unit 1. Was this part of a deck house from the ship? Despite our team's many years of cumulative experience studying wrecks, no one could understand what we had found in Unit 2. With this unsatisfactory result, we back-filled our trenches and ended the first period of work on the site.

Figure 2.2. *The shipwreck excavation on the Southampton Beach. This photograph was taken shortly after the start of digging in 2004. Note the use of an archaeological grid system with standard 1-meter-square archaeological units being excavated in 50-centimeter increments. The grid system on the site covered a 20- by 30-meter area of the beach. Also note the submersible pumps operating in 8-foot-deep pipes to draw the ground water off the site. The photograph provides an excellent view of the site where the wreck was buried with Chantry Island and its restored Imperial Lighthouse in the distance. (Photo by Larry LePage.)*

Two weeks later we returned, armed now with the results of remote sensing data recorded during the excavation of the first two units. The ground penetrating radar (GPR) information provided us with the apparent northern, southern, and eastern limits of whatever was under the sand. These limits suggested that the entire structure extended over an area 75 feet (23 m) long and 30 feet (10 m) wide. Whatever this oddly shaped vessel was, it appeared to be fairly large.

We dug our third trench, Unit 3, at the southern limit of the GPR readings. Buried a little more deeply here we found the obvious end of a vessel—whether bow or stern we were not immediately sure—with wood type and construction similar to that found in Unit 1. The fourth trench, Unit 4, was excavated at the northeastern limit of the GPR-recorded material. Here we quickly found the end of another structure, but one that had nothing in common with the vessel end seen in Unit 3. From its box-like appearance, it looked like another part of what we had uncovered in Unit 2. We remained completely confused by the four pieces of this archaeological jigsaw puzzle.

With our excavation time winding down and the puzzle still unsolved, we established a 1-meter-wide excavation unit to start at the exposed frame ends and dig fore and aft. To the south, we uncovered more timbers until we had a continuous line of frames running to the vessel end found in Unit 3. The same pattern

2001/2002 Site Plan

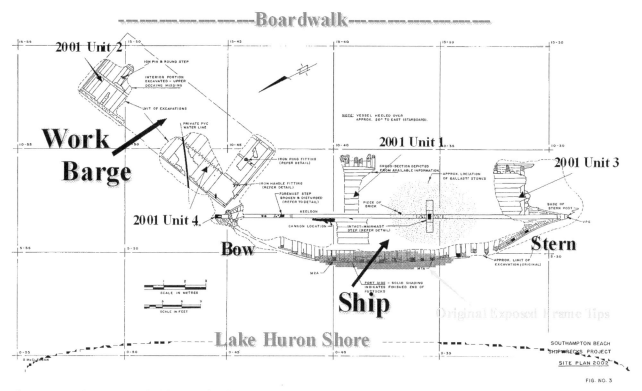

Figure 2.3. Southampton Beach Shipwreck site plan, 2001–2002. This shows the test excavations that revealed two vessels buried end to end and almost touching. One end of the stone-hooker work barge (circa 1870–90) rests over the starboard bow of the ship. Note the two mast steps and the swivel cannon found in the test trench excavated along the keelson of the ship in 2002. These discoveries provided evidence of an early sailing vessel and incentive for full excavation. (Drawing by Stan McClellan based on site survey measurements and photos by Julie Cassavoy.)

of excavation to the north uncovered a line of frames leading not only to the other end of the framed vessel but also the end of a *separate* vessel of very different construction. The two were almost touching (fig. 2.3). We had been excavating not one large vessel but two smaller ones, buried end to end under the sand!

We now determined that the vessel with the exposed frame tips was approximately 55 feet (16.76 m) long and 17 feet (5.18 m) in breadth. From its dimensions, fasteners, and construction features, we were quite certain this wreck was an early Great Lakes vessel. The second, box-like wreck to the north was clearly some kind of work barge about 29 feet (8.8 m) long and 12 feet (3.65 m) wide. From construction evidence and from late-nineteenth-century photographs, we determined that the barge was almost certainly from a period of intensive construction between the 1850s and the 1890s when the Southampton "Harbour of Refuge" was

built.[3] Ultimately, we were satisfied that there was no historical connection between the two wrecks.

2002 Keelson Excavation

In 2001 we determined that the older wreck had a keelson and that it appeared to be intact from bow to stern. This was good news, because the keelson can provide archaeologists with important clues about a vessel's design and history. The 2002 research plan therefore focused on excavating a 6.56-foot-wide (2 m) unit along the extrapolated centerline of the hull. Our objective was to find evidence of the vessel's propulsion, evidence such as support timbers for a steam engine or mast steps that would indicate that this was a sailing vessel. At the same time, we planned to look for the presence of a centerboard, a device widely used on lake sailing ships by the second quarter of the nineteenth century.

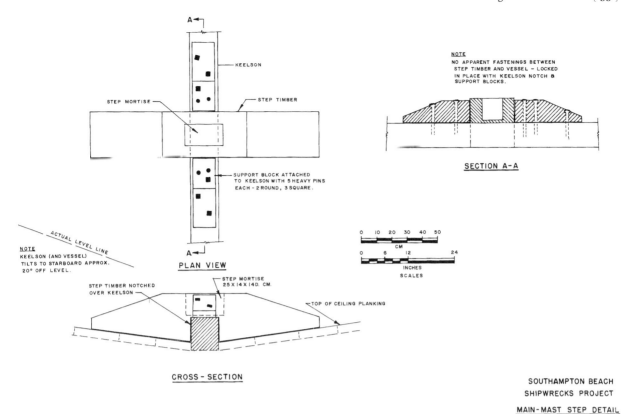

Figure 2.4. *The saddle-type mainmast step found on the Southampton Beach Shipwreck. There are no fasteners in the step, but it is held in place by a notch on its underside and by support blocks fastened atop the keelson. The step was easily lifted off the keelson for full examination and then put back in place afterward. (Drawing by Stan McClellan based on measurements of the wreck and photos by Julie Cassavoy.)*

In the event, our excavation quickly uncovered two mast steps along the keelson. The smaller foremast step was located about 10 feet (3 m) from the bow; it consisted of a timber fastened atop the keelson with a step opening that overlay a mortise in the top of the keelson. The mainmast step farther aft was a large block of wood—a saddle-type step—set perpendicular to the keelson (fig. 2.4). Saddle steps have been found on lake ships dating from the 1750s to the 1840s but appear to be more common on earlier vessels.[4]

During the penultimate hour of the 2002 excavation, we made a totally unexpected and tremendously exciting discovery: a small cannon with a swivel mount that lay along the port side of the keelson, a short distance abaft the foremast step (fig. 2.5). The cannon presented all kinds of interesting possibilities for the origin of our wreck. Most importantly, it suggested that the vessel might predate the Rush-Bagot Agreement of 1817, which limited naval armament on the Great

Lakes.[5] Certainly the cannon fit nicely into our evolving theories about the relatively early date of the ship.

Concurrent with these finds on the wreck was the discovery of a document describing the loss of a small commercial schooner near the Saugeen River in 1798. The vessel, named *Weazell,* was built in Detroit in 1786 for merchant John Askin and transported goods on the Upper Lakes for the Askin family for a dozen years before its loss.[6] *Weazell* reportedly wrecked in the general area of modern-day Southampton. The dimensions, construction features, and fasteners of the wreck all suggested a ship built in the late eighteenth or early nineteenth century, while the presence of the cannon hinted that this ship sailed prior to 1817. We also found documents confirming that Askin's commercial vessels typically carried at least one cannon, probably used primarily for signaling.[7] Given the very limited numbers of ships on the Upper Lakes at that time, what were the possibilities of two ships from the same

Figure 2.5. *A significant discovery. During the 2002 excavation, a small, 1-pounder swivel cannon was found on the port side of the keelson, aft of the foremast step. (Photo by Julie Cassavoy.)*

terior structural details but did recover some exterior hull information, especially at the bow and stern. Based on this data, we were able to extrapolate with a comfortable degree of certainty many exterior features that we could not reach during the 2004 project.

The wreck, which lists to starboard at 19 degrees, consisted of the full length of the vessel's bottom, a smaller portion of the port side, and a larger portion of the starboard side (figs. 2.6 and 2.7). Parts of the starboard hull extended above the turn of the bilge to the actual side. The existing hull had an overall length of 53 feet 10 inches (16.41 m), and its maximum width at the probable midship frame was 16 feet 10 inches (5.14 m). The timbers used in the construction of the vessel were quite heavy, and all appeared to be oak, probably white oak. We noted a high level of craftsmanship throughout the hull.

Although we were not able to excavate major sections of the wreck's exterior (the keel was not examined in 2004), we did uncover selected external timbers (fig. 2.8). During our work at the bow and stern, carved draft numbers (III and IV) were noted, but only on the port side of the stem and the starboard side of the sternpost. The draft marks provided very useful information for calculating the location and dimensions of the keel and, together with other evidence, allowed us to estimate the keel's probable dimensions as 16 inches molded by 10 inches sided (40.6 by 25.4 cm).

The stem consisted of three curved timbers, the main post, an outer post (or gripe), and the apron. During a later stage of the hull's construction, the stem assembly and the bow's cant frames were reinforced internally by a large two-piece breast hook. The starboard half of this piece was found in situ, with a notch at its forward end that showed where it fit with the now-missing port-side timber.[8]

The stern had a main post (eroded and split at the top) and a shorter outer post, reinforced by a very simple assembly of four horizontally oriented deadwood timbers stacked atop the keel. During the exterior excavation around the stern, no part of the rudder or its hardware was found, although the locations of two missing gudgeons were determined from fastener holes, ridges in the wood, and some barely discernible staining on the posts.

The frames were doubled, of generous proportions, and placed very closely together with a room and space of 24 inches (60 cm). The substantial framing suggested

period wrecking in the same place? All the evidence seemed to point to *Weazell* as a good candidate for our wreck. Whatever its identity, we were now certain this was a very early Great Lakes ship, one that clearly would contain a storehouse of detailed construction information from the period. With this knowledge, we proceeded to plan for a major excavation in 2004.

2004 Excavation of the Hull's Interior

The full excavation of the hull's interior in 2004 covered an overall site area of 98.4 by 65.6 feet (30 by 20 m). Units 3.28 feet (1 m) square were excavated in 19.6-inch-deep (50 cm) levels (plate 4a), with all overburden sand carried off the site and screened for small finds. Once the ship's hull was reached, provenience for artifacts was tied into established points on the wreck. During this work, we focused on recording in-

Photos & composite, redone 2007.
Larry LePage

Figure 2.6. *A photomosaic of the fully excavated interior of the hull. Note the small deck for the after cabin or a storage locker and the fragmentary bulkhead that separates the stone ballast from the cabin or locker. Limber boards on the port and starboard sides of the keelson have been removed to allow recording of the keelson and lower frames. (Photos and mosaic by Larry LePage.)*

that the vessel was built to naval standards and, with this kind of structural strength, was capable of mounting a number of cannon. The frame timbers varied in their sided dimensions, ranging from 8 to 10 inches (20 to 25.4 cm). At the keel the frames were 9 inches (22.8 cm) molded, tapering to 6 to 7 inches (15.2 to 17.8 cm) molded at their upper ends. The gap between the frame sets was 5 to 6 inches (12.7 to 15.2 cm). The wreck had twenty-four frame sets, including eighteen square frames (ending at H in the bow and 9 at the stern), two pairs of cant frames notched into the apron at the bow, and four half frames notched into the deadwood at the stern (fig. 2.9).[9]

Only the floor timber in each square frame crossed the keel, while the heels of the first futtocks were located approximately 9 inches (22.8 cm) from the keel. Where we could observe their construction, the frames were fastened together with wooden treenails, indicating that the frames were assembled prior to being set in place on the keel.[10] Square frames A through H were assembled with the first futtocks abaft the floor, while square frames Ⅺ through 9 were assembled with the first futtocks forward of the floor. Each floor had a pair of limber holes—drains for bilge water—cut through its base, one on each side of the keel. The floors were not notched to fit over the keel, and the keel was not

notched to fit the floors. Roughly split wooden pieces were placed along the keel between the floors to act as spacers for positioning the frames. Some of these spacers were left in place as construction proceeded and were found still in position during the excavation.

The single-piece keelson measured 7½ inches sided by 10 inches molded (19 by 25.4 cm) and had an overall length of 39 feet (11.9 m). The underside of the keelson had shallow, ¾-inch-deep (1.9 cm) notches over the floors, and the timber was fastened to the floors and keel by a pair of iron bolts located at every other frame set.

Seven strakes of ceiling planking (including the limber boards) survived on the port side of the wreck, and ten remained on the starboard side. The ceiling varied in width since the planks tapered over their lengths. The widest plank was 13 inches (33.2 cm) across, and the longest individual piece measured 29 feet 9½ inches (9.1 m). Where they could be measured, the ceiling planks were found to be 2 inches (5 cm) thick (the limber boards were 1¾ inches [4.4 cm] thick). Most of the joints between ceiling planks were still tight and uniform.

Between frames D and 6 in the central part of the hull, the planks alongside the keelson were not fastened to the frames, allowing them to be taken up for

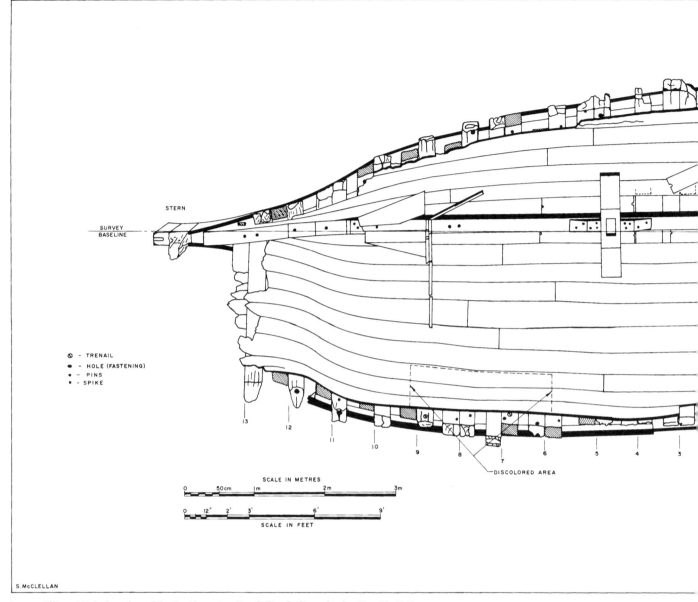

STERN

SURVEY
BASELINE

⊘ - TRENAIL
● - HOLE (FASTENING)
• - PINS
▪ - SPIKE

13   12   11   10   9   8   7   6   5   4   3

DISCOLORED AREA

SCALE IN METRES
0   50cm   1m   2m   3m

0   12"   2'   3'   6'   9'
SCALE IN FEET

S. McCLELLAN

Figure 2.7. A plan view of the Southampton Beach Wreck. (Drawing by Stan McClellan based on measurements of the wreck and photos by Larry LePage.)

cleaning the bilges. These removable limber boards had finger notches at each end for lifting, and the edges between the limber boards and adjacent ceiling strakes were beveled for easier lifting and a tighter fit. There were five such removable boards on each side of the keelson, including smaller ones directly forward of the mainmast step. The aftermost limber boards on each side of the keelson were overlain by the step.

Enough of the starboard hull was left to include portions of the lowest wale. The wale section toward the stern measured 16½ feet (5 m) long, the section closer

to the bow measured 11½ feet (3.5 m), and both were 3 inches thick by 6 inches wide (7.6 by 15.2 cm). Hull planking averaged 2 to 2½ inches (5 to 6.3 cm) thick.

The two mast steps discovered during the 2002 excavation differed greatly in their construction. The foremast step consisted of a mortise in the top of the keelson, surmounted by a timber with a step opening cut into it; we believe the four protruding bolts forward of the mortise were used to fasten the step and stem framing, framing which now has been broken and eroded away. The saddle-type mainmast step was

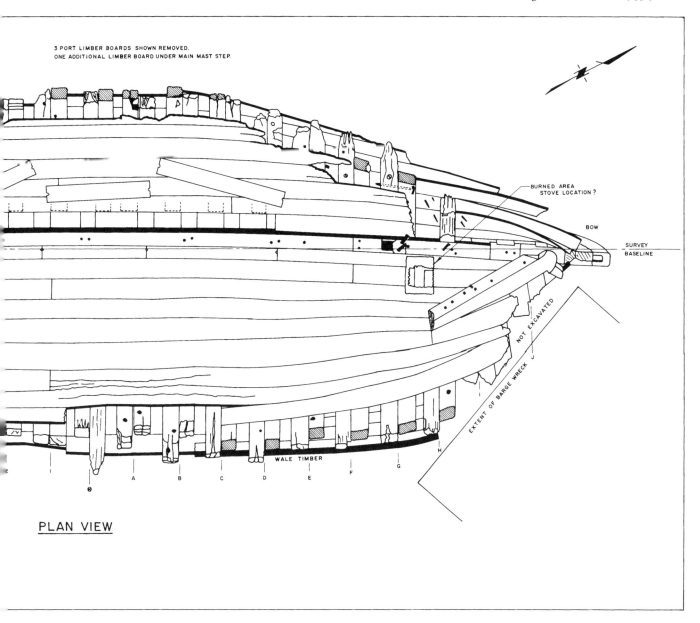

3 PORT LIMBER BOARDS SHOWN REMOVED.
ONE ADDITIONAL LIMBER BOARD UNDER MAIN MAST STEP.

BURNED AREA
STOVE LOCATION ?

BOW

SURVEY
BASELINE

NOT EXCAVATED

EXTENT OF BARGE WRECK

WALE TIMBER

A   B   C   D   E   F   G   H

PLAN VIEW

notched over the keelson and locked into place by a pair of tapering blocks. The two blocks were bolted and spiked to the keelson, but the step itself had no fasteners in it. The deep notch in the bottom of the saddle step prevented it from moving sideways on the keelson, and the tapered blocks kept it from moving forward or aft. We suspect that the saddle may have been left unfastened to allow repositioning of the step in case the angle or location of the mainmast needed to be adjusted.[11] This type of step may also have distributed the mast's weight and allowed some movement

and stress relief, which would take some strain off the keelson. During the excavation, a careful search was made of both steps for a dated coin, which, by tradition, might have been placed in the step as a good luck token. No such coin was found.

The limber boards immediately forward of the mainmast step, on both the port and starboard sides of the keelson, were significantly shorter than all of the other limber boards. Each of these anomalous planks covered the space between two frames and may possibly indicate the location of bilge pumps, although

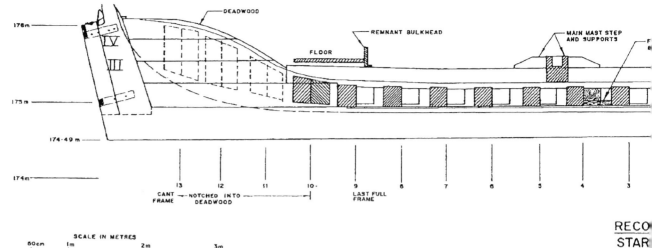

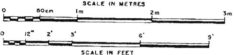

S. McCLELLAN

Figure 2.8. *A longitudinal profile of the Southampton Beach Wreck. The assembly of the keel, end posts, frames, and keelson is partially revealed in this plan. The builders ensured correct frame spacing by placing small pieces of scrap wood between the frame sets to provide a reference; the pieces were still in place two hundred years later. (Drawing by Stan McClellan based on measurements of the wreck and photos by Larry LePage.)*

pump tubes or fittings were not found during the excavation. An alternative explanation for these short boards, posited by shipwreck recorder Stan McClellan, is that at some point in the ship's life the mainmast step may have been slightly forward of its present location and above the short limber boards. The step width and the length of the boards match very closely.

There were two obvious areas of damage on the wreck. One was at the port bow, where cant frames, ceiling, and the port section of breast hook were missing and the exterior planks were broken and pulled away from the frames. The second was an area with shattered frame timbers amidships on the starboard side. Here and elsewhere on the wreck many of the frame ends and planks were charred, providing strong evidence that the upper hull burned at some point in time. Toward the bow, a rectangular charred area was found on the starboard ceiling planking. Since we discovered what appeared to be parts of a cast iron stove in the same vicinity, it is likely that the charring indicates the stove's location before the vessel wrecked.

Fasteners in sizes ranging from small, tack-sized nails to large spikes and bolts were found by the hundreds in all areas of the hull. All of the metal fasteners, both those we recovered and those seen in place on the

wreck, were made of iron. No manufacturing or identifying marks such as the British government's broad-arrow stamp were found on any of the fastenings that we examined. Many of the recovered loose nails and smaller brads were clenched. Since these were often found among large numbers of unclenched nails, we do not, as yet, have any acceptable explanation for this clenching. Some of the larger nails had a red coating (hematite) that indicates that they likely had been exposed to high heat, which would have occurred if the ship was burned.[12]

Wooden fasteners were also noted in parts of the wreck. The floor and futtocks of each frame were held together by treenails approximately 1 inch (2.5 cm) in diameter, driven through sideways in several locations along the frames. Treenails were also used, in combination with iron spikes, to fasten exterior and ceiling planking to the frames. This use of treenails was noted in several locations on the hull, especially in the bow and stern. While fasteners of various types were observed and recorded during the excavation, we did not identify uniform nailing or fastening patterns.

Fastener types, sizes, and manufacturing methods changed relatively slowly over a long period and generally are not helpful in providing specific dating infor-

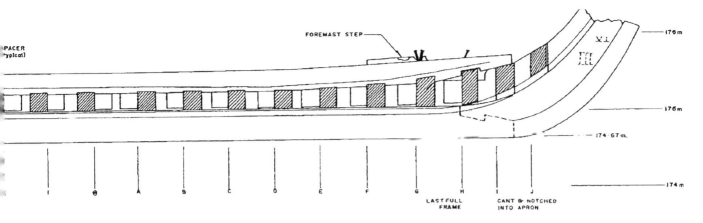

SPACER
(typical)

FOREMAST STEP

XI

III

176 m

176 m

174·67 m.

174 m

I   θ   A   B   C   D   E   F   G   H   I   J

LAST FULL
FRAME

CANT & NOTCHED
INTO APRON

RUCTED SECTION ALONG
RD SIDE KEEL/KEELSON

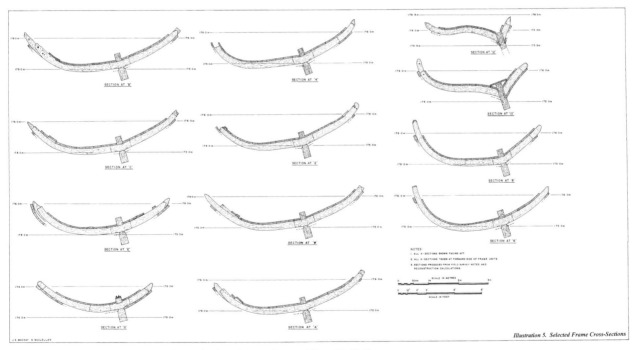

Figure 2.9. *Selected frame sections. (Drawing by John Mackay and Stan McClellan based on measurements of the hull and photos by Larry LePage.)*

mation. However, the presence of forged nails in the wreck is consistent with construction materials used on the lakes in the late eighteenth or early nineteenth century. The extensive use of wooden fasteners in the building of the vessel also accords with known construction practices during this period.

Artifacts

Over the course of the excavations, hundreds of artifacts were recovered from the shipwreck site. With a few notable exceptions, the recovered artifacts were relatively small objects, such as buttons, ceramic pieces, bones (including pig, cow, sheep, duck, and fish bones), lead shot, and various small miscellaneous items, as well as the hundreds of iron fasteners mentioned earlier.[13] The larger artifact finds consisted of the swivel gun, the remains—in several large pieces—of what we believe was an iron stove, and four iron cannon balls. During the excavation, we were somewhat surprised at the relative paucity of artifacts in the hull, especially in terms of larger objects. Later, we would come to understand why we found so little material on the wreck.

Some of the small finds were critically important in the dating and identifying of the wreck, especially the military buttons, which proved to be, by far, the most important category of artifacts found on the site (fig. 2.10). Four of the buttons were from British units: the Royal Newfoundland Fencibles, the 10th Royal Veterans Battalion, the 41st Regiment, and the 37th Regiment. Seventeen of the buttons were US Army issue, including three different styles of infantry buttons and at least two buttons from artillery units, one with no regiment indicated but the other from the 1st Artillery Regiment. The only coin found associated with the wreck is in very poor condition, but the Canadian Conservation Institute staff identified it as a Spanish half Real, which appears to date to the reign of Charles IV (1788–1808).

While the buttons turned out to be important for identifying the wreck, the most intriguing artifact was the small swivel cannon discovered during the 2002 excavation. It was found lying against the port side of the keelson about 3 feet (1 m) abaft the foremast step. The cast-iron gun is 40½ inches (103 cm) long from cascabel button tip to muzzle face and weighs 178 pounds (80.7 kg). Although considerably worn, the reinforce-

Figure 2.10. *US and British military buttons found on the Southampton Beach Wreck. These proved vital in identifying the wreck. The two buttons on the left are US army buttons; the upper one is a general service button; the lower one with the ornate "I" is a general-issue Infantry button, indicated by the star in the circle below the "I" where a specific regiment could be shown instead of the star; the two buttons on the right are from British Army units, including the Royal Newfoundland Regiment (above) and the 10th Royal Veterans Battalion (below). (Photo by Julie Cassavoy.)*

ments, astragals, vent, and other features of the cannon can still be seen. The bore measures 2.279 inches (5.845 cm) in diameter, which, allowing for windage, indicates a one-pound gun.[14] The wrought-iron swivel yoke is 15¾ inches (40 cm) long and has a noticeable bend in the pintle below the collar.

When recovered, the gun was completely covered with corrosion products and the swivel yoke was solidly concreted to the tube. The gun was cleaned and restored to its operational appearance by the Canadian Conservation Institute (CCI) in Ottawa. During the cleaning, the CCI team established that the gun's bore and vent had not been obstructed and it was in working order when the ship went ashore. The cannon has no distinguishable identifying marks and appears to have been a basic type in common use during the eighteenth and early nineteenth centuries (fig. 2.11). The worn features of the gun suggest many years of use before it was lost. Although the gun certainly could be used for defensive purposes, we expect it was principally used to signal—with a powder charge only—

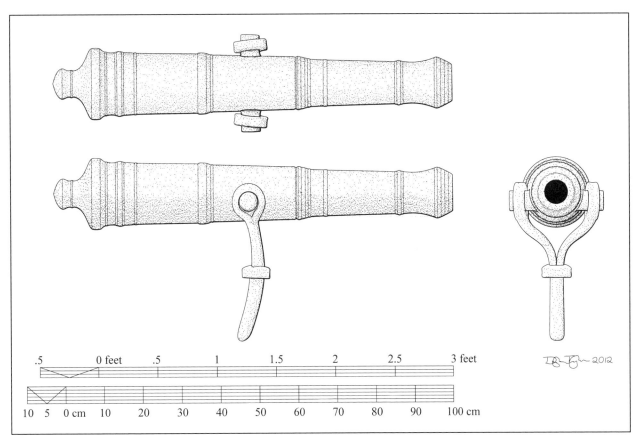

Figure 2.11. *The swivel cannon found on the Southampton Beach Wreck. (Drawing by Douglas Inglis.)*

other ships, shore parties, and ship's boats or to let residents in remote and isolated areas know that the ship was offshore. The cannon is now the centerpiece of the shipwreck exhibit at the Bruce County Museum and Cultural Centre in Southampton.

It is interesting to note that if we had dug our initial test trench in 2001 just a few inches to the north, we would have found the cannon during the very first day of work on the site. As it was, the discovery of the cannon in 2002 came as a tremendous surprise to all of us. Such a find is extremely rare on shipwrecks in the Upper Lakes. Of course, in 2002 we still had no idea of the identity of the wreck and the cannon provided no answers but, rather, raised a number of new questions.

The four cannon balls, found in separate locations in the ballast pile, were all far too large for the 1-pound swivel gun. Two of the balls were the correct diameter for a 12-pounder cannon, and two were for an 18-pounder. We believe the balls were lost or discarded in the ballast during an earlier period in the ship's career.[15]

There seems little doubt that the large iron pieces we found in the wreck are the broken pieces of a stove (although we have not been able to reconstruct it). Near these pieces we found several hardened spatters of molten lead, suggesting that the stove might have been used to cast lead shot. In various locations throughout the wreck, but primarily in the bow area, we found a total of thirty pieces of lead shot in three distinct sizes: sixteen small (0.28 inches [0.7 cm] in diameter), six medium (0.5 inches [1.3 cm] in diameter), and eight large (0.65 inches [1.65 cm] in diameter). These could have been for pistols, muskets, or, in the case of the largest size, possibly even grapeshot.

Other weaponry finds include a musket bayonet, three other possible pieces of a musket or pistol, and two gun flints of different sizes. A large military cross-belt plate (for uniform straps worn across the chest) and a walking stick of the size and type favored by British officers were also found on the wreck.[16] Collectively, the munitions, small arms, uniform buttons, and other military items made it clear to the excavation crew that we were working on a ship that had served at least some part of its life as a military vessel.

Identifying *General Hunter*

But what ship was it? After the 2004 excavation, the wreck's probable military background became the central focus of the identification effort. The military buttons indicated who might have sailed in the vessel and the period when that sailing took place. One early button discovery—from a Royal Newfoundland Fencibles uniform—was particularly significant. It immediately suggested to project historian Patrick Folkes that our wreck could not be John Askin's *Weazell*.[17] Lost in the Southampton area in 1798, *Weazell* had initially been considered a good candidate for the wreck under the beach.[18] However, the Royal Newfoundland Fencibles Regiments were formed in 1803, first ordered to Quebec in 1807, and sent to Upper Canada in 1812 to serve as seamen and marines with the Great Lakes naval squadrons.[19] This means *Weazell* was lost fourteen years before a member of the Royal Newfoundland Fencibles could have been on a vessel sailing the Upper Lakes.

Now that the strong military connection was established, Folkes drew our attention to another possible candidate, the brig *General Hunter*.[20] A June 11, 1885 article in the trade paper *Marine Record* reported the loss of *General Hunter* in August 1816.[21] Among other details, the article reported the ship "ashore and wrecked" in the general area of present-day Southampton. With the information from the recovered artifacts and the initial analysis of the hull providing support for the *General Hunter* identification, we began to steer our historical investigation in this direction.

General Hunter packed a lot of activity into its decade-long career on the lakes. Initially rigged as a schooner, the Canadian Provincial Marine vessel spent the tense and uncertain years leading up to the War of 1812 transporting troops and supplies between British posts on Lake Huron and Lake Erie.[22] As was often the case with wooden vessels built on the salt-free lakes, rot set in quickly; in a report dated December 7, 1811, the schooner *General Hunter* was described as "the only really serviceable vessel on the Lake," but was "falling fast into decay."[23] Regardless of the hull's condition, the British government needed every warship it had to counter the US invasion of Canada in 1812, and

the cannons mounted on *General Hunter*'s deck were welcome at this critical hour.

During the first summer of the war, *General Hunter* contributed greatly to British successes in the west. In one of the initial naval confrontations on the Upper Lakes, the brig's commander Lt. Frederic Rolette and six of his crew members captured the US packet schooner *Cuyahoga* in the Detroit River off Amherstburg on July 2, 1812. *Cuyahoga* yielded papers belonging to US Army Gen. William Hull that outlined the size and disposition of US forces in Detroit poised for the invasion of Upper Canada.[24] In August, *General Hunter* seized twelve US boats and bateaux after the repulse of US troops at Maguaga.[25] During the same month, the brig supported British Gen. Isaac Brock's bold and successful attack upon General Hull's army at Detroit.[26]

In the spring of 1813, *General Hunter,* now a Royal Navy ship, was one of the transports that carried Gen. Henry Proctor's forces across Lake Erie to lay siege to Fort Meigs in Ohio.[27] And in its final act as a British warship, the brig sailed as part of Comm. Robert H. Barclay's line of battle when the Royal Navy met the US Navy on September 10, 1813. The ensuing action, the Battle of Lake Erie, was one of the truly decisive naval actions fought on the lakes during the War of 1812. Stationed between the two principal British warships *Detroit* and *Queen Charlotte* at the start of the battle, *General Hunter* was in the thick of the prolonged, bloody engagement (fig. 2.12). During the battle, two seamen and a private from the 41st Regiment were killed on *General Hunter* and five others on board were wounded. Significantly, *General Hunter*'s commander Lt. George Bignell was among those severely wounded, seriously affecting the ship's ability to maneuver and fight effectively as the battle raged on.[28] With the British defeat in that battle, the brig became, along with the rest of Barclay's squadron, a prize of the US Navy (fig. 2.13).[29]

The brig—now simply known as *Hunter*—saw little use while in US hands, probably due to its "much decayed" condition. Laid up at Presque Isle (present-day Erie, Pennsylvania) with an overload of captured stores during the winter of 1813–14, the vessel went aground, tipped over, and filled with water. *Hunter* was refloated in the spring but apparently never sailed in 1814.[30] After the war ended in early 1815, the government sold the vessel to a private citizen, John Dickson.[31] During

Figure 2.12. *A conjectural painting of* General Hunter *at the Battle of Lake Erie.* Hunter *is shown during the initial phase of the battle, with the British squadron's flagship* Detroit *ahead and the ship* Queen Charlotte *astern; three vessels in the US battle line can be seen in the distance. (Courtesy of Peter Rindlisbacher and Bruce County Museum and Cultural Centre.)*

Figure 2.13. *Ken Cassavoy examines the flag of the Royal Navy brig* General Hunter. *Captured at the Battle of Lake Erie along with the brig, this flag was sent to Washington, DC, as a trophy of the US Navy's victory. In 2012 the US Naval Academy loaned the flag to the Bruce County Museum and Cultural Centre in Southampton, Ontario, for inclusion in a War of 1812 bicentennial display on the war and the archaeological discoveries from the wreck of* General Hunter. *(Photo by Sandy Lindsay of the* Saugeen Times.*)*

that summer, the vessel, still called *Hunter,* made at least three or four voyages carrying private merchandise and US military stores and troops between Buffalo, Detroit, and Mackinac.[32]

Sometime in the late fall or early winter of 1815, the US Army purchased *Hunter* for use as a transport vessel.[33] During the spring and summer of 1816, the vessel made several trips carrying military supplies, troops, and passengers to Mackinac at the northern end of Lake Huron.[34] It was while returning in ballast from one of these supply runs that the brig met its fate when it was overwhelmed by a powerful gale and wrecked on a remote Canadian beach on August 19, 1816.

The full and productive ten-year life of *General Hunter,* both as a warship and as a transport vessel, speaks to its construction pedigree. The hull was built at the British government's naval yard at Amherstburg (Fort Malden) in 1806, one of numerous ships and gunboats launched by the talented Master Builder William Bell.[35] In fact, two-thirds of the British squadron lost in the Battle of Lake Erie—the ships *Detroit* (19 guns) and *Queen Charlotte* (17 guns), the brig *General Hunter* (10 guns), and the schooner *Lady Prevost* (13 guns)— were built by the prolific Bell.[36] Bell's contributions did not end when he was ordered to leave Fort Malden with the retreating British forces in the fall of 1813.[37] He was placed in charge of the Royal Navy's yard at

Kingston in October 1813 and superintended work on the largest lake warships built by the British during the War of 1812, including *Princess Charlotte* (40 guns), *Prince Regent* (58 guns), and *St. Lawrence* (102 guns).[38] Sadly, the architect of so much British naval firepower received few rewards in his time and remains largely unrecognized in Canadian popular history.[39] However, *General Hunter* clearly was built under skillful and experienced direction, something we recognized in the construction of our wreck long before we discovered the builder's identity.

Although several anecdotal reports and at least one published source suggest that an Admiralty draft plan of *General Hunter* drawn by William Bell exists in Archives Canada, we do not believe any identified plan of the ship has been found.[40] We do know of two unidentified ship plans in the archives, drawn by Bell, one of which is widely believed to be for *Hope,* built in 1803.[41] It is known that *General Hunter* was built to replace

Hope after it was lost in 1805. Thus, it seems logical and likely that the *Hope* plan was used to construct *General Hunter.* Regardless of whether or not they are for *General Hunter,* the Bell plans provide a basis for understanding the general design and appearance of the ship. One plan shows a vessel around 54 feet (16.45 m) on the keel, 18 feet (5.48 m) in breadth, of 70 to 74 tons burden, and capable of carrying up to 10 guns.[42] Our wreck had a surviving hull length of 53 feet 10 inches (16.4 m), with a remaining breadth of 16 feet 10 inches (5.12 m). The number of frames and their configuration also fit closely with the other unidentified and undated vessel plan located in the William Bell Papers.[43] During the excavation we noted the considerable size and high quality of the timbers and the obvious precision of the shipbuilder's work in shaping and fitting those timbers, all of which suggested to us the vessel had been constructed in a navy yard to exacting military standards.[44] Later, as we will see, the hull remains would provide even more evidence in support of the *General Hunter* identification.

As indicated earlier, during the excavation we became convinced by the artifacts we were uncovering that the wreck had spent a considerable part of its life as a military vessel. The identified and dated buttons, in particular, indicated use of the ship by British and US military personnel during the War of 1812 period. All of the dated buttons spanned the period from immediately prior to the War of 1812 to some years following the close of the conflict. Furthermore, historical documents placed soldiers from at least two of the British units represented by shipwreck buttons—the 41st Regiment and the Royal Newfoundland Regiment—on board *General Hunter.*[45] As well, we have documentation showing US Army units, which used both the general service and foliated script "I" for "Infantry" buttons, traveling on *Hunter.*[46] At least one document also confirms the presence of two members of a US artillery unit, which used the foliated script "A" buttons, on *Hunter* in 1815.[47]

As part of the historical research on the wreck, an annotated list was prepared of all naval and military vessels on the Upper Lakes from 1806 to 1816.[48] The list included details on all known government vessels, both British and US—thirty-four in total—active on the lakes during that ten-year period. Particular attention was paid to the final disposition of each. Of the ships

listed, there are only two whose ultimate fate is unknown or uncertain.[49] In neither of those two cases is there anything that would link them to the Southampton wreck. Based on this research, the conclusion was reached that there was only one ship of the period that the historical record supports as a candidate for the wreck at Southampton—and that is *General Hunter.*[50]

The hull, the artifacts, and the historical record together presented an almost irresistible combination in support of the *General Hunter/Hunter* identification. Still we had not yet found our "smoking gun." Enter Washington, DC, researcher Jonathan Webb Deiss. I had met Deiss on the internet while searching for information on individual crew members from *Hunter.* The crew names in the 1885 *Marine Record* story included a man named John Webb. Deiss was working on a family Web site, documenting information on members of the Webb family who had been involved in military units and activities. My enquiry about *Hunter* crew member John Webb led to a growing interest in our wreck on the part of Deiss. Ultimately, his research provided the key items in the *General Hunter/Hunter* story.

In September 2005, while searching at the US National Archives, Deiss located original documents concerning the loss of *Hunter.*[51] His finds included a letter from Gen. Alexander Macomb to Secretary of War William Crawford reporting *Hunter*'s misfortune, accompanied by an account by crew members of the events leading to the wrecking on August 19, 1816.[52] Macomb's letter is dated September 7, 1816, and the attached legal declaration was sworn on August 29, 1816. The documents provide convincing evidence that our wreck and *General Hunter/Hunter* are the same vessel.

Macomb's letter tells Crawford of *Hunter* being "cast away on the Canadian shore," and further states, "I have dispatched two boats to save the rigging, anchors and cables and to burn the wreck so as to secure the iron of the hull." In our excavation, we found no rigging, anchors, or cables and very little else of any size, suggesting that the wreck was salvaged. The hull showed clear evidence of burning in all upper sections, especially on the frame ends. As well, the appearance of many of the iron fasteners found on the wreck indicated they had been exposed to extreme heat. Although we have no historical documentation yet, it appears that the two boats sent by Macomb found the beached wreck and carried out his orders to salvage what they could and then burn the vessel in order to more easily recover metal fixtures and fasteners from it.

In the legal declaration by John Davis, the master of *Hunter,* and two other crew members, there are a number of details that match the evidence from the Southampton wreck. In his statement, Davis says the brig left Michilimackinac for Detroit on August 15, 1816, "having taken on the necessary ballast. . . . there being no lading of any kind for said brig." We recovered over seven tons of ballast from the hull at Southampton but found nothing that could be identified as possible cargo.

Davis stated that the gale struck the vessel on August 17 and continued through the next two days, pushing the brig toward the east side of Lake Huron (plate 4b). The crew's struggle to stay off the lee shore was hampered by the aged and unsound condition of the mainmast, which Davis declared was "sprung and very rotten in the partners." This echoes a report written seventeen months earlier by US Navy Captain Arthur Sinclair, wherein *Hunter* was said to be "very old and rotten and unfit for service," with its "sails and rigging equally bad."[53] Some repairs may have been done on the vessel during the intervening time, but they apparently did not include the mainmast or the deck timbers around it.

Davis stated that as the storm continued to force *Hunter* toward the Canadian shore, "at twelve of the clock of midnight . . . it being very dark . . . we found ourselves in among the breakers . . . [we decided to] put the helm hard a weather and run her in head foremost . . . when she struck in a few minutes." About 0.93 mile (1.5 km) directly out from where the wreck lies on Southampton beach, a series of shoals create a breaker line running parallel to the shore for a little over half a mile (1 km). An inward-bound ship would have to cross through these breakers before reaching the shore just a few minutes later.

After the ship ran on the shore, the mainmast went over the side, enabling Davis, the seven other crew members, and two young passengers to crawl to land "by the wreck of the mainmast."[54] During our excavation we found serious hull damage in two places, the port bow and amidships on the starboard side. The port bow damage must have happened as the ship struck the beach and then was pounded continually by the

storm waves. Certainly the vessel could not have sailed at all with the damage now evident at the bow. Given the present orientation of the wreck—parallel to the water's edge with the bow to the north—the damage at the starboard amidships area is most likely where the mast, mentioned in the crew's statement, came crashing down as the ship hit the shore.

The crew and passengers spent a day and a half on the beach, struggling to recover food from the wreck—which had filled with water—and presumably waiting for the wind and waves to abate. They left in the ship's boat at 4:00 p.m. on August 21, heading for Detroit: "compelled to leave said brig . . . about one hundred miles in a northern and eastern direction from the rapids of St. Clair, surrounded by rocks, buried in the quick sands, her seems [*sic*] open and in such a situation as being rotten above the light water mark, as to render any probable efforts to save her useless." The beach at Southampton is almost exactly 100 nautical miles, or 116 statute miles (186.7 km), north and east of the St. Clair rapids where Lake Huron funnels into the St. Clair River. The location of the wreck is at the head of a gradually curving beach bay. This is a favorite present-day swimming location with a bottom of mostly smooth sand and with water that deepens more quickly than locations just 150 feet (45 m) or so on either side. It is also relatively free of the rocks, some very sizeable, that cover the bottom immediately north and south of the wreck location. The words "surrounded by rocks, buried in the quick sands" perfectly describe the very specific beach environment at the wreck site. Clearly, we had found our historical "smoking gun." The wreck buried under the beach at Southampton is the same vessel built in 1806 as the Provincial Marine's (and later the Royal Navy's) *General Hunter,* then lost in 1816 as the US Army's transport *Hunter.*

While the Southampton beach shipwreck has been identified, we remain intrigued by certain questions about the brig and its life. For instance, why was *Hunter* still sailing in 1816? The historical evidence suggests that it was not seaworthy by this time. As we have seen, in March 1815 the vessel was described as "very old, rotten and unfit for service," and at the time of the wrecking seventeen months later, its mainmast was "sprung and very rotten in the partners" and the hull was "rotten above the light water mark." So, the record indicates that by 1816, *Hunter*'s upperworks and at least some of its spars were suffering from years of exposure to extremes of weather and were in need of extensive repairs or replacement. In contrast, however, and intriguingly, the hull remains we excavated and recorded—largely below the light water mark—appeared to be in remarkably good condition, with most interior seams solid and tight.

Also intriguing is the question of why *Hunter*'s wrecking seems to have received little attention in the public press or in British records. It is possible that the loss of a US military vessel on a Canadian shore in 1816 was something the United States preferred to keep quiet. Tension between these two recent combatants continued to exist on the lakes in the early years after the war. For example, in 1815 a British ship was seized at Sacket's Harbor and held by the United States under questionable circumstances.[55] In 1816 the British illegally boarded and inspected a US vessel off Fort Malden.[56] In this environment, the US Army may have wanted to handle the loss of *Hunter* with a minimum of fuss and official notice. It is equally possible that the wrecking was considered just not to be newsworthy: *Hunter* was a worn-out old brig, there was no cargo of value on board, and no lives were lost in the wrecking.

There is much more to be learned about the life and times of the remarkable shipwreck buried under the Southampton beach. The *General Hunter* story remains a work in progress, and plans are still under consideration for the recovery, conservation, and display of the shipwreck in a museum setting.[57] In the meantime, a 90-foot-long (27.43 m) stone breakwater on the Southampton beach helps protect the *General Hunter*'s buried hull while a large descriptive plaque serves as a headstone on the gravesite of this unique War of 1812 veteran.

NOTES

1. The Ontario Marine Heritage Committee (OMHC) is a volunteer organization formed in 1976 to help protect the province's shipwrecks and other marine-related sites. OMHC members who played a major role in the initial investigation include shipwreck reconstructor Stan McClellan, historian Patrick Folkes, and archaeologists Scarlett Janusas, Leslie Currie, and Burke Penny. McClellan, Folkes, and Currie continued to play vital roles in the later work, especially the 2004 excavation. The author also acknowledges the critical role played by the Southampton Marine Heritage Society—particularly Michael Sterling, Ken Rothenberg, and Project Photographer Larry LePage—as well as over two hundred community volunteers who assisted with all periods of excavation.

2. The *General Hunter* is reported by various sources as built and launched in 1805: John R. Stevens, "H.M. Provincial Marine Schooner *General Hunter, 1805*," *Nautical Research Journal* (October 1951), p. 1; or in 1806: William S. Dudley, ed., *The Naval War of 1812: A Documentary History,* vol. 2 (Washington, DC: Naval Historical Center, 1992), p. 506; or in 1807: Robert Malcomson, *Warships of the Great Lakes: 1754–1834* (London: Caxton Editions, 2003), p. 45. To date, we have found no primary source that provides a definitive date for the launch of *General Hunter.* However, it seems clear from the correspondence of Alexander Grant that the vessel was laid down in the fall of 1806; Alexander Grant, March and May of 1806, vol. 727, pp. 14, 15, 21–22, series C, record group 8 (RG 8), Library and Archives Canada (LAC). It is not clear if it entered service late that year or in the spring of 1807.

3. The Harbour of Refuge was constructed at Southampton during the last half of the nineteenth century to provide a protected area for sailing vessels traveling the largely open and unprotected eastern shore of Lake Huron. The Harbour was enclosed by two sections of a massive breakwater rising 7½ feet (2.28 m) above the lake's mean water level. One section formed a 1600-foot (488 m) landward arc out from the northern end of Chantry Island, where an Imperial Lighthouse had been built. A second section was built in a slightly curved line extending 1800 feet (549 m) out from the shore. A 450-foot (137 m) gap between the two breakwater sections formed the entrance.

4. The author has found information on nine other "saddle" mast steps located on the following wrecks: the British sloop *Boscawen* (1759); the schooner *Nancy* (1786); two unidentified wrecks near Savannah, Georgia, one at the "Fig Channel Site" (mid-to-late 18th century) and the other at the "Derelict Site" (first third of the nineteenth century); the "Clydesdale Wreck" in the Savannah Back River (1780 to 1820 period); the Royal Navy frigate *Burlington,* ex–*Princess Charlotte* (1814); the Millecoquins/Naubinway Sands Wreck (ca. 1833); the Mepkin Abbey Wreck (ca. 1825–50); and the schooner *Alvin Clark* (1846). The mast step on our wreck closely resembles the earlier examples—especially that found on *Boscawen*—and is markedly different from the much later *Alvin Clark* step.

5. The Rush-Bagot Agreement limited the British and the US to one armed ship each on Lakes Ontario and Champlain and two ships each on the Upper Lakes. All other ships on the lakes, including naval vessels, were banned from carrying any cannon. See John W. Foster, *Limitation of Armaments on the Great Lakes,* pamphlet no. 2 (Washington, DC: Carnegie Endowment for International Peace, Division of International Law, 1914).

6. Milo M. Quaife, ed., *The John Askin Papers,* vol. 2 (Detroit: Detroit Library Commission, 1931), pp. 608–10; Fred C. Hamil, *The Valley of the Thames 1640 to 1850* (Toronto: University of Toronto Press, 1951), p. 67.

7. Quaife, ed., *The John Askin Papers,* vol. 2, p. 256.

8. J. Richard Steffy, *Wooden Ship Building and the Interpretation of Shipwrecks* (College Station, TX: Texas A&M University Press, 1994), p. 180. A similar breast hook can be seen on the Revolutionary War US privateer brig *Defence* (1779), although *Defense*'s breast hook was shaped from a single piece of timber.

9. At the time of writing, the location of the midship frame remains under discussion. The configuration of the frames would theoretically allow either the frame indicated or the one immediately aft of it to be the midship frame. Thus, the indicated location of the midship frame remains tentative, pending further study of the recorded hull information.

10. There would not have been room between frames to drill the holes and drive the treenails if the frames were assembled in place on the hull.

11. However, no obvious evidence was found on the keelson to indicate that the wedge-shaped blocks supporting the mast step had ever been fixed to the keelson in another location.

12. This possibility is being tested by the Canadian Conservation Institute in Ottawa during the ongoing cleaning and conservation of the fasteners.

13. Katherine Patton (Department of Anthropology, University of Toronto), preliminary faunal analysis, personal communication, August 2010.

14. Mendel Peterson, *History Under the Sea: A Handbook for Underwater Exploration* (Washington, DC: The Smithsonian Institution, 1965), p. 116. The bore of our swivel gun measures about ¼ inch (.63 cm) larger than the diameter of a 1-pound ball, a comfortable fit between shot and cannon. Neither the considerably smaller ½-pound shot nor the larger 1½-pound ball would be suitable for this gun.

15. We know that at different points in its Provincial Marine and Royal Navy service *General Hunter* carried both 18- and 12-pounder guns. See David C. Skaggs and Gerard T. Altoff, *A Signal Victory: The Lake Erie Campaign 1812–1813* (Annapolis: Naval Institute Press, 1997), p. 187.

16. Brian L. Dunnigan, *The British Army at Mackinac 1812–1815: Reports in Mackinac History and Archaeology,* no. 7 (Lansing, MI: Mackinac Island State Park Commission, 1980), p. 28.

17. John Askin was a well-known merchant, landowner, and public figure in Upper Canada in the late eighteenth and early nineteenth centuries. His "Askin Papers," edited by Milo M. Quaife and published in two volumes, provide a wealth of information on trade as well as the general state of affairs in the country at the time.

18. Quaife, ed., *John Askin Papers,* vol. 2, pp. 608–10.

19. J. Mackay Hitsman, *The Incredible War of 1812: A Military History,* rev. ed. (1965; repr. Toronto: Robin Brass Studio, 1999), pp. 13, 19, 42.

20. The vessel was named for Peter Hunter, lieutenant governor of Upper Canada from 1799 until his sudden death in 1805. *Dictionary of Canadian Biography Online,* s.v. "Hunter, Peter" (Laval University, 2000, http://www.biographi.ca/009004-119.01

-e.php?&id_nbr=2471&interval=25&&PHPSESSID=ae3vue16dkshnfprbv4rspnoho, accessed February 2013).

21. *Marine Record* (Cleveland), June 11, 1885. This article reported details of the loss of *General Hunter* nearly seventy years earlier. The paper credited the *St. Ignace Republican* as the source of the story but provided no date or further information on the original report. To the best of our knowledge, copies of the *St. Ignace Republican* from that early period have not survived. However, the story did contain considerable detail on the events leading up to the shipwreck and the date and circumstances of the wrecking. It also provided the names of the master and the members of the crew and reported that all on board, including two passengers, were saved. The article was clearly a credible account of the loss and included the statement, "[*Hunter*] went ashore and was wrecked on the eastern shore of Lake Huron, about one hundred miles from the St. Clair rapids." That location would place the wreck in the Southampton area. The *Marine Record* story, published seven decades after the event, rang true but could only be verified after the discovery in 2005 of the official US Army report on the loss of the vessel.

22. Quaife, ed., *John Askin Papers,* vol. 2, pp. 568, 636, 696, and *passim.*

23. William Wood, ed., *Select British Documents of the Canadian War of 1812,* vol. 1 (Toronto: The Champlain Society, 1920), pp. 239–41.

24. Wood, ed., vol. 1, pp. 29, 558; Donald R. Hickey, *The War of 1812: A Forgotten Conflict* (Urbana: University of Illinois Press, 1989), pp. 81–84.

25. Wood, ed., *Select British Documents,* vol. 1, p. 558.

26. Skaggs and Altoff, *Signal Victory,* pp. 30–31, 92.

27. William Wood, ed., *Select British Documents of the Canadian War of 1812,* vol. 2 (Toronto: The Champlain Society, 1923), p. 38.

28. Vol. 730, p. 150; series C, RG 8, LAC. Bignell was just one of the commanders or first officers killed or wounded on five vessels of the six-ship British squadron. This critical loss of command capability in the squadron is considered to have been an important factor in the British loss of the battle.

29. Skaggs and Altoff, *Signal Victory,* pp. 118–48.

30. Michael J. Crawford, ed., *The Naval War of 1812: A Documentary History,* vol. 3 (Washington, DC: Naval Historical Center, 2002), pp. 453–54, 543, 574. *Hunter*'s dimensions were recorded by the US Navy as 70 feet (21.33 m) on deck, 18 feet (5.48 m) beam, and 10 feet (3.14 m) depth of hold, with an armament of ten 4-pounder cannon and a prize value of $20,600. Crawford, ed., *Naval War of 1812,* vol. 3, pp. 374–75.

31. According to a letter held by researcher Michael Spears, the original registration document transferring ownership of *Hunter* from the US Navy to John Dickson on July 8, 1816 is missing from the National Archives and Records Administration (NARA) files but the entry for the registration does appear on the pertinent Master Abstract held in the Washington archives. A copy of the (clearly authentic) registration is held by the author,

but the original source remains unknown. The author acknowledges the assistance of Detroit, Michigan, researcher Michael Spears and Dearborn, Michigan, researcher Fred Neuschel in providing many of the NARA references found in this chapter.

32. *Buffalo (NY) Gazette,* August 1, 1815; F. S. Belton, General Orders Fifth Military District (General Orders), November 10 and September 19, 1815, Records of United States Army Commands, 1784–1821, record group 98 (RG 98), National Archives and Records Administration (NARA).

33. Peter B. Porter Papers, Buffalo and Erie County Historical Society, Buffalo, NY. Henry B. Brevoort to Peter B. Porter, January 2, 1816. Brevoort wrote: "The Government has purchased the Hunter" and went on to request a position on the ship, presumably as master.

34. *Buffalo (NY) Gazette,* May 28, 1816; NARA, RG 98, Records of US Army Command 1784–1821, F. S. Belton, General Orders, April 18, June 16, and July 28, 1816, RG 98, NARA. In contemporary documents the fort and village on Michilimackinac Island are variously referred to as Mackinac, Fort Mackinac, Michilimakinac, and Fort Michilimackinac. This apparently caused no confusion. The various names continue in use today.

35. Stevens, "Schooner *General Hunter,*" p. 1; Dudley, ed., *Naval War of 1812,* vol. 2, p. 506; Malcomson, *Warships of the Great Lakes,* p. 45.

36. William Bell Papers, p. 96, Military Group 24 (MG 24), LAC; Malcomson, *Warships of the Great Lakes,* p. 85.

37. William Bell Papers, p. 96; Malcomson, *Warships of the Great Lakes,* pp. 101, 112.

38. William Bell Papers, p. 96.

39. William Bell Papers, *passim.*

40. Eiko Emori, *Shipbuilding at Fort Amherstburg 1796–1813* (Ottawa: Parks Canada, 1978), p. 14. In fact, this plan is apparently a copy of one prepared by John R. Stevens for his 1951 *Nautical Research Journal* article on the *General Hunter.* Stevens' plan, in turn, was apparently redrawn from one done by William Bell in 1803 (William Bell Ship Plans, vol. 726, p. 77, series C [I], RG 8, LAC), probably for *Hope* but not labeled as such.

41. In a number of existing ship and shipwreck publications this vessel is identified as *General Hope,* but historian Patrick Folkes suggests the primary references he has seen refer to the vessel as *Hope,* e.g., vol. 726, p. 188 and vol. 727, p. 15, series C, RG 8, LAC.

42. William Bell Ship Plans, p. 77.

43. William Bell Papers, Folio 3, p. 5; MG 24, LAC.

44. J. Richard Steffy, personal communication, 2005. Steffy, a leading authority on wooden ship building, concurred with the members of the excavation team who made this same observation during the excavation.

45. Dudley, ed., *Naval War of 1812,* vol. 2, p. 485; Wood, ed., *Select British Documents,* vol. 1, p. 558.

46. Francis S. Belton, General Orders, April 18, June 16, and July 28, 1816, RG 98, NARA; Ernest A. Cruikshank, "The Contest for the Command of Lake Erie," in *The Defended Border: Upper Canada and the War of 1812,* Morris Zaslow, ed. (Toronto: MacMillan Company of Canada, 1964), p. 85.

47. Francis S. Belton, General Orders, September 28 and November 10, 1815, RG 98, NARA.

48. Ken Cassavoy, "Southampton Beach Shipwreck Project: 2004/2005 Excavation & Preliminary Research Report" (archaeological report, Peterborough, ON, December 2005), Appendix II, List of Ships.

49. Cassavoy, "Southampton Beach Shipwreck Project." The two vessels in question are the *General Wilkinson/Amelia* and the *Caledonia/General Wayne.*

50. Patrick Folkes, personal communication, 2005.

51. Washington-based researcher Warren Deiss located the critical documents in the US Army Quartermaster General's papers at the US National Archives in Washington. Deiss's hourly research consultant fees were made available to the author through the Symons Trust Fund at Trent University in Peterborough, Ontario, Canada.

52. Alexander Macomb to William Crawford with attached Legal Declaration by *Hunter* Master and two crew members, September 7, 1816, entry 18, letter 302, letters received 1801–89, Records of the Secretary of War: RG 107, NARA.

53. Comm. Arthur Sinclair to unknown addressee, March 24, 1815, microcopy 625, roll 77, Naval Records Collection of the Office of Naval Records and Library 1775–1910: RG 45, NARA.

54. Macomb to Crawford, RG 107, NARA.

55. Comm. Edward Owen to Edward Laws, October 19 and 28, 1815, Comm. Sir Edward Owen Letterbook, Queen's University Archives, Kingston, ON. The letters discuss a British "dockyard schooner" detained and held at Sacket's Harbor by the American authorities.

56. The *Canton Ohio Repository* of July 4, 1816 published the sworn legal declaration of George B. Larned, a passenger on *Hunter,* to George McDougall (J. P.) concerning the boarding and inspection of the vessel, its cargo, and its passengers by a British naval officer off Fort Malden on June 8, 1816.

57. Kenneth A. Cassavoy, "The Southampton Beach Shipwreck Project: Recovery, Conservation and Display, Preliminary Study" (archaeological report, Peterborough, ON, 2005). A major new *General Hunter* and War of 1812 exhibit opened in June 2012 at the Bruce County Museum and Cultural Centre in Southampton, Ontario, commemorating the bicentennial of the start of the war.

3 "A PERFECT MASTERPIECE OF WORKMANSHIP"

His Majesty's Hired Transport Schooner *Nancy*

CHRISTOPHER R. SABICK

Introduction

The story of His Majesty's Schooner *Nancy* begins where the vessel's career ended: at the south end of Lake Huron's Georgian Bay, in the little town of Wasaga Beach. The town is renowned for its beautiful sandy shoreline, a feature that attracts thousands of tourists each summer. Not far from the beach is a small museum, the Nancy Island Historic Site, where the remains of *Nancy*'s hull are displayed (fig. 3.1). Originally built as a transport for the fur trade, *Nancy* enjoyed twenty-five years of service that encompassed many important events on the Great Lakes. *Nancy* was one of the earliest merchant vessels built on the Upper Lakes, and for years it was also the largest, despite its modest size.[1] The British government pressed the schooner into service during the War of 1812, and it was ultimately set ablaze to avoid capture by the United States. Excavated and recovered from the Nottawasaga River in the late 1920s, *Nancy*'s charred and eroded lower hull has survived into the twenty-first century. The ship is the earliest example of a Great Lakes merchant schooner—and the oldest veteran of the 1812–14 naval campaigns—to be documented by archaeologists.

Nancy in Peace and War

In the aftermath of Britain's conquest of French Canada in 1760, the trade in fur burgeoned. The flow of pelts out of the Canadian interior had to be met by an inflow of goods in exchange, and this led to the development of trading routes along the waterways. The majority of cargoes were shipped via the Ottawa River in large canoes propelled by voyageurs.[2] The Ottawa route involved more than thirty portages, where merchandise and canoes were carried around rapids and other obstacles in the water. This required a large number of men, an average of eight to ten voyageurs per canoe, and reduced the amount of goods that could be carried. There was, however, another way to reach

Figure 3.1. *The lower hull of the merchant schooner–turned–naval transport* Nancy. *One of the earliest commercial vessels to sail the Upper Lakes,* Nancy *is also the oldest surviving vessel from any of the 1812-era naval squadrons on the North American lakes. (Courtesy of Wasaga Beach Provincial Park.)*

the continental interior—sailing the Great Lakes. Merchandise could be sent in privately owned sailing vessels by the lakes route as far as Grand Portage on western Lake Superior. This route was less direct and slower than that of the Ottawa River but it was more cost effective, particularly for items such as heavy barrels, stoves, and ironware that were difficult to carry in canoes. For the lake route, schooners like *Nancy* were a necessity.

With the outbreak of the American Revolutionary War, the British placed severe restrictions on lake commerce. Fearing that trade items might find their way to rebel colonists, authorities ordered that all goods be carried in government vessels.[3] For the fur traders of Montreal, this was a setback for their thriving businesses. The King's vessels were kept busy transporting troops and supplies to the military posts around the lakes, and the government had little time or space for commercial cargoes. Goods were often delayed for

months and in some cases even a year or more.[4] Thus, traders were forced to rely heavily on the Ottawa River route, which greatly increased labor costs and cut into profits. Merchants were willing to put up with these restrictions during wartime, for they were, after all, transporting the weapons and stores desired by the Americans: muskets, powder, shot, blankets, and food-stuffs. They were outraged, however, when the restrictions remained in place after the war ended in 1783.

With trading areas now extending to the Canadian Rockies, merchants were desperate to reduce shipping costs in any way possible. To this end, they petitioned for the removal of controls on lake shipping. As their business generated more than £20,000 a year in taxes, traders carried considerable political weight, and in 1788 the government finally relented and opened Lake Ontario to private navigation. The following year saw this right extended to all the Great Lakes.[5]

The first fur trading company to take advantage of the lifting of restrictions on the Upper Lakes was Forsyth Richardson and Company. This small firm was formed in 1787 to directly compete with the much larger and wealthier North West Company. A sailing vessel was deemed necessary to reduce their shipping costs, and company partner John Richardson elected to oversee the construction of the ship at Detroit.

Richardson, whose knowledge of ships included service as the supercargo on the British privateer *Vengence* during the American Revolution, arrived in Detroit on June 20, 1789 with a master shipwright and party of carpenters.[6] The crew set up its yard in a protected location on the banks of the River Rouge just south of Detroit. This location, adjacent to the Detroit River, allowed builders to float large rafts of excellent timber directly to the shipyard. White oak was harvested from nearby lake shores for the keel, frames, and planking of the new ship; white pine was gathered from the shores of Lake Huron for the masts and beams; and red cedar was cut from the islands of Lake Erie for the upperworks of the hull.[7]

The North West Company's vessel was large for a lake merchantman, measuring 80 feet (24.4 m) in length by 22 feet (6.7 m) in beam, with an estimated burthen of 120 tons (the hold reportedly could carry up to 350 standard-sized wooden barrels). According to Richardson the bow was adorned with a figurehead of "a lady dressed in the present fashion, and with a hat and feather."[8] Richardson described the new schooner

Figure 3.2. *The schooner* Nancy *under sail.* Nancy *was built to support the thriving trade in furs that was so important to the economy of late-eighteenth-century Canada. In this conjectural painting by Peter Rindlisbacher, the vessel is passing the fur-trading post of Moy Hall on the Canadian side of the Detroit River. (Courtesy of the artist.)*

to his partners as "a perfect masterpiece of workmanship and beauty," declaring that "the cost to us will be great but there will be the satisfaction of her being strong and very durable."[9] This assertion was borne out by the vessel's quarter-century-long career.

Completed in late summer and launched in November, the new schooner was named *Nancy* (fig. 3.2). The outfitting and rigging were finished in the spring of 1790, and the vessel departed on its maiden voyage to Fort Erie at the eastern end of Lake Erie on June 19. It was the first of scores of journeys the schooner would make on the lakes.[10] Although historical documentation of *Nancy*'s merchant career is limited, it is clear that most passages were between Fort Erie, Detroit, and Michilimackinac, the fortified post at the Straits of Mackinac that join Lakes Huron and Michigan.

A table of freight rates for cargoes shipped on *Nancy* in 1790 shows the variety of provisions and merchandise, including pickled meat, alcohol, powder and shot, candles, soap, stoves, oil, and paint, that was carried on lake vessels of this period. *Nancy* was not used exclusively for commercial trade, however. On at least two occasions, in 1794 and again in 1801, the schooner was hired to carry government dispatches to outposts around the Lakes.[11]

Nancy also worked as a troop transport. In 1794 the schooner carried members of the 5th Infantry Regiment from Fort Erie to Detroit, and in 1803 the ship transported elements of the 49th Regiment of Foot to Amherstburg.[12] Additionally, the journal of trader Thomas Duggen at Michilimackinac reported that in July 1796, *Nancy* arrived from Lake St. Clair carrying a Native American chief and his family who were to receive presents from the British government.[13] *Nancy* worked as a trading vessel for Forsyth Richardson and Co. until 1798, when the firm merged with other small competitors of the North West Company to form the XY Company. Competition from this new firm escalated prices dramatically. As this was harmful to both groups, members of the North West Company advocated a union with the competition, and in July 1804 the XY Company and *Nancy* were absorbed into the larger concern.[14]

Tensions between the United States and Great Britain mounted through the early years of the nineteenth century, ultimately drawing *Nancy* into a conflict more violent than the struggle of rival trading companies. As early as January 1812, the British Army's Provincial Marine explored the possibility of arming merchant ships for the coming war. A letter dated in that month from the North West Company to Capt. Andrew Gray of the Provincial Marine inventoried the firm's assets and their potential for military use. The company listed two vessels on Lake Superior, one of 120 tons capable of mounting six to eight guns and a second of 60 tons capable of being run down the rapids at St. Marys and into Lake Huron. In addition, the North West Company had two vessels on the Upper Lakes, *Nancy* and *Caledonia,* each suitable for four guns.[15]

Nancy remained a merchant ship until word of the declaration of war by the United States reached British military commanders on the lakes in July 1812. They immediately took control of *Nancy,* which was docked at Moy just across from Detroit. A letter from Lt. Col. Thomas St. George in Amherstburg to Maj. Gen. Sir Isaac Brock dated July 8, 1812 reported, "On receiving your letter of the 28th I ordered the Nancy belonging to the NW Co. of about 70 tons, waiting for a wind to take her up from Moy to the upper lake, down here, where she remains."[16] From this location *Nancy* sailed on July 30 in convoy carrying troops to reinforce Fort Erie. *Nancy* spent the remainder of the summer of 1812 transporting troops and supplies throughout Lakes Erie and Huron, and then overwintered in British-occupied Detroit.

In the campaigns of 1813, the British Army commander in Upper Canada, Maj. Gen. Henry Proctor, focused his attention on gaining control of the Ohio shore. Proctor's first goal was to attack and capture Fort Meigs on the Maumee River as soon as the lake was free of ice. The departure of the British was delayed by several weeks of constant rain, and the Americans used the time to improve the fort's defenses and

greatly increase the garrison's numbers. Proctor's force, consisting of 978 troops carried in *Nancy, Lady Prevost,* four other sailing vessels, two gunboats, and several bateaux, finally sailed from Amherstburg on April 24.[17] In addition to the crew, *Nancy* was packed with twenty-eight men of the Royal Artillery, three officers of the 41st Regiment, and fifty-six men of the Royal Newfoundland Regiment.[18] On April 27, the expedition landed on the western shore of the Maumee River, where it was joined by one thousand two hundred Native American warriors. The British found Fort Meigs fully prepared to meet them, and despite a steady bombardment through the end of April and into early May, they were unable to force a breach. Realizing that his opportunity to capture the fort had passed, Proctor lifted the siege and returned with his ships and men to Amherstburg on May 9.[19] A second British expedition against Fort Stephenson on the Sandusky River in late July also failed.[20]

Completing its stint as a troop transport on Lake Erie, *Nancy* then hauled supplies and troops to the isolated fort at Michilimackinac. The schooner departed Detroit on August 31, arriving at the northern fort ten days later. After unloading, *Nancy* spent the rest of September moving supplies between the British posts on Lake Huron. During the first week of October, *Nancy* was ordered to return to Amherstburg with a load of sugar, gunpowder, and cannon.[21]

The tide of war on the western frontier had turned while *Nancy* was away. Unbeknownst to the captain and crew of the schooner, on September 10, 1813 the US and British naval forces met in combat near Put-in-Bay, Ohio. After a hard-fought three-hour battle, the US Navy ships captured the entire Royal Navy squadron. *Nancy* was now in the precarious position of being the only British naval vessel on the Upper Lakes. The United States followed up this victory by recapturing Detroit and taking Amherstburg, effectively seizing control of the waterway between Lakes Erie and Huron.

Nancy's crew discovered this change of fortunes when they entered the St. Clair River on October 5. The schooner was challenged by a small band of US militia, and after a brief firefight, *Nancy* quickly returned to the open waters of Lake Huron, sailing for Michilimackinac to inform the garrison of the defeat on Lake Erie.[22] After passing nearly the full length of Lake Huron, the schooner encountered a violent storm that forced it to turn and run before the gale for three days. *Nancy* was carried back to within 80 miles (128 km) of the St. Clair River before the storm was over. With tattered sails and a badly leaking hull, *Nancy* limped northward once more. Upon arrival at Michilimackinac, the vessel and its crew were sent to St. Marys for the winter.[23]

In February 1814, British naval authorities replaced *Nancy*'s civilian captain with Royal Navy Lt. Newdigate Poyntz. Because Lake Erie and the St. Clair River were now closed to the British, the lieutenant traveled via a newly established supply route to the northern lake. This led overland from York (modern-day Toronto), north to Lake Simcoe, and from there to the headwaters of the Nottawasaga River, leading to Georgian Bay, where transit to Michilimackinac was supplied by *Nancy*.[24]

Poyntz took command of *Nancy* in early May and clashed immediately with Lt. Col. Robert McDouall, the British Army's commander at Michilimackinac. Their feud escalated until Poyntz was relieved of his command and Lt. Miller Worsley was sent in his stead.[25] Worsley also took the overland route, reaching the mouth of the Nottawasaga River in mid-July, where he waited for *Nancy* to arrive. When the schooner appeared at the end of the month, Worsley and crew set about loading the vessel with supplies for the fort that had been stockpiled on the river.[26] *Nancy*, however, was fated never to leave the Nottawasaga.

It was then that a powerful US force commanded by Army Lt. Col. George Croghan and Navy Capt. Arthur Sinclair entered Lake Huron. The ships of the naval force—the 20-gun brigs *Niagara* and *Lawrence,* the brig *Caledonia,* and the schooners *Tigress* and *Scorpion*—were filled with over seven hundred troops intent on capturing Fort Michilimackinac.[27] When the US squadron appeared off Mackinac Island on July 26, McDouall sent word to Worsley via canoe that the long anticipated American attack was imminent.[28] US troops stormed ashore on August 4 but were beaten back by determined opposition from British troops and their native allies. Seeing that the fort could not be captured without a protracted siege, Croghan embarked his troops and the US squadron went in search of easier prey: the schooner *Nancy.* Having learned of the supply depot on the Nottawasaga, the Americans reasoned that if they destroyed it and *Nancy,* Michilimackinac would quickly fall.[29]

McDouall's warning to Worsley recommended that *Nancy* be defended from land: the schooner was armed with only four guns, two 6-pounder long guns and two 24-pounder carronades, and thus had no chance of standing up to the US vessels on the open lake.[30] Worsley and his crew warped the schooner about a mile (1.6 km) upstream from the river mouth and anchored in the channel, leaving *Nancy* separated from Georgian Bay by a narrow spit of sand. They then hastily constructed a log blockhouse on a hill overlooking the schooner and armed it with the vessel's guns.[31]

The US squadron appeared off the Nottawasaga on August 13. Although the brigs *Lawrence* and *Caledonia* had returned to Detroit with soldiers wounded in the abortive attack on Michilimackinac, Worsley and his crew were still greatly outnumbered. The United States had *Niagara, Tigress, Scorpion,* and four hundred soldiers, against which the British could field only twenty-one seamen and ten Native American allies.[32] The landing took place the following morning. Lieutenant Worsley and his men put up a spirited defense, fending off the attackers until mid-afternoon. The Americans then landed an 8½-inch (21.6 cm) howitzer and began dropping explosive shells on and around the blockhouse. One of these shells found its target, detonating the powder supply and blasting the building to pieces.

Recognizing a hopeless situation, Worsley ordered the destruction of *Nancy,* setting the schooner afire as the British defenders slipped into the surrounding forest.[33] Fully laden with a cargo of flour and other stores, the vessel burned furiously before sinking beneath the waters of the river. Worsley and his sailors escaped with one man killed, four wounded, and *Nancy,* the long-serving and able schooner, destroyed.[34]

The loss of the schooner and the vital stores in its hold was a blow to the garrison at Fort Michilimackinac, but one from which the isolated British forces on Lake Huron soon recovered. Not long after the skirmish on the Nottawasaga, Lieutenant Worsley brought two small boats laden with supplies to Mackinac Island, evading the pair of US Navy schooners left by Captain Sinclair to interdict British craft. In early September Worsley turned the tables on the blockaders by leading four boatloads of sailors and soldiers that boarded and captured first *Tigress* and then *Scorpion.*[35] These schooners formed the nucleus for a second Royal Navy Upper Lakes squadron to be built in 1815 at the newly

Figure 3.3. *The excavation of* Nancy *in 1925. The salvage of the schooner's hull, led by a dentist named F. J. Conboy, yielded the crew possessions, ships equipment, weaponry, and barrels of pork and flour left behind when the vessel was scuttled in 1814. Unfortunately, not much is known about the provenience of the artifacts within the hull, the composition of the collection, and the present-day location of these finds. (Courtesy of the Ontario Archives.)*

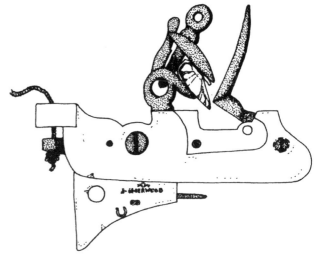

Figure 3.4. *A British cannon lock from the War of 1812 era. According to a report on* Nancy's *excavation, the wreck produced a lock made by Thomas Ashton (or Aston) of London. The present location of the* Nancy *gun lock is not known; however, we know from a somewhat blurry photograph that it resembled this contemporary example made by J. Sherwood. (M-68, A-1980–0399, National Museum of American History, Smithsonian Institution, drawing by Kevin J. Crisman.)*

established base at Penetanguishene on Georgian Bay. The war ended before these plans could be realized.

Salvage and Study of *Nancy*

Nancy's charred hull formed an obstruction in the narrow Nottawasaga River, and in the years after 1814 silt accumulated on and around the timbers, eventually forming a small island. Parts of the vessel remained visible until the late nineteenth century, when mud and vegetation had nearly swallowed up the wreck. In the following years, the beaches around the mouth of the river became a vacation destination, attracting tourists from across Canada. With increased tourism came increased interest in local history, particularly in the story of the dramatic fight of August 1814.

During a visit to the area in 1912, Canadian historian C. H. J. Snider located the hull of the schooner protruding from the side of the island.[36] Word of this discovery spread, and during the summer of 1925 a local amateur group led by a dentist named Dr. F. J.

Conboy began to excavate the remains (fig. 3.3). Conboy's group recovered numerous artifacts, including ship's equipment and rigging elements, pieces of a cast-iron stove, ceramic plates and cups, lead and cast-iron shot, weapons parts (among them a brass cannon lock made by Thomas Ashton of London, fig. 3.4), and hundreds of pig bones from the provisions that had been stowed in the hold. Excavators even unearthed clumps of flour from the casks that were to be shipped to Michilimackinac.[37] In keeping with the practice of many amateur excavations of the time, most of these items found their way into private collections and few can be located today.

The largest artifact, the schooner's hull, avoided this fate (fig. 3.5). The waterlogged remains were removed from the mud during the summer of 1928 and immediately placed in an enclosed museum built on the island that *Nancy*'s hull helped create. Since its salvage the timbers have been kept continuously covered at the Nancy Island Historic Site, a measure of care that has preserved *Nancy*'s remains in better condition than most other 1812 wrecks raised from the lakes during the twentieth century. In the decades since 1928,

Figure 3.5. Nancy's bow shortly after the salvage of the hull. The wreck of Nancy *was considered an important part of Canada's commercial and naval heritage and the structure was accordingly placed in an enclosed exhibit soon after the recovery. This careful treatment has kept the hull in good condition up to the present day. (Courtesy of Queen's University Archives.)*

the wreck has been periodically studied by naval historians and architects, but full-scale archaeological documentation and analysis of the structure was belated, taking place sixty-nine years after the recovery.[38]

During the summer of 1997, archaeologists from Texas A&M University's Nautical Archaeology Program recorded the hull remains. The study included detailed measurements of individual timbers, the taking of offsets and triangulation measurements, and photography. A digital goniometer was used to determine the curvature of the hull at nine frames. The recording project was followed by historical research in the National Archives of Canada, the Public Record Office in London, and libraries and archives throughout the Great Lakes region.

Construction and Reconstruction

The lower portion of *Nancy*'s hull is the impressive centerpiece of the museum display depicting the ship's story and the War of 1812 on Lake Huron. Enclosed in a glass structure at the Nancy Island Historic Site, the remains of the schooner are 68 feet (20.7 m) long, with a beam of 22 feet (6.7 m) at its widest point (fig. 3.6). The well-preserved wood retains much of its structural integrity. The hull is supported transversely by two concrete cradles and longitudinally by a steel "I" beam running under the keel. Unfortunately there is some

minor sagging between the concrete cradles. While most of the timbers retain their original surfaces, many of the upper hull members are eroded from their long immersion in the flowing waters of the Nottawasaga River. Erosion has destroyed almost all evidence of the fire that brought about *Nancy*'s end.

The keel of *Nancy* is preserved for its entire 59 foot 9-inch (18.2 m) length. From its forward end, the keel swells to its greatest dimension, 14¾ inches (37.5 cm) molded by 9½ inches (24 cm) sided at its scarf with the stem, and then gradually tapers toward its after end. The upper surface of the keel's after end is mortised to accept the tenons of the main and inner posts, neither of which are present. A pair of dovetail plates, now missing but whose impressions are visible on either side of the keel, gave the juncture of the keel and main post added strength. The same reinforcing elements are found at the forward end of the keel, where two pairs of iron dovetail plates secure the hook scarf of the keel and stem. The keel is rabbeted for the garboards from the juncture with the stem to a point 14 inches (35.6 cm) from its aftermost end.

The underside of the keel is pierced in twenty-four places. Seventeen of these holes are for iron through bolts that attach keel, floor, keelson, apron, and deadwood. It appears that most of these holes once had plugs that have dried and fallen out, revealing that the bolts are recessed about 2 inches (5 cm). The other seven holes on the underside of the keel do not correlate with through bolts and may be attachment points for a shoe. Such a feature protected the lower surface of the keel in the event of grounding, a common enough hazard on the Great Lakes.

Although neither the main post nor inner post remain, a portion of the other principal stern element, the stern deadwood, still exists. This is one of several impressive pieces of timber used in the construction of *Nancy*. The deadwood sits atop the keel and grows taller as it extends aft over a length of 17 feet 9⅝ inches (5.4 m), terminating only 16 inches (40.6 cm) from the keel's end. Aft of the notch for frame 15, the timber becomes trapezoidal in shape, with the remainder of its lower third beveled to accept the garboard strakes. The deadwood was attached to the keel by five iron bolts, two of which pass through frames 13 and 14. From what survives of the deadwood's after end, it is clear that it had a large, naturally curved upright extension (per-

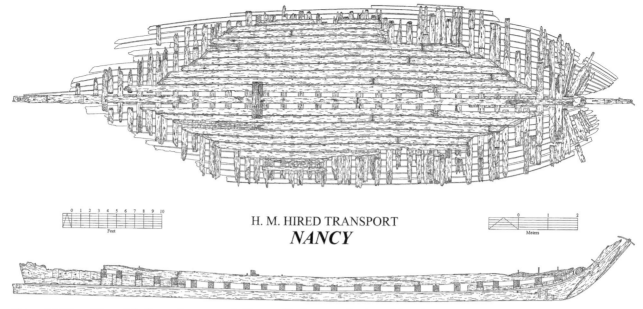

H. M. HIRED TRANSPORT
NANCY

Figure 3.6. *Plan of* Nancy's *hull remains as recorded in 1997. The fire set at the time of the schooner's scuttling burned away the upperworks, and decay and ice further reduced the structure. Nevertheless, the surviving lower hull was a mine of information on the design and construction of the vessel in 1789 and also bore evidence of* Nancy's *long service and many repairs between 1789 and 1814. (Drawing by Christopher R. Sabick.)*

haps originally a protruding branch on a tree trunk) that fit the inboard face of the inner post. The single timber thereby acted as both a stern deadwood and a stern knee, giving *Nancy* an extra measure of strength in this part of the hull.

The stem is another sizable piece of naturally curved timber. The hook scarf that joins the stem to the keel has the two pairs of dovetail plates noted above, as well as a stopwater across the seam to prevent water from leaking into the hull. The stem itself reaches a maximum molded dimension of 23½ inches (59.7 cm) at the gripe and then tapers slightly toward its heavily eroded upper extremity. The starboard surface has the roman numerals "IV" and "V" carved into it to show the crew how much water the schooner was drawing. There may have been more numbers above these two, but they have been eroded away by the river. The lower end of the knee of the head is scarfed to the forward face of the stem; the missing upper section of the knee supported the head rails and figurehead of the vessel.

The stem-keel join was reinforced above by an apron. This piece is notched on its sides and top to seat five floors and is also notched on the sides to fit two cant frames. The apron's forward end is heavily eroded, making it impossible to determine its original length.

Five iron bolts join the stem, keel, apron, keelson, and knee of the head into a single unit.

With the exception of the half frames at the stern, the lower portions of *Nancy*'s framing system are extensively preserved, including parts of all twenty-five full (or square) frames (fig. 3.7). Two types of square frames were evident in *Nancy*'s construction, mold frames (ten total) and regular frames (fifteen total). The former consist of the forwardmost and aftermost full frames (I and 18) and every third frame in between (F, C, Midship, 3, 6, 9, 12, and 15). The mold frames helped the shipwrights to define the fore-and-aft shape of the hull and were preassembled by fastening floors and futtocks together and then mounting the complete frames on the keel, apron, and deadwood. The regular frames between the mold frames were added in separate pieces as the hull was planked, starting with the floor timbers and then continuing with the futtocks. The individual elements of the regular frames were not attached to one another, but only to the planking.

All twenty-five of the original floors are present, though those in the stern are heavily eroded (fig. 3.8). These timbers range in size from 7½ to 9 inches (19 to 22.9 cm) molded and 8 to 9 inches (20.3 to 22.9 cm) sided at the keel. All are notched down over the apron,

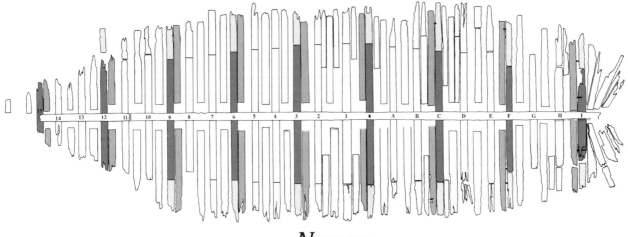

Nancy
Molded Frames

Figure 3.7. *Plan of* Nancy's *lower frames, showing molded frames and filler pieces. The shipwrights working in 1789 preassembled every third frame, fastened each to the keel, and then added the intermediate floors and futtocks as separate pieces, a style of construction seen on the 1759 British Lake Champlain sloop* Boscawen *and the 1814 US Navy schooner* Ticonderoga. *The additional futtock timbers at the turn of the bilge on each side of* Nancy *were added during a later rebuilding of the schooner. (Drawing by Christopher R. Sabick.)*

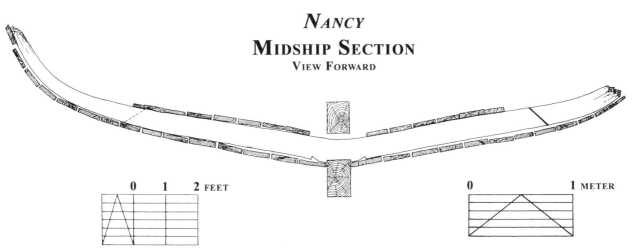

NANCY
MIDSHIP SECTION
VIEW FORWARD

Figure 3.8. *Section of* Nancy's *surviving lower hull at the midship frame. The section shows modest rise to the floors and slack bilges, a form intended to optimize cargo capacity while still providing good sailing characteristics. Note the simple V-shaped cuts that created a pair of limber holes in the bottom of the floor. (Drawing by Christopher R. Sabick.)*

keel, and deadwood on 25-inch (63.5 cm) centers, and all but six (F, 1, 3, 4, 9, and 11) are, or were, attached to the keel or keelson (or both) with iron bolts. A pair of small, triangular limber holes cut into the underside of every floor timber allowed bilge water to flow to the pump well.

Forward of the midship frame, the first futtocks are located aft of the floors, while aft of the midship frame they are forward of the floors, a standard framing pat-tern on ships of the period. The first futtocks of both the molded and the regular frames average 8 inches (20.3 cm) molded and sided, and their heels are located 7 to 10 inches (17.8 to 25 cm) from the sides of the keel. The dimensions of the second and third futtocks were harder to determine (most were eroded or covered by ceiling), but they were similar in size to the first fut-tocks.

The remains of four pairs of radial cant frames

are present in the bow. One of the cant frame pairs is seated in notches on the sides of the apron; the heels of the remaining six timbers simply butt up against it. The heels of the aftermost cant timbers taper to a point, and their sides parallel the forwardmost floor.

Nancy's framing system showed numerous signs of repairs, alterations, and additions, which is hardly surprising in a wooden vessel with such a long career. Wooden treenails were extensively used in the schooner's construction, but by the time of the vessel's loss in 1814, most if not all were replaced by iron spikes and bolts. Floors and futtocks throughout the hull had empty holes for treenails that attached the outside planking. The treenails that fastened the floor and futtock of each mold frame were later reinforced or replaced by diagonally driven iron bolts (there was no room between the frames in the assembled ship to drive the bolts horizontally). Finally, filler timbers were dropped in between the frames to reinforce the turn of the bilge amidships (ten were found on the port side and five on the starboard). The filler pieces had no treenail holes, suggesting that they were a later addition to the schooner's structure; it is possible that they were added to strengthen the hull when *Nancy* was armed with cannon.

The keelson is composed of two timbers hook-scarfed together; it extends for 53 feet (16.2 m) and is molded 12 inches (30.5 cm) and sided 9 inches (22.9 cm). The underside of the keelson has shallow notches that fit over each of the floors. At nearly every floor a bolt was driven through the keelson, floor, and keel (as well as the apron in the bow and the deadwood in the stern). Between frames 7 and 8, a semicircular notch was cut out of the port side of the keelson to fit the schooner's single pump. The base of the wooden pump tube was recorded by John R. Stevens in 1946, although it is no longer displayed with the wreck.[39] Curiously, the top of the keelson did not have mortises for deck beam–supporting stanchions, a common feature on many larger lake vessels of this era; this apparent lack of stanchions may have limited *Nancy*'s ability to carry many guns without straining the deck.

Just forward of the pump well, between floors 6 and 7, are the remains of the mainmast step (fig. 3.9). Known as a "saddle" mast step, this consists of an eroded, large semicircular chock of wood notched to fit over the keelson, with its lower surfaces cut at an

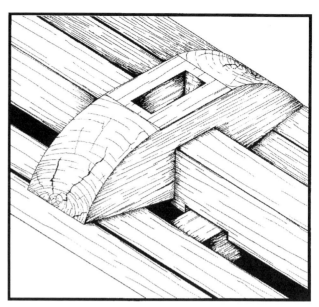

Figure 3.9. Nancy's saddle-type mast step. This style of step has been found on the wrecks of British-built ships dating from the middle of the eighteenth century to the second quarter of the nineteenth century. Saddle steps could be moved forward or aft on the keelson with little difficulty, allowing changes in the location or rake of a mast. (Drawing by Christopher R. Sabick and Adam Loven.)

angle to rest on the ceiling. A large rectangular mortise measuring 13 by 5 inches (33 by 12.7 cm) is cut into its upper surface to receive the squared heel of the mainmast. The foremast step was nothing more than a mortise cut into the keelson. Unfortunately, the forward end of the keelson is heavily eroded and only a single worked surface is visible, making it impossible to determine the dimensions of the mortise.

The hull planking averages 2 inches (5 cm) thick, with individual timbers ranging from 6 to 10 inches (15 to 25 cm) in width. Each strake is comprised of two planks, and all are fastened to the frames with iron spikes. A total of seventeen graving pieces—patches and repairs to the planking—were found, most of them quite small, with the largest being 15¾ inches (40 cm) long and 3 inches (7.6 cm) across. In all cases the decayed or damaged wood was cut out and the graving piece was then fastened with iron spikes.

The ceiling planking is well preserved, averaging 1½ inches (3.8 cm) thick and from 7 to 9 inches (17.8 to 22.9 cm) wide. Individual ceiling strakes are composed of one to three planks, with two planks on the port side reaching 36 feet (11 m) in length. The ceiling is attached to the frames with iron spikes. Four limber boards are present along each side of the keelson. These planks were not fastened to the floors to allow access to the bilges for cleaning. Unlike the hull planking, the ceiling showed no evidence of repair or patching, suggesting that these planks had been replaced not long before the schooner's demise.

Reconstruction and Analysis

The study of *Nancy* adds significant data to the relatively small pool of information relating to eighteenth century lake vessels, highlighting the similarities and differences between *Nancy* and its contemporaries from both freshwater and saltwater environments. *Nancy* has features common to other, slightly later lake vessels in its construction details. The framing pattern suggests a construction sequence that began with the laying of the keel and the addition of the stem-apron and sternpost-deadwood assemblies. Once the backbone was complete, the mold frames were assembled with treenails and attached on 75-inch (1.9 m) centers along the keel. Thin wooden battens were probably used to fair the shape of the mold frames and achieve some level of symmetry. With the shape of the hull defined by these ten frames, the other fifteen intermediate floors were installed and planking of the vessel began using treenails to fasten the planks to the schooner's skeleton. As planking reached the ends of the floors, the futtocks of the regular frames were added by fastening them to the planks.

A nearly identical framing arrangement was found on the British Army sloop *Boscawen* built in 1759 on Lake Champlain.[40] The use of mold frames has also been noted on the remains of the War of 1812 schooner *Ticonderoga* (see Chapter 9). Originally laid down as a steamboat on Lake Champlain, *Ticonderoga*'s unfinished hull was purchased and converted to a sailing warship by the US Navy in 1814. *Ticonderoga*'s hull shape was defined by mold frames located at every fourth frame station; as on *Nancy,* the intermediate (or regular) frames were added separately, with the futtocks attached only to the planking.

Notching the keelson down over the tops of the floors was a common practice on British-built ships of the eighteenth and early nineteenth centuries. It has been noted on many wrecks, including the 1812-era lake warships *General Hunter, Newash,* and *Tecumseth,*

the Browns Bay Vessel, and *Linnet* (see Chapters 2, 4, 8, and 11).[41] Notching the keelson undoubtedly provided a measure of extra strength and resistance to hogging but required more labor in construction as well.

The schooner's saddle-type mainmast step is comparable to steps found on the 1759 sloop *Boscawen* and the brig *General Hunter,* built by the Provincial Marine in 1806 (see Chapter 2).[42] On all three vessels the timber was notched to fit over the keelson. Both *Boscawen* and *General Hunter* had a pair of small, wedge-shaped timbers spiked to the top of the keelson to hold the step in place, but there is no evidence of these pieces on *Nancy*. The mortise in *Boscawen*'s step passes completely through the wood so that the heel of the mast sat on the keelson, which is not the case with *Nancy* and *Hunter*. *Nancy* and *General Hunter* also had similar foremast steps, which consisted of a mortise cut directly into the keelson (*Boscawen,* a sloop, was never fitted with a foremast).

Nancy's unusual longevity was apparent in several repair and reinforcement features. The filler pieces between the frames at the turn of the bilge were almost certainly later additions intended to strengthen the hull amidships. The original treenail fastenings of the mold frames were replaced or reinforced by diagonally driven iron bolts, perhaps during the replacement of rotted frame elements. And there can be no doubt that *Nancy* was replanked at least once, since the frames displayed old treenail holes but the planking currently on the hull is all iron fastened. The use of treenails for fastening frames and planking in 1789 was probably due to the expense of iron fasteners at Detroit, which had to be shipped from eastern sources.

Nancy's twenty-five-year career is surprising, since rot forced the retirement of most lake ships after only six to eight years of service. The fact that this hull lasted three or four times longer than average suggests two things: that the timber in the original structure was well selected and seasoned (the red cedar in the upper hull may have been an especially good choice) and that the vessel was well maintained by its owners. It is also possible that salt was packed between *Nancy*'s frames as a preservative. In the pre-war era, salting experiments were carried out on a number of vessels, including the US brig *Adams* (built in 1797 on Lake Erie) and the Provincial Marine ship *Earl of Moira* (built in 1805 on Lake Ontario); in 1808 the frames of *Adams*

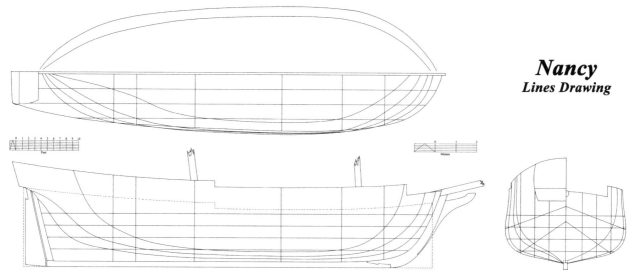

Nancy
Lines Drawing

Figure 3.10. *Reconstructed lines of the Royal Navy schooner* Nancy. *The surviving lower portion of the hull provided a starting point, indicating keel length, the rake of the lower stem and stern, the placement of the mast steps, and frame deadrise to the turn of the bilges. Determining the shape of the upper hull began with upward projections from the existing structure, with supporting evidence drawn from plans of similar late-eighteenth-century merchant schooners, archaeological investigations of the lake schooners* Hamilton *and* Scourge, *and contemporary descriptions of* Nancy. *(Reconstruction by Christopher R. Sabick.)*

were said to be "as sound as the day she was launched," while in 1811 *Earl of Moira*'s timbers were "perfectly sound and free from decay."[43] Whatever combination of factors extended the life of the schooner, *Nancy* proved to be remarkably durable.

The nine hull frame sections recorded in 1997 are the basis for reconstructing *Nancy*'s hull form (fig. 3.10). The well-preserved lower hull, combined with historic descriptions of the schooner's basic dimensions, has allowed for a re-creation of the ship's lines, although the form and arrangement of the upper works is necessarily speculative. The reconstruction reveals a vessel with a relatively bluff entry but with a surprisingly fine run at the stern and a nearly U-shaped midship section with moderate deadrise. The full hull form allowed *Nancy* to carry a large amount of cargo in a stable, seaworthy—but not necessarily speedy or weatherly—vessel. *Nancy*'s hull shape is probably typical of many small lake and coastal merchant schooners of the period.

The reconstructed lines show the vessel as it likely appeared during its working life. These lines, in conjunction with the measurements taken during recording, provided the foundation for a reconstruction of the upper hull (fig. 3.11). The timbers of the lower hull needed minimal adjustment for inclusion on the re-construction drawing, requiring only corrections for the hull distortion that has occurred since the vessel's sinking. This included correcting for the sagging between the concrete supports on which *Nancy* rests, adjusting for timber erosion, and compensating for timbers that have pulled away from their original positions. The upper works were re-created through a comparison to similar vessels from the late eighteenth and early nineteenth centuries, including the Lake Ontario schooners *Hamilton* and *Scourge* (see Chapter 5), examination of primary historic sources that describe *Nancy,* descriptions of the excavation of the hull, and contemporary art depicting vessels of this type. Because nothing survived of the main deck and bulwarks, some guesswork was involved and certain elements may require revision if new information is found.

The reconstruction of *Nancy*'s living spaces is based on the historical record and Snider's description of the hull excavation in 1925. *Nancy*'s stern cabin was one of the schooner's most notable features, as several passengers mention the "admirable cabin."[44] Snider gives an idea of the cabin's size in his description of the artifact assemblage found during the excavation. He describes finding china and other artifacts associated with the cabin to a point 20 feet (6.09 m) forward of the stern. At this spot, Snider and Conboy uncov-

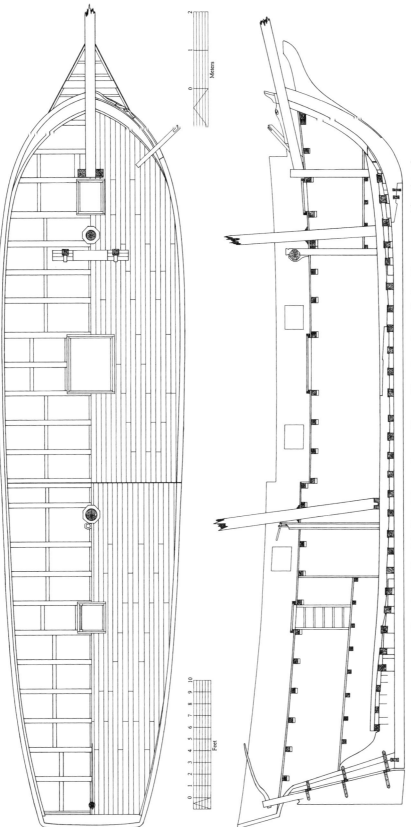

Figure 3.11. Reconstructed deck plan and interior profile of the Royal Navy schooner Nancy. These two views relied on the same combination of evidence used to prepare Nancy's lines: the surviving lower hull, plans and records of similar vessels, archaeological data, and contemporary descriptions of Nancy. Some details are based on informed conjecture. (Reconstruction by Christopher R. Sabick.)

Meters

Feet

0 1 2 3 4 5 6 7 8 9 10

ered the remains of a bulkhead separating the cabin from the cargo hold.[45] Unfortunately, no evidence of this bulkhead remains on the hull today.

The reconstructed deck plan is an educated guess based on the layouts of *Hamilton, Scourge,* and other plans and wrecks and on hints gleaned from the historical record. The windlass is mentioned in *Nancy*'s log during the storm of October 1813: "We then took in sail & handed them, clinched the best & small bower around the mainmast, chocked the windlass from the deck and between the foremast & windlass bit. . . ."[46] This passage also tells us that the windlass is located aft of the foremast.

The inclusion of planked bulwarks and gunports on *Nancy* is based on the after-action report written by Captain Sinclair to Secretary of the Navy William Jones on September 3, 1814. In describing the artillery used by *Nancy*'s defenders, Sinclair says, "There were three guns on the block-house, two twenty-four pounders and one six pounder. I cannot say what was on the vessel as all her ports were closed."[47] The bulwarks and ports on *Scourge* were used to reconstruct those on *Nancy.* These would have offered minimal protection to the crews while they worked the guns, but they are more substantial than *Hamilton*'s open rail.

Hatch placement is based on comparison with contemporary plans and wrecks and on logic. An "admirable cabin" undoubtedly had its own entrance from the quarterdeck. Forecastles invariably had a small companion hatch to allow access to the quarters below. The placement of the large cargo hatch is in the only logical location, above the main hold.

Conclusions

The diminutive size of *Nancy* is inversely proportional to its importance in the history of early Great Lakes shipping. This schooner is the oldest vessel from the Upper Lakes to be archaeologically documented, and it opens a window on the expansion of trade in this region. Gradually, an archaeological and historical perspective on *Nancy* has materialized, revealing aspects of its building, lengthy peacetime service, and short but active career during the War of 1812. The number of freshwater merchant ships with which to compare *Nancy* is quite small, and therefore it is not entirely clear how the schooner fits into the evolution of this vessel type. As more watercraft from this region and

period are discovered and analyzed, a better understanding of the ship may become apparent.

What can be fully gleaned from the history of this reliable little fur trader turned military transport is the important role that sailing vessels played in the survival of the far-flung outposts of the old northwest. *Nancy* was present for many events affecting the political and social development of the Great Lakes region. From its time carrying the merchandise of fur traders, to its fiery demise on the Nottawasaga, to the wreck's raising and display in Wasaga Beach, *Nancy* witnessed the Great Lakes grow from an obscure backwater to one of the most important commercial waterways in the world.

NOTES
1. William S. Dudley, ed., *The Naval War of 1812: A Documentary History,* vol. 1 (Washington, DC: Naval Historical Center, 1985), p. 308.

2. Voyageurs, the canoe men who carried out the wilderness trade, were mostly French Canadians employed by English trading firms after 1761. Marjorie Wilkins Campbell, *The Northwest Company* (Toronto: Macmillan, 1957), pp. 22–23.

3. Harold A. Innis, *The Fur Trade* (New Haven: Yale University Press, 1930), pp. 166–67.

4. Innis, *Fur Trade,* p. 182.

5. Gordon Charles Davidson, *The North West Company* (New York: Russell and Russell, 1967), pp. 29–31.

6. C. H. J. Snider, "A Report on the Schooner *Nancy,* 1789–1925" (manuscript report, Archives of Ontario, n.d.), p. 38.

7. Snider, "Report on the Schooner *Nancy,*" p. 212.

8. Barry Gough, *Through Water, Ice & Fire: The Schooner* Nancy *of the War of 1812* (Toronto: The Dundurn Group, 2006), p. 19; Barry Gough, *Fighting Sail on Lake Huron and Georgian Bay* (Annapolis: Naval Institute Press, 2002), p. 59.

9. Snider, "Report on the Schooner *Nancy,*" p. 38.

10. E. Cruikshank, "An Episode of the War of 1812: The Story of the Schooner *Nancy*" *Ontario Historical Society Papers* 9 (1910), p. 75.

11. England to Simcoe, May, July, August 1794, in John Graves Simcoe, *The Correspondence of Lieutenant Governor John Graves Simcoe,* vol. 2, ed. E. A. Cruikshank (Toronto: Ontario Historical Society, 1923), pp. 237, 242, 365.

12. Ormsby to Green, November 15, 1803, record group 8 (RG 8), Library and Archives Canada (LAC).

13. Thomas Duggan Journal, July 19, 1796, Clements Library, University of Michigan, Ann Arbor, Michigan.

14. Davidson, *North West Company,* p. 86.

15. William Wood, ed., *Select British Documents of the Canadian War of 1812,* vol. 1 (Toronto: The Champlain Society, 1920), pp. 286–87.

16. Wood, ed., *Select British Documents,* vol. 1, p. 364.

17. Alec R. Gilpin, *The War of 1812 in the Old Northwest* (East Lansing: Michigan State University Press, 1958), pp. 182–83.

18. England to Baynes, April 23, 1813, RG 8, LAC.

19. Gilpin, *War of 1812 in the Old Northwest,* p. 190.

20. Gilpin, *War of 1812 in the Old Northwest,* p. 206; Donald R. Hickey, *The War of 1812: A Forgotten Conflict* (Urbana: University of Illinois Press, 1989), p. 136.

21. C. H. J. Snider, ed., *Leaves from the War Log of the Nancy: Eighteen Hundred and Thirteen* (Toronto: Huronia Historical Development Council, 1967), p. 16.

22. Snider, ed., *War Log of the* Nancy, pp. 16–21.

23. Snider, ed., *War Log of the* Nancy, pp. 21–38.

24. Drummond to Prevost, January 28, 1814, RG 8, LAC.

25. Drummond to Prevost, June 16, 1814, RG 8, LAC.

26. Prevost to Bathurst, July 10, 1814, and Worsley to Crookshank, August 2, 1814, RG 8, LAC.

27. Cruikshank, "An Episode of the War of 1812," p. 81.

28. Lieutenant Colonel McDouall to Lieutenant Worsley, July 28, 1814, RG 8, LAC.

29. Michael J. Crawford, ed., *The Naval War of 1812: A Documentary History,* vol. 3 (Washington, DC: Naval Historical Center, 2002), pp. 568–70.

30. McDouall to Drummond, May 26, 1814, RG 8, LAC.

31. Snider, ed., *War Log of the* Nancy, p. 47.

32. Snider, ed., *War Log of the* Nancy, p. 47.

33. There are conflicting opinions as to who destroyed *Nancy* during the battle. Worsley says that an American shell demolished the blockhouse and that he ordered the schooner fired. American sources suggest that the schooner was accidentally set on fire when an exploding shell ignited a powder train that led to the vessel. The author accepts the British view due to the fact that Worsley was on the scene while US commanders Croghan and Sinclair did not land with their troops and relied on the accounts of subordinates. For the British viewpoint see Cruikshank to Turgund, August 21, 1814 (RG 8, LAC), and Worsley to Worsley, October 6, 1814 (Snider, ed., *War Log of the* Nancy, p. 47). For the American view see Croghan to McArthurs, August 23, 1814 and Sinclair to the Secretary of the Navy, September 3, 1814 in E. Cruikshank, "An Episode of the War of 1812," pp. 112–15).

34. Snider, ed., *War Log of the* Nancy, p. 47.

35. Crawford, ed., *Naval War of 1812,* vol. 3, pp. 604–607.

36. Nancy Island Historic Site Personnel, personal communication, 1999.

37. Snider, "Report on the Schooner *Nancy,*" pp. 113, 118, 122, 127.

38. Christopher R. Sabick, *His Majesty's Hired Transport Schooner* Nancy (Master's thesis, Texas A&M University, 2004). Readers wishing to know more about the history and architecture of *Nancy* may download this thesis as a PDF file from the Texas A&M University Anthropology Department Web site.

39. John R. Stevens, personal communication with Kevin Crisman, July 28, 2008; see John R. Stevens, *The Construction and Embellishment of Old Time Ships* (Toronto: Printed for the Author, 1949), p. 46, for a sketch of the tube base. Captain Mackintosh mentions this pump in his log entries when *Nancy* was buffeted by the storm in October 1813; see Snider, ed., *War Log of the* Nancy, p. 27.

40. Kevin Crisman, "Struggle for a Continent: Naval Battles of the French and Indian War," in *Ships and Shipwrecks of the Americas,* ed. George F. Bass (New York: Thames and Hudson, 1988), pp. 142–47.

41. Kellie Michelle Vanhorn, *Eighteenth-Century Colonial American Merchant Ship Construction* (Master's thesis, Texas A&M University, 2004), p. 192.

42. Vanhorn, *Colonial American Merchant Ship Construction,* pp. 193–96.

43. George Herriot, *Travels Through the Canadas Containing a Description of the Picturesque Scenery on Some of the Rivers and Lakes* (Rutland, VT: Charles E. Tuttle, 1971), p. 132; Wood, ed., *Select British Documents,* vol. 1, pp. 242–43; United States National Archives, record group 45, entry 148, Observations by William Gamble, November 12, 1808; Robert Malcomson, *Lords of the Lake: The Naval War on Lake Ontario 1812–1814* (Toronto: Robin Brass Studio, 1998), p. 26.

44. Snider, "Report on the Schooner *Nancy,*" p. 35.

45. Snider, "Report on the Schooner *Nancy,*" p. 113.

46. Snider, ed., *War Log of the* Nancy, p. 28.

47. Cruikshank, "An Episode of the War of 1812," p. 114.

ECHOES OF A NAVAL RACE

The Royal Navy Schooners *Tecumseth* and *Newash*

LEEANNE GORDON, SARA HOSKINS, AND ERICH HEINOLD

Introduction

In August 1953, the tangled, skeletal remains of a ship were raised from the harbor in the Lake Huron town of Penetanguishene, Ontario. Excavations at the nearby War of 1812–era naval base inspired town leaders to raise a contemporary wreck for exhibition. It was only after the salvaging that historians identified the hull as the armed transport *Tecumseth,* one of a pair of Royal Navy schooners built on the Upper Lakes in 1815. Recent research on *Tecumseth* and its sister ship *Newash* (still sunk in the harbor) has illuminated the ships' shadowy past. Conceived and built in the immediate aftermath of the War of 1812, the vessels sailed for only two years before being rendered obsolete by the Rush-Bagot disarmament agreement. Despite their short service, these vessels offer a unique perspective from which to view the postwar period on the Great Lakes.

"Ready to Repel Any Act of Insult or Aggression"

At the close of 1813, the British situation on the upper Great Lakes looked bleak, even unsalvageable. Oliver Hazard Perry's sweeping victory over the Royal Navy on Lake Erie in September left the British with only a handful of small supply vessels. The defeat of Gen. Henry Proctor's army in October resulted not only in the death of the powerful Native American leader Tecumseh but the weakening of the British-Indian alliance and the disorganization of military forces in the west as well. The loss of mobility on the lakes and lack of adequate roads greatly hampered British efforts to maintain the small garrison of Fort Michilimackinac at the western end of Lake Huron.[1]

Despite these daunting circumstances, British leaders were unwilling to cede naval control of the Upper Lakes. Plans to launch an incendiary raid on the US base at Erie during the winter of 1813–14 came to naught, but over the following year a series of opportunistic attacks deprived the US squadron of most of its smaller warships. A British foray on Buffalo, New York, in December 1813 resulted in the burning of the schooners *Chippewa* and *Ariel* and the sloops *Little Belt* and *Trippe*. In August and September 1814, boarding parties in small boats captured the US Navy schooners *Somers, Ohio, Scorpion,* and *Tigress.* Although three small British transports—including *Nancy*—were taken or destroyed in 1814, the garrison at Fort Michilimackinac was sustained with supplies and successfully repelled an American attempt to capture the island in August 1814.

British forces on the western frontier held on in 1814, and there was promise of greater things to follow. A naval yard was established in November 1814 at Penetanguishene, a remote harbor at the southern end of Georgian Bay, Lake Huron, and men and supplies were sent to construct a 44-gun frigate. The new vessel surely would have initiated a new round of building by both sides, but shortly before construction began news of peace reached Canada and the frigate was cancelled.[2]

The war may have been over, but supply and communication were still vital to British forces. In the spring of 1815, the Royal Navy's commissioner of the dockyards on the Great Lakes, Capt. Sir Robert Hall, ordered the building of two 150-ton schooners to serve as transports and gunboats on Lake Erie. Shipwright Robert Moore was appointed to design the vessels and to construct them at Streets Creek, a tributary of the upper Niagara River.[3] Moore's task was daunting: due to the pressing need for transports, he had to convert standing timber to sailing vessels as quickly as possible.[4]

Moore enlarged Hall's proposed ships to slightly over 166 tons. Admiralty plans show a vessel 70 feet 6 inches (21.49 m) long on deck carrying two 32-pounder carronades and two 24-pounder long guns (fig. 4.1). The schooners were given moderate deadrise, considerable rake to the stem and the sternpost, a fine entrance, a full run, and noticeable drag to the keel—features that suggest Moore was seeking a balance between capacity and sailing speed. Moore brought a number of craftsmen to the frontier shipyard and was joined by those who had been sent to Penetanguishene in 1814 to build the frigate.[5]

A commander and several lieutenants were appointed to the renascent squadron by Comm. Edward Owen, commander-in-chief of the British naval forces on the Great Lakes. For the senior officer, Owen chose Capt. William Bourchier, a "firebrand" who fit the mold of many nineteenth-century naval officers: ambitious, self-promoting, and contentious. Also appointed were two lieutenants who would actually command the schooners, Henry Kent and Thomas Bushby.[6] The wartime complement of each schooner would have been around forty men, but for peacetime patrol and transport service this number was reduced to thirty. This number included twenty seamen and warrant officers, a Royal Marine sergeant and six privates, and three ship's boys for each vessel.[7]

Accommodations on the ships were cramped. The sailors berthed in the fore part of the vessel, which also served as the galley. The greater part of the below-deck space was given over to the hold, placed in the middle and widest part of the vessel to maximize cargo capacity. The after accommodations were divided into two compartments. The first, just abaft the mainmast, contained lockers for ship's stores as well as berths for the pilot and master; the after compartment contained berths for the captain and other officers, as well as a storage cupboard. Aft of this compartment were the bread room and magazine.[8]

By August, the schooners were ready to be launched. A watercolor of the vessels standing end to end on one set of stocks (fig. 4.2) illustrates their plain appearance.[9] Each had an unadorned stem with a gammoning knee but no headrails, and their decks were enclosed by open rails instead of bulwarks. The schooners were steered by a tiller instead of a wheel. Curiously, there is no evidence of a windlass in the painting, the Admiralty plans, or the archaeological remains, but a windlass was apparently installed on each foredeck for raising the anchors.[10]

On August 13, 1815, the two hulls were launched and commissioned *Tecumseth* and *Newash* in honor of two Native American allies who had assisted the British in the fight against the United States between 1812 and 1814. Over the next two weeks, the schooners were rigged and outfitted, and they finally set sail on August 26. After five days working upriver against the Niagara's fierce current, they finally wet their keels in Lake Erie.[11]

The schooners' first months were not easy. Shortly after launching, *Tecumseth* ran aground in the Niagara River, and a week later *Newash* struck bottom near Tur-

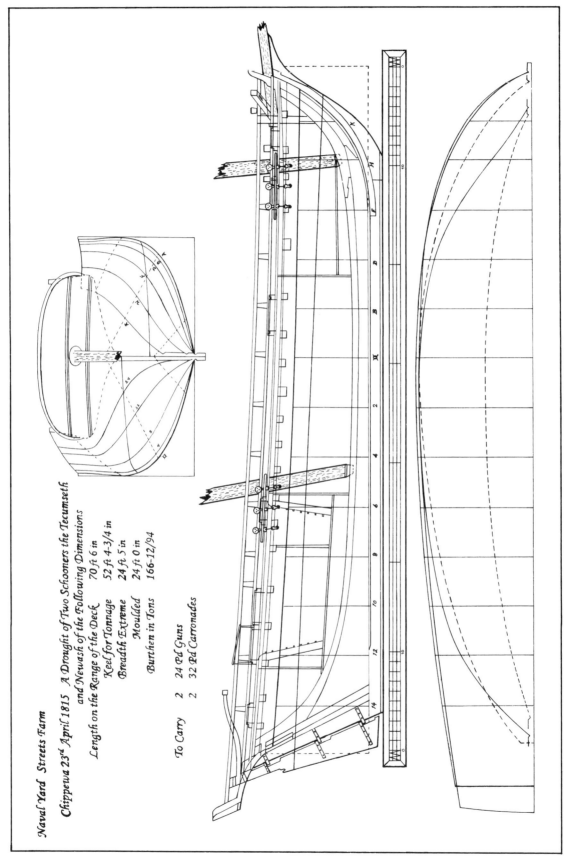

Naval Yard Streets Farm

Chippewa 23rd April 1815 A Draught of Two Schooners the Tecumseth
and Newash of the Following Dimensions

Length on the Range of the Deck   70 ft 6 in
Keel for Tonnage   52 ft 4-3/4 in
Breadth Extreme   24 ft 5 in
Moulded   24 ft 0 in
Burthen in Tons   166-12/94

To Carry   2   24 Pd Guns
       2   32 Pd Carronades

Figure 4.1. Lines of the Royal Navy schooners Tecumseth and Newash. These lines are based on an original plan of the vessels and on archaeological measurements of the two wrecks at Penetanguishene, Ontario. They show a design with considerable drag to the keel, steeply raking end posts, and pronounced rise to the floors, all suggesting a desire for speed and handiness under sail; the full, slack bilges, on the other hand, hint that capaciousness was also wanted in these two transports. (Drawing by LeeAnne Gordon; plan on file in the Public Record Office, Admiralty Fonds, ADM, Reg. No. 4562, Box 64.)

Figure 4.2. Newash *and* Tecumseth *on the slipway at Streets Creek on the upper Niagara River. The schooners appear ready for their launching, which took place on August 13, 1815. This contemporary watercolor by an unknown but accomplished artist nicely illustrates the sleek form, near-flat sheer, and open rails evident in the builder's lines. (With permission of the Royal Ontario Museum, 967.106.2.)*

key Point on Lake Erie. *Tecumseth*'s log notes a draft of 8 feet 5 inches (2.56 m) fully loaded, slightly deeper than the 8 feet (2.43 m) on the lines drawing. This was a problem on the shallow Niagara and Grand Rivers, and the crews would often resort to kedging the ships over the bars.[12]

The schooners also encountered rig-related problems in the capricious, often volatile weather on the Great Lakes. The two were cruising Lake Erie on the afternoon of September 2 when the wind suddenly increased to gale force. *Tecumseth* was unable to reduce sail in time to prevent the bowsprit and both masts from being carried overboard, fortunately without loss of life. *Newash* sprang its foremast despite the crew's efforts to quickly strike sails, yards, and the fore topmast. Lieutenant Bushby of *Newash* wrote that the seas "began to pitch so violently as to render it impossible to lay at anchor without carrying away our masts."[13] These problems were exacerbated by the ships' canvas-heavy rigs: large fore-and-aft sails as well as square topsails and topgallant sails on both masts.[14] The crew of *Newash* attempted to repair the foremast by fishing it with wooden splints and a tight wrapping of rope, but the crack continued to spread until the shipwrights cut

6 feet (1.83 m) off the mast.[15] Meanwhile, *Tecumseth*'s crew rigged jury masts to return to Streets Creek.

After repairs, *Tecumseth* and *Newash* continued operating through the fall of 1815, carrying supplies and passengers between Fort Erie at the entrance to the Niagara River, the naval establishment at Grand River, and Amherstburg on the Detroit River. On one of its passages, *Newash* encountered the US merchant schooner *Mink* near Middle Island in Canadian waters. After *Mink* refused to heed Bushby's request to board, musket shots fired across the bow forced it to stop. *Mink*'s captain was ordered aboard *Newash* and questioned about the ship's origin and destination.[16]

Under other circumstances the event might have been insignificant, but not at this time and place. US newspapers ran scathing articles decrying the "British outrage" as a "renewal of those insults and injuries which led to the late war."[17] The fragile peace was further threatened when US vessels detained or harassed British merchant craft on Lakes Ontario and Champlain.[18] These incidents prompted Commodore Owen to order his officers to "be continually on their guard . . . ready to repel any act of insult or aggression which may be offered them; remembering that the honor

Figure 4.3. *Glass lenses, known as "deck lights" or "patent illuminators," from the wreck of* Tecumseth. *The example on the left bears a British government–property broad arrow mark. A relatively new invention at the time of the War of 1812, deck lights were inset into planks or gunport lids, allowing natural light to illuminate a ship's interior during the daytime. Deck lights were also found on the wrecks of the US Navy lake warships* Jefferson *and* Allen. *(Photo by Erich Heinold.)*

of the British character as well as of its flag is in their hands."[19]

Fortunately, the early onset of winter forced the squabbling navies off the lakes before a more serious breach of the peace could occur. *Tecumseth* and *Newash* were laid up at Grand River and Owen used the winter to re-rig the schooners with different sail configurations. *Tecumseth* was given a gaff-rigged main topsail instead of the square topsail and topgallant, and a trysail mast was fitted abaft the foremast for the foresail. *Newash* was converted to a brigantine by removing the fore-and-aft foresail and by restepping the foremast farther aft. The crews recaulked both vessels, scraped the decks, painted the sides, tarred the rigging, and repaired sails in the winter and early spring of 1816. In addition, they mounted sweeps on which the 24-pounder long guns pivoted, and shipwrights installed deck lights, two examples of which were recovered from the wreck of *Tecumseth* (fig. 4.3).[20]

By late April 1816, *Tecumseth* and *Newash* were ready to begin what would prove to be an eventful sailing season.[21] The Treaty of Ghent stipulated that all territories occupied during the war be returned to their original owners, but the United States and Britain continued to dispute the boundary between Detroit and Amherstburg. At issue was Bois Blanc Island, separated from Amherstburg by a 400-yard-wide (365.76 m)

channel, which the United States claimed and began to occupy in 1815. Captain Bourchier considered the island British territory and the channel to be a British waterway and ordered his naval forces—including *Newash* and *Tecumseth*—to stop and search all passing US vessels for contraband and deserters.[22] A storm of diplomatic protests followed, leading to an admiralty inquiry into Bourchier's actions. The captain was reprimanded and ordered to stop immediately. Neither country wanted war, and the crisis quickly passed.[23]

Falling water levels ended the schooners' careers on Lake Erie. By the summer of 1816, the depth at the mouth of Grand River was only 5 feet 6 inches (1.68 m). In September, Owen decided to transfer the two ships to Lake Huron, where deeper water would allow them to operate with less likelihood of grounding; the smaller schooners *Surprise* and *Confiance* were ordered to Lake Erie in exchange. Due to the late season, *Tecumseth* and *Newash* were laid up for the winter at Grand River and did not reach Lake Huron until June 1817.

After a last transport mission, the vessels sailed for their new station at Penetanguishene. Here their officers and crews learned of the Rush-Bagot Agreement, wherein the United States and Great Britain agreed to limit their respective naval forces on the Upper Lakes to two vessels not exceeding 100 tons, each armed with nothing more than one 18-pounder cannon.[24] At 166 tons apiece, *Tecumseth* and *Newash* were too large to remain in service under the terms of the agreement, and they were therefore decommissioned. After only two years of service, they were stripped of rigging, spars, and guns and placed in ordinary on June 30, 1817.[25]

For the next two years, *Tecumseth* and *Newash* remained at anchor, maintained by a small contingent of sailors (fig. 4.4). In 1819 orders were sent to refit *Tecumseth* for the transport of 200 soldiers to Drummond Island. A survey of the schooner revealed that her timbers had rotted extensively, and a thorough repair was ordered.[26]

Small repairs were probably done over the next several years in an effort to keep the vessels afloat, but they continued to decay. By 1827, *Tecumseth* was listed as "completely rotten" and "sunk." *Newash* was also described as "completely rotten" and apparently had been driven aground. In 1831, the Admiralty decided to close the Great Lakes establishments, and *Tecumseth* and *Newash* were abandoned, their names stricken

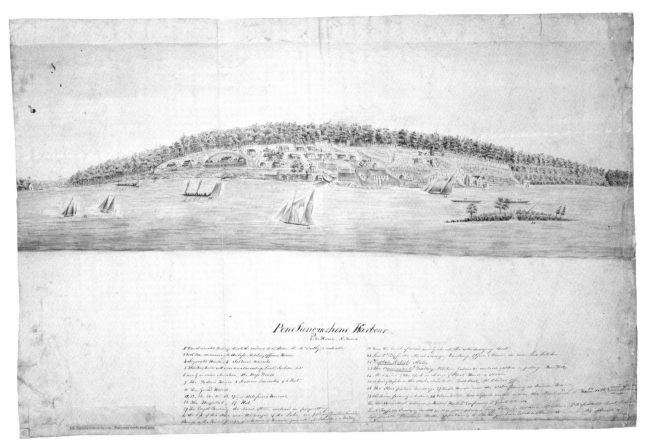

Figure 4.4. Penetanguishene Harbour Lake Huron No. America. *This watercolor identifies the principal structures and vessels at the Royal Navy's base in the southeastern corner of Lake Huron's Georgian Bay. The dismasted hulls of* Tecumseth *and* Newash *are visible on the right, behind the small island; their presence here indicates that the painting postdates their decommissioning in June 1817. (Courtesy of the Toronto Public Library.)*

from the Royal Navy list. Later that year, Comm. Robert Barrie recommended selling most of the lake warships. An advertisement in the newspaper *Canadian Freeman* announced a public auction at Penetanguishene on March 15, 1832. No bids were received for either schooner.[27]

The Raising of *Tecumseth*

For 120 years, the vessels lay on the bottom of Penetanguishene harbor. Interest in Lake Huron's naval history was revived in the 1950s when Dr. Wilfred Jury, an archaeologist from the University of Western Ontario, began excavating and reconstructing the former naval establishment at Penetanguishene. The local Chamber of Commerce, hoping to capitalize on public interest in the War of 1812, approached Jury with a plan to recover one of the wrecks in the harbor, preferably the Royal Navy schooner *Confiance* (ex–US Navy *Scorpion*).[28]

In 1953, Jury set about raising a wreck with a clam-shell dredge (fig. 4.5). Thousands of people lined the shore to watch the operation, which at first only succeeded in snapping off frames and planking. Additional attempts to grab the wreck damaged frames in the bow, but the clamshell finally got a solid grip on the structure and lifted it from the water. It was the lower hull, including the complete keel and keelson, portions of the stem and stern, and the lower frame timbers.[29]

The wreck was left on shore as an impromptu exhibit (fig. 4.6). Historians concluded the vessel was too large to be *Confiance* and that it corresponded closely with the Admiralty plans for *Tecumseth* and *Newash*. Three chainplates on the hull's side for foremast shrouds suggested a schooner rig, and on this basis the hull was identified as *Tecumseth*.[30]

The salvaged wreck was eventually moved to a more permanent display on the grounds of the old naval establishment, now known as Discovery Harbor

Figure 4.5. *The bow of* Tecumseth *rises from the lake in 1953. The techniques employed to recover the wreck were crude and ended up damaging frames and planking at the forward end of the hull. This loss of hull structure and archaeological information was a common feature of the enthusiastic but ill-planned efforts to salvage 1812-era wrecks during the twentieth century. (Courtesy of Discovery Harbour Collection, Penetanguishene, Ontario.)*

Figure 4.6. Tecumseth *on the shore at Penetanguishene after the salvage. The photograph provides a good idea of the extent of the surviving hull and the good condition of the timbers at the time of the recovery. (Photo by John R. Stevens.)*

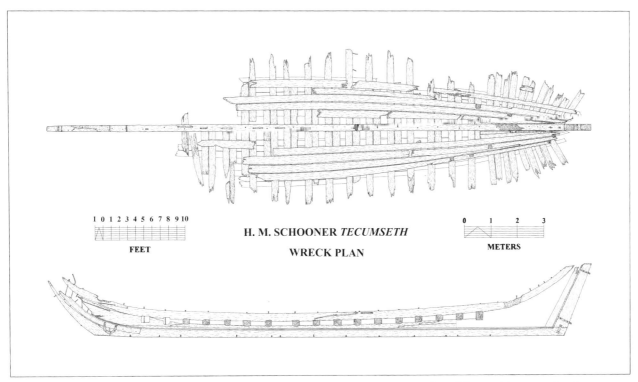

Figure 4.7. *Plan and profile of* Tecumseth. *This drawing was prepared from measurements taken off the wreck in 1997 and 1998.*
(Drawing by Erich Heinold.)

(Havre de la Découverte). In 1976 a study of *Tecumseth*'s condition was carried out by conservator and archaeologist Charles Hett, who reported signs of continuing deterioration due to exposure to the elements. Five samples of wood from the ship were identified at this time; four of them, from the keel, keelson, Frame 9, and the fourth strake on the port side, proved to be white oak, while the fifth sample, from the starboard garboard strake, was identified as ash.[31]

Renewed Study of *Tecumseth* and *Newash*

In 1997 archaeologists from Texas A&M University examined and recorded the remains of *Tecumseth* and assessed the feasibility of recording *Newash. Tecumseth* was, predictably, suffering from rot and exposure but appeared to be holding its shape. The entire lengths of the keel and keelson and approximately half the original lengths of the stem and sternpost were preserved. In the stern, the frames, half frames, and ceiling planking, which obscured some frames, remained well preserved almost to the turn of the bilge (fig. 4.7). In the bow, notches in the apron indicated the locations of

the cant frames and several full frames destroyed during the 1953 salvage.

After recording *Tecumseth,* its sister ship was examined (fig. 4.8). *Newash* lay in shallow water, 6 to 12 feet (1.83 to 3.65 m) deep, at the town's public beach. Its sides and bow had been ripped off by ice, exposing many features obscured on *Tecumseth.* Most of the stem and ceiling planking and all of the deck structure were missing, but much of the lower hull was complete. In 1998 the team surveyed the exposed portions of *Newash* and generated a basic wreck plan (fig. 4.9). Excavation of buried timbers was not permitted under the terms of the project permit, and so the documentation of this hull is not complete.

The Construction of the Schooners

The studies of the schooners' hulls show that they closely match the 1815 plans, making them rare examples of War of 1812 ships with good contemporary documentation. The archaeological studies revealed assembly details not in the plans, as well as modifications made during the building to make better use

Figure 4.8. *Erich Heinold recording the wreck of* Newash *in 1998.*
He is employing a digital goniometer (an angle-measuring device)
to reconstruct the three-dimensional shape of the hull. (Photo by
Oscar Blasingame.)

of available timber.[32] The following description of the
ships' construction relies principally on data from the
wreck of *Tecumseth,* but in areas where measurements
could not be obtained, the 1815 plans and the remains
of *Newash* provide missing information.

Originally, a false keel, or shoe, was fastened underneath the keel, but all that remains of it are impressions of sixteen staples with widely varied spacing.
Based on the 1815 plans, the piece ran the entire length
of the keel and protruded forward of it to protect the
gripe. There is no evidence of staples connecting the
false keel to the gripe.

The keel of *Tecumseth* is a single piece of timber
over 55 feet (17 m) long, tapering slightly in its sided
dimension fore and aft, with rabbets cut into its sides
for the garboard strakes. The recorded measurements
correspond with the 1815 plans.[33] The gripe abuts the
keel and the timber is cut to receive a trapezoidal
chock that fills the gap between keel, gripe, and stem
(fig. 4.10). A boxing scarf joins the stem and keel. The
bow assembly of gripe, stem, chock, and keel is held
together by a pair of iron horseshoe brackets, positioned in a U-shape and fastened by five iron bolts. The
stem tapers toward its existing upper extremity, and
rabbets cut along each side accepted the strake ends.

In the stern, the main post sits atop the keel and
rakes aft approximately 25 degrees. It appears to be
held in place with a tenon. The post is further secured
by a pair of iron dovetail plates holding six bolts, three
through the keel and three through the post. Four iron
bolts fastened the main post, inner post, and stern

deadwood together. The forward corners of the main
post are rabbeted to fit the hood ends of the planking,
and its after corners are beveled to accommodate the
swing of the rudder. According to the plans, three gudgeons supported the rudder, although the uppermost
gudgeon is now missing. The lowest gudgeon is fastened to the post by three iron bolts headed over iron
rings; a fourth bolt pierces the first strake above the
garboard and connects the gudgeon to the inner post.
The middle gudgeon is fastened to the main post by
two bolts and to the inner post by a single bolt.

The rising wood consists of three timbers bolted
atop the keel. The forward piece connects with the
after upper and lower pieces with a double flat scarf.
The rising wood is notched to accommodate the floors
and lock them in place. On *Newash* it appears that the
rising wood scarfs into the deadwood at the stern. The
sides of the stern deadwood are assumed to be notched
for the half frames, although on both wrecks these
areas were not accessible for examination. In the bow,
the apron connects to the forward rising wood with a
flat Z-scarf and is notched to fit the two forward-most
floors.

Tecumseth originally had 17 square frames (fig. 4.11).
Frames A through F forward of amidships and the midship frame itself had the first futtocks attached to the
after faces of the floors, a pattern that reverses on the
aftermost ten square frames. Aft of frame 10, six half-
frames form the shape of the stern.

The floor dimensions are consistent throughout.
The heads of the floors were cut at an angle to permit a
flat scarf with the heels of the second futtocks. Pairs of
triangular watercourses are cut into the floor and first
futtocks of each frame, allowing bilge water to drain to
the pump wells. The futtocks are similar in dimensions
to the floors. The heels of the first futtocks are notched
to fit over the rising wood and butt over the vessel's
centerline. On many of the frames, a small triangular
chock fits into the V-shaped space above each pair of
first futtock heels, creating a flat surface for seating the
keelson.

The keelson consists of two timbers hook-scarfed
together just forward of the mainmast step. The keelson's underside is notched down over the floors, and
the assembly is fastened to the keel by through bolts,
one through each floor timber. Abaft frame 10 (the
aftermost floor), the keelson is bolted to the top of the
deadwood and flat scarfed to a large, curving stern-

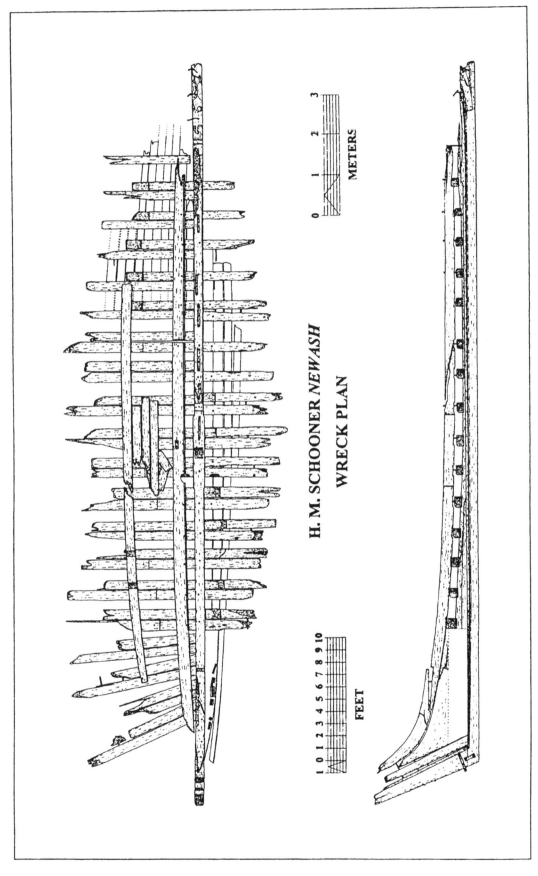

H. M. SCHOONER *NEWASH*

WRECK PLAN

METERS
0 1 2 3

FEET
0 1 2 3 4 5 6 7 8 9 10

Figure 4.9. Plan and profile of Newash. This drawing was prepared from measurements taken off the wreck in 1997 and 1998. (Drawing by Erich Heinold.)

Figure 4.10. Tecumseth's bow assembly, starboard side. The schooner shows a relatively complex arrangement of timbers, fastened together with a pair of semi-circular horseshoe plates. (Photo by John R. Stevens.)

son; the sternson continues above the deadwood and is through-bolted to the inner and main posts. The forward end of the keelson is hook-scarfed to a stemson that sits atop the apron. According to the 1815 plan, this piece continued to the level of the main deck, but now only a short section survives.

A mortise for the mainmast step was cut into the top of the keelson. To lend extra support to Tecumseth's step, a pair of iron plates was bolted through the keelson's sides. On Newash, the builder increased the keelson's sided dimension by 2 inches (5.08 cm) instead of attaching plates. The 1815 plans show the foremast stepped atop the stemson. Additionally, nine rectangular mortises were chiseled into the top of the keelson between the foremast and mainmast steps to fit stanchions to support the deck beams. On Newash, the keelson contains six such mortises.

Nine strakes of hull planking survive on Tecumseth's port side, with the garboard wider and thicker than the other strakes. Planks are fastened with two spikes per strake at each frame. Only five strakes of ceiling planking remain on Tecumseth, each fastened to the frames in the same manner as the hull planking.

Part of Tecumseth's remaining starboard side consists of two wales, a clamp, a deck shelf, three chainplates, and scuppers. The upper wale and clamp were originally bolted together through the frames, which no longer remain. The interior face of the clamp met a deck shelf, a longitudinal timber that reinforced the join between the sides of the ship and the deck, serving the same purpose as hanging knees, but with less timber and topside weight. The clamp contains six notches along its upper surface to seat deck beams; portions of two beams were recovered. Attached to each is an eyebolt, one still containing an iron ring. Three chainplates were originally attached to the lower wale and would have contained deadeyes for securing the shrouds for one of the masts.

It is clear that Moore and his shipwrights followed a shipbuilding tradition emphasizing frugality with

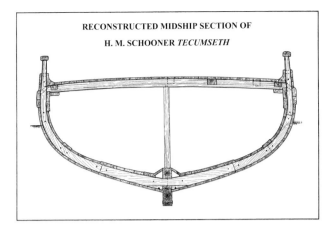

RECONSTRUCTED MIDSHIP SECTION OF
H. M. SCHOONER *TECUMSETH*

Figure 4.11. *Reconstructed midship section of* Tecumseth. *(Drawing by Erich Heinold, based on a reconstructed section of the schooner prepared by John R. Stevens.)*

Figure 4.12. *Reconstructed schooner mast, spar, and rigging profile. This drawing was based on evidence from the wrecks as well as contemporary treatises and documents. Among the most useful sources was an 1815 rigging warrant for* Newash *prepared by Lt. Thomas Bushby of the Royal Navy. (Reconstruction by LeeAnne Gordon.)*

timber. Since the seventeenth century, European ship-yards had suffered shortages of good timber, a problem that became ever more acute. War exacerbated this, both from the increased demand for ships and from interruptions in the timber supply. By 1815, after over two decades of war, British shipwrights were in the habit of cutting, fitting, and bending short pieces of timber to create larger components.[34] The increased number of individual elements and associated scarfs and joints made for weaker hulls. To compensate, ship-builders relied on elaborate joints, overlaps, and the notching of the frames and keelson. The construction of *Tecumseth* and *Newash* is noteworthy for these and for other features, such as the three-piece rising wood and the boxing scarf of the keel and stem. The two ships were plainly labor intensive in their assembly. Like many of the ships built on the lakes during the war, the schooners apparently lacked lodging, hanging, or dagger knees in their deck assemblies. Instead, they employed the clamp and deck shelf arrangement that required less wood, weight, and construction time.

Reconstructing the Schooner Rig

The rig arrangement and sailing characteristics of *Newash* and *Tecumseth* have long intrigued maritime scholars. The eminent naval historian John R. Stevens published a rigging plan for *Tecumseth* in 1961 based on archival evidence and hull elements observed in 1954.[35] Recently, LeeAnne Gordon undertook a new reconstruction and analysis of the original rig. Gordon, who served as a mate on the brig *Niagara* (see chapter 1), combined her knowledge of lake sailing with archaeological and historical data to generate a hypothetical rig that accorded with available evidence (fig. 4.12).

One key source of information on the two schooners, found in the Penetanguishene Public Library, was a copy of the 1815 rigging warrant for *Newash* prepared by Lt. Thomas Bushby.[36] Other major sources used for Gordon's reconstruction were the 1794 rigging treatise of David R. Steel and another treatise prepared in 1829 by John Fincham.[37] Specifications for many elements were found in Darcy Lever's *The Young Sea Officer's Sheet Anchor* of 1819.[38]

Bushby's rigging warrant lists the sails of the schooners' first configuration, the sizes and lengths of the standing and running rigging, as well as the number and sizes of the associated blocks. From this, it is

known that the schooners carried nine sails in their original configuration: flying jib, standing jib, gaff-rigged foresail, square sail (foresail), fore topsail, fore topgallant, boom mainsail, main topsail, and main topgallant. In Gordon's reconstruction, the lengths of individual sticks were adapted from a series of proportions created by Howard I. Chapelle, which are based on the extreme breadth of a vessel and its load water-line length.[39] Diameters of the lower masts were derived from Robert Moore's draft of the schooners, and the other spars were extrapolated from these measurements. The taper of the masts was taken from Steel's treatise.

MAIN RIGGING

The schooner rig presented a challenge in interpreting the main rigging. On a fully square-rigged vessel, the main stay led directly to the deck without interfering with any other sails. Such a stay, however, would have interfered with the operation of the fore-and-aft rigged foresail. A stay leading between the heads of the main and fore lower masts would not have the proper downward angle and needed to be carefully placed to avoid interfering with the main topsail.

The proposed rigging arrangement combines these two types of stays. Bushby's warrant lists a "Main Mast Head Stay" and two "Main Mast Deck Stays."[40] From this, it is assumed that two stays were rigged from the main lower mast hounds, one to either side of the ship. The main runners, or breast backstays, opposed the main stays and were given as much of an aft lead as possible. Moore's drawings indicate the mainmast carried three shrouds on either side.[41] The forward two legs were made from the same line while the after legs were single legs, each with an eye spliced into one end. Each shroud had a deadeye at its lower end, connected by a lanyard to another deadeye attached to the hull with a chainplate. A series of smaller lines between shrouds provided ratlines for sailors to climb.

FORE RIGGING

Bushby does not list a fore stay, but there must have been one for the vessel to sail. James Childs' logbook contains an entry on setting up a "preventer fore stay," indicating that the original fore stay was insufficient, but not that it was absent.[42] The primary fore stay was rigged to the end of the bowsprit and secured with hearts to the stem. Since the jibboom was hove out over the bowsprit, the fore stay was offset to starboard. After *Tecumseth*'s dismasting, a preventer fore stay was rigged with a horse collar, as the port bee block would have already accommodated the fore topmast stay. A horse collar acted in the same manner as a pair of hearts or deadeyes but allowed space for the jibboom to pass underneath it. The rest of the fore rigging included running backstays and shrouds and was set up in a manner similar to the main rigging.

BOWSPRIT RIGGING

The bowsprit can be imagined as a mast leaned forward. Like the mainmast and foremast, it had shrouds and stays—here called *bobstays*—and these led to the ship's stem. Bobstays had hearts or deadeyes seized into their upper ends and supported the bowsprit by pulling it downward. Because of the bowsprit's low angle, the bobstay bridles were placed near the waterline. Shortly after it was re-rigged, *Tecumseth*'s crew shifted the bobstays "a foot [0.30 m] further down."[43] This may have meant the bobstays were submerged—perhaps continually.

TRESTLETREES, CROSSTREES, AND MAST CAPS

To be properly secured by the standing rigging, each mast was shaped with an enlarged shoulder for the eyes of the rigging to be placed over and tightened against. A wooden framework of trestletrees and crosstrees, supported underneath by cheeks, was placed at the shoulder of the masts. This provided a base to seat the heels of the topmasts and to secure the deadeyes of the topmast shrouds, as well as other rigging elements.

At the upper end of each lower mast and outer end of the bowsprit, the topmasts and jibboom were secured with a cap. Rectangular in shape, the caps contained a mortise in the after or lower half for a tenon in the head of the lower mast or bowsprit. A circular hole was cut in the other half of the cap, to fit the topmast or jibboom. The overlap of the two masts was called the *doubling.*

TOPMAST RIGGING

With the lower rig in place, the topmasts were swayed. To avoid overburdening the ship with a heavy rig aloft, topmasts were smaller in dimension than the lower masts, the standing rigging was smaller, and there were fewer pieces. The fore and main topmasts had

only two shrouds on each side, one stay leading forward and a pair of backstays. The fore topmast also had a flying jib stay. The main topmast stay led to the hounds of the fore lower mast. The topmasts were not secured to each other; either could be swayed up or taken down independent of the other. The main topmast backstays fell at a plumb line, perpendicular to the load waterline shown on Moore's draft, and were secured to the outside of the hull.

As with the lower shrouds, the lower ends of the topmast shrouds were seized around a deadeye, and a corresponding deadeye was secured at the crosstrees. To keep the full strain of the topmast shrouds from falling on the crosstrees alone, futtock shrouds were rigged. These were short lengths of rope that ran from the underside of the lower topmast deadeyes to a wooden batten, or futtock stave, which was secured to the lower shrouds below. Tension on the topmast shrouds transferred through the deadeyes and lanyards to the futtock and lower shrouds.

TOPGALLANT RIGGING

Newash's and *Tecumseth*'s topmasts and topgallant masts were made from a single piece of wood, meaning that when the topmast was swayed, the topgallant pole was as well. The topgallant standing rigging had to be placed before the topmasts were rigged. The main and fore topgallant mast had one stay and two backstays but no shrouds. The topgallant sails were not permanently rigged but were set from the decks.

The main topgallant stay led to the fore lower mast cap and was secured at the fore trestletrees. The main topgallant backstays fell at a plumb line to the hull, where they were secured with deadeyes. The fore topgallant stay led to the end of the jibboom, and its backstays also fell at a plumb line to the hull. A short pole stuck out above each topgallant mast and a flag halyard used to hoist signal flags was placed at the truck of the mast.

JIBBOOM RIGGING

After the topmasts were swayed, the jibboom was rigged. Before it could be secured, a martingale had to be made and placed. This was a short spar projecting downward from the forward side of the bowsprit cap and was rigged just before the jibboom was run out. Because of the low angle and long length of the bowsprit and jibboom, it was difficult to get a downward pull on jibboom stays, more appropriately called martingale stays. By adding the martingale and reeving rigging through its lower end, a better angle was achieved.

The jibboom had two shrouds—one to either side. The jibboom also supported the fore topgallant mast, whose stay ran through a notch, or dumb sheave, in the end of the jibboom, through the martingale, and then to the hull.[44] The jibboom's inboard end was secured by a heel rope and lashing to prevent the boom from sliding down the bowsprit.

The flying jib stay had a separate stay that prevented the strain of the sail from falling on other pieces of the rig. An iron ring, or traveler, with a thimble or shackle attached at its upper side was placed over the jibboom before it was hove out.[45] The flying jib stay ran through this ring and through a sheave in the jibboom. Aloft, the stay ran through a single sheave block at the fore topmast hounds. At either end of the stay, two more single sheave blocks were secured. A separate line ran through those blocks along with another, creating a gun tackle purchase at both ends.[46] The tackles meant that the flying jib stay could be tensioned from either its upper or lower end, and the traveler allowed the stay to be moved along the length of the jibboom. Additionally, the entire jibboom could be moved inboard toward the bow.[47]

MAINYARDS AND SPARS

Dimensions for the yards were derived from John Fincham's treatise. The yard lengths on the foremast and mainmast are identical, although the difference in mast heights yields larger sails on the latter. The yards, gaffs, and booms share similar characteristics, both to each other and to other ships of the time, but each is rigged slightly differently. To best illustrate these differences, the yards and spars are considered by mast.

The mainsail was a hoisting sail stretched between a gaff at the head, or top, of the sail and a boom at the foot, or bottom. The gaff was raised with throat and peak halyards. The throat halyard assembly included a double and a single sheave block.[48] The double sheave block was lashed to the underside of the main trestletrees, and the single block was lashed to the main gaff. The peak halyard was hauled at the same time as the throat halyard to raise the sail and was rigged with a double sheave and a single sheave block.[49] To allow the peak of the gaff to be raised higher than the throat,

the double sheave block was secured to the mainmast above the doubling and the single one to the gaff. The end of the halyard was made off to the end of the gaff. To control the gaff when lowering the sail, both throat and peak halyards had a downhaul. The throat downhaul block had a single sheave while the peak downhaul block had two sheaves. The extra sheave was probably not for purchase but for a separate flag halyard to be rove. Because the main gaff was hoisted to the same position on a regular basis, chafe appeared on the mast from the transverse motion of the gaff. To prevent a weak spot from forming there, one or more pieces of copper were placed around the mast.[50] The copper was generally greased, which kept the gaff from squealing. The jaws of the gaff were sheathed in leather for this same purpose.[51] The rest of the main lower mast was greased to ensure easy motion of the main gaff.[52]

The boom topping lifts were comprised of three parts. A rope was hitched around the boom's end and rove through two single sheave blocks lashed to the underside of the mainmast trestletrees, one to either side. Each end of the lifts was seized around a double sheave block. The topping lift falls were rove as a single luff tackle between the double sheave block and a single sheave block lashed on deck.

When the mainsail was set, the leeward lift was slackened to allow the sail to fill while the weather lift remained taut to prevent the boom from falling. To make slacking the leeward lift easier, a lazy guy was rigged. This was a line that ran through a block made along the run of the topping lift.[53] When this line was hauled on, the topping lift would become slack faster and easier than if the line were simply left hanging loose. Like the peak downhaul, one of the lazy guy blocks had a single sheave while the other was a double sheave block carrying a separate halyard for the ensign to be raised when the mainsail was not set.

Above the main gaff, the mainyard was hoisted and its center lashed to a sling, a line running around the hounds of the mainmast.[54] Lines called trusses helped pull the yard toward the mast. The yard ends were supported with lifts hitched around their ends, which then led over the mast cap and down through the trestle and cross trees on the opposite side.[55]

Two single and two double sheave blocks were used in the lift assemblies, allowing them to be rigged with a fall having a single luff purchase.[56] The lifts supported the ends of the yardarms, keeping them level or cockbilled as necessary to be used as cranes to load cargo. The yard lifts could also help achieve proper sail shape, as hauling on the leeward lift lowered the weather yardarm. When a stack of square sails was set, this stretched their weather edges.

Also attached to the yardarm ends were braces, set up in opposition so that by hauling on one brace and easing the other, the yard could rotate around the mast. Changing the angle at which the yards encountered the wind gave the schooners a wider arc of favorable winds. The amount yards can be braced up is limited by the stays and shrouds of their masts, and as a yard rotates around, it will encounter, and lay heavily on, the shrouds and the stay.

Only two single sheave blocks, placed in the foremast rigging to act as turning blocks, were used in the brace assemblies. The main braces were hitched around the mainyard, led forward to the fore rigging, run through the single sheave turning blocks, and then run down to the deck.

The topsail yard was crossed on the main topmast and, unlike the mainyard, had to be raised to stretch the main topsail. It was rigged with a halyard for hoisting and lifts for supporting the yardarms. Unlike the lifts on the mainyard, the main topsail yard lifts were not rigged with tackles leading to the deck. It is likely that these lifts were hitched around the yardarms, run through a single block, and secured to the trestle or crosstrees or lower mast cap. The rigging warrant gives the dimensions for the cordage of the topsail lifts but does not list any blocks for these.[57] The cordage used, of approximately ¾ inch (1.91 cm) diameter, seems large for a simple thimble, and so sister blocks seized between the legs of the topmast shrouds are shown in the reconstruction.[58]

Footropes, or horses, were run under the yards to give sailors working aloft secure footing. The footropes hung from stirrups placed at each quarter of the yard on either side and were laced between them. Footropes were also rigged on the main topsail yard with stirrups fixed at approximate thirds across each side, as the topsail yard was shorter than the main.

Both fore and main topgallants were set flying or from the deck, meaning that there was no standing rigging for these yards. Their halyards ran through a sheave in the topgallant mast and down to the deck. To set the sail, the halyard was tied to the center of the yard. A downhaul was also attached, usually at one yardarm. Without braces of their own, the topgallant yards simply followed the topsail when the crew braced the yards.

FOREYARDS AND SPARS

The foresail, like the mainsail, was fore-and-aft rigged, although in a different configuration. The sail was loose-footed (there was no boom) and when not in use was brailed in to the gaff and foremast. Because there was no boom, there was no need for topping lifts or lazy guys, although the gaff still required a throat and peak halyard to hoist it. These were set up similar to those on the main with the same arrangement of blocks, although the sizes were slightly smaller. Unlike the main gaff, the fore gaff did not have peak and throat downhauls, as it was not lowered each time the sail was taken in. The foreyard was rigged in a manner similar to the mainyard.

The fore lower mast carried a square sail, unlike the main lower mast, and Bushby lists slings for the yard and a halyard for the sail. This would seem redundant, as slings would already support the bulk of the yard and sail, but the halyard may have been ready in case of need. Bushby lists only a single sheave block.[59]

The fore topsail yard was rigged much like the main topsail yard, with a halyard, lifts, and braces. The topgallant yard was set from deck with a halyard and downhaul. As on the main, the topgallant yard followed the topsail yard when bracing up or in.

RUNNING RIGGING

Most lines used as running rigging occur in opposing pairs. Halyards and downhauls can be attached to the same point on a spar but work in opposite ways. On fore-and-aft sails, sheets perform the same function as braces on a square sail and control the attitude, or the way a sail encounters the wind. Square sails had several types of running rigging. One line, called a clueline, opposed both the halyard and sheet. A clueline ran to the bottom corner, or clue of the sail.[60] When the sheet was in operation, drawing the clue down, the clueline was left slack. To bring a sail back in, the opposite was done: the sheet was left slack and the clueline was hauled on, bringing the clues back up to the yardarm. *Newash*'s and *Tecumseth*'s original rigging configuration included cluelines on the topsails but not on topgallants, as they were set from deck.

Just as lifts can keep the weather edge of a square

sail taut, bowlines could be used for the same purpose. These were comprised of several short lines, called bridles, rove through semi-circles of rope, or cringles, attached to the boltrope along the vertical edges of a square sail.[61] The bowline ran parallel to the fore topmast stay through a block at the bowsprit cap and was hauled on and made fast on deck. When sailing, the weather bowline was tensioned, stretching the weather edge of the sail, while the other bowline was left slack.

One type of running rigging curiously absent from Bushby's warrant was buntlines. A buntline was tied to the bottom edge of a square sail, the "bunt," from where the line ran through one or more thimbles, small doughnut-shaped pieces of wood sewn into the forward side of a sail. These took in square sails, and there were usually an equal number of buntlines on the port and starboard sides of the sail. The buntline then ran through a turning block placed high in the rigging and down to the deck. When the sail was being set, buntlines were left slack. Once a square sail's halyard had been eased, hauling on the buntlines brought the bulk of the canvas up to the yard. Bushby's omission of buntlines may indicate that the small size of the square sails on *Tecumseth* and *Newash* made them unnecessary.

An interesting configuration in the original sail plans is seen when comparing the gaff-rigged main and foresails. Both were fore-and-aft sails suspended from gaffs and hoisted with throat and peak halyards. The bottom edge, or foot, of the foresail was not attached to any other spar, while the foot of the mainsail was attached to the main boom. This meant that the entirety of the mainsail and gaff had to be hoisted each time the sail was set. The sheet was attached to the boom, which controlled the attitude of the sail. The foresail, however, being loose-footed was set and taken in with brails, small lines tied off at various points of the after edge, or leech, of the sail. When the brails were hauled on, the foresail could be drawn up and in to the foremast, much like a curtain can be drawn back. Because the gaff generally remained in a hoisted position, two lines called vangs controlled its movement. These were tied to the gaff and led to a tackle at deck level. Tension or slack of the vangs allowed the gaff to pass from one side of the vessel to the other, or kept it parallel to the ship's centerline.

Rigging and Manpower on Great Lakes Warships

This rigging reconstruction is speculative, but Bushby's rigging warrant provides an excellent basis for speculation. No records of the actual dimensions of the vessels' masts and spars could be found, although such documents once existed.[62] One thing that can be interpreted from the rigging warrant with a measure of certainty is the way purchase blocks were used. Single sheave blocks were used more frequently than double sheave blocks on these ships, limiting the possible setup of the rigging.

Rigs are designed for specific functions, and some features of rigs match certain hulls better than others. It makes little sense to put a small, short rig on a large vessel or an enormous pile of canvas on a tiny, shallow hull. An ideal sail plan might consist of one extremely large sail to utilize the maximum amount of available wind.[63] An obvious problem with this utopian plan is that the sail would be so heavy it would require an enormous crew to handle it. Indeed, the vessel might well be full of the sailors needed to manage the sail, without any space for cargo, guns, equipment, or provisions. A way around this is to split the sail into several smaller ones on multiple masts, an arrangement that requires far less manpower. However, an increase in the number of sails makes quick maneuvers difficult, and naval craft needed to be nimble to overtake or evade an enemy. The art of rigging *Tecumseth* and *Newash* involved finding the appropriate balance between sail area, manpower, and maneuverability.

Historical evidence suggests the schooners could carry a tremendous amount of canvas, although the total sail area may be somewhat misleading as there were few times when all the canvas was piled on (fig. 4.13). Nevertheless, *Tecumseth* and *Newash* were naval vessels with large crews capable of setting large sails quickly and handling them efficiently with a minimum of purchase blocks.

Flexibility in sail area is arguably more important than sail area alone. The Great Lakes are prone to all types of weather. Autumn brings squalls, strong winds, and high seas. The spring carries similar dangers, while summer can bring months of near calm. Ships operating on these waters needed flexibility in sail area, windage, and weight aloft. In autumn and spring, sail area was kept to a minimum, and the most

Figure 4.13. *A hypothetical sail plan for the reconstructed schooner rig.* Tecumseth *and* Newash *were naval vessels, with a need for speed and handiness under sail if they were to be effective in their missions. The sail area shown here would be excessive for a merchant vessel, but the larger crews of the Royal Navy schooners made it possible to effectively use such a rig. (Reconstruction by LeeAnne Gordon.)*

commonly used sails were those set low and close to the center of a ship. In summer's calm weather sailors set nearly every stitch of canvas they could.[64]

A good working sail plan for *Tecumseth* and *Newash* might have included the mainsail, foresail, standing jib, and fore and main topsails. In lighter winds or to increase speed, topgallants and flying jib were added. The square sail was used when running before the wind. As winds increased, sail area was reduced from the outer edges and working inward; topgallants and flying jib were taken in, and topsails were reefed or taken in entirely. During the winter of 1815–16, sailors on *Tecumseth* made points—pieces of line sewn to the front and back of a sail to secure its unused part—for

several new reef bands in the mainsail and others.[65] These allowed more control over the amount of set canvas, as reefing reduces a sail's size by folding or rolling an edge. On the main, foresails, and standing jib, the bottom edges were rolled up and tied off. On the fore and main topsails as well as the fore course, the top of the sail was rolled up and tied off. The addition of reef bands was probably due to observations from the first sailing season when *Tecumseth* was dismasted in a squall and later caught in another storm. In addition to reef points, both vessels were fitted with a topmast studdingsail, or stuns'l, after the 1815 season, yielding a greater sail area when winds were light or speed was needed.[66]

The hypothetical sail plan, including all nine sails, was calculated to have a total area of 7284.50 square feet (677.00 m²).[67] This figure is not necessarily accurate as it includes both the foresail and fore course, and these were not commonly used together. Chapelle calculated ideal sail area as 3.6 times that of the "load waterline section."[68] The reconstructed sail area is over one and a half times larger than the proportions recommended by Chapelle's formula.

It is evident from the hypothetical sail plan and its calculations that *Newash* and *Tecumseth* were unique vessels, as underscored by Robert Moore's draft of the ships. The foremast placement alone was unusual. John Fincham gave specific proportions based on the midpoint of the load waterline for the placement and rake of masts in schooners and brigantines. From this, Chapelle devised a range of values for mast placement that have been applied to *Tecumseth* and *Newash*.[69]

The mainmast of each vessel falls almost directly in the center of the prescribed range, but the foremast is out of its predicted range as it is far forward and placed atop the stem. This placement gave the vessels a distinctive appearance. There are no records to indicate why Moore placed the foremasts so far forward, but it is possible the placement was a result of the chosen rigging plan. When a vessel has two or more square-rigged masts, it is necessary to space them apart properly. Usually square sails are braced into the wind to some degree, and when set this way air flows on both sides, creating an airfoil shape, providing lift and drive. If two square-rigged masts are placed closely together, the air flowing off the sails on the forward mast can cause the sails on the after mast to receive a breeze on the wrong side, distorting their shape and reducing their effectiveness. Another problem is blanketing, where sail areas overlap, causing one to steal wind from the other. The best example of this effect can be seen on a square-rigged vessel with the wind dead astern: no matter how the foresails are braced, those on the mainmast almost always blanket them. These concerns may have caused Moore to place the masts a wide distance apart.

Echoes of a Naval Race

Tecumseth and *Newash* are not, strictly speaking, examples of wartime construction on the lakes, but they were designed, hurriedly built, and launched within six months of the war's end, at a time when the Royal Navy badly needed to reestablish itself on the Upper Lakes. While the ships were intended principally as transports, their great sail area and heavy guns made them formidable opponents in the event of renewed fighting. In a sense, they were an echo of the frantic wartime shipbuilding effort. Their short careers illustrate the uncertainties of the immediate postwar era, when navies established peacetime routines while retaining a readiness for hostilities.

The Rush-Bagot Agreement forced *Newash* and *Tecumseth* into retirement after very short sailing careers. Ironically, hostile interactions between the schooners and US merchant vessels affected the way the agreement was framed; in a sense, *Newash* and *Tecumseth* acted as architects of their own demise. Royal Navy Capt. William Bourchier had thought his post on Lake Erie a distant and obscure corner of Canada; Penetanguishene, the harbor where the schooners were retired, truly was on the edge of nowhere. Disarmed and neglected as peace prevailed, the ships simply rotted away.

In recent decades, with the introduction of nautical archaeology and the incorporation of various disciplines that it demands, the story of *Tecumseth* and *Newash* has been reexamined and explored. The history of the two vessels, while short, is intriguing; analysis of the architecture and rigging shows that they were, in fact, remarkable vessels that illustrate the transition from war to peace on the Great Lakes of North America.

NOTES

1. J. MacKay Hitsman, *Safeguarding Canada, 1763–1871* (Toronto: University of Toronto Press, 1968), pp. 101, 104, 110, 119–20; C. P. Stacey, "The Myth of the Unguarded Frontier, 1815–1871," *The American Historical Review* 56, no. 1 (October 1950), pp. 2, 3, 11; L. Farrington, "The Decline of Naval Bases on the Lakes of Canada, 1815–1834" (paper presented for the Barry German Naval History Prize, 1955), pp. 2–3; Extracts from Bourchier to Owen, March 2, 1816, vol. 738, series C (I), record group 8 (RG 8), Library and Archives Canada (LAC).

2. Robert Malcomson, *Warships of the Great Lakes 1754–1834* (Great Britain: Chatham Publishing, 2001), p. 138; Hitsman, *Safeguarding Canada, 1763–1871*, pp. 108–109.

3. LeeAnne Elizabeth Gordon, "*Newash* and *Tecumseth*: Analysis of Two Post-War of 1812 Vessels on the Great Lakes" (Master's thesis, Texas A&M University, 2009), p. 14; Malcomson, *Warships*

of the Great Lakes, p. 138 says the designer was William Bell; Hits-man, *Safeguarding Canada, 1763–1871,* pp. 105, 109; Hall to Navy Board, November 29, 1814, Admiralty Fonds, ADM 106/1997, The National Archives of the UK (TNA): Public Record Office (PRO); Owen to Owen, October 21, 1815, ADM 1/2264, TNA: PRO.

4. "Draft of Schooners," reg. no. 4562, Box 64, Admiralty Fonds, ADM, TNA: PRO; Owen, Statement of the Naval Forces on Lake Erie and Huron, June 1, 1815, ADM 1/2262, TNA: PRO.

5. Gordon, "*Newash* and *Tecumseth,*" p 14

6. Henry Kent to E. W. C. R. Owen, June 11, 1815, ADM 1/2262, LAC.

7. Owen, December 11, 1815, ADM 1/2265, TNA: PRO; A. L. Burt, *The United States, Great Britain, and British North America: From the Revolution to the Establishment of Peace After the War of 1812* (New York: Russell & Russell, 1961), p. 386; Capt. Thomas Bushby, Officer's Service Record, Admiralty Fonds: ADM 196/3, TNA: PRO; Capt. Henry Kent, Officer's Service Record, ADM 196/5, pt. 1, TNA: PRO; H. F. Pullen, ed., *March of the Seamen* (Halifax, Nova Scotia: Maritime Museum of Canada, 1961), pp. 16–17.

8. Owen to Drummond, April 14, 1815, vol. 370, series C (I), RG 8, LAC; Hall to Navy Board, May 18, 1815, ADM 106/1997, TNA: PRO; Rowley Murphy, "Resurrection at Penetanguishene," *Inland Seas* 10 (1954), p. 3; Farrington, "The Decline of Naval Bases on the Lakes of Canada," p. 9.

9. Owen, "General Instructions for the Commander of the Naval Establishment upon Lake Erie," October 12, 1815, ADM 1/2264, TNA: PRO; Owen, "Table of Peace Compliment of His Majesty's Ships and Vessels on the Lakes of Canada under the Command of Commodore Sir E. W. C. R. Owen," ADM 1/2264, TNA: PRO.

10. Gordon, "*Newash* and *Tecumseth,*" p. 49 notes that a wind-lass is mentioned in *Tecumseth*'s log, but only once, suggesting that most of the lifting of cables and anchors was done by hand with the schooners' relatively large crews. "Log of the Proceed-ings on Board HM Schooner/Brigantine *Newash* on Lake Erie, 13 August 1815–30 June 1817" (hereafter "Log of the *Newash*"), Au-gust 13–26, 1815, ADM 51/2607, TNA: PRO. The watercolor paint-ing *The Dual Launching of the* Newash *and the* Tecumseth (cata-logue number 2205) can be found in Mary Allodi, ed., *Canadian Watercolours and Drawings in the Royal Ontario Museum,* vol. 2 (Toronto: The Royal Ontario Museum, 1974).

11. "Log of the *Newash,*" August 13–31, 1815, ADM 51/2607, TNA: PRO.

12. Abraham Whitehead, "Log of the Proceedings of H.M. Schooner *Tecumseth* Commencing November 14th 1816 and end-ing June 30th 1817" (hereafter "Log of the *Tecumseth,* 1816–1817") May 30, 1817, ADM 51/2072, TNA: PRO; "Log of the *Newash*" Au-gust 30 and September 4, 1815, ADM 51/2607, TNA: PRO.

13. "Log of the *Newash,*" September 2, 1815, ADM 51/2607, TNA: PRO.

14. C. H. J. Snider, "Recovery of H.M.S. *Tecumseth,*" *Ontario History* 46, no. 2 (1954), p. 104.

15. "Log of the *Newash*" September 2 and 5, 1815, ADM 51/2607, TNA: PRO.

16. Farrington, "The Decline of Naval Bases on the Lakes of Canada, 1815–1834," p. 3; Owen to Drummond, October 15, 1815 and Bushby to Bourchier, November 9, 1815, vol. 736, series C (I), RG 8, LAC.

17. "British Outrage!" extract from the *Niagara Journal,* Octo-ber 17, 1815, enclosed in E. W. C. R. Owen to Baker, October 23, 1815, ADM 1/2264, TNA: PRO.

18. John Robson, "Statement of the circumstance which took place on board the *Julia* Schooner of the Dock Yard Kingston, previous to and after her seizure by the Custom House Officers of the United States lying off the Farm of Sheppard Esq. about seven miles from Sackets Harbor," October 15, 1815; "Account of Cyrus Smith," October 24, 1815; Baumgardt to Owen, Decem-ber 4, 1815, vol. 736, series C (I), RG 8, LAC.

19. Owen to Respective Captains and Commanders of His M. Ships and Vessels on the Lakes of Canada, November 1, 1815, vol. 370, series C (I), RG 8, LAC.

20. "Log of the *Newash,*" October 14, 1815, ADM 51/2607, TNA: PRO; Owen, "General Instructions No. 2 for the Commander of the Naval Establishment upon Lake Erie," October 12, 1815, ADM 1/2264, TNA: PRO.

21. "Log of the *Newash,*" April 22 and May 1, 1816, ADM 51/2607, TNA: PRO; Farrington, "The Decline of Naval Bases on the Lakes of Canada, 1815–1834," p. 10.

22. Owen to Croker, October 16, 1815, ADM 1/2265, TNA: PRO; Burt, *The United States, Great Britain, and British North America,* p. 385.

23. Burt, *The United States, Great Britain, and British North America,* p. 386.

24. A transcript of the Rush-Bagot Agreement can be found in Gordon, "*Newash* and *Tecumseth,*" Appendix C, pp. 265–67.

25. Whitehead, "Log of the *Tecumseth,* 1816–1817," June 9, 23, and 30, 1817, ADM 51/2072, TNA: PRO; Farrington, "The Decline of Naval Bases on the Lakes of Canada, 1815–1834," pp. 10–11.

26. Gordon, "*Newash* and *Tecumseth,*" pp. 83–84.

27. Gordon, "*Newash* and *Tecumseth,*" p. 85.

28. Murphy, "Resurrection at Penetanguishene," p. 4; Snider, "Recovery of H.M.S. *Tecumseth,*" p. 99.

29. Murphy, "Resurrection at Penetanguishene," p. 4; Snider, "Recovery of H.M.S. *Tecumseth,*" p. 100.

30. Snider, "Recovery of H.M.S. *Tecumseth,*" pp. 101, 103.

31. Charles E. S. Hett, "Report on Visit to Penetanguishene" (letter, *Tecumseth* and *Newash* Archival and Field Record Collec-tion, Texas A&M University, October 6, 1976).

32. Mary-Lou Florian (Conservator, Biological Studies on Collections, Environment and Deterioration Research) to Charles E. S. Hett, "Wood Samples from *HMS Tecumseth,*" November 5, 1976 (*Tecumseth* and *Newash* Archival and Field Record Collection, Texas A&M University).

33. P. T. Nation (transcriber), "Contracts, Approved Tenders and Other Documents: The Royal Naval Dockyard, Kingston,

Upper Canada, 1815–1824," Document 17 (*Tecumseth* and *Newash* Archival and Field Record Collection, Texas A&M University, 1992 copy), p. 2.

34. C. Nepean Longridge, *The Anatomy of Nelson's Ships* (London: Percival Marshall, 1955); William Hookey, "Improved Method of bending Timber for building large Ships of War," *The Repertory of Arts, Manufactures, and Agriculture,* 2nd series, 28 (1816), pp. 37–42. Hookey wrote, "The constant want of compass timber, and the difficulty of obtaining it, is apparent, and seems to increase every year."

35. John R. Stevens, "The Story of H.M. Armed Schooner *Tecumseth,*" in H.F. Pullen, *March of the Seamen,* pp. 23–29.

36. Thomas Bushby, "An Account of Rigging and Sails Belonging to His Majesty's Schooner Newash," September 19, 1815, vol. 5, series 3a, record group 8, LAC. The rigging warrant is reproduced in Appendix E of Gordon's thesis.

37. David R. Steel, *Steel's Elements of Mastmaking, Sailmaking, and Rigging* (Largo, FL: Edward W. Sweetman, 1982); John Fincham, *A Treatise on Masting Ships and Mast Making* (London: Conway Maritime Press, 1982).

38. Darcy Lever, *The Young Sea Officer's Sheet Anchor, or A Key to the Leading of Rigging and to Practical Seamanship* (London: John Richardson, 1819; Facsimile edition, Mineola, NY: Dover Publications, 1998).

39. Howard I. Chapelle, *The Baltimore Clipper* (Salem, MA: The Marine Research Society, 1930), pp. 161, 179–85. All of the dimensions of the spars correspond to the ratios provided by Chapelle except the bowsprit and jibboom. Chapelle's ratios, which were based on Fincham's various examples, are far shorter than the actual numbers reported in Fincham's treatise. For this reconstruction, both bowsprit and jibboom were lengthened to a dimension closer to those given by Fincham directly.

40. Later schooners referred to this as a "triatic stay."

41. In Bushby's logbook, the two sides of a ship were referred to as "starboard" and "larboard" rather than the later "starboard" and "port."

42. James Childs, "Log of the Proceedings onboard H.M. Schooner *Tecumseth* on Lake Erie Between the 13th of August 1815 and 13th November 1816," September 7, 1815, ADM 52/3933, TNA: PRO.

43. James Childs, "Log of the Proceedings onboard H.M. Schooner *Tecumseth* on Lake Erie Between the 13th of August 1815 and 13th November 1816" (hereafter "Log of *Tecumseth,* 1815–1816"), September 20, 1815, ADM 52/3933, TNA: PRO.

44. Tension on the fore topgallant stay kept the line in the jibboom notch. Although the notch would have added more friction than a sheave, it was much simpler and quicker to rig than a regular sheave.

45. Lever, *Young Sea Officer's Sheet Anchor,* p. 60, Figs. 333–36.

46. Lever, *Young Sea Officer's Sheet Anchor,* p. 60, Fig. 337.

47. Henry Kent, "Log of the Proceedings of H.M. Brigantine *Newash* on Lakes Erie and Huron Between the 14th of Novem-

ber 1816 and 30th June 1817" ("*Newash* on Erie and Huron, 1816–1817"), May 19, 1817, June 5, 1817, ADM 52/4548, TNA: PRO.

48. Thomas Bushby, "An Account of Rigging and Sails Belonging to His Majesty's Schooner Newash," September 19, 1815, vol. 5, series 3a, RG 8, LAC.

49. Bushby, "Rigging and Sails," September 19, 1815, vol. 5, series 3a, RG 8, LAC.

50. Childs, "Log of *Tecumseth,* 1815–1816," June 7, 1816, ADM 52/3933, TNA: PRO.

51. Childs, "Log of *Tecumseth,* 1815–1816," August 28, 1816, ADM 52/3933, TNA: PRO.

52. Childs, "Log of *Tecumseth,* 1815–1816," June 12 and July 12, 1816, ADM 52/3933, TNA: PRO.

53. Lever, *Young Sea Officer's Sheet Anchor,* p. 44.

54. Lever, *Young Sea Officer's Sheet Anchor,* p. 35.

55. Lever, *Young Sea Officer's Sheet Anchor,* p. 34, Fig. 221.

56. These are the blocks listed in Bushby's rigging warrant for the foreyard. The warrant does not mention any of the gear necessary for the mainyards, since they were going to be replaced with a gaff topsail. The rigging for the mainyards here has been taken from the rigging for the foreyards, assuming that the blocks and lines used were identical or similar.

57. Curiously, the rigging warrant lists 28 fathoms (168 feet [51.22 m]) of 2½-inch (6.35 cm) cordage for the fore topsail lifts, an extraordinarily long length of rope for lines that were apparently rigged without falls.

58. Lever, *Young Sea Officer's Sheet Anchor,* p. 47. Lever describes a setup whereby the lifts ran through thimbles that were seized to the forward legs of their respective shrouds. It has been supposed that the sister blocks were considered differently than the other blocks listed in the rigging warrant, perhaps due to the permanency of their placement.

59. Lever, *Young Sea Officer's Sheet Anchor,* p. 39, Fig. 248.

60. Also spelled "clew."

61. On the lower parts of the sail, cringles were used for bowline bridles. There was always one more cringle than there were bridles. The first bridle was rove through an eye in the second bridle, and the ends of the first were attached to the highest two bowline cringles. The second bridle, one end being a splice to accommodate the first bridle, was rove through an eye in the third bridle and attached to the third cringle. Additional bridles were rove in the same manner. Finally, the last bridle was not attached to the sail at all; an eye at one end accommodated the previous bridle. Lever, *Young Sea Officer's Sheet Anchor,* p. 57, Figs. 321, 322, 324.

62. Several contemporary naval documents mention enclosures of rigging dimensions, but the enclosures could not be located.

63. Of course, if this sail were square rigged, its versatility would be limited by the rigging that supported it. A fore-and-aft sail also has restrictions on its use, since it is not the preferred sail for certain conditions.

64. William Bourchier to Baumgardt, enclosed in William

Baumgardt to Bagot, September 5, 1816, Sir Charles Bagot Fonds, vol. 1, series A13, Military Group 24, LAC.

65. Childs, "Log of *Tecumseth,* 1815–1816," February 22, 1816, ADM 52/3933, TNA: PRO.

66. Childs, "Log of *Tecumseth,* 1815–1816," September 3, 1815, ADM 52/3933, TNA: PRO; Kent, "*Newash* on Erie and Huron, 1816–1817," November 22, 1816, ADM 52/4548, TNA: PRO.

67. Howard I. Chapelle, *Baltimore Clipper,* pp. 162–63. Individual sails were drawn using proportions in this book that provided ratios of leeches, luffs, heads, and feet of sails.

68. Chapelle, *Baltimore Clipper,* p. 160.

69. Chapelle, *Baltimore Clipper,* p. 160.

Part II

The Naval War of 1812 on Lake Ontario

KEVIN J. CRISMAN

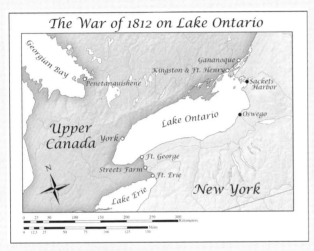

Figure II.1. *The Lake Ontario region during the War of 1812.*
(Map by Douglas Inglis.)

If any single location could have been called the epicenter of the War of 1812, it was Lake Ontario (fig. II.1). Geography, not size, conferred strategic significance: Ontario is the easternmost Great Lake, and the navy that held supremacy here controlled the principal supply routes for all military forces operating along the western frontier of the United States and Canada. The lake was particularly vital for the British, whose forces in Upper Canada relied on a slender supply line that extended up the St. Lawrence River from Montreal and Quebec. For the United States, the lake's outlet offered an invasion route to Montreal and the heart of Lower Canada (the British Army demonstrated this in 1760 when it descended the St. Lawrence to conquer New France).[1] Both belligerents had powerful incentives to command Lake Ontario, and throughout the War of 1812 both would apply their greatest ship building and outfitting efforts to achieve this end.

Ontario is the smallest of the five Great Lakes in area (193 miles [311 km] in length by 53 miles [85 km] in maximum breadth), but it was the only lake where both the United States and Great Britain had naval vessels in service at the start of the war. The British Army had over a half-century of experience building and operating ships on Lake Ontario, a record that extended back to the French and Indian War and the American Revolution.[2] In 1812 the Army Quartermaster Department's Provincial Marine had the nearly new 20-gun ship *Royal George* (fig. II.2), the 14-gun ship *Earl of Moira*, the new 12-gun schooner *Prince Regent,* and the worn-out 6-gun schooner *Duke of Gloucester*.[3] They were based at Kingston, a town near the head of the St. Lawrence River that served as the principal Canadian commercial and military entrepôt on the lake in the early nineteenth century.

The United States had the 16-gun brig *Oneida* on Lake Ontario at the start of the war, the only US Navy warship in service on any lake (fig. II.3). *Oneida* was

Figure II.2. *The Provincial Marine (later Royal Navy) 20-gun ship* Royal George. *The largest warship on Lake Ontario (or any of the lakes) at the start of the war,* Royal George *would continue to serve throughout the conflict. (Drawing by Kevin J. Crisman.)*

launched at Oswego, New York, in March 1809 to enforce a US embargo on trade with Britain. Actual commissioning was delayed until 1810, but the brig thereafter patrolled Ontario's waters, sailing out of the tiny port of Sackets Harbor, New York, at the eastern end of the lake.[4]

With four warships and 40-plus guns, the Provincial Marine should have been more than a match for one US Navy vessel mounting 16 guns, but during the summer and fall of 1812, superiority in numbers and firepower did not result in the kind of easy victories that the British Army achieved at Mackinac Island and Detroit in the far west. Quite the contrary: the Lake Ontario squadron accomplished almost nothing. The problem was obvious to contemporary observers: the Provincial Marine had functioned as a peacetime transport service for three decades, and its personnel were unprepared for war. The crews were under strength, lacked knowledge of their profession, and showed little dedication to the cause (one Royal Army officer

dismissed them as "totally incapable for any hasardous [sic] undertaking").[5] The British squadron made one half-hearted, abortive attack on *Oneida* at Sackets Harbor on July 19 but thereafter avoided contact with the US Navy.[6]

The commander of *Oneida,* Lt. Melancthon T. Woolsey, showed more initiative and as soon as he learned of the war's declaration began rounding up merchant schooners to convert into naval vessels. During the summer of 1812, the US Navy Department provided little guidance or material support. Woolsey faced shortages of cannon, stores, and sailors and was forced to rely on militia volunteers to fill out his crews. The lieutenant particularly coveted a collection of merchant schooners blockaded at the St. Lawrence River port of Ogdensburg, New York, by the Provincial Marine. A temporary regional truce in early September allowed Woolsey to bring the schooners to Sackets Harbor, where preparations were begun to arm them.[7]

The US Army's string of disasters in the far west,

Figure II.3. *The US Navy 16-gun brig* Oneida. *The only American naval vessel in commission on any of the lakes at the start of the conflict, this vessel remained in service throughout the War of 1812. (Drawing by Kevin J. Crisman.)*

and the dawning recognition that naval forces were needed on the border lakes, finally goaded the US government into action in late August of 1812. The Navy Department selected Captain Isaac Chauncey to take charge, instructing him to build and outfit two squadrons and sweep the British off both Lake Ontario and the Upper Lakes. It was a tall order, but Navy Secretary Paul Hamilton now held nothing back in terms of resources: "The object must be accomplished; and all the means which you may judge essential, must be employed."[8]

The forty-year-old Chauncey was an experienced seaman who had commanded a merchant ship by the age of nineteen (fig. II.4). He entered the fledgling US Navy as a lieutenant in 1798 and served with distinction through the Quasi-War with France and the suppression of the Barbary corsairs. Promoted to master commandant in 1804, two years later he rose to the rank of captain, then the highest rank in the US Navy. He took a one-year leave of absence from the navy to

sail a merchant ship to China and upon his return in 1807 was assigned to the command of the New York naval yard, a post he held until called to the lakes in 1812.[9]

After the receipt of his orders, Chauncey launched into his new duties with a will, requesting intelligence reports; requisitioning or purchasing tons of ordnance, ship's equipment, and miscellaneous stores; hiring shipwrights and laborers; and seeking out volunteers among the officers and sailors stationed at New York. Obtaining the materials and people he required was merely the beginning, for everything had to be transported, on short notice and at very great cost, up the Hudson River to Albany, transferred to small boats, and then poled up the Mohawk River and finally down the Oswego River to Lake Ontario. September was late in the year to launch a naval offensive, but Chauncey gamely set out to drive the British off Lake Ontario by the close of the 1812 navigation season. In just three weeks he had most of what he needed en route to Sack-

Figure II.4. *Isaac Chauncey, commodore of the US Naval squadron on Lake Ontario. Chauncey accomplished miracles of logistics in building, outfitting, and manning his squadron during the war, but he was unable to win the decisive victory that his countrymen expected. (Painting by Gilbert Stuart, courtesy of the US Naval Academy Museum.)*

ets Harbor: Master Shipwright Henry Eckford (the builder of *Oneida*) and 140 shipwrights; seven hundred sailors and marines; and nearly everything required to outfit a 24-gun ship as well as to arm the schooners that Woolsey had so diligently gathered.[10]

Chauncey arrived at Sackets Harbor on October 6 and over the next two months presided over a whirlwind of preparations, excursions, and naval actions on the lake (fig. II.5). Eckford started on the new ship and promised to have it launched in six weeks, while five merchant schooners underwent conversion into warships. At the end of the month four more schooners were purchased at Oswego to carry shipments of guns and stores to Sackets Harbor, where they were then armed for employment in the US squadron.[11]

Chauncey, mindful of Hamilton's instructions to gain control of the lake before the year was out, repeatedly sailed against the British in November, first with *Oneida* alone and then on November 8 with *Oneida* and six schooners that collectively mounted 25 guns.[12] Dur-

ing this cruise, the US squadron burned one merchant vessel, captured two others, and chased the Provincial Marine's *Royal George* into Kingston and engaged in a brisk—though inconclusive—cannon duel with the ship and several shore batteries.

Gales, snow, and the freezing of the lake made sailing increasingly difficult, and the US ships were laid up for the winter at the beginning of December.[13] The 1812 campaign was over, but Chauncey had no doubt that he now controlled Lake Ontario. The US squadron's outlook for 1813 was brightened by Eckford's launch on November 26 of the 24-gun ship-rigged corvette *Madison*, built from standing timber in forty-five days.[14]

Over the winter, both sides prepared for a renewed contest in the spring. Of particular significance for 1813 was the British government's decision to turn the lake squadrons over to the Royal Navy. The Provincial Marine's feeble performance in 1812 made it clear that unless drastic changes were made, Ontario was certain to become a US lake the following year, a disaster that could lead to the loss of all of Upper Canada. On March 19, 1813, the Admiralty ordered Captain Sir James Lucas Yeo to assume command of naval forces on the North American lakes.[15]

The thirty-year-old Yeo had a long and distinguished record of service that began when he entered the Royal Navy as a midshipman at the age of ten (fig. II.6). He served on numerous ships and stations, was promoted to post captain at the age of twenty-five, led a bold campaign that captured French Guiana in 1809, and earned a knighthood from Britain's Portuguese allies. Yeo's appointment to the lakes owed much to the accidental wrecking of his previous command in the Bahamas in November 1812.[16] He returned to England for a court of inquiry into the loss of the frigate *Southampton*, and after being absolved of blame for that incident, he was directed to proceed to Canada and the Great Lakes.[17] The entry of the Royal Navy greatly changed the nature of the freshwater naval war: it was now a match between two professional services with more or less equal experience and zeal.

Each side initiated the construction of new warships during the winter of 1812–13. The British started first but divided their efforts between Kingston, where work got underway on a 22-gun ship, *Wolfe*, and York (modern-day Toronto), where a 30-gun frigate was laid down. The latter location was perhaps not the best choice; although York was judged to have a better har-

SOUTH EAST VIEW OF SACKETT'S HARBOUR

Figure II.5. *Sackets Harbor during the War of 1812. A small town located on a well-protected harbor before the War of 1812, Sackets Harbor grew exponentially during the war years. The town experienced two unsuccessful British attacks in 1812 and 1813 and by 1814 was the home port of the most powerful US naval squadron to sail during the conflict. (View by Thomas Birch, etching by Thomas Strickland, collection of Kevin J. Crisman.)*

Figure II.6. *Capt. James Lucas Yeo, commodore of the Royal Navy squadron on Lake Ontario. A competent and experienced officer, he was ordered to the Great Lakes after the accidental wrecking of his frigate* Southampton *in 1812. Like his adversary Isaac Chauncey, Yeo was proficient at preparing a squadron for action, but he proved equally cautious about gambling on the outcome of a battle. (Courtesy of the Toronto Public Library, JRR 1184, Repro T 15241.)*

Figure II.7. *Henry Eckford, designer and builder of the US Navy's warships on Lake Ontario. US commodore Isaac Chauncey said of Eckford, "There is not his equal in the U. States or perhaps in the World." (Painting attributed to Henry Inman, courtesy of the Adirondack Museum, Blue Mountain Lake, NY.)*

bor for a squadron, it was much farther from the St. Lawrence supply line and its defenses were weak.[18]

In late January, four British deserters from *Royal George* brought news of the building in Canada to Sackets Harbor. "The information . . . is unquestionably correct," Chauncey wrote newly appointed Secretary of the Navy William Jones. "It will therefore require correspondent exertions on our part to defeat their plans and destroy their hopes." The commodore recommended another corvette the size of *Madison,* and Jones was quick to approve its construction, adding, "you are to consider the absolute superiority on all the lakes, as the only limit to your authority."[19] During a trip to New York City in February, Chauncey once more contracted with Henry Eckford to assemble his new ship.[20]

If ever a person epitomized the American immigrant success story, it was Henry Eckford (fig. II.7). Born in Kilwinning on the west coast of Scotland in 1775, he moved to Canada at age sixteen and served a five-year shipbuilding apprenticeship under an uncle. Eckford spent most of this time at Kingston in Upper Canada,

the beginning of an association with Lake Ontario that would last almost a quarter century. In 1796, his apprenticeship now over, he left Canada for New York City, which was then rising from the ashes of the Revolutionary War and becoming the principal port and shipbuilding center of the United States. For Eckford it was a place of opportunity, and he made the most of it. By 1799 he had established his own yard on the East River and was launching merchant vessels and building a reputation.[21]

Henry Eckford's approach to shipbuilding was empirical. "He never frittered away his time or the money of his employers in daring experiments, which so often extort applause from the uninformed multitude," said a contemporary biographer, "he preferred feeling his way cautiously, step by step."[22] When one of his new ships returned to port, Eckford questioned the crew about its sailing qualities and then incorporated what he learned into the next. "In this way he proceeded," the same biographer continued, "successively improving the shape of each, until those constructed by him, or after his models, firmly established the character of New York built ships over those of any other port in the union." His prewar experience as a contractor for the US Navy included the building of *Oneida* on Lake Ontario and gunboats for the defense of New York.[23] During the war Eckford's genius for organization and construction shortcuts allowed him to turn out a rapid succession of naval vessels.

In the spring of 1813, Eckford began work at Sackets Harbor by running up a small, loftily rigged, and very sharp 1-gun schooner, *Lady of the Lake*; launched on April 6, this nimble vessel would become indispensible to Chauncey for spying on the British squadron. Eckford then laid down the keel for a 26-gun corvette that would be christened *General Pike* after its launch on June 12 (fig. II.8). One more warship would be added to the US squadron in August, when Eckford completed the sharp-hulled 16-gun schooner (later brig) *Sylph* in just twenty-one days, which was very fast work indeed.[24]

Chauncey's strategy for the 1813 campaign initially called for a bold coup de main, a sudden descent upon Kingston by combined army and navy forces. After one thousand "picked troops" were debarked west of town, the US ships and soldiers would attack simultaneously by water and land, overwhelming the British defenses. This plan promised at one stroke to make the British

Figure II.8. *Sail plan of the US Navy corvette* General Pike. *This vessel was flagship of the US Navy's Lake Ontario squadron during the summer and fall of 1813. (Painting by Charles Ware, USN, Sailmaker, NH57006, National Archives and Records Administration.)*

situation on the Great Lakes untenable. As the thawing of the lake approached, however, intelligence from Canada suggested Kingston had been strengthened and that any attempt to take it would result in fearsome casualties. In late March, Chauncey chose to attack elsewhere, first at York and then on the Canadian side of the Niagara River.[25] Although less risky than the Kingston expedition, the revised plan concentrated on the peripheries rather than the core of British defenses in Upper Canada.

The US offensive went well at first. The 14-ship squadron bearing one thousand seven hundred US Army troops took York after a short, sharp battle on April 27. Retreating British troops burned the nearly completed 30-gun ship on the stocks, along with stores intended for the Royal Navy squadron on Lake Erie (their loss would be much lamented by Comm. Robert Barclay later that summer).[26] This was a raid only, and no effort was made to permanently occupy York. One month later, Chauncey's ships landed the army on the Canadian side of the Niagara River's outlet. This attack

also went well: the British Army abandoned its positions along the Niagara and retreated into the interior, allowing Comm. Oliver H. Perry to extract five small vessels from the upper river for use in the US Lake Erie squadron.[27]

While the US warships were occupied at the western end of the lake, a significant change took place in the British squadron at Kingston. The first contingent of Royal Navy officers and sailors arrived in late April, and Yeo took command in mid-May. The navy inherited five vessels: the 22-gun *Wolfe,* launched in April, as well as *Royal George* (20 guns), *Earl of Moira* (18 guns), *Lord Beresford* (ex–*Prince Regent,* 12 guns), and *Sir Sidney Smith* (ex–*Governor Simcoe,* 12 guns). A sixth vessel, the 14-gun brig *Lord Melville,* was under construction at Kingston and would be launched in July.[28] Most of the Provincial Marine's officers resigned, but about seventy of its sailors continued in service under the new regime. Yeo still considered his ships to be critically short of sailors and detached only a handful for the Royal Navy's Lake Erie squadron.[29]

The prolonged absence of the US squadron from its base in May inspired Lt. Gen. Sir George Prevost, Governor-in-Chief of Canada, to undertake a raid of his own. Most of the regular forces in Kingston, nearly nine hundred in total, boarded the squadron on May 27, and that evening the ships set sail, towing a flotilla of small craft for landing the troops. Unfavorable winds delayed the British arrival at Sackets Harbor until the next afternoon, and squally weather led Prevost to call off the landing until the next day. Given a bonus of extra time to prepare, the US defenders managed to assemble 750 regulars and 700 militiamen to meet the British.[30]

The Battle of Sackets Harbor on the morning of May 29 was a victory for the defenders, but only by the narrowest of margins. Accompanied by both Prevost and Yeo, the British expeditionary force landed under withering fire, dispersed the militia defenders, and fought its way to the outskirts of the heavily fortified town, suffering casualties all the way. US defenses were on the verge of collapse when the cautious Prevost took stock of his depleted troops, hesitated, and then sounded the retreat and withdrew to the squadron. "It was a scandalously managed affair," lamented one British Army officer. "We gained a surprise and threw it away."[31] For the victors, Sackets Harbor was a pyrrhic success: the US Navy lieutenant in charge of the shipyard's defense panicked and set fire to the squadron's naval stores, although the unfinished *General Pike* was spared the flames.[32]

The near-success of the British attack on Sackets Harbor rattled Isaac Chauncey, reinforcing an innate caution that would become more evident as the war progressed. After his return to Sackets Harbor on June 1, the US commodore, aware of the edge in firepower that the new *Wolfe* gave to the British squadron, firmly declined to sortie until *General Pike* was launched, outfitted, and manned. The US Navy thus remained harbor-bound for all of June and most of July. During this time, the British squadron roved the length of the lake, supporting British Army counterattacks on the Niagara frontier that rolled the US Army back to the border and attacking ports along the New York shore to destroy or carry off US government supplies.[33]

On July 21, the US squadron finally sailed from Sackets Harbor to the western end of Lake Ontario to interdict British Army supplies and lure the Royal Navy into action. The Royal Navy squadron sailed on July 31, also bound for the head of the lake. The two navies met one week later and began a complicated dance around each other, and around the lake, that would continue intermittently for the next two months.[34]

This reluctance to come to grips was due, in part, to marked differences in each squadron's capabilities, for although the total number of guns was similar (97 British versus 112 American guns at the beginning of August), the proportion of gun types varied, as did the qualities of the ships that carried them. Yeo's six ships were all built from the keel up as naval vessels, had similar sailing qualities, and carried a high proportion of powerful but short-range carronades. They maneuvered well as a group but in battle had to quickly close with the US ships to effectively use their guns. Chauncey's squadron included only three purpose-built warships, the other ten being armed merchant schooners.[35] Besides offering no protection for their crews in battle, the schooners often lagged behind the rest of the squadron in moderate winds and pitched too heavily in rough weather to employ their guns.[36] The US squadron carried a high proportion of long guns and could achieve its best results (with the least hazard to the frail schooners) by staying out of British carronade range and disabling its foe from a distance.

The first confrontation between the two squadrons since the previous year began on August 7 and lasted over four days. It featured a confusing succession of sailing maneuvers and long-range exchanges of shot as the winds favored first one side and then the other. Throughout it all, the US schooners repeatedly demonstrated how unsuited they were for this kind of service. Four of the ten were lost: a sudden squall in the early morning hours of August 8 upset the over-gunned *Scourge* and *Hamilton* and sent them to the bottom with most of their crews, and on the night of August 10–11, *Julia* and *Growler* became separated from the US squadron and were captured.[37]

More maneuvering followed, with further encounters on September 11 and 28. On the latter occasion, the flagships narrowed the range and *General Pike's* long 24-pounders toppled *Wolfe's* main and mizzen topmasts, but the brisk intervention of *Royal George,* the bursting of a gun on *Pike's* foredeck, and rapidly deteriorating weather combined to give Yeo's flagship and the rest of his squadron the opportunity to escape from the pursuing Americans. One week later, Chauncey's ships surprised and captured five small transport vessels but otherwise met with no significant success against the Royal Navy.[38]

Chauncey and Yeo blamed each other for refusing to meet under fair terms, but both were widely criticized for the lack of results in 1813. Britons and Americans expected bold, decisive action from their navies, and all the dodging and feinting around the lake suggested that the rival commodores lacked fighting spirit. Chauncey attracted more scorn, since his tactics of engaging from beyond British carronade range and holding back to wait for the laggardly schooners could be interpreted as cowardice. By the end of the summer, Chauncey's leadership of the squadron was being derided by friend and foe alike. A US midshipman on *Madison* described the commodore as "thunderstruck (and no doubt frightened)" when he turned away from oncoming British ships on August 7, and Royal Navy officers considered Chauncey "a coward or a jackass" for failing to follow up his initial success in the September 28 duel.[39]

In truth, both commodores had cause to hesitate before risking the ships they prepared with such expense and effort. As the squadrons grew in numbers and weight of broadsides, it was increasingly apparent that the losing side in a battle had scant possibility of ever regaining parity with the victor. There would be no second chances. And with the loss of Lake Ontario, the losing side's armies would be hard-pressed to hold the western frontier. In short, here, as in no other place, the outcome of the entire war along the US-Canadian border might hinge on a single, split-second decision by one man.[40] It is little wonder that Chauncey and Yeo were skittish about sailing into battle without a decisive edge in ships, firepower, or wind direction.

The 1813 campaign season on Lake Ontario concluded in late October with the launch of a US Army offensive from Sackets Harbor. The original objective was Kingston, a project for which Chauncey expressed his support. At the last minute, however, the expedition's commanders concluded that the town's defenses were too formidable and instead opted to descend the St. Lawrence and attack Montreal. The poorly planned offensive fizzled after a skirmish with a smaller British force, and the invading army instead went into winter quarters.[41] Yeo and Chauncey laid their ships up for the winter season and began a new and ambitious round of ship construction.[42]

The year 1814 on Lake Ontario featured more and much bigger ships. Yeo got a head start on construction for the Royal Navy squadron in the fall of 1813 by laying down two frigates, launched the following spring as the 58-gun *Prince Regent* and the 40-gun *Princess Charlotte*.[43] They were a challenge that Chauncey could not ignore if he hoped to remain in the contest. Early US intelligence reports suggested that the British were building a frigate and two brigs, so Chauncey matched them by having Eckford build the 58-gun *Superior* and the 20-gun brigs *Jefferson* and *Jones.* The three US vessels were completed over the winter, and all were in the water by May 1. Parity with the new British ships was insured by a second US frigate, the 42-gun *Mohawk,* begun in April and launched in June.[44] In terms of their size, number, and fast assembly, the ships built at Kingston and Sackets Harbor in 1814 were collectively the most impressive feat of naval construction of the entire War of 1812.[45] Nor did it end with these six ships, for during the late winter of 1814, Yeo elected to build a 102-gun first rate, *St. Lawrence.* Begun in April and launched in September, it was the largest warship ever to sail on a North American lake.[46]

Getting the new ships built was only the start of the challenges that beset Yeo and Chauncey that year: manning and outfitting them proved as much if not more of a headache. Every sailor, every cannon, every piece of equipment needed on Lake Ontario had to be shipped by river and by road at great cost. By the spring of 1814, Britain's long struggle against Napoleon was winding up in Europe, allowing the Royal Navy to send spare naval vessels to Quebec, where they were stripped of crews, guns, stores, rigging, and even ballast. The US Navy had fewer resources to spare but nonetheless emptied crews and equipment from ships blockaded in ports along the Atlantic seaboard.[47]

The Royal Navy squadron was the first to enter the lake that spring, sailing from Kingston on May 4 to interdict the flow of supplies to Sackets Harbor. Its efforts met with mixed success. An amphibious landing at Oswego on May 6 netted guns, shot, rigging, and provisions intended for the US squadron, but the landing party paid a stiff price—125 casualties—storming the old fort that overlooked the harbor (plate 5a).[48] Three weeks later, on May 30, a British expedition in small boats entered Sandy Creek on the New York shore to seize a flotilla of US supply bateaux laden with naval equipment. Ambushed in the narrow river by US Army riflemen and Oneida Indians, the entire 183-man expedition—including two post captains and four lieutenants—was killed or captured. When Yeo gave up his blockade of Sackets Harbor on June 5, he had little to show for the injury or loss of over three hundred men during the previous month.[49]

The contest for the lake now entered a period of relative inactivity that lasted until the beginning of August. Yeo kept his largest ships at Kingston to await the completion of the new first rate; Chauncey stayed put in Sackets Harbor while the rigging, outfitting, and manning of his new ships dragged on. The US commodore initially planned to sail during the first week of July but delays in completing *Mohawk* and sickness among the shipyard workers pushed the sailing date back, and finally, in mid-July, Chauncey himself was laid low with a fever that kept him bedridden for two weeks.[50]

For the US squadron, the timing could not have been worse. A major US Army offensive led by Gen. Jacob Brown crossed the Niagara River and defeated the British Army at the Battle of Chippewa on July 5. Brown subsequently sent Chauncey an appeal for naval support: "we have between us the command of sufficient means to conquer Upper Canada within two months . . . now is our time, before the enemy can be greatly reinforced."[51] Sick, unwilling to sortie without all of his new ships, and fearing an attack on Sackets Harbor during his absence, Chauncey chose not to meet the army, and on July 25–26, Brown's offensive was blunted at the Battle of Lundy's Lane. The only significant US attempt to invade Canada in 1814 was over, and Brown's widely published pleas for assistance made it appear that the navy's inaction was largely to blame. Chauncey was enraged, writing Secretary Jones: "I perceive, Sir, with regret . . . that General Brown has succeeded in deceiving you as well as the president and the nation, by his *insidious letters.*"[52] The commodore would spend much time and ink over the next few months trying to repair the damage to his reputation.

The squadron that finally left Sackets Harbor on August 1 consisted of two frigates, two corvettes, two brig-rigged sloops of war, and two smaller brigs; it was by far the most potent US Navy force to sail during the war. The Americans went first to the western end of the lake, where the Royal Navy's 11-gun schooner *Magnet* (ex–*Sir Sidney Smith*) was chased ashore and then blown up by its crew. After detaching three brigs

to blockade British supply vessels inside the mouth of the Niagara River, Chauncey proceeded back down the lake and began a close watch on Kingston that would continue (with short interruptions) until the beginning of October. Yeo was challenged to come out and fight, but with his first rate nearing completion, the British commodore saw no point in taking on the more powerful US squadron.[53]

The situation reversed itself on October 7 when the US squadron returned to Sackets Harbor to avoid confronting a British squadron strengthened by *St. Lawrence.* Chauncey fully expected an attack upon his base, but Yeo had another mission to fulfill. In an exchange of letters that curiously paralleled the difficulties between the US Army and Navy commanders, Lt. Gen. Gordon Drummond and his superior General Prevost insisted that Yeo transport troops and supplies to Drummond's embattled army on the Niagara River. Concerned that he might be blamed for the collapse of the British position, Yeo acquiesced and used what little time was left in the waning navigation season to make two runs to the west between October 16 and November 10.[54] And with that, the 1814 campaign on the lake came to an end; nothing had changed from the previous year except that a great deal of money had been spent to build many large ships. Unlike 1813, there were not even any skirmishes on the lake between the two squadrons.

Yet another round of shipbuilding got underway. Chauncey was authorized to build two first rate ships mounting over 100 guns apiece as well as another large frigate, a construction program that utterly dwarfed the previous year's efforts. Henry Eckford was again the chief builder, but the project was too much for one person, and Adam and Noah Brown were contracted to run up one of the first rates. The new ships required eight hundred carpenters and laborers to construct and over two thousand tons of cannon and stores to outfit, and the station needed 2898 more officers, sailors, and marines, a massive commitment of the navy's thin resources.[55] The ceaseless building gave many in Washington qualms, most notably Navy Secretary Jones, who wrote President James Madison: "If we have hitherto maintained a vacillating superiority, on Lake Ontario, by the greatest exertions . . . we ought not to delude ourselves with the belief that these can be extended indefinitely."[56]

The Royal Navy also remained committed to maintaining the contest despite the mounting costs. During the summer and fall of 1814, the hull of a frigate sent over in pieces from England was hauled up the St. Lawrence River; its assembly at Kingston began in November. Named *Psyche,* the 56-gun ship was launched on December 25.[57] Two more first rates similar in size to *St. Lawrence,* named *Canada* and *Wolfe,* were also laid down at Kingston, and substantial progress was made over the course of the winter on their framing and planking. Once more the Royal Navy routed men, cannon, and ship stores to Quebec and Montreal to complete the newest freshwater warships in its fleet.

Then, suddenly, the contest was over: on February 16, 1815, news of peace reached Sackets Harbor. When it was confirmed one week later, sailors and soldiers celebrated by illuminating the town with bonfires while the naval officers held a grand ball aboard *Superior.* Chauncey passed the glad tidings along to Commodore Yeo at Kingston and then began shutting down the construction work and transferring carpenters and crews back to the seaboard. The ships of the squadron were stripped of rigging, cannon, and stores, and the massive ships of the line nearly ready for launching—Eckford's *New Orleans* and the Brown Brothers' *Chippewa*—were left unfinished on the stocks.[58] Across the lake at Kingston, the Royal Navy followed suit, leaving *Canada* and *Wolfe* high and dry, never to wet their keels in the lake. The rival squadrons, suddenly of little consequence to their creators, began a long slide into decay and abandonment.

Lake Ontario's role in the War of 1812 was paradoxical. Considered the most important of all the border lakes from a strategic point of view, both sides made it the focus of their military and naval campaigns. Yeo and Chauncey were the recipients of a vast quantity of men and materials, and as the highest-ranking naval commanders on the Great Lakes, they were also given wide latitude to plan and carry out their objectives in concert with, but not under the direct orders of, the commanders of their respective armies.

Conditions proved ideal for a stalemate. After 1812, the two navies were about evenly matched when it came to quality of leadership, seamanship, supply, and ships. Furthermore, in the tightly contained theater that was lake warfare, it was difficult to surprise one's foe. The steady flow of intelligence across the border allowed the two commodores to weigh the odds on a near-daily basis, to tally every ship, gun, and sailor and calculate the material strength of each squadron. And unlike naval commanders on Lakes Erie and Champlain, neither Chauncey nor Yeo ever faced a crisis or orders that forced them to act. Acutely aware of the potential costs of losing, both stuck firmly to the side of caution, opting to fight their war in the shipyards rather than risk everything on the lake. The result was a series of impressive logistical and shipbuilding accomplishments but not the glorious, sanguinary, decisive battle expected by the public.

For nautical archaeologists, the legacy of the War of 1812 on Lake Ontario has been a varied collection of ships and excellent opportunities for studying naval construction and naval life. The following four chapters examine the seven wrecks that have thus far been discovered and investigated. These provide examples of the principal vessel types used on Ontario during the war: a mysterious small vessel, very likely a Royal Navy gunboat (the Browns Bay Vessel); two commercial schooners converted into warships (*Hamilton* and *Scourge*); a US Navy 20-gun brig built by Henry Eckford (*Jefferson*); two Royal Navy frigates (*Prince Regent* and *Princess Charlotte*); and the largest ship to sail any lake during the war (the first rate *St. Lawrence*). The construction of these vessels varies widely: the Browns Bay Vessel's lapstrake assembly is unique among known 1812-era shipwrecks, and *Prince Regent, Princess Charlotte,* and *St. Lawrence,* although built at the same place and during the same year, show very different approaches to frame assembly. The seven wrecks also demonstrate the full range of preservation possibilities: *Hamilton* and *Scourge* are nearly complete, with guns still lining their decks and masts standing, while *St. Lawrence* consists of only a long fragment of one side (which side of the hull has not been determined). Whether complete or in pieces, all of these wrecks have much to tell us about the greatest shipbuilding effort in North America during the War of 1812.

NOTES

1. Fred Anderson, *Crucible of War: The Seven Years' War and the Fate of Empire in British North America, 1754–1766* (New York: Alfred A. Knopf, 2000), pp. 387–88, 400–404.

2. Robert Malcomson, *Warships of the Great Lakes, 1754–1834* (Chatham Publishing, 2001).

3. William Wood, ed., *Select British Documents of the Cana-*

dian War of 1812, vol. 1 (Toronto: The Champlain Society, 1920), pp. 242, 246–47, 253–54; Robert Malcomson, *Lords of the Lake: The Naval War on Lake Ontario, 1812–1814* (Toronto: Robin Brass Studio, 1998), pp. 327–30. The appendices in Malcomson's book provide a useful, year-by-year summary of the opposing squadrons on Lake Ontario.

4. "Contract with Eckford & Bergh for Building a Gun Brig on Lake Ontario," July 26, 1808, Contracts of the US Navy, entry 235, vol. 1, no. 348, Naval Records Collection of the Office of Naval Records and Library, record group 45 (RG 45), National Archives and Records Administration (NARA); Woolsey to Hamilton, October 6, November 19, and December 16, 1810, Letters received by the Secretary of the Navy from Officers below the rank of Master Commandant, entry 148, RG 45, NARA; Malcomson, *Lords of the Lake,* pp. 17–20.

5. Malcomson, *Lords of the Lake,* pp. 31, 36; William Wood, ed., *Select British Documents of the Canadian War of 1812,* vol. 2 (Toronto: The Champlain Society, 1923), pp. 116–17; William S. Dudley, ed., *The Naval War of 1812: A Documentary History,* vol. 2 (Washington, DC: Naval Historical Center, 1992), pp. 413–17.

6. Dudley, ed., *Naval War of 1812,* vol. 2, pp. 283–84; Malcomson, *Lords of the Lake,* pp. 31–34.

7. Dudley, ed., *Naval War of 1812,* vol. 1, pp. 286–93, 295, 305.

8. Dudley, ed., *Naval War of 1812,* vol. 1, pp. 297–301.

9. Allen Johnson and Dumas Malone, eds., *Dictionary of American Biography,* vol. 4 (New York: Charles Scribner's Sons, 1930), pp. 40–41; Malcomson, *Lords of the Lake,* pp. 38–42.

10. Dudley, ed., *Naval War of 1812,* vol. 1, pp. 301, 311–17, 322–24.

11. Dudley, ed., *Naval War of 1812,* vol. 1, pp. 338–42.

12. Malcomson, *Lords of the Lake,* pp. 329–30.

13. Dudley, ed., *Naval War of 1812,* vol. 1, pp. 343–53, 361–64.

14. Dudley, ed., *Naval War of 1812,* vol. 1, pp. 348, 353.

15. Wood, ed., *Select British Documents,* vol. 2, pp. 76–78.

16. David J. Hepper, *British Warship Losses in the Age of Sail: 1650–1859* (Rotherfield, East Sussex: Jean Boudriot Publications, 1994), p. 143.

17. J. K. Laughton, s.v. "Yeo, James Lucas (1782–1818)," Rev. Michael Duffy, *Oxford Dictionary of National Biography* (Oxford University Press, 2004, Online Edition, http://dx.doi.org/10.1093/ref:odnb/30217, accessed February 22, 2013); William James, *The Naval History of Great Britain: During the French Revolutionary and Napoleonic Wars, vol. 5: 1808–1811* (London: Conway Maritime Press, 2002), pp. 206–13; John W. Spurr, s.v. "Yeo, Sir James Lucas," *Dictionary of Canadian Biography,* vol. V (University of Toronto Press, 1983, Online Edition, http://www.biographi.ca/009004-119.01-e.php?&id_nbr=2722, accessed February 22, 2013).

18. Malcomson, *Lords of the Lake,* pp. 59–60, 66–70, 94–97.

19. Dudley, ed., *Naval War of 1812,* vol. 2, pp. 417–20.

20. Dudley, ed., *Naval War of 1812,* vol. 2, pp. 425–27.

21. Steven M. Selig, *Draughts: The Henry Eckford Story* (Scottsdale, AZ: Agreka History Preserved, 2008). This book contains a detailed account of Eckford's life; chapters 1–3 tell the story of his career from birth to the War of 1812.

22. Henry Howe, *Memoirs of the Most Eminent American Mechanics* (New York: Alexander V. Blake, 1841), pp. 211–12.

23. Selig, *Draughts,* pp. 34–36; Howard I. Chapelle, *The History of the American Sailing Navy* (New York: W. W. Norton, 1949), pp. 225, 229–32.

24. Kevin Crisman, "The *Jefferson:* The History and Archaeology of an American Brig from the War of 1812" (PhD diss., University of Pennsylvania, 1989), pp. 37–38, 43–44, 47.

25. Dudley, ed., *Naval War of 1812,* vol. 2, pp. 417–20, 430–35.

26. Robert Malcomson, *Capital in Flames: The American Attack on York, 1813* (Montreal: Robin Brass Studio, 2008), pp. 138–261.

27. Dudley, ed., *Naval War of 1812,* vol. 2, pp. 460–66; an excellent summary of the two US landings can be found in Malcomson, *Lords of the Lake,* pp. 102–12, 124–29.

28. Malcomson, *Warships of the Great Lakes,* pp. 78, 81.

29. Malcomson, *Lords of the Lake,* pp. 122–23, 333; Malcomson, *Warships of the Great Lakes,* pp. 77–78.

30. Patrick A. Wilder, *The Battle of Sackett's Harbour 1813* (Baltimore: The Nautical and Aviation Publishing Company of America, 1994), pp. 71–83.

31. Donald E. Graves, ed., *Merry Hearts Make Light Days: The War of 1812 Journal of Lieutenant John Le Couteur, 104th Foot* (Ottawa: Carlton University Press, 1994), p. 117; see also Wilder, *Battle of Sackett's Harbour,* pp. 85–123; Don Bamford & Paul Carroll, *Four Years on the Great Lakes, 1813–1816: The Journal of Lieutenant David Wingfield, Royal Navy* (Toronto: Natural Heritage Books, 2009), pp. 62–67; Wood, ed., *Select British Documents,* vol. 2, pp. 123–34.

32. Dudley, ed., *Naval War of 1812,* vol. 2, pp. 477–79.

33. Dudley, ed., *Naval War of 1812,* vol. 2, pp. 492–512.

34. Dudley, ed., *Naval War of 1812,* vol. 2, pp. 523–24, 534.

35. Malcomson, *Lords of the Lake,* p. 169.

36. Malcomson, *Warships of the Great Lakes,* p. 65; Dudley, ed., *Naval War of 1812,* vol. 2, pp. 537–41.

37. Dudley, ed., *Naval War of 1812,* vol. 2, pp. 537–41; Wood, ed., *Select British Documents,* vol. 2, pp. 196–99.

38. Dudley, ed., *Naval War of 1812,* vol. 2, pp. 579–90; Wood, ed., *Select British Documents,* vol. 2, pp. 206–11.

39. Dudley, ed., *Naval War of 1812,* vol. 2, pp. 536–37; Graves, ed., *Merry Hearts Make Light Days,* p. 148.

40. Lt. Frederick John Johnston of Yeo's flagship *Wolfe* declared in July 1813, "The Fate of Canada depends upon us" (M. K. Ritchie and C. Ritchie, "A Laker's Log," *American Neptune* 17 [1957], p. 207), while a Philadelphia merchant wrote that fall, "The feelings of our citizens are all alive respecting a reported engagement between Com. Chauncey & Yeo" (Emlin & Howells to Messrs J & I Townsend, October 11, 1813, Townsend Papers, Box 1, Folder 2, New York State Archives, Albany). Chauncey and Yeo were feeling the glare of the stage lights.

41. Dudley, ed., *Naval War of 1812,* vol. 2, pp. 592–99; Don-

ald R. Hickey, *The War of 1812: A Forgotten Conflict* (Urbana: University of Illinois Press, 1989), pp. 143–46.

42. Chauncey to Jones, December 11, 1813, Isaac Chauncey Letter Books (CLB), vol. 1, New York Historical Society (NYHS); Dudley, ed., *Naval War of 1812,* vol. 2, pp. 591, 612–15; Wood, ed., *Select British Documents,* vol. 2, pp. 217–18.

43. Malcomson, *Warships of the Great Lakes,* pp. 100–102.

44. Crisman, "The *Jefferson*," pp. 55, 62–64, 69–71, 97, 109.

45. Chauncey, writing of the four new US ships, challenged anyone to "produce a parallel instance, in which the same number of vessels of such dimensions have been built and fitted in the same time by the same number of workmen." Chauncey to Jones, August 10, 1814, CLB, vol. 2, NYHS.

46. Michael J. Crawford, ed., *The Naval War of 1812: A Documentary History,* vol. 3 (Washington, DC: Naval Historical Center, 2002), p. 440; Malcomson, *Warships of the Great Lakes,* pp. 111–16.

47. Malcomson, *Warships of the Great Lakes,* p. 102; Crawford, ed., *Naval War of 1812,* vol. 3, pp. 404, 409–12, 433–37, 495–96.

48. Hickey, *The War of 1812,* p. 185; Crawford, ed., *Naval War of 1812,* vol. 3, pp. 463–79.

49. Major Appling, the commander of the American riflemen, listed a total of 183 British captured or killed at Sandy Creek, while Yeo reported the loss of 220 men. Crawford, ed., *Naval War of 1812,* vol. 3, pp. 508–12, 518–23; Malcomson, *Lords of the Lake,* p. 282.

50. Crisman, "The *Jefferson*," pp. 109–21.

51. Paris M. Davis, *An Authentic History of the Late War Between the United States and Great Britain* (New York: Ebenezer F. Baker, 1836), pp. 156–57.

52. Chauncey to Jones, August 19, 1814, William Jones Papers, Uselma Clark Smith Collection (UCSC), Historical Society of Pennsylvania (HSP), see also Crawford, ed., *Naval War of 1812,* vol. 3, pp. 549–57, 577–88.

53. Crisman, "The *Jefferson*," pp. 123–34; Crawford, ed., *Naval War of 1812,* vol. 3, pp. 617–24.

54. Malcomson, *Lords of the Lake,* pp. 297–98, 303–10.

55. Chauncey to Jones, November 5, 1814, and "An Estimate of the Number of Officers and Men Required to Man the Fleet on Lake Ontario," ca. November 1814; microcopy 125, roll 40, RG 45; NARA.

56. Jones to Madison, October 26, 1814, William Jones Papers, UCSC, HSP.

57. Malcomson, *Warships of the Great Lakes,* pp. 115, 117–18.

58. Chauncey to Agents and Shipbuilders, February 23, 1815, and Chauncey to Crowninshield, March 8, 1815, CLB, vol. 2, NYHS.

5

FORE-AND-AFTERS AT FIFTY FATHOMS
The Wrecks of *Hamilton* and *Scourge*

JONATHAN MOORE

Introduction

In a period characterized by flourishing trade on Lake Ontario, ineffective American efforts to curb smuggling, and heightened political tension between Britain and the United States, two new schooners, *Diana* and *Lord Nelson,* joined the lake's commercial fleet. *Diana* was launched at Oswego, New York, in 1809 and *Lord Nelson* at Niagara, Upper Canada, in 1811. Although hailing from opposite sides of the border, both were part of a fledgling commercial system that scarcely noticed national boundaries. Trade succumbed to national rivalry in 1812, however: *Lord Nelson* was seized on June 5 by US authorities on suspicion of smuggling, and two weeks later the outbreak of war disrupted the careers of all lake craft, including *Diana.* By October both were part of a small squadron of schooners converted into makeshift gunboats by the US Navy. The war ended in 1815, but *Diana* and *Lord Nelson* never resumed their peacetime routines. Sent to the bottom by a sudden squall on August 8, 1813, they rested, invisible, as successive generations of merchant ships passed overhead.

Diana and *Lord Nelson*:
Coasting Schooners on Lake Ontario

Well before the launch of the *Diana* and *Lord Nelson,* the schooner had emerged as the preferred vessel type for trade and passenger service on North American waters. On Lake Ontario, schooners worked in conjunction with the bateaux and Durham boats that ferried goods up and down the rivers that linked the lake with tidewater ports. Although the lake's early schooners varied significantly in size and proportions, all were shoal drafted to permit passage across river bars and into shallow harbors and channels. The fore-and-aft schooner rig offered good windward ability in the confined waters and lee shores of the lake, and their small crews made them economical (plate 5b).[1]

British customs records from 1803 reveal at least eleven American and British commercial vessels navigating the lake, ranging from 15 to 90 tons. Two years later, a Royal Navy timber procurer observed ten or twelve vessels from 40 to 120 tons passing between Kingston and the head of the lake. A US official who visited Oswego in 1810 reported that most of the eleven vessels belonging to the village were carrying salt from Salina (near Syracuse, New York) to US and Canadian markets around the Great Lakes. British customs records show that by 1810, at least thirty-two schooners and sloops, averaging about 50 tons, were regularly calling at Canadian ports.[2]

When the United States government began enforcing its Embargo Act in 1808, the firmly established commercial links across the lake and porous border made it nearly impossible to stem the flow of smuggled goods.[3] In 1808, US Navy Lt. Melancthon Woolsey was ordered to build a brig at Oswego to enforce the act. New York shipbuilder Henry Eckford and his assistant Henry Eagle accompanied Woolsey to supervise the shipbuilding.[4] The embargo was repealed in March 1809, the same month Woolsey's *Oneida* was launched.

Keen to take advantage of improved prospects for trade and the availability of an experienced shipwright, Oswego merchants Matthew McNair, Daniel Hugunin, and Peter Hugunin contracted with Henry Eagle to build a schooner at Oswego in the summer of 1809. Later that year the three merchants contracted with Porter Barton & Co. to operate the schooner. Their agreement noted that *Diana* was "about eighty tons burthen" and stipulated that the schooner was to run exclusively between Oswego and its environs to Lewiston, New York, where Porter Barton & Co. ran the US portage around Niagara Falls. Augustus Porter's business records show that *Diana*'s regular run was between the two ports; typically the schooner carried salt (four hundred to five hundred barrels) or mixed cargoes of salt, flour, pork, merchandise, and liquor. Porter's accounts also minutely detail the schooner's operating expenses between 1810 and 1811, from crew staples such as bread, pork, and whiskey to shipboard supplies like candles, rope, and paintbrushes.[5]

In 1808 Porter Barton & Co. contracted the Hudson, New York, shipbuilding firm Stannard & Clark to build a schooner at Lewiston named *Ontario*. Asa Stannard subsequently established his own shipyard at Black Rock (now Buffalo, New York), and in the autumn of 1810, brothers James and William Crooks, merchants based at Niagara, Upper Canada (now Niagara-on-the-Lake, Ontario) engaged him to build a schooner. Accounts drawn up by the Crooks provide a detailed record of the materials used for construction and fitting out. Tons of manufactured gear for the schooner were shipped from the United States via Oswego, and local timber and plank were cut and hauled to the Niagara building site by August 1810. Stannard began work in October, and the completed schooner, of "about 50 tons," was launched on May 1, 1811 as the *Lord Nelson*. The vessel began a regular run between Niagara and Prescott, Upper Canada.[6]

There is little historical information concerning the design, dimensions, and construction of the *Diana, Lord Nelson,* and other lake schooners of the period. Many of the men who owned and built them had roots in coastal shipping along the Atlantic seaboard or along the Hudson River, and their designs likely reflected this heritage. We know that in addition to their hold space, these craft typically had passenger accommodations under raised quarterdecks. The cabin of the 53-ton schooner *Experiment,* built at Ogdensburg, New York, in 1809 was "large, & very Convenient for Passengers its height is just sufficient for every person not above 6 feet to Stand Straight in."[7] The *Hunter,* a 59-ton schooner launched at Great Sodus in 1814 of slightly more tonnage than the *Lord Nelson,* measured 61 feet 6 inches (18.7 m) in length and 20 feet (6 m) in breadth and had a depth of hold of 5 feet 9 inches (1.8 m).[8] The 82-ton *Fair American,* launched at Oswego by 1810, was "schooner-rigged, with a fore and main topsail, and modeled much like the Albany [Hudson River] sloops," Robert Hugunin later recollected.[9] *Fair American*'s tonnage appears to have been slightly greater than *Diana*'s, and a postwar enrollment lists her dimensions as 64 feet (19.5 m) in length and 18 feet 6 inches (5.6 m) in breadth, with a depth of hold of 8 feet (2.4 m).[10] By tonnage, the largest US commercial vessel on the lake in 1812 was the 99-ton *Charles and Ann,* launched in 1810 with a length of 70 feet (21.3 m), a breadth of 22 feet (6.7 m), and a depth of hold of 7 feet 6 inches (2.3 m).[11]

"Fitting for Guns": Summer and Autumn 1812

In anticipation of the coming war, Congress reinstated the Embargo Act on April 4, 1812. Upon receiving this news, Lieutenant Woolsey entered the lake with *Oneida* and on June 5 seized the *Lord Nelson* on suspicion of smuggling. According to co-owner James Crooks, "Lord Nelson was a fast sailer, and being ahead of several others in Company, beating up the Lake against a headwind from Prescott, the *Oneida* made for her first."[12] Crooks traveled to Sackets Harbor to seek the release of his vessel, but fate had other plans in mind: the new schooner was taken just thirteen days prior to the declaration of war by the United States on June 18, 1812.[13] The Crooks brothers would never recover *Lord Nelson.*

Although *Lord Nelson* had not yet been purchased into the Navy, its conversion for naval service commenced not long after the capture: Woolsey reported to Secretary of the Navy Paul Hamilton on July 4 that "Lord Nelson is fitting for six guns."[14] Throughout August and September, Henry Eagle and other carpenters worked intermittently on the rigging, raised bulwarks, and made gun carriages. An acute shortage of ordnance at Sackets Harbor delayed the arming, however.[15]

Comm. Isaac Chauncey (who assumed command of US Navy forces on the Great Lakes in late August) and Lieutenant Woolsey spent much of September and October creating a squadron of gunboats to sail in company with *Oneida.*[16] Merchant schooners were purchased and taken to Sackets Harbor, and guns and stores were shipped up from New York to convert them into warships (Table 5.1). Chauncey himself arrived at Sackets Harbor on October 6, five days after *Lord Nelson* was purchased for $2999.25 from the United States Marshal. The schooner was still not ready for service.[17]

The schooners were typically armed with one or two long 12, 24, or 32 pounders mounted on centerline pivots, supplemented on some vessels by smaller-caliber guns mounted on regular carriages.[18] One exception was *Diana,* which bristled with short-range carronades. This vessel was purchased at Oswego from Mathew McNair for $5250 and arrived at Sackets Harbor on November 3 with a full load of guns and stores. Chauncey informed Secretary Hamilton on November 4 that he had *Diana*'s hold emptied and "commenced the alteration to mount 10–18 pounders Carronades upon her."[19] The schooner, renamed *Hamilton* in honor of the Navy secretary, was swiftly readied, for two days later Chauncey set out in search of the British Provincial Marine squadron with *Oneida* and six converted schooners, including *Hamilton. Lord Nelson*

had been renamed *Scourge* but would not take part in Chauncey's first cruise because the fitting out was not yet complete.[20]

"The brig went out in company with the Conquest, Hamilton, Governor Tompkins, Pert, Julia and Growler, schooners," recounted Edward (Ned) Myers, a seaman temporarily aboard *Oneida.* "These last craft were all merchantmen," he recalled, "mostly without quarters, and scarcely fit for the duty on which they were employed." Long after the war, Myers described his adventures on the lake to American author James Fenimore Cooper, who published the story as *Ned Myers; or, a Life Before the Mast.* Myers was ultimately assigned to *Scourge.* Unimpressed, he considered the schooner "unfit for her duty, but time pressed, and no better offered. Bulwarks had been raised on her, and she mounted eight sixes, in regular broadside."[21]

Although Myers's scornful assessment of the merchant schooners was undoubtedly justified, later events proved them to be potent gun platforms when working close to shore in support of troop landings.[22] Chauncey's schooners immediately demonstrated their worth during a long, slow running engagement on November 10, 1812. Chauncey boasted that "Oneida and 4 Small schooners fitted as gunboats [*Conquest, Hamilton, Julia, Growler*]" were able to chase the Provincial Marine's ship *Royal George* into Kingston harbor. There was no grave damage to either side and *Hamilton* sustained only "1 gun disabled" and a few shot through her sails. During the return of the squadron to Sackets Harbor on November 11, the British schooner *Simcoe* narrowly evaded capture. "She escaped by running over a Reef of Rocks under a heavy fire," Chauncey reported, "Hamilton chased her into 9 feet water before she hawled off" (plate 6a).[23] *Scourge*'s fitting out was completed after November 13, and the schooner sailed in convoy to Niagara with ordnance and supplies before the squadron went into winter quarters in December.[24]

"Fights and Flights": Spring and Summer 1813
The principal US objectives at the opening of navigation in 1813 were York (present-day Toronto) and Fort George at the outlet of the Niagara River. On April 22, the new US corvette *Madison,* the brig *Oneida,* and twelve schooners began embarking US Army troops at Sackets Harbor and the next day set sail for York. Myers recalled: "A company came on board the *Scourge,* and

Table 5.1. *Tonnage, armament, and crew compositions of United States Navy armed schooners on Lake Ontario, June 1813; ranked by tonnage*

USN SCHOONER	PRE-WAR NAME	TONNAGE, ARMAMENT, AND CREW COMPOSITION					
		Tons	*Guns*	*Type*	*Sailors*	*Marines*	*Total Crew*
Governor Tompkins	*Charles & Ann*	96	6	1 × 32 1 × 24 1 × 9 2 × 24*	53	11	64
Lady of the Lake	—	89	1	1 × 9	29	0	29
Fair American	*Fair American*	82	2	1 × 32 1 × 24	52	11	63
Conquest	*Genesee Packet*	82	3	2 × 24 1 × 6	37	9	46
Ontario	*Ontario*	81	2	1 × 32 1 × 12	26	3	29
Hamilton	*Diana*	76	9	1 × 12 8 × 18 *	44	9	53
Asp	*Elizabeth*	57	2	1 × 24 1 × 12	27	0	27
Julia	*Julia*	53	2	1 × 32 1 × 12	35	1	36
Growler	*Experiment*	53	5	1 × 32 4 × 4	30	1	31
Pert	*Collector*	50	3	1 × 32 2 × 6	26	9	35
Raven	*Mary Hatt*	50	1	1 × 18	16	0	16
Scourge	*Lord Nelson*	45	8	4 × 6 4 × 4	32	1	33

*Indicates carronades

they filled us chock-a-block. It came on to blow, and we were obliged to keep these poor fellows, cramped as we were, most of the time on deck, exposed to rain and storm."[25] The stormy weather Myers alluded to drove the troop-laden vessels back to Sackets Harbor. The condition of *Scourge* was particularly perilous, accord-

ing to Myers: "Her accommodations were bad enough, and she was so tender, that we could do little or nothing with her in a blow. It was often prognosticated that she would prove our coffin."[26]

The squadron set out again and early on the morning of April 27 anchored off York to land the troops in small boats. Thereafter, Chauncey deployed some of his schooners, including *Scourge,* to engage the British fortifications.[27] The schooners crept along the shore, and Myers remembered, "We were the third from the van, and we all anchored within canister range . . . We now had some sharp work with the batteries, keeping up a steady fire."[28] Chauncey, who was circulating among the schooners in his gig, came aboard *Scourge,* as Myers recollected:

> While he was on the quarter-deck, a hot shot struck the upper part of the after-port, cut all the boarding-pikes adrift from the main-boom. . . . Two of the trucks of the gun we were fighting had been carried away, and I determined to shift over its opposite. My crew were five negroes, strapping fellows. . . . Shoving the disabled gun out of the way, these chaps crossed the deck, unhooked the breechings and gun-tackles, raised the piece from the deck, and placed it in the vacant port. The commodore commended us, and called out, "that is quick work, my lads!"[29]

On May 8, Chauncey crossed the lake to land troops near the Niagara River in preparation for the attack on Fort George. The US squadron spent two weeks transporting troops and supplies and then regrouped on the morning of May 27. Troops were embarked into nearly 140 boats, and each schooner moved along the shore to predetermined positions to cover the landing and engage the British batteries. Calm conditions forced the schooners to move along the lake using their sweeps.[30] Myers observed:

> The schooners were closest in, and some of them opened on Fort George, while others kept along the coast, scouring the shore with grape and canister as they moved ahead. The *Scourge* came to anchor a short distance above the place selected for the landing, and sprung her broadside to the shore. We now kept up a steady fire with grape and canister, until the boats had got in-shore and were engaged with the enemy, when we threw round-shot, over the heads of our own men, upon the English.[31]

The fire of *Hamilton,* commanded by Lt. Joseph Mac-Pherson, was directed with the assistance of Mstr. Cmdt. Oliver Perry and was equally effective. Sometime since November of 1812 the schooner had two

of its carronades removed and replaced by a long 12 pounder mounted on a pivot. Perry related:

> I went on board the Hamilton, of nine guns . . . and opened a tremendous fire of grape and canister . . . the enemy could not stand the united effect of the grape and canister from the schooner, and of a well-directed fire from the troops, but broke and fled in great confusion, we plying them with round shot.[32]

By all accounts, the punishing fire of the schooners contributed to the light US casualties, the silencing of the British batteries, and the successful capture of the fort. Myers contrasted this assault with the attack on York: "This affair, for our craft, was nothing like that of York. . . . We had no one hurt, though we were hulled once or twice. A little rigging was cut."[33]

While still off the Niagara, Chauncey learned of Comm. Sir James Lucas Yeo's descent upon Sackets Harbor. After sitting out two days of storms, he set sail and arrived at his base on June 1 to survey the damage inflicted by the British attack of May 29. Shaken by this near catastrophe, Chauncey kept the squadron huddled at Sackets Harbor for the next two months until the new corvette *General Pike* was fitted out, leaving Yeo free reign of the lake (fig. 5.1).[34] A squadron roster prepared by Chauncey at this time and dated June 15, 1813 shows the change in *Hamilton*'s armament (table 5.1). In mid-July, Lt. Walter Winter took command of the schooner and its complement of forty-four sailors and nine marines. *Scourge* was commanded by Sailing Master Joseph Osgood and had a complement of thirty-two sailors and one marine. The roster lists *Scourge*'s armament as eight guns: four 6-pounder and four 4-pounder long guns. Myers recalled, however, that "we got two small brass guns at York, four-pounders, I believe, which Mr. Osgood clapped into our two spare ports forward. This gave us ten guns in all, sixes and fours."[35]

"She's Gone!": The Sinking of *Hamilton* and *Scourge*

General Pike emerged from Sackets Harbor on July 22 to join the rest of the US squadron on the lake (*Madison, Oneida,* and ten schooners, including *Scourge* and *Hamilton*). Nine days later, Yeo ventured out with his six vessels (*Wolfe, Royal George, Earl of Moira, Lord Mel-*

Figure 5.1. Sackets Harbor, 1813. *In this conjectural painting by Peter Rindlisbacher, the US Navy armed schooner Hamilton sails out of the crowded anchorage at the US naval base on Lake Ontario. (Courtesy of the artist.)*

ville, Beresford, and *Sir Sidney Smith).* The stage was set for a confrontation, and at dawn on August 7 the rivals finally crossed paths near the mouth of the Niagara River.[36]

The two squadrons that met that morning differed markedly, and their commanders sought to engage each other on different terms. Yeo had a greater number of short-range, quick-firing carronades, and he needed the weather gauge and close action to use them to best advantage. The greater number of long guns in Chauncey's squadron gave him an edge at long range in light winds. The ten US Navy schooners carried half of the squadron's long-gun broadside weight, and they were the only US vessels mounting long 32 pounders.[37] Yeo knew that in light airs the schooners could maneuver with sweeps to ply him with shot from beyond carronade range: "Sir James . . . is fully impressed with

the necessity of having a *commanding* breeze," wrote a British officer, because "in a light one or calm the enemy's flotilla of small vessels would have an incalculable advantage." The US schooners, on the other hand, were sluggish under sail and unstable in rough weather. Chauncey called their performance "dull," and Mstr. Cmdt. Arthur Sinclair of *General Pike* noted that the British ships sailed alike and could fight in sea conditions "when our Gunboats dare not cast their guns loose." Myers stated that "Our squadron sailed very unequally, some being pretty fast, and others as dull as droggers" and added, "Throughout the day, the *Scourge* had as much as she could do to keep anywhere near her station."[38]

The first meeting between Yeo and Chauncey did not result in the much-anticipated duel. The two squadrons harmlessly passed each other well beyond long-gun range. Chauncey was forced to regroup after some of his schooners lagged 6 miles (9.7 km) behind the van. Yeo turned north to avoid losing the weather gauge as Chauncey made all sail in chase. The US commodore later reported, "In the afternoon the Wind became very light and towards night quite calm, the Schooners used their Sweeps . . . to close with the Enemy, but without Success." For schooner crewmen it was trying work in the hot summer weather. "We were sweeping, at odd times, for hours that day," Myers recalled. He added, "Towards evening, all the light craft were doing the same, to close with the commodore. Our object was to get together, lest the enemy should cut off some of our small vessels during the night." The American line re-formed before nightfall, and Myers and his crewmates on *Scourge* could rest when "A little before sunset, Mr. Osgood ordered us to pull in our sweeps, and to take a spell."[39]

The crew of *Scourge* was still at quarters and the guns were cleared for action, as they had been all day. "It was a lovely evening," Myers recalled, "not a cloud visible, and the lake being as smooth as a looking-glass." Both squadrons lay becalmed, the Americans some 9 miles (14.5 km) south by east of the British. One of *Scourge*'s crew members, George Turnblatt, asked Myers whether it would be advisable to secure the guns for the night. Myers remembered saying "I would gladly secure mine if he would get an order for it; but as we were still at quarters, and there lay John Bull, we might get a slap at him in the night."[40] Turnblatt went aft to consult with *Scourge*'s commander:

> He . . . met the captain (as we always called Mr. Osgood) at the break of the quarter-deck. When George had told his errand, the captain looked at the heavens, and remarked that the night was so calm there could be no great use in securing the guns, and the English were so near we should certainly engage, if there came a breeze; that the men would sleep at their quarters, of course, and would be ready to take care of their guns; but that he might catch a turn with his side-tackle-falls around the pommelions of the guns, which would be sufficient.[41]

Osgood assembled the crew at the break of the quarter-deck and ordered them to take their suppers and a ration of rum and then to catch some sleep. Myers re-counted the state of the rig and guns when the tired crew settled for the night:

> The schooner, at this time, was under her mainsail, jib, and fore-top-sail. The foresail was brailed, and the foot stopped, and the flying-jib was stowed. None of the halyards were racked, nor sheets stoppered. This was a precaution we always took, on account of the craft's being so tender . . . Each gun's crew slept at the gun and its opposite, thus dividing the people pretty equally on both sides of the deck. Those who were stationed below, slept below.[42]

Myers and his messmate Tom Goldsmith were awakened late that night by drops of rain. The lake was motionless, and there was a not a breath of wind. Myers got up to fetch some liquor stowed below in a chest, little noticing a "strange rushing noise" from the starboard side as he made his way to the forward companionway. "One hand was on the bitts, and a foot was on the ladder," Myers recalled, "when a flash of lightening almost blinded me. The thunder came at the next instant, and with it a rushing of winds that fairly smothered the clap." As the squall struck, Myers instantly cast loose the jib sheet and port-side fore topsail sheet and, with a seaman named Leonard Lewis, began to clew up the fore topsail. Others let run the mainsail halyards; Myers cried to the man at the tiller to put the helm "hard down" into the wind. But in the minute that elapsed since Myers let fly the jib sheet, it was already too late; he was up to his chest in water and "knew the schooner must go over."[43] Myers recalled:

> I heard no hail, no order, no call; but the schooner was filled with the shrieks and cries of the men to leeward, who were lying jammed under the guns, shot-boxes, shot, and other heavy things that had gone down as the vessel fell over. The starboard second gun, from forward, had capsized, and come down directly over the forward hatch, and I caught a glimpse of a man struggling to get past it.[44]

Myers made his way to the starboard fore channel, where he came upon William Deer, the boatswain, and Joseph Philips, the powder-boy for his gun. Myers cried, "She's gone!" as Deer scrambled up the shrouds towards the mast head ("He probably had some vague notion that the schooner's masts would be out of water if she went down," Myers reflected). Myers himself crawled aft atop the starboard bulwarks, amid the "din of thunder, and shrieks, and dazzling flashes of lightning; the wind blowing all the while like a tornado." As he moved aft he put his foot through the port of his gun, "thinking to step on the muzzle of the piece; but it had gone to leeward with all the rest, and I fell through the port, until I brought up with my arms."[45] Abaft the mainmast he came upon four sweeps stowed in beckets outboard of the bulwarks:

> I could not swim a stroke, and it crossed my mind to get one of the sweeps to keep me afloat. In striving to jerk the becket clear, it parted, and the forward ends of the four sweeps rolled down the schooner's side into the water. This caused the other ends to slide, and all the sweeps got away from me.[46]

Water was pouring into the aft companionway "like a sluice" when Myers reached the fashion piece, and he caught a glimpse of Mr. Osgood trying to get out one of the stern windows. A man clinging to the end of the mainsail boom cried to Myers, "Don't jump overboard!—don't jump overboard! The schooner is righting" (fig. 5.2). Myers paid no heed and leapt as the schooner slipped under the water. Fortunately, he jumped within reach of the schooner's boat, which someone had managed to cast off. Once aboard, Myers began sculling the boat to pick up other survivors and rescued seven, including his friend Tom Goldsmith, seamen Leonard Lewis and Lemuel Bryant, Mr. Osgood's steward, Master's Mate Peter Bogardus, ship's cook Ebenezer Duffy, and a local mariner who had served as the schooner's pilot all summer.[47]

Myers and his seven companions soon fell in with the schooner *Julia* and once aboard were given a glass of grog and a change of clothes. *Julia*'s commander, Sailing Master James Trant, sent out a boat to search for survivors and brought back four men belonging to *Hamilton* who had been floating on sweeps and gratings. Myers learned from them that just prior to *Hamilton*'s sinking the topsails were set, the sheets stopped, and she was "ready, in all respects, for action."[48] Chauncey later reported the incident to the Secretary of the Navy:

> at 2 a.m. missed Two of our Schooners at daylight discovered the missing Schooners to be the *Hamilton* & *Scourge,* Soon after Spoke the *Govr.*

Tompkins who informed me that the *Hamilton* and *Scourge* both over-set and sunk in a heavy Squall about 2 O'Clock, and distressing to relate every Soul perished except 16—this fatal accident, deprived me at once of the Services of two valuable Officers . . . and two of my best Schooners, mounting together 19 Guns. . . .[49]

When Myers awoke the next morning on *Julia,* the weather was very warm and the lake calm again. The US squadron had not moved far from the scene of the accident, or had crossed back over the area since "we now passed many relics . . . floating about in the water. I saw sponges, gratings, sweeps, hats, &c., scattered about."[50]

The slow-paced sparring match between Chauncey and Yeo resumed at first light. There was little fighting, however, until August 10, when Chauncey lost two more of his schooners after *Julia* and *Growler* were separated from their companions and captured by Yeo's squadron. Yeo learned of the fate of *Hamilton* and *Scourge* from captured US sailors. "I am also happy to acquaint you," Yeo reported to Sir George Prevost, "that two of [Chauncey's] largest schooners, the *Hamilton,* of nine guns, and the *Scourge,* of ten guns, upset the night before last in carrying sail to keep from us, and all on board perished, in number about one hundred." Ned Myers and the crews of *Julia* and *Growler* were marched off to prison, while back at Sackets Harbor, US Navy Purser Edward Fitzgerald closed out the musters for *Hamilton* and *Scourge.*[51]

Yeo was not pleased with *Julia* (renamed *Confiance*) and *Growler* (renamed *Hamilton*) and retired them from active service in mid-September. *Confiance,* he wrote, "only retards me when the enemy have the weather-gage . . . [and] gives me more anxiety and trouble than she is worth." In the opposite camp, Arthur Sinclair was equally disdainful of the schooners. Chauncey, he believed, "has had rather too high an opinion of those confounded gunboats, which he now finds of very little service, as they are a mere drag upon the ships. We have them constantly in tow, and as soon as cast off they drift out of the line." The statements of Sinclair and Yeo underscore the shortcomings of gunboats on the open lake, but during the first year of the war Chauncey had little choice in the matter: he needed schooners that could carry guns, for it would take time to build better warships.[52]

Figure 5.2. *Ned Myers leaps from the stern of the sinking US Navy schooner* Scourge.
(Painting by Richard Schlecht, image 284977, courtesy of the National Geographic Stock.)

Archaeology at Arm's Length: Remote Surveying at 300 Feet

Chauncey's squadron made sail on the morning of August 8, 1813, leaving *Hamilton* and *Scourge* behind, stranded in place and time on the lake bottom. It was not until 1971, 158 years later, that the first serious effort to find them began, when the Royal Ontario Museum (ROM) initiated a search spearheaded by Dr. Daniel A. Nelson, a museum research associate. Nelson cleverly used the August 8, 1813 log entry from Yeo's *Wolfe* to define a search area north of Port Dalhousie, Ontario, and with technical support from the Canada Centre for Inland Waters (CCIW), a remote sensing search was begun in 1972.[53] In 1973 one promising target was located using side-scan sonar, and when the sonar hunt resumed in July 1975, two wrecks were discovered.[54] Sonar images showed the vessels lying upright on the lakebed, each with two standing masts, intact bowsprits, as well as distinct reflectors on their decks that resembled guns. Several months later, in November 1975, CCIW deployed a remotely operated vehicle (ROV) at the stern of one of the wrecks. The ROV's video camera recorded a rudder, a ship's boat, spars, a platter, skeletal remains, and, importantly,

cannon shot, which undoubtedly pointed to a warship. There was now little doubt that *Hamilton* and *Scourge* had been found (fig. 5.3).[55]

In 1976 the wrecks were designated as a National Historic Site of Canada and the project's steering committee began preparations for a survey and evaluation of the sites. Aimed at providing the information needed to manage the wrecks, the project had four objectives: an environmental study, an acoustic survey to accurately position both wrecks and generate basic site plans, a photographic survey, and recovery of samples for conservation analysis. The first two were achieved in 1978, but murky water conditions and technical hurdles limited the team's ability to carry out the latter two objectives.[56]

Following several years of negotiations, title to the wrecks was transferred from the US Navy to the City of Hamilton, via the ROM, on May 1, 1980. That year photographic images of *Hamilton* were captured during a visit to Lake Ontario by French explorer Jacques Cousteau's research vessel *Calypso*; dives were conducted in September and October using *Calypso*'s submersible *Soucoupe*. Color photographs and movie footage vividly proved the full extent of the preservation

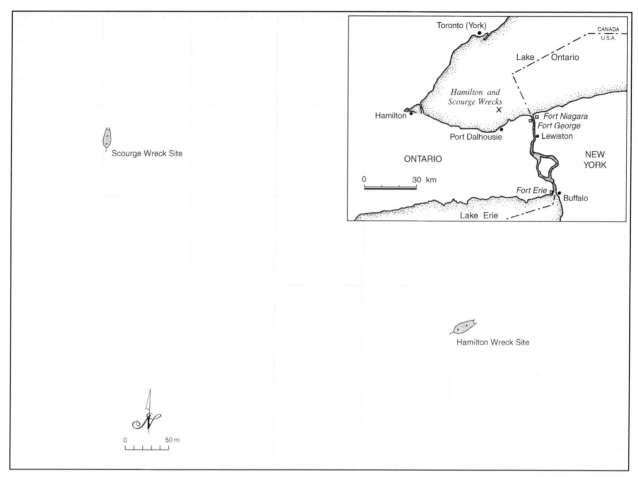

Figure 5.3. *Map of* Hamilton *and* Scourge *site location, showing their positions relative to one another. (Drawing by Dorothea Kappler, Parks Canada, inset based on map in Nelson 1983.)*

and confirmed that *Hamilton* mounted eight carronades and a pivoting long gun.[57]

The sites were photographed again during an April 1982 project directed by Nelson in conjunction with the Hamilton and Scourge Foundation Inc. (a fund-raising and organizing body created by the City of Hamilton) and the National Geographic Society. An ROV equipped with an array of cameras recorded high-quality color slides and video of both wrecks. This marked the first time that *Scourge* had been observed and showed that this schooner had ten long guns and that it also shared *Hamilton*'s excellent preservation. Worldwide exposure was given to the project with the publication of an article by Nelson in the March 1983 issue of *National Geographic,* an article that featured spectacular reconstructed views by artist Richard Schlecht, pieced together from photographic and video records (fig. 5.4).[58] The photographs were also published in the

1983 book *Ghost Ships* Hamilton *and* Scourge: *Historical Treasures from the War of 1812* by project researcher and coordinator Emily Cain. The book included reconstruction drawings of both schooners by marine heritage specialist Ian Morgan. The 1982 images and the 1978 sonar data allowed three distinct sets of project researchers (Daniel Nelson, Dr. Peter Sly of the Canada Centre for Inland Waters, and Kenneth Cassavoy and Kevin Crisman of Texas A&M University) to calculate preliminary wreck dimensions, inventory and identify visible artifacts, explore artifact distribution, and create preliminary sketch plans and elevations of the wrecks.[59] Limitations in technology did not permit the creation of scale site plans (figs. 5.5 and 5.6).[60]

Analysis showed that both schooners righted as they sank to the lake floor 295 feet (90 m) below. They struck the nearly flat and featureless bottom approximately one-quarter mile (450 m) apart, where they pierced a

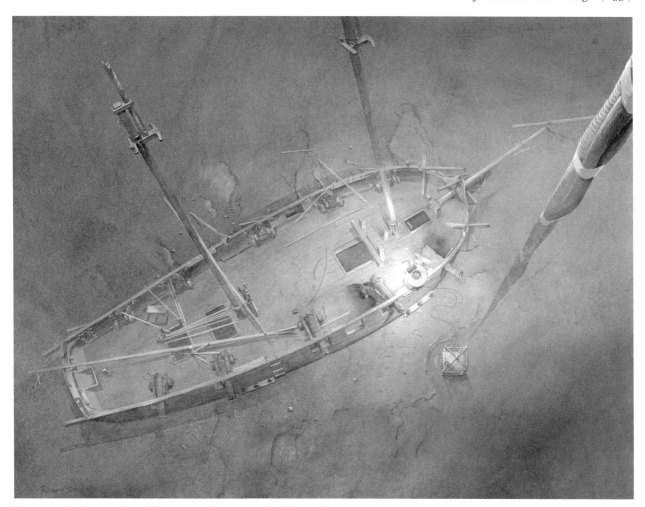

Figure 5.4. *Conjectural view of* Scourge *on the bottom of Lake Ontario, 1982.*
(Painting by Richard Schlecht, image 284970, Courtesy of the National Geographic Stock.)

firm surface crust and penetrated into the relatively soft underlying sediments. The impact spilled artifacts and ship's equipment onto the lakebed around the hulls, more through *Hamilton*'s open rail than *Scourge*'s planked-in bulwarks. The ordnance on both schooners, well secured by side-tackles and breechings, remained more or less in place after the impact, despite the heel to port of both schooners. Enclosed parts of the wrecks began to fill with fine, current-born silt while more exposed surfaces were swept clean by the same currents. Halyards, yard slings, lifts, and sheets that had not broken during the sinking rotted, dropping yards, booms, rigging blocks, rope, and canvas fragments to the decks and lakebed. Crew members dragged under during the sinking were reduced to skeletons. Further decay was so slow that when the

schooners were discovered, they appeared much like they did the day after their sinking.

In 1986, a technical study team of experts was charged with formulating a comprehensive plan for raising and conserving *Hamilton* and *Scourge*. Planning was supported by the work of researchers Ian Morgan and John Ames, who revised site plans and artifact inventories. In October 1988, the technical study team submitted a plan for precise site mapping and conservation studies to conclusively determine the state of the hulls, vital information for either in situ management of the schooners or their recovery and preservation.[61]

An opportunity to obtain additional data came in 1990 when the Woods Hole Oceanographic Institution and the Jason Foundation for Education carried out a

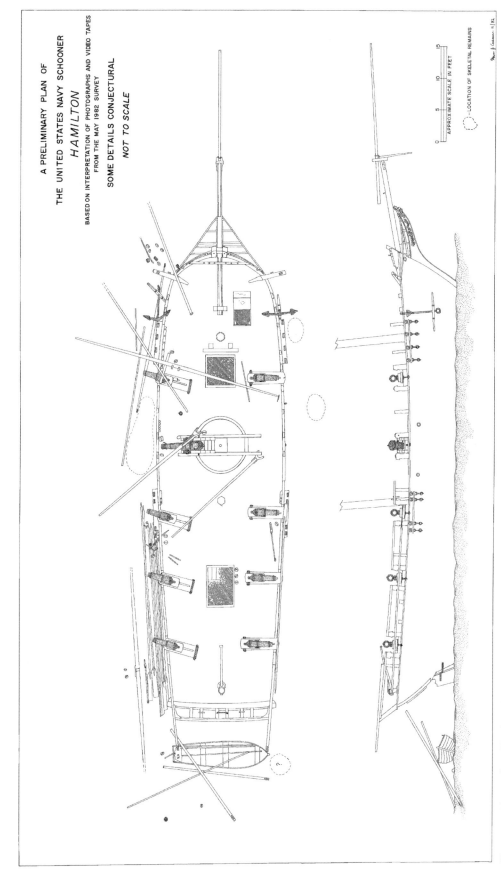

A PRELIMINARY PLAN OF
THE UNITED STATES NAVY SCHOONER
HAMILTON
BASED ON INTERPRETATION OF PHOTOGRAPHS AND VIDEO TAPES
FROM THE MAY 1982 SURVEY

SOME DETAILS CONJECTURAL

NOT TO SCALE

APPROXIMATE SCALE IN FEET

0   5   10   15

◯ — LOCATION OF SKELETAL REMAINS

Figure 5.5. *Plan and profile of Hamilton on the bottom of Lake Ontario. These unscaled views are based on 1982 survey photographs. (Drawing by Kevin J. Crisman and Kenneth Cassavoy.)*

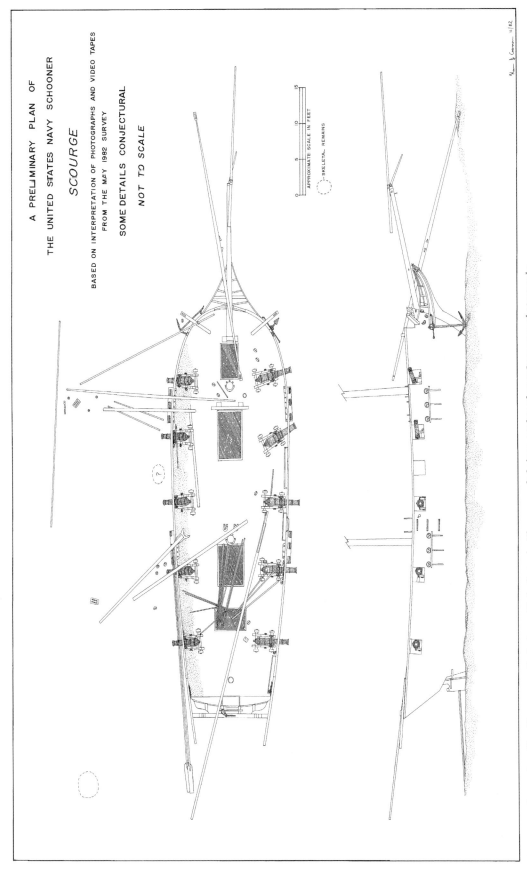

Figure 5.6. Plan and profile of Scourge on the bottom of Lake Ontario. These unscaled views are based on 1982 survey photographs. (Drawing by Kevin J. Crisman and Kenneth Cassavoy.)

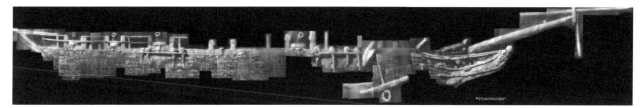

Figure 5.7. *Electronic still camera mosaic of* Hamilton's *starboard side. The images for the mosaic were recorded during the 1990 survey. (Mosaic by Woods Hole Oceanographic Institution, courtesy City of Hamilton.)*

combined scientific and educational study of *Hamilton* and *Scourge* using state-of-the-art ROVs. Archaeological objectives included photomosaic mapping of the sites and their debris fields using both acoustic and visual imaging systems. The project, which drew financial support from the City of Hamilton and other governmental agencies, took place in April and May 1990. The two-week-long effort was plagued by poor underwater visibility (usually about 6.5 feet [2 m]), but digital images and video were collected. A mosaic of the starboard side of *Hamilton* was assembled from 120 images (fig. 5.7), but no measured site plans were prepared.[62]

In 2000–2001, technical divers visited *Hamilton* and *Scourge* and found that the wrecks had been colonized by an invasive mollusk species, quagga mussels (relatives of the more widely known zebra mussels). This revelation, as well as the realization that the wrecks were now accessible to technical divers, led to a renewed effort on the part of the City of Hamilton to conduct a condition assessment of the wrecks. This materialized in a series of environmental studies, remote sensing surveys, and ROV dives between 2005 and 2009. This collaborative effort involved a range of Canadian governmental organizations and a private-sector partner, ASI Group Ltd. of St. Catharines, Ontario, with archaeological direction provided by Parks Canada.[63]

In 2007, the project team completed a side-scan sonar survey of the wrecks and their surrounding debris fields.[64] In May 2008 and 2009, ROV dives to the wrecks revealed near-total exterior cover by mussels and that modern polypropylene lines were entangled with the mainmast of each wreck. Although both wrecks had remained generally intact since the last ROV dives in 1990, change was evident, in particular deterioration of *Scourge*'s transom and the separation of its jibboom and bowsprit.

An important objective of the ROV dives was to col-

lect video of the hull interiors. In 2008, *Hamilton*'s after hatch was inspected with a video probe attached to an ROV; this revealed a rack holding muskets as well as bulkheads and possible berths in the stern cabin.[65] In 2009, a micro-ROV entered all of *Hamilton*'s hatches and companionways, capturing fleeting views of the schooner's starboard side. The ROV showed that interior structures were substantially covered by mussels and the hull bottom was covered by a layer of silt, obscuring stores, ballast, and other artifacts. On the port side, the silt reached almost to the deck beams due to the heel of the wreck. ROV inspections of *Scourge* revealed that it is almost entirely filled with silt, apart from the after end of the stern cabin, which could not be penetrated by the micro-ROV.[66]

Another important goal of the 2008 and 2009 condition assessments of the wrecks was to accurately determine their dimensions and the angles at which they listed (figs. 5.8 and 5.9). A dual-axis scanning sonar system developed by ASI Group was used to record both schooners in three dimensions, resulting in the collection of over one hundred sixty thousand point measurements. Meticulous examination of these measurements as well as other sonar data determined that *Hamilton* measures 66.9 feet (20.4 m) from the knightheads to the taffrail and that its maximum breadth is 19 feet (5.8 m). The respective measurements for *Scourge* are 58.7 feet (17.9 m) and 16.4 feet (5 m). The distance between the schooners' knightheads and taffrails has been employed for dimensioning since they are clearly discernible in sonar records and their separation approximates the schooners' length on deck. The heel of the wrecks to port, eighteen degrees for *Hamilton* and twelve degrees for *Scourge,* has made it difficult to accurately determine their maximum breadths; however, it is clear that on both vessels this occurs one-quarter of their hull length aft from the knightheads.[67] It has also not been possible to determine accurately

Figure 5.8. *Side-scan sonar image of* Scourge, 2007. *The sonar cast an acoustic shadow of the wreck, revealing its longitudinal profile—complete with gunports—at the far left. (Courtesy of the Underwater Archaeology Service, Parks Canada.)*

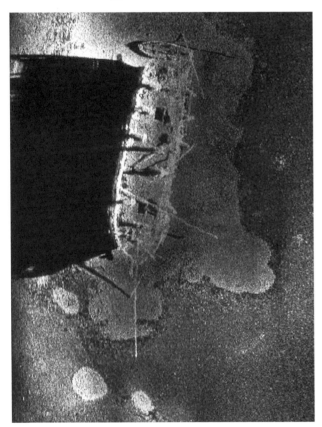

Figure 5.9. *Side-scan sonar image of* Hamilton, 2007. *The schooner's small boat is clearly visible under the stern. (Courtesy of the Underwater Archaeology Service, Parks Canada.)*

the schooners' depths of hold, given that they are partially embedded in the lakebed, although preliminary estimates put them at about 7 feet (2 m).

"Relics of the Scene": A Closer Look at the Schooners

In the absence of surviving half-models, lines plans, or building contracts, we are left with little historical evidence of the schooners' assemblies. Construction accounts for *Lord Nelson* (later *Scourge*) describe the purchase of timber and planks and payment of a blacksmith, a joiner, sawyers, caulkers, and painters. Other materials included oakum and pitch for caulking, kegs of black, red, and yellow paint powder, and the lead and oils needed to mix the paint. Over 3000 pounds (1360 kg) of steel and iron went into the hull, including "bolt iron" for the framework, 5-inch spikes for the hull planking, 4-inch deck nails, and brads for fastening the interior work. Surviving accounts of *Diana* (later *Hamilton*) deal with repair and maintenance work and are even less informative.[68]

The archaeological record, to which we now turn, is of course far more informative.[69] In terms of their overall hull shape, sonar data from 2007–2009 and the collective photography and video archive suggest that each hull has a relatively fine entry and run, slack bilges, and pronounced tumblehome abaft of amidships. Interior video of *Hamilton* confirmed that it has a shallow depth of hold. The maximum breadth for both vessels is well forward of amidships, lending their hulls a distinctive cod's head and mackerel tail shape; this feature of early lake vessels would later disappear in the canal era and would be supplanted by parallel hull sides. *Hamilton* and *Scourge* appear to be moderate merchant vessel designs, with features that balanced sailing speed, capacity, and seaworthiness. Suitable for the prosaic demands of merchant service, they could never keep up with the sharp-hulled, loftily rigged warships built for Chauncey during the war.

Each schooner has a raised quarterdeck with the break immediately forward of the mainmast, providing increased headroom in the stern cabin.[70] The decks are pierced by small hatches and companionways with high coamings notched inside to fit gratings or covers. Neither wreck retains any hatch covers, which were undoubtedly lost during the sinking (Myers observed some of them floating on the lake the next day). *Hamilton* has two companionways and a hatch. A steep companion ladder leads down from the port side of the quarterdeck companionway to the stern cabin. The forecastle companionway has raised sides and a cover that folds back upon itself. The deck of *Scourge* is pierced by three companionways and a small hatch. The two quarterdeck companionways are obscured by fallen pikes, making it difficult to observe ladders, but the aftermost companionway does have wooden rail stanchions mounted on each of its inside corners.

The present configuration of hatches and companionways does not reflect the original deck layouts. On *Hamilton*'s deck, interruptions in the planking runs and changes in the planking widths between the mainmast and foremast indicate that a cargo hatch was decked over to mount the pivot gun. The forward hatch was reduced in size athwartships to provide room to work the forward carronades. On *Scourge* discontinuous deck planking immediately forward of the break indicates that one hatch was covered over.[71] The fore hatch is open but partially obstructed by the bitts above its forward end—this must have been the hatch Myers was about to descend when the storm struck *Scourge*.

In 2009, a micro-ROV attempted to complete Myers's descent into *Scourge*'s hatch, but accumulated silt blocked its path. ROV insertions into *Hamilton* in 2008 and 2009 were more successful and revealed how the interior space was arranged on this schooner. *Hamilton* has three compartments—a forecastle, hold, and stern cabin—defined by two transverse bulkheads, one positioned forward of the aft companionway and one at the foremast. The aft bulkhead is pierced by two low passageways connecting the stern cabin and hold. There is no passageway through the forward bulkhead that separates the forecastle and hold. At the foot of *Hamilton*'s stern cabin ladder is a fore-aft rack supporting an estimated ten muskets, all of them heavily encrusted with corrosion and mussels (fig. 5.10). Farther aft, along the starboard side of the stern cabin, are what appear to be two berths, one atop the other. Due to the silt accumulation and mussel attachment, no additional cabin fittings, furniture, or artifacts have been observed and we can only speculate on the other items that are buried in the cabin.[72] *Scourge*'s construction accounts list walnut planks and hardware such as hinges, drawer locks, drawer handles, and a cupboard lock, all of which hint at built-in drawers

Figure 5.10. *A stand of muskets in the stern cabin of* Hamilton, *facing starboard, 2009. Invasive mussels have partially encrusted the firearms and plank bulkheads inside the hold. (Video frame capture by Jonathan Moore, courtesy of City of Hamilton.)*

and compartments. Some of the items that might fill such cupboards can be inferred from naval records that show equipment obtained for the schooners between November 1812 and April 1813. Teapots, a coffee pot, a tureen, dishes, plates, cups, saucers, knives, forks, spoons, a pitcher, a decanter, and tumblers were purchased for *Hamilton.* A teakettle, teapot, coffee pot, as well as cups, knives, and forks were purchased for *Scourge.*[73] The crew's meals would have been prepared on a cast iron stove or camboose. Outfitting records tell us that the Crooks purchased a "comboos" for *Lord Nelson,* and what might be a stovepipe is visible on the starboard side of the main deck, slightly abaft the foremast. No pipe is evident on *Hamilton*'s deck, although the schooner must have had some type of stove.[74]

The accumulation of trapped silt has given the hold the appearance of an expansive, open space with no observable equipment, stores, or ballast. One interesting feature is a stanchion with attached footholds at the forward end of the hatch that allowed the crew to climb in and out of the hold. A brief glimpse into *Hamilton*'s forecastle companionway revealed a small wooden shelf or box on the starboard side. In it are a wooden shot gauge and a small block, possibly for gun tackle, among other unidentified items, all of which could be a set of gunner's tools.

Hamilton's double framing and frame space were clearly observed in the schooner's hold but could not be measured. In both the hold and stern cabin, deck beams appear to be numerous, and dual-axis sonar that penetrated the stern cabin revealed their room and space to be 1.6 feet (0.5 m). The deck beams are supported along the hull's centerline by stanchions, and at least two lodging knees (but no hanging knees) were observed where beams met the side of the hull. The 2009 survey of the hold recorded a carling notched over the undersides of the deck beams and supported below by a row of stanchions. This centerline carling was probably added during the navy's refit to prevent *Hamilton*'s deck from buckling under the weight of the pivot gun.[75]

Both schooners originally had open decks enclosed by stanchions and rails. Forward of the quarterdeck, toe rails rise to form low bulwarks surmounted by weatherboards at the bows. On *Hamilton* the toe rail begins at the quarterdeck break, but on *Scourge* it begins at the middle of the fore channels. There is ample evidence of the changes made to the bulwarks of both schooners during their conversion to warships at Sackets Harbor.

When taken into naval service, *Diana* had light-weight rails and stanchions stretching from the foremast to the taffrail. Something heavier was needed to secure the carronade breechings, however. The rails were taken up and five pairs of stout timbers were installed on each side of the deck. Stop cleats were attached near the head of each new stanchion to prevent the breechings from riding up on recoil (rounded grooves under the cleats are probably wear from the breechings). The rails were reattached after the installation of the heavier stanchions, with openings left at the carronade positions (fig. 5.11). The rail was entirely removed amidships, probably when the pivot gun was added.[76]

Scourge's bulwarks extend from immediately abaft the catheads to the taffrail and were assembled by nailing thin planks to both the inboard and outboard faces of stanchions, some of which were presumably newly installed heavy timbers like those on *Hamilton*. The bulwarks were then covered by a thin cap rail, which has a uniform height along the entire length of the schooner.[77] The bulwarks are pierced by six gunports on each side, although the pair of empty ports in the waist was not fitted with gun tackle and breeching bolts. The extra ports may have been added to allow the mounting of extra guns, to provide a measure of flexibility in the ordnance configuration, or to allow

Figure 5.11. *A carronade on the starboard side of* Hamilton, *1982. Also visible in this photograph are the pair of heavy stanchions with stop cleats that secured the carronade's breechings, the cut-through rail, the blade of a sweep lying atop the carronade bed, and (in the foreground) the main channel and two of the deadeyes for the mainmast shrouds. (Photo by Emory Kristof, courtesy of City of Hamilton.)*

Figure 5.12. *One of* Scourge's *starboard-side long guns extends through its port, 1982. The makeshift appearance of the port's framing is evidence of its hasty conversion from merchant vessel to warship in 1812. (Photo by Emory Kristof, courtesy of City of Hamilton.)*

the schooner's trim to be adjusted.[78] Thin pieces of plank were nailed to the sides of some of the ports to protect the end grain of the bulwark planks (fig. 5.12). Sills were installed at the bottom of each port, except in the two forward positions where the toe rails could be used as sills. On the quarterdeck, the upper bulwark plank and rail were modified for the two aftermost pairs of ports to provide clearance for the gun barrels, since the deck-to-rail height is less than on the foredeck. Given the restricted size of the quarterdeck gunports, it is probable that 4 pounders were mounted there instead of 6 pounders.[79]

Figure 5.13. *The starboard bow of* Hamilton's *boat, 1982. An oar lies parallel with the boat's keel, its blade alongside the forefoot. (Photo by Emory Kristof, courtesy of City of Hamilton.)*

The taffrails of both schooners are partially open with a rail affixed to the tops of the counter timbers (which form the taffrail stanchions). *Scourge* has a boom bolster at each end of its taffrail to support the main boom, and each schooner has davits with two sheaves attached to the after ends of their rails for suspending a small boat astern. *Scourge*'s boat was cast off during the sinking (saving Ned Myers and his companions), but *Hamilton*'s went down with the schooner and fell to the lakebed when its tackles broke or rotted. The boat, measured in 2008 and 2009, is 14.8 feet (4.5 m) long, 4.9 feet (1.5 m) in breadth, transom sterned (the rudder is still attached), and carvel planked in a fashion known as "banana peel" construction (fig. 5.13). The planking is mostly intact and three thwarts are still attached, the forwardmost of which is pierced by a centerline hole that is likely for a mast. A small spar with a hole in one end lies over the starboard side and may be the pole mast for the boat. Three oars lie atop the thwarts, and two others are on the lakebed nearby, indicating that the boat could accommodate at least two oarsmen per side. Since one thwart appears to be missing, it is more likely that the boat had six oarsmen and a helmsman.[80]

Below the bulwarks and taffrails, the sides of both schooners exhibit some interesting features. Wooden footholds—boarding steps—were fitted immediately forward of the main channels on the port and starboard sides of both schooners. This location allowed the main channels to also be used as steps and the main shrouds as handholds. *Hamilton* has one step per side, while *Scourge* has three to allow entry over the

bulwarks. On *Scourge*'s starboard side, two iron pullovers were fitted to the rail above the steps, each with a ring at the top for handlines. There are sockets for two pullovers above the port side steps, but no pullovers are present. Immediately forward of *Scourge*'s boarding steps are keyhole-shaped apertures through the bulwarks that have perplexed researchers since their discovery. They may have allowed a boat crewman to hold fast to the schooner's side with a boathook while loading and unloading passengers. Both schooners drained water from their decks by small, lead-lined scuppers located in the waist just forward of the quarterdeck break. *Scourge* has one scupper per side, while *Hamilton* has two per side.

The transoms of both schooners share certain characteristics, including a pronounced tumblehome, a slight fore-aft curvature, a high, arching crown, and decorative moldings and trim. The transom planking is pierced by four small windows separated into port and starboard pairs and offset from the center to make room for the rudder trunk inside the cabin. There are subtle differences between the schooners' sterns, however. *Hamilton*'s hull and transom planking hood ends are rabbeted into the fashion pieces, whereas *Scourge*'s planking is more crudely executed and extends over the fashion piece, where it laps the transom planking, leaving the end grain of the hull planks exposed. *Hamilton* has a carved chock fairlead for mooring lines neatly fit in each quarter and a carved star mounted on the both port and starboard corners of the transom planking. *Scourge* has a lead-lined drain under the port counter, a feature that probably originates from a toilet or sink in the cabin. *Hamilton* and *Scourge* both have stern window sashes that slide up into pockets inside the transom crown. It appears that all windows were open at the time of wrecking, which is to be expected given the weather preceding the squall.[81] As Ned Myers was about to jump from the starboard fashion piece of the sinking schooner, he saw *Scourge*'s captain Joseph Osgood struggling to escape through one of these windows (fig. 5.14).[82]

Hamilton and *Scourge* were steered by a rudder fitted with a tiller. Each rudder is now turned to starboard, and their blades are mostly buried in the silt, revealing only the uppermost gudgeons and pintles. *Hamilton* has a plug-stock rudder with the stock centered over the pintles; it passes up through the rudder trunk and

Figure 5.14. *The starboard stern cabin window of* Scourge, *1982. The photograph clearly shows the partly opened window sash with intact glass and putty. On the night of August 7–8, 1813, as the schooner was sinking, Ned Myers looked down from the starboard fashion piece and spotted* Scourge's *captain Mr. Osgood attempting to escape through one of these windows. Myers survived but Osgood did not. (Photo by Emory Kristof, courtesy of City of Hamilton.)*

Figure 5.15. *The tops of* Scourge's *two pump tubes, 1982. The pumps were located immediately forward of the mainmast; a fallen spar is wedged between the starboard tube and the mast. The pump handles (or brakes) were removed prior to the sinking, probably because they obstructed movement on the crowded deck. A cutlass was inserted into the near (port) tube, and an unidentified object, possibly a cannon rammer, was left in the starboard tube. (Photo by Emory Kristof, courtesy of City of Hamilton.)*

Figure 5.16. Hamilton's *port-side anchor in its stowed position, 1982. The anchor's crown is perched on the fore channel, and one fluke is hooked on a timberhead. (Photo by Emory Kristof, courtesy of City of Hamilton.)*

a round wooden gasket at deck level. The tiller has a gentle S-shaped curve, and its heel passes through a slot in the rudder stock's head, where it is secured by an iron brace. *Scourge*'s rudder is of the older rule-joint style, with the pintles set forward of the stock, which turns in an arc and requires a relatively wide rudder trunk and opening at deck level. Although there is a tiller slot in the head of the stock and possible fastening holes for a brace, *Scourge*'s tiller is missing. Neither schooner shows any clear sign of a binnacle near the tiller. Compasses were purchased to outfit the *Diana* and *Lord Nelson,* but we do not know what navigational aids were on board during their naval service other than lake pilots.[83]

Each schooner has two pumps situated between the mainmast and the quarterdeck break. Made from hollowed-out tree trunks, the pump tubes are octagonal in section with a single discharge hole near the top.[84] In service, the pump handles (or "brakes") extended forward, but the brakes are not attached. On *Scourge* the brakes were stowed at the time of the sinking, since a cutlass had been placed deliberately in the top of the port pump tube and there appears to be a rammer or sponge inserted into the starboard tube (fig. 5.15). The tube may simply have been a convenient

place for stowage, although it is also possible that the rammer and cutlass were inserted to stop the pump spears from rattling within the tubes and disturbing the crew's sleep.[85]

Farther forward, each schooner has two iron anchors, one on each side of the bow (fig. 5.16). *Hamilton*'s are similar in size and have wooden stocks that are secured by iron hoops and treenails. The puddenings that wrapped each anchor ring to lessen cable chafing still survive. Each of *Hamilton*'s cathcads has a thumb cleat for securing the anchor ring with a stopper, two boxed sheaves for the catting tackle, and a carved cat-face decoration with red glass inserts for eyes.[86] *Lord Nelson*'s construction accounts list the purchase of three anchors weighing 392, 318, and 171 pounds (178, 144, and 78 kg), as well as two anchor cables.[87] The two anchors visible on *Scourge* are both of the folding-stock variety. *Scourge*'s catheads have a single sheave at their head and are undecorated, although the port cat-head has lost the cap that boxed in the sheave. A horn cleat is mounted on the forward face of each cathead to secure the cat tackle falls. The lead-lined hawse holes of both schooners show telltale grooves worn by the anchor cables.

Precisely how the anchors were raised remains a mystery, since no windlass or similar equipment for hauling in anchors can be seen on either schooner. Neither is there clear evidence of a removable windlass stowed below decks. It is possible that a windlass was not required aboard the schooners during their naval service, given the large number of sailors on board, but some sort of mechanical assistance would surely have been needed by the smaller pre-war merchant crews.

Each schooner has a projecting beakhead that culminates in a carved softwood figurehead. On *Hamilton* the quality of Henry Eagle's work shines: the bow and beakhead are blended together beautifully by the hair brackets, cheek pieces, and head rail, all of which have beaded and molded decoration (fig. 5.17). On each side the upper cheek and the head rail neatly frame the hawse hole and its bolster, and the after end of the head rail blends into a sculpted knee under the cathead. There are scroll and garland decorations between the hair brackets, a gammoning slot with bolster, and a standing gammoning knee.[88] The artistically well-executed figurehead, mounted onto the mainpiece, represents Diana, the Greek goddess of the hunt. She wears an Empire dress draped over her right side, and there is a quiver over her left shoulder with a strap running across her half-bare chest. At her waist is a rose and on either side a garland of leaves, each of which overlies a large scroll. *Scourge*'s beakhead is comparatively cruder in execution, lacking the decora-

Figure 5.17. *Hamilton's bow showing its figurehead, headrails, and carved decorations, 1982. (Photo by Emory Kristof, courtesy of City of Hamilton.)*

Figure 5.18. *Scourge's bow and figurehead, 2008. This photograph clearly shows the extent to which the now-ubiquitous quagga mussels cover both wrecks. (Photo by ASI Group, courtesy of City of Hamilton.)*

tive touches (fig. 5.18). The figurehead on *Scourge* is a male in a striding pose wearing stylish Hessian boots, his hair in "an unfashionable, but sailorly queue." His right arm is crossed over his chest, and his left arm reinforces the pose. The figurehead listed in the *Lord Nelson*'s construction accounts was shipped from New York and must have been an off-the-shelf model not intended to precisely depict Lord Horatio Nelson (who lost his left arm in 1797).[89]

Sailing Rigs and Sweeps

There are no known pre-war depictions of *Hamilton* or *Scourge* to show their merchant rig, but business records provide some evidence. Accounts for the construction of *Lord Nelson* mention the purchase of spars and a main boom, mast hoops, and bar iron for dead-eye straps and chains. Sails and blocks came from the United States through Oswego, and much of the cordage was purchased from Augustus Porter. *Diana*'s operating accounts are less detailed but do itemize purchases such as rope, blocks, several hundred pounds of rigging, a spar, and payments to a blacksmith for "Making Studdinsail Boom Irons."[90]

A contemporary watercolor of *Hamilton, Governor Tompkins,* and *Julia* chasing *Simcoe* into Kingston harbor on November 11, 1812 shows each US schooner with a gaff mainsail and foresail, gaff main topsails, square fore topsails, and fore topgallant sails, as well as a fore staysail and jib (see plate 6a). Myers's description of *Scourge*'s rig on the night of its sinking agrees with this arrangement, although he does not mention a gaff main topsail. His narrative also noted that "the only square-sail we had, was made out of an English marquée we had laid our hands on at York" (this was probably the fore topsail).[91]

Archaeological evidence largely confirms the rigs described in the historical sources.[92] Upon their discovery, each schooner had two intact masts still joined at the doubling to topmasts, as well as a bowsprit and jibboom at each bow; spars, blocks, and deadeyes did not fall far from their original positions after the ropes holding them in place decayed. During the latter stages of the 1982 project, the foremast of *Hamilton* was broken off just above deck level, apparently when it became entangled with a cable from the survey barge. The mast and attached topmast now lie 330 feet (100 m) from the schooner's starboard bow.[93] Recent sonar mapping of the in situ masts as well as *Hamilton*'s dislocated foremast has allowed approximate measurement of the main and foremast deck-to-masthead heights: 51 feet (15.6 m) and 69 feet (21 m) for *Hamilton* and 52 feet (16 m) and 49 feet (15 m) for *Scourge*.[94]

Hamilton's masts are octagonal from the deck level (where the securing wedges are in place) to the boom saddles, whereas *Scourge*'s are round. Cleats attached to each mast's front and sides secured halyard falls. There are no mast hoops resting on the saddles of either schooner, although *Scourge*'s construction accounts record payment for them. The hoop fasteners may have deteriorated, allowing the hoops to open and fall off, or it is possible that the sails were bent to the masts with lashings that have since perished.[95] Above the saddles the lower masts of both schooners

are round in section up to the squared-off mast heads. The mast doublings on both schooners are well preserved, with the mast caps, cross trees, trestle trees, and fids still joined. Standing halyard blocks and partial remains of parceled and served shroud or stay collars are evident. There are minor variations: *Hamilton*'s mast caps are iron with an integral horizontal eye for a standing halyard block, while *Scourge*'s caps are made of wood. All of the topmasts sustained damage during or shortly after wrecking. *Hamilton*'s main topmast and *Scourge*'s fore topmast both snapped off just above the cap during wrecking. A spar with octagonal hounds lying off *Hamilton*'s port quarter might be the broken topmast. The upper portion of *Scourge*'s fore topmast lies across the port rail: its hounds supported the collars of the fore topmast stays and shrouds, and there is a sheave slot below the hounds for the tye of the topsail yard. *Scourge*'s main topmast did not break but appears to have slipped down through the cap and fallen to the deck after its fid fell out or broke.

Hamilton and *Scourge* have channels extending out from their sides below the sheer, a feature that disappeared later in the nineteenth century when lake vessels had to pass through narrow canal locks. There is one channel for each mast per side, to which four pairs of deadeyes were attached on *Hamilton* (see figs. 5.7 and 5.11) and only three on *Scourge*. The lower deadeyes are firmly secured by their iron straps and chains, but the upper deadeyes fell to the lakebed as the shrouds and lanyards rotted. Smaller deadeyes scattered around the site are likely from the topmast shrouds.

The heels of the bowsprits are secured by two bowsprit bitts with a crosspiece. *Hamilton*'s jibboom was aligned along the bowsprit centerline, while *Scourge*'s was offset to the starboard side. When first photographed in 1982, it was observed that both had shifted from their original positions after the lashings that secured their heels to their jibboom saddle had given way. They were held by their bowsprit cap alone (crafted from wood for *Hamilton* and iron for *Scourge*). The dolphin strikers, attached with two large iron staples, were partially dislodged from each bowsprit. The 2008 ROV dives revealed that *Scourge*'s iron bowsprit cap gave way, dropping the jibboom and dolphin striker to the lakebed.

Hamilton's foreyard, which lies across the port-side fore channel, has sling cleats attached to its octagonal central section, and at each yardarm there is a boxed

Figure 5.19. *The jaws of either the main boom or gaff atop the pivot gun on* Hamilton, *1982. The photograph is facing the port side of the wreck. (Photograph by Emory Kristof, courtesy of City of Hamilton.)*

sheave for the fore topsail sheets, as well as a studdingsail boom iron. The fore topsail yard lies farther forward and also has an octagonal central section with sling cleats and a metal band visible on one yardarm, possibly a studdingsail iron. Two small spars resembling studdingsail booms lie in the concentration of rigging materials off the port side adjacent to the foremast. Two spars lying near the pivot gun, each with a well-preserved leather-lined jaw, could be the main boom and main gaffs, although it has not been possible to identify them unequivocally (fig. 5.19). What might be *Hamilton*'s broken fore gaff lies on the bottom off the port side, its jaws near the forwardmost carronade. The mainyard lies parallel to the port side and has an octagonal central section and broken ends. A smaller yard with fitted sheaves, possibly the main topgallant yard, lies alongside the stern.

Identification of *Scourge*'s spars is more straightforward and corroborates Myers's rig description. The long main boom extends lengthways along the quarterdeck with its jaws projecting over the break. The standing block for the main sheet (with an iron bail) is still attached to the sheet horse on the taffrail, and a batten cleat for the main sheet is fastened to the taffrail. A gaff, probably the main gaff, lies over the port bulwarks with its peak embedded in the lake bottom, and a similar spar, likely the fore gaff, lies on the port side of the deck. Off the port side farther forward is an as-

semblage of spars for the foremast, as well as halyard blocks, topmast shroud deadeyes, and shroud or stay fragments. The fore topsail yard, which has parrel or sling cleats, lies under the broken fore topmast. Two small spars nearby are probably studdingsail booms. The large spar lying over the bow is the foreyard, which has fitted sheaves for topsail sheets and studdingsail boom irons mounted on both yardarms.

In summary, archaeological evidence for each schooner's rig points to a gaff mainsail with boom, a gaff foresail, and a square fore topsail with studdingsails. Fittings on the bowsprit and jibboom suggest at least a fore staysail and jib. The *Hamilton* appears to have carried a square main topsail, but *Scourge*'s main topsail rig remains enigmatic. There is no clear evidence for fore topgallants on either schooner, although contemporary watercolors show many of the schooners with fore topgallants (see plate 6a).[96] The number of booms present on the sites and the fact that other spars have not been found off the wrecks suggest that the foresails had no booms at the time of sinking, despite the presence of boom saddles on the foremasts. The fore booms may have been removed to facilitate working the midship guns, a measure that was surely necessary for *Hamilton*'s pivot gun.[97] Indeed, two contemporary drawings of the US schooners by US Navy Acting Midshipman Peter Spicer clearly show all of the US schooners with loose-footed foresails. In describing the rig of *Julia* on August 10, Myers stated, "I never saw a studding-sail in any of the schooners, the *Scourge* excepted."[98] This is curious, given the historical sources and the spar remains on *Hamilton* that show it was so equipped. It is possible that Myers's memory was faulty or that studdingsails were not regularly employed on schooners other than *Scourge*.

The rig modifications made by the Navy were probably less significant than the addition of sweeps, which marked a fundamental change in the way the schooners could be propelled. On *Hamilton* there are eight sweeps on the port side and four on the starboard. They were evidently stowed on the outboard ends of the carronade slides when the schooner sank, but after the beckets holding them broke or rotted, all fell to the lakebed. One sweep, on the starboard side quarterdeck carronade slides, is missing half its blade and points forward, unlike the others that point aft, suggesting that it was singled out as unserviceable.

Thus, at least eleven serviceable sweeps were aboard, and others might have been lost as *Hamilton* sank. The sweep handles were small and designed to be used by one man. Determining where and how sweeps were employed is difficult. The rail stanchions and two pairs of short timberheads per side (resembling mooring bitts) could have served as thole pins, and some are pierced by holes that may have secured thole rings. It is possible that the sweeps could have been braced by the shrouds as well. Given the available evidence, at least six sweeps per side could have been used by as few as twelve sailors. Only two sweeps have been observed on *Scourge,* both lying on the lakebed off the port side. Without a doubt there are none on the starboard side since Ned Myers released the four he found there from their beckets. There are few clues on *Scourge* pointing to how the sweeps were employed, but they must have been placed either atop the cap rail, through gunports, or against the shrouds.

"Ready, in all Respects, for Action": The Armament

Hamilton and *Scourge* are conspicuous among 1812-era warship wrecks for their preserved assemblages of guns, carriages, gunports, and gun tackle. Truly, the guns and carronades appear to have been frozen at the instant the squall struck the schooners, although breeching and side-tackle ropes have mostly rotted away since 1813. Their decks were crowded with ordnance, with little space between and behind them, especially for guns situated abreast hatches or companionways.[99]

Hamilton has eight carronades mounted in broadside, six on the quarterdeck and two at the bow, identified as 18 pounders in Chauncey's June 1813 roster (Table 5.1) and by an identification plate on a carronade slide photographed in 1980 that reads "1·8 US" (plate 6b).[100] Their cascabels form an eye designed to be used with an elevating screw, although wooden quoins with turned wooden handles were substituted aboard *Hamilton.* Each carronade is secured by a two-piece mount consisting of the bed (to which the carronade's mounting lug is bolted) and the slide. The bed recoiled atop the slide and is held in place by means of a bolt fitted through a slot in the top of the slide. The outboard end of each slide is secured to a pintle mount, while two small trucks mounted under the in-board end allowed it to traverse in a narrow arc. To prevent the carronade slides from traversing when not in use, small sheet metal chocks were placed under the trucks. Given the proximity of the enemy, the carronades were probably run out and ready to be fired at the time of the sinking, but at present all of the carronades are on the port ends of their slides due to the heel of the wreck. None have tompions in their muzzles, and built-up iron corrosion makes it difficult to tell if aprons are fitted over the vent holes. Empty pintle mounts for a pair of carronades can be seen amidships, which accords with the June 1813 roster that tells us two 18-pounder carronades were removed from *Hamilton* that spring and replaced by a pivoting long gun.

The long gun in the waist is a 12 pounder, according to the roster.[101] Its 360-degree pivot mount consists of a carriage, a slide, and a wooden circle fastened directly onto the deck (see fig. 5.5). The carriage appears to be standard other than the fact that the cheek pieces are parallel and do not taper forward (a feature typical of broadside carriages). The underside of each cheek was notched to fit into corresponding dovetail notches in the two slide rails. The slide has three cross pieces, one at the center to hold the pivot bolt and one at each end; it appears to have been held in place on top of the circle by the weight of the gun. The schooner's violent foundering threw the gun, carriage, and slide assembly off the pivot bolt and circle about 1 foot (30.5 cm) toward the port side. In all probability, traversing tackles and muzzle lashing (which is partially preserved) prevented the gun from crashing through the port rail stanchions. The cannon now lies with its muzzle resting on the deck and breech pointing upward. There is no tompion in the muzzle, nor is there an elevating quoin, so both were probably lost as the gun upset. A sheet lead apron covers the vent.

The shipwrights at Sackets Harbor created shot racks on *Hamilton* by attaching shallow battens to the deck planking beside the carronades. The racks were emptied when the canister, grapeshot, and round shot stored in them were sent tumbling as the schooner went over. A dozen or so shot are still visible around the port side: four canister shot lie on the main channel, two others are near the pivot circle, and a small cluster of loose grapeshot, canister shot, and a round shot lies inboard near the vacant carronade port. Outboard, at least one stand of grapeshot lies on the port sweeps, and at least two other stands lie off the port side near the fore gaff.

The ten cast-iron long guns on *Scourge* were mounted on standard broadside carriages (plate 7a). The guns occupying the forward ports are not brass, as Ned Myers stated, so either he was mistaken or the brass pieces mounted by Sailing Master Osgood were later replaced by iron guns. All appear to be 4 or 6 pounders. Wooden quoins with turned handles, similar to those used for *Hamilton*'s carronades, are still wedged between the breeches and carriage beds of some guns; sheet lead vent covers and tompions are also evident. Gun tackle hardware such as eyebolts, ringbolts, blocks, and hooks are preserved, and even short segments of the breeching lines survive at points of contact with the guns or iron fittings.

Myers tells us that when *Scourge*'s crew bedded down for the night, the guns had their side-tackles fastened.[102] This is supported by the present position of the starboard side guns, which are run out with their outboard trucks still very close to the gunport sills. If the side-tackles had not been secured, these guns would have rolled to the port side to the limits of the breechings. This contradicts Myers statement, "The starboard second gun . . . had capsized, and come down directly over the forward hatch, and I caught a glimpse of a man struggling to get past it."[103] The twelve-degree list of the sunken schooner caused all of the port-side guns to tip into their ports. Their rear trucks are suspended above the deck, the forward ends of the carriages are wedged against the port sills, and the gun muzzles point down at the lakebed.

Myers recalled that he and his fellow crew members went to sleep "with our heads on shot-boxes." He added, "There was a box of canister, and another of grape, at each gun, besides extra stands of both, under the shot racks. There was also one grummet of round-shot at every gun, besides the racks being filled."[104] As *Scourge* fell over, he heard "the shrieks and cries of the men to leeward, who were lying jammed under the guns, shot-boxes, shot, and other heavy things."[105] Apart from a solitary round shot in the starboard quarter rack, the starboard side has no round shot, grapeshot, or canister shot, nor are there any shot boxes. Eight stands of grapeshot have been observed on the lakebed along the port side. Although it is unlikely that the guns crushed anyone, shot falling to the port side may have inflicted injury before they either fell through the ports or collected inside the bulwarks. Silt and mussels now obscure the interior of the port-side bulwarks, but it is probable that shot (and possibly the remains of crewmen) lie buried there.

Few examples of gun tools are evident, suggesting that the majority were lost overboard. On *Hamilton,* three powder ladles (with nonferrous scoops) have been observed (see plate 6b), and on *Scourge* visible items include a ladle (also with a nonferrous scoop), a possible rammer and worm, a combination rammer and sponge, as well as a possible rammer or sponge inserted into the starboard pump tube.

Edged weapons and pole arms are particularly well represented on *Scourge* since they were stowed in ready-use mounts. Two crossed cutlasses are mounted above six of the gunports, and another port has a solitary cutlass above it (see plate 7a). Seven boarding axes are mounted inside the bulwarks at the port and starboard quarters and appear to have been held in place by line that has since rotted, leaving them fused together by corrosion. Lastly, there are approximately nineteen pikes and the remains of a retaining rack lying over the two aftermost hatches.

Hamilton has a concentration of five cutlasses and partial cutlasses lying near the quarterdeck carronades on the port side, and nearby about a dozen broken cutlasses lie among the sweeps. Eight pikes (or presumed pikes) are concentrated near the foremast, mostly in the debris area off the port side, and three pikes or gun tools lie under the sweeps on the port side. To date the only firearms observed on the wrecks are the ten or so muskets in *Hamilton*'s stern cabin. These were lined up on a stand attached to a fore-and-aft partition at the foot of the aft companionway ladder and were held in place by what appears to be a strap or bar (see fig. 5.10). Clearly the muskets were stowed below deck to protect them from the elements, and one can imagine them being passed up through the hatch to the deck during a call to arms.

"That Is Quick Work, My Lads!": Crew Composition and Gunnery

Archaeological observations have told us a great deal about the hull, rig, and ordnance of *Hamilton* and *Scourge,* but to date we have learned little about the sailors. Evidence of their personal possessions, diet, and health currently lies beyond our reach. On each wreck three skeletons or concentrations of bones have been observed on the lakebed (none have been seen on the decks). This accounts for only six sailors, and it is likely that others floated away when the schooners sank, settled farther out in the debris zones, or were trapped within the hulls.

Historical evidence for the number of men aboard the schooners is contradictory. The schooners' final musters list a total of sixty-seven men, of whom fifty-two were lost and fifteen saved, eight from *Hamilton* and seven from *Scourge.* Statements by Chauncey and Myers indicate that Mr. Osgood's steward was overlooked in the final muster, however, yielding eight survivors from *Scourge* for a total of sixteen saved. Arthur Sinclair of the US squadron reported seventy men lost and twelve saved, while Ned Myers recalled "about 45 souls" on *Scourge* in the fall of 1812 and that the schooners had "near a hundred souls on board them" prior to sinking.[106] Researcher Daniel Nelson has questioned the accuracy of the official musters, arguing that sixty-seven men would not have been enough to sail the schooners and fight all of their guns. He speculated that at least thirty supernumeraries such as soldiers, dockyard workers, and landsmen were overlooked in the musters, and that ultimately more than fifty-two men were lost.[107]

Although it is possible that unrecorded marines were on board, it seems less likely that additional landsmen escaped notice, given that they are singled out on the musters. Furthermore, the muster figures are roughly consistent with payrolls for February 1813 and, more importantly, Chauncey's June 1813 roster. Over the period from February to August, the crew size for *Scourge* varied little, but there is a marked increase in *Hamilton*'s complement between February and June 1813, which may reflect the installation of the more labor-intensive pivot gun. The minimum crew required merely to sail the vessels would have been about four or five, given that the crew of the typical Lake Ontario schooner at the time consisted of only a master with three or four men.[108]

During the naval war on the lakes, crew numbers were dictated not by ideal complements but by the harsh reality of availability. To compensate for shortfalls, guns could be manned selectively. Myers recalled that *Julia*'s crew deigned not to use their 6 pounders in favor of their 24- and 32-pounder pivot-mounted long guns. Myers's own gun crew on *Scourge* consisted of five plus himself, assigned to a pair of guns in opposite

ports.[109] The number of men required to fight a gun was flexible in cases of crew shortages. Louis de Tousard's *American Artillerist's Companion,* published in 1809, lists the typical gun crew for 12-, 6-, and 4-pounder long guns as eight, five, and four men, respectively. He added, "In practice, this calculation is not strictly adhered to, and is rather subordinate to the number of men who compose the crew, as one man may perform the duty of two or three men working pieces of small calibers."[110] This consideration is particularly valid for *Scourge,* which mounted only small-caliber guns. Indeed, Jack Mallet, Ned's friend on *Julia,* jokingly referred to *Scourge*'s ordnance as "pop-guns."[111] Applying Tousard's figures to each schooner yields gun crew totals of twenty-four to forty-two men for *Hamilton* and twenty-four to forty-four men for *Scourge.* A comparison of these figures with the crew musters suggests that *Hamilton* was comparatively better manned than *Scourge,* which could probably fight only one broadside at a time. The present evidence does not tell us the number of men assigned to each gun and the number of pieces each schooner could effectively work at one time. Hope of answering these questions, as Nelson has pointed out, still lies in the crew remains and personal possessions preserved in and around the wrecks.[112] The recent ROV hull penetration dives have revealed that much of this evidence most probably lies undisturbed and well preserved under silt in the hull interiors.

The heavy deck loads of guns on *Hamilton* and *Scourge* have been singled out as the prime culprits behind their capsizing. It would appear that *Scourge*'s guns indeed doomed it to sink, as Myers and his colleagues predicted. *Scourge* carried an estimated 18,816 pounds (8535 kg) of ordnance (not including carriages, shot, and powder), almost as much as the estimated 21,952 pounds (9957 kg) on *Governor Tompkins,* a schooner of more than double the reported tonnage. Furthermore, *Scourge*'s planked-in bulwarks likely caught the onrush of wind and trapped water on the deck as the schooner went over. The real mystery is why *Hamilton* sank, given that its ordnance weight-to-tonnage ratio was more moderate; other schooners carried proportionately heavier loads, so why did they not sink? This forces us to look at other factors beyond cannon weight to explain the fate of all of the schooners, including the characteristics and condition of each hull; the number of sails set; the positions of the guns; relative loads of shot, provisions, and powder; whether vigilant watches detected the approaching squall; the reaction time of the crews; local variations in the squall's intensity; and a vessel's orientation relative to the direction of the squall. Sinclair of *General Pike* recalled his crew not "at all distrest by the wind in this Ship, [and] did not even suspect that [*Hamilton* and *Scourge*] had upset until late in the morning; but as we had been carrying hard sail all night to try and weather the Enemy, we supposed they had drifted out of sight."[113] It also appears *Hamilton*'s and *Scourge*'s guns were run out at the time of sinking, while the broadside guns on other schooners might have been secured inboard. Finally, if we assume that the gun configurations listed in June 1813 remained unchanged by August 8, the schooners with heavy gun loads such as *Pert, Governor Tompkins,* and *Growler* had only about 45 percent of their gun weight in broadsides. The other schooners had their ordnance on centerline pivots exclusively. *Scourge,* on the other hand, carried all its guns on broadside mounts, while *Hamilton*'s carronades accounted for 68 percent of the ordnance load, making them both more prone to capsizing.

In the Wake of *Hamilton* and *Scourge*

Forty years have elapsed since the discovery of *Hamilton* and *Scourge,* and the two-hundredth anniversary of their sinking is upon us. The archaeological secrets still guarded by the wrecks continue to fascinate the public, divers, and nautical archaeologists. The skeletons lying around and inside the hulls can tell us about the lives and ultimately the deaths of the crews. The schooners' hulls offer anatomy lessons of a different kind: lines and construction details that are available nowhere else.

In the past four decades the debate over the fate of the schooners has at times been intense and has centered on arguments for and against their recovery, rights of access to the wrecks, and how they can best be preserved. The constituencies in these debates all share a desire to retrieve archaeological information. The method and timetable by which these goals are accomplished have been the principal points of discussion, factors that are at the mercy of financial and technological limitations. How we ultimately answer all of our archaeological questions regarding *Hamilton* and *Scourge* remains to be seen.

NOTES

1. For discussion of the prevailing state of affairs of Lake Ontario navigation, see Emily Cain, *Ghost Ships* Hamilton *and* Scourge*: Historical Treasures from the War of 1812* (Toronto: Musson; New York: Beaufort Books, 1983), pp. 24–28; Emily Cain, "Customs Collection—and Dutiable Goods: Lake Ontario Ports 1801–1812," *FreshWater* 2, no. 2 (Autumn 1987), pp. 22–27; and Emily Cain, "Early Schoonerdays on Lake Ontario: Building Lord Nelson" (manuscript, Hamilton-Scourge Project, City of Hamilton, n.d.), pp. 5–15. An abridged version of the latter paper was published as Emily Cain, "Building the *Lord Nelson*," *Inland Seas,* 41.2 (Summer 1985), pp. 121–29.

2. Thomas Mossington Papers, May 7, 1805, Diaries vol. 2, F527, Archives of Ontario, Toronto; Richard F. Palmer, "The Forwarding Business in Oswego, 1800–1820 (Part I)," *Inland Seas* 41, no. 2 (Summer 1985), pp. 100–105; Cain, "Customs Collection," p. 27.

3. Cain, "Customs Collection," pp. 23–24; Cain, *Ghost Ships,* pp. 38–39; Harvey Strum, "Virtually Impossible to Stop: Smuggling in the North Country—1808–1815," *The Quarterly* 27, St. Lawrence County Historical Society (July 1982), pp. 21–23; Palmer, "Forwarding," pp. 105–107.

4. Cain, *Ghost Ships,* pp. 38–40.

5. Cain, *Ghost Ships,* p. 40; Augustus Porter Papers, 200.029, 200.033, 200.035, 200.064 ("Articles of Agreement . . . ," October 14, 1809), 200.069, 200.086, 200.092, 202.044, 202.047–050, 202.052, 202.069, 202.094, 202.096–098, 202.133, Buffalo and Erie County Historical Society Library & Archives, Buffalo, NY (BECHS). Gary Gibson kindly provided copies of selected Augustus Porter Papers.

6. Cain, "Early Schoonerdays," pp. 4–5, 15–33; Emily Cain, "Naval Wrecks from the Great Lakes," in *History from the Sea: Shipwrecks and Archaeology, from Homer's Odyssey to the Titanic,* ed. Peter Throckmorton (London: Mitchell Beazley, 1987), p. 208; Cain, *Ghost Ships,* p. 125.

7. Cain, "Early Schoonerdays," p. 24; Cain, "Customs Collection," p. 27.

8. *Hunter,* Oswego, no. 4 of 1816, May 8, 1816, Certificates of Enrollments 1815–1866, Headquarters (Washington Office Copies), entry 119, Records of the Bureau of Marine Inspection and Navigation, record group 41 (RG 41), National Archives and Records Administration (NARA).

9. Palmer, "Forwarding," p. 104; Anthony M. Slosek, *Oswego: Hamlet Days, 1796–1828* (Oswego, NY: Slosek, 1980), p. 38; Paul E. Fontenoy, *The Sloops of the Hudson River: A Historical and Design Survey* (Mystic, CT: Mystic Seaport Museum and Hudson River Maritime Museum, 1994), pp. 42–49, 60, demonstrates that from the mid-eighteenth century onwards Hudson River sloops grew to be larger than typical coastal sloops and reached 60 to 80 tons in size. They were beamy and shoal-drafted with capacious passenger accommodations under a raised quarterdeck with a stern gallery. They were steered with a tiller, and in a calm they could be propelled by sweeps. By 1807 some were built bigger

(120 tons) with deeper yet still broad-beamed hulls specifically to provide increased passenger accommodations.

10. *Fair American,* no. 8 of 1815, November 22, 1815, entry 119, RG 41, NARA.

11. Palmer, "Forwarding," p. 108; Slosek, *Oswego,* p. 177; *Charles & Ann,* no. 4 of 1815, June 12, 1815, entry 119, RG 41, NARA.

12. Cain, *Ghost Ships,* pp. 54–55.

13. Emily Cain, "Merchant Schooners Converted for War: Lake Ontario, 1812" (manuscript, Hamilton-Scourge Project, City of Hamilton, n.d.), pp. 22–23.

14. William S. Dudley, ed., *The Naval War of 1812: A Documentary History,* vol. 1 (Washington, DC: Naval Historical Center, 1985), Woolsey to Hamilton, July 4, 1812, p. 280.

15. Vouchers of John Young, September 21, 1812, Samuel McClary, September 25, 1812, James Pierce, September 26, 1812, and Henry Eagle, September 26, 1812, Woolsey Family Papers, Box 1, 1744–1812, Burton Historical Collection, Detroit Public Library (DPL); Woolsey, M. T., July 29, 1812, August 12, 1812, and August 16, 1812, Fourth Auditor Settled Accounts, Alphabetical Series, Records of the Accounting Officers of the Department of the Treasury, record group 217 (RG 217), NARA; Robert Malcomson, *Warships of the Great Lakes: 1754–1834* (Chatham Publishing, London: 2001), pp. 62, 66–67. Copies of the Woolsey "Settled Accounts" kindly provided by Gary Gibson.

16. Cain, *Ghost Ships,* pp. 60–63; Robert Malcomson, *Lords of the Lake* (Toronto: Robin Brass Studio, 1998), pp. 38–48.

17. Dudley ed., *Naval War of 1812,* vol. 1, Chauncey to Hamilton, October 8, 1812, p. 336; "Vessels purchased by Commodore Chauncey prior to March 3rd, 1813" (National Archives Microfilm Publication), Area File of the Naval Records Collection, 1775–1910: M625, roll 76, frames 59–60, Naval Records Collection of the Office of Naval Records and Library: RG 45, NARA, provided by Gary Gibson.

18. Malcomson, *Warships,* pp. 66–67.

19. Chauncey to John Bullus, October 26, 1812, Issac Chauncey Letterbook, September 3, 1812 to March 18, 1813, William L. Clements Library, University of Michigan; Dudley, *Naval War of 1812,* vol. 1, Chauncey to Hamilton, November 4, 1812, p. 341; Lt. Jesse D. Elliott, USN, stated that in late 1812 *Diana* was armed with 11 guns, a long 24 pounder (possibly on a pivot mount) and 10 18-pounder carronades (Elliott to Porter, November 3, 1812, Peter B. Porter Papers, roll 2, item A-152, BECHS).

20. Cain, *Ghost Ships,* pp. 65–66.

21. James Fenimore Cooper, ed., *Ned Myers; or, a Life Before the Mast* (1843; repr. Annapolis: Naval Institute Press, 1989), pp. 52–53, 56. Note that the armament attributed to *Scourge* varies over time and between Myers's and Chauncey's accounts.

22. Cain, *Ghost Ships,* p. 81.

23. Dudley ed., *Naval War of 1812,* vol. 1, Chauncey to Hamilton, November 13, 1812, pp. 344–46 and "Return of Damage sustained by the Squadron under the Command of Commodore Isaac Chauncey in his attack upon the Royal George and the Batteries at Kingston on the 10th Novr.," p. 351. Chauncey noted that *Governor Tompkins* and *Pert* played a limited role in the chase of *Royal George* into the harbor.

24. Dudley ed., *Naval War of 1812,* vol. 1, Chauncey to Hamilton, November 17, 1812, p. 348.

25. Cooper, *Ned Myers,* p. 59.

26. Cooper, *Ned Myers,* p. 56.

27. Malcomson, *Lords of the Lake,* pp. 104–107.

28. Cooper, *Ned Myers,* pp. 60, 64.

29. Cooper, *Ned Myers,* pp. 60–61.

30. Malcomson, *Lords of the Lake,* pp. 110–12, 124–27; Cain, *Ghost Ships,* pp. 89–90.

31. Cooper, *Ned Myers,* p. 66.

32. Cain, *Ghost Ships,* p. 90.

33. Cooper, *Ned Myers,* p. 67; Malcomson, *Lords of the Lake,* pp. 126–28; Cain, *Ghost Ships,* pp. 91–92.

34. Malcomson, *Lords of the Lake,* pp. 129, 141.

35. Isaac Chauncey, "A Return of Vessels of War belonging to the United States upon Lake Ontario exhibiting their force in Guns and Men" ("Return of Vessels"), June 15, 1813 (National Archives Microfilm Publication M625, roll 76, frames 201–203), RG 45, NARA; Cain, *Ghost Ships,* pp. 96–97; Cooper, *Ned Myers,* p. 75.

36. Malcomson, *Lords of the Lake,* pp. 162–69.

37. The schooners had a combined single-shot, long-gun broadside of 413 pounds, out of a squadron total of 779 pounds. The broadside figures are from Malcomson, *Lords of the Lake,* Appendix E, Tables 2, 3, pp. 335–36.

38. Malcomson, *Lords of the Lake,* pp. 169–70; Malcomson, *Warships,* pp. 82–83; Cooper, *Ned Myers,* pp. 75, 77.

39. Malcomson, *Lords of the Lake,* pp. 168–69; William S. Dudley, ed., *The Naval War of 1812: A Documentary History,* vol. 2 (Washington, DC: Naval Historical Center, 1992), Chauncey to Jones, August 13, 1813, p. 538; Cooper, *Ned Myers,* pp. 77–78.

40. Cooper, *Ned Myers,* p. 78; Daniel A. Nelson, "*Hamilton & Scourge*: Ghost Ships of the War of 1812," *National Geographic Magazine* 163, no. 3 (March 1983), p. 298; Daniel A. Nelson, "Status Report Hamilton-Scourge Project September, 1978" (manuscript report, Hamilton-Scourge Project, City of Hamilton, 1978), p. 8.

41. Cooper, *Ned Myers,* pp. 78–79.

42. Cooper, *Ned Myers,* pp. 79–80. For a visual representation of Myers's description of *Scourge*'s rig at this time, see the illustration by Richard Schlecht in Nelson, "*Hamilton & Scourge,*" p. 300.

43. Cooper, *Ned Myers,* pp. 81–82.

44. Cooper, *Ned Myers,* p. 82.

45. Cooper, *Ned Myers,* p. 82.

46. Cooper, *Ned Myers,* pp. 82–83.

47. Cooper, *Ned Myers,* pp. 83–87.

48. Cooper, *Ned Myers,* p. 93.

49. Dudley ed., *Naval War of 1812,* vol. 2, Chauncey to Jones, August 13, 1813, p. 538.

50. Cooper, *Ned Myers,* p. 90.

51. Malcomson, *Lords of the Lake,* pp. 173–79; Cain, *Ghost Ships,* pp. 112–13, 116; Cooper, *Ned Myers,* pp. 99–107.

52. Malcomson, *Lords of the Lake,* p. 195; Robert Malcomson, *Sailors of 1812: Memoirs and Letters of Naval Officers on Lake Ontario* (Youngstown, NY: Old Fort Niagara Association, 1997), p. 49; Cain, "Merchant Schooners," pp. 1–2, points out that Chauncey's schooners "performed good service . . . as floating batteries to cover troop landings, . . . as transports, or, when not weighed down, as nimble messengers."

53. Nelson, "Status Report," pp. 4–5; Nelson, "*Hamilton & Scourge,*" pp. 294–98.

54. Nelson, "Status Report," pp. 6–8; Daniel A. Nelson, "Deep Water Archaeology in Lake Ontario," paper presented at the First Annual Canadian Ocean Technology Congress, Toronto, March 11–14, 1982 (manuscript, Hamilton-Scourge Project, City of Hamilton), pp. 5–6; Daniel A. Nelson, "The Hamilton-Scourge Project," *International Journal of Nautical Archaeology and Underwater Exploration* 8, no. 3 (August 1979), pp. 245–49.

55. Nelson, "*Hamilton & Scourge,*" pp. 298, 306–308; Cain, *Ghost Ships,* pp. 130–31; Nelson, "Deep Water," pp. 6–7. This wreck later proved to be *Hamilton.*

56. Peter G. Sly, "Side Scan Sonar Survey and Study of Red and White Targets in Lake Ontario—1978. Report to the Hamilton-Scourge Committee" (Environment Canada, National Water Research Institute, February 1982), pp. 1–14; Nelson, "Status Report," pp. 11–19, 23–24; Nelson, "Deep Water," p. 7 ff. This project was supported by the ROM, CCIW, Parks Canada, and the Ontario Ministry of Culture and Recreation.

57. Cain, *Ghost Ships,* pp. 131–32; Nelson, "Deep Water," p. 7.

58. Nelson, "*Hamilton & Scourge,*" pp. 292–93, 310–13; Daniel A. Nelson, "Report of the Photographic and Videotape Investigation of the Armed Schooners Hamilton and Scourge in Lake Ontario during May, 1982" (manuscript report, Hamilton-Scourge Project, City of Hamilton: Aqua-Probe, May 1982), pp. 1–4. The project team included photographer Emory Kristof of the National Geographic Society and archaeological licensee Kenneth Cassavoy, a research associate at the Institute of Nautical Archaeology of Texas A&M University.

59. Sly, "Side Scan," pp. 24–34 and Appendix 28; Kenneth A. Cassavoy, "Hamilton/Scourge May, 1982 Survey Preliminary Archaeological Report" (archaeological report, Ontario Ministry of Culture and Recreation, Toronto, October 1982), pp. 8–22; Daniel A. Nelson, "Homeward Bound—The Hamilton and Scourge Project—A Personal View" (manuscript report, Hamilton-Scourge Project, City of Hamilton: Aqua-Probe, December 1984), pp. 15–45; Nelson, "Photographic and Videotape Investigation," p. 3.

60. Cassavoy, "Preliminary Archaeological Report," pp. 36–37; Nelson, "Photographic and Videotape Investigation," pp. 1–7; Aqua-Probe, "The Remote Survey of Deep Water Archaeological Sites Referencing and Scaling" (manuscript, Hamilton-Scourge Project, City of Hamilton, April 1983, including "Additional Notes," May 1983).

61. Phillip J. Wright, "Armed Schooners from the War of 1812: *Hamilton* and *Scourge,*" in *Excavating Ships of War, International Maritime Archaeology Series 2,* ed. Mensun Bound (Oswestry: Anthony Nelson, 1998), pp. 273–74; Ian L. Morgan and John H. Ames, "[Notes] made during an analysis of Hamilton-Scourge Project slide and videotape records, fall 1986" (manuscript report, Hamilton-Scourge Project, City of Hamilton, March 23, 1987); and John Ames, "Hamilton-Scourge Project Artifact Inventory Second Draft" (manuscript report, Hamilton-Scourge Project, City of Hamilton, September 1987). In 1988 Nelson updated his site plans that first appeared in "Homeward Bound."

62. Wright, "Armed schooners," pp. 274–75; Jonathan C. Howland, Stephen R. Gegg, and Steven Lerner, "Archaeological Data from the 1990 Jason Project Surveys of the Hamilton and Scourge Using the Jason ROV" (Woods Hole Oceanographic Institution, October 2001); Margaret Rule, "Work on the Hamilton-Scourge Site, Lake Ontario, April–May 1990, Preliminary report of the Project Archaeologist Margaret Rule" (manuscript report, Hamilton-Scourge Project, City of Hamilton, n.d.).

63. Darren Keyes and Jonathan Moore, "The *Hamilton* and *Scourge* Shipwreck Site Condition Survey 2008: Rationale, Organization, and Objectives," in *ACUA Underwater Archaeology Proceedings, 2009,* eds. Erika Laanela and Jonathan Moore (Advisory Council on Underwater Archaeology, 2010), pp. 129–38; Michael F. McAllister, "Museum under the Waves: Preserving and Interpreting the *Hamilton* and *Scourge* National Historic Site of Canada," in *ACUA Underwater Archaeology Proceedings, 2009,* eds. Erika Laanela and Jonathan Moore (Advisory Council on Underwater Archaeology, 2010), pp. 181–86. Jonathan Moore served as the project's archaeologist for 2007–2009, with ASI Group serving as project managers. The project also drew technical and logistical support from the Canadian Hydrographic Service, Canadian Navy, Canadian Coast Guard, Canadian Conservation Institute, and Environment Canada.

64. Ryan Harris, Andrew Leyzack, and Brandy M. Lockhart, "Recent Multibeam and Side-Scan Sonar Surveys of the *Hamilton* and *Scourge* Shipwreck Site," in *ACUA Underwater Archaeology Proceedings, 2009,* eds. Erika Laanela and Jonathan Moore, pp. 139–46.

65. Jonathan Moore and Darren Keyes, "Initial Visual Results from the *Hamilton* and *Scourge* Shipwreck Site Condition Survey 2008," in *ACUA Underwater Archaeology Proceedings, 2009,* eds. Erika Laanela and Jonathan Moore, pp. 147–55; Nancy E. Binnie, "Overloaded? Mussels, Biofouling, and Material Condition Observations for the *Hamilton* and *Scourge* Shipwreck Site," in *ACUA Underwater Archaeology Proceedings, 2009,* eds. Erika Laanela and Jonathan Moore, pp. 157–72.

66. Jonathan Moore, Brandy Lockhart, Ryan Harris, Nancy E. Binnie, and Darren Keyes, "Hamilton and Scourge National Historic Site: A Condition Survey of Two War of 1812 Shipwrecks (AhGt-9) in Lake Ontario" (survey report, Underwater Archaeology Service, Ontario Service Centre, Parks Canada, Ottawa, 2011).

The British attack on Oswego, May 6, 1814. This print is one of a series of engravings that show the course of the combined British Navy and Army assault on the US fort. The Royal Navy's two new Lake Ontario frigates Prince Regent *and* Princess Charlotte *are prominently featured on the right-hand side of this view. (Courtesy of Library and Archives Canada, C-793.)*

Harbour at Niagara, 1811. *In this conjectural painting by Peter Rindlisbacher, the Canadian merchant schooner* Lord Nelson *sails wing-and-wing past Fort Niagara at the mouth of the Niagara River. (Courtesy of the artist.)*

An early naval action on Lake Ontario. This contemporary watercolor, Chase of the British Schooner *Simcoe* by the U.S. Schr. Hamilton, Gov. Tompkins, *and* Julia, *depicts three of the newly armed US schooners chasing the Provincial Marine schooner* Simcoe *on November 11, 1812. (By an unknown artist, courtesy of the Sackets Harbor Battlefield State Historic Site, New York State Office of Parks, Recreation, and Historic Preservation.)*

One of Hamilton's starboard-side carronades, 1982. The photograph shows the bed-and-slide carriage, the wedge-shaped quoin under its breech, and on the deck aft of the carriage, a powder ladle. (Photo by Emory Kristof, courtesy of City of Hamilton.)

A port-side long gun on Scourge, 1982. The photograph shows the gun's broadside carriage, a cutlass stowed above the port, and atop its right rear truck, the butt of a pike. (Photo by Emory Kristof, courtesy of City of Hamilton.)

Detail from Attack on Fort Oswego, Lake Ontario, N. America, May 6th, 1814, Noon. . . . *The print features the Royal Navy's two new frigates,* Prince Regent *(left foreground) and* Princess Charlotte *(middle foreground). (Library and Archives Canada, C-00794.)*

Kingston from Fort Henery [sic] by James Gray, 1828. Of the six ships on the stocks in 1828, only four are shown in this color aquatint. Only Wolfe *and* Canada *can be positively identified, side by side near the left margin.* St. Lawrence *is shown in the same position as in Figure 7.7. The three ships on the right are probably* Kingston, Burlington, *and* Montreal. *(Library and Archives Canada, C-2041.)*

Parks Canada conservator Flora Davidson inspects the Browns Bay Vessel in 2011. The view is from the sternpost facing toward the bow. Shortly after this photograph was taken, the hull was moved from the St Lawrence Islands National Park in Mallorytown, Ontario, to its new home at Fort Wellington in Prescott. (Courtesy of the Underwater Archaeology Service, Parks Canada.)

67. The values herein incorporate data collected in 2009 and are updated dimensions first presented in Brandy M. Lockhart, Jonathan Moore, and Robert Clarke, "New Insights into the Nautical Archaeology of the *Hamilton* and *Scourge,*" in *ACUA Underwater Archaeology Proceedings, 2009,* eds. Erika Laanela and Jonathan Moore, pp. 173–80. A full list of dimensions determined by Brandy Lockhart is presented in Jonathan Moore et al., "Underwater Archaeology at *Hamilton* and *Scourge* National Historic Site of Canada," pp. 120–21.

68. Cain, "Early Schoonerdays," pp. 17–31; Augustus Porter Papers, 202.098, BECHS.

69. This and the following three sections provide the author's synthesis of archaeological information in Sly, "Side Scan"; Cassavoy, "Preliminary Archaeological Report"; Nelson, "Homeward Bound"; Morgan and Ames, "Notes"; and Ames, "Artifact Inventory"; as well as associated site plans, reconstruction drawings, and feature illustrations. These sources are supplemented by recent findings from the 2005–2009 fieldwork, presented in Jonathan Moore et al., "Underwater Archaeology at *Hamilton* and *Scourge* National Historic Site of Canada," in *ACUA Underwater Archaeology Proceedings, 2009,* eds. Erika Laanela and Jonathan Moore, and the author's own research and examination of the project's archaeological archive over a fourteen-year period. Findings and observations made by previous researchers overlap, and their site plans and drawings do not agree in all details. An attempt has been made to present a balanced archaeological picture of the wrecks, provide references to archaeological discussion by subject, and cite specific and notable archaeological observations.

70. Ian Morgan and John Ames first observed the schooner's quarterdeck steps; see "Notes," October 31, 1986.

71. For hatch modifications and configuration, see Cassavoy, "Preliminary Archaeological Report," pp. 14–16; Morgan and Ames, "Notes," October 20, 1986 for *Hamilton* and November 14, 1986 for *Scourge*; and Nelson, "Homeward Bound," pp. 20–23.

72. Moore and Keyes, "Initial Visual Results," pp. 150–53.

73. Cain, "Early Schoonerdays," pp. 17–33; Isaac Chauncey, *Hamilton,* November 10, 1812, December 5, 1812, and April 18, 1813, *Scourge,* November 10, 1812 and December 3, 1812, Fourth Auditor Settled Accounts, Alphabetical Series, Records of the Accounting Officers of the Department of the Treasury: RG 217, NARA. Copies of the "Settled Accounts" provided by Gary Gibson.

74. Yet other stern cabin features can be inferred from the wreck of a small schooner found near the mouth of the Millecoquins River in northern Lake Michigan. Believed to date to the 1830s, the vessel had an overall length of 62 feet (18.9 m) and a breadth of 17 feet 5 inches (5.3 m). It exhibited single, double, triple, and quadruple frames, irregularly spaced with an average room and space of 17 inches (43.2 cm). With its hull divided between passenger quarters and a cargo hold, it appears to have been used for the same purposes as the *Diana* and *Lord Nelson* twenty years earlier. The stern cabin had built-in berths and a U-shaped settee that followed the shape of the

stern. Small lockers packed with personal belongings were positioned under the settee, and there was a cabinet at the forward end of the cabin. The forecastle cabin also had a settee, berths, and evidence of a cooking stove. Whether *Hamilton* and *Scourge* shared similar arrangements other than the berths remains to be seen. Frank J. Cantelas, "A Portrait of an Early 19th-Century Great Lakes Sailing Vessel," in *Underwater Archaeology Proceedings from the Society for Historical Archaeology Conference, Kansas City, Missouri, 1993,* ed. Sheli O. Smith (Tucson: The Society for Historical Archaeology, 1993), pp. 13–17; Henry N. Barkhausen, *The Riddle of the Naubinway Sands* (Manitowoc, WI: Association of Great Lakes Maritime History, 1991), pp. 7–10, 17; Cain, "Early Schoonerdays," pp. 17, 19–20.

75. An Admiralty deck plan of the Royal Navy schooners *Tecumseth* and *Newash* depicts carlings under the deck beams at the pivot gun and carronade positions. "*Tecumseth* (1815), *Newash* (1815) deck" (ZAZ 6138, reg. no. 4563, Admiralty ship plan collection, National Maritime Museum, London).

76. Nelson, "Homeward Bound," p. 23; Morgan and Ames, "Notes," October 20, 1986.

77. Morgan and Ames, "Notes," November 6, 1986.

78. The rationale for the extra ports is explained in Nelson, "Homeward Bound," p. 21.

79. Morgan and Ames, "Notes," October 31, 1986.

80. The boat is described in Ames, "Artifact Inventory," p. 42, and Morgan and Ames, "Notes," December 8, 1986, the latter entry observing that one of the oars lies along the boat's keel with its blade end flush with the forefoot. Viewed side-on, this oar gives the appearance that it is an unusual extension of the keel. The boat has been drawn separately by both Nelson and Morgan.

81. Nelson, "Homeward Bound," p. 20 reached this conclusion for *Scourge.*

82. In 1982, the outboard starboard sash of *Scourge* was found half open, revealing that it originally had four window-panes, one of which was missing, apparently blown out cleanly by air escaping from the sinking schooner. Putty was clearly visible around the three in situ panes. Construction accounts for *Scourge,* outlined in Cain, "Early Schoonerdays," pp. 25–27, mention the purchase of 9 pounds of putty and twenty-four panes of glass. The schooner's windows required sixteen panes, leaving eight extra panes as replacements. In 2008 the window sash was found collapsed.

83. Cain, "Early Schoonerdays," p. 30; Augustus Porter Papers, 202.098, BECHS; Cooper, *Ned Myers,* p. 79.

84. Cain, "Merchant Schooners," p. 3.

85. Morgan and Ames, "Notes," October 29, 1986; Ames, "Artifact Inventory."

86. The starboard decoration was accidentally knocked off by Cousteau's *Soucoupe* in 1980.

87. Cain, "Early Schoonerdays," pp. 30–33.

88. Kenneth Cassavoy and Kevin Crisman, Daniel Nelson, and Ian Morgan have separately drawn the schooners' beakheads in

considerable detail; the *Hamilton*'s beakhead is well depicted in the Woods Hole Oceanographic Institution's 1990 mosaic of the schooner's starboard side.

89. Cain, *Ghost Ships,* p. 40; Cain, "Naval Wrecks," p. 208; Cain, "Early Schoonerdays," pp. 30, 35.

90. Augustus Porter Papers, 202.098, BECHS (Buffalo and Erie County Historical Society Library & Archives, Buffalo, NY); Cain, "Early Schoonerdays," pp. 21, 25–26, 31–33. Cain (p. 23) suggests that the *Lord Nelson*'s spar dimensions were probably close to those of the similarly proportioned schooners *Experiment* and *Collector,* for which spar dimensions survive.

91. Cain, *Ghost Ships,* pp. 114–15; Cooper, *Ned Myers,* p. 75; Nelson, "Homeward Bound," p. 26.

92. For descriptions of rigging remains, see Cassavoy, "Preliminary Archaeological Report," pp. 6–13; Nelson, "Homeward Bound," pp. 25–29; Morgan and Ames, "Notes," August 21, 1986; and Ames, "Artifact Inventory," November 5, 1986, pp. 10–23, 35–37, 43–48, 73–75, 77–79; as well as the site plans and drawings associated with these sources. There is considerable uncertainty about the dimensions and identification of spars and rigging elements on both schooners, in particular *Hamilton.*

93. Aqua-Probe, "Supplemental Report," September 1982, in Cassavoy, "Preliminary Archaeological Report." The detached foremast was imaged by sonar in 1983, McQuest Marine Sciences Limited, "Report on Hamilton-Scourge Project Side Scan Sonar Survey" (manuscript report, Ontario Ministry of Culture and Recreation, Toronto, September 1983). The foremast was imaged again in 2007 and inspected by ROV in 2008, Harris, Leyzack, and Lockhart, "Recent Multibeam and Side-Scan Sonar Surveys," p. 144; and Moore and Keyes, "Initial Visual Results," p. 149.

94. Moore et al., 2011; Sly, "Side Scan," p. 29 also estimated the mast dimensions from 1978 side-scan sonar records. Note that the figures provided in the text represent surviving heights and could include parts of the broken topmasts extending beyond the doubling.

95. Cain, "Early Schoonerdays," pp. 25–27; Nelson, "Homeward Bound," p. 26.

96. National Geographic Society artist Richard Schlecht, working with Nelson, reconstructed the *Scourge*'s sail plan in Nelson, "*Hamilton & Scourge,*" pp. 299–300. Nelson, "Homeward Bound," p. 29 suggests that *Hamilton* carried topsails and topgallants on both masts and each schooner could have set three headsails. The sail plans were reconstructed by Morgan and appear in the frontispieces of Cain, *Ghost Ships.* Colan D. Ratliff, "Early Running Square Sails Used by the Navy on Schooners and Sloops," *Nautical Research Journal* 30, no. 4 (December 1984), pp. 187–200 presents reconstructions of the rig of *Scourge*; elements of Ratliff's reconstructions are at odds with the archaeological evidence.

97. Cain, "Early Schoonerdays," p. 23; Nelson, "Homeward Bound," p. 26.

98. Cooper, *Ned Myers,* p. 97. The Peter W. Spicer drawings are reproduced in the endsheets of Dudley ed., *Naval War of 1812,* vol. 2.

99. For descriptions of the ordnance, see Nelson, "Homeward Bound," pp. 30–33 (and associated drawings) and Ames, "Artifact Inventory," pp. 24–30, 71. The drawings by Schlecht in Nelson, "*Hamilton & Scourge,*" pp. 301–307 are particularly demonstrative of the scale and configuration of *Scourge*'s guns.

100. Nelson, "Homeward Bound," p. 33.

101. Nelson, "Homeward Bound," p. 32, states that it is a long 24 pounder and argues that "A twelve pounder, which is only six or seven feet long, simply does not fit the reconstruction geometry." Nevertheless, in Spencer Tucker, *Arming the Fleet: U.S. Navy Ordnance in the Muzzle-Loading Era* (Annapolis: Naval Institute Press, 1989), p. 125, contemporary sources provide near-identical lengths for 12-, 24-, and 32-pounder long guns at 10-0, 10-0, and 9-6 feet and inches, respectively. Nelson, "*Hamilton & Scourge,*" p. 307, identifies the pivot gun as a long 32 pounder.

102. Cooper, *Ned Myers,* p. 80.

103. Cooper, *Ned Myers,* p. 82.

104. Cooper, *Ned Myers,* p. 80.

105. Cooper, *Ned Myers,* p. 82.

106. Dan Nelson, "The Sinking of the *Hamilton* and *Scourge*—How Many Men Were Lost?" *FreshWater* 2, no. 1 (Summer 1987), pp. 5–7; Cooper, *Ned Myers,* pp. 56, 90; Malcomson, "Sailors," p. 51.

107. Nelson, "Sinking," pp. 4–7.

108. Emily Cain, "Provisioning Lake Ontario Merchant Schooners, 1809–1812: *Lord Nelson* (*Scourge*), *Diana* (*Hamilton*), *Ontario* and *Niagara,*" *FreshWater* 3, no. 1 (Summer 1988), p. 21.

109. Cooper, *Ned Myers,* pp. 75–76, 80, 91–92. In "Homeward Bound," p. 31, Nelson noted that each *Scourge* gun crew fought two guns.

110. Louis de Tousard, *American Artillerist's Companion, or Elements of Artillery,* vol. 1 (Philadelphia: 1809; New York: Greenwood Press, 1969), p. 396.

111. Cooper, *Ned Myers,* p. 75.

112. Nelson, "Sinking," p. 7; Nelson, "Homeward Bound," p. 35.

113. Malcomson, "Sailors," p. 51.

6

"ANTICIPATED LAURELS"

The US Brig *Jefferson*

KEVIN J. CRISMAN

Introduction

Joseph Delafield found Sackets Harbor, New York, a sad, sodden refuge in the gray dawn of September 16, 1818. A member of the Anglo-American commission charged with establishing the boundary between the United States and Canada, he had spent the summer surveying the islands of the upper St. Lawrence River. The work was over, but Delafield's trek back to New York City was starting badly. His passage to Sackets Harbor in a schooner had been long and miserable due to autumn storms on Lake Ontario. The inn where he stayed the previous night hosted a muster-day "frolic" for local militiamen that lasted far into the night. "The Indian war dance and war whoop was their particular amusement," the sleep-deprived Delafield noted with irritation.[1] Rain now dripped from the overcast skies above.

Adding to Delafield's somber mood was the dilapidated appearance of the US Navy's station at Sackets Harbor (fig. 6.1). It was the largest on the Great Lakes, but the yard appeared nearly deserted. Weather-stained warships rolled and jerked at their moorings, their lower masts protruding starkly through the board roofs that capped every hull. All showed signs of neglect. "The public vessels here are fast going to decay," Delafield wrote. "One, the Jefferson, lies sunk, others are badly hog'd and look like ruins."

So much had changed in such a short time. Only four years earlier these ships were newly built, their sides freshly painted, their masts towering far above the water. Cannon bristled from gunports, ready to unleash a hailstorm of iron shot. Decks and rigging swarmed with hundreds of officers and sailors. The naval force that filled the harbor in 1814 was the culmination of the most concentrated building effort undertaken by the US Navy during the War of 1812. Its glory was fleeting, however, and the passage of time between a squadron poised for greatness and a row of ruined

Figure 6.1. *A view of Sackets Harbor in 1817 by French tourist Jacques Milbert. This print captures the swiftly deteriorating postwar appearance of the US Navy's Lake Ontario squadron one year before Joseph Delafield's visit in 1818. (From Milbert,* Picturesque Itinerary of the Hudson River and the Peripheral Parts of North America, *plate 39.)*

hulks proved to be remarkably brief. As Delafield could plainly see, the ships were not holding up well under the peace, particularly the listing, half-awash brig *Jefferson.*

"Exertions on the Part of Mr. Eckford"

The brig *Jefferson* began its existence as an idea in the mind of Capt. Isaac Chauncey, the harried commodore of the US naval squadron on Lake Ontario. In the autumn of 1813 intelligence reports told Chauncey of renewed Royal Navy shipbuilding on the lake; he wrote Navy Secretary William Jones on October 8: "From the best information I can get there is materials prepared at Kingston for three vessels—one of these vessels is to be a Frigate—the other two are to be 20 Gun Ships or Brigs." Although still hopeful that the existing British squadron could be defeated before the onset of winter, the commodore saw only one recourse if the stalemate continued: "We must build vessels of an equal class."[2]

By late November the writing was on the wall: there would be no decisive action on Lake Ontario in 1813. Chauncey's spies also confirmed the earlier intelligence from Kingston, reporting that two of the enemy's new vessels were framed and ready for planking and that carpenters were getting started on the third. How many guns would these ships mount? The spies could not say with certainty, but Chauncey warned Navy Secretary Jones that whatever the number of British guns, "It will become absolutely necessary to increase our

naval force on this lake, so as to be ready to meet the enemy upon equal terms in the spring."[3]

Jones, fully committed to the success of Chauncey's squadron, already had the wheels in motion. The first order of business was to hire shipwrights. Pleased with their work on Lake Erie in 1813, Jones recommended the brothers Adam and Noah Brown to Chauncey for this new race with the adze, a suggestion that met with little enthusiasm from the commodore. "Altho I have the highest opinion of the talents of Messrs. A. & N. Brown," Chauncey wrote, "Mr. Eckford has built 4 vessels at this place and has become acquainted with the resources and people of this country . . . as to his talents as a Ship Carpenter I am bold to say that there is not his equal in the U. States or perhaps in the World. Such exertions on the part of Mr. Eckford I should humbly hope would intitle him to a share of the public patronage."[4]

Chauncey's enthusiasm for his shipwright is understandable. In less than one year, and working in a small, remote lake port, Eckford and his carpenters launched the 24-gun corvette *Madison,* the 1-gun dispatch schooner *Lady of the Lake,* the 26-gun corvette *General Pike,* and the 16-gun schooner *Sylph.* These vessels set new construction records, only 45 days on the stocks for *Madison* and a mere twenty-one days for *Sylph; Niles Weekly Register* considered the latter "an instance of expedition, perhaps, unknown to the history of shipbuilding."[5]

During the winter of 1813–14 Chauncey was given a carte blanche from Secretary Jones to hire Eckford and build the squadron he needed. On the basis of the sketchy intelligence from Kingston, the commodore decided to construct three ships to match the British in 1814: a 44-gun frigate and two 20-gun, brig-rigged sloops of war.[6] This simultaneous building of three large warships was the most ambitious construction project yet attempted by the US Navy on the lakes. The logistics were staggering. It required no less than four hundred wood cutters, shipwrights, and laborers; a minimum of six hundred naval officers and sailors to man the new ships; and over 1000 tons of iron bolts and spikes, guns, gun carriages and shot, cables and anchors, rigging and canvas, and ships' stores of every description. Iron ballast—500 tons of it—had to be cast or purchased. Not only did the people and materials have to be hired or procured, but they also had to be transported overland to Sackets Harbor. Transportation costs alone would reach about $200,000, an enormous sum in 1814 dollars.[7] Only the ship timber could be obtained locally.

Eckford returned to Lake Ontario on January 11, 1814 and set to work. Within a few days three oaken keels were laid down, the stems were scarfed in place, and the carpenters began to cut and assemble hundreds of frame timbers. In September 1813, when Navy Secretary Jones first discussed the building program on Lake Ontario, he recommended copying the design for the navy's ship-rigged sloop of war *Peacock* (fig. 6.2). Intended as high-seas commerce raiders, *Peacock* and its sister ships mounted enough heavy guns to defeat anything in their class (*Peacock* mounted twenty 32-pounder carronades and two long 12 pounders), and they were swift enough to outrun heavier warships in most sea conditions. The design was greatly admired by Jones, who described *Peacock* as "a noble and elegant vessel 118 feet Gun Deck & 32 feet Beam. . . . Her form combines all the properties of fleetness stability and accommodation."[8]

Eckford may have been issued copies of *Peacock*'s plans and he surely must have seen the vessel during its construction at the Brown Brothers' yard in New York, but Chauncey's new brigs bore only a superficial resemblance in their length, breadth, and topside appearance. Below the waterline, *Peacock* and the two sloops of war building at Sackets Harbor were vastly different vessels, reflecting differences in sailing and fighting conditions on the oceans and Lake Ontario. Everything about the design of the freshwater brigs spoke of a desire for speed under sail: they were much shallower than *Peacock* and sharp in the extreme, with pronounced frame deadrise, a sharp entrance, a long, tapering run, and considerable drag to the keel. Plainly, wartime conditions on the lakes allowed Eckford to freely experiment with hull forms that would have been considered impractical for high-seas warships.

Despite frigid weather and widespread sickness at Sackets Harbor, Eckford pushed the work ahead rapidly, and by the end of February—six weeks after commencing construction—the two brigs were planked, half-caulked, and nearly ready to launch. Belatedly, Chauncey learned that the British were completing not one but two large frigates at Kingston, threatening to make his squadron inferior in 1814. Eckford increased the US frigate's beam so it could carry more guns, but

it was too late to upgrade the brigs. "They will be the same as the Peacock as you first ordered," the commodore reported to the navy secretary. Eckford was therefore instructed to build a second frigate as soon as the brigs were launched. Pleased with progress at the yard, Chauncey reported that his new ships were "in a fine state of preparation."[9]

The same could hardly be said of the matériel needed to outfit the squadron. The incredible weight and quantity of equipment, and the distance over which it had to travel, completely overwhelmed the crude transportation system. Rivers were the most efficient way to carry supplies to Lake Ontario, but they were frozen over; roads, the slower and costlier alternative, became quagmires during winter thaws. Wagons hauling cannon became stranded near Poughkeepsie, New York, and other shipments bogged down along the route to Sackets Harbor. By early April the supply situation was still in a tangle, prompting Chauncey to write in desperation to his shipping agents, "figure to yourselves my situation and then judge whether I have not cause for anxiety and almost for *mental derangement*."[10]

Iron ballast contributed to Chauncey's mental derangement. In late February the foundry casting the squadron's ballast reported that it could deliver only one-fourth of the amount promised. Secretary Jones recommended stone ballast as a cheap substitute, but this was impossible in the sharp, shallow vessels. Stone took up too much hold space, Chauncey wrote, leaving no room for provisions, and it was too light to counteract the weight of cannon mounted on the new ships. An officer was dispatched to a second foundry to place an order for 200 tons of cast iron, and the naval agent at New York was directed to send 100 tons of ballast as well.[11]

The new brigs were completed by early March, but the ice that covered Sackets Harbor made it impossible to launch them. One month later, impatient to clear the ways for building his second frigate, Chauncey had the ice cut away from behind one brig and floated it on April 7. The vessel was christened *Jefferson* to honor the nation's third president. Stores and cannon were on hand to outfit this vessel, and crews went to work stepping masts, setting up rigging, and mounting guns. Six days after *Jefferson*'s launch, its sister brig, named *Jones* after the navy secretary, also went into the water. *Jones* was rigged but there were no guns to mount on the vessel. Neither of the brigs had a crew.[12]

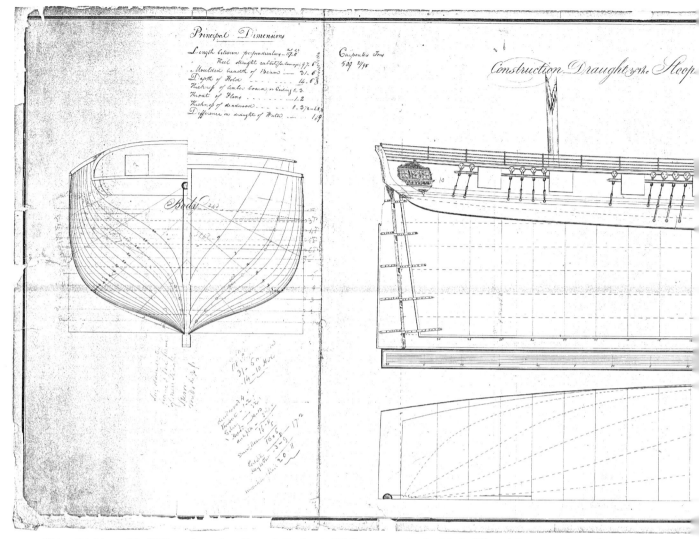

Figure 6.2. *Lines of the US Navy sloop of war* Peacock. *In 1813 the US Congress authorized the building of six 20-gun sloops of war. Peacock was one of them. The vessel had an excellent balance of armament, seaworthiness, speed under sail, and endurance. The US Navy brig-rigged sloops of war Jones and Jefferson on Lake Ontario were similar in length, beam, and armament but had a vastly different hull form below the waterline. (Ship plan 41-5-6E, Record Group 19, National Archives and Records Administration.)*

"Anticipated Laurels"

On the day that *Jefferson* slid down the ways into the lake, the US Navy's new 22-gun sloop of war *Erie* returned to Baltimore after an unsuccessful attempt to run the British blockade of Chesapeake Bay (fig. 6.3). Far from discouraged, *Erie*'s captain, Mstr. Cmdt. Charles Goodwin Ridgely, proposed an alternative plan. "If you should determine to lay [*Erie*] up for the summer," he wrote the navy secretary, "I should be happy if it were done immediately, that I may the sooner go for the lakes with my officers and crew, in hope to obtain some of the anticipated laurels that may be won in that quarter." William Jones was only too happy to honor this re-

quest—most officers tried to avoid lake service—and he immediately ordered *Erie*'s complement to proceed to Sackets Harbor.[13] Chauncey's brig *Jefferson* now had a crew.

Like his colleague Oliver Hazard Perry, Master Commandant Ridgely personified the US Navy's officer corps in its first quarter century (fig. 6.4). A native of Baltimore, he joined the service as a midshipman at the age of fifteen, saw action against the corsairs of Tripoli, was commissioned a lieutenant in 1807, and took a two-year leave of absence to gain experience on a merchant voyage to India. When war came in 1812, he was the first lieutenant on a frigate at Norfolk but

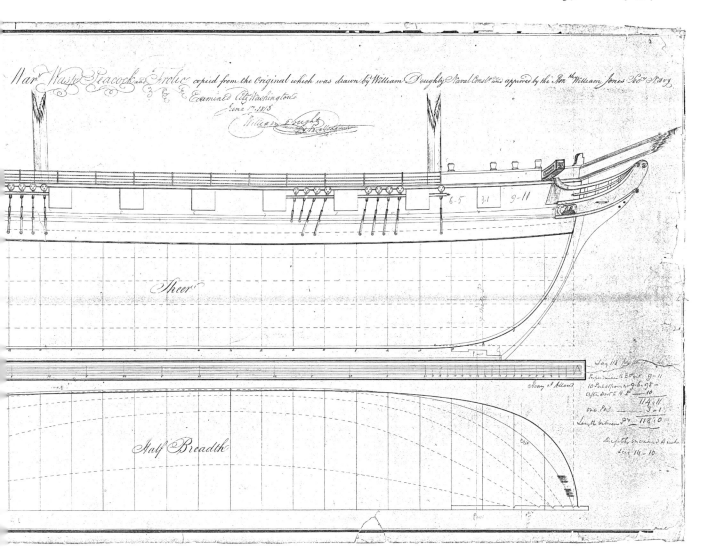

was promoted to master commandant the following year and given command of *Erie.* By 1814 Ridgely was thirty and had spent half his life absorbing the nascent traditions of the service. Ambitious and competent, he was admired by subordinates and esteemed by superiors; Chauncey commented, "I have seen nothing in him but a correct deportment and uncommon zeal."[14] Great things were expected of Charles G. Ridgely, not least by himself. If he could not sail to glory in *Erie* in 1814, a role in the impending naval battle on Lake Ontario would serve equally well.

Jefferson's new crew numbered about 160 men, full strength for a sloop of war. The complement of com-

missioned and warrant officers included four lieutenants, a sailing master, a surgeon and surgeon's mate, a purser, and eight midshipmen. There was a boatswain, a carpenter, a gunner, and a sailmaker, as well as mates to assist them. Finally, there were forty-five to fifty able seamen, an equal number of ordinary seamen, one landsman, eight boys, and twenty marines. The high proportion of able seamen reflected Ridgely's efforts to find skilled sailors. How *Erie*'s crew felt about their transfer to freshwater is unknown, but they did have the consolation of a pay increase recently authorized by Congress for lake service: $3 for able seamen to $15 per month, and $5 for ordinary seamen to $12 per month.[15]

Figure 6.3. *The US Navy sloop of war* Erie. *The Royal Navy's blockade of the US coast prevented* Erie *from getting to sea in 1814, and so the vessel's captain, officers, and crew were transferred to Comm. Isaac Chancey's new 20-gun sloop of war* Jefferson *on Lake Ontario. (Image courtesy of Independence Seaport Museum, Philadelphia, PA.)*

Bidding adieu to Baltimore on April 11, the crew proceeded to New York, then up the Hudson River to Albany, and finally westward along the Mohawk River. There were plenty of opportunities for desertion, and twelve sailors succumbed to the temptation; this problem was by no means unusual, for many contingents of sailors bound to the lakes lost men along the way, despite the vigilance of the officers. Ridgely clearly took to heart Secretary Jones's admonition to "lose no time in forwarding the whole of your crew," for half of his men reached Sackets Harbor on April 29 and the balance, including Ridgely, arrived on the evening of May 1.[16]

Erie's crew found *Jefferson,* at first glance, much like the ship they left behind in Baltimore (fig. 6.5). *Jefferson* had only two masts, but the two vessels were similar in length and breadth and both were flush decked,

with a raised forecastle deck at the bow. The lake brig had less freeboard and was painted black all over, without a decorative white stripe below the gunports.[17] Up close *Jefferson* undoubtedly appeared rougher in assembly and finish than *Erie,* for it was built in six weeks and outfitted at a wilderness station, whereas *Erie* took six months to build and five months to outfit in a well-supplied port. The living space on the berth deck was similar in breadth and headroom. Any similarities ended below the berth deck, however, for the lake vessel had a small hold and could stow only a six-week supply of provisions. There was no need to carry water in casks, since the lake provided for all needs.

The armament of *Jefferson* exceeded anything ever mounted on a vessel of this class: sixteen carronades firing 42-pound shot (the heaviest shot used by the US Navy), four long 24 pounders, and a pivoting long 18

Figure 6.4. *Mstr. Cmdt. Charles Goodwin Ridgely. In this portrait, painted around the time he was outfitting his new sloop of war* Erie *at Baltimore, Ridgely proudly displays the single epaulet signifying his recent promotion to the rank of master commandant. (Painting by John Wesley Jarvis, courtesy of Randall Hunt Norton.)*

pounder on the forecastle deck. Altogether these guns could fire 402 pounds (182.34 kg) of shot in a broadside, a weight of metal guaranteed to devastate any ship of equal size. At carronade range, this broadside was even more potent than the next two largest ships in Chauncey's fleet, the 26-gun ship *General Pike* (336 pounds [152.4 kg]) and the 23-gun ship *Madison* (272 pounds [123.37 kg]). *Jefferson*'s firepower came at a price, however: the weight of cannon, carriages, and gun equipment on the brig's topsides was approximately 41.35 tons (37.6 mt), an immense load for such a shallow design.[18]

Jefferson and *Jones* were a remedy for the unwieldy mix of warships and armed merchant schooners that plagued the Lake Ontario squadron in 1813. In 1814, the US squadron would be composed entirely of Eckford-built warships designed to outsail and outgun their British counterparts. The intended recipient of all this

firepower was unimpressed. Commenting on intelligence reports about the new US ships, Comm. James Yeo of the Royal Navy dismissed *Jefferson* and *Jones* as impractical: "I perceive two of the Enemy's new Vessels are *brigs*—and, however formidable they may be as to *weight of metal,* should any accident befall their Gaff or Main Boom—they become for the time unmanageable. Brigs have never been esteemed so effective as Ships in Battle."[19]

And what did Master Commandant Ridgely think of his new brig? His observations, if he wrote them down, have not been found, but he made two significant modifications about one month after taking command, changes that suggest problems with the brig's handling and stability. First, he shifted the mainmast 3 feet (.91 m) abaft the original step, probably to move the rig's center of effort aft and thereby improve steering. Second, he removed the long 18 pounder from the forecastle deck and deposited it on shore. The cannon and its pivot mount weighed around 5500 pounds (2494.78 kg), and their removal surely improved stability and lessened the strain on the narrow bow. The same modifications were later made to *Jones* (fig. 6.6).[20]

Jefferson was ready to sail and fight by early May, but completing the other ships took much longer, thoroughly disrupting Chauncey's timetable. *Jones* did not receive a captain and crew until June 16. The 58-gun frigate *Superior* was launched on May 1, and the 42-gun frigate *Mohawk* was launched on June 11. However, outfitting required many more weeks. The Royal Navy squadron, led by the new frigates *Prince Regent* and *Princess Charlotte,* took to the lake in early May, seizing guns and stores intended for Chauncey's frigates and blockading Sackets Harbor. Deliveries of supplies were held up or laboriously rerouted. Sickness among the shipyard workers caused further delays, and Chauncey himself became seriously ill during the second half of July. For the one thousand nine hundred officers and sailors of the US squadron it was a season of profound frustration, perhaps best summed up by a lieutenant on *Superior* who wrote a friend, "We have seen the foe but they are *not* ours, neither could we meet them."[21]

Jefferson was not immune to the discontent that infected the ships. On the night of June 28, the brig's senior midshipman John Chew assaulted a sailor, an incident that began when Chew, commanding a small boat patrolling the harbor, decided that Seaman John

Figure 6.5. *Interior profile of the US Navy sloop of war* Jefferson. *When the full complement of 160 officers and sailors was on board, crew members had neither personal space nor privacy. In this drawing, we see* Jefferson *shortly after noon on a windy day in 1814. On the main deck a gang of sailors "stamps the capstan 'round," hauling in the anchor cable in preparation for sailing. Below hatches, the berth deck is the scene of much activity: up forward, carpenters and sailmakers return to work; between the masts, the cook and his assistants clean up from the meal, off-watch men linger to chat with their mess mates, and sailors stow the anchor cable in the hold (a messy job); abaft the mainmast, three off-duty officers share a story over the wardroom table, and in the captain's cabin, Charles Ridgely and a clerical assistant try to keep up with the ship's paperwork; below the berth deck, the gunner and his assistants fill and stow flannel powder cartridges in the brig's sheet copper–lined magazine. (Reconstruction by Kevin J. Crisman.)*

Harris was malingering at his oar. He cursed and punched Harris, who protested that he was convalescing from a recent illness and would tell the captain of Chew's behavior. Chew then called Harris a "Damned French son of a bitch" and commenced beating him with both the flat of his sword and its scabbard. Holding the point of the sword against Harris's chest, Chew declared, "Were it not for the law I would run you through the body and throw you overboard." A short time later Chew ran the boat onto a secluded shore and gave Harris thirty lashes on his bare back with a knotted rope's end.

The outburst cost Midshipman Chew his naval career. Captain Ridgely ordered him arrested for "cruelty and oppression" and confined until a court martial could be convened. At the trial, two of *Jefferson*'s lieutenants characterized Chew as "irritable, rude and overbearing," and this, combined with the eye-witness testimony of Seaman Harris and his companions, effectively sank the midshipman's defense. The court found Chew guilty and ordered him cashiered.[22]

The US squadron was finally ready to sail on the last day of July 1814. Early the next morning the ships weighed anchors and set out for the Niagara River at the western end of the lake. Chauncey's command was now comprised of eight large vessels, all built from the keel up as warships. This impressive display of naval might included the frigates *Superior* (58 guns) and *Mohawk* (42 guns), the corvettes *General Pike* (26 guns) and *Madison* (23 guns), the sloops of war *Jefferson* (20 guns), *Jones* (20 guns), and *Sylph* (18 guns), and the brig *Oneida* (14 guns). These ships mounted a total of 221 cannon, making the squadron the most powerful US naval force ever assembled during the War of 1812.[23]

Despite the many predictions of a titanic naval battle on Lake Ontario in 1814, the cruise that followed was

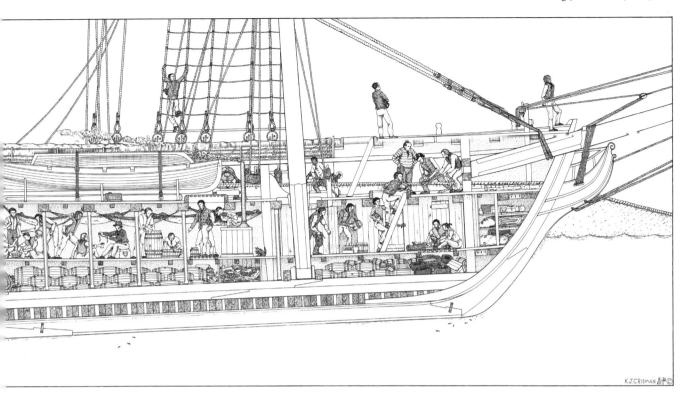

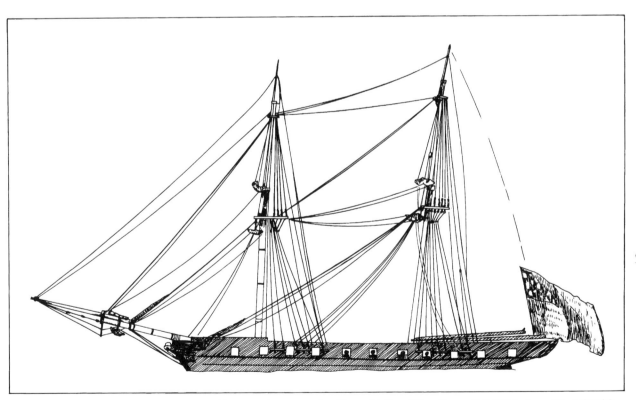

Figure 6.6. *Jefferson's sister brig* Jones, *traced from an 1815 watercolor. The artist, Royal Navy Purser E. E. Vidal, showed the brig with an all-black hull, a small and apparently simple arrangement of cutwater and headrails, and a slight rise in the sheer to indicate the existence of a raised forecastle deck. He shortened the rig in order to fit it within the painting. (Traced by Kevin J. Crisman from the original at the Royal Military College, Kingston, Ontario.)*

mostly anti-climax for the simple reason that Commodore Yeo refused to fight. Indeed, he had every incentive to avoid action at this time, for the next addition to his squadron, the 102-gun *St. Lawrence,* was nearing completion at Kingston. Without its new first rate warship, the Royal Navy would fight at a disadvantage against the greater number of long guns the US ships carried; with *St. Lawrence* the strength of the British squadron would be overwhelming.[24]

The US squadron arrived off the Niagara River on August 5 to find several smaller enemy vessels transporting provisions and munitions to the British Army fighting on the Niagara frontier. One of them, the schooner *Magnet,* was chased ashore and then blown up by its crew. The other transports visible inside the river (two brigs and a schooner) were blockaded by detaching *Jefferson, Sylph,* and *Oneida* from the squadron. The remainder of the US force sailed east to commence a blockade of Kingston.[25] *Jefferson* and its consorts kept watch for twenty days, until a lack of provisions forced them to rejoin the squadron off Kingston on August 27. Chauncey ordered them to Sackets Harbor to revictual and then dispatched *Jefferson* back to the Niagara, this time in company with *Jones.*[26]

The two brigs took up their station off the river mouth on September 10 but had no sooner settled into a routine when, early on the morning of September 12, the wind picked up from the northeast and the lake grew increasingly rough. By 4 a.m. it was blowing a full gale. The two-day storm that followed gave Charles Ridgely and his crew their first experience with the fierce autumnal storms that sweep the Great Lakes.[27] Aboard *Jefferson* and *Jones* the topgallant yards were sent down, topgallant masts housed, and lower sails reefed to reduce the strain on the rigs; at the same time shot and gun equipment were stowed below to reduce weight on the topsides. The brigs faced a perilous situation: there were no safe havens at Lake Ontario's western end (all protected anchorages were in British hands), and the nor'easter gale was inexorably driving them toward the shore under their lee. Wrecking could be avoided only by carrying enough sail to claw off the land, yet the last thing the warships needed under these conditions was more sail aloft. *Jefferson* pounded through the waves, straining every timber. Blasts of wind twice laid the vessel over on its side, and the waterways that secured the main deck began

to tear free of their bolts, allowing water to pour into the ship.

With his ship threatening to capsize, flood, or twist itself to pieces, Captain Ridgely saw only one remedy: reduce topside weight by dumping cannon. Ten of the brig's 42-pounder carronades were unbolted from their mounts and levered through the ports, a hazardous operation that required careful timing. One gun after another splashed overboard, relieving the main deck of 13 tons of iron. It was an expensive decision but it saved the ship, for *Jefferson* safely rode out the remainder of the storm. The winds finally abated on the morning of September 14, and the two brigs, in no condition to resume the blockade, sailed for Sackets Harbor.

Jefferson replaced its lost carronades and both brigs rejoined the US squadron, but the period of US naval supremacy on Lake Ontario in 1814 was over: Yeo's 102-gun *St. Lawrence* had completed its outfitting at the Royal Navy yard. When this vessel crossed its topgallant yards in preparation for sailing, Chauncey ordered his ships to return to their base and prepare for a British assault on the harbor.[28] The attack failed to materialize, nor did Commodore Yeo even bother to establish a blockade of Sackets Harbor; Chauncey, for his part, entertained no thoughts of sailing to meet the British but instead prepared to build more ships. When the lake froze in early December, all of the warships were laid up for the winter, while shipwrights in Kingston and Sackets Harbor began sharpening their adzes for the next round of construction.

Peace, Decay, and Abandonment

The strategic importance of Lake Ontario in 1815 mattered little to the two thousand young men facing confinement and cold aboard the ice-bound ships in Sackets Harbor. The squadron's sailors had no choice but to endure the winter, but many officers sought to escape by furlough or transfer. Their reasons varied. One supplicant, Midshipman David R. Stewart of *Jefferson,* patriotically offered to exchange his current "inactivity and idleness" on the lake for "service to my country" on the seaboard. *Jefferson*'s second lieutenant Lawrence Rousseau was more cryptic, stating only that "business of a private nature" called him home to New Orleans. Midshipman Harrison Cocke of *Jones* claimed that the lake's climate was giving him "the diarrhoea, leprosy, and other diseases . . . rendering life quite irksome."[29]

The station could not spare officers, however compelling their requests, and few transfers were approved.

Among the unhappiest of officers at Sackets Harbor that winter was *Jefferson*'s captain, Charles G. Ridgely. Neither *Erie* nor *Jefferson* fought a glorious action in 1814, and in late November Ridgely learned that several officers of lower seniority had been promoted above him on the basis of their success in battle. Chauncey wrote Secretary Jones on his friend's behalf, earnestly recommending that Ridgely be either promoted or given command of a seagoing cruiser. When there was no response to this request, Ridgely sent a bitter reminder to the Navy Department in early 1815: "if any junior officer should get to sea and be fortunate enough to flog the enemy I do suppose I shall again be overlooked." Chauncey finally dispatched Ridgely to Washington in early February, ostensibly to convey intelligence but also to plead his case for promotion directly with the new Secretary of the Navy, Benjamin Crowninshield.[30]

Charles G. Ridgely never returned to *Jefferson*. Sometime during his trip south he learned of the peace agreement that ended the war, and while in Washington he received his long-sought promotion to the rank of captain. Ridgely was ordered to Baltimore to prepare his former command *Erie* for sea, and Chauncey was directed to send *Jefferson*'s complement to *Erie* as soon as possible. Their return to Baltimore was marred by tragedy. In late March the brig's crew reached New York, where Lieutenant Rousseau arranged for the privateer schooner *Surprise* to transport them on the final leg of the journey. The schooner was only a few hours out of New York on April 3 when its crew, stupefied by too much drinking, bungled a simple tack and ran their vessel aground off New Jersey. *Surprise* broke up the next day, drowning thirteen of *Jefferson*'s sailors; thirty-five others deserted after getting ashore. Altogether, nearly one-third of the crew was lost to death and desertion on the passage between Lake Ontario and Baltimore. Despite this disaster, Ridgely managed to rebuild his crew and get to sea in May.[31]

The mothballing of the squadron and facilities at Sackets Harbor was accomplished in a matter of months in the spring of 1815. Merchant schooners acquired during the war were sold, perishable stores were shipped back to New York, and spare ship timber was gathered for resale. The schooner *Lady of the Lake* and brig *Jones* remained in commission, while *Jefferson* and the other large ships were placed in ordinary and moored inside the harbor (fig. 6.7). Chauncey recommended sinking the ships to preserve their hulls, but the navy elected to keep them afloat and house their decks for protection against the elements. The unfinished first rates were covered on the stocks by gigantic, warehouse-like structures. The reduction was completed under the direction of Mstr. Cmdt. Melancthon T. Woolsey, who assumed command of the station and its 134 men when Chauncey departed for the last time on July 4, 1815.[32]

The next ten years saw a rapid decline in the condition and importance of the station and its ships. The Rush-Bagot Agreement of 1817 reduced the US Navy's presence on Lake Ontario to a single armed vessel, the schooner *Lady of the Lake.* The number of personnel dwindled each year (sixty-four men were on the station rolls in 1818 and only thirty-six in 1820). The green-timbered hulls, housed though they were, swiftly deteriorated. Open plank seams above the waterline allowed water to flow in when the ships rolled at their moorings, causing *Sylph* to sink in 1816 and *Jefferson* to go down in 1818. Woolsey left them on the bottom until their seams had swollen tight and then pumped them dry again. Sailors steadily pumped and caulked, but it was a losing battle and by 1821 all of the large warships were said to be "sunk and decayed."[33]

The Board of Naval Commissioners, responsible for the building and maintenance of the navy's ships and stations, advised the Secretary of the Navy in January 1821 that the vessels at Sackets Harbor were unworthy of repair.[34] The wheels of peacetime naval bureaucracy turned slowly, however, and it was not until 1825 that the sunken ships and surplus stores were sold. Robert Hugunin, a businessman from Oswego, New York, offered to purchase the wrecks as they lay for the sum of $8000, and the Navy Department approved the sale with the condition that he return any equipment found within the hulls.[35] Four of the navy's old ships were rebuilt and used as merchant vessels in the late 1820s, including *Lady of the Lake, Oneida, Sylph,* and a cut-down *Madison*; four others, *Superior, Mohawk, General Pike,* and *Jones* disappear from the records and were probably broken up.[36] For unknown reasons, Hugunin never salvaged *Jefferson* and left the wreck sunk on the harbor bottom.

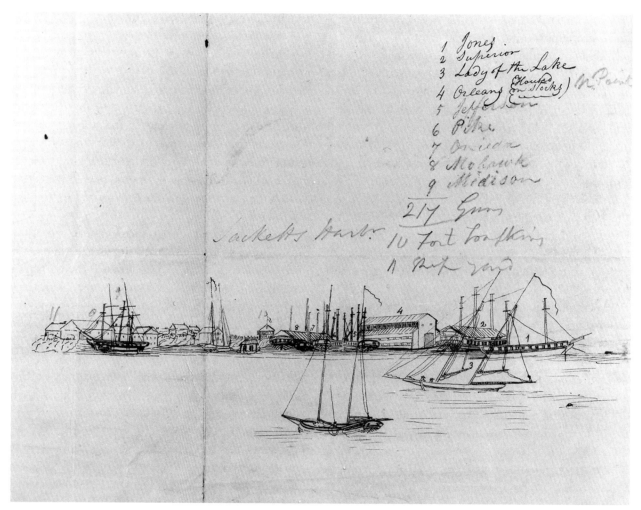

Figure 6.7. *A pen-and-ink sketch of the US squadron in ordinary at Sackets Harbor in 1816. The schooner on the right foreground is the fast-sailing* Lady of the Lake *(3), the brig on the far right in the background is* Jones *(1), and the vessel immediately below the ship house is* Jefferson *(5) (the brig is sunk in the same location today). Other identified ships in this sketch include:* Superior *(2),* New Orleans *(4, housed),* General Pike *(6),* Oneida *(7),* Mohawk *(8), and* Madison *(9). (From the Charles Wilkes Papers, courtesy of the Wisconsin Historical Society.)*

Melancthon Woolsey left Sackets Harbor for a seagoing assignment in 1825, but the navy retained the station's buildings and grounds, first as a sort of rest home for worn-out officers and later as a base for the New York State Naval Militia. The two unfinished ships of the line remained, *Chippewa* until it was broken up in 1833 and *New Orleans* an astounding 70 years, until it too was scrapped in 1884 (fig. 6.8). *Jefferson* also remained, visible to residents and tourists as a line of frames that protruded above the lake surface during periods of low water. Historian Benson Lossing saw and remarked upon the wreck during a visit to the harbor in 1860, and the hull appears in a lithograph and numerous photographs from the late nineteenth and early twentieth centuries.[37] Low lake levels in 1931 exposed the stem and forward ends of the keel and keelson, inspiring local historian and newsman David Lane to extensively photograph the structure.[38]

In its semi-exposed location, the wreck suffered from steady deterioration and occasional vandalism. The high and dry starboard side of the hull rotted and fell apart by the middle of the nineteenth century. Naval reservists dynamiting obstructions in the harbor blew the upper part of the port stern to pieces in the early twentieth century.[39] According to a local resident, the bow's oaken timbers were occasionally set on fire to warm ice skaters in the winter. During the period of low water in 1931, Sackets Harbor residents tried to

Figure 6.8. *An 1878 lithograph of the ship house over the unfinished New Orleans at Sackets Harbor. The row of frames protruding from the water in front of the house is the starboard side of the "sunken hulk" Jefferson. (From Samuel W. Durant and Henry B. Peirce,* History of Jefferson County, New York, *p. 411.)*

Figure 6.9. *The exposed bow of Jefferson during low water in 1931. The greater part of the stem had survived the elements up to this time, but over the next three decades it would be repeatedly set on fire to warm ice skaters. Very little of the bow structure was left by the 1950s, and the forward end of the keel and keelson were subsequently torn from the wreck during the construction of a marina in the 1960s. (From the collection of Kevin J. Crisman.)*

interest the New York Park Commission in salvaging and displaying the timbers, but no action was taken by the state (figs. 6.9 and 6.10).[40] Two surveys by naval historians in the 1950s showed that the wreck had much to tell about 1812-era ships, but unfortunately techniques for archaeological hull recording had not been developed at this time (fig. 6.11).[41] In the early 1960s, before further study could be undertaken, developers purchased the harbor spit from the state and, despite an outcry from local historians, built a marina on top of the wreck. *Jefferson* was reportedly buried by tons of stone fill during the construction.[42]

The Archaeology of *Jefferson*

The rediscovery and study of *Jefferson* began as an outgrowth of the 1981–83 project to record the 20-gun brig *Eagle* in Lake Champlain (see chapter 12). *Jefferson*'s purported destruction was much regretted by the *Eagle* research team, since we hoped to compare the workmanship of the Brown brothers with that of Henry Eckford. A glimmer of hope came in 1983, however, when archaeologist James Duff reported seeing a wreck several years earlier in Sackets Harbor during the testing of an underwater camera. He described bulwarks with gunports poking out of the harbor bottom, some with pier pilings driven through them. Encouraged by the possibility that *Jefferson* survived after all, Arthur Cohn and I went to Sackets Harbor in May 1984 to look at Duff's wreck.

Our scuba-diving search may hold the record as the shortest ever: we suited up, slid off a marina pier, and

Figure 6.10. Watertown Daily Times *newsman David Lane inside the bow of Jefferson in 1931. The forward end of the brig's port side was still well preserved at this time. Lane's left foot is on the forwardmost diagonal rider, the charred ends of the two keelson timbers can be seen above his shoulder, and the two crosspieces of the foremast step are visible on the right side of the photograph. (Courtesy of the* Watertown Daily Times, *Watertown, NY.)*

landed on the keelson. Our initial impression was one of chaos: detached timbers, partially buried structure, and modern debris. Visibility was quite poor, especially when the silty bottom was disturbed (fig. 6.12). An hour of exploration showed that a surprising amount of the hull survived, however. The wreck lay heeled over to port at a forty-five-degree angle; the starboard side was gone, but much of the port side seemed to be preserved

Figure 6.11. *Souvenirs from Jefferson, April 1958. Frogmen from the Gillman's Club, amateur archaeologist Jackson Jenks (seated on right), and curious residents of Sackets Harbor gather around a pair of deadeyes and chainplates pried from the wreck. (Courtesy of the* Watertown Daily Times, *Watertown, NY.)*

beneath the mud (fig. 6.13). An arc of bulwark sections protruding from the bottom contained nine gunports, eyebolts, and ringbolts for gun tackle and part of the cap rail. The tops of the sternposts showed above the mud aft, along with a transom timber. The keel and keelson were broken amidships, slightly forward of the mainmast step, and their forward ends were missing, along with the stem. The port-side frame floors were also missing forward of amidships. The wreck was in rough condition, but there was clearly enough of it left to warrant further study.

Was it *Jefferson*? Local tradition said it was, but in 1984 there was no way to be certain. It was unquestionably a warship (the gunports were proof of that) and it was a vessel of moderate size, but Chauncey's squadron had several ships that met this description, including *Jefferson, Jones, Sylph,* and *Madison.* In 1984 it did

not really matter to us which vessel it was, for nothing much was known about any of the ships Eckford built during the war.

From the start, our research strategy was to excavate only what was necessary for reconstructing the vessel's lines and assembly since we lacked the budget and time needed to uncover the entire wreck (fig. 6.14a–d). This ship was laid up, rather than lost in service, but we still hoped to find artifacts that would tell us about the interior layout and daily life on an 1812-era naval vessel. Cohn and I began in 1985 with a week-long reconnaissance, a short project that allowed us to measure and sketch the bulwarks and gunports and to record a frame section amidships.[43] We selected a frame located slightly forward of the mainmast step that was complete on its port side from the keel centerline to the sheer (frame 15). The excavation of a

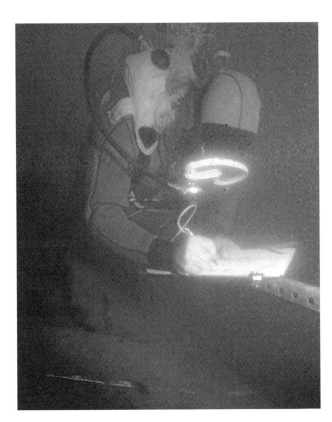

Figure 6.12. *Arthur Cohn records exposed timbers on* Jefferson. *The wreck was in shallow water, but murky water conditions and soft bottom sediments often severely limited visibility. This photograph was taken during a rare time of clarity on the site. (Photo by John Butler,* Jefferson *project files of Kevin J. Crisman.)*

Figure 6.13. *A section of the sunken* Jefferson *at frame 26, view forward. The wreck settled on its port side when it sank for the final time, preserving portions of the hull up to the level of the gunports and cap rail. A series of dock pilings were driven through the hull during the construction of the marina at Navy Point in Sackets Harbor. (Drawing by Kevin J. Crisman.)*

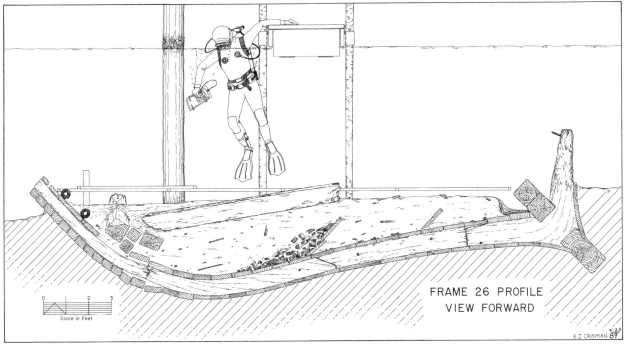

FRAME 26 PROFILE
VIEW FORWARD

Scale in Feet

K.J. CRISMAN 89

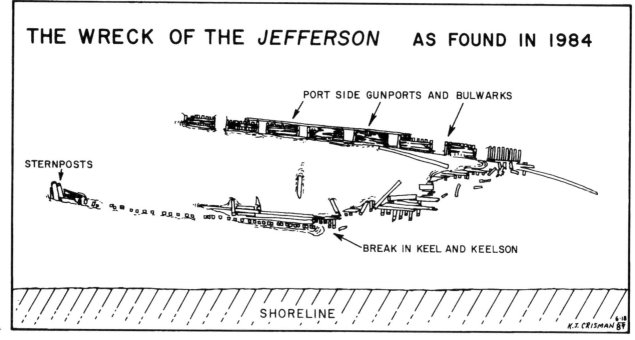

THE WRECK OF THE *JEFFERSON*   AS FOUND IN 1984

PORT SIDE GUNPORTS AND BULWARKS

STERNPOSTS

BREAK IN KEEL AND KEELSON

SHORELINE

K.J. CRISMAN 84

A

Figure 6.14. *Excavations on the wreck of Jefferson between 1984 and 1988. (a) The wreck of Jefferson was first examined by Kevin J. Crisman and Arthur Cohn in 1984, when it was determined that much of the port side was preserved up to the level of the gunports. (b) In 1985 a test trench was excavated across the hull at frame 15, to learn what might be buried under the sediments and to record the shape of the hull at this location. (c) In 1987 excavators uncovered the mainmast step, the after end of the keelson, and the sternpost and deadwood assembly; a trench was also opened at half-frame 36 to record a section. (d) Finally, in 1988 trenches allowed the recording of sections at frames 26 and 4, and the clamp and waterway timbers between the two frames were exposed and measured. (Drawings by Kevin J. Crisman.)*

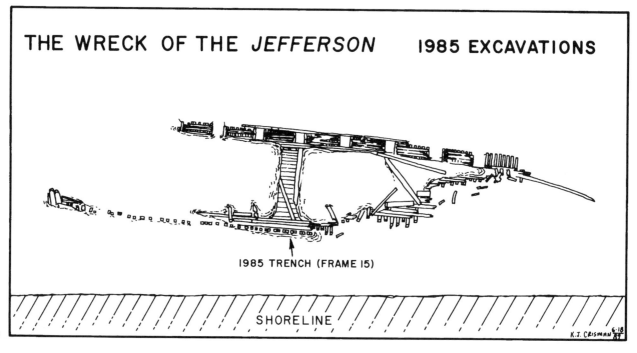

THE WRECK OF THE *JEFFERSON*   1985 EXCAVATIONS

1985 TRENCH (FRAME 15)

SHORELINE

K.J. CRISMAN 84

B

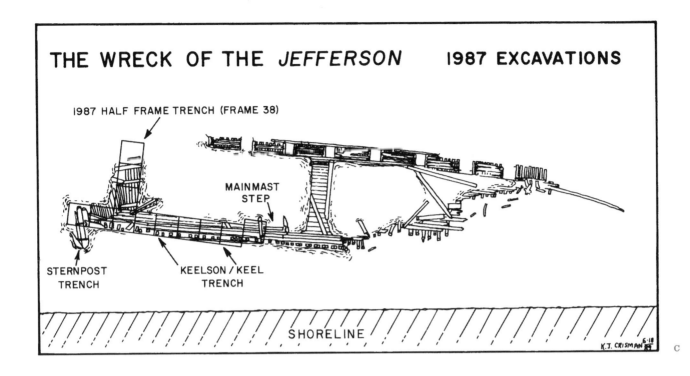

THE WRECK OF THE *JEFFERSON*   1987 EXCAVATIONS

1987 HALF FRAME TRENCH (FRAME 38)

MAINMAST STEP

STERNPOST TRENCH

KEELSON/KEEL TRENCH

SHORELINE

K.J. CRISMAN 6-18-89

C

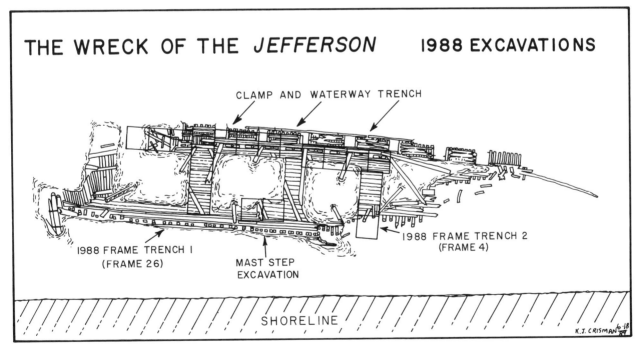

THE WRECK OF THE *JEFFERSON*   1988 EXCAVATIONS

CLAMP AND WATERWAY TRENCH

1988 FRAME TRENCH 1 (FRAME 26)

MAST STEP EXCAVATION

1988 FRAME TRENCH 2 (FRAME 4)

SHORELINE

K.J. CRISMAN 6-18-89

D

3-foot-wide (91 cm) trench from keelson to bulwarks yielded loose berth deck planking, small artifacts of ceramic and iron, and two small wooden grates, one of which was incised with the letter "F" (fig. 6.15a–d). A cluster of cast-iron grapeshot and grapeshot stands, iron canister shot, and lead shot suggested that an ammunition locker had been located directly forward of the mast step.

The next phase in the investigation was a three-week project in May of 1987, when we systematically uncovered what was left of the wreck's "spine": the after ends of the keel and keelson, as well as the stern deadwood and sternpost assembly.[44] A trench was excavated over a half frame (frame 38) at the stern to obtain a hull section. All of the structure exposed during excavation was drawn and measured, and the curvature of frame 38 was recorded. The digging produced debris both old and modern, detached timbers (fig. 6.16), and clues to stowage spaces on the ship. Fragments of sheet copper and numerous copper tacks from the vessel's copper-lined magazine were found atop the deadwood in the stern (the typical location for gunpowder storage on sloops of war).[45] Alongside the keelson excavators found cast-iron ballast, a wooden mallet, and a small cask. Finally, the trench over frame 38 yielded a silver US 25-cent piece dated 1806.

The final phase of the fieldwork was a four-week study in September 1988. The goals for this season were ambitious and included recording two more frame sections, documentation of the clamp and waterway timbers that supported the main deck's port side, and a closer look at the mainmast step. The season was extraordinarily productive of hull data and artifacts and helped to fill out our understanding of Eckford's work and the crew's daily lives.

The excavations around the mainmast step turned up curious finds, including a conical shot plug of pine, prepared by the carpenter as an emergency stopper for shot holes in the hull. Two 5¼-inch (13.33 cm) diameter disks of blue-green glass, flat on one side and convex on the other, were later identified as "patent sky lights"; these lenses were set into the main deck with the convex side up to allow natural light into the living spaces on the berth deck. Deck lights were patented in England in 1807, and these lenses are among the earliest examples to be found on a shipwreck.[46] Also in the vicinity of the mainmast step were crew-related artifacts such as discarded beef bones, glass London Mus-

tard bottles, and a brass, eagle-and-anchor US Navy uniform button manufactured by Peasley of Boston (fig. 6.17a–d).

The most significant find near the step was a metal spoon with the owner's name "J New" scratched inside the bowl. *Jefferson*'s muster roll listed an ordinary seaman named James New, a veteran of the Battle of Lake Champlain who was transferred to Lake Ontario and *Jefferson* in October 1814. New served on the brig until the war's end but deserted from the navy after he survived the wrecking of the privateer *Surprise* in April 1815. The hull configuration and gunport arrangement had already convinced us that the wreck was either *Jefferson* or *Jones,* but New's spoon provided strong evidence that this was indeed *Jefferson.*

The first frame trench excavated in 1988 was located abaft the mainmast step, over frame 26. This area originally had partitioned, decked stowage space in the hold and quarters for the officers on the berth deck. Many partition and deck planks were found. On the berth deck was a pile of bricks, batten boards, and a cast-iron stovetop, the collapsed remnants of a temporary brick stove used to heat the officer's wardroom during the winter of 1814–15. Artifacts from the berth deck included two small pearlware bowls, a broom handle, a brass thermometer scale, a second pine shot plug, and an 1805 copper one-cent piece. The hold space beneath the berth deck contained a complete wooden bucket and an iron marlin spike.

The port-side clamp and waterway timbers were either exposed or slightly buried, and it required little effort to excavate them. Abaft of frame 26 we discovered that two gunports and their associated bulwarks were missing, probably as a result of blasting operations in the early twentieth century. Our second frame trench in 1988 was centered over frame 4, which (like all frames forward of amidships) had its lower timbers torn off when the marina was built. Atop the ceiling we found a length of cast-iron ballast, an oaken cradle for supporting a small boat, a large but eroded wooden grating, and a broad-bladed shovel carved from a single piece of pine and edged with a strip of iron; the letters MTTP were carved on the blade. The shovel was likely used for clearing *Jefferson*'s deck of snow during the winter of 1814–15.

The recording of sections at frames 26 and 4 and details of the deck assembly wrapped up our work on *Jefferson* in 1988. There is much more to be learned

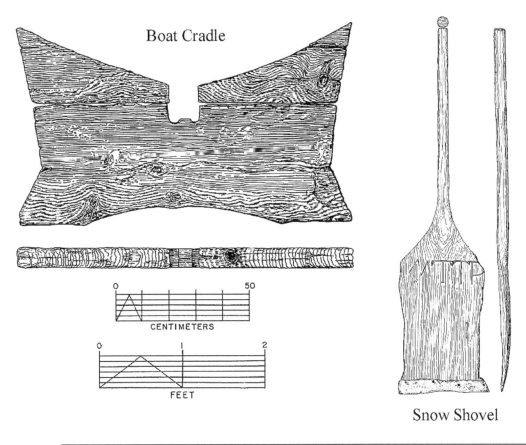

Boat Cradle

Snow Shovel

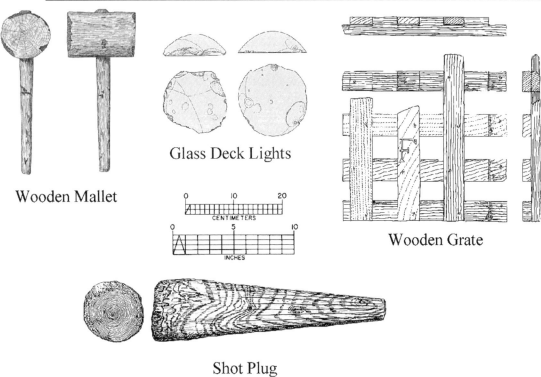

Wooden Mallet

Glass Deck Lights

Wooden Grate

Shot Plug

Figure 6.15. *Ship's equipment discovered on the wreck of* Jefferson. *The finds included: boat cradle, snow shovel, wooden mallet, glass deck lights, wooden grate, and shot plug. (Drawings by Kevin J. Crisman, Daniel Laroche, and Heidi Shauliss.)*

Figure 6.16. *Daniel Laroche and Virginia West record a timber found on* Jefferson. *Excavators found numerous detached timbers within the port side of the wreck, many of them pieces that fell from the starboard side of the hull as it disintegrated. (Photo by John Butler,* Jefferson *project files of Kevin J. Crisman.)*

from this wreck, but the work provided us with an understanding of its construction and enough data to carry out an on-paper reconstruction.[47] Artifacts recovered from the hull were conserved by the New York Bureau of Historic Sites, and an exhibit on *Jefferson* was subsequently opened at the Sackets Harbor State Historic Site.

The Assembly of *Jefferson*

Degraded by nearly 200 years of water, sun, and organic decay, blasted by naval reservists, burned by ice skaters, speared by pilings, and otherwise mangled by marina construction, *Jefferson* now bears little resemblance to the sloop of war launched by Henry Eckford and his carpenters. Archaeological recording and historical research have allowed us to regain much of what has been lost, however. The following

is a summary of *Jefferson*'s construction, following the sequence used by the shipwrights during the six-week assembly of the hull in January and February of 1814.

Only the aftermost 60 feet (18.28 m) of *Jefferson*'s keel remained. Fashioned from a single piece of white oak, it measured 1 foot 11 inches (58.4 cm) molded and 11½ inches (29.2 cm) sided and tapered to 7 inches (17.78 cm) sided at the sternposts. Photos taken in 1931 show that the keel's forward end was composed of two pieces, the lower being approximately 3 inches (7.62 cm) molded. No scarfs were found in the existing keel, nor are any visible in the 1931 photographs, suggesting that the brig's keel had a single scarf amidships. Amidships, the rabbets for the garboard planks were about 2 inches (5.08 cm) below the keel's top corners, but abaft the mainmast step the rabbets sloped down the side of the keel until they met the sternpost. The aftermost 3 feet 9 inches (1.14 m) of the keel was cut down 7 inches (17.78 cm) to fit the sternposts.

Nothing survived of *Jefferson*'s stem, but fortunately many visitors to the wreck sketched or photographed the timbers prior to their destruction by fire and marina builders. These show that the lower stem was slightly curved over its length and had a pronounced forward rake. Three timbers can be seen: the apron, the main stem, and an outer stem (or gripe). The stem was hook-scarfed to the keel's forward end and secured with a pair of iron dovetail plates; the stem had a flat scarf at its upper end to fit the upper post. The sides of the apron were deeply notched to fit the heels of the cant frames. The entire assembly was heavily fastened with round iron bolts (*Jefferson*'s hull seems to have been entirely fastened with iron).

Jefferson's stern was comprised of the deadwood and three sternposts (fig. 6.18). The deadwood was assembled from six straight-grained oak pieces, all laid parallel to the keel. In a departure from the standard practice on seagoing ships, there was no stern knee joining the top of the deadwood to the posts. The second and third deadwood timbers are extensions of the keelson (the second overlies six frame floors), a highly unusual way of constructing the stern, for shipwrights typically terminated the keelson at the forward end of the deadwood. Extending the keelson aft to the posts meant that the deadwood was completed only after the framing of the hull, an unusual construction sequence. The sides of the deadwood had thirteen pairs of rectangular mortises, averaging 1¼ inches (3.17 cm) deep,

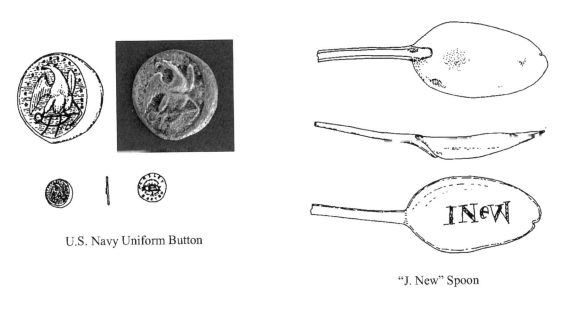

U.S. Navy Uniform Button

"J. New" Spoon

Hand-Painted Pearlwear Bowl

London Mustard Bottle

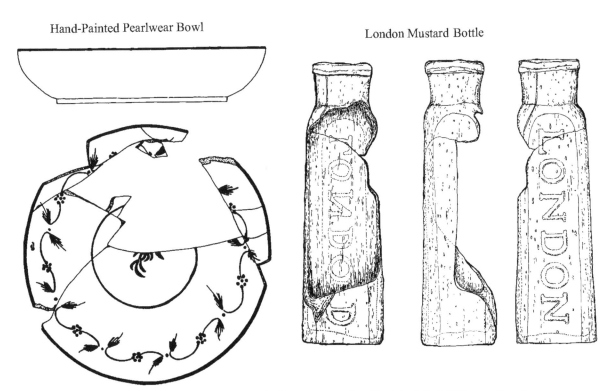

Figure 6.17. *Personal possessions found on the wreck of* Jefferson; *crew-related finds included: US Navy uniform button, "J. New" spoon, hand-painted pearlware bowl, and London Mustard bottle. The sailor's name on the spoon provided strong corroborating evidence that the wreck was indeed that of* Jefferson *and not one of the squadron's other medium-sized ships. (Drawings by Kevin J. Crisman, Anne Erwin Cohn, and Heidi Shauliss.)*

The Stern Assembly of Jefferson

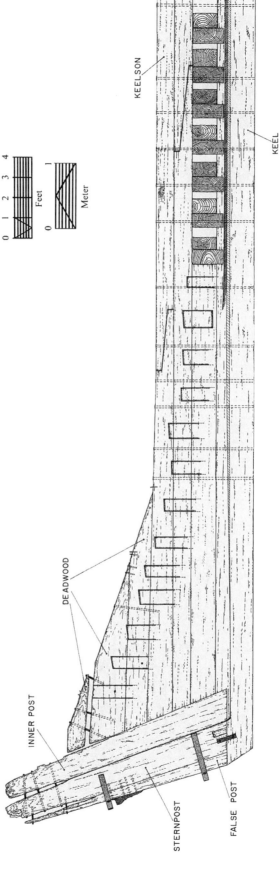

Figure 6.18. The stern assembly of Jefferson. The timbers that composed Jefferson's spine were of substantial dimensions and heavily fastened. The stern deadwood incorporated the aftermost keelson timbers and did not include a stern knee. (Drawing by Kevin J. Crisman.)

to fit the heels of the half frames. The entire assembly was heavily bolted to the keel and posts.

The three white oak sternposts, the inner, main, and false posts, were fastened together with many square iron bolts, and the main post was secured to the keel by a pair of through-bolted iron dovetail plates (the inner and main posts were probably tenoned to the keel as well, but this could not be verified). A round dowel or stopwater was driven into a hole drilled across the seam of the main post and keel to deflect water traveling along the seam. The three posts raked aft at an angle of about seventy degrees.

The inner post served as the attachment surface for the planking, and the rabbets for the hood ends were cut into the forward corners of the main post. Above the deadwood, the inner post had shallow notches on its forward face to fit the stern transoms. Two iron rudder gudgeons were spiked to the posts (there was a third gudgeon above them, but it is now missing). A triangular dumb brace for supporting the weight of the rudder on a pintle was spiked slightly below the second gudgeon.

The keel and end posts defined the overall length of the hull, but it was the frames that defined its maximum breadth and overall form. Photographs suggest that the frames on *Jefferson*'s port side were nearly intact prior to the 1960s, but the ripping out of the keel and stem also resulted in the loss of the lower frame timbers forward of amidships; the damage is more profound forward, and at the foremast channels only the top timbers have survived. Our knowledge of the forward end of the hull relies on photos taken of the wreck in the early twentieth century and on presumed continuity of construction practices seen in the hull's after end.

Sections of *Jefferson*'s hull were recorded at frames 4, 15, 26, and 38, and the room and space of the surviving frames was measured at the keel. The brig was estimated to have been built with sixty-six frames in its hull: forty-seven square frames, six pairs of cant frames at the bow, and thirteen pairs of half frames that fit into the mortised sides of the deadwood. A variety of woods were used for floors and futtocks, predominantly white oak but also hard maple and American elm, and the top timbers included softwoods such as hemlock, pine, and spruce.

The square frames had a room and space that averaged 1 foot 9 inches (53.34 cm), with a space of 4 to 6 inches (10.16 to 15.24 cm) between frames. Each was composed of seven timbers: the floor, two first futtocks (which butted over the keel's centerline), two second futtocks, and two top timbers (fig. 6.19). Floors and futtocks were fastened to one another at the heads and heels with ¾-inch (1.9 cm) square bolts. The frames were of substantial molded dimensions at the floors (frame 15 measured 13½ inches [34.29 cm] at the keel and 16 inches [40.64 cm] at the rabbet) but had a pronounced upward taper. At the bulwarks the top timbers averaged only about 4½ inches (11.43 cm) molded. There was also modest taper in the sided dimensions of the frames, from an average of about 9 inches (22.86 cm) at the floors to 6 inches (15.24 cm) at the top timbers. Filler pieces were inserted between the top timbers to create solid bulwarks.

The system of bilge water removal on *Jefferson* departed from the pattern seen on most wooden ships of its era: quite simply, there was no way to remove water from between the frames. Limber holes were not cut into the bases of the floors and first futtocks to allow water to flow to the pump wells, the limber boards alongside the keelson were spiked down to the frames, and there was no sign of any pump wells in the vicinity of the mainmast step (where we would expect to find them). Evidently the pumps were seated atop the ceiling, and *Jefferson*'s bilges always held pools of stagnant water between the frames. Was this standard practice on all Eckford-built ships or just a wartime expedient? We do not know yet.

Jefferson's keelson was of unusually large dimensions for a vessel of its class and was obviously intended to strengthen the brig's spine. Only the aftermost 57 feet (17.37 m) of the structure survived for study, but this, plus the series of photographs taken during low water in 1931, provided a good idea of its original configuration. The keelson had an estimated original length of 109 feet 3 inches (33.29 m), was 10½ inches (26.67 cm) sided and 21 inches (53.34 cm) molded, and was composed of two courses of white oak timbers set one atop the other. The lower course was comprised of three pieces, all molded 11 inches (27.94 cm) and flat scarfed end to end; the upper row had four flat-scarfed timbers, all molded 10 inches (25.4 cm). The keelson was heavily bolted to the floors and keel, and its top surface contained a series of long, rectangular notches intended to fit the heels of deck-supporting stanchion posts.

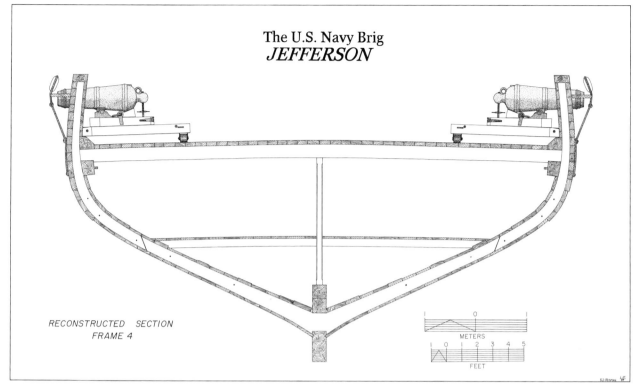

The U.S. Navy Brig
JEFFERSON

RECONSTRUCTED   SECTION
FRAME 4

Figure 6.19. *A reconstructed section of* Jefferson *at frame 4. This frame, located slightly abaft the hull's widest point, shows the brig's sharp angle of frame deadrise and shallow form. (Drawing by Kevin J. Crisman.)*

Jefferson's deck assembly differed significantly from the pattern seen on most seagoing vessels of this period.[48] Henry Eckford skipped the wooden knees commonly used to impart strength and rigidity to wooden hulls: there were no lodging, hanging, or dagger knees to reinforce the join of the deck beams to clamps and frames. Instead, he installed unusually large white oak clamps that were 11 inches (27.94 cm) molded and sided, beveled to fit the inside surfaces of the frames below the gunports, and fixed in place by 1-inch-diameter (2.54 cm) iron bolts. The tops of the clamps were notched down 1 inch (2.54 cm) to fit each deck beam.

The beams of *Jefferson*'s main deck were fitted in a readily discernable pattern of one beam beneath every gunport and one between every port. Obviously, it made good sense to support the weight of each gun directly upon a substantial timber (the beams were 10 inches [25.4 cm] molded and between 10 and 14 inches [25.4 to 35.56 cm] sided). The spaces between the ends of each deck beam contained a pair of filler pieces, each 6 inches (15.24 cm) square, bolted one behind the other to the frames. These locked the beam ends in place. The inboard filler pieces each had a single notch in the

center to fit a small, intermediate deck beam known as a ledge. Curiously, only the white oak beams beneath the gunports were found on the wreck; the ledges and beams between the ports may have been salvaged for reuse after *Jefferson* was sold, or they may have been of a weaker wood that did not survive.

The deck beam ends and filler pieces were capped over by white oak waterways that were 10 inches (25.4 cm) molded and sided. These timbers were heavily fastened with ¾-inch (1.9 cm) square bolts to the frame tops, beam ends, and clamps. The top inside corners of the waterways were deeply chamfered between the gunports, perhaps as a weight-saving measure.[49] Only a single scupper hole was found in the port-side waterway, directly outboard of the mainmast. Amidships, two waterway timbers met with a flat butt over frame 5; the forward piece was markedly different, being only 4½ inches (11.43 cm) molded and without chamfering. This waterway section was probably a replacement fitted after the gale of September 1814, when Captain Ridgely reported that *Jefferson* "opened in her waterways and leaked much forwards."[50]

Jefferson's main deck was attached to the sides of the

Figure 6.20. *Model of* Jefferson *showing the series of angled riders. Taken during the assembly of the model, this photograph shows the riders extending from the undersides of the clamps to the sides of the keelson. They greatly stiffened the hull longitudinally and helped to support the considerable weight of the guns. (Model by Glenn Grieco, Center for Maritime Archaeology and Conservation, Texas A&M University.)*

hull by clamps, filler pieces, and waterways, but Eckford saw the need for something more to stiffen the long, shallow hull and support the tremendous weight of guns. His solution was to install ten pairs of diagonal riders, angled timbers that fit between the sides of the keelson and the undersides of the clamps (fig. 6.20). The white oak riders were each comprised of a single timber 9 inches (22.86 cm) molded, between 7 and 10 inches (17.78 and 25.4 cm) sided, and drift bolted through the ceiling to every frame they crossed. The riders slanted away from the midship frame, with six angling aft and four angling forward.[51]

The practice of strengthening the hulls of wooden warships with riders dates back at least as far as the sixteenth century. Until the late eighteenth century, however, riders were fitted transversely, at a right angle to the keelson and parallel to the frames. Transverse riders helped the sides of a hull support the weight of guns but did little to counteract hogging. By the 1790s the increase in the length and armament of warships was reaching the point where something more was needed. One solution to the problem appeared in Philadelphia shipwright Joshua Humphreys's design for the US Navy's new 44-gun frigates, submitted in 1794. Humphreys specified the addition of six pairs of diagonal riders, extending from the keelson to lower deck. They were fitted in *Constitution, United States,* and possibly other vessels.[52] The Royal Navy got in on the

act in 1800, when the frigate *Glenmore* was strengthened with diagonal timbers.[53] By the second decade of the nineteenth century the use of diagonal riders had spread, and Naval Constructor Robert Seppings of the Royal Navy had developed a latticework system that was highly effective for preventing hogging.[54]

Below the turn of the bilge, *Jefferson* was planked with wide strakes of white oak that averaged 2 inches (5.08 cm) thick and 10 to 15 inches (25.4 to 38.1 cm) in width; one strake measured an astounding 24 inches (60.96 cm) wide. From the turn of the bilge up, the planks increased in thickness to between 3 and 4 inches (7.62 and 10.16 cm) but narrowed to an average of 8 to 9 inches (20.32 to 22.86 cm). Softwoods, including white pine, were selected for certain strakes above the turn of the bilge. Amidships, *Jefferson* had a total of seventeen ceiling strakes between the keelson and clamp, ranging from 10 to 13 inches (25.4 to 33.02 cm) in width and 2 to 2½ inches (5.08 to 6.35 cm) in thickness; the two strakes nearest the keelson and the four beneath the clamp were slightly thicker (about 3 inches [7.62 cm]) and entirely of white oak, and those in between were a mixture of oak and white pine. Iron spikes were used to fasten planks to frames inside and outside. The discovery of bolt heads clenched over iron rings on the ceiling suggested that plank butts outside the hull may have been reinforced in the manner seen on the US Navy schooner *Ticonderoga* (see chapter 9).

Jefferson's oak mainmast step consisted of two contiguous steps: the original and a second step added in the early summer of 1814 when Captain Ridgely moved the mast 3 feet (91.44 cm) farther aft (fig. 6.21). The original step was composed of two 9-foot-long (2.74 m) timbers notched down transversely over the keelson, fayed to the ceiling, and bolted securely in place (the keelson had shallow notches on its top surface to fit these pieces). The transverse timbers each had a pair of notches to fit the two side pieces of the step between them, creating a 10-inch-wide (25.4 cm) by 2-foot-8-inch-long (81.28 cm) space to hold the heel of the mast atop the keelson. When it became necessary to restep the mast farther aft, a third transverse timber (slightly shorter than the first two) was fashioned and bolted across the keelson (the keelson was not notched this time), and notches were cut to fit two more side pieces. The second step opening was the same width as the first but for some reason was 11

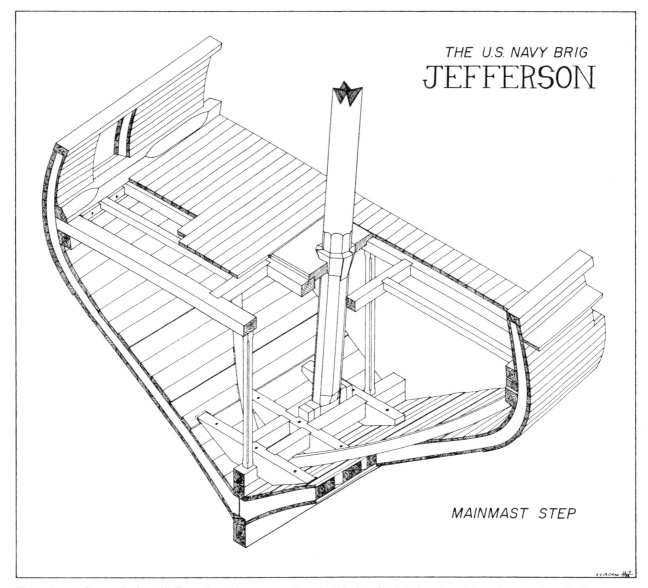

THE U.S. NAVY BRIG
JEFFERSON

MAINMAST STEP

Figure 6.21. *An isometric view of Jefferson's mainmast steps. Captain Ridgely shifted the location of the mainmast aft and had a new step added to the back of the existing step. (Drawing by Kevin J. Crisman.)*

inches (27.94 cm) longer, for a total length of 3 feet 7 inches (1.09 m).

The brig's port-side bulwarks and nine surviving gunports contained a trove of information about the weaponry, rigging, and topside appearance of the brig (the bridle port at the bow and the two aftermost ports were gone). The port openings varied slightly but averaged about 3 feet 2 inches (96.52 cm) wide by 3 feet 6 inches (1.06 m) high. Bulwark sections were 6 feet 6 inches (1.98 m) in length and composed of a nearly solid mass of frame tops and filler pieces. The frame tops at the side of each port opening were higher than the other frames and fit into mortises cut into

the underside of the cap rail. The white pine rail was 6 inches (15.24 cm) thick and 12 inches (30.48 cm) wide and was fastened to the frame tops by diagonally driven square bolts, with about three to four bolts per bulwark section.

The bulwarks held a profusion of iron eyebolts, some with their rope-protecting thimbles still attached. Most of the eyebolts held training tackle and breechings for *Jefferson*'s guns, although some may have been rigging related. Two of the ports, the third and eighth abaft the stem, differed from the others by having a horizontally oriented eyebolt midway up each side (six other ports had these bolts, but at the base of

Figure 6.22. *Prepared for serious recoil. Jefferson's bulwarks had lead-lined round openings midway up the side of each gunport to allow the fitting of breeching ropes around the top timbers; this system was better able to resist the heavy recoil of the brig's 42-pounder carronades and long 24 pounders. (Photo by Kevin J. Crisman,* Jefferson *model by Glenn Grieco, Center for Maritime Archaeology and Conservation, Texas A&M University.)*

the port); the pair of anomalous ports may have held the two 24-pounder long guns that were interspersed with the eight 42-pounder carronades of *Jefferson's* port broadside.

Circular openings were cut through the bulwarks on either side of each gunport, halfway between the cap rail and waterway (fig. 6.22). The lead-lined holes had an interior diameter of 2½ inches (6.35 cm), with a 4-inch-diameter (10.16 cm) lead flange nailed to the inside of the bulwarks. The openings were an enigma until a contemporary print of a US Navy *Peacock*-class sloop of war finally answered the mystery: it showed a loop of breeching at the side of every port. Naval historian William James observed that US Navy ships sometimes secured guns with double breechings, with one pair spliced around the frame tops. James considered

this a very good idea, for when eyebolts alone were used to check the recoil of heavy guns, they often pulled out of the bulwarks after repeated firing. Smaller classes of warships with their lighter upperworks seem to have been particularly prone to drawing their bolts.[55] *Jefferson's* big guns surely required this reliable means of checking their recoil.

Evidence of *Jefferson's* rig could also be gleaned from the interior and exterior of the bulwarks. The foremast and mainmast shrouds and stays were anchored to the hull by three channels on a side (five were still preserved on the port side). The two forward channels for each mast extended the full length of a bulwark section and consisted of a 2-inch-thick (5.08 cm) by 14½-inch-wide (36.83 cm) timber edge-bolted to the frame tops 9 inches (22.86 cm) below the cap rail.

The aftermost channel for the foremast was shorter, narrower, and thicker than the two forward channels (this was probably the case for the missing aftermost channel of the mainmast as well). The deadeyes for the shrouds were 12 inches (30.48 cm) in diameter, 6 inches (15.24 cm) thick, and bolted to the hull by two lengths of iron chainplate that measured 2 feet 9 inches (83.82 cm) in length, 3 inches (7.62 cm) wide, and 1¼ inch (3.17 cm) thick.

"Not His Equal . . . in the World"

Isaac Chauncey described Henry Eckford as a shipwright with no equal in the United States, "or perhaps in the World." Judging from the comments of contemporary observers and later biographers, Chauncey was not alone in his opinion. Lines exist for several of Eckford's ships, but *Jefferson* has been, to date, the only chance to see his workmanship firsthand.

Jefferson proves once again that even badly battered, incomplete hulls have much to tell us about the shipbuilders and seafarers of an earlier era. The wreck yielded a remarkably complete picture of Henry Eckford's approach to building warships, at least as he was building them on Lake Ontario in 1814. The study of the wreck provided us with four hull sections abaft the midship frame, as well as data on the keel, framing system, stern deadwood and lower sternposts, keelson, mainmast step, clamps, riders, deck assembly, planking, bulwarks, and gunports. In order to prepare a set of lines and construction plans, it was necessary to build upon the existing hull to determine the form, assembly, and appearance of the missing bow and transom. Besides the wreck itself, we had several good sources to draw upon for a reconstruction, including a contemporary watercolor of *Jones,* plans of post-1815 ships built by Eckford, and the photographs of the bow taken in 1931.[56]

As I have reconstructed *Jefferson*'s hull (fig. 6.23), the keel measured 108 feet 9 inches (33.14 m), with an overall length between perpendiculars of 122 feet 11 inches (37.46 m). At the midship frame, the hull measured 32 feet 6 inches (9.9 m) molded beam (without planking) and 33 feet 2 inches (10.1 m) extreme beam (with planking).[57] These dimensions gave the brig a length-to-beam ratio of 3.78:1. The depth of hold, from the top of the floor to the top of the main deck beam at the midship frame, was 10 feet 5 inches (3.17 m), and the midship rabbet-to-sheer height was 15 feet 7 inches

(4.74 m). Altogether, these dimensions indicate a moderately narrow, shallow-drafted vessel. What they do not show is the extreme sharpness of *Jefferson*'s design: the angle of deadrise at the midship frame was estimated to be twenty-five degrees, a high angle that gave the vessel a V-shaped hull. The 1931 photos of the wreck clearly show a steeply raking stem and narrow entrance, while the sections taken off the wreck show the stern had a long, tapering run and posts that raked aft at a pronounced angle. There was considerable drag to the keel, probably around 4 feet (1.21 m) between the bow and stern when the vessel was properly trimmed.

Jefferson was no carbon copy of contemporary US Navy seagoing designs such as *Peacock* but was tailored specifically for Lake Ontario. Unlimited fresh water for the crew and the ability to frequently replenish stores allowed Eckford to dispense with the hold space required for long cruises and concentrate on the design elements that conferred sailing speed, maneuverability, and firepower.[58] With its sharp, shallow form and keel drag, *Jefferson* most resembled the celebrated Baltimore Clipper designs used by US privateer schooners during the War of 1812, but it was much larger and more heavily armed than the average privateer. In moderate winds and seas *Jefferson* was probably capable of an impressive turn of speed, and the handy brig rig would have given it an edge when maneuvering for position against a foe (fig. 6.24). Certainly the broadsides of ship-smashing 42-pounder carronades would have dealt terrible destruction to any target unlucky enough to sail into range.

Eckford's choices of timbers, fasteners, and assembly techniques also tell us of the special circumstances the navy faced on the lakes. Speed of assembly was a prime consideration. One significant time-saving practice was the omission of knees and compass timber—nearly every piece in the hull was fashioned from straight-grained wood.[59] This approach lent itself well to mass-production: little time was wasted selecting, cutting, and fitting timbers to match complex curves, and loggers had only to keep a steady supply of wood on hand for the builders to get the job done. The kneeless deck assembly technique might have been a fatal weakness on a seagoing ship, but for a brief career on an inland lake the tradeoffs were acceptable.

Other vital considerations in *Jefferson*'s construction were reducing the hull's topside weight and providing sufficient longitudinal strength. The combination of

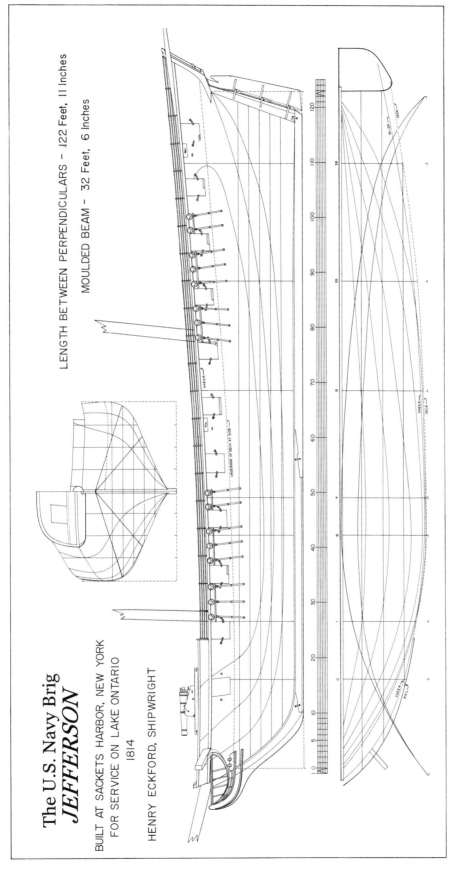

The U.S. Navy Brig
JEFFERSON

BUILT AT SACKETS HARBOR, NEW YORK
FOR SERVICE ON LAKE ONTARIO
1814

HENRY ECKFORD, SHIPWRIGHT

LENGTH BETWEEN PERPENDICULARS - 122 Feet, 11 Inches

MOULDED BEAM - 32 Feet, 6 Inches

Figure 6.23. *The reconstructed lines of the US Navy brig Jefferson. These are the only plans we have for any of the wartime-built US Navy ships constructed by Henry Eckford for Lake Ontario. Everything about the design of this hull speaks of a desire for speed under sail, maneuverability, and overwhelming firepower. Jefferson and its sister brig Jones were also dangerously top heavy. (Reconstruction by Kevin J. Crisman.)*

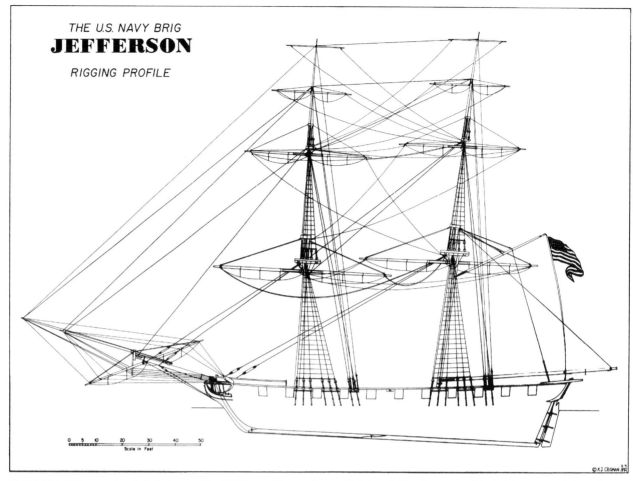

Figure 6.24. *The reconstructed rigging profile of* Jefferson. *The wreck provided clues to the placement of the brig's masts and shrouds. The reconstruction also relied on a set of postwar US Navy rigging proportions, and a contemporary rig profile prepared by Sailmaker Charles Ware for the Eckford-built Lake Ontario ship* General Pike. *(Reconstruction by Kevin J. Crisman.)*

a shallow draft and a heavy battery made the brig top heavy, a problem that could be remedied to some extent by adding ballast, but Eckford took other measures to lessen weight above the waterline. He made the upperworks lighter by using softwood top timbers and by tapering the frames by two-thirds in their molded dimensions and one-third in their sided dimensions between the keel and cap rail. The lack of knees in the deck assembly must have saved weight as well.

Jefferson's heavy battery of guns, narrow ends, and shallow draft in proportion to its length would have exacerbated the built-in tendency of wooden warships to hog. Eckford dealt with this problem in two ways. First, he gave the brig a heavier-than-usual backbone: the keel and keelson were much greater in molded dimensions than was typical for a sloop of war of this size.[60] Second, he installed the ten pairs of diagonal riders be-

tween the keelson and clamps. Diagonal riders were a relatively new innovation that worked remarkably well for stiffening a hull, particularly when used in the numbers found in *Jefferson*. Shaping them was, however, a laborious and time-consuming task.[61]

Jefferson combined fast assembly, speed, maneuverability, and lethal armament in one package, but these qualities came at a cost in strength, stability, and seaworthiness. Henry Eckford's creation was a fair-weather warship that operated on a narrow margin of safety, a truth that was amply demonstrated by the gale of September 1814. The high winds and waves of the storm caused the shallow hull to make too much leeway, and to keep from drifting onto the shore *Jefferson*'s crew spread more sail than was otherwise prudent. The combination of a shallow draft, weighty guns, and too much canvas twice sent the brig over on its beam ends. Even with diagonal riders the strain on the overburdened hull was too much, and the waterways began tearing loose. The situation was saved by jettisoning half the guns, but this was a drastic and costly solution.

Despite *Jefferson*'s close shave with disaster, Eckford's overall experience with sharp designs on Lake Ontario during the War of 1812 seems to have been positive. His postwar designs showed a strong predilection toward this form of hull, and he designed many famous fast-sailing ships, including the US Navy schooner *Grampus,* the corvette *Bolivar* (which bears a strong resemblance in form and dimensions to *Jefferson*), and the fast corvette *United States.*[62] Eckford died in Constantinople in 1832 while building ships for the Turkish government, but his influence would carry over to the next generation of shipwrights. His protégé Isaac Webb purchased his New York yard, and Webb's apprentices William Webb, John Griffiths, and Donald McKay became the preeminent designers of the legendary clipper ships of the 1840s and 1850s.[63]

Capt. Charles Ridgely and *Jefferson* were never "fortunate enough to flog the enemy" during their brief career on Lake Ontario, and Ridgely (much to his regret) never entered the pantheon of American naval heroes. *Jefferson*'s legacy has been more subtle than a heroic naval engagement, but no less important. It is a monument to—and an archaeological snapshot of—a prodigious feat of ship designing, building, and outfitting during the War of 1812. It has been a means for us to examine the people behind the events, the shipbuilders, the officers, and the sailors, to see the tools and materials of their daily existence, to understand the lives they lived, and to discover how they adapted to the demands of naval service on a remote freshwater lake.

NOTES

1. Joseph Delafield, *The Unfortified Boundary, A Diary of the First Survey of the Canadian Boundary Line from St. Regis to the Lake of the Woods by Major Joseph Delafield,* eds. Robert McElroy and Thomas Riggs (New York: Privately Printed, 1943), pp. 212–13.

2. Chauncey to Jones, October 8, 1813, Isaac Chauncey Letter Books (CLB), vol. 1, New York Historical Society (NYHS).

3. Chauncey to Jones, November 25, 1813, entry 125, Naval Records Collection of the Office of Naval Records and Library, record group 45 (RG 45), National Archives and Records Administration (NARA).

4. William Dudley, ed., *The Naval War of 1812: A Documentary History,* vol. 2 (Washington, DC: Naval Historical Center, 1992), pp. 581–82; Chauncey to Jones, October 8, 1813, CLB, vol. 1, NYHS.

5. *Niles Weekly Register,* vol. 5, no. 1, September 4, 1813 (Baltimore), p. 12; Chauncey to Jones, October 8, 1813, CLB, vol. 1, NYHS. The *Register* stated that *Sylph* was built in thirty-three days "from the stump," while Chauncey, who provided over the building, said it was twenty-one days.

6. Chauncey to Jones, December 12, 1813, entry 125, RG 45, NARA; Jones to Samuel Evans, November 30, 1813, entry 441, RG 45, NARA; Jones to John Bullus, December 13, 1813, entry 209, RG 45, NARA; Jones to Samuel T. Anderson, December 13, 1813, entry 441, RG 45, NARA.

7. Jones to President James Madison, May 25, 1814, William Jones Papers, Uselma Clark Smith Collection (UCSC), Historical Society of Pennsylvania (HSP).

8. Howard I. Chapelle, *The History of the American Sailing Navy* (New York: W. W. Norton, 1949), pp. 255–63; Dudley, ed., *Naval War of 1812,* vol. 2, pp. 581–82.

9. Chauncey to Jones, February 24, 1814, entry 125, RG 45, NARA.

10. Chauncey to Samuel T. Anderson, March 4, 1814 and Chauncey to J. Walton, April 9, 1814, CLB, vol. 1, NYHS.

11. Chauncey to Jones, February 28, March 11, and March 29, 1814, entry 125, RG 45, NARA. Chauncey to Melancthon T. Woolsey, March 1, 1814, Chauncey to Mathew Brown Jr., March 24, 1814, Chauncey to John Bullus, March 29, 1814, CLB, vol. 1, NYHS.

12. Chauncey to Jones, April 8, 1814, entry 125, RG 45, NARA; Chauncey to Jones, April 14, 1814, and Chauncey to Noah Brown, April 9, 1814, CLB, vol. 1, NYHS.

13. Ridgely to Jones, April 2, 1814, entry 147, RG 45, NARA; Jones to Ridgely, April 4 and April 10, 1814, entry 149, RG 45, NARA.

14. Kevin Crisman, "The *Jefferson*: The History and Archaeology of an American Brig from the War of 1812" (PhD diss., University of Pennsylvania, 1989), pp. 73–94; Chauncey to Jones, November 29, 1814, CLB, vol. 2, NYHS. During a visit to Baltimore in January 1814, Chauncey invited Ridgely to bring his crew to Lake Ontario if *Erie* was unable to get to sea.

15. Crisman, "The *Jefferson*," pp. 83–84, 88–90; US Brig *Jefferson* Muster Rolls, 1814, RG 45, NARA; Jones to Ridgely, April 4, 1814, entry 149, RG 45, NARA.

16. Jones to Ridgely, April 10, 1814, entry 149, RG 45, NARA; Ridgely to Jones, April 11, 1814, entry 147, RG 45, NARA; Chauncey to Jones, April 30 and May 2, 1814, CLB, vol. 1, NYHS.

17. Watercolor paintings of the sloop of war *Erie* dated 1817 and 1824 show the vessel with a white stripe down each side, directly below the gunports. Painting entitled *United States Corvete* [sic] *Erie Cap^n Ch^s Gamble,* Philadelphia Maritime Museum; painting by Camilierre, *Erie, 1824,* in Richard Hough, *Fighting Ships* (London: Michael Joseph, 1969), p. 172.

18. The estimated weight of the original armament on *Jefferson* was 82,700 lbs (41.35 tons), derived from the following calculations:

Cannon	Carriage	Combined	Total on Jefferson
42-pounder carronade			
2500 lbs	600 lbs	3100 lbs	× 16 = 49,600 lbs
24-pounder long gun			
5800 lbs	800 lbs	6600 lbs	× 4 = 26,400 lbs
18-pounder pivot gun			
4700 lbs	800 lbs	5500 lbs	× 1 = 5500 lbs
Gun tools and tackle		1200 lbs	1200 lbs
		TOTAL:	82,700 lbs (41.35 tons)

Captain Ridgely landed the 18-pounder pivot gun and its pivot mount by early June of 1814, reducing the weight of armament to 77,200 lbs (38.6 tons). These weights are derived from Spencer Tucker, *Arming the Fleet: U.S. Navy Ordnance in the Muzzle-loading Era* (Annapolis: Naval Institute Press, 1989), p. 125 and from estimates by Capt. Walter Rybka in Chapter 1 of this book.

19. William Wood, ed., *Select British Documents of the Canadian War of 1812,* vol. 3, pt. 1 (Toronto: The Champlain Society, 1926), p. 45.

20. "Exhibit of the Nature & Force of the Squadron on Lake Ontario under the Command of Commodore Isaac Chauncey," July 15, 1814, William Jones Papers, UCSC, HSP; "Journal of the US Brig Jones," entries from June 17–19, 1814, Melancthon Woolsey Papers, Detroit Public Library (DPL).

21. Lt. John Elton to Purser William Chew, May 16, 1814, Chew Family Papers, Clements Library, University of Michigan. The travails of the US Navy squadron from May to July are described in Crisman, "The *Jefferson*," Chapter 5, and in Robert Malcomson, *Lords of the Lake, The Naval War on Lake Ontario, 1812–1814* (Toronto: Robin Brass Studio, 1998), Chapters 15–17. The number of sailors in the Lake Ontario squadron in August 1814 was 1961 according to a muster roll of all naval stations and the ships attached to them, dated August 31, 1814, William Jones Papers, UCSC, HSP.

22. Midshipman John Chew Court Martial Record, November 1814, entry 273, RG 45, NARA.

23. "Exhibit of the Nature & Force of the Squadron on Lake Ontario under the Command of Commodore Isaac Chauncey, July 15, 1814," William Jones Papers, UCSC, HSP.

24. Malcomson, *Lords of the Lake,* p. 342.

25. Chauncey to Capt. Charles G. Ridgely, August 6, 1814, and Chauncey to Maj. Gen. Jacob Brown, August 7, 1814, CLB, vol. 2, NYHS.

26. Chauncey to Jones, August 29 and September 5, 1814, and Chauncey to Ridgely, September 4, 1814, CLB, vol. 2, NYHS.

27. The description of the storm and its effects on *Jefferson* and *Jones* is based on entries in the "Journal of the US Brig Jones," Melancthon Woolsey Papers, DPL; Chauncey to Jones, enclos-ing Ridgely to Chauncey, September 18, 1814, entry 125, RG 45, NARA. There is a curious discrepancy here: *Jones* mounted only 6600 pounds (3.3 tons) less weight in cannon than *Jefferson* yet did not jettison any guns during the storm. Was *Jones* a stronger or more stable ship, or was its commander Melancthon Woolsey more willing to risk capsizing?

28. Chauncey to Jones, October 8, 1814, CLB, vol. 2, NYHS; Chauncey to Jones, October 8 and 12, 1814, entry 125, RG 45, NARA.

29. Lt. Lawrence Rousseau to Jones, October 11, 1814, Midshipman Harrison H. Cocke to Jones, October 12, 1814, Midshipman David R. Stewart to Benjamin Homans, December 7, 1814, entry 148, RG 45, NARA.

30. Chauncey to Jones, November 29, 1814, CLB, vol. 2, NYHS; Ridgely to Homans, January 8, 1815, entry 147, RG 45, NARA; Chauncey to Benjamin Crowninshield, January 31, 1815, CLB, vol. 2, NYHS.

31. *American and Commercial Daily Advertiser* (Baltimore), vol. 31, no. 4941, April 8, 1815; vol. 31, no. 4942, April 10, 1815; NARA, RG 45, entry 125, Ridgely to Crowninshield, April 8 and n.d. [circa April 12], 1815, entry 125, RG 45, NARA.

32. Chauncey to Crowninshield, March 8, 1815, CLB, vol. 2, NYHS; Chauncey to Crowninshield, March 26, May 18, and July 1, 1815, entry 125, RG 45, NARA; Woolsey to Crowninshield, June 13, 1815, entry 147, RG 45, NARA; Woolsey to Capt. John Rodgers, July 20 and August 26, 1815, entry 220, RG 45, NARA.

33. The history of the naval station at Sackets Harbor between 1815 and 1825 is described in Crisman, "The *Jefferson*," Chapter 8. See also Delafield, *Unfortified Boundary,* p. 213 and United States Department of State, *A Register of Officers and Agents Civil, Military, and Naval in the Service of the United States on the 30th of September, 1821; Together with the Names, Force, and Condition of all the Ships and Vessels Belonging to the United States and When and Where Built* (Washington City: Davis and Force, 1822), p. 116.

34. United States Congress, *American State Papers-Document, Legislative and Executive, of the Congress of the United States: Class VI, Naval Affairs* (Washington, DC: Gales and Seaton: 1834), p. 713.

35. Robert Hugunin to Capt. William Bainbridge, March 23, 1825, and Lt. Samuel Adams to Hugunin, April 26, 1825, entry 220, RG 45, NARA.

36. James Van Cleve, "Reminiscences of Early Steam Boats, Propellers and Sailing Vessels" (manuscript, 1877), Buffalo Historical Society Collection. *Freeman's Advocate* (Sackets Harbor, NY), May 31, 1827. Courtesy of the *Watertown* (NY) *Daily Times.*

37. A description of *Jefferson* between 1825 and 1984 can be found in Crisman, "The *Jefferson*," Chapter 9; Benson Lossing, *The Pictorial Fieldbook of the War of 1812* (New York: Harper and Brothers, 1868; repr. New Hampshire Publishing Company, 1976), p. 616.

38. David Lane's photographs of *Jefferson* in 1931 are on file at the Watertown (NY) *Daily Times.*

39. *Watertown* (NY) *Daily Times,* April 22, 1931. Courtesy of Robert Brennan, Sackets Harbor, NY.

40. *Watertown* (NY) *Daily Times,* October 19 and 22, 1931. Courtesy of Robert Brennan.

41. John Stevens, "Naval Dockyards on Lake Ontario in the War of 1812–14," *Nautical Research Guild Secretary's Monthly Letter* 3, no. 2 (February, 1950); Jackson Jenks to Howard I. Chapelle, April 24, 1958, National Museum of American History, Division of Transportation Records, circa 1927–73: Record Unit 239, Box 28, Smithsonian Institution Archives.

42. Richard C. Van Gemert, "Ships of the Great Lakes," in *A History of Seafaring Based on Underwater Archaeology,* ed. George F. Bass (London: Thames and Hudson, 1972), pp. 291, 302.

43. Kevin Crisman and Arthur Cohn, "The 1985 Underwater Archaeological Survey of the War of 1812 Brig in Sackets Harbor, New York," excavation report (Bureau of Historic Sites, New York State Office of Parks, Recreation, and Historic Preservation, June 1985).

44. Kevin Crisman and Arthur Cohn, "The 1987 Archaeological Investigation of the US Navy Brig *Jefferson,*" excavation report (Bureau of Historic Sites, New York State Office of Parks, Recreation, and Historic Preservation, April 1988).

45. Isaac Chauncey, "Estimate of Materials and Stores Required to Be Sent from the Atlantic Ports to Build and Equip Three Ships, Two of Which of the Line & One Frigate" (undated manuscript circa October 1814), William Jones Papers, UCSC, HSP; magazines and cartridge filling rooms can be seen in "Deck Plans of the Sloop of War Erie," August 9, 1815, and untitled deck plan and interior profile of the sloop of war *Peacock,* dated July 27, 1813, RG 19, NARA.

46. Kevin Crisman, "Two Deck Lights from the US Navy Brig *Jefferson* (1814)," *Seaways' Ships in Scale* 3, no. 6 (November/December 1992), pp. 48–50. Deck lights have also been found on the 1814 Lake Champlain row galley *Allen,* the 1815 schooner *Tecumseth,* and the 1824 schooner *Cleopatra's Barge* sunk in Hawaii.

47. The results of the 1988 excavation are described in Crisman, "The *Jefferson,*" Chapter 13.

48. Details of the deck assembly of the US Navy's 1813 *Peacock* can be found in Howard I. Chapelle, *The History of American Sailing Ships* (New York: W. W. Norton, 1935), pp. 371–74.

49. Glenn Grieco of the Center for Maritime Archaeology at Texas A&M University calculated that the total weight of wood removed from *Jefferson*'s waterways by chamfering amounted to between 1500 and 2000 pounds (679.5 and 906 kg).

50. Ridgely to Chauncey, September 18, 1814, enclosed in Chauncey to Jones, September 20, 1814, entry 125, RG 45, NARA.

51. The photographs taken of *Jefferson*'s bow during low water in 1931 by David Lane clearly show the forward-angling riders (now missing from the wreck). Photographs courtesy of the *Watertown Daily Times.*

52. United States Government, *American State Papers,* *Naval Affairs,* vol. 1 (Washington, DC: Gales and Seaton, 1860), pp. 10–13; Donald L. Canney, *Sailing Warships of the U.S. Navy* (Annapolis: Naval Institute Press, 2001), pp. 26–29, 35–36, 42, 206; Richard Eddy, "'. . . Defended by an Adequate Power': Joshua Humphreys and the 74-Gun Ships of 1799," *The American Neptune* 51, no. 3 (Summer 1991), pp. 185–87.

53. William James, *The Naval History of Great Britain, from the Declaration of War by France in February 1793 to the Accession of George IV in January 1820,* vol. 6 (London: Harding, Lepard, 1826), pp. 596–99.

54. Samuel Humphreys apparently added five pairs of diagonal riders when he built the US Navy's 74-gun *Franklin* in 1813–15; see Wharton and Humphreys Notebook, Joshua Humphreys Papers (JHP), Historical Society of Pennsylvania (HSP), p. 308. Other sources on diagonal riders include Robert Seppings, "On a New Principal of Constructing Ships," *The Repertory of Arts, Manufactures, and Agriculture* 27, 2nd series (1815), pp. 217–34; Robert Gardiner, *Warships of the Napoleonic Era* (London: Chatham Publishing, 1999), p. 22; Peter Goodwin, *The Construction and Fitting of the English Man of War, 1650–1850* (Annapolis: Naval Institute Press, 1987), pp. 101–105.

55. The profile of the *Peacock*-class sloop of war showing through-bulwark breechings was first published in William James's *A Full and Correct Account of the Chief Naval Occurrences of the Late War* (1817) and is reprinted in Robert Gardiner, ed., *The Naval War of 1812* (London: Chatham Publishing, 1998), p. 84. William James's observations on gun breechings are published in his *Naval History of Great Britain,* vol. 6, pp. 317, 426, 428.

56. *Jones* is in the foreground of a panoramic watercolor of Sackets Harbor painted on September 20, 1815 by Royal Navy Purser Emerich Essex Vidal; there are distortions due to Vidal's perspective and he shortened the rig to fit it on the page, but his rendition of *Jones* agrees with what we know of *Jefferson*'s appearance and provides important clues to missing features. Vidal's painting is in the collections of the Royal Military College in Kingston, Ontario. Plans of the Eckford-built ships *Grampus, Hercules* (ex-*Bolivar*), and *Ohio* may be seen in Chapelle, *American Sailing Navy,* pp. 313 (plan 20), 331, 333; Howard I. Chapelle, *The Search for Speed Under Sail* (New York: W. W. Norton, 1967), p. 268 (Plate V); and Canney, *Sailing Warships of the U.S. Navy,* pp. 98–100, 177–79.

57. The reconstruction plans of *Jefferson* were prepared in 1988 from the available archaeological and historical evidence, which did not include any reliable contemporary dimensions. In 2002, the dimensions of *Jefferson* and *Jones* were discovered in the Wharton and Humphreys Notebook, JHP, HSP, wherein they were listed as "121˜feet" (36.8 m) between perpendiculars, 31 feet 6 inches (9.6 m) beam, and 5 feet 4 inches (1.62 m) "waist" (this last was apparently the distance from waterline to gunport sill amidships). The tilde after "121" suggests that this figure was an approximation.

58. Ridgely's 20-gun sloop of war *Erie* (similar to *Peacock* but slightly sharper) carried a fourteen- to sixteen-week supply of

water and provisions on a seagoing cruise, but the Lake Ontario warships carried at most a four- to six-week supply of provisions. *Erie*'s crew required 160 to 180 gallons (605.5 to 681.3 L) of fresh water per day while at sea. Ridgely to William Jones, March 11, 1814, entry 147, RG 45, NARA; Chauncey to Jones, March 29, 1814, entry 125, RG 45, NARA; "Journal of Charles G. Ridgely, 1815–21, On Board *Erie, Independence,* and *Constellation,*" June 22, 1815, Manuscripts Division, Library of Congress.

59. The fact that *Jefferson* could be assembled almost entirely of straight-grained timbers was determined by Glenn Grieco during his construction of a 1:36-scale wooden model for the Center for Maritime Archaeology and Conservation at Texas A&M University.

60. For dimensions of *Peacock*'s keel, see Chapelle, *American Sailing Ships,* pp. 365–76.

61. These observations on riders are based on Glenn Grieco's experience building the 1:36-scale *Jefferson.* The riders imparted great rigidity to the model's previously flexible hull and presumably did the same thing for the original *Jefferson.*

62. Chapelle, *American Sailing Navy,* pp. 340–41. Eckford also submitted plans for a 124-foot (37.79 m) sharp-modeled sloop of war to the Navy Department in 1819 (it was never built). Chapelle observed, "It might be suggested that [Eckford] became converted to this form of hull through his experiences with the lakes but, of course, there is no proof." *Jefferson* provides the proof that Chapelle lacked, for it does indeed bear a strong resemblance to the 1819 design.

63. Chapelle, *Search for Speed,* p. 321.

7 FRONTIER FRIGATES AND A THREE-DECKER

Wrecks of the Royal Navy's Lake Ontario Squadron

JONATHAN MOORE

Introduction

On April 10, 1815, the US Navy schooner *Lady of the Lake* sailed into Kingston harbor, the Royal Navy's base on Lake Ontario. On board were Comm. Isaac Chauncey, Maj. Gen. Jacob Brown, and other US officers. A line of warships lay anchored adjacent to the King's Yard, but rather than resisting the American incursion, they were awaiting inspection by the visitors. At noon the next day, following a tour of the squadron, Chauncey debarked from the British commodore's colossal flagship *St. Lawrence* to the sound of a thirteen-gun salute. The war between Britain and the United States was over, and the day proved to be a remarkably friendly ending to a bitter rivalry.[1]

Peace abruptly ended the shipbuilding race that for nearly three years had consumed the rival dockyards at Kingston and Sackets Harbor. It was the start of a steady decline in the lake's naval dockyards and squadrons. Within six months, most of the ships at Kingston would be laid up; in two years they would be in ordinary; in five they would be condemned as rotten; after fifteen they would be half-sunk nuisances; and after twenty-five years their rotten hulls would be put up for auction and the dockyard closed. The *St. Lawrence* would be sold off to serve as a cordwood dock in Kingston, and two of the large frigates, *Prince Regent* and *Princess Charlotte,* would be abandoned in nearby Hamilton Cove. One hundred years later, local legend would assert that the hulls had been intentionally sunk following the war to be raised again if hostilities resumed. Lying in shallow, silty water, obscured by weeds and winter ice, the bones of these ships from the War of 1812 would be visited by antiquarians, hard-hat divers, "frogmen," and marine archaeologists.

"Indefatigable Zeal and Exertions"

At the outbreak of the War of 1812, Britain's naval force on the Great Lakes was the Provincial Marine, an insti-

Figure 7.1. *Detail from "Plan of Kingston and It's [sic] Vicinity," June 1816. The map shows, from left to right, the town of Kingston, the mouth of the Cataraqui River forming Kingston Harbor, Point Frederick, Navy Bay, Point Henry, and Hamilton Cove. (United Kingdom Hydrographic Office, B718.)*

tution loosely modeled upon the Royal Navy but administered by the Quartermaster General's Department of the British Army. The Provincial Marine's Lake Ontario dockyard had been established in 1789 at Kingston, a small commercial and military center strategically situated where eastern Lake Ontario meets the headwaters of the upper St. Lawrence River. The yard was situated on a peninsula called Point Frederick, separated from Kingston to the west by the mouth of the Cataraqui River. It was flanked to the east by Navy Bay, which provided an anchorage exposed to the prevailing southwest winds (fig. 7.1). The town, dockyard, and anchorage were overlooked by the high ground of Point Henry to the east. All of this was surrounded by a sparsely populated wilderness penetrated by few roads.

During the first year of the war, the Provincial Marine demonstrated a singular lack of effectiveness due to inexperienced officers and inadequate crews. The switch to Royal Navy command of the squadron, which began over the winter of 1812–13, resulted in a radical change in the way the naval war was fought, as well as a dramatic increase in the size and firepower of vessels launched at Kingston. Comm. Sir James Lucas Yeo and the first contingent of Royal Navy officers and sailors took charge of the lake squadrons in May 1813, inheriting a Lake Ontario force that consisted of the sloops of war *Wolfe* and *Royal George,* the brig *Earl of Moira,* the armed schooners *Prince Regent* and *Gover-*

nor Simcoe, and the unfinished brig *Lord Melville.* Built of unseasoned timber and armed with carronades mounted on flush decks, these small, shoal-drafted vessels could maneuver in shallow, confined waters but were by some accounts dull and leewardly sailers.

Not long after his arrival, Commodore Yeo sought the approval of his military superior, Lt. Gen. Sir George Prevost, Commander-in-Chief of British forces in North America, to build a frigate at Kingston. The need for a "large-class" vessel was the result of two events: the launch of the new US corvette *General Pike* and the loss of the unfinished sloop of war *Sir Isaac Brock,* burned on the stocks at York by the Americans in April 1813.[2]

Local conditions also influenced Yeo's plan to improve his squadron. Despite its relatively small size, Lake Ontario imposed no limitations on the size of vessel Yeo could build; confined and shallow channels such as the upper St. Lawrence River could always be navigated by the squadron's smaller vessels. More to the point, Navy Bay, with 18 to 24 feet (5.5 to 7.3 m) of water at the end of the launching slips, was deep enough for launching large warships. The advantage of building lake vessels with a deeper draft for better sailing to windward had been noted almost three decades earlier in a report dating to 1788:

Vessels sailing on these waters being seldom for any length of time out of sight of land; the navigation must be considered chiefly as pilotage. . . . Gales of wind or squalls rise suddenly upon the lakes, and from the confined state of the waters, or want of sea room (as it is called), vessels may in some degree be considered as upon a lee shore, and this seems to point out the necessity for their being built on such a construction as will best enable them to work to windward.[3]

Yeo knew that any new warships he built could be given sharp, V-shaped hulls for speed and better windward performance, as voluminous holds were not required for stowing provisions and water. Although Lake Ontario can be treacherous, particularly at the end of the navigation season, its relatively short fetch does not generate the mountainous waves of the open ocean. During the war, the Royal Navy learned that ships could be more heavily gunned than normal, given the "sea" conditions: "The port of Kingston and the general navigation upon Lake Ontario, are free for Ships of any size. . . . Ships being on the lake in the Summer only when little but fine weather is expected should mount the heaviest guns."[4]

There were two important obstacles to Yeo's expansion of the Lake Ontario squadron. The first was that apart from timber, all shipbuilding materiel, ordnance, and supplies had to be shipped up the St. Lawrence River from Quebec, Montreal, and Halifax; a navy captain later commented, "Kingston is too much in its Infancy to make any thing of the kind which was usually supplied by the Americans previous to the War."[5] From Montreal, the limit of seagoing navigation, stores were loaded aboard flotillas of 20- to 30-foot-long (6 to 9 m) flat-bottomed bateaux for the arduous 180-mile (290 km) journey up the St. Lawrence. After the close of navigation in December, stores had to be hauled on sleighs over snow-covered roads.

The second obstacle was an acute shortage of shipwrights and artificers in Upper Canada that persisted throughout 1813 and 1814. The nearest port where they could be found in any number was Quebec, from where gangs of mostly French Canadian artificers were contracted to work at Kingston. This skilled but sometimes divided workforce would build Yeo's new ships, but not without intermittent strikes and work stoppages. The task of overcoming these obstacles, regulating the dockyard, supervising the shipbuilding, and making supply requisitions fell to Cmdr. Richard

O'Conor, whom Yeo appointed acting commissioner. The dockyard's master builder was George Record, also a newcomer to Kingston. He had come from Quebec in February 1813 and received his appointment in March during the construction of *Wolfe* (later *Montreal*).[6]

Yeo's dream of a new frigate began to take shape in late May 1813, but it would not be realized until the following spring. He wanted ship-rigged vessels mounting enough heavy guns to overwhelm Chauncey's *General Pike,* so he requested that a master shipwright and men be sent to Kingston to lay down a new frigate with a length on deck of 136 feet (41.45 m).[7] In June Prevost asked Quebec shipbuilder John Goudie to bring four hundred artificers to work at the Kingston dockyard. Goudie's first one hundred men arrived at the dockyard by the end of the month but were put to work on other tasks, such as building gunboats, barracks, and stores and fitting-out the new brig *Lord Melville*.[8]

Late in July, when Yeo learned that the US Navy had laid down yet another vessel at Sackets Harbor, he pressed Prevost to increase the proposed frigate to 160 feet (48.76 m) on deck.[9] Prevost approved the plan, and O'Conor ordered the keel for *Ship No. 1* (later *Prince Regent*) laid down by Goudie's men. Requisitions for ordnance and equipment were immediately dispatched.[10] This frigate was designed by Patrick Fleming, a master shipbuilder who had come as one of several foremen from Quebec with Goudie's first gang; Goudie soon returned to Quebec, and under the supervision of Fleming the work at Kingston progressed when material could be procured.[11]

While Yeo's squadron was on the lake in September 1813 and O'Conor was absent from the yard, work on a brig intended to serve as either a transport or warship was initiated by Record. Before the building got started, however, two gangs of artificers from Quebec struck and only resumed work after receiving promises of pay advances and better living conditions. The second new vessel (first called *Ship No. 2,* then *Vittoria,* and finally *Princess Charlotte*) had its keel laid down, and by late September shipwrights were busy squaring timbers for the building effort.[12] The objective was to complete both ships by the following spring; the monumental task of getting their guns and equipment to Kingston would require most of the winter.

In the second week of October, one gang of fifty-two shipwrights and choppers supervised by Fleming was building *Ship No. 1.* They had the "Floors and frames in hand Stem and Stern up & half the floor timbers laid," while thirty sawyers were cutting plank for the ship. The forty-five shipwrights, choppers, and caulkers under Record, who had been working on the brig *Ship No. 2,* were temporarily diverted to building barracks and a floating battery.[13] While at Kingston in early October, Capt. Augustus Vere Drury of the troopship *Dover* noted that although the keel of *Ship No. 1* had been laid in July, little progress had been made:

> the Timber for this vessel was of Oak and not Fir which might be more easily worked, and as durability was not the present Object, she might have been ready for launching in August provided those Artificers who were at work on the Barracks, had been placed upon her, and Fir substituted for Oak. I observed that much time and labour was thrown away by cutting crooked Timber out of straight, when Timber for the purpose grew about seven Miles from the spot.

The decision to build in oak was probably a result of the large stocks of unseasoned oak on hand in the yard. Drury concurred with Yeo's desire for large warships, reasoning that it was "more preferable to build vessels upon the same scale as at home, which would give stability and prevent the necessity of bearing up for a port in a gale by reason of their being leewardly."[14]

Unable to defeat Chauncey in 1813, Yeo requested in October that *Ship No. 2* be enlarged to a frigate with a keel length of 110 feet (33.52 m). In correspondence to Prevost, he argued that "The Enemy I have no doubt (if they do not succeed in their designs on Upper Canada this year) will build another ship capable of carrying heavy metal," adding that "If they do, I have only to assure your Excellency that had I any number of Brigs they would not be the smallest service against ships mounting such metal."[15] Prevost approved the conversion of the brig into a George Record–designed frigate and urged that progress on both ships be made with "all possible dispatch."[16]

The yard's workforce, however, was now in complete disarray. Dissatisfied with living conditions at Kingston and aware of their importance in the naval race, the artificers demanded exorbitant wages. Others simply broke their contracts and returned to Quebec.[17] Workers were also at odds with each other because they had been contracted on different pay scales: "Mr. Goudies Men will not attend to Mr. Record, and

Mr. Records Men will not work without the same Pay Mr. Goudies have," Yeo complained, "I sincerely wish any effort or persuasion of mine could cause a proper exertion to be made at our Dock Yard, or that I could hold out any hope of the new Ships, being ready early in the Spring."[18] To control costs and steady the workforce, Yeo and O'Conor attempted to complete each ship by contract. They recommended that Goudie (still in Quebec) be contracted for the construction rather than superintendence of *Ship No. 1,* since "he is not to be relied on unless bound down by an agreement."[19] Record and a partner entered into a contract to build *Ship No. 2* at £10 per ton. They were to privately contract for labor and submit timely requisitions to the navy for materiel and timber. *Ship No. 2* was to be completed by May 1, 1814 under penalty of £1000.[20]

The new contractual arrangement for *Ship No. 2* eased labor troubles. O'Conor's first weekly report for November 1813 noted that the building "goes on very satisfactory, and gives me great hopes of executing by the ensuing spring the important services required."[21] By the second half of November the framing of *Ship No. 1* was nearly completed, and *Ship No. 2* would be framed by the end of the month. A spirit of competition between the two gangs developed, much to the satisfaction of O'Conor.[22] Goudie was still absent from the yard, however, and the men who had come to Kingston with him considered themselves "neglected, foresaken, and ill treated" as construction proceeded without his assistance.[23] It is probable that Fleming and the other master shipbuilders who had come to the yard in July 1813 as foremen supervised assembly of *Ship No. 1* until its completion, for the government ultimately abandoned its attempt to enter into a contract with Goudie.

By the time *Ship No. 1* was named *Prince Regent* in mid-December, its keelson had been bolted down, the planking was in hand, and the gun deck beams had been dressed and scarfed. *Princess Charlotte,* formerly *Vittoria* and *Ship No. 2,* was mostly timbered and partially planked.[24] The tone of Commissioner O'Conor's reports to headquarters continued to improve as the frigates took shape:

> The Prince Regent, promises to be, as fine, and formidable a Frigate, as any, sailing on the Atlantic. The Princess Charlotte (late Vittoria) has likewise every appearance of being a most desirable vessel,

in size equal to our small frigates, but in force superior from the heavy metal she is intended to carry.[25]

Over the winter, everything necessary to arm and fit out the frigates was stripped and scrounged from Royal Navy ships at Quebec, principally from the frig-ate *Æolus* and ship sloop *Indian*.[26]

By early February 1814, *Prince Regent* was planked and ready for caulking, the deck beams were being in-stalled, and the masts and spars were one-third com-plete. *Princess Charlotte* was still being planked and deck beams were ready to go into the hull.[27] The num-ber of artificers at the dockyard frequently exceeded three hundred, and the crews of the squadron were employed picking oakum, making wads and paint, and fitting sails and gun tackle. Seamen also provided labor in the yard and rigging house, and others helped transport supplies.[28]

Prince Regent and *Princess Charlotte* were nearing completion in March when word of three new US ves-sels on the stocks at Sackets Harbor prompted the start of another ship "of far greater force than any the Enemy can launch at Sacketts Harbour . . . of a descrip-tion to look down all opposition." Designed by William Bell, formerly the master shipwright of the dockyard at Amherstburg, Lake Erie, *Ship No. 3* was originally conceived as a heavy frigate but would rise from the stocks as a three-decker. In April, O'Conor reported the progress on this latest entry in the shipbuilding race: "Moulds made, Keel laid, stern and stem newly fin-ished, dead wood made, four frames made, and timber sided for ten frames." At this time Yeo received word that the Admiralty had given him a command indepen-dent of Prevost. He was also informed that the frames for two ships and two brigs were being shipped to him from Chatham in England. This scheme met with im-mediate objections from Kingston, for it threatened to interfere with shipments of vital material for *Ship No. 3* and thereby delay the launch scheduled for late sum-mer. Furthermore, there were barely enough stocks of timber on hand and artificers to complete the current work. These objections would arrive at the Admiralty long after the frames left England.[29]

The good news was that the frames were accompa-nied by enough sailors to man the four vessels and a large civil establishment party. The latter, over 100 men strong, was under the direction of Commissioner Sir Robert Hall and included a naval storekeeper, clerks, shipwrights, smiths, and sailmakers. Two quartermen of the shipwrights at Chatham, Thomas Strickland and Robert Moore, had been selected to serve as master shipwright and master attendant in Canada, no doubt because they had worked at Chatham to prepare the frames.[30]

"A Reasonable Prospect of Success"
As the ice was breaking up in Kingston harbor in early April, the crews of *Prince Regent* and *Princess Charlotte* were scraping and painting the hulls of their new frig-ates. The day before their launch, Yeo considered his options against the United States for the coming sea-son: "We never have been so confident to engage them with a reasonable prospect of success as at present,— For, altho' the enemy have a greater number of guns of heavy calibre—but, my having two ships of such effec-tive strength as the Prince Regent & Princess Charlotte closely to support each other may give me an advan-tage in the early part of an action."[31] He believed he could bring Chauncey to a "decisive engagement," but if the US squadron was too strong, he would retire to Kingston until the completion of *Ship No. 3*.

Launched on April 14, 1814, almost one year after Yeo first proposed constructing a large warship, the frigates were immediately hauled alongside the wharves on the west side of Navy Bay. All hands went to work removing the launching cradles, stowing pig iron and shingle ballast, stepping and rigging masts, sending up yards, and loading ordnance and supplies. Master Attendant Michael Spratt (who replaced Robert Moore when he became foreman of the shipwrights) later recollected that a shortage of cast iron for ballast necessitated greater reliance on bulky stone. This no doubt was a problem given the limited hold space and top-heaviness inherent in the frigates' sharp, V-shaped hulls (figs. 7.2 and 7.3): "The large ships had a propor-tion of cast Iron, old guns, shot, and stones. . . . The difficulties that occurred in procuring substitute for cast Iron ballast was, that . . . shingle (composed of lime stone) . . . filled their holds so much that little or no room was left for provisions or stores except on the Decks."[32]

Despite a shortage of seamen to man his warships, Yeo armed his flagship *Prince Regent* with 58 guns, in-cluding 28 long 24 pounders on the gun deck and 2 long 24 pounders, 20 32-pounder carronades, and 8 mas-

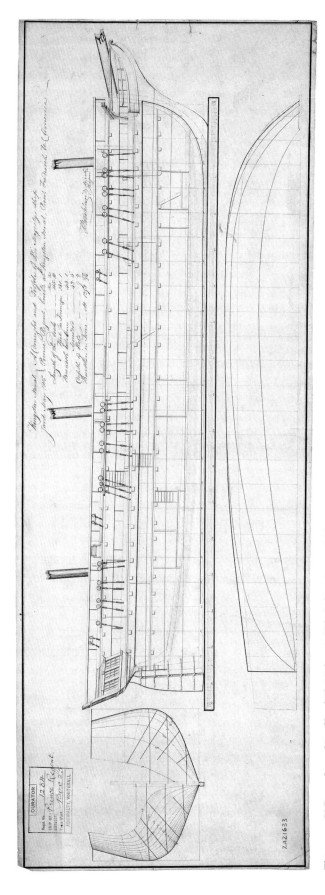

Figure 7.2. "A Draught and Profile of His Majesty's Ship Prince Regent." These contemporary plans were prepared by Thomas Strickland in May 1815. (Courtesy of National Maritime Museum, Greenwich, U.K., ZAZ1633.)

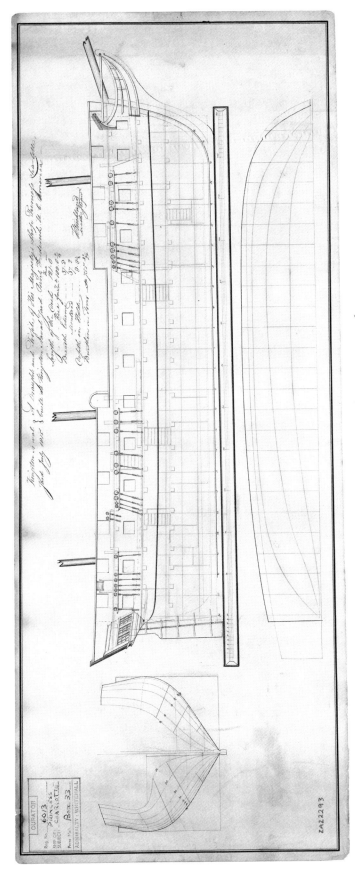

Figure 7.3. "A Draught and Profile of His Majesty's Ship Princess Charlotte." These contemporary plans were prepared by Thomas Strickland in May 1815. (Courtesy of National Maritime Museum, Greenwich, U.K., ZAZ2293.)

sive 68-pounder carronades on its flush spar deck (appendix A). Henry Kent, the first lieutenant of *Princess Charlotte,* wrote that "the Regent is about eight feet longer than our 38-gun frigates, having fifteen ports on each side of her main-deck, and guns on her gangways." The frigate had a complement of 550 men. *Princess Charlotte* was to have 40 guns, including 24 long 24 pounders on the gun deck, ten 32-pounder carronades on the quarterdeck, and six 32-pounder carronades on the forecastle. Kent added that his ship was "about the length of a 32-gun frigate, but 18 inches (45 cm) more beam, pierced for thirteen ports on her main deck." This frigate had a complement of 330 men.[33] Although contemporary documents clearly refer to *Princess Charlotte* as having a quarterdeck and forecastle, the vessel appears to have had a flush spar deck but with neither guns nor bulwarks in the waist, a precaution against the hull being overgunned, overstrained, and unsteady (fig. 7.3).

Yeo's squadron sailed on May 4, vastly improved by the addition of the two heavy frigates. Despite his desire for a decisive engagement, US Navy Comm. Chauncey did not venture out upon the lake and Yeo's summer cruise was limited to a raid on Oswego, New York, and a blockade of Sackets Harbor, which he maintained until June 6 (plate 7b). Finishing *Ship No. 3* became Yeo's chief concern at this time. Chauncey, for his part, completed preparation of his squadron and sailed on August 1 with four new warships: the brigs *Jefferson* and *Jones,* with 20 guns each, and the frigates *Mohawk* and *Superior,* with 42 and 58 guns, respectively. Temporarily outgunned, Yeo kept his ships in Kingston to await the completion of *Ship No. 3.*[34]

In earlier reports to the Admiralty, Yeo stressed the difficulties of shipbuilding under primitive frontier conditions: "It would be endless to detail the substitutes used and the difficulties to be overcome in constructing vessels of force in a country so new and deficient of materials."[35] Throughout the summer, every article needed to equip *Ship No. 3* was taken from warships laid up at Quebec.[36] Yeo would implore the captain of the 74-gun *Centaur* for his long 32 pounders: "I have written for Your lower Deck Guns which I hope to God You will be able to spare me, or otherwise all my exertions will be lost in having built a three Decker."[37]

The monumental difficulty of shipping heavy ordnance and materiel up the St. Lawrence River was not the only factor that delayed the launch of the three-decker. The work stalled at the end of May when many of the laborers, freed from their contracts by the launch of *Prince Regent* and *Princess Charlotte,* left Kingston and returned to Lower Canada.[38] Relief was on the way, however. Three shipbuilders who had worked at Kingston since 1813 were contracted to assist with *Ship No. 3,* and they in turn recruited seventy-five shipwrights at Quebec.[39] The first party of artificers sent out from England under Sir Robert Hall arrived at the lake on June 23.[40] Finally, all available hands at Kingston were called to assist. A lieutenant of the British Army's 104th Regiment recorded in his diary, "The *whole* of our regiment ordered to work at the new Line-of-battle Ship, 104 Guns—in compliment to our number of course she sh[oul]d be called the 104th—a pleasant job for Soldiers."[41] After the squadron returned to Kingston in the last week of June, the ships' crews were also put to work on *Ship No. 3.*[42]

Huge quantities of unseasoned timber were drawn to Kingston by settlers and lumbermen. The yard's records show that *Ship No. 3* was mostly composed of oak, supplemented with elm for frames and white and red pine for planking. Oak, elm, and spruce knees were particularly in demand.[43]

At the end of August, with the launch of *Ship No. 3* approaching, the United States intercepted letters from shipwrights at Kingston. Chauncey, writing from *Superior* while blockading Kingston, reported to the navy secretary that:

> These letters state her to be longer than the Nelson of 120 guns, that she is to have three complete decks with 34 guns on each deck but that she is slight built. They express apprehension for her safety in launching as they have no means of laying her ways below the water so that when she tips she will be water borne and it is thought her great weight may break her in two, this is also the opinion of Mr. Eckford.[44]

These fears might have had more to do with the absence of suitable ways than any hull weakness, and in any event the three-decker, named *St. Lawrence,* was successfully launched on September 10. The ship was armed with 34 long 32 pounders on the gun deck, 34 long 24 pounders on the middle deck, and 34 carronades, 32 pounders, on the flush spar deck, a total of 102 guns (fig. 7.4 and appendix A). Following a month-long

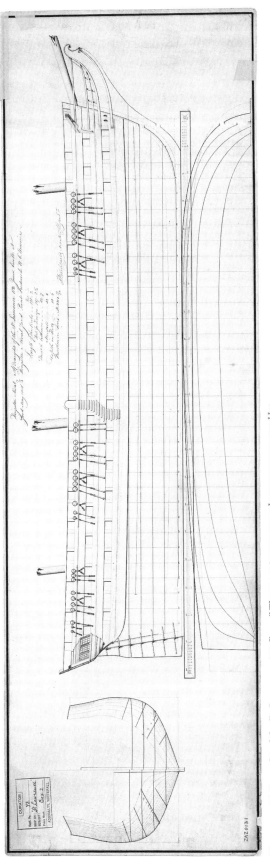

Figure 7.4. "A Draught of the St. Lawrence 112 Guns." These contemporary plans were prepared by Thomas Strickland in May 1815. (Courtesy of National Maritime Museum, Greenwich, U.K., ZAZ0131.)

period of fitting out, *St. Lawrence* made its maiden voyage on October 16, delivering supplies to troops on the Niagara Peninsula. Yeo thought his new flagship "very superior" to any other vessel on the lake, and in terms of sheer firepower he was right; the Royal Navy would control the lake for the remainder of 1814.[45]

Yeo believed Chauncey would again attempt to outbuild him in 1815, so construction continued under the supervision of Commissioner Sir Robert Hall. The workforce was bolstered by the arrival of over two hundred artificers from Portsmouth and Chatham. The single ship to be assembled from the frames shipped from England, the frigate *Psyche* of 54 guns, was launched on December 25, only five weeks after the keel was laid.[46] The Treaty of Ghent was signed the day before *Psyche*'s launch. Nevertheless, news of it would not reach Yeo for two months, and work continued unabated during that time. Two more three-deckers (*New Ship No. 1* and *New Ship No. 2,* later *Wolfe* and *Canada*) were laid down, the latter contracted to John Goudie. They were well advanced when Yeo received a copy of the Treaty of Ghent from Chauncey on February 25, 1815. With the cessation of hostilities, Yeo was recalled to England, ending his eventful two-year association with the lake.[47]

"As Great Bulk as Any on the Ocean": Measuring the Lake Warships

Yeo's replacement as commodore, Sir Edward Campbell Rich Owen, arrived at Kingston in March to find the squadron partially dismantled and *Psyche* being fitted for service. The first steps toward a peace establishment had already been made, since Goudie's contract for *New Ship No. 2* was cancelled and the Canadian shipwrights discharged.[48] Commodore Owen studied the state of the Royal Navy on the lakes and sent voluminous reports to England, which provide interesting glimpses on how he and his contemporaries viewed the naval squadron on Lake Ontario.

Comparing the construction of the British and US ships, Owen noted that the latter "kept a greater quantity of timber in their ships, which gives them greater strength, and their people better shelter, whilst it diminishes in some degree the labour of the building; for the American Artificers fashion their timbers &c principally with the Axe."[49] Joseph Bouchette, Surveyor General of Lower Canada, who served in the Provincial Marine in the 1790s, compared the fabric of the British ships favorably against the US ships but also identified differences in their modes of construction:

> The Americans build their ships much faster than we do on our side, and for this reason, strength is the chief object with them, and if that be obtained they care but little about beauty of model or elegance of finishing; in fact, they receive no other polish than what is given them by the axe and the adze. On the other hand, we employ as much time upon ours as we should in the European dock-yards: they are undoubtedly as strong as the Americans, they are handsomer and much better finished, but they are far more expensive, and will not endure a longer period of service.[50]

Neither of the squadrons would last longer than the other, Bouchette noted, because both were built of un-seasoned timber; Owen predicted that "there can be little doubt that all the ships which have been run up by both parties in such haste will be attacked by the Dry rot."[51]

Over a three-month period in 1815, Thomas Strickland surveyed the squadron and drafted plans of each of the larger warships to send to England. He reported the hulls of *St. Lawrence* and *Prince Regent* "Sound & Serviceable" but regarded the hull of *Princess Charlotte* as "Perfectly sound, but being put together very bad and not sufficient fastening occasions weakness." Recommended repairs included refastening the knees and shelf pieces to the deck beams and adding knees and carlings to the quarterdeck, waist, and forecastle.[52] A later inspection revealed the forecastle and quarter-decks lacked carlings and ledges and that "Chocks & Iron Knees to Shelf Pieces" were required for the gun deck since they were "Not Strong enough to Support the weight of the Guns."[53]

Further insights into the Kingston-built ships can be gleaned from a few surviving sailing qualities reports required of each ship's captain by the *Additional Regulations and Instructions 1813*. Capt. Henry Thomas Davies of *Prince Regent* considered his ship "as weatherly as any except the Psyche" and "Equal to the St. Lawrence on all points & superior to every other ship on the Lake before the wind but inferior to the Psyche by the wind." Despite these generally favorable sailing qualities, Davies considered that the frigate was "By no means a strong built ship And I think shews great signs of weakness" (appendix B).

Two of the squadron's three frigates were renamed by the Admiralty in England at this time to avoid duplication of names already in the *List of the Navy*. In 1814 Yeo was instructed to change *Prince Regent*'s name to *Kingston* and *Princess Charlotte*'s name to *Burlington*. Due to the loss of outgoing mail destined for Kingston in January and February of 1815, it took nearly two years for the Admiralty's orders to reach Canada, and it was not until October 1816 that the renaming actually occurred in the yard books.

In considering the design, construction, and armament of the three large ships built at Kingston in 1814, it is worth examining how they fit within the wider context of the Royal Navy and how they compared to their opposite numbers in the US squadron. The Admiralty's original ratings of the ships, entered into the *List of the Navy* in 1814, must have been based on incomplete information, for they greatly underestimated their actual strength (*Kingston* was rated as a 28-gun sixth rate, *Burlington* as a 24-gun sixth rate, and *St. Lawrence* as a 98-gun second rate). In 1816 the ships were rated at Kingston based upon the *New Naval Instructions of 1806*, and these were more appropriate to the armament and crew (appendix A). In arriving at these ratings, Owen observed that "the ships upon the Lake have been Rated for more men, proportionately to other ships of the same size in His Majesty's Service in consequence of the greater weight of metal which they carry."[54]

The practice at Kingston was to mount unusually heavy long gun batteries on the gun decks (as well as the middle deck in the case of the *St. Lawrence*) and to place batteries composed almost exclusively of 32-pounder carronades on the spar decks. In arming his frigates in this manner, Yeo mirrored the Royal Navy's trend of giving seagoing frigates increasingly heavy guns, in particular the 24-pounder frigates hastily built to meet the threat posed by their spar-decked American opponents. Robert Malcomson and Robert Gardiner have identified close similarities between the form and armament of the 56-gun *Kingston* and the Royal Navy's 24-pounder, 60-gun fourth rate frigates *Newcastle* and *Leander*, hastily launched in 1813. Although their armament was similar to *Kingston*'s, their hulls did not possess a V-shaped bottom and they had a narrower breadth.[55]

The closest US vessel to *Kingston* on Lake Ontario was *Superior* of 58 guns, which was 180 feet (54.86 m) between perpendiculars and, as the British were painfully aware, carried heavier guns: 30 long 32 pounders on the gun deck and 26 42-pounder carronades and 2 long 24 pounders on the upper deck, which gave a broadside weight of 1048 pounds (475.4 kg) versus 952 pounds (431.8 kg) for *Kingston*.[56] Owen observed that while the United States built its ships nominally of the same class, it gave them greater armament once the intended firepower of British ships on the stocks was known. They could accomplish this, according to Owen, due to their much shorter supply lines: "The Americans have been thus enabled to proportion their force upon this Lake to ours in such a manner as that each ship should be superior to her opponent in our squadron."[57]

Like *Kingston*, *Burlington* (ex–*Princess Charlotte*) had a firepower far greater than its initial Admiralty rating would suggest. O'Conor stated it was "in size equal to our small frigates, but in force superior from the heavy metal she is intended to carry." *Burlington* was about the length of the US brigs *Jefferson* and *Jones* but had a greater depth of hold and two gun decks. Its closest US rival in terms of armament was *Mohawk* of 42 guns, which was 155 feet (47.24 m) long between perpendiculars and 1200 tons. Although *Burlington* was considerably smaller in length and tonnage, it carried an armament very close to the US frigate's 26 long 24 pounders and 16 32-pounder carronades, and the two ships had comparable broadsides (568 pounds [257.6 kg] for *Mohawk* versus 544 pounds [246.7 kg] for *Burlington*).[58]

St. Lawrence was also a hybrid design, even more difficult to pigeonhole into traditional Royal Navy ship categories. Following his arrival at Kingston, Commodore Owen remarked that *St. Lawrence* and the two three-decker ships on the stocks had "as great bulk as any on the Ocean."[59] Yeo compared *St. Lawrence* with the 120-gun *Caledonia,* and the English shipwrights whose letters were intercepted by Chauncey compared it to *Nelson* of 120 guns.[60] American design influence is suggested by one contemporary observer, who stated that "The St. Lawrence is built in the American style, without any poop deck."[61] *St. Lawrence* was in fact closest in dimensions with the 100- to 110-gun first rates *Ville de Paris* and *Hibernia*.[62] Robert Malcomson has shown that while it was slightly smaller in size than the 120-gun first rates, *St. Lawrence* carried a heavier broadside. In contrast to the seagoing three-deckers, *St. Lawrence* had much finer lines, with a

sharper V-shaped midship deadrise (versus flat midship floors), a flush spar deck without a forecastle or quarterdeck, and a modest stern gallery that provided only one deck with lighted officer accommodations.[63]

Deck plans, profiles, and a midship section prepared by Strickland in 1815 illustrate some of the assembly techniques used in the construction of *St. Lawrence* (figs. 7.4 and 7.5).[64] The floors were formed from two straight lengths of timber attached at their heels by a squared vertical scarf secured with four bolts. This mode of fashioning floors was undoubtedly faster and more economical than seeking out grown timber for one-piece floors, but it also resulted in frames that were potentially weaker along their centerline. The joints between the floors and futtocks were reinforced by chocks, and the floor head line was overlain by four thick footwales. Later in the construction sequence, after the installation of the keelson and ceiling, the lower hull was strengthened by the addition of eleven large floor riders.

The Strickland plans show that few knees were fitted, probably due to the ship's accelerated construction and a shortage of grown knees. The plans instead exhibit internal design features akin to the methods being devised in Britain's shipyards to overcome a lack of grown knees, chiefly the use of short, straight-grained filler pieces and many iron bolts.[65] By the early nineteenth century, many shipyards, especially European yards, employed iron straps and knees as substitutes for traditional wooden knees and riders, but iron reinforcements appear to have been minimal in *St. Lawrence,* probably due to a general shortage of iron at Kingston in 1814. A small iron strap securing the head of the stern knee to a carling can be seen in the longitudinal profile, but no other iron reinforcing is evident.

The midship section shows that a great deal of care was taken to secure the deck beams to the hull framing in proportion to the weight of ordnance carried on each deck (see fig. 7.5). The lower gun deck beams supported the immense 32-pounder long guns and thus were heavily fastened by many iron bolts. The beams were supported below by a three-strake clamp and a longitudinal shelf that was through-bolted to the uppermost clamp and tenoned to the undersides of the beams. The clamps and shelf formed, in effect, a rudimentary L-shaped hanging knee running the entire length of the hull. The spaces between beam ends each contained three short, straight pieces of timber that

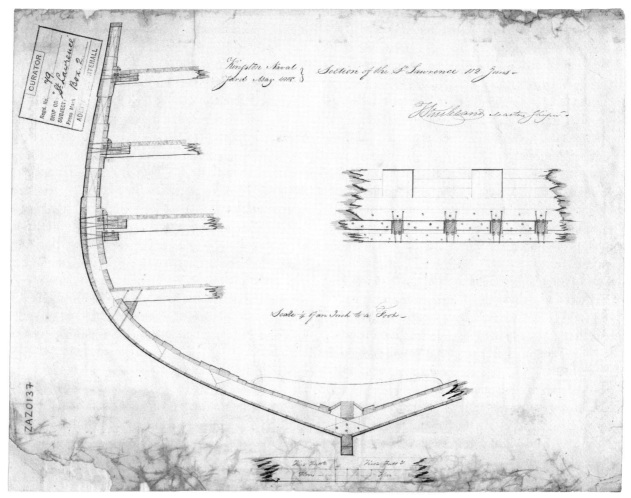

Figure 7.5. *"Section of the St. Lawrence 112 Guns."* *This section was prepared by Thomas Strickland in May 1815. (Courtesy of National Maritime Museum, Greenwich, U.K., ZAZ0137, Reg. No. 79.)*

functioned like lodging knees to prevent the beams from shifting horizontally. Finally, a large waterway was through-bolted to the beams and shelf and further secured to each beam with tenons. The arrangement was unconventional but substantial. The middle and upper deck beams were secured in a similar manner but with only a single clamp, no shelf, and no tenons. The orlop deck had a single clamp reinforced with a triangular chock under each beam, as well as a single lodging knee positioned between each beam.

Were these design features conceived locally, or were they introduced by the shipwrights from Chatham? The frames, at least, seem to have been the work of local shipwrights, including William Bell (who initiated the work), since Thomas Strickland, Robert Moore, and the rest of the English shipwrights arrived at Kingston in late June 1814, when the framework of

St. Lawrence was already well advanced. Both Bell and George Record left the lake in July 1814 for England, two months before the launch of *St. Lawrence,* and the senior English shipwrights were therefore left to superintend the construction at a time when the deck beams would have been installed.

To what extent did the lessons learned during the building and sailing of *St. Lawrence* influence the designs of the three-deckers prepared by Strickland in late 1814? Although modeled after *St. Lawrence,* *Wolfe* and *Canada* were to be slightly smaller but more heavily armed, with 118 guns, in a manner that Charles P. Stacey has termed "typical of the determination of the Ontario builders to pile on every weapon the ships could carry."[66] The new three-deckers were given a slightly fuller midship body and a flatter bottom, as well as a quarterdeck, thereby providing additional stowage space in the hold and two decks of lighted officer accommodation; it is possible that these features corrected perceived deficiencies in *St. Lawrence*.[67]

"Chiefly in a Half-Sunken State": The Squadron in Ordinary, 1815–34

When Master Shipwright Thomas Strickland completed his survey of the squadron in July 1815, *St. Lawrence, Kingston,* and *Burlington* were swinging at their moorings in Navy Bay and their top masts had been removed. A major reduction to the establishment took effect in October, by which time the entire squadron had been laid up along the shore around the new sheer and careening wharves, and almost all were housed over (figs. 7.6 and 7.7).[68] Comm. Edward Owen was reassigned to command *Royal Sovereign* and left for England in November 1815 to be replaced by his brother Capt. William Fitz William Owen. Captain Owen resigned shortly after his appointment to concentrate on surveying duties, so in September 1816 Commissioner Robert Hall took command. Although it was laid up and housed over, *Kingston* remained in commission and served both as Hall's headquarters and a barracks; all of the other vessels, including *St. Lawrence* and *Burlington,* were out of commission.[69] Following the signing of the Rush-Bagot Agreement in April 1817, Hall received orders from the Admiralty to place the squadron in ordinary. Thereafter only a small establishment of naval personnel remained to maintain the ships and the yard.[70]

Sir Robert Hall died in 1818, and the following year his replacement, Capt. Robert Barrie, took over as acting commissioner. In briefing Barrie on his new assignment, the Navy Board instructed him to maintain the ships before they became unserviceable but without attracting the attention of the United States.[71] A survey of the ships in 1819 revealed dry rot in all of them, despite the fact that they had been housed over and that every effort had been made to keep them dry and well ventilated. All of the ships leaked, and the thirty seamen of the establishment spent much of their time pumping.[72] Barrie asked the Navy Board for the establishment to be increased to sixty or seventy seamen, but the board refused, asserting that "no increase in the number of men will tend to preserve the ships laying in ordinary there considering that they were built of green materials of a bad quality."[73] Two Navy Board surveyors sent to inspect the vessels in July 1820 also painted a bleak picture: extensive dry rot was found in most of the vessels, including *St. Lawrence, Kingston,* and *Burlington.* The board favored gradual rebuilds; in the coming years, *Psyche, Niagara, Star,* and *Netley* were hauled out, never to return to the water.[74] Through the 1820s, the estimates for the naval force on the Great Lakes steadily diminished despite the objections of Barrie. A Royal Navy lieutenant who visited the squadron in 1826 reported that the warships were "chiefly in a half-sunken state."[75]

By 1828, *Kingston* and *Burlington,* as well as another old veteran, *Montreal* (ex-*Wolfe*), had been moved from the berths they had occupied since 1815 to a position abreast of the mast pond (plate 8a). Shipwright Thomas Mossington, who had served at Kingston during the war, revisited the yard in 1830 and remarked that the "place now looks a desert, as it respects business" and observed that *St. Lawrence* was "shored up along side the wharf, but much broke at the Miz. chains, I apprehend they will never be able to move her, except by breaking her up where she lies."[76]

In 1831 the Admiralty declined to make any further expenditures and ordered *St. Lawrence, Kingston,* and *Burlington* to be broken up.[77] Barrie recommended auctioning off the vessels as a more economical way to clear the yard.[78] The Navy Board approved, and an advertisement for the sale appeared in the *Kingston Gazette* in November 1831, offering *St. Lawrence, Kingston, Burlington,* and *Montreal* "as they now lay on the shore off the King's Dock Yard at Kingston." Each hull was to be sold separately and removed at the expense of the purchaser.[79]

The auction resulted only in the sale of *St. Lawrence,* which was purchased for £25 by Robert Drummond, a Kingston shipbuilder and brewer. The vessels that did not sell were to be broken up and the iron removed as opportunities offered.[80] The 1833 *List of the Navy* records that *Kingston* was "Broken up November 1832 or Jany. 1833" and "Sold £30.0.0." *Burlington* is recorded in a similar fashion as "Supposed to be taken to pieces Jany. 1833" and "Sold £21."[81] It is not known exactly when or to whom *Kingston* and *Burlington* were sold, but in any event, for the time being, they remained in Navy Bay. *St. Lawrence,* however, was stripped down to the water's edge, and in January 1833 Drummond's new side-wheel steamer *Rideau* pumped out the hull with the help of Barrie's men. Described by the *Kingston Gazette* as an "immense uncouth Ark,"

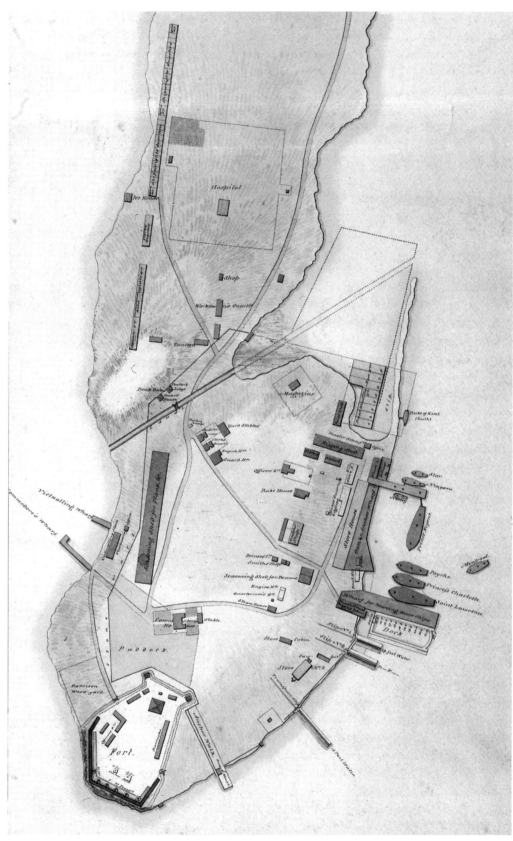

Figure 7.6. *"Plan of Point Frederick with the Proposed Alterations for the Dock-Yard Establishment"*
from "Plan of Kingston and Its Vicinity," June 1816. (United Kingdom Hydrographic Office, B718.)

Figure 7.7. *The Royal Navy dockyard at Kingston from atop Point Henry. Prepared by Hugh Irvine circa 1815–16, this view shows the squadron laid up as in Figure 7.6. The ship under sail at the left may be* Montreal. *(Library and Archives Canada, C-2041.)*

St. Lawrence was towed out of Navy Bay to the site of Drummond's brewery on the outskirts of Kingston. Immediately afterwards a storm blew the hulk aground, where Drummond used it as a wharf.[82]

Clearing the dockyard of stores and old hulls was one of Barrie's last duties before the Admiralty ordered the place closed in 1834. When he and his men departed Kingston, they left behind *Psyche, Star, Niagara, Netley,* and ten gunboats, all of them in frame on slips. The unfinished three-deckers *Wolfe* and *Canada* had been broken up on the stocks. The transport *Charwell* (launched in 1816 as *Beckwith*) and a schooner named *Brock* were reportedly hauled aground and condemned. *Kingston, Burlington,* and *Montreal* were still aground in Navy Bay, their housings totally dilapidated. The only serviceable vessels were two small schooners, *Cockburn* and *Bullfrog.*[83]

John Marks, a veteran Royal Navy purser left in charge of the facility, organized another auction in the summer of 1836. He offered for sale all of the vessels in the water and on the shore, including "four Old Ships of War laying aground on the mud in the harbour," which undoubtedly included *Kingston, Burlington,* and *Montreal.*[84] The results of the sale are uncertain, although after 1838 all of the vessels of the Lake Ontario squadron had disappeared from the *List of the Navy.*[85]

The closure of the dockyard did not last long. Following the Upper Canada Rebellion in 1837, Capt. William Sandom was sent to reestablish a naval force on the Great Lakes, arriving at Kingston in April 1838. Regardless of the fact that some of the ships aground in Navy Bay were reported to have been sold or taken to pieces, the abandoned hulks were still there in June 1839. Sandom complained:

> Navy Bay on the east side of the peninsula, or Point Frederick, is considerably injured as an Anchorage, for large vessels, in consequence of the three old frigates, and two smaller vessels, (which were sold out of the service) having been allowed to fall to decay, where they lay—and their wrecks now remain in a manner materially to injure that, which was, formerly, a good and safe port.[86]

Capt. David James Ballingall, a Royal Marine who arrived at Kingston in 1841 to serve with Sandom, recorded in his diary that the old ships "after crumbling to pieces, have been broken up, some sold as old timber, and others sunk."[87] It is unfortunate that Ballingall's entry is so vague. Evidence suggests that sometime after June 1839 and before the departure of the Royal Navy detachment from the lake in 1843, Sandom had two of the above-mentioned hulks pumped out and towed around to a small adjacent inlet called Hamilton Cove (later renamed Deadman Bay) and had another one sunk off the mouth of Navy Bay.[88] Paintings and drawings of Navy Bay from the early to mid-

1840s show that the old hulks had disappeared from sight. In 1853 the dockyard closed for good.

Antiquarian and Archaeological Studies, 1909–2012

Following several decades of intermittent military and naval use after the departure of Captain Sandom, Point Frederick was transferred to the Dominion of Canada in 1870, and in 1876 the Royal Military College of Canada opened on the grounds of the former Royal Navy dockyard. At the end of the nineteenth century, the locations of the abandoned ships in Deadman Bay and Navy Bay had not been forgotten but their identities had become a mystery. One early college cadet recollected that in the early 1880s "some of the wrecks of the old war vessels could be seen near the bottom of Deadman's Bay, and at least one of them was also visible in Navy Bay." He also recalled seeing in a shed "detailed plans of the old men-of-war. Some of them were on the shelves and some on the floor, and I have no doubt that there was much valuable historical material, which went into the fire or was thrown out as waste paper."[89]

Charles Henry Jeremiah Snider of the *Toronto Telegram* newspaper first sought to rescue the wrecks from obscurity, beginning in 1909 when he visited the wreck of *St. Lawrence*.[90] From conversations with local people, Snider learned that the ship had been used as a cordwood dock to fuel steamers at Drummond's brewery. Over the years, southwest gales and ice had reduced the warship to a small segment of hull lying in shallow water near the old brewery: "I secured a rowboat and pikepole," Snider wrote, "and after methodical soundings struck what appeared to be the upper face of her keelson or some of her ceiling, six feet under water. I traced it along in a straight line westwards for a hundred feet until the water became deeper than my sounding pole." Snider's book *In the Wake of the Eighteen-Twelvers,* published in 1913, excited public interest in the naval actions on the Great Lakes during the War of 1812, and through the 1930s and 1940s he shared his findings at Kingston in his weekly column "Schooner Days." In a report on *St. Lawrence*'s wreck written in 1950, Snider described seeing "a great many straight timbers, floor-frames, or lower futtocks apparently and a large quantity of planking and waling, for sides and ceiling and deck, all broken and in disorder." Snider raised timbers and fasteners, as well as

1830s coins and bank tokens, which he suggested were small change lost during the traffic in firewood. In 1920 a small iron swivel gun and its wooden mount were raised from the wreck site.

In 1912 Snider visited a wreck in shallow water at the head of Deadman Bay. Since most of the wreck was under water, he was not able to make detailed observations other than measuring the distance between the end posts at 160 feet (48.76 m). During very low lake levels in 1935, Snider and Maj. L. F. Grant of the Royal Military College were able to map the remains of a wreck in Navy Bay that Snider believed (incorrectly) to be the schooner *Netley*.[91]

In February 1938, a salvage operation on a second, deeper wreck in Deadman Bay was organized by museum official Ronald Way, who employed a hard-hat diver to collect artifacts for a display at nearby Fort Henry (fig. 7.8). No definitive information concerning the wreck's identity was found. Two newspaper articles and some photographs are the only known records from this salvage operation. The artifacts raised included about 18 iron guns of various types found along the keelson (some of the guns had their trunnions struck off or were otherwise damaged), cast-iron gun carriage wheels, iron ballast blocks, a three-sided copper ship's lantern (manufactured by Collinson and Son, Southwark, England), a copper magazine tray, round and canister shot, bayonets, boarding pikes, blocks and deadeyes, and several anchors. Elements of the ship were also raised, including two saddle-type mast steps, hull planking, futtocks, and a large quantity of lead sheeting. Several of the guns proved to be French pieces spiked by the British in 1758 when they captured Fort Frontenac at Kingston.[92] No doubt they were among the old guns that Master Attendant Michael Spratt said were being used as ballast in 1814.

In 1951 a group of staff members from the Royal Military College of Canada set out to conclusively identify the wrecks in Deadman Bay with the assistance of a Royal Canadian Navy "frogman" employing the latest scuba diving gear. The group named the hull at the head of the bay (visited by Snider in 1912) "Wreck Able" and the one in the middle of the bay (salvaged in 1938) "Wreck Baker." The Navy Bay wreck surveyed by Snider and Grant in 1935 was named "Wreck Charlie" (fig. 7.9). The diver, Lt. Cmdr. W. H. Willson measured Wrecks Able and Baker as 93 and 134 feet (28.34 and 40.84 m) long, respectively, counting this

Figure 7.8. *Wintertime salvage of the 1812 wrecks in Deadman Bay, 1938. Diver Dennis Coffey stands beside one of the guns raised through the ice. Note that the trunnions of this gun are missing. (Courtesy of the Fort Henry Museum, St. Lawrence Parks Commission.)*

amongst the earliest underwater archaeological surveys to take place in Canada. The research was published in a paper by Professor Richard Preston titled "The Fate of Kingston's Warships." Preston narrowed down the candidates for the wrecks in Deadman Bay to *Kingston, Burlington,* and *Montreal.* Since Preston believed that the 1833 *List of the Navy* said *Burlington* had been "taken to pieces," rather than the actual entry of "Supposed to be taken to pieces," he reasoned that this vessel was never towed to Deadman Bay. Preston therefore concluded that Wreck Able was *Montreal* and that Wreck Baker was *Kingston.* Wreck Charlie in Navy Bay remained unidentified.[93]

By 1960 Preston had begun to doubt his wreck identifications when the measurements taken by Willson in 1951 proved incorrect (Wreck Able is in fact longer than Wreck Baker). John R. Stevens, curator of the Maritime Museum of Canada in Halifax, visited Wreck Able in 1960 and produced a detailed sketch plan from the water's surface. He believed that Wreck Able was not *Montreal* but rather *Kingston*; the identification of Wreck Baker remained unresolved.[94]

Archaeological recording resumed in 1987 when the *St. Lawrence* and Deadman Bay wrecks were surveyed by a Kingston-based marine heritage organization called Preserve Our Wrecks.[95] Further historical and archaeological investigations were conducted by me between 1995 and 2002 with assistance from volunteer divers for site recording.[96] In 2000 and 2001, a team of Texas A&M graduate students under the direction of Daniel Walker conducted detailed survey work on Wreck Baker, which resulted in a site plan, frame profiles, and scale drawings of the ship's construction features.[97] Since the wrecks are mostly exposed above the bottom, these projects did not involve excavation and were limited to survey recording and photography. Finally, from 2002 to the present, Parks Canada's Underwater Archaeology Service, based in Ottawa, Canada (a team to which I belong), has been surveying the waters surrounding the dockyard, including Navy Bay and Deadman Bay. This ongoing work has revealed that yet another War of 1812 wreck rests in deeper water off the mouth of Navy Bay and that a smaller wreck lies in the bay itself.[98]

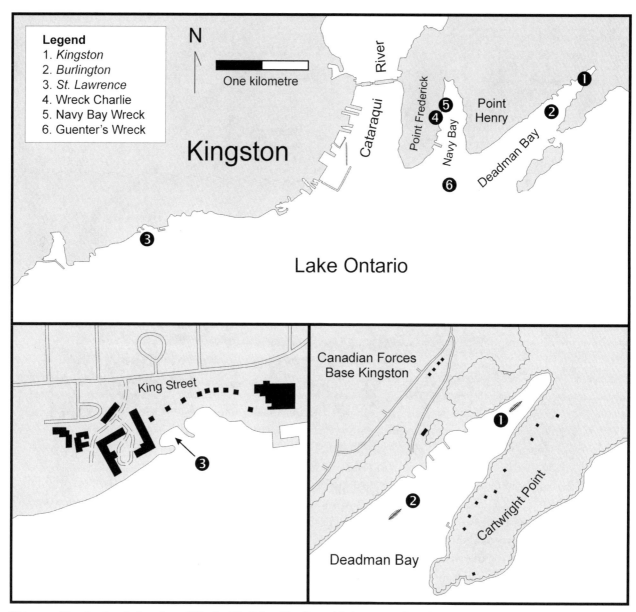

Figure 7.9. *Map showing the locations of Wrecks Able, Baker, Charlie, and* St. Lawrence. *(Map by Jonathan Moore.)*

Many features that could have helped to identify the Deadman Bay wrecks have been removed over the years. The challenge has therefore been the same as that faced by Professor Preston's team in 1951—to identify the ships from approximately one-tenth of their original structure—although we have the advantage of a much clearer archaeological picture of the wrecks. This work has not been limited to examining the remains of the ships: countless "dives" in archives and libraries in search of further clues have settled many questions. Captain Williams Sandom's correspondence, which Preston had not seen in 1951, states

that "three old frigates" were still in Navy Bay in 1839, so we now know that *Burlington* cannot be ruled out as a candidate, notwithstanding the statements in the 1833 *List of the Navy*. The possible identities of the two Deadman Bay wrecks can be chosen from the three large ships believed to be in the water during Sandom's tenure, namely *Kingston, Burlington,* and *Montreal.* The extant lengths of the wrecks and their construction features have been compared with the lines plans and profiles drawn by Thomas Strickland in 1815. Fortunately, enough of each wreck survives to permit a reasonable basis for comparison.

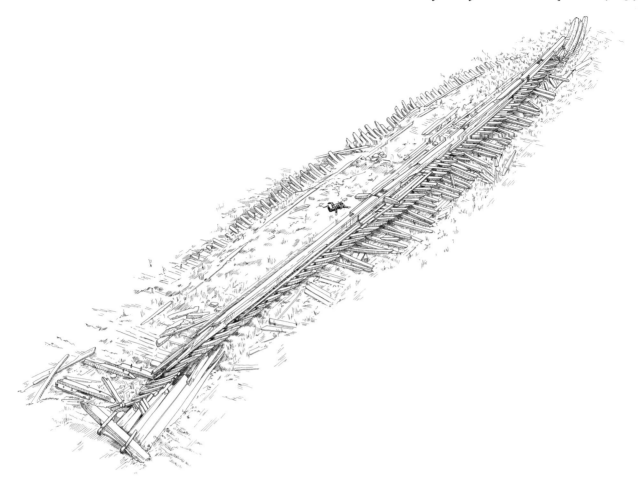

Figure 7.10. *Perspective view of Wreck Able* (Kingston/Prince Regent)*, view from the stern. (Drawing by Carol Pillar based on scale archaeological drawings and photos by Jonathan Moore.)*

Wreck Able at the head of Deadman Bay can be identified with some certainty as *Kingston* (ex–*Prince Regent*), since the overall length of the surviving wreck structure is 160 feet 9 inches (49 m), close to the recorded gun deck length of 155 feet 10 inches (47.83 m). The wreck is too long to be *Burlington* or *Montreal*. Furthermore, the positions of the mast steps and the steep frame deadrise correlate closely with *Kingston*'s lines plan. Wreck Baker, which has a maximum length of 131 feet 11 inches (40.2 m), is too long to be *Montreal* and has therefore been identified as *Burlington* (ex–*Princess Charlotte*).[99]

Archaeological Snapshots of the War of 1812 Wrecks at Kingston

Situated in shallow water only 100 feet (30.48 m) from shore at the head of Deadman Bay, *Kingston* (Wreck Able) survives from the gripe to the sternpost (fig. 7.10). At one time the upright hull would have projected above the water's surface, but the combined forces of decay, wave action, and ice have broken off the hull's upperworks. When *Kingston* sank for the final time it settled on its port bilge, and thus most of the surviving structure is on that side of the hull. Closer inspection of the wreck reveals that it is totally covered by zebra and quagga mussels, foreign species introduced to the Great Lakes in the 1980s. They obscure timber edges and fasteners, making the job of piecing together the construction of the wreck more difficult. The water-filtering action of billions of these thumbnail-sized creatures has dramatically improved underwater visibility in the years since they first arrived in Kingston waters, however, making it possible to see far more of the wreck than was formerly possible.

The keel of *Kingston* is mostly buried (the surfaces are visible in a few locations), but it nevertheless appears to be complete. The principal keel assembly consists of a row of heavy, flat-scarfed timbers rabbeted at

Figure 7.11. *Zebra and quagga mussels encrust the stern of Wreck Able* (Kingston/Prince Regent). *The hull is heeled to port. Two rudder gudgeons, one pintle stop, the sternpost, and the hood ends of hull planking are clearly visible. (Photo by Jonathan Moore.)*

the top corners. Above the lower keel, three layers of timbers were stacked to form a deadwood of considerable molded height, a configuration intended to accommodate the extreme frame deadrise in *Kingston*'s design. Not much is left of the stem assembly due to the shallow depth of water over the bow. Only a small section of the forefoot and the iron horseshoe plates that attached it to the keel are left. The stern structure is in deeper water and is accordingly more complete. It consists of the keel, stern deadwood, and inner and outer sternposts. The rudder is missing. Three iron gudgeons are attached to the sternpost, along with an iron pintle stop or "dumb brace" that is bolted to the post under the uppermost gudgeon (fig. 7.11). The inner sternpost has two small transoms attached directly above the deadwood. The stern deadwood appears to consist solely of horizontally stacked lengths of timber, with no evidence of a stern knee in its assembly. The base of the sternpost and the after end of the keel are buried, obscuring construction details in this location.

The preservation of the frames has been highly uneven. There are no surviving cant frames on either the port or starboard sides, and the starboard sides of the square frames now consist of only the floor heads and (detached on the lake floor) the first futtocks, which have fallen away in an orderly fashion, taking some of the planking with them. The square frames of the port side are much more complete but mostly obscured by ceiling planking, silt, plants, and debris. The eroded futtock ends visible at the upper margin of the port side curve up slightly, indicating that this side of the hull now terminates at the turn of the bilge. The port side of the wreck has not, unfortunately, survived to the level of the orlop deck and its supporting timbers, for these timbers could have told us much about how the decks were assembled on this ship.

The floors and first futtocks appear to form double frames, although wood erosion, the corrosion of iron fasteners, and overlying mussels, silt, and algae have made this difficult to determine conclusively. Collectively, the lower framing timbers have a great molded

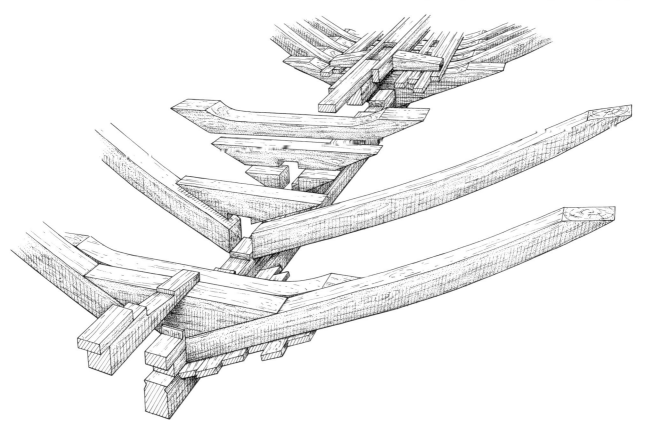

Figure 7.12. *Wreck Able (Kingston/Prince Regent), near the midship frame. The foreground shows the assembled arrangement of the floors, first futtocks, keel, keelson, and rider keelson, as well as the typical keelson scarf. Note the deadwood construction of the keel. The mid area shows the vertically expanded components of the floors and first futtocks. Note also the mast step arrangement in the background. No fasteners are shown. (Drawing by Fred Werthman and Carol Pillar based on scale archaeological drawings and photos by Jonathan Moore.)*

height and sharp deadrise. The floors themselves are made from four constituent parts: two large timbers that lie one atop another and form the floor proper and a pair of triangular chocks attached to the underside of the lower timber on opposite sides of the keel that shaped the floor to meet the keel rabbet (fig. 7.12). The heels of each pair of first futtocks butt the sides of the thick keel deadwood and are bolted to a large, overlying chock that straddles the keel centerline. This complex and labor-intensive system of assembling individual frame elements from numerous smaller pieces of timber provides archaeological corroboration for Captain Augustus Drury's complaint that in building the frigates, "much time and labour was thrown away by cutting crooked Timber out of straight." The floors and first futtocks show no evidence of limber holes, and given the tight spacing of the frames, it is evident that the ship's bilge pumps were seated atop the frames alongside the keelson.

For most of its length the keelson is flat, with only a slight rise at the bow and stern. It consists of a lower row of five large timbers joined by hook scarfs, overlain by a thinner upper row of timbers. The three surviving mast steps were all made in an unconventional fashion (fig. 7.13). They are not formed from timbers positioned atop the keelson but rather by gaps in the upper row of keelson timbers; each gap has a pair of thick fore-and-aft timbers bolted alongside the keelson to form the sides of the step. Crutches bolted on either side of the step provide additional lateral support. The ceiling planking in the vicinity of the mainmast step is mortised to receive upright stanchions for shot lockers or bulkheads (see fig. 7.12). The upper and lower rows of keelson timbers have broken apart at the mizzen step due to the twisting of the hull. The major structural components and frames of *Kingston* were joined with round iron bolts, and the planking was attached with iron spikes. The eleven wood samples collected

Figure 7.13. *Wreck Able* (Kingston/Prince Regent) *mainmast step and bolsters, facing starboard. The heads of the floor cross-chocks are visible in the background. (Photo by Jonathan Moore.)*

from the wreck for species identification all proved to be oak (appendix C).

The remains of *Burlington* (Wreck Baker) are situated near the entrance to Deadman Bay, some 200 feet (61 m) from the north shore. The depth of water here is greater than over *Kingston* and averages about 14 feet (4.26 m). The orientation and condition of *Burlington* are quite similar to *Kingston,* for it also settled on the port side when scuttled for the final time (fig. 7.14). The backbone of the wreck is nearly complete from just forward of the gripe to the sternpost, and the port side is more complete than the starboard side. The starboard side framing has separated from the rest of the hull along the side of the keel, which allows direct observation of the floor assembly and the keel's starboard surface. A jumble of detached planking and structural timbers surrounds the wreck's intact structure. Like *Kingston, Burlington*'s timbers are covered with layers of mussels.

Burlington's keel appears to be complete, although uneven and twisted. It is composed of a row of timbers

scarfed end to end, topped above by a single row of keel deadwood timbers and protected below by a false keel. A significant percentage of *Burlington*'s stem assembly has also survived and currently consists of eight timbers that make up the outer stem, gripe, main stem, and apron. The entire assembly is heavily through-bolted in the conventional manner, and its lower end is secured by a pair of circular iron plates, a variation on the dovetail or horseshoe plates more typically seen on the forefoot of a wooden ship (fig. 7.15).

The stern assembly is also well represented and stands proud of the lake bed, although at a slightly different angle of list from the rest of the hull due to a twist in the keel and keelson just forward of this location. The straight sternpost is secured to the top of the keel by a pair of iron fish plates (and probably a tenon, too, although this was not visible); with only one degree of rake, the post is at a near right angle to the run of the keel. Outer planking covers most of the stern structure, but it is evident that the assembly included an inner post (notched at the top for transoms), a stern knee,

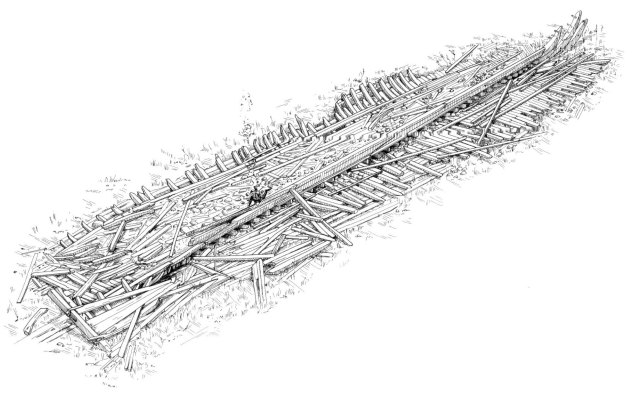

Figure 7.14. *Perspective view of Wreck Baker* (Burlington/Princess Charlotte), *view from the stern. (Drawing by Carol Pillar based on scale archaeological drawings and photos by Jonathan Moore and a scale site plan by Daniel Walker and Amy Borgens.)*

and a stack of deadwood timbers. The ship's rudder is missing, but associated features may still be seen: two iron rudder gudgeons as well as an iron dumb brace positioned under the uppermost gudgeon. A small skeg projects from the after end of the keel to protect the rudder in the event of a grounding.

The detached starboard side's framing survives to the second or third futtocks. The port sides' half-floors and first futtocks are still bolted to the ship's spine and are visible alongside the keelson, but beyond the limber strake the framing is covered by ceiling planking, wooden debris, and angular ballast stones. The port frames survive out to their fourth or fifth futtocks, and triangular chocks are evident where the heads and heels of futtocks join (see fig. 7.14). More of the hull at the turn of the bilge is preserved than on *Kingston,* but not enough to show us the manner of securing the orlop deck to the hull.

The floors were assembled from straight lengths of timber, with dimensions and a mode of construction markedly different from what we saw on the wreck of *Kingston* (fig. 7.16 and appendix C). Each was made from a pair of long half floors that notch down over the

side of the keel deadwood, with heels that meet over the centerline of the keel. The third element in each floor was a cross-chock that was vertically scarfed to the heels of the half floors and fastened with round iron bolts. The heels of the first futtocks also meet over the keel centerline, and a small unfastened chock fitted above them forms a flat surface for seating the keelson. No limber holes are evident in any of the frame timbers, and like *Kingston,* the bilge pumps must have been seated atop the floors and futtocks next to the keelson.

The keelson is formed of five principal pieces flat scarfed end to end and four thinner timbers that form the keelson's top surface. The five principal pieces sit flush atop the frames (the underside of the keelson is not notched), and the entire assembly is bolted to the keel through the half-floor chocks. *Burlington*'s foremast and mainmast steps were salvaged from the wreck in 1938, and the third has not been located. The two salvaged examples are the saddle-type steps often seen on British vessels of the eighteenth century: large blocks of wood with tapered ends, mortised in the center to fit the heel of the mast. The steps were reinforced

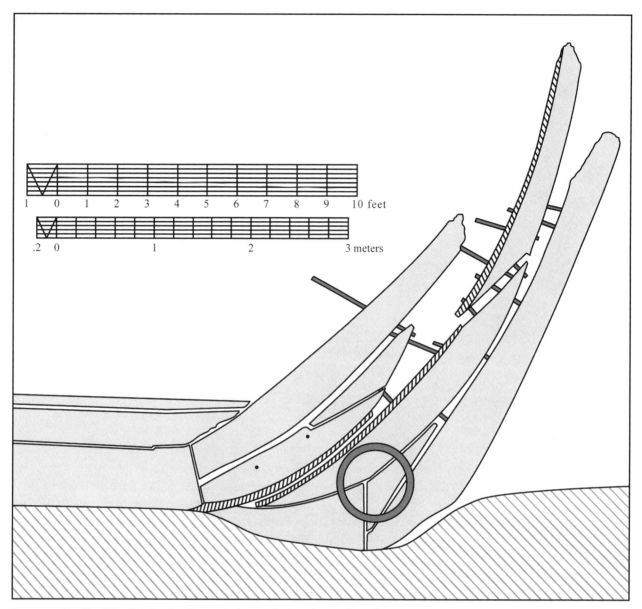

Figure 7.15. *Profile of Wreck Baker* (Burlington/Princess Charlotte) *stem. (Drawing by Daniel Walker.)*

by two pairs of iron dovetail plates bolted to their fore and after surfaces. The steps were positioned transversely across the keelson and secured in place, but the points where they were originally mounted have not been determined (see fig. 7.16).

Structural timbers and framework are fastened with round iron bolts, and the planking is attached with iron spikes. Thirteen wood samples were collected from the wreck, one from each of the principal hull components. All were of oak except for one sample from a hull plank and one from the false keel, both of which were of chestnut. The angular ballast stones that

overlie the port side of the hull are not the rounded shingle ballast reportedly used in 1814, but they might be some of the stone that Master Attendant Michael Spratt said was used to partially ballast the large ships of the squadron.

The remains of the great three-decker *St. Lawrence* lie near old buildings from Robert Drummond's brewery, within a small, artificial cove formed by twentieth-century breakwaters. The shoreline in this vicinity is exposed to the prevailing southwest winds and ice floes, but the cove offers some protection to the wreck. The articulated structure lies in an east-west orientation in

Figure 7.16. *Wreck Baker (Burlington/Princess Charlotte) frame assembly. The extreme foreground shows the arrangement of the rising wood, keel, and false keel. Atop this assembly is a floor gusset that unites the half-floors. In the middle area a mast step raised from the wreck in 1938 has been positioned atop the keelson, rider keelson, and bilge ceiling. Only selected fasteners are shown. (Drawing by Fred Werthman and Carol Pillar based on scale archaeological drawings and photos by Jonathan Moore.)*

water between 5 and 8 feet (1.52 and 2.43 m) deep. The shoreline's gentle southward slope continues offshore for several hundred feet, and where the water reaches about 30 feet (9.14 m) deep there is a scatter of other timbers that are probably from the wreck.

The remains of *St. Lawrence* consist of a 105-foot-long (32 m) segment of one side of the lower hull that was once adjacent to the keel and keelson (fig. 7.17). Nothing remains of the hull's keel or keelson, nor has enough of the wreck survived for us to say with any certainty that this is the port or starboard side. The hull segment consists of the half-floors, first futtocks, and second futtocks from thirty-six double frames, fastened in the manner depicted in Strickland's midship section (see fig. 7.5). The frames overlie at least a dozen

hull strakes, some of which project out from under the framing at the eastern end of the site. The vertically scarfed half-floor heels were fastened with round fore-and-aft iron bolts that were headed over washers, and the first futtocks and half-floors are fastened together with both round and square bolts (figs. 7.18 and 7.19). Several chock-scarfs at the floor heads survive, although they are highly eroded and the chocks themselves have disappeared. A short piece of the limber strake survives, as does part of a ceiling plank, but the rest of the structure is otherwise devoid of ceiling. A few loose planks lie along the south side of the wreck, partially buried by sand. Iron frame bolts that project from the upper surfaces of the half-floors and futtocks likely fastened footwales and some of the 11 floor

Figure 7.17. *Perspective view of the* St. Lawrence *from the south. (Drawing by Fred Werthman and Carol Pillar based on scale archaeological drawings and photos by Jonathan Moore.)*

riders shown in Strickland's section. The hull planking is attached with iron spikes (see fig. 7.19).

Although only a small portion of this once large warship still survives, the remains are important because they corroborate many of the lower-hull construction features and scantlings recorded in Strickland's midship section (see fig. 7.5 and appendix C). The remains also show that, like *Kingston* and *Burlington,* the three-decker had timber scantlings that compare favorably against contemporary tables of design scantlings; this is important in light of the contemporary descriptions of *St. Lawrence* being "slight built." Like Wreck Able and Wreck Baker, there are no limber holes on the wreck. Five wood samples have been collected from the wreck, one each from a half-floor, first futtock, hull plank, limber strake, and ceiling plank. Four are of oak, the exception being the rock elm half floor. The latter wood species is not unexpected, for the dockyard advertised for rock elm in February of 1814 when preparations were underway for the construction of *St. Lawrence,* and timber inventories show that elm was used for the hull's framework.[100]

Wooden Walls in a Wilderness: The Frigates and Three-Decker in Perspective

Travelers who visited Kingston after the war invariably commented on the presence of a Royal Navy squadron at such a remote frontier post: "[when] you come by water, uncultivated lands, and an uninterrupted line of wooded shore, seem conducting you to the heart of a wilderness, known only to the hunter, and his prey: you emerge from a wood, double a headland, and a fleet of ships lies before you, several of which are as large as any on the ocean."[101] The efforts of the Royal Navy at Kingston are indeed astonishing, for within a year of its arrival at this remote freshwater port, two powerful frigates had been launched and construction of a three-decked ship of the line was well underway. *Kingston* (ex–*Prince Regent*), *Burlington* (ex–*Princess Charlotte*), and *St. Lawrence* were tailored by shipwrights George Record, Patrick Fleming, and William Bell to the local navigational conditions and Yeo's imperative to either defeat the US squadron in a decisive engagement on Lake Ontario or blockade it in Sackets Harbor. Besides the unusually large number of guns they mounted, all three were designed both sharper and shallower than was typical for seagoing ships of similar dimensions and rating.

Archaeological surveys of the three wrecks revealed some similarities in their materials and construction techniques. They were assembled from relatively short lengths of straight-grained oaken timbers with numerous scarfs and chocks at the timber joins. Iron bolts and spikes were used for fastening all timbers and planks, with iron horseshoe plates at the keel-gripe scarf and iron dovetail plates at other vital scarfs and joins. The

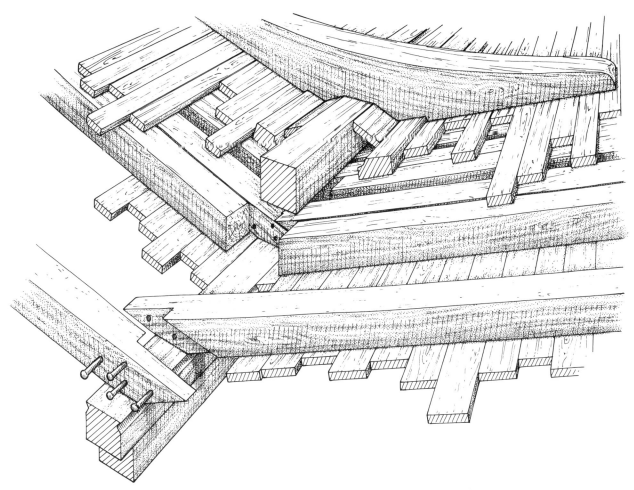

Figure 7.18. St. Lawrence *frame assembly, based on both Figure 7.6 and archaeological evidence. The expanded view in the extreme foreground shows the lapped construction (including bolt fastenings) of the floors. Note also the limber strake, limber boards, bilge ceiling, bilge rider, double timbered keel, and the first futtock heels falling short of the keel rabbet line. Only the half-floors, futtocks, and planking are represented archaeologically. Only selected fasteners are shown. (Drawing by Fred Werthman and Carol Pillar based on scale archaeological drawings and photos by Jonathan Moore.)*

archaeological studies also highlighted significant differences in construction practices, and there can be little doubt that each hull represents the work of different supervisors, each of whom had his own ideas on how the job should be done. *Kingston*'s keel deadwood was a massive structure, whereas the other two vessels had more modest deadwoods. The stern assemblies of *Kingston* and *Burlington* differed in many respects, including the apparent lack of a stern knee in the former. Curiously, while all three ships had floors assembled from straight timbers, the assembly patterns were different in every case. *St. Lawrence*'s two-piece floors had their arms vertically scarfed over the hull's centerline, and the floors were not notched to fit over the top of the keel; *Kingston*'s floors were assembled from a stack of four timbers and were let down quite deeply over the keel deadwood; the heels of *Burlington*'s floor arms, notched down over the shallow keel deadwood, butted over the keel and were vertically scarfed to a crosschock that spanned the keel. Finally, the mast steps of *Kingston* and *Burlington* were surprisingly different in design.

During and after the war, unfavorable comments circulated regarding the structural strength of the three Royal Navy warships. Archaeological observations suggest that while the ships were comparable to their seagoing counterparts in their construction, shortcuts were taken and certain types of reinforcing elements were omitted. The lack of compass timber in the framing, the dearth of grown knees or iron knees in the deck structure, and the tendency to build by cutting and fitting shorter lengths of timber would all

Figure 7.19. *Kingston diver Ken Fuller lends scale to the east end of* St. Lawrence *during survey work. In the right foreground, hull planks project out from under alternating half-floors and first futtocks. (Photo by Jonathan Moore.)*

have shortened the working life of the hulls. The ship-wrights were taking a calculated risk, but there was little choice: during the furious shipbuilding race in 1814, the Royal Navy was not in a position to construct ships that would last for long. They may have been built to a lower standard than their seagoing cousins, but these ships were nevertheless strong enough to bear the weight of their heavy guns and challenge the US Navy on Lake Ontario.

NOTES

1. *Princess Charlotte,* April 11, 1815, Admiralty Fonds, ADM 51/2700, The National Archives of the UK (TNA): Public Record Office (PRO).

2. Robert Malcomson, *Warships of the Great Lakes: 1754–1834* (Annapolis: Naval Institute Press, 2001), p. 100.

3. Emily Cain, *Ghost Ships* Hamilton *and* Scourge*: Historical Treasures from the War of 1812* (Toronto: Musson; New York: Beaufort Books, 1983), p. 24.

4. Owen, "Observations Relative to the Defence of the Lake Frontier," November 5, 1815, ADM 1/2264, p. 394a, TNA: PRO.

5. Drury to Melville, January 1, 1814, GD 51/2, p. 496, National Archives of Scotland, Edinburgh (NAS).

6. Freer to Pearson, March 18, 1813, vol. 1220, p. 213, series C (I), record group 8 (RG 8), Library and Archives Canada (LAC).

7. Yeo to Prevost, May 31, 1813, vol. 729, pp. 201–202, series C (I), RG 8, LAC.

8. J. Bélanger, June 22, 1813, Contracts, Notary Public J. Bélanger (M173/37), Bibliothèque et Archives nationales du Québec (BAnQ), cited by Eileen Marcil in Francess G. Halpenny, *Dictionary of Canadian Biography,* vol. 6 (Toronto: University of Toronto Press, 1987), pp. 289–92; Goudie to Drummond, April 20, 1816, vol. 737, pp. 187–89, series C (I), RG 8, LAC. Prevost made repeated attempts in the autumn of 1813 to formalize a contract for the construction of *Ship No. 1.* Goudie initially offered to build the frigate for £20 per ton exclusive of materials. This offer was rejected, and eventually Goudie agreed to simply superintend the building for £700, Goudie to Freer, September 22, 1813, vol. 1708, pp. 79–80, series C (I), RG 8, LAC; Prevost to Yeo, October 12, 1813, vol. 1709, pp. 15–16 and undated note, vol. 1221, p. 182, series C (I), RG 8, LAC.

9. Yeo to Prevost, July 22, 1813, vol. 730, pp. 55–56, series C (I), RG 8, LAC; Malcomson, *Warships of the Great Lakes,* p. 100.

10. Prevost to Yeo, July 23, vol. 1221, p. 6, series C (I), RG 8, LAC; Prevost to Commissioner Woodhouse (Halifax), August 1, 1813, enclosing (pp. 19–23) requisition by O'Conor, July 28, 1813, vol. 1221, p. 18, series C (I), RG 8, LAC; O'Conor to Yeo, July 23, 1813, vol. 730, pp. 61–62, series C (I), RG 8, LAC.

11. Goudie to Drummond, April 20, 1816, vol. 737, pp. 187–89, series C (I), RG 8, LAC.

12. Record to Freer, September 21, 1813, vol. 730, p. 181, series C (I), RG 8, LAC; Darroch to Prevost, September 17, 1813, vol. 730, pp. 182–84, series C (I), RG 8, LAC; "Receival and Expenditure of Oak Timber," vol. 59, Admiralty Lake Service Records (series 3a), RG 8, LAC.

13. Capt. Thomas McCulloch (acting commissioner in O'Conor's absence), "Report and Progress of the Naval Yard at Kingston in Upper Canada up to 10th October 1813," vol. 731, p. 18, series C (I), RG 8, LAC.

14. Drury to Melville, January 1, 1814, GD51/2, pp. 494–97, NAS.

15. Yeo to Prevost, October 8, 1813, vol. 731, pp. 8–9, series C (I), RG 8, LAC.

16. Prevost to Yeo, October 12, 1813, vol. 1221, p. 182, series C (I), RG 8, LAC. A draught and profile of a ship (97256, National Map Collection [NMC], LAC) labeled "John Goudie Marine Architect 1813 Quebec Canada" and signed in another hand "Princess Charlotte" displays a full, rounded hull in the body plan, unlike the postwar draughts of the *Princess Charlotte* by Strickland. The circumstances surrounding the creation of this plan and its intended purpose are unknown. On the plan, the ship's gun deck length is approximately 130 feet (39.62 m). Since Goudie evidently had nothing to do with the design and construction of *Princess Charlotte,* it is possible that this plan in fact depicts an early design for the 136-foot (41.45 m) frigate first requested by Yeo in June 1813, O'Conor to Freer, October 14, 1813, vol. 731, pp. 29–34, series C (I), RG 8, LAC.

17. Yeo to Prevost, October 17, 1813, vol. 731, p. 50, series C (I), RG 8, LAC.

18. Yeo to Prevost, October 22, 1813, vol. 731, pp. 60–61, series C (I), RG 8, LAC.

19. Yeo to Prevost, October 22, 1813, vol. 731, p. 62, series C (I), RG 8, LAC; O'Conor to Freer, October 22, 1813, vol. 731, pp. 64–72, series C (I), RG 8, LAC; Prevost to Yeo, November 2, 1813, vol. 1221, p. 218, series C (I), RG 8, LAC.

20. Record to Drummond, August 31, 1815, vol. 735, pp. 147–49, series C (I), RG 8, LAC. The contract's terms are noted in O'Conor to Freer, October 30, 1813, vol. 731, p. 91, series C (I), RG 8, LAC.

21. O'Conor to Freer, November 5, 1813, vol. 731, p. 101, series C (I), RG 8, LAC.

22. O'Conor to Freer, November 19, 1813, vol. 731, pp. 131–32, series C (I), RG 8, LAC.

23. O'Conor to Freer, November 24, 1813, vol. 731, p. 134, series C (I), RG 8, LAC.

24. O'Conor, "Return of the State of Forwardness of His Maj-

esty's Ships Prince Regent and Princess Charlotte," December 16, 1813, vol. 731, p. 178, series C (I), RG 8, LAC.

25. O'Conor to Prevost, December 17, 1813, vol. 731, p. 179, series C (I), RG 8, LAC.

26. Malcomson, *Warships of the Great Lakes,* p. 102.

27. O'Conor, "A Statement of His Majesty's Naval Force on Lakes Ontario & Champlain," enclosed in Yeo to Bathurst, February 9, 1814, vol. 1219, p. 192, series C (I), RG 8, LAC.

28. *Princess Charlotte,* January 1, 1814 to June 28, 1814, ADM 52/3928, TNA: PRO; the February 8, 1814 edition of the *Kingston Gazette* promised artificers "liberal encouragement" if they applied to O'Conor's office for work.

29. The foregoing paragraph is based on Robert Malcomson, "HMS *St. Lawrence*: The Freshwater First-Rate," *The Mariner's Mirror* 83, no. 4 (November 1997), pp. 420–23; Robert Malcomson, *Lords of the Lake* (Toronto: Robin Brass Studio, 1998), pp. 237–39.

30. February 4 and 15, 1814, ADM 3/181, TNA: PRO.

31. Yeo to Prevost, April 13, 1814, vol. 683, pp. 20–22, series C (I), RG 8, LAC. In this letter Yeo underscored his preference for ship-rigged warships over brigs and stated, "Brigs have never been esteemed so effective as ships in battle."

32. Spratt to Barrie, October 26, 1821, ADM 106/1999, TNA: PRO.

33. Yeo to Prevost, "Statement of the Force of His Majesty's Fleet on Lake Ontario as It Will Appear in the Spring of 1814," p. 78, ADM 1/2737, TNA: PRO. Kent's comments, dated June 20, 1814, appear in Robert Malcomson, ed., *Sailors of 1812: Memoirs and Letters of Naval Officers on Lake Ontario* (Youngstown, NY: Old Fort Niagara Association, 1997), pp. 79–80. Kent records a slightly different armament for both vessels than Yeo. According to David Lyon, *The Sailing Navy List: All the Ships of the Royal Navy—Built, Purchased and Captured—1688–1860* (London: Conway Maritime Press, 1993), pp. 118–23, 126–28, 38-gun frigates were fifth rates with main batteries of long 18 pounders and 32-gun frigates were also fifth rates armed with either 18 or 12 pounders on the gun deck.

34. Malcomson, *Lords of the Lake,* pp. 290–93, 328, 341–42. The armament of these vessels is summarized in Appendix H, Table 2, p. 341.

35. Yeo to Croker, May 21, 1814, p. 100, ADM 1/2737, TNA: PRO.

36. Malcomson, *Lords of the Lake,* pp. 294–95.

37. Malcomson, "HMS *St. Lawrence,*" p. 423.

38. Drummond to Prevost, May 31, 1814, vol. 683, p. 215, series C (I), RG 8, LAC.

39. Contract signed by Notary Public J. Bélanger and master shipbuilders Patrick Fleming, Peter Leitch, and John Want, as well as artificers, June 7, 1814, vol. 0, pp. 101–102, series C (I), RG 8, LAC.

40. Thomas Mossington, Papers, June 23, 1814, Diary vol. 2, F527, Archives of Ontario, Toronto (AO). Quarterman Mossington recorded that he found the three-decker in frame only. The

shipwrights from Quebec had attached five strakes of the bottom planking, which was 3½-inch (8.9 cm) pine except for the fore-and-aft shifts, which were oak, and there was one tier of internal staging or "cross spawls" in place. To spall is "To fix (ship-frames) at the proper breadth by means of cross-spalls," C. T. Onions, ed., *Shorter Oxford English Dictionary on Historical Principles,* 3rd ed., vol. 2 (Oxford: Clarendon Press, 1970), p. 1955.

41. Donald E. Graves, ed., *Merry Hearts Make Light Days: The War of 1812 Journal of Lieutenant John Le Couteur, 104th Foot* (Ottawa: Carleton University Press, 1993), p. 162.

42. *Prince Regent,* June 10–September 30, 1814, ADM 51/2641, TNA: PRO; *Montreal,* June 26–November 3, 1814, ADM 52/4189, TNA: PRO; throughout the summer of 1814 Naval Storekeeper Edward Laws contracted artificers from Quebec and the yard books attest to the huge sums spent on extra wages. See "No. 1104 Extra Pay List for the Extra Quartermen Artificers & Labourers for the Months of July, August and September 1814," ADM 42/2167, TNA: PRO, and Contracts from June 24, June 30, July 7, July 14, August 18, September 8, and September 15, 1814, Notary Public W. F. Scott (CN 301, S 253), BAnQ.

43. "Receival and Expenditure of Oak Timber" and "Receival and Expenditure of Red Pine," vol. 59, series 3a, RG 8, LAC; later, more detailed records documenting the construction of the *Psyche, New Ship No. 1,* and *New Ship No. 2* show that oak and elm were used throughout the hulls and white and red pine were used for some members, including floors, frames, plank, clamps, spirketting, waterways, and shelves. It is not possible to state at present the extent to which softwood was used in the *St. Lawrence* for purposes other than planking. See "An Estimate of Materials Required to Finish the Psyche after Part of Her Had Arrived from England," June 10, 1815, Thomas Mossington Papers, 1, AO; Laws, Spratt, Strickland to Navy Board, January 6, 1815, ADM 106/1997, TNA: PRO; "Receival and Expenditure of White Pine," vol. 59, series 3a, RG 8, LAC; *Kingston Gazette,* June 2, 1814, p. 3.

44. Chauncey to Jones, August 10, 1814, entry 125, Naval Records Collection of the Office of Naval Records and Library, record group 45, National Archives and Records Administration. Transcribed courtesy of Robert Malcomson.

45. Malcomson, "HMS *St. Lawrence,*" pp. 424, 426.

46. Malcomson, *Lords of the Lake,* p. 314; Hall to Navy Board, December 6, 1814, ADM 106/1997, TNA: PRO.

47. Thomas Strickland, "Statement of the Naval Force on Lake Ontario," March 23, 1815, p. 137, ADM 1/2262, TNA: PRO; Malcomson, *Lords of the Lake,* pp. 317–19.

48. Owen to Croker, March 25, 1815, p. 110, ADM 1/2262, TNA: PRO.

49. Owen to Croker, October 10, 1815, p. 123b, ADM 1/2263, TNA: PRO.

50. Joseph Bouchette, *A Topographical Description of the Province of Lower Canada with Remarks Upon Upper Canada* (London: W. Faden, 1815), pp. 600–601.

51. Owen, "Observations," November 5, 1815, p. 398, ADM 1/2264, TNA: PRO.

52. Thomas Strickland, "Statement," March 23, 1815, p. 137, and "State of the Hulls, Masts, and Yards, of His Majesty's Ships and Vessels on Lake Ontario," enclosed with Owen to Croker, June 21, 1815, p. 353, ADM 1/2262, TNA: PRO.

53. Robert Moore, "A Survey of His Majesty's Ships at this Port Taken by Order of Commissioner Sir Robt. Hall," December 31, 1816, ADM 106/1997, TNA: PRO.

54. Laws, Moore, Spratt to Navy Board, October 10, 1816, enclosing "War Complement of the Ships and Vessels on Lake Ontario June 1816," ADM 106/1997, TNA: PRO, signed by W. F. W. Owen. It appears that the 1816 ratings were devised by W. F. W. Owen but that the remarks on the rating, cited here, were a "True Extract from the Orders of Commodore Sir E.W.C.R. Owen K.C.B."

55. Robert Gardiner, *Warships of the Napoleonic Era* (Annapolis: Chatham Publishing, 2000), pp. 45–55; Malcomson, *Warships of the Great Lakes,* p. 102.

56. See Malcomson, *Warships of the Great Lakes,* pp. 101, 106 for the dimensions and armament of the *Superior*; "Ship Mohawk Building Sacketts Harbor," p. 156, Joshua Humphreys Papers, Wharton and Humphreys Notebook, Historical Society of Pennsylvania.

57. Owen, "Observations," November 5, 1815, p. 397, ADM 1/2264, TNA: PRO; O'Conor to Freer, March 7, 1814, vol. 732, pp. 54–55, series C (I), RG 8, LAC. See Malcomson, *Lords of the Lake,* Table 3, p. 342, which shows that on July 31, 1814 the US squadron's broadside strength was greater than that of the Royal Navy and that it had a significantly greater number of long guns.

58. For the wartime armament and dimensions of the US ships, see Malcomson, *Lords of the Lake,* p. 328, and Malcomson, *Warships of the Great Lakes,* p. 101.

59. Owen, "Observations," November 5, 1815, p. 394a, ADM 1/2264, TNA: PRO.

60. Malcomson, "HMS *St. Lawrence,*" p. 427.

61. John M. Duncan, *Travels Through Part of the United States and Canada in 1818 and 1819,* vol. 2 (New York: W. B. Gilley, 1823), p. 115.

62. Lyon, *The Sailing Navy List,* pp. 105–107.

63. Malcomson, "HMS *St. Lawrence,*" pp. 428–31.

64. Thomas Strickland, "*St. Lawrence* (May 1815)" ZAZ 0131–ZAZ 0137, Reg. Nos. 93–78, Admiralty ship plan collection, National Maritime Museum (NMM), London.

65. Malcomson, "HMS *St. Lawrence,*" p. 431; Gardiner, *Warships,* p. 89.

66. C. P. Stacey, "The Ships of the British Squadron on Lake Ontario, 1812–14," *Canadian Historical Review* 34 (1953), p. 316. For a good comparison of the Kingston three-decked ships with those at Sackets Harbor, see pp. 315–16.

67. Thomas Strickland, "*Wolfe* & *Canada* (May 1815)" ZAZ0138–ZAZ0139, Reg. Nos. 131–32, Admiralty ship plan collection, NMM.

68. Watercolor by E. E. Vidal, *Kingston Harbour. Lake Ontario Taken July 1815,* Massey Library, Royal Military College of Canada; "Situation of the Ships in Ordinary in Kingston Harbour 15 Oct. 1815," p. 86, ADM 1/2264, TNA: PRO.

69. "Statement of HM Naval Force on the Lakes of Canada, 1st Sept. 1816 Lake Ontario," vol. 738, p. 139, series C (I), RG 8, LAC.

70. Hall to Navy Board, May 29, 1817, ADM 106/1998, TNA: PRO.

71. Navy Board to Barrie, April 16, 1819, series 3a, vol. 31, RG 8, LAC; "Most Secret" memo to Barrie, n.d., ADM 106/1998, TNA: PRO.

72. Barrie to Navy Board, August 24, 1819 (Letters Number 7 and 8), ADM 106/1998, TNA: PRO.

73. Memo by Navy Board on Barrie to Navy Board, August 24, 1819 (Letter Number 7), ADM 106/1998, TNA: PRO.

74. The hauling out of these vessels is documented in ADM 106/1999–2002, TNA: PRO.

75. Lt. F. F. De Roos, *Personal Narrative of Travels in the United States and Canada in 1826—With Remarks on the Present State of the American Navy* (London: W. H. Ainsworth, 1827), pp. 160–63.

76. Mossington to Edwards, January 13, 1830, Thomas Mossington Papers, I, AO.

77. Barrie to Navy Board, May 30, 1831, ADM 106/2002, TNA: PRO.

78. Barrie to Navy Board, July 2, 1831, ADM 106/2002, TNA: PRO.

79. Barrie to Glover, November 14, 1831, series 3a, vol. 49, RG 8, LAC; *Kingston Chronicle,* November 19, 1831, p. 3.

80. *Kingston Chronicle,* January 21, 1832, p. 2; Barrie to Navy Board, January 25, 1832, ADM 1/2002, TNA: PRO.

81. "Ships and Vessels on the Lakes in America," p. 67, *List of the Navy 1833,* Admiralty Library, London (AL). These entries are imprecisely quoted in Richard A. Preston, "The Fate of Kingston's Warships," *Ontario History* 44, no. 3 (July 1952), p. 98.

82. *Montreal Gazette,* January 5, 1833, p. 2. This newspaper citation was kindly provided by Rick Neilson.

83. *List of the Navy, 1833,* p. 67, *List of the Navy, 1834,* p. 60; Edward Charles Frome, R.E., *View of Kingston Looking Over the Dockyard from Fort Henry,* Ink Drawing, 1833, Agnes Etherington Art Centre, Queen's University.

84. *Kingston Chronicle and Gazette,* May 7, 1836, p. 3.

85. Preston, "The Fate of Kingston's Warships," p. 97. See *List of the Navy, 1837,* p. 60, *List of the Navy, 1838,* p. 52, *List of the Navy, 1839,* p. 61, AL.

86. Sandom to Paget, April 21 1838, and Sandom to Wood, June 7, 1839, ADM 1/2563, TNA: PRO.

87. David James Ballingall Diary, "Fifteen Months on Lake Ontario Upper Canada in the Years 1841 and 1842," p. 60, A. Arch. 2403, Queen's University Archives, Kingston (QUA).

88. This conclusion was reached by Preston, "The Fate of Kingston's Warships," pp. 98–99.

89. "Further Notes on the Early History of the College," *Royal Military College of Canada Review* 8 (June 1927), pp. 43–44.

90. Snider's archaeological observations of the wrecks can be found as follows: LAC, C. H. J. Snider, *The Silent* St. Lawrence: *An Angel of Enduring Peace* (Toronto: Rous & Mann Press, 1948), enclosing "Memoranda on Remains of HMS St. Lawrence by C.H.J. Snider," 1950; *Toronto Telegram,* April 21, 1934, November 16, 1935, November 23, 1935, December 7, 1935, and March 26, 1949; C. H. J. Snider, "Memoranda Regarding Wreck in Navy Bay, Point Frederick, Kingston, Ont," and "Memoranda Regarding Wreck in Deadman's Bay, Kingston, Ont.," Box 2, C. H. J. Snider Papers, A. Arch. 2215, QUA; "The Wreck in Navy Bay," *Royal Military College of Canada Review* 16 (December 1935), p. 28.

91. The *Netley* had been hauled out and was on shore in frame when Sandom arrived at Kingston in 1838. This vessel was then renamed *Niagara,* commissioned, and became the namesake of Sandom's Kingston establishment. Sandom to Paget, April 21, 1838, ADM 1/2563, TNA: PRO.

92. *Globe and Mail,* February 4, 1938; *Kingston* (ON) *Whig-Standard,* February 8, 1938. Photographs of the diving operations are held by the Fort Henry Museum. All of the recovered artifacts are held by the Fort Henry Museum and the Marine Museum of the Great Lakes at Kingston.

93. Preston, "The Fate of Kingston's Warships," p. 99. See also Preston Papers, Box 5, pt. 1, 1951–54, and pt. 2, 1959–1962, Royal Military College of Canada Archives, Kingston (RMCA).

94. Preston to Stevens, October 12, 1960, Stevens to Preston, October 15, 1960. Preston Papers, Box 5, pt. 2, RMCA; Stevens noted in this letter that Ronald Way believed that Wreck Baker was the *Burlington.*

95. Susan M. Bazely, "Preserve Our Wrecks (Kingston), Underwater Survey License No. 88–42" (manuscript report, Ontario Ministry of Culture, Toronto, 1988). This group tentatively agreed with the identification of Wreck Able as *Kingston* and suggested that Wreck Baker was *Psyche.* The latter identification is dubious because as late as 1836 *Psyche* was in frame on a slip and was never replanked and relaunched.

96. Jonathan Moore, "Archaeological and Historical Investigations of Three War of 1812 Wrecks at Kingston, Ontario: HMS *St. Lawrence,* HMS *Kingston* and HMS *Burlington*: Report for Province of Ontario License to Conduct Archaeological Exploration or Fieldwork 1999–096 at Sites BbGd-6, BbGc-45 and BbGc-46" (archaeological report, Ottawa, 2006); Jonathan Moore, "Kingston's Bicentennial Warships: A Century of Exploration," in *Sideshow or Main Event: Putting the War of 1812 into Regional Contexts,* eds. Brian S. Osborne and Robert J. Andrews (Kingston, ON: Kingston Historical Society, 2012), pp. 93–108.

97. Daniel Robert Walker, "The Identity and Construction of Wreck Baker: A War of 1812 Era Royal Navy Frigate" (Master's thesis, Texas A&M University, 2007).

98. Jonathan Moore, "Fort Henry National Historic Site of Canada Submerged Cultural Resource Inventory: 2004, 2006 & 2007 Surveys" (manuscript report, Underwater Archaeology Service, Parks Canada, Ottawa, 2008). The *Montreal* (ex-*Wolfe*) is a candidate for the identity of the wreck off the mouth of Navy

Bay known as Guenter's Wreck; this possibility does not affect the identification conclusions presented in this chapter. For details on the wreck in Navy Bay, see Nadine Kopp, "The Navy Bay Wreck: An Unidentified Wreck in Kingston, Ontario," in *ACUA Underwater Archaeology Proceedings, 2009,* eds. Erika Laanela and Jonathan Moore (Advisory Council on Underwater Archaeology, 2010), pp. 195–200.

99. The gun deck lengths of the *Montreal* and *Charwell* were 109 feet 9 inches (33.45 m) and 107 feet 5 inches (32.74 m), respectively. For more detailed discussion of the wrecks' identities and a photographic record, see Moore, "Archaeological and Historical Investigations of Three War of 1812 Wrecks at Kingston." The identity of Wreck Baker is also discussed in Walker, "The Identity and Construction of Wreck Baker," pp. 84–97.

100. *Kingston Gazette,* March 1, 1814, p. 3.

101. Francis Hall, *Travels in Canada and the United States, in 1816 and 1817* (London: Longman, Hurst, Rees, Orme & Brown, 1818), pp. 161–62.

8 "SMALLER VESSELS ARE OF NO LESS CONSEQUENCE"

The Browns Bay Vessel

CHRISTOPHER AMER

Introduction

The War of 1812 saw the construction of different vessel types for service on the high seas, in coastal regions, and on the inland lakes. The rapid escalation of the naval war on the lakes created a need for greater numbers of ships, and as the freshwater campaigns wore on, both the Royal and US Navies built increasingly larger and more heavily armed ships. There were exceptions to this trend, however. The frigates and sloops of war that ranged the lakes in 1813 and 1814 were open-water ships, ill-suited to navigating and fighting in extremely shoal areas, especially in rivers, creeks, and the near-shore margins of the lakes. For this reason, both navies produced gunboats—small, shallow, lightly armed, and highly maneuverable oared vessels—to defend or attack supply routes and harbors, patrol strategic passageways, and land troops on hostile shores. This, presumably, was the purpose of the diminutive vessel found on the bottom of Browns Bay, a shallow inlet on the north shore of the St. Lawrence River some 30 miles (48 km) from the eastern end of Lake Ontario.[1]

Like many wrecks sunk close to shore, the hull was known to local boaters, fishermen, and bird hunters, and its waterlogged timbers generated speculation about its origins. According to one popular legend, the wreck was abandoned in Browns Bay by a smuggler named Patterson in the nineteenth century. And, like many shipwrecks, this one had the power to summon up romantic images of ruined fleets and long-lost treasures. Typical of this is the reminiscence of one old-timer who recalled, "When I was a youngster we used to go skating in Browns Bay in the winter time, and if the ice was clear of snow and the moon was full, you could see a ship frozen in the ice with its copper fasteners shining like gold!"[2] In addition to entertaining skaters, the wreck was said to have been used as a blind

Figure 8.1. *The salvage of the Browns Bay Vessel in 1967. Suspended on slings beneath a heavy support structure, the hull has just been raised from the water. This was one of the earliest Canadian government projects to excavate, recover, and conserve a historic wooden shipwreck. (Courtesy of the Underwater Archaeology Service, Parks Canada.)*

by duck hunters, and, after the introduction of scuba diving to the lakes, it was a site where exploring divers could collect copper fittings and other souvenirs.

In the early 1960s, a diver reported the vessel to the National Historic Sites Service (NHSS) of the Canadian Department of Indian Affairs and Northern Development (now Parks Canada). In 1967, after historical research tentatively identified the wreck as a British gunboat dating to the 1812 era, the NHSS raised and conserved the vessel (fig. 8.1). It was later placed on public display at nearby Mallorytown Landing, Ontario.

In 1985 I began a program of archival research, hull recording, and architectural analysis that supported the vessel's identification as a former Royal Navy gunboat. My research also showed that no other British gunboats of this type had ever been archaeologically studied.[3] While many of its features suggested naval origins, the wreck was found to contain elements not characteristic of early-nineteenth-century British gunboats, including a centerboard, a wide-bladed rudder, and a heavy keelson. These features, together with the absence of a gun platform or ordnance-related fittings

in the bow, implied that the hull was modified for reuse as a sailing merchant vessel.

Gunboats on the Lake and River

Armies and navies operating along the margins of land and water have long depended on small, oar-propelled warships. Roman armies defending the empire's northeastern frontier along the Rhine River, for example, built flotillas of pocket-sized galleys to patrol the river and keep hostile Germanic tribes in check.[4] Later European history is replete with examples of small boats being employed on rivers, lakes, estuaries, and coasts to support military and naval operations and harass enemy shipping and troops.[5] The addition of cannon to vessels of this type created the gunboat, a craft that combined shallow-water mobility with concentrated firepower.

"Gunboat" is a general term that covers many different forms of warships, but common characteristics of eighteenth- and early-nineteenth-century gunboats included modest dimensions, light scantlings, and a shoal draft; vessels intended to navigate extremely shallow waters often had flat bottoms to further reduce their draft. Because they frequented narrow waterways and relied on stealth, maneuverability, or bursts of speed to surprise their foes, most were equipped with oars or sweeps and most carried large numbers of men to row them. To conserve the strength of the crew, some gunboats had one or two masts with simple, handy gaff, lugger, or lateen rigs for sailing when conditions permitted. The size of these craft limited their armament, which typically consisted of a single cannon mounted on a platform in the bow (fig. 8.2). Larger gunboats sometimes mounted one or two additional cannon in the waist or in the stern.

Service on gunboats seems to have been universally unpopular, and for good reasons. Rowing them was hard work, living conditions were often cramped and uncomfortable, and except perhaps for a canvas awning, crews had little protection from the sun, wind, and rain. Nor did these frail craft offer much protection against enemy shot, and in battle exposed crews could be picked off individually by sharpshooters or mowed down en masse by cannon fire. Some naval tacticians, usually nonprofessionals, envisioned flotillas of nimble gunboats attacking and even capturing larger warships when the latter were becalmed, but in

Figure 8.2. *A skirmish between Royal Navy and US Navy gunboats. This conjectural sketch by Peter Rindlisbacher shows an engagement on the North American lakes during the War of 1812. (Courtesy of the artist.)*

practice this was rarely successful, and under most circumstances gunboats avoided tangling with heavily gunned foes.[6] Despite their disadvantages, these craft could go almost anywhere that had enough water to float them, a characteristic that made them indispensable on the inland waters of North America.

The first widespread use of gunboats on the northern lakes occurred during the Anglo-French conflict known as the French and Indian War (the "Seven Years War" in Europe). Between 1755 and 1760, the opposing sides relied on rivers and lakes to transport armies and their supplies through the interior of the continent. Gunboats were constructed on Lakes Champlain and Ontario and were widely employed in the successful British offensives of 1759 and 1760 that ended with the conquest of New France.[7] During the War of the American Revolution between 1775 and 1783, gunboats were again widely used; in 1776, for example, they fought in both the British and the Continental Army flotillas at the Battle of Valcour Island on Lake Champlain.[8]

At the outbreak of the War of 1812, neither the United States nor Britain possessed many gunboats on the lakes, and it was apparent that more would be needed. The British were faced with the particularly difficult task of defending a long and exposed line of supply and communication between Upper and Lower Canada. Nearly all of the matériel consumed by their naval and military forces in the Great Lakes region—provisions, naval stores, tools, ordnance, and munitions—had to be hauled up the St. Lawrence River in fleets of bateaux. For much of the distance between

Montreal and Kingston, the river is also the boundary between the United States and Canada, and it did not take a genius to understand just how precarious the British situation in Upper Canada could become if the United States made a concerted attempt to disrupt the flow of supplies along this corridor.

Six months before the start of hostilities, the Provincial Marine had only six gunboats on the lower St. Lawrence River, and the lists of the naval forces on Lakes Erie or Ontario do not mention gunboats. The deficiency in small warships was recognized by military authorities, for among the proposals for putting Canada on a wartime footing was an increase of the gunboat flotilla to a total of thirteen craft.[9] The Provincial Marine, overwhelmed by events after the declaration of war, seems to have done little to protect the river transports, but fortunately for the British cause, their foe made no serious effort to cut communications on the St. Lawrence in 1812.

The naval situation on the lakes underwent a profound sea change in early 1813 when the Royal Navy superseded the Provincial Marine. One of the first saltwater officers to reach Kingston, Cmdr. Robert Barclay, saw the need for shoal-draft warships and immediately began building six new gunboats, commenting: "Although a large ship may be necessary, the smaller vessels are of no less consequence."[10] Capt. Sir James Lucas Yeo, commander of all British naval forces in the interior of Canada, agreed with this assessment and continued to add more gunboats to his forces. In July of 1813, he outlined a plan for the defense of the supply convoys that called for three divisions of three boats apiece, based at Kingston, Gananoque, and Prescott, to escort bateaux and patrol the upper St. Lawrence River.[11] By January 1814, the Royal Navy had over twenty gunboats in service between Kingston and Montreal.[12] The undermanned Lake Ontario squadron could not spare skilled sailors for duty on the river, and throughout the war the greater part of the gunboat crews were made up of soldiers and militiamen.

Lines or construction plans of the British gunboats used during the war have not been found, and so our knowledge of them depends heavily on the lists of the lake squadrons that were periodically sent to the Admiralty. The detailed January 26, 1814 "List of His Majesty's Gun Boats" on the St. Lawrence and Lake Ontario shows that the twenty then in existence varied greatly in their dimensions, armament, and condition. Most appear to have been purpose-built vessels, but others were probably small merchant craft converted to gunboats as a wartime expedient. A few of them were sloop or schooner rigged, but the majority were luggers. The smallest, the lugger-rigged *Thunder,* was 40 feet (12 m) in length, 8 feet (2.4 m) in breadth, and propelled by twenty-two sweeps and mounted a long 6-pounder cannon and a 24-pounder carronade. The largest gunboats in the flotilla were around 60 feet (18 m) in length and 14 to 16 feet (4.2 to 4.8 m) in breadth, had 36 sweeps, and were armed with a long 24 pounder and a 32-pounder carronade. It is clear from the list that by 1814 the Royal Navy was beginning to build the gunboats according to a standard design, which measured about 55 by 12 feet (16.5 by 3.6 m) and had thirty-six oars, a long 18 or 24 pounder, and a 32-pounder carronade.[13] In 1814 at least three of the gunboats had their 32 pounders replaced by a 68-pounder carronade, then the largest gun in regular use by the Royal Navy.[14]

The wooded islands and many passages of the upper St. Lawrence offered ample cover for American raiding parties and British commanders expected attacks, but their fears were only occasionally realized.[15] In July 1813, two US privateer sloops, *Neptune* and *Fox,* captured the gunboat *Spitfire* and a convoy of fifteen bateaux laden with provisions and munitions.[16] One year later, in June 1814, a US Navy small-boat expedition surprised the British gunboat *Black Snake*; the gunboat's crew were taken prisoner, but *Black Snake* was scuttled during a close pursuit and later recovered by the Royal Navy.[17] Aside from minor incursions like these, the US Army and Navy made no serious attempt to interrupt the convoys between Montreal and Kingston, and British forces in Upper Canada continued to receive needed supplies throughout the war.

The Royal Navy's gunboat flotilla also provided vital near-shore firepower for military actions and amphibious landings. Several gunboats accompanied the abortive British attack on Sackets Harbor in May 1813. Here they blasted the enemy shore in advance of the disembarking troops, but their unprotected crews suffered greatly from the fire of the US defenders.[18] Other combined operations followed. In 1813 gunboats from Yeo's flotilla bombarded US Army positions at 40-Mile Creek at the western end of Lake Ontario and at the Battle of Crysler's Farm on the northern bank of the St.

Figure 8.3. Storming Fort Oswego, *May 6, 1814. This detail from the print shows Royal Navy gunboats transporting troops and supporting the assault on the US fort at Oswego, New York. The ability of these small warships to work close to shore and provide covering fire with their guns made them invaluable for amphibious operations such as this one. (Library and Archives Canada, C-00793.)*

Lawrence.[19] The following year, on May 6, 1814, they covered the landing of a British force at Oswego, New York, where cannon, naval stores, and provisions for the US fleet at Sackets Harbor were seized and taken to Kingston (fig. 8.3).

It was also in May 1814 that the hazards of gunboat duty were vividly demonstrated in the Sandy Creek debacle. This incident began when a British cutting-out expedition consisting of two gunboats, five ships' boats, and 183 seamen and marines attempted to capture eighteen US supply bateaux bound from Oswego to Sackets Harbor. The bateaux sheltered in narrow and heavily wooded Sandy Creek, where they were defended by about three hundred US Army riflemen, Oneida Indians, and sailors. The expedition imprudently pushed up the creek, the lead gunboat firing grapeshot and canister shot into the dense foliage, until it floated into a well-concealed ambush. Hunters became the hunted in the sharp ten-minute fight that followed, and over one-quarter of the British fell dead or wounded. The exposed survivors had no choice but to surrender to the hidden sharpshooters who surrounded them. It was the greatest single loss of personnel that the Royal Navy experienced on Lake Ontario during the war.[20]

After news of peace reached Canada in early 1815,

the gunboats of the Lake Ontario–St. Lawrence flotilla assisted in the demobilization of the British forces. In June the gunboat flotilla was officially decommissioned and ten of the boats were laid up at Kingston.[21] The laid-up boats (augmented by an eleventh, *Radcliffe,* completed and launched in 1817) saw little use, maintenance, or repair and were reported to be in a dilapidated condition by 1820.[22] Periodic repairs were authorized after 1823, and the boats were pulled onto a slip at the naval yard and housed over to further protect them from the elements. In 1831, however, the Admiralty elected to dispose of its decayed fleet on Lake Ontario. It was not until five years later, in 1836, that the last of the Royal Navy's 1812-era warships, including the old gunboats, were broken up or sold out of the service.[23]

Of all the gunboat flotillas operating on the coastal and inland waters of North America between 1812 and 1815, the British force on the St. Lawrence River and Lake Ontario was probably the most active and in many ways the most successful. The primary duty of these boats was to defend the river shipping that supplied Upper Canada, and they were able to do this throughout the war. That the United States made few attempts to cut this lifeline might be ascribed, at least in part, to the deterrent effect of the escorting flotilla. The gunboats also served during the war as mobile gun platforms that closely supported amphibious landings and shore-side battles, a role for which they were well suited, although the vulnerable crews might have disputed this assessment. The work of the gunboats has been overshadowed in the historical record by the larger ships of Yeo's Lake Ontario squadron, but their contributions to the defense of Canada were of no less consequence.

Excavation, Conservation, and Investigation

The fate of the Royal Navy's gunboats after their disposal in the 1830s has not been adequately traced, but we can be certain that repairable hulls were attractive to St. Lawrence River merchants and ship owners. The boats were, after all, built to operate in a shallow riverine environment, and for their size they were strongly built. At least one former gunboat entered a new career as a commercial carrier. This hull, now known as the Browns Bay Vessel, saw an extended period of use, although we do not know exactly how long, and then sank in Browns Bay on the north shore of the river between Gananoque and Brockville, Ontario.

The wreck settled on a sandy bottom, 300 feet (90 m) from shore in approximately 6 feet (1.8 m) of water, deep enough to cover most of the hull. Some of the uppermost structure of the hull was subsequently lost to decay and human activity. The action of ice in the river probably loosened and removed timbers, and over time the upper extremities of the stem, sternpost, frames, and centerboard trunk succumbed to rot induced by continuous waterlogging and drying as the river rose and fell with the seasons. There is no evidence of any salvage attempts prior to the 1950s, but following the wreck's discovery by scuba divers, artifacts and souvenir timbers were removed. The rudder, for example, was salvaged in 1957.

After research showed that the vessel was likely a survivor of the 1812-era naval fleet, the NHSS elected to lift, conserve, and display the remains. During the 1967 excavation, NHSS divers worked for over eight hundred hours digging, recording, and preparing the hull for recovery. During this process they recovered a collection of artifacts that provided clues to the boat's career. Objects relating to the preparation and consumption of food suggest that there was a small galley in the stern.[24] These included several two-pronged forks with bone handles, a pewter plate, a bottle, two iron pot lids, and a cast-iron stove door bearing the name of a New York manufacturer. Clay pipe fragments were also recovered, including one stem stamped "J. Nimmo, Glasgow"; one or more pipe makers with this name lived in Glasgow between 1834 and 1865.[25] Other artifacts included a caulking mallet, a chisel, a whetstone, a leather boot, and two shovels. A quantity of nineteenth- and twentieth-century cartridge primers found within the hull attests to the wreck having been used as a hunting platform after sinking.

After the excavation was completed, a wooden cradle was fabricated to lift the wreck, which was then floated 2½ miles (4 km) upstream to Mallorytown Landing. Here, the structure, weighing an estimated 22 tons, was lifted from the water. A bath was constructed around the vessel, and an 11,000-gallon (41,800 L) solution of polyethylene glycol was added to immerse the hull. Two years after the recovery the vessel was removed from preservative treatment and moved to

Figure 8.4. *The Brown's Bay Vessel is lowered into its support cradle. In the spring of 1969, after one and a half years of immersion in a solution of polyethylene glycol, the hull was removed from treatment and placed on exhibit at Mallorytown Landing in the St. Lawrence Islands National Park, Ontario. (Courtesy of the Underwater Archaeology Service, Parks Canada.)*

the nearby St. Lawrence Islands National Park, where it was placed on public display in a building located on the St. Lawrence River. The hull was supported by a wooden cradle shaped to conform to the reconstructed hull lines (fig. 8.4).[26]

In the fall of 1985, a team from Parks Canada and the Canadian Conservation Institute performed a visual and physical examination of the hull. They concluded that while the overall condition was good and the remains appeared reasonably stable, severe shrinkage and warping had affected individual timbers. Rot, which probably first developed during the service period of the vessel, was also evident in parts of the structure.[27]

The port side survived to a greater extent than the starboard side, and the central portion of the hull was in better condition than the ends. The keel and keelson were complete. The upper extremities of both the bow and stern were missing, leaving only the lower ends of

the posts, apron, and stern knee. The transom was suspended from the ceiling by wires and reattached to the starboard plank ends with nails (the port planks were eroded short of the transom). The rudder was complete.

Cant frames in the bow and stern did not fare well, and many were degraded or absent. Square frames, each composed of a floor and two pairs of futtocks, were for the most part represented in their entirety, although they exhibited varying degrees of shrinking, warping, and rot. The external planking was nearly complete, if somewhat broken and eroded at the ends of the hull. Ceiling on the port side was well represented and the planks were solidly attached to frames, but only four ceiling planks remained attached to the frames on the starboard side. Deck remains included two deck beams with attached lodging knees and one lodging knee still fastened to the top of the port side. Added-on features, including a centerboard, a second layer of planking, and an enlarged keelson timber, all pointed to an extensive refit later in the boat's career.

The hull was documented between March 31 and June 1, 1985.[28] I decided to take frame sections from the starboard side because port sections had previously been measured during the hull recording in 1967. The starboard sections could serve as a check for the sections recorded on the port side and provide additional information about the hull's construction. When the starboard sections were converted to a body plan, they closely followed the existing port-side lines. A revised wreck plan was created by adding information to, and redrawing, the 1966 plan (fig. 8.5). Since the vessel was most likely built by shipwrights using the English system of measurement, all dimensions were recorded in feet and inches.

The Construction of the Gunboat

The Browns Bay Vessel had a clinker-built lower hull and was thus assembled in a very different manner from all of the other ships described in this book. In clinker construction the planking of the sides precedes the framing; the edges of strakes are lapped and then fastened together with metal rivets. The principal strength of the hull lies in the plank shell, not in the frames. Clinker-style construction originated in Northern Europe, where it had a long history (the Vikings built their ships this way), but was largely superseded in the early sixteenth century by frame-based assembly techniques, which featured an internal skeleton covered with flush-laid carvel planking. The clinker tradition has survived in many forms of small craft, however, because boats built in this manner are relatively lightweight yet strong and flexible.

The hull of the Browns Bay Vessel measured 54 feet 2 inches (16.25 m) in length, with a beam of 16 feet 5¾ inches (4.95 m), measurements that are probably very close to the boat's original dimensions. The structure is almost exclusively composed of white oak, although the stern knee, midship beam, and lodging knees were fashioned from larch. Futtocks installed during a refit included at least one piece of ash. The ceiling planks are reused white pine boards.

The straight, single-piece keel measured 49 feet 3½ inches (14.79 m) from the forward end of the stem scarf to the keel scarf at the heel of the sternpost; its dimensions are modest, averaging 8¾ inches (22.23 cm) molded and 6 inches (15.24 cm) sided. The upper surface was notched to receive twenty-six floor timbers that were fastened in place with iron bolts. The bolt ends were recessed into the lower surface of the keel and the holes sealed by wooden plugs. The lower surface of the keel is gouged and abraded and in some places split, a consequence of many years of active service and the wood drying after raising. Rabbets were cut 2 inches (5.08 cm) below the keel's upper corners to fit the garboard strakes of the inner (original) planking layer.

The stem consists of a single post and an apron (fig. 8.6). Only the lower 3 feet (90 cm) of the stem's estimated length of 6 feet (1.8 m) survives. The stem joined the keel in a complex vertical scarf with horizontal tables and was fastened by four iron bolts and a treenail. The scarf's horizontal and vertical seam each had a single, 1-inch-diameter (2.54 cm) stopwater to tighten the seams and deflect water. Here, as at other scarf locations, the seams were heavily caulked and tarred. The apron, seated atop the scarf and fastened in place with iron bolts, reinforced the join of the stem and keel.

The stern of the vessel is more complete than the bow (fig. 8.7). Surviving elements include the heel timber, sternpost, stern knee, and transom. The heel is an external knee that forms the connection between the keel and sternpost; it is an unusual piece that has not been seen on any of the other 1812-era hulls described in this book. The heel's 3-foot-long (90 cm) lower arm is joined to the keel by a 15-inch-long (38.1 cm) vertical flat scarf, the seam of which has two ½-inch-diameter (1.27 cm) stopwaters. The vertical arm of the heel is 1 foot 11 inches (57.94 cm) high and terminates at its upper end in a 1-foot-long (30 cm) scarf with the base of the sternpost. Stopwaters were not considered necessary in this scarf. Less than half of the sternpost's estimated original height of 5 feet 3 inches (1.58 m) survives. The post rakes aft at an angle of eighteen degrees and has square rabbets cut into its forward corners to fit the ends of the inner planking strakes. The final element in the lower stern assembly, the stern knee, was bolted atop the keel, heel timber, and sternpost to provide reinforcement to the scarfs. The top of the knee was notched to receive two floors.

The transom was made up of three planks edge-joined with iron bolts. The upper edge of the transom was beveled to accept deck planks while its outboard edges form a graceful curve from the sternpost

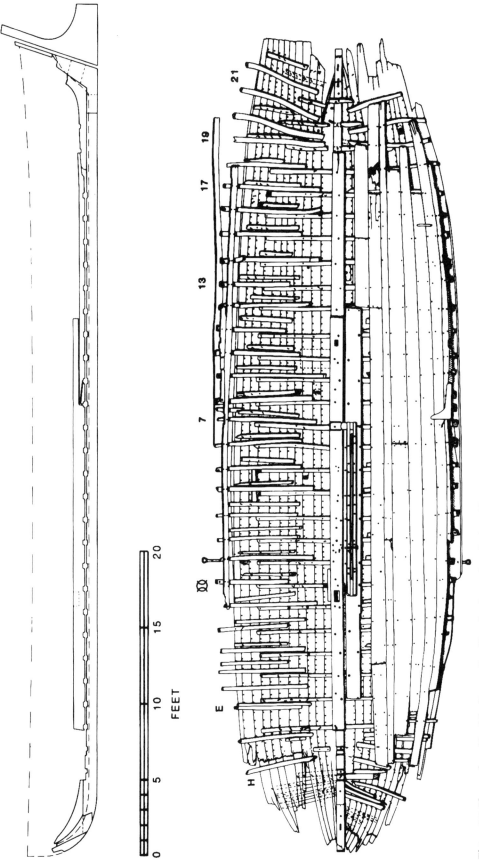

Figure 8.5. Plan and profile of the Browns Bay Vessel as it was found. The ceiling planking has been removed from the starboard side of the hull to show the framing pattern. (Drawing by Christopher Amer and C. Piper.)

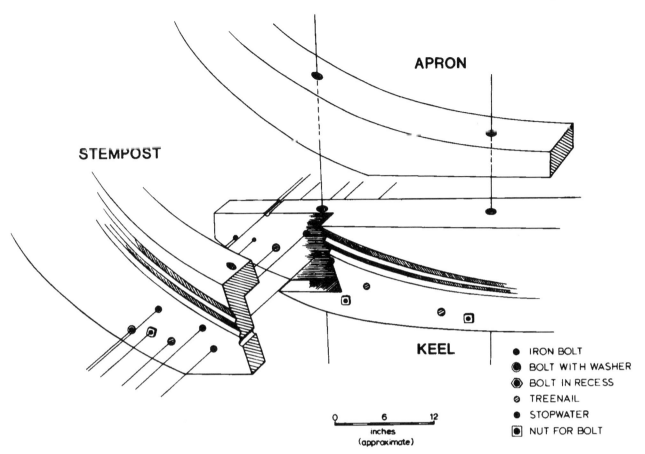

Figure 8.6. *An isometric view of the Browns Bay Vessel's bow timbers. This diagram shows the assembly of the keel, stem, and apron. (Drawing by C. Piper.)*

to deck level, thus defining the shape of the stern. The sternpost was let into a 6-inch-wide (15.24 cm) vertical groove in the forward face of the transom and fastened to it with iron spikes.

As noted above, the assembly of the Brown's Bay Vessel's sides began with the lapping and riveting of the planking; the framing elements were added later to provide additional strength to the plank shell. The hull was clinker planked from the garboard to the eleventh strake, while the three uppermost rows of planks, strakes 12 to 14, were carvel planked (fig. 8.8). The lapstrake planks of the lower hull averaged 8½ to 9½ inches (21.59 to 24.13 cm) wide amidships, taper-ing slightly toward the ends, and were ¾ inch (1.9 cm) thick (the garboards were 1 inch [2.54 cm] thick). The outboard edge of each strake lapped over the edge of the adjacent plank and was fastened at 6-inch (15.24 cm) intervals with copper nails riveted over square cop-per roves. The clinker strakes were also fastened to the floors and original futtocks with copper nails clenched over the inboard faces of the frames. The seams be-tween the garboards and keel rabbets were caulked with a fibrous material, while at the stem a thick layer of pine tar mixed with hog bristles and other fibers filled the spaces between the garboards and apron.

The shipwright was obliged to scarf planks together to make up the strakes, many of which exceed 55 feet (16.5 m) in length. Riveted vertical flat scarfs joined the clinker planks, while the carvel planks of strakes 12 through 14 were butt-joined over the frames. Strakes are fastened to frames by two nails at each futtock and by three nails at butt joints. Strake 14, the upper-most and heaviest of the carvel strakes, measured 10 inches wide (25.4 cm) by 1½ to 1¾ inches (3.81 to 4.44 cm) thick and consisted of two planks joined by a 4-foot-long (1.2 m) hook scarf. This strake strength-ened the sides of the hull above the waterline and also served as the attachment point for the chainplates, two of which were found still secured to the wreck.

At some point in the boat's career, a second layer

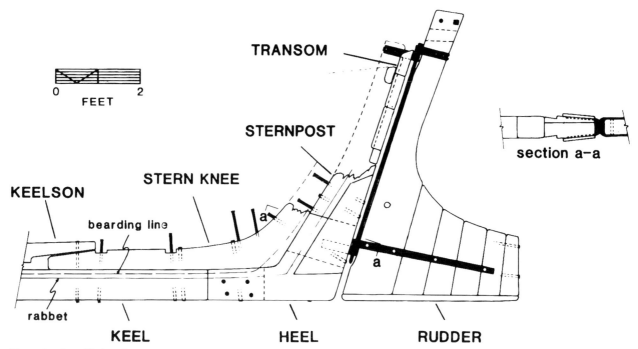

Figure 8.7. *A profile drawing of the Browns Bay Vessel's stern. The assembly includes the keel, an external knee or heel, a sternpost, a stern knee, and the keelson; the boat's complete rudder is also shown here. (Drawing by A. E. Wilson and Christopher Amer.)*

of clinker planking was fastened with iron nails to the outsides of strakes 1 to 11. The widths and thicknesses of these planks parallel those of the inner strakes. Rabbets were cut into the stem and forward end of the keel to fit the garboards of the outer planking layer. Abaft the bow, however, there were no rabbets for the garboards; they were nailed directly to the keel, and the seams were heavily caulked. Each strake of the outside layer is made up of two to four planks butt-joined over frames, with many planks as short as 4 feet (1.2 m) in length. It was not as critical to use long planks in the outer layer because the inner layer provided much of the strength and short planks were easier to acquire and fit on the hull, saving on refitting costs. The planks on the port side are both fewer and longer, which may indicate an attempt on the part of the shipwright to compensate for the weakness created when the floor timbers and planks were cut through for the installation of the centerboard.

The planking showed evidence of efforts to extend the life of the vessel. The hull was heavily sealed with pine tar; much of the coating on the outside of the hull was removed prior to conservation in 1967, but a thick layer remains between the inner and outer clinker strakes. Graving pieces in the planks attest to repairs; while wooden dowels replaced knots in the planking,

dowels in the stern plugged drain holes, some of which predated the second layer of planks. Three-quarter-inch-thick (1.9 cm) oak boards were nailed to either side of the sternpost to secure the hood ends of the planks and perhaps to seal leaks. Nail holes in the stem suggest similar boards were nailed over the planking ends in that location.

The Browns Bay Vessel originally contained a total of twenty-nine square frames and several pairs of cant frames in the bow and stern (see fig. 8.5). The floor timbers, on 18-inch (45.72 cm) centers, were notched underneath to fit corresponding notches in the top of the keel and stern knee. The floors vary from 2½ to 3½ inches (6.35 to 8.89 cm) sided and 3½ to 4½ inches (8.89 to 11.43 cm) molded and average about 11 feet (3.3 m) in length between frames F and 18. The notches on the bottoms of the floors were cut wider than was necessary to fit into the keel notches and thereby formed limber holes on either side of the keel. The floors were also notched on their undersides to fit the laps of the clinker planking.

The ninth square frame abaft the stem is the midship frame, which defined the maximum breadth of the hull. At some point in the vessel's history, most likely during the refit, a section of the midship frame directly above the port garboard was removed, perhaps

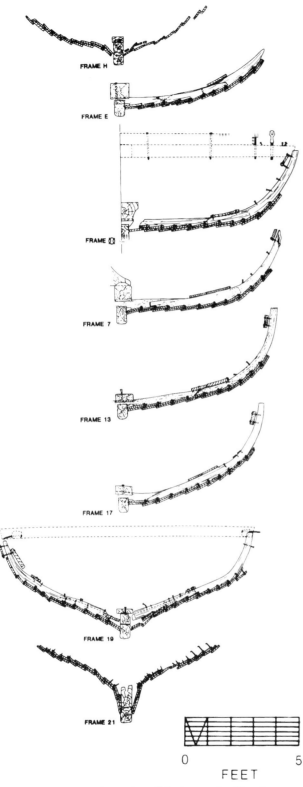

Figure 8.8. *Frame sections taken off the Browns Bay Vessel. The lapstrake assembly of the lower hull planking and the light framing are evident in these sections. (Drawings by Christopher Amer and Kevin J. Crisman.)*

to facilitate a repair to the inner garboard plank (a section is missing directly below the midship frame) or to create a pump well.[29] The midship floor and floor timbers 1 through 7 were cut through on the port side of the keel to permit the installation of the centerboard.

Fastening patterns and timber dimensions together indicate that the boat's futtocks were added at two different times: during the original construction and during a refit. The original futtocks are similar to the floor timbers in dimension and are more or less centered between floors, which they overlap by as much as 3 feet (90 cm). The exterior surfaces of the futtocks were joggled to closely fit the clinker planking. The upper ends of the original futtocks terminated at or below the eleventh strake, the uppermost strake of clinker planking on the hull.

Futtocks from the later rebuilding of the hull are represented on the starboard side by twenty-seven timbers between frames G and 19. These futtocks are more robust than those of the original construction. They were placed against the after sides of floors from frames D to 19 and forward of the floors from frame D to the bow; the floors and refit futtocks were not fastened to each other, however. These futtocks were also joggled to fit the clinker planks up to strake 11, and above this their outer surfaces were dubbed flat to seat three strakes of carvel planking.

The keelson is composed of three timbers installed at different periods in the vessel's history. The original keelson consisted of two pieces, 4½ inches molded by 10½ inches sided (11.43 by 26.67 cm), flat scarfed together amidships. The 16-foot-10-inch-long (5.05 m) after section is complete, but only a short piece of the forward section survives at the scarf. The forward section was replaced during the refit by a much heavier timber that measures 10 inches (25.4 cm) square and 27 feet 5½ inches (8.24 m) long. Extraneous fastener holes and features suggest that this piece may have been reused from some other hull or structure. The replacement keelson had a mortise cut into its upper surface to serve as a mast step, and all three keelson timbers were notched underneath to fit over the floors.

The vessel once contained eight ceiling strakes per side, each composed of three to four planks that were butt-joined over frames. Intact planks are 6 to 13½ inches (15.24 to 34.29 cm) wide and 1 to 1½ inches (2.54 to 3.81 cm) thick and vary in length from 4½ feet to almost 40 feet (1.35 to 12 m). Like the replacement keelson timber, some of the ceiling planks may have been reused pieces, as suggested by fastening holes and cutouts that do not match frame locations or hull features. The interior surfaces of many ceiling planks are heavily scored by extensive use. There is an imprint on the ceiling in the port quarter matching the stove recovered with the wreck.[30]

The port and starboard clamps were well preserved for approximately half their length. At least two and probably three sections once abutted to form the estimated 54-foot (16.2 m) stem-to-stern length of the clamps. Clamps are 5½ to 6½ inches (13.97 to 16.51 cm) wide, average 1½ to 2 inches (3.81 to 5.08 cm) thick, and were notched at the top to accept the ends of deck beams.

Two complete beams were raised with the hull, one from just forward of the midship frame and the other from the stern. The midship beam, 6 inches (15.24 cm) molded and 11¼ inches (28.58 cm) sided, was slightly cambered over its length and was originally secured to the hull with four lodging knees. The beam contains evidence of various functions, including notches to support the mast, carlings, and forward end of the centerboard trunk; a 12-foot-long (3.6 m) section of main hatch coaming was bolted to the beam's upper surface. Iron fittings include eyebolts to secure rigging and a centrally located collar to secure the mast. At least one of the eyebolts is stamped with a British broad arrow, indicating that it was originally government property. The second beam, located above frame 20, is 6 inches (15.24 cm) sided and 5½ inches (13.97 cm) molded and also has a very slight camber. Small, ¼-inch (6.35 mm) nails and nail holes along the beam's after edge provide evidence for an after deck. Similar holes near the forward edge, within 2½ feet (75 cm) of the beam ends, suggest the presence of gangways extending along the sides of the vessel amidships.

The vessel was fitted with a pivoting centerboard designed to increase lateral resistance and reduce leeway while under sail. The centerboard structure was installed against the port side of the keelson and consists of three components: the sill, the trunk, and the centerboard (see fig. 8.5). The centerboard sill is a single timber, 26 feet 2 inches (7.85 m) long, which extends from frame E to frame 12. Between the midship frame and frame 7, the sill was notched underneath to fill the spaces between floors and planking, and a slot 10 feet (3 m) long and 3½ inches (8.89 cm) wide was cut vertically through the midline of the sill, the floor timbers, and both layers of hull planks to allow the centerboard to be raised and lowered.

The centerboard trunk, composed of edge-fastened plank sides and two vertical end posts, measured 11 feet 9 inches (3.53 m) long and 7 to 8½ inches (17.78 to 21.59 cm) wide. It is fitted into mortises in the top of the sill and secured to the keelson by a knee; the trunk's end posts also abutted deck beams forward and aft. The centerboard itself was made up of six planks edge-joined with iron bolts. The complete board was 9 feet 7 inches (2.88 m) long, 4 feet 4 inches (1.3 m) wide, and 1½ inches (3.81 cm) thick. It pivoted on an iron pin inserted through the forward end of the trunk and was raised and lowered by means of a chain attached to the after end of the board.

The boat's wide-bladed rudder had a 7-foot-long (2.1 m) stock and a 4-foot-3-inch-long (1.28 m) blade, as measured along the sole piece (see fig. 8.7). It hung from the sternpost by four gudgeons, two of which were on the post and two on the rudder stock; a long, 1-inch-diameter (2.54 cm) iron rod passed through both pairs of gudgeons and served as the pintle. The upper end of the rudder stock was slotted to fit the tiller.

From Gunboat to Sailing Merchant Vessel

Restudy of the Browns Bay Vessel confirmed what earlier research suggested: the boat had two careers and underwent modifications during a rebuilding. The refit left the basic shell untouched but changed many features and altered the original appearance. Despite these changes and despite the fact that no evidence of a cannon platform was found in the bow or stern, there is little doubt that this craft was a British gunboat dating to the early nineteenth century.[31]

Several lines of evidence point to naval origins. First, the presence of broad arrow marks on fittings and blocks shows that numerous items of equipment on the boat were once property of the British government. Second, copper fastenings were rarely used in commercially built vessels on the lakes. Nails and spikes of copper were much more expensive than their iron counterparts and unnecessary because iron corrosion is not a problem in freshwater. The US Navy knew this and employed copper fastenings only for pump fittings and gunpowder magazines. Admiralty suppliers, far from the scene of the building and apparently ignorant of conditions on the lakes, simply drew on available stocks of materials and shipped copper fasteners and fittings across the Atlantic. As late as 1820, Royal Navy surveyors in Canada were reminding naval commissioners back home that "copper is not necessary in the construction of Ships which are not exposed to the corroding effects of Salt water."[32]

Finally, key elements in the boat's design and construction provide strong evidence that the Browns Bay Vessel was intended for a naval career (fig. 8.9). With its shallow, low-freeboard design and clinker construction, the wreck simply does not resemble any of the common varieties of commercial craft built on Lake Ontario and the Upper St. Lawrence River in the nineteenth century. Furthermore, the challenging repair requirements of clinker-constructed vessels—it is very difficult to replace rotted or damaged planks—made this sort of hull impractical for a purpose-built merchant vessel. It does, however, closely resemble certain types of Admiralty launches and gunboats of the period, craft that were intended to carry a large crew and do most of their maneuvering and fighting under oars.[33] The hull's size and general form also share common characteristics with plans and descriptions of British gunboats used in Europe and North America during the late eighteenth and the early nineteenth centuries.[34]

Can we link this particular hull with a name on the Royal Navy's lists of gunboats in Upper Canada? Possibly. All the vessels on the postwar navy list are too long, too short, or too narrow to match the Browns Bay Vessel, with the exception of a 56-ton gunboat named *Radcliffe.* This craft, authorized after the war and launched in March 1817, was apparently laid up with the rest of the Lake Ontario gunboat flotilla soon after its completion. In 1831 the hull was deemed beyond repair, the only one of eleven gunboats at Kingston to be selected for disposal that year (which suggests that its construction may have differed from the others).[35] *Radcliffe* had a length on deck of 54 feet (16.2 m), an extreme breadth of 15 feet 8 inches (4.7 m), and a depth of hold of 3 feet 3 inches (98 cm), measurements that are very close to those of the wreck (the slightly greater breadth of the latter is likely the result of the hull spreading after the loss of the upper stem and transom). In all, there is a strong possibility that *Radcliffe* and the Browns Bay Vessel are the same craft.[36]

When the vessel was rebuilt, it changed from an

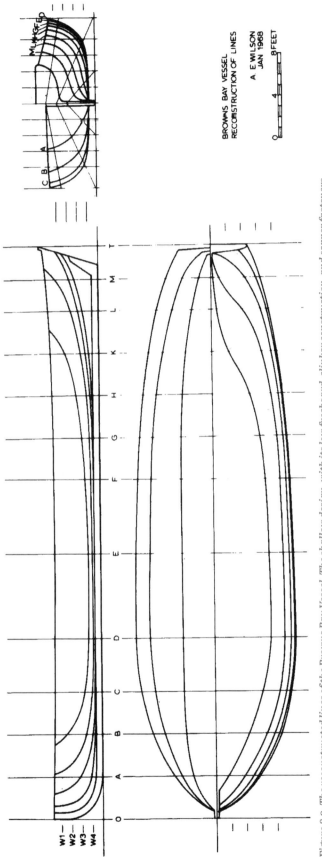

Figure 8.9. The reconstructed lines of the Browns Bay Vessel. The shallow design, with its low freeboard, clinker construction, and copper fasteners in the planking, strongly suggests that this craft was originally a Royal Navy gunboat. (Drawing by A. E. Wilson and C. Piper.)

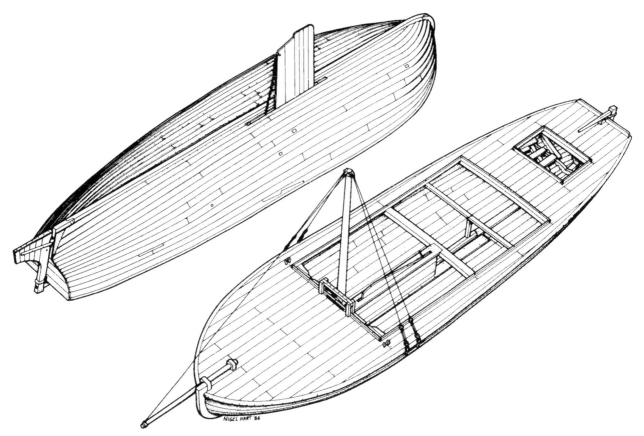

Figure 8.10. *Underside and deck reconstruction of the Browns Bay Vessel. The second layer of planking, the heavy coating of tar on the outside, and particularly the addition of the centerboard trunk and centerboard on the port side of the keel indicate that the hull was modified sometime after its construction to serve as a commercial cargo carrier. (Drawing by Nigel Mart.)*

oar and sail–propelled warship designed to carry one or two cannon and a large crew to a decked cargo-carrying vessel that could be sailed by a small crew (fig. 8.10). The features inherent in a lapstrake hull, longitudinal strength, thin planking, and light framing, were retained and enhanced during the refit. The original futtocks appear to have been cut off at the eleventh strake and the structure above that point removed, perhaps due to rot in the upperworks or because the hull needed strengthening. Larger futtocks that carried up to the sheer were added between floor timbers and existing futtocks. The upperworks were then replanked with three carvel strakes, the uppermost and thickest of which acted as a wale.

I believe that the topsides of the hull were always carvel planked. Although most of the original futtocks were cut off short during the refit, some in the stern were left complete, and their outer faces were dubbed flat above the eleventh strake. The outboard edges of the transom also showed no evidence of notch-

ing above the eleventh strake. This combination of a clinker-planked bottom and carvel sides seems to have been common in vessels of this type and is shown in a plan of a gunboat built in Ipswich, England in 1809.[37] While the gunboat in the plan is not as flat bottomed as the Browns Bay Vessel, it too has eleven overlapping strakes from the keel to above the turn of the bilge.

Clamps fastened to the inboard faces of the futtocks just below the sheer line provided additional longitudinal strength and supported the deck beams that stiffened the hull laterally. Only two deck beams survived on the wreck, but notches in the clamp show the locations of five more beams. In its gunboat configuration the hull probably would have been fitted with strengthened cannon platforms at the bow and stern, with an open area amidships for the rowers' stations. Nail patterns on the tops of the surviving beams suggest that the boat was flush decked with gunwale-to-gunwale fore and quarter decks and narrow, 2-foot-wide (60 cm) gangways on each side of a large central hatch.

During the refit, the forward section of keelson was removed and replaced by a larger timber. This no doubt added longitudinal strength to the flexible hull and enhanced its cargo-carrying ability. The larger timber also distributed the weight of the mast, which may have been of greater dimensions and carried a heavier press of sail than the vessel's previous rig.

The shallow keel and minimal draft necessitated the addition of a centerboard to reduce leeway when sailing close to the wind. The pivoting centerboard was ideally suited for navigation of shoal waters and for beaching to load and unload cargo. The centerboard structure was probably installed at the same time as the replacement keelson section but prior to the addition of the second layer of hull planking. The rectangular slot cut in the outer plank layer for the centerboard opening is significantly larger than the slot in the inner planking, and there are no cut marks on the latter. If the exterior strakes had been in place when the centerboard was installed, there would likely have been a single cut through both layers.

More than any other feature, the centerboard truly signaled the change in careers for the vessel. A centerboard was not vital in a gunboat that depended primarily on its oars and oarsmen for maneuvering in tight spots, and centerboards do not appear on plans or descriptions of gunboats from the 1812 era. The pivoting centerboard was a very recent invention at the time of the war (it was reportedly developed in 1809), and it did not come into widespread use in North America until the 1820s.[38]

A new rudder may also have been part of the refit. The shape of the rudder found on the wreck does not conform to contemporary plans and illustrations of rudders on early-nineteenth-century gunboats. The wide blade would not have been necessary in a vessel where oarsmen could provide maneuverability, but for a sailing vessel navigating confined waterways, the wide-bladed rudder must have greatly improved steering.

The second layer of strakes spiked over the original planking was added during or sometime after the major refit, probably after the installation of the centerboard. The hull was also heavily coated with tar to inhibit decay and seal the seams. The first application of tar may have been in the 1820s, while the boat was still government property. Commissioner Robert Barrie, responsible for maintaining the laid-up warships at

Kingston, requested information from the Admiralty in 1820 on the application of tar to preserve the boats, a procedure that apparently had not been previously adopted.[39] It was not until 1822 that Surveyor of the Navy Sir Robert Seppings provided directions on how to scrape the wood and apply warm tar.[40] The exterior coating of tar removed from the outside of the hull in 1967 was clearly added after the refit.

The modifications to the hull are characterized by the use of wrought-iron fastenings throughout, whereas the original construction included many of copper. As we have seen, the Admiralty was advised by one of its surveyors in 1820 that copper was unnecessary in freshwater hulls. The presence of wrought-iron threaded bolts in the vessel also suggests a date after 1820 for the refit, since threaded bolts apparently came into widespread use in shipbuilding between 1820 and 1850.[41]

Conclusions

The hull of the Browns Bay Vessel has many similarities with Royal Navy launches and related types of clinker-built boats of the eighteenth and early nineteenth centuries; it also has many features in common with known British gunboats in operation on North American waterways during the first half of the nineteenth century. It was a broad, shallow-draft craft with a slight rise in the sheer at the bow and stern, a moderately full bow, and a transom stern. The archaeological study of the hull demonstrated that it was a well-built boat, strong, light, and flexible. The hull form is well suited to navigation in shallow or confined waters, for use as a floating gun platform, for transportation of men, and for landing troops and equipment. Under oars the original vessel may have been quite fast and maneuverable.

The conversion of the rowed gunboat into a sailing cargo vessel was probably carried out sometime after 1820, perhaps by the Royal Navy but more likely by civilian owners who purchased the hull after 1831. The modifications did not alter the basic hull form and retained many of the features that made the vessel a useful naval craft. The elimination of oars as a principal mode of propulsion made the boat more practical and economical as a cargo carrier. The extremely shallow draft was not an ideal feature for a sailing craft, however, particularly in the narrow passages of the St. Lawrence River, for it gave the vessel scant lateral resistance to the force of the wind. This problem was solved by the addition of a centerboard and larger rudder, which counteracted the vessel's tendency to fall off to leeward.

The Browns Bay Vessel had a long career, beginning as one of His Majesty's warships built around the time of the War of 1812 and ending its days as a commercial cargo carrier. The many repairs to the hull and its collection of artifacts all suggest the aging vessel sank in Browns Bay around the middle of the nineteenth century. It is, at present, the only known Royal Navy gunboat from the period of the War of 1812 (plate 8b). The fact that the hull shows repairs and modifications attaches additional significance to this unique craft. Of the sixteen warships described in this book, it is the only one that seems to have successfully transitioned from naval to commercial use in the decades following the war.[42]

NOTES

1. A. McKennon, "The H.M.S. Radcliffe" (manuscript, St. Lawrence Islands National Park, Mallorytown, ON, 1973), p. 3; Walter Zacharchuk, "The Raising of the Mallorytown Wreck," in *The Conference on Historic Site Archaeology Papers, 1967*, vol. 2, pt. 1, ed. Stanley A. South (Raleigh, NC: Conference on Historical Archaeology, 1968), p. 85.

2. Walter Zacharchuk, "One of a Thousand Wrecks" (manuscript, National Historic Parks and Sites Branch, 1969), p. 1.

3. A wreck described as an "Old British Gunboat" was raised from the Thames River, Ontario, around the beginning of the twentieth century. It is believed to have been one of General Proctor's vessels that were scuttled in 1814. A photograph and brief description are all that could be found relating to the vessel. James Oliver Curwood, *The Great Lakes* (New York: G. P. Putnam's Sons, 1909), pp. 212–13.

4. Boris Rankov, "Fleets of the Early Roman Empire, 31 b.c.–a.d. 324," in *The Age of the Galley: Mediterranean Oared Vessels since Pre-Classical Times*, ed. John Gardiner (London: Conway Maritime Press, 1995), pp. 80–82.

5. Pekka Toivanan, "The Burial Grounds of the Russian Galley Fleet in the Gulf of Bothnia (Finland) from 1714," in *Underwater Archaeology Proceedings from the Society for Historical Archaeology Conference*, ed. John Broadwater (Rockville, MD: Society for Historical Archaeology, 1991), pp. 65–70.

6. The comments of Capt. J. B. Irwin, assistant quartermaster general of the British Army in Canada, stand as an example of the amateur's enthusiasm for gunboats. He wrote in March of 1813, "They are calculated for the calms so prevalent in the Lake Ontario, and by taking prompt advantage of such a moment, *one of the boats in question could teaze and cut up the largest vessel in such a way as to force it to shift its station, if not perhaps to capture it.*" Irwin to Noah Freer, March 29, 1813, series C, 729, p. 148, record group 8 (RG 8), Library and Archives Canada (LAC).

7. Robert Malcomson, *Warships of the Great Lakes 1754–1834* (London: Chatham Publishing, 2001), pp. 18–19; Kevin Crisman, "Struggle for a Continent: Naval Battles of the French and Indian Wars," in *Ships and Shipwrecks of the Americas*, ed. George F. Bass (London: Thames and Hudson, 1988), pp. 147–48.

8. John R. Bratten, *The Gondola* Philadelphia *and the Battle of Lake Champlain* (College Station, TX: Texas A&M University Press, 2002); John W. Jackson, *The Pennsylvania Navy, 1775–1781: The Defense of the Delaware* (New Brunswick, NJ: Rutgers University Press, 1974).

9. William Wood, ed., *Select British Documents of the Canadian War of 1812*, vol. 1 (Toronto: The Champlain Society, 1920), pp. 246–47.

10. William Wood, ed., *Select British Documents of the Canadian War of 1812*, vol. 2 (Toronto: The Champlain Society, 1923), pp. 114–16.

11. Judith Beattie, "Gunboats on the St. Lawrence River (1763–1839)" (manuscript report no. 15, National Historic Sites Service, 1967), p. 12.

12. Beattie, "Gunboats on the St. Lawrence," p. 64.

13. Beattie, "Gunboats on the St. Lawrence," p. 64.

14. Beattie, "Gunboats on the St. Lawrence," p. 66; Adrian B. Caruana, *The History of English Sea Ordnance 1523–1875, Volume II: The Age of the System, 1715–1815* (East Sussex: Jean Boudriot Publications, 1997), pp. 178–81.

15. Beattie, "Gunboats on the St. Lawrence," p. 23.

16. Robert Malcomson, *Lords of the Lake, The Naval War on Lake Ontario, 1812–1814* (Toronto: Robin Brass Studio, 1998), pp. 161–62.

17. Isaac Chauncey to William Jones, June 20, 1814, Isaac Chauncey Letter Book, vol. 2, New York Historical Society, New York.

18. Malcomson, *Lords of the Lake*, pp. 129–34; William S. Dudley, ed., *The Naval War of 1812, A Documentary History*, vol. 2 (Washington, DC: Naval Historical Center, 1992), pp. 470–73.

19. Beattie, "Gunboats on the St. Lawrence," pp. 11–12, 17.

20. William Wood, ed., *Select British Documents of the Canadian War of 1812*, vol. 3, pt. 1 (Toronto: The Champlain Society, 1926), pp. 78–79; Michael J. Crawford, ed., *The Naval War of 1812: A Documentary History*, vol. 3 (Washington, DC: Naval Historical Center, 2002), pp. 508–12; Malcomson, *Lords of the Lake*, pp. 278–82.

21. Beattie, "Gunboats on the St. Lawrence," pp. 24–25, 68.

22. Beattie, "Gunboats on the St. Lawrence," p. 73.

23. Beattie, "Gunboats on the St. Lawrence," pp. 32–34.

24. Walter Zacharchuk, "Architectural Report on The Browns Bay Gunboat" (manuscript report, National Historic Parks and Sites Branch, Parks Canada, 1981).

25. Zacharchuk, "Architectural Report"; Iain C. Walker, *Clay Tobacco-pipes, with Particular Reference to the Bristol Industry*, Canada National Historic Parks and Sites Branch History and

Archaeology Series 11C (Ottawa: Parks Canada, 1977), pp. 1025–26; Peter Davey, ed. *The Archaeology of the Clay Tobacco Pipe, Vol. 10: Scotland,* BAR British Series, 178 (Oxford: B.A.R., 1987), pp. 105–106.

26. Walter Zacharchuk and John M. Rick, "The Mallorytown Wreck," *Historical Archaeology* 3 (1969), p. 11.

27. Moisture contents of timbers from various areas on the hull were as follows: hull planks and keelson, 9.5 to 11.0 percent; frames, 8.25 to 10.0 percent; and ceiling, 9.0 to 15.5 percent. Lorne D. Murdock, "Examination and Maintenance Recommendations for Browns Bay Shipwreck on display at St. Lawrence Islands National Park, Mallorytown, Ontario" (manuscript report, Conservation Division, Parks Canada, 1985).

28. The 105 hours of recording was carried out by Chris Amer, with two days of participation by Kevin Crisman.

29. Zacharchuk and Rick, "The Mallorytown Wreck," p. 10.

30. Zacharchuk, "Architectural Report."

31. Beattie, "Gunboats on the St. Lawrence," pp. 23–127; Zacharchuk, "The Raising of the Mallorytown Wreck," p. 85.

32. Beattie, "Gunboats on the St. Lawrence," p. 101; vol. 31, pp. 118–23, series 3a, RG 8, LAC.

33. Brian Lavery, *The Ship of the Line, Vol. 2: Design, Construction and Fittings* (Annapolis: Naval Institute Press, 1984), p. 126, Fig. 1; Robert Gardiner, *Warships of the Napoleonic Era* (London: Chatham Publishing, 1999), p. 98.

34. Chapelle, *The History of the American Sailing Navy* (New York: W. W. Norton, 1949), p. 94, Fig. 11b, RN gunboat 1776; 81203/44, items 2 and 3, National Map Collection, record group 24M, LAC. In 1808 the Royal Navy began building scores of clinker-hulled gunboats for use in European waters that were based on a plan prepared by Capt. Thomas Hamilton; this design was similar in length and breadth to the Browns Bay Vessel but had a much sharper hull. See Gardiner, *Warships of the Napoleonic Era,* pp. 73–74.

35. Admiralty Order, signed by Second Naval Lord Admiral George Dundas and J. G. Barrington, Admiralty, London, March 29, 1831, series 3a, Admiralty Lakes Service, vol. 42, RG 8, LAC. Courtesy of Dana Ashdown.

36. Beattie, "Gunboats on the St. Lawrence," p. 126. A plaque bearing the name of the gunboat *Radcliffe* was displayed over the Browns Bay Vessel when it was exhibited at Mallorytown. Dana Ashdown (February 15, 2010, personal communication with Kevin Crisman) has suggested a second possible identity for the wreck, the 60-ton *Bullfrog* of 1833, which was referred to as a yacht, a yard boat, and a tender for the naval facilities at Kingston.

37. 78903/44, item 5, National Map Collection, RG 24M, LAC.

38. Chapelle, *American Sailing Navy,* p. 237. The earliest dated archaeological example of a pivoting centerboard-equipped vessel in North America is the wreck of the Lake Champlain canal schooner *Troy,* sunk in November 1825 near Westport, New York; see Kevin Crisman, "Sails on an Inland Sea: The Evolution of Lake Champlain's Sailing Merchant Fleet," in *The Philosophy of Shipbuilding: Conceptual Approaches to the Study of Wooden Ships,* eds. Fredrick M. Hocker and Cheryl Ward (College Station, TX: Texas A&M University Press, 2004), pp. 143–47.

39. ADM 106/1999, TNA: PRO.

40. F 66, vol. 2, pp. 79–83, MG 12, LAC.

41. David Lyon, personal communication, 1985.

42. After forty years in a boathouse at the St. Lawrence Islands National Park site at Mallorytown Landing, the hull of the gunboat was inspected, stabilized, packed for shipment, and then moved to a new location on August 4, 2011. The gunboat is now on display in the visitor's center at Parks Canada's Fort Wellington National Historic Site in Prescott, Ontario. *Ottawa Sun,* August 17, 2011.

Part III

The Naval War of 1812 on Lake Champlain

KEVIN J. CRISMAN

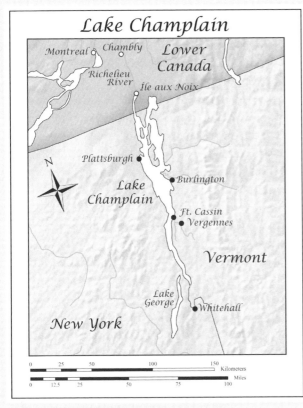

Figure III.1. *Lake Champlain in the War of 1812.*
(Map by Douglas Inglis.)

The first two years of the War of 1812 saw little naval activity on Lake Champlain, a curious fact in light of the American government's stated intentions when it declared war (fig. III.1). This region was the obvious starting gate for any serious US effort to invade Canada. The lake's northern terminus at the Richelieu River was close to Montreal and Quebec, Canada's centers of trade, communications, government, and defense. Indeed, from a British viewpoint, Montreal was perilously close, only 40 miles (64 km) distant from the US border. Lake Champlain's southern end (and head of navigation) at Whitehall, New York, was but a short overland distance from the upper Hudson River and hence much closer to sources of naval and military supplies than the Great Lakes. And there were precedents for using the Champlain-Richelieu corridor to invade Canada, successfully when the British conquered New France in 1760 and almost successfully when rebelling American colonists attempted to wrest Canada from the British in 1775–76.

Despite the encouragement provided by geography and history, the direct route into Canada was given short shrift by the war's planners in Washington. Instead, as we have seen in the previous chapters, US efforts focused on Canada's western frontier. To a great degree this was a default strategy, the momentum of regional enthusiasm: the Republican western states were far more interested in prosecuting the war than the Federalist New England states.

Efforts to invade Lower Canada were not entirely lacking. Two expeditions were launched against Montreal, one in late 1812 headed by Gen. Henry Dearborn and the other in late 1813 by Gen. James Wilkinson and Gen. Wade Hampton; both floundered badly due to poor planning, inadequate resources, and the ineptitude of their commanders.[1] The leadership and the professional army needed to conquer Canada were missing during the war's first two years, and by 1814 the window of opportunity was effectively closed.

Whereas the opposing navies on Lake Ontario started the war with purpose-built warships and rapidly added more and much larger vessels to their squadrons over the next year and a half, the naval forces on Champlain got by in 1812 and 1813 with the bare minimum: armed merchant sloops and small gunboats. Both navies adopted a defensive posture in this theater of operations, with protection of the border being the first priority. Waterborne raids took place on a limited, opportunistic basis, but it was only in 1814 that one navy made a concerted effort to dominate the waters on the other side of the border.

Besides its separate location far to the east of the Great Lakes, Champlain had different navigational and logistical parameters. The lake is relatively narrow (12 miles [19.3 km] at its widest point) in proportion to its overall length of 120 miles (193 km). The northern reaches are broken up by islands and shallows, while the southern one-third of the lake tapers to a channel that resembles a river. Compared to the western lakes, Champlain offered far less room for opposing naval squadrons to maneuver. And unlike Lakes Ontario, Erie, and Huron, with their shorelines more or less equally divided between US and Canadian territory, nearly all of Lake Champlain lies inside the United States, with New York to the west and Vermont to the east. A British naval force sailing on its waters could regard every shore as hostile.

Conditions for building and outfitting US naval vessels also differed from the challenges faced by Perry on Lake Erie and Chauncey on Lake Ontario. Lake Champlain had several good locations for establishing a shipyard, sites that were sheltered from the open lake, near centers of population, transportation, and industry, and easily defended against surprise attacks. In 1813–14, the US Navy built its ships at Vergennes, Vermont, located 6 miles (9.65 km) up a narrow, winding river—Otter Creek—and adjacent to forests of good oak and pine, as well as to water-powered saw mills. A fully functioning foundry, the Monkton Iron Works, lay directly across the river from the government's shipyard. Thus the raw materials necessary for building vessels, timber, iron fasteners, and iron ballast, were close at hand; the Monkton Iron Works also produced much of the shot needed by the squadron, although it was incapable of casting cannon.[2] Naval stores not

available in the region could be shipped up from New York City in short order.

The British naval force on Lake Champlain also operated in circumstances notably different from the Great Lakes squadrons. Here the Royal Navy's "home waters" consisted of the Richelieu River, the lake's 106-mile-long (171 km) outlet to the St. Lawrence River. The course of the Richelieu was interrupted by rapids at Chambly that prevented vessels on the St. Lawrence from sailing directly up to the lake. Small gunboats could be hauled around the rapids, but large warships had to be built from scratch on the upper river, and once launched their cruising range within Canada was limited to the 25 miles (40 km) of channel between the lake and Chambly.

In 1813–14, the Royal Navy's shipbuilding took place on Isle aux Noix, a fortified island base about 11 miles (17.4 km) below the US-Canadian border. The Richelieu River yard was close to sources of naval supply in Montreal and Quebec, as well as to shipments of ordnance and equipment sent from Britain, but its output was given a lower priority than the building effort on Lake Ontario. Good shipbuilding timber was also hard to get at Isle aux Noix, and shipwrights there had to settle for second-rate woods or shipments of frame timbers, planks, masts, and yards smuggled across the border from Vermont forests.[3]

Thomas Macdonough commanded the US Navy's forces on Lake Champlain throughout the war (fig. III.2). A native of Delaware who entered the navy as a fifteen-year-old midshipman in 1798, Macdonough saw considerable action in the Mediterranean against the Barbary States as a young man. He was promoted to lieutenant in 1807, the rank he still held when ordered to Lake Champlain on September 28, 1812 (he was rapidly promoted, first to master commandant in 1813 and then captain in 1814). Although described as "a very mild & pleasant man," Macdonough demanded much of himself and of the men he commanded and, like his colleague Oliver H. Perry, was relentlessly single-minded when it came to achieving his goals. A professional through and through, he had little patience for naval officers who did not know how to manage a ship or showed lack of dedication to the service. Nevertheless, he was widely respected by most subordinates; one midshipman serving on the lake commented, "I like him very much he is . . . a fine sailor & a real gentleman."[4]

Figure III.2. Thomas Macdonough, commander of the US squadron on Lake Champlain, 1812–14. Dedicated to the service, knowledgeable about the building, outfitting, and sailing of warships, and relentless in his pursuit of objectives, Macdonough proved to be a good choice for this assignment. Like his colleague Oliver Hazard Perry on Lake Erie, he was also supremely lucky, surviving a very bloody battle virtually unscathed. In this portrait, painted after his victory at Plattsburgh Bay, Macdonough wears the two epaulets of a captain. (National Museum of American History, Smithsonian Institution.)

Macdonough arrived at the lake in October 1812 and found that the vessels at his disposal included two old gunboats and six merchant sloops recently purchased by the US Army. Only three of the sloops were suitable for arming, and one of them first had to be extracted from the grasp of General Dearborn, who aspired to command his own naval force.[5] Macdonough temporarily repaired and armed his five-vessel squadron at Whitehall, New York, that fall, and once winter closed the lake he had the sloops redecked and strengthened to carry more guns. When the lake thawed in the spring of 1813, the US Navy sailed with *President* (12 guns), *Growler* (11 guns), and *Eagle* (11 guns).[6]

When the year 1813 began, the British had only three gunboats (2 guns each) on the upper Richelieu, and there seemed scant prospect of their threatening US control of the lake. However, this situation drasti-

cally changed on the morning of June 3, when during Macdonough's temporary absence from the squadron, his senior lieutenant ordered *Growler* and *Eagle* to sail down the Richelieu River to challenge the enemy. It was a foolish move. A south wind and the river's current made it difficult to work back up to the lake, and inside the narrow channel the sloops were easy targets for the combined fire of the gunboats and of troops lined along the shore. The surrender of the US sloops after a lengthy shooting match instantly altered the balance of forces on the lake.[7]

While Macdonough hurried to arm more vessels at Burlington, Vermont, the British assembled an expeditionary force and sailed up the lake in late July with their newly acquired sloops (renamed *Shannon* and *Broke*), the three gunboats, forty-seven bateaux, and a contingent of about one thousand troops. The raiders landed without opposition at Plattsburgh, New York, to capture or burn US government property, briefly bombarded Burlington, and destroyed or carried off a handful of merchant sloops.[8] Macdonough reconstituted his squadron and returned to the lake by late summer. He kept the British bottled in the river for the remainder of the year, but the overall performance of the US Navy on the lake in 1813 was not impressive.

By late 1813 it was apparent that Lake Champlain's time as the quiet sector of the inland naval war was over. A shipbuilding race got underway and quickly gained the momentum that characterized activity on the other lakes. That fall the senior Royal Navy officer at Isle aux Noix, Lt. Daniel Pring, received permission to expand his squadron with five new gunboats and a 16-gun brig, *Linnet*; the latter vessel constituted a serious challenge to the US Navy's armed sloops. Macdonough initially planned to build more gunboats at his winter quarters at Vergennes, but news of the British brig led to the construction of more substantial vessels, a 26-gun ship, *Saratoga,* and a 17-gun schooner, *Ticonderoga*. Six large two-gun row galleys rounded out the new US squadron.[9]

Saratoga served as Macdonough's flagship throughout the summer and early fall of 1814. Built by Noah Brown of New York City (the celebrated shipwright who created Perry's squadron on Lake Erie the previous year), the vessel was laid down on March 7 and launched only 35 days later. According to a set of existing plans *Saratoga*'s hull measured 143 feet 6 inches (43.7 m) between perpendiculars, had a molded beam of 36 feet 4 inches (11 m), featured a very shallow draft and moderate deadrise to the floors, and had a nearly flat sheer (fig. III.3). The ship mounted 26 guns on its flush main deck: eight long 24 pounders on truck carriages, twelve 32-pounder carronades, and six 42-pounder carronades.[10]

On Lake Champlain, as on the other lakes, military and naval intelligence flowed easily across the border, and by April 1814 both protagonists knew, more or less, what the other was preparing.[11] Because the Royal Navy's new brig would be outclassed by the new US vessels, Pring made a point of getting on the water first. In early May, the British squadron sailed up the lake to the mouth of Otter Creek with the intention of either destroying the unfinished US ships or blocking the river by sinking sloops in the channel. Delayed by contrary winds, the expedition lost the element of surprise and found the entrance to the river defended by an earthwork-protected artillery battery and the US row galley flotilla. After a brief exchange of fire, Pring called off the attack and the British ships returned to Canada.[12] The enlarged and improved US Navy squadron sailed in late May and held uncontested control of the lake for the next three months.[13]

Momentous events taking place on the far side of the Atlantic that spring had repercussions in the Champlain Valley later in the summer. The collapse of Napoleon Bonaparte's armies and his abdication in April 1814 ended a decade of continuous fighting in Europe and allowed Great Britain, for the first time, to direct full attention and greater resources to the war in North America. The desire to chastise those who started this sideshow conflict was powerful. The 12th Earl of Eglinton, Hugh Montgomerie, succinctly stated the view widely shared by British political and military leaders in the wake of Napoleon's fall. "The only thing now is those cursed Americans," he wrote on May 1, 1814, "I hope a sufficient force will be sent to crush them at once."[14] Opinions varied upon the extent of the chastisement to be meted out, but most agreed that it must be severe. Royal Navy Adm. Sir David Milne, assigned to the blockade of New England's coast, was confident that:

The Americans must now yield to any terms we may please to offer them. I really think we ought even now oblige them to have a new form of government, for certainly the present one cannot

remain. At all events they must be made to give up all the lakes in Canada, [and] both Florida and Louisiana to us.[15]

Conquest of the United States was not seriously contemplated—the country was too big to occupy, and after the lengthy war in Europe the British had no wish to see this conflict continue indefinitely. Instead, a total of forty-four regiments from the Duke of Wellington's seasoned army in Spain, from England, and from overseas garrisons were sent to serve in Canada or to work in conjunction with the Royal Navy along the eastern seaboard of North America.[16] These forces were to attack shipping, ports, industries, military and naval depots, as well as capture strategic territory, the goal being to destroy the credibility of James Madison's government and shatter the US will to fight. Formal negotiations to end the war were scheduled to begin at Ghent in the Austrian Netherlands (modern-day Belgium), and a string of crushing US defeats on land, lakes, and sea, along with the occupation of selected territory, would ensure that British diplomats could impose the harshest possible peace terms.

The British government's instructions to Gov. Gen. Sir George Prevost, dated June 3, outlined the priorities for the 1814 campaign in the north. Prevost was to provide for the "protection . . . and ultimate security" of Canada by the destruction of the US naval establishments on Lakes Ontario, Erie, and Champlain, to occupy Detroit and parts of the Michigan Territory, and to seize "any advanced position" on the Lake Champlain frontier. The last objective was intended both to protect Montreal and Lower Canada and to provide further leverage in the peace negotiations. Prevost was warned not to advance too far into US territory and thereby risk having his army encircled and destroyed.[17] These orders provided the strategic basis for the British invasion of the Champlain Valley later that summer.

Even before Prevost received his instructions, the Royal Navy took steps to regain the initiative on Lake Champlain by commencing work on a frigate to mount 37 guns (27 long 24 pounders, six 24-pounder carronades, and four 32-pounder carronades). The keel was laid at Isle aux Noix in early June. Named *Confiance* upon its launch on August 25, the vessel was the largest warship ever built on Lake Champlain (fig. III.4). The hull measured 147 feet 6 inches (44.95 m) in length on

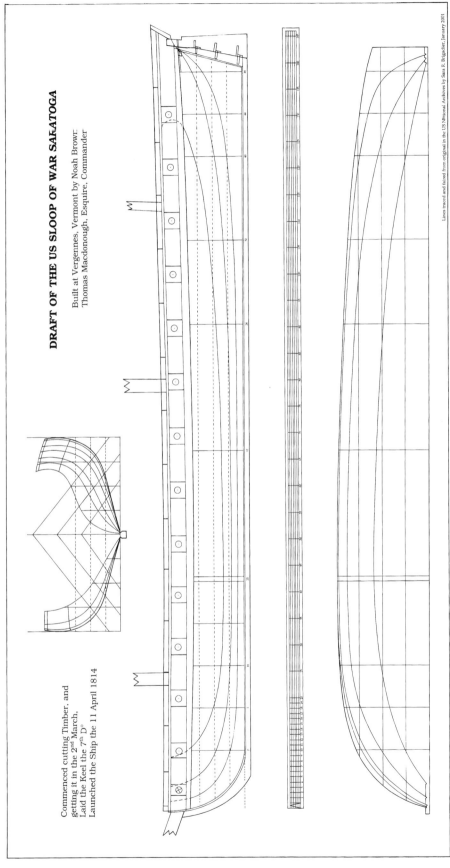

DRAFT OF THE US SLOOP OF WAR SARATOGA

Built at Vergennes, Vermont by Noah Brown.
Thomas Macdonough, Esquire, Commander

Commenced cutting Timber, and
getting it in the 2nd March,
Laid the Keel the 7th Do
Launched the Ship the 11 April 1814

Lines traced and faired from original in the US National Archives by Sara R. Brigadier, January 2001

Figure III.3. *The US Navy corvette Saratoga, built at Vergennes, Vermont, in 1814. The 26-gun Saratoga served as Macdonough's flagship from May through September 1814 and bore the brunt of the fighting during the Battle of Lake Champlain. This is the only known contemporary set of lines for any of the fourteen large US Navy warships built on the North American lakes during the War of 1812. (Lines traced and faired by Sara R. Brigadier from ship plan 41-5-6B, Record Group 19, National Archives and Records Administration.)*

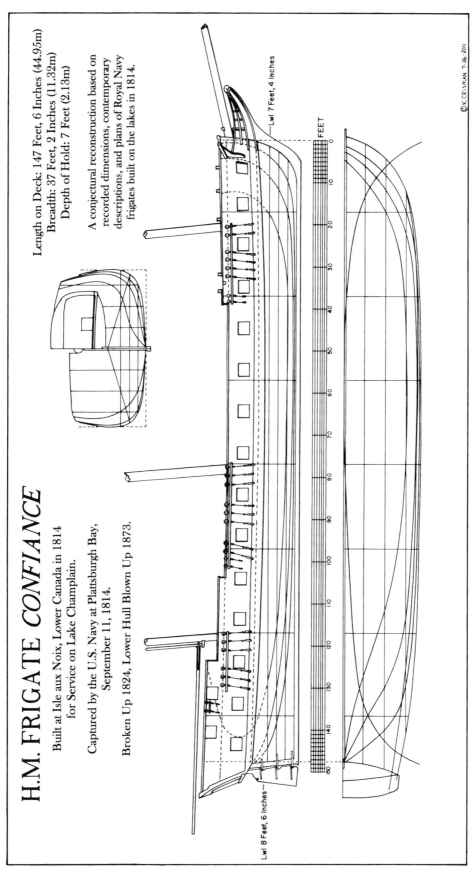

H.M. FRIGATE *CONFIANCE*

Built at Isle aux Noix, Lower Canada in 1814
for Service on Lake Champlain.

Captured by the U.S. Navy at Plattsburgh Bay,
September 11, 1814.

Broken Up 1824, Lower Hull Blown Up 1873.

Length on Deck: 147 Feet, 6 Inches (44.95m)
Breadth: 37 Feet, 2 Inches (11.32m)
Depth of Hold: 7 Feet (2.13m)

A conjectural reconstruction based on
recorded dimensions, contemporary
descriptions, and plans of Royal Navy
frigates built on the lakes in 1814.

Lwl 7 Feet, 4 Inches

Lwl 8 Feet, 6 Inches

FEET

© K. CRISMAN 7-26-2011

Figure III.4. A conjectural reconstruction of the Royal Navy frigate Confiance. This vessel had a very short career: Confiance was launched less than three weeks before the confrontation at Plattsburgh Bay, and carpenters were still working aboard the frigate until the morning it sailed into battle. The length, beam, depth of hold, and draft of the hull were recorded, and we know something about the distribution of guns on its two decks but not much more. No original plans of Confiance are known to exist. This is a "best guess" of the vessel's design and appearance based on the available information. (Reconstruction by Kevin J. Crisman.)

the gun deck and 37 feet 2 inches (11.35 m) in beam and had a depth of hold of 7 feet (2.13 m), making it extraordinarily long and broad in proportion to the shallow depth.[18] It was described as being framed with flat, long floor timbers, which made the hull quite full in section. *Confiance*'s construction was rushed and, according to a postwar assessment, incorporated "the very worst timber for building ships."[19]

It did not take long for spies and deserters to bring news of the new British frigate to the US squadron. In early June, with the paint barely dried on his expensive new ships and gunboats, Macdonough asked Navy Secretary William Jones for permission to build yet another large warship. At this point in the war, the US government was fast running out of money and the navy was stretched painfully thin. Jones was not enthusiastic, particularly when Macdonough noted that on Lake Champlain, "there is no knowing where [the British] building may stop."[20] Goaded by President James Madison, however, the secretary reluctantly approved this addition to the squadron, and on a later-than-last-minute schedule, Noah Brown's brother Adam completed and launched the 20-gun brig *Eagle* in time for the climactic encounter on the lake.

The contest for the Champlain Valley formally began on September 1, when an army of ten thousand British troops—the largest ever to enter the United States during the War of 1812—crossed the border on the New York side of the lake and began to march southward.[21] Sir George Prevost was following his instructions to seize an "advanced position." He faced trifling opposition—only three thousand four hundred US Army regulars and local militia under Brig. Gen. Alexander Macomb.[22] Seeing no future in an uneven fight in the open, Macomb did little to oppose the British advance from the border to Plattsburgh and instead positioned his troops in earthwork fortifications south of town. Macdonough, meanwhile, withdrew his squadron from its watch on the border and anchored the ships in a line ahead across Plattsburgh Bay. The US forces on land and water would succeed or fail within sight of one another. Prevost's army occupied Plattsburgh, but the British general delayed further attack on the US defenses until his lakeside flank was protected. By September 6 the stage for a decisive battle was set, but one player was needed before the curtain could rise: the Royal Navy.

The carpenters and naval personnel working on the frigate at Isle aux Noix during the summer of 1814 endured numerous setbacks, including shortages of timber and other building supplies, a lack of sailors, and last-minute changes in leadership. Most of all, there was a shortage of time. Sir George Prevost, under orders to achieve spectacular results with his large army before cold weather ended the campaign season, relentlessly hurried the final stages of *Confiance*'s preparation. The general wrote to Capt. George Downie, the newly arrived commander of the British squadron on September 8, "I need not dwell with you on the Evils resulting to both services from delay."[23] Shipwrights labored aboard the frigate until the very last minute, and the hastily amalgamated crew of soldiers and sailors were hurriedly trained at the guns. The arrival of *Confiance* and the rest of the British warships at the entrance to Plattsburgh Bay early on September 11 signaled the start of a battle between two squadrons that were nearly equal in terms of ships, cannon, and men. There can be no doubt, however, that Downie's frigate was poorly prepared for the death match that followed.

The Battle of Lake Champlain was the second decisive naval action to be fought on freshwater during the War of 1812, and like the first on Lake Erie the previous year, it would end in a US triumph (fig. III.5). Unlike Lake Erie, it was a defensive rather than an offensive victory, reflecting the changing circumstances of the two belligerents in 1814. The consequences were both immediate and far-reaching. General Prevost, dispirited and now concerned about his lakeside flank, cancelled the attack on Plattsburgh and ordered his army back to Canada. Macdonough's victory, and the earlier repulse of a British attack on Baltimore, made it amply clear to the British government that crushing the "cursed Americans" might be more difficult than anticipated. At the peace talks in Ghent, British negotiators dropped their demands for American concessions and settled for a neutrally worded treaty on Christmas Eve, 1814. Naval historian and US President Theodore Roosevelt termed Lake Champlain "the greatest naval battle of the war" and pronounced Macdonough "down to the time of the Civil War . . . the greatest figure in our naval history."[24]

Thirty ships and gunboats took part in the battle at Plattsburgh Bay, ranging from a ship as large and new as the not-quite-completed 37-gun *Confiance* to boats as small and old as the 1808-built, one-gun *Ludlow*

Figure III.5. The Battle of Lake Champlain, *a watercolor by Thomas Birch. The perspective is from the northern end of the US line near the conclusion of the engagement. Five large warships were present: on the left are the British brig* Linnet *and frigate* Confiance *and on the right are the US corvette* Saratoga *and, partially obscured by smoke, the schooner* Ticonderoga *and brig* Eagle. *Lateen-rigged US gunboats are shown in the foreground and on the right, and the recently surrendered British sloop* Chub *is being towed from the battle on the far right. In order to fit the entire scene on one page, Birch has placed the ships in closer proximity to one another than was actually the case; otherwise this is a reasonably accurate depiction of the fight. (Collection of the New York Historical Society, Accession # 1925.135.)*

and *Wilmer.* Remarkably, no vessels were sunk in the fight, although the two largest British warships were in a near-sinking condition when the shooting stopped. What round shot could not destroy, however, time and decay would eventually overcome. To date, four participants in the battle are known to have survived into the twenty-first century: the US Navy 17-gun schooner *Ticonderoga,* the US Navy 2-gun row galley *Allen,* the Royal Navy 16-gun brig *Linnet,* and the 20-gun US Navy brig *Eagle.*

The following chapters tell the stories of these four warships, from the building of their hulls, to active service in 1814, to laid-up hulks, to sunken wrecks, to archaeological sites. The reader will notice that here, more than in the previous two sections, the accounts of these vessels closely parallel one another. Three were built at the same place, three were designed and built from the keel up to be warships, all were launched

within four months of one another in the spring and summer of 1814, and all took part in the second great naval battle on the North American lakes. And when the battle and the war were over, these four ships all passed into oblivion as a group, in the same location. Yet, as the reader will see, each differs in significant ways from the others, and each has its own unique tale to tell.

NOTES

1. Donald R. Hickey, *The War of 1812: A Forgotten Conflict* (Urbana: University of Illinois Press, 1989), pp. 80, 88–90, 143–46; Allen S. Everest, *The War of 1812 in the Champlain Valley* (Syracuse, NY: Syracuse University Press, 1981), pp. 88–92, 123–39.

2. Norman Ansley, *Vergennes, Vermont and the War of 1812* (Severna Park, MD: Brooke Keefer Limited Editions, 1999), pp. 2–3.

3. Michael J. Crawford, ed., *The Naval War of 1812: A Documentary History,* vol. 3 (Washington, DC: Naval Historical Cen-

ter, 2002), pp. 537–38; James T. Leonard to Board of Navy Commissioners, November 13, 1819, entry 220, record group 45 (RG 45), National Archives and Records Administration (NARA).

4. William S. Dudley, ed., *The Naval War of 1812: A Documentary History,* vol. 1 (Washington, DC: Naval Historical Center, 1985), pp. 319–20; Rodney Macdonough, *Life of Commodore Thomas Macdonough U.S. Navy* (Boston: The Fort Hill Press, 1909); David Curtis Skaggs, *Thomas Macdonough: Master of Command in the Early U.S. Navy* (Annapolis: Naval Institute Press, 2003), Christopher McKee, *A Gentlemanly and Honorable Profession: The Creation of the U.S. Naval Officer Corps, 1794–1815* (Annapolis: Naval Institute Press, 1991), pp. 290–92; Macdonough to the Board of Navy Commissioners, May 6, 1815, Subject File NI, RG 45, NARA; Midshipman Joel Abbot to Jonathan T. Patten, April 29, 1814, manuscript letter, Lake Champlain Maritime Museum, Vergennes, VT. Courtesy of Arthur B. Cohn.

5. Dudley, ed., *Naval War of 1812,* vol. 1, pp. 325–26.

6. Dudley, ed., *Naval War of 1812,* vol. 1, pp. 370–71; William S. Dudley, ed., *The Naval War of 1812: A Documentary History,* vol. 2 (Washington, DC: Naval Historical Center, 1992), pp. 424–25, 460.

7. Dudley, ed., *Naval War of 1812,* vol. 2, pp. 488–92, 513, 516.

8. Everest, *War of 1812 in the Champlain Valley,* p. 116; Dudley, ed., *Naval War of 1812,* vol. 2, pp. 513–514, 516–520.

9. Kevin J. Crisman, *The Eagle: An American Brig on Lake Champlain During the War of 1812* (Shelburne, VT: The New England Press; Annapolis: The Naval Institute Press, 1987), pp. 14–23; Robert Malcomson, *Warships of the Great Lakes, 1754–1834* (London: Caxton Editions, 2003), pp. 124–29.

10. Crawford, ed., *Naval War of 1812,* vol. 3, pp. 428, 461; Plan of Corvette *Saratoga,* Ship Plan 41–5–6B, record group 19, NARA; "A Report on the State and Condition of the Naval Force . . . Under the Command of Thomas Macdonough, Esquire on the 31st day of August 1814," manuscript document, Lake Champlain Maritime Museum. Courtesy of Arthur B. Cohn.

11. *More or less*: at the end of April, Macdonough believed that the new British brig mounted 20 32 pounders and 4 68-pounder carronades, a broadside nearly five times greater in weight of metal than *Linnet*'s actual armament of 16 long 12 pounders. William Jones to James Madison, June 6, 1814, James Madison Papers, Library of Congress. See also Macdonough's comments on intelligence in Macdonough to Jones, June 8 and 11, 1814, entry 147, RG 45, NARA.

12. Macdonough to Jones, May 13 and 14, 1814, entry 147, RG 45, NARA.

13. Macdonough to Jones, May 29, 1814, entry 147, RG 45, NARA.

14. Hugh Montgomerie to Sir Thomas M. Brisbane, May 1, 1814, Sir Thomas Makdougall Brisbane Papers, Clements Library, University of Michigan.

15. Edgar Erskine Hume, "Letters Written During the War of 1812 by the British Naval Commander in American Waters (Admiral Sir David Milne)," *William and Mary College Quarterly Historical Magazine,* 2nd ser., 10, no. 4 (October, 1930), p. 293.

16. John R. Grodzinski, "The Duke of Wellington, the Peninsular War and the War of 1812: Part II: Reinforcements, Views of the War and Command in North America," *The War of 1812 Magazine,* no. 6 (April 2007, http://www.napoleon-series.org /military/Warof1812/2007/Issue6/c_Wellington1.html, accessed July 4, 2008).

17. J. Mackay Hitsman, *The Incredible War of 1812: A Military History,* rev. ed. (Toronto: University of Toronto Press; reprint, Toronto: Robin Brass Studio, 1999), pp. 289–90.

18. Dimensions and armament of prize frigate *Confiance,* entry 169, RG 45, NARA.

19. James T. Leonard to the Board of Navy Commissioners, November 19, 1819, and January 10, 1820, entry 220, RG 45, NARA. With its combination of hurried construction, second-rate timbers, flat floors, and shallow form, *Confiance* not surprisingly became badly hogged within five years of its construction.

20. Macdonough to Jones, June 11, 1814, entry 147, RG 45, NARA.

21. Donald R. Hickey, *Don't Give Up the Ship! Myths of the War of 1812* (Urbana: University of Illinois Press, 2006), pp. 75–77.

22. Hickey, *War of 1812,* pp. 189–90.

23. William Wood, ed., *Select British Documents of the Canadian War of 1812,* vol. 3, pt. 1 (Toronto: The Champlain Society, 1926), pp. 378–83.

24. The course of the peace negotiations is summarized in Chapter 11 of Hickey, *War of 1812,* pp. 281–99; Roosevelt's remarks on Macdonough can be found in Theodore Roosevelt, *The Naval War of 1812* (Annapolis: Naval Institute Press, 1987), pp. 337, 356.

9

"LT. CASSIN SAYS THERE IS A NEW BOAT NEAR VERGENNES"

The US Schooner *Ticonderoga*

KEVIN J. CRISMAN

Introduction

In 1958 the town of Whitehall, New York, celebrated the bicentennial year of its founding by raising the remains of an old wooden ship from the nearby Poultney River and placing them on display outside the new Skenesborough Museum in downtown Whitehall (fig. 9.1). Among the artifacts recovered from the wreck were lead musket shot, cast-iron cannon shot, and the leather flap from a cartridge pouch bearing the crest of King George III. One of the timbers was carved on its upper surface to hold round shot. With all of this evidence, the Whitehall Bicentennial Committee and the town historical society had little doubt the hull was once a warship; the question was, which one? The surviving structure was about 114 feet (34.7 m) in length, larger than anything built on Lake Champlain during either the French and Indian War or the Revolutionary War. The lake's 1812-era warship squadrons contained at least one vessel of about this length, however—the US Navy's 120-foot-long (36.6 m) schooner *Ticonderoga*.

One day a few years after the salvage, a group of self-proclaimed experts appeared at the Skenesborough Museum and closely inspected the hull. After examining the keel, end posts, and frames, they reached a startling conclusion and informed the museum staff that the Whitehall Historical Society had made an error in identification. This wreck could not possibly be the 17-gun schooner *Ticonderoga,* for it was the hull of a steamboat, not a sailing vessel.[1]

Architecturally speaking, the "experts" were right: they *were* looking at the hull of a steamboat. And the Whitehall Bicentennial Committee and the Whitehall Historical Society were equally correct in their identification: this *was* the wreck of a War of 1812 schooner. Therein lies the unusual tale of *Ticonderoga,* a vessel begun as Lake Champlain's second steamer but com-

Figure 9.1. *The hull of the US Navy 17-gun schooner* Ticonderoga *in 1981. Found in the graveyard of Lake Champlain's War of 1812 naval squadron, the wreck contained a wooden shot garland, numerous cannon and musket shot, and an unusually deep keel, evidence that it was once a sailing warship. The assembly and shape of the lower hull, however, suggest that it was designed for a very different career. This view, taken from the stern, looks forward along the keelson. (Photo by William Noel,* Ticonderoga *project files of Kevin J. Crisman.)*

pleted as a sailing warship, a veteran of the naval action at Plattsburgh Bay with a service career of less than one year.

"A New Boat Near Vergennes"

Steam propulsion was still a novelty when the war between the United States and Britain began in 1812. The first commercially successful steamboat in the world, Robert Fulton's *North River Steamboat,* made its inaugural voyage on the Hudson River only five years earlier in 1807. *North River* heralded a new era in waterborne transportation, when the power of steam, generated and contained in a boiler, could be harnessed by a reciprocating piston engine and transformed by a crank into rotary power that turned a pair of paddle wheels. With this machinery installed in its hold a vessel could navigate at will, no longer dependent on the limited power of human muscles or the fickle forces of the wind. Steam propulsion was especially useful in early-

nineteenth-century North America, where the lack of good roads meant that most people and goods traveled around the continent on rivers, lakes, and coastal waters.

At least part of the incentive that drove Fulton and his partner Robert Livingston to complete *North River* in 1807 was a prize offered by the State of New York to the first persons to build and operate a reliable steamboat. This prize, meant to encourage inventive efforts and investment in a risky new technology, was a monopoly on all future steam navigation on state waters. By the early nineteenth century, New York, particularly New York City, was becoming the center of trade and finance in the United States, and for Fulton and Livingston the domination of a lucrative new means of transportation was a powerful incentive indeed. *North River*'s success ensured that every steamboat plying the Hudson River or any other state waterway was owned by the monopolists or ran under the terms of a license agreement. By 1811 Fulton and Livingston had two additional boats paddling between New York City and Albany and were drawing off passengers and trade from the sloops that had dominated river transportation since the seventeenth century.[2]

One owner of Hudson River sloops, Elihu Bunker, refused to sit idly by while steamers drained away his customers. With the financial backing of businessmen from Albany, Bunker's Albany Steamboat Company mounted a direct challenge to the Fulton-Livingston monopoly in 1811 by putting the steamboats *Hope* and *Perseverance* into service on the river. The monopolists immediately challenged these competitors in court and in September 1812 won a judgment in their favor. *Hope* and *Perseverance* were retired and broken up, and Bunker turned his attention to building steamboats on Long Island Sound. Bunker's Albany backers, who included Abraham Lansing, Isaiah Townsend, and Julius Winne Jr., had other plans and managed to wring a concession out of the Fulton-Livingston monopoly in the court settlement: the right to operate steamboats on the New York waters of Lake Champlain.

Their new venture, The Lake Champlain Steamboat Company, expanded its circle of investors to include several Vermont businessmen and was officially granted the Lake Champlain steam monopoly by the New York Legislature in March 1813. The company faced a mountain of problems in its immediate future, not least of which was the War of 1812. Much of the profit to be made by Lake Champlain steamboats was in carrying people between the United States and Canada, and the conflict brought that traffic to a standstill. There was little fighting on the lake in the first year of the war, but that could change quickly and threaten the safety of commercial shipping. Furthermore, the court agreement settling the Hudson River dispute stipulated that the company had to put a boat in service no later than eighteen months after the conclusion of the war. The new steamer needed to be completed in a timely manner. Finally, there was the problem of existing competition, namely the steamer *Vermont*. This vessel began operating on the lake in 1809, and because it was Vermont owned, *Vermont* could not be barred from service by the New York monopoly. The Lake Champlain Steamboat Company had to surmount all of these military and commercial obstacles if it was to survive and prosper.

The new steamboat company did have two assets:

the *Perseverance*'s captain and engine. The former, Captain Jahaziel Sherman, was sent to the lake in 1813 to oversee the construction and outfitting of the company's first boat. The little town of Vergennes, Vermont, 6 miles (9.65 km) up the winding Otter Creek from Lake Champlain, was selected as the building site. This remote location offered protection from British naval raids, and the town was also the home of the Monkton Iron Works, a firm that could provide spikes, bolts, and other ironwork for building the hull and installing its machinery. The company engaged the services of shipwright John Lacy, who had originally been called to the lake during the winter of 1812–13 to rebuild several of the navy's armed sloops.[3]

Ways for building the steamboat were prepared and details of the hull's design and materials were worked out, presumably by Sherman and Lacy. Their choice of design was significant. Only six years had passed since Fulton's *North River* was launched, but steamer hulls were undergoing profound modifications in their form. *North River* reflected Fulton's belief that steamships should resemble canal boats, with extremely high length-to-beam ratios, flat floors, a "chine" (a hard angle where the bottom met the side), a flat deck with little or no sheer (rising ends), and light scantlings throughout. *Vermont*, built two years later, emulated many of *North River*'s characteristics. By 1813, however, practical experience had exposed flaws in Fulton's design. Long, narrow, flat-sheered, and lightly framed hulls proved weak and over time developed wavy profiles, hogging at the ends and sagging amidships from the weight of the machinery. The extreme length, combined with the flat bottom and shallow draft, made these boats difficult to steer; *Vermont* had to be assisted in making turns by deck hands who rolled heavy barrels from side to side in the bow.[4] These characteristics made early-style boats unsuitable for open, unprotected waters.

Elihu Bunker's Long Island Sound steamboat *Fulton* established a new standard for steamer hulls when it was built in 1813 (fig. 9.2). The vessel did not represent a revolution in ship design but merely incorporated more of the elements that made a good seagoing hull. *Fulton* featured a more moderate length to breadth ratio, slight deadrise to the frames, and a rounded rather than angled turn of the bilge (although the hull still had what naval architects would term "hard bilges"). The ends of the deck were raised, giving the

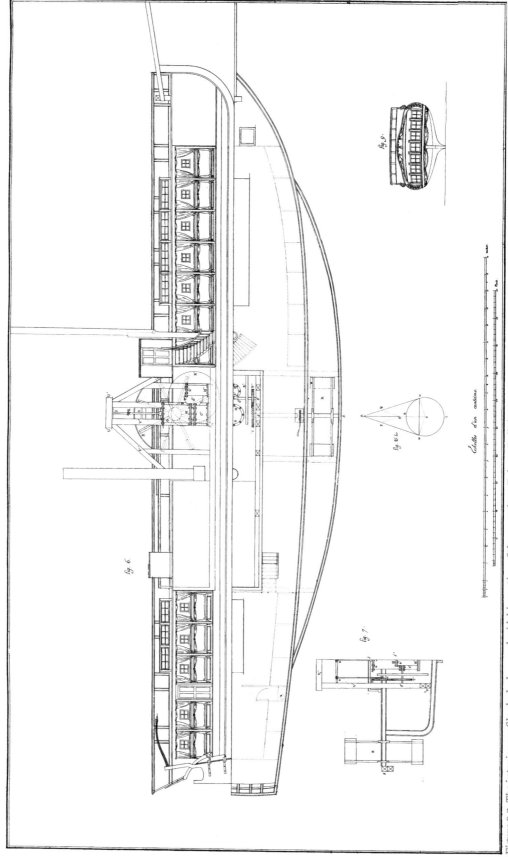

Figure 9.2. The interior profile, deck plan, and midship section of the steamboat Fulton. Built in 1813, Fulton is credited with establishing a new model for the design and construction of North American steamboats. (From Jean Baptiste Marestier, Memoir on Steamboats of the United States of America, Plate II, Courtesy of Cushing Library, Texas A&M University.)

steamer a more pronounced sheer. In most ways *Fulton* was a stronger and more seaworthy vessel than its predecessors. Someone in the Lake Champlain Steamboat Company, probably Jahaziel Sherman, was paying attention to Bunker's modifications, for the hull begun at Vergennes had much more in common with *Fulton* than with the earlier style of steamboat.

The work of Lacy and Sherman was well underway in late December 1813 when Comm. Thomas Macdonough sailed his flotilla of four sloops and four gunboats into Otter Creek and laid them up for the winter. Macdonough had come to Vergennes to do some building of his own, and the unfinished steamer on the stocks surely caught his eye. However, what he saw must not have been to his liking, for he said nothing about it to Navy Secretary William Jones. It was only in late February 1814 that Lt. Stephen Cassin, Macdonough's senior officer, told Jones of the hull during a sojourn in Washington. The secretary wrote the commodore, "Mr. Cassin says there is a new boat, 120 feet long, near Vergennes, intended for a steamboat, if she will answer, you are authorized to purchase her for the use of the Navy." Macdonough's response was noncommittal: "The [new warships], and the force we already have, I calculate will be sufficient; but should it not be, the Steam Boat can then be purchased, finished, and fitted."[5]

Why did the commodore hesitate? Perhaps it was because of the characteristics described above. Though more seaworthy than earlier designs, the steamer's hull was still long, narrow, and shallow, with timbers of modest dimensions that were ill suited for a warship. Macdonough may have been concerned that the hull, built to carry boilers and engines low in the hold, might be too unstable and too weak in its upperworks and main deck to safely support a battery of heavy iron guns. After getting by for two years with armed merchant sloops, he was probably reluctant to add another ill-adapted commercial vessel to his squadron, especially when Noah Brown was cutting timber for a stout new 26-gun ship and six row galleys, vessels designed from the keel up to be warships.

Events now took a curious turn. For reasons that are not entirely clear, the owners of the Lake Champlain Steamboat Company decided that they wanted to unload their boat on the navy. They sent a letter to John Lacy in Vergennes, communicating the company's interest in selling the unfinished steamer, and the directors asked New York's Governor Daniel Tompkins to use his influence with the Navy Department. The governor accepted the role of salesman, writing Navy Secretary Jones on March 10:

> Sir
>
> The Steamboat Company of Lake Champlain, who have an exclusive privilege of navigating that lake with boats propelled by steam, are building a boat at Vergennes, of 125 feet keel and 24 beam of the strength of a vessel of 400 tons at least. They have an engine and machinery ready for her equipment at Vergennes. They are now about laying her deck timbers. The Company would, I believe, have no objection to dispose of her to the government in her present state with all the machinery at an expense of from $15,000 to $17,000 dollars. At this time she is capable of being equipped as a war vessel, with very little alteration, & to be so bulwarked, without impeding her navigation, as to protect vessel, machinery, & men from the assaults of row gallies or other vessels. She may be made to carry 4 long 32 pdrs. & 10 12- or 18's at an expense of $37,000 including the price above mentioned. The importance of such a vessel on Lake Champlain is obvious. She can move when no other vessels can, is at all times capable of firing hot shot, can tow gallies or other vessels in a calm, will require but 100 men, at most, for the 14 guns above mentioned & to navigate her. She will transport men and warlike stores & tow batteaux, etc with more certainty & in less time than they can otherwise be conveyed down Lake Champlain.
>
> At the conclusion of the war, gun brigs, row gallies, & all the usual naval equipments will be worth little or nothing whilst the steamboat and her machinery will sell to great advantage for carrying passengers through the lake, which has in time of peace been a lucrative business. The company with this boat, will, I understand convey a right of running her under their exclusive privilege, as well as during the war as after the conclusion of a peace.[6]

Tompkins added to this, "I have reflected on this subject maturely & the result is, that in my opinion the Government ought not to omit having the use of that boat for public purposes."

Why was the company so anxious to sell? We can

only speculate, but there is enough evidence to make an informed speculation. The desire to dispose of the boat may reflect, at least in part, the deteriorating military situation in the Champlain Valley. The rush of naval shipbuilding at Vergennes and at Isle aux Noix in Canada portended a violent summer on the lake. The performance of the US Army and Navy in the region during the previous year had been lackluster at best, and there was no reason to assume things would be different in 1814. Tompkins' letter to William Jones and the company's subsequent actions also plainly indicate a desire to profit by selling the unfinished hull at a substantial markup in price and by charging the navy a fee for operating a steamer under the "exclusive privilege" granted to the company by the Fulton-Livingston monopoly and the state of New York. By selling, the company avoided any risk and still made money.

Noah Brown made splendid progress on the navy's new vessels at Vergennes and by late April had the ship *Saratoga* launched, rigged, and ready to mount cannon. Despite this powerful new addition to his squadron, Macdonough decided to increase his margin of superiority on the lake in 1814 by accepting the steamboat company's offer to sell the unfinished hull. Governor Tompkins and Secretary Jones may have been enthusiastic about the US Navy having its first steam-powered warship, but Macdonough saw it from a different perspective. His arguments were compelling. "I have advised with Mr Brown and with the carpenter who is building the Steam Boat," he wrote Jones at the end of April, "on the practicability of having this boat prepared in due time in the manner you have suggested and they assure me it cannot be done within two months."[7] The machinery was not complete, nor were spare parts readily available.

The commodore was equally pessimistic about the usefulness of a steam warship even if it was completed in a timely fashion: "I have scarcely known the Steam Boat, now running here [*Vermont*], to pass through the lake without something happening to her, and they have to send to Albany to replace what was damaged." These concerns, he concluded, "have induced me to abandon the idea of fitting this vessel to be propelled by steam, but to have her directly fitted for twenty guns in the rig of a schooner." Macdonough needed to put as many guns on the lake as possible in 1814, and he needed reliable vessels to carry them. The US Navy's

adoption of steam propulsion would have to await a less-critical time and place.

Noah Brown and Macdonough estimated the value of the framed but incomplete hull to be about $5000, and since time was running short and the company obviously intended to sell, they decided to start work and negotiate the price at a later date. Brown set about modifying the hull to meet its new mission. We know that he somehow shifted or lifted the hull on the stocks and bolted on more keel timbers, adding 14 inches (35.6 cm) to the keel's depth. Besides adding longitudinal strength to the hull, the extra timbers increased the keel's "bite" into the water and thereby improved both stability and resistance to lateral drift—sliding off to leeward—when under sail. We can be sure that the main deck John Lacy constructed for the steamer was too weak to support the tons of iron cannon it was now required to bear and that Brown added extra deck-supporting timbers, and more or larger deck beams, to enable it to take the strain. Steamers of the time typically had an open rail around the main deck, and Brown therefore must have raised bulwarks between the gun positions on each side of the deck. Whatever the extent of the modifications, by May 12 Brown had the vessel completed, launched, and rigged. The next day Macdonough informed Secretary Jones that the new schooner, *Ticonderoga,* was afloat, "and had she men she could enter the lake with all the force in ten days at farthest."[8]

"Her Full Share of the Action"
Cannon, sailors, and officers were three vital elements in critically short supply for the Lake Champlain squadron in 1814. For *Ticonderoga*'s guns, Macdonough initially planned on eight to ten long 24 pounders, mounted on pivots down the centerline of the deck. This was powerful armament for a warship of this class, and pivot mounts permitted the guns to be aimed port or starboard, effectively increasing firepower while halving the number of guns on the main deck. There were no long 24 pounders to be had in Vergennes, however, and Macdonough could only shuffle his available cannon, noting to Jones, "her armament will be composed of two of the sloops guns (these sloops being miserable sailers) and some spare guns which we have here, and the guns of the four old gallies, thus making a much more efficient force." In the end, *Ticonderoga*

was armed with 17 guns in conventional broadsides: 8 long 12 pounders and 4 long 18 pounders, all on truck carriages, and 5 32-pounder carronades on the traversing bed-and-slide mounts typically used by these light, powerful guns. The combined weight of cannon, carriages, and gun equipment totaled around 70,000 pounds (31,752 kg) or 35 tons—a considerable load on the topsides of a shallow, narrow vessel.[9]

Ticonderoga's crew was composed principally of sailors transferred from the four old gunboats. Only one set of muster books was kept for the entire squadron (rather than crew lists for individual ships), and sailors were shifted between ships on a regular basis. As a result, we do not know the names of most of the men who served on *Ticonderoga*. We do know that there were not enough of them. Macdonough originally intended a crew of 150 to sail the schooner and work its guns, but the total, including officers, sailors, and soldiers acting as marines, does not appear to have exceeded 110. Macdonough held a low opinion of the majority of the sailors in his squadron, noting that they were "very indifferent" and "such as the command of this lake should not be trusted to."[10]

And then there was the problem of obtaining enough officers, particularly lieutenants. The wartime navy's demand for experienced officers rapidly outstripped the supply, with the result that captains on every ship and station were forced to rapidly promote, on an "acting" basis, officers who were young, inexperienced, and sometimes incompetent. To add to Macdonough's woes, the navy maintained no centralized recruiting bureau but followed the tradition of European navies by expecting captains and commodores to find their own crews. The squadron's most mature and persuasive officers were therefore detached for several weeks at a stretch to scour the waterfronts of cities along the eastern seaboard. Thanks to this system of enlisting seamen, Macdonough lost the services of some of his best officers when he most needed them on the lake.

Command of *Ticonderoga,* the second largest vessel in the squadron, was given to Macdonough's second in command, Lt. Stephen Cassin (fig. 9.3). The son of a respected senior captain in the US Navy, Cassin joined the navy as a midshipman in 1800 and had seen service in the Mediterranean against the Barbary States. Unlike most naval lieutenants of the time, he was married and had a large family. At thirty-one years of age, Cas-

STEPHEN CASSIN.

Figure 9.3. *Stephen Cassin, captain of the US schooner* Ticonderoga. *Lieutenant Cassin's command of* Ticonderoga *during the summer of 1814 and in the Battle of Lake Champlain on September 11 met with the full approval of Commodore Macdonough. In this mid-nineteenth-century print he is shown with the epaulets of a captain, the rank he eventually attained in the US Navy. (From Charles J. Peterson,* The American Navy, *p. 483.)*

sin was slightly older than Macdonough, but he seems to have been a good second-in-command: neither brilliant nor flamboyant, but solid, steady, and reliable. Macdonough considered him "a man of firmness, when put to the test, as good a seaman as Most Men of his age and experience[,] whose Judgement is good."[11]

Lieutenant Cassin's subordinate officers on *Ticonderoga* were few, mostly young, and mostly inexperienced. The senior (and only other) lieutenant aboard was John Stansbury, who joined the schooner after a term of recruiting for the Lake Champlain squadron in Boston. Stansbury had been appointed midshipman in 1809 and was a relatively new lieutenant, having received his commission in July 1813. Sailing Master Joseph Lindsay, *Ticonderoga's* third-ranking officer, was also a new appointee with a warrant that dated from March 1814. During the War of 1812, the rank of sailing master was used by the navy to obtain skilled professional seamen from the merchant service. At 45 years of age, Lindsay seems to have been typical of the older, experienced mariners who entered the navy's officer corps through this back door. He was described by Macdonough as "a steady careful man . . . of good habits and a good seaman." Finally, *Ticonderoga* had three midshipmen, Hiram Paulding, William Boden, and James Freeman. A newly warranted midshipman in the summer of 1814, Freeman was probably so inexperienced as to be useless, but Macdonough regarded sixteen-year-old Paulding and seventeen-year-old Boden as industrious, very promising young men.[12]

Ticonderoga entered the lake with the rest of Macdonough's new squadron on May 26, 1814. Noah Brown's modifications to the steamer hull seem to have resolved any potential problems with its strength and stability. Macdonough had little to say about *Ticonderoga*'s sailing qualities, but that little was positive: "The schooner is a fine vessel and bears her metal full as well as expected."[13]

There was still the matter of settling with the Lake Champlain Steamboat Company. In late May, the company presented Macdonough with an invoice for $22,000, a price the commodore considered "extraordinary" but that the directors claimed as fair compensation for damages and for "anticipated profits in running the boat." Noah Brown's appraisal of $5000 fell far short of what the company thought its hull was worth, and the decision to finish the vessel as a schooner had torpedoed their plan to charge a fee for the "exclusive privilege" of operating a steamer on the lake. Warning Navy Secretary Jones that a steamboat company agent was on his way to Washington to present the bill directly to the navy, Macdonough also passed along a copy of the company's letter to John Lacy announcing their intention to sell the hull, observing, "There appears a great inconsistency in their wishing so anxiously to dispose of their vessel, to their own loss, as they wish to make it appear."[14]

The agent sent to Washington was none other than Jahaziel Sherman, the steamboat company's would-be captain. The details of the negotiations between Sherman and Jones are not known, but on June 9 they compromised on a price of $12,000 to be paid through a New York bank. Jones authorized the payment on July 1, but the process of remuneration was slow. On July 20 Sherman wrote from Albany to complain: "As

I am under positive orders from the Company to commence building another boat immediately on receiving the money . . . you will much oblige them by immediate attention to the liquidation of their claim."[15]

Ticonderoga's story fades in the historical record after the schooner entered the lake with Macdonough's squadron in late May. We know that all through the summer months the vessel's officers and crew were active in patrolling the northern lake and preparing to meet the British, but we know almost nothing about the daily routines or personal lives of those aboard the schooner. *Ticonderoga*'s logbook has never come to light, and Stephen Cassin, respectful of Macdonough's prerogative as commodore of the squadron, did not carry on a lengthy correspondence with the Navy Department in Washington. The lack of references to the vessel in Macdonough's letters and other contemporary records is probably a positive sign, suggesting that Cassin ran a tight ship.

On Sunday, September 11, 1814, the day of the battle in Plattsburgh Bay, *Ticonderoga* was anchored third in the US line of battle, with *Saratoga* and the brig *Eagle* ahead and the sloop *Preble* astern (fig. 9.4). The plan of attack outlined by British Comm. George Downie called for his two largest vessels, *Confiance* and *Linnet*, to engage *Eagle* and *Saratoga*, while his gunboats were to close with *Ticonderoga* under oars, fire one volley with their cannon, and then board the schooner "with the greatest expedition." The attack of the gunboats was to be supported by the 11-gun sloop *Finch*.[16]

The twelve British gunboats were each armed with one or two cannon, and their combined complements outnumbered the men on *Ticonderoga* by a substantial margin. Downie's plan to carry the US schooner by boarding therefore had a reasonable chance of success, but only with certain prerequisites: brave and skillful leadership of the gunboats, resolute crews who were prepared to suffer casualties, and effective covering fire from *Finch*. Unfortunately for the Royal Navy, all of these elements were conspicuously lacking in the gunboat flotilla and *Finch*.

Naval history shows that boarding actions by small craft against a larger warship, unless carried out with complete surprise, tended to be bloody, ugly affairs, especially for the people in the small boats. This reality must have been uppermost in the mind of Lieutenant Raynham, commander of the gunboat flotilla, as he regarded the black muzzles of *Ticonderoga*'s star-

Figure 9.4. Ticonderoga *holds the southern end of the US line. This detail from an 1816 engraving of the Battle of Lake Champlain shows* Ticonderoga *and the sloop* Preble *firing upon the British gunboats.* Saratoga *and* Confiance *are closely engaged ahead of* Ticonderoga, *while the British sloop* Finch *is aground off Crab Island to the right. Gunboats of the US galley flotilla, in the foreground, provide supporting fire. In his after-action report Commodore Macdonough reported that Lieutenant Cassin's schooner "gallantly sustained her full share of the action." (From Barber Badger,* The Naval Temple, *"Plate Sixth," p. 179.)*

board battery in the early morning sunshine. As the gunboats closed to within 600 yards (550 m) of the US schooner, Raynham ordered nearby boats to lower their sails in preparation for action, raised a flag signaling "board enemy ship," lowered the flag, and then turned his gunboat around and rowed off in the opposite direction. Of the remaining gunboats, only three continued to advance under oars toward *Ticonderoga,* one attacked the US sloop *Preble,* and the rest began "dropping off to leeward in great confusion." The odds now swung strongly in favor of the US schooner.

Captain Cassin's view of the action was limited by the closely packed gun crews and by bulwarks and hammock rails, so he climbed to a commanding but exposed position on the taffrail of *Ticonderoga.* Here,

"perfectly cool and unconcerned," he directed the schooner's fire against the gunboats. Midshipman Hiram Paulding, who commanded the eight guns of the second division on the schooner, found that the slow matches for firing the cannon were defective and resorted to firing his guns by flashing a pistol at the priming in their touch holes. Disorganized as the British gunboats were, some of their guns were effectively served, for shot and splinters took a toll on the sailors on *Ticonderoga*'s deck. Twelve men fell as casualties, half of them fatally wounded. Lt. John Stansbury was among the latter—while attending to the spring lines in the bow, he was cut in half by a round shot and flung overboard.[17]

Cassin ordered his guns loaded with grapeshot,

and with each discharge, nine 1- or 2-pound iron balls showered the advancing British. In the face of *Ticonderoga*'s steady fire, the already enfeebled gunboat attack stood little chance of success. On some of the boats the oarsmen sought shelter by lying flat in the bilges. Lt. Christopher Bell of the gunboat *Murray* lost his right leg to a round shot from *Ticonderoga,* and "Mr. Pym," commander of the gunboat *Blucher,* was hit on the arm by a grapeshot and then bowled over when the base of a grapeshot stand struck him on the shoulder. The British sloop *Finch,* far from supporting the attack, merely sailed by at the beginning of the action, fired one ineffective broadside from a distance, and subsequently ran aground off Crab Island. According to the first lieutenant of *Confiance,* once the attack of the gunboats and *Finch* fizzled out, *Ticonderoga* pivoted on its spring lines and began a "steady, deliberate, and raking fire" on the British frigate that continued until *Confiance* lowered its flag.

Cassin's after-action report to Macdonough was notable for its brevity: "It is with great pleasure that I state, that every officer and man under my command did their duty yesterday." Macdonough found nothing lacking on the lieutenant's part, either, reporting to the secretary of the navy that under Cassin's leadership, *Ticonderoga* "gallantly sustained her full share of the action." The commodore paid Cassin a further compliment two days after the battle by selecting him to carry the official reports of the victory and the captured British flags to Washington. It was a naval tradition that the bearer of good news and trophies be rewarded for his role in a victory, and captains and commodores usually sent officers whom they considered deserving of recognition. And so it proved: Cassin was promoted to the rank of master commandant (effective from the day of the battle), given leave to visit his family in Philadelphia, and then ordered to take command of the schooner *Spitfire* at New York City.[18] It was the end of his service on the lake and on *Ticonderoga.*

Ticonderoga's career on Lake Champlain also ended soon after the battle. The schooner underwent repairs to its shot-damaged hull and rigging, then sailed with a greatly reduced crew to Whitehall, New York, in mid-October, where, along with the rest of the squadron, it was laid up over the winter of 1814–15. When news of peace reached the lake in February 1815, Macdonough had all of the navy's large warships cleared of bulk-

heads below, whitewashed inside and out, and housed over with board roofs. After ten months of active service, *Ticonderoga* now began ten years of inactivity as an empty hulk, "in ordinary" at the Whitehall naval station. A small contingent of sailors—including *Ticonderoga*'s former sailing master Joseph Lindsay—was retained to keep the ships pumped out and to maintain the squadron's equipment. The Lake Champlain Steamboat Company wasted no time replacing the hull it sold to the government, launching the 147-foot (44.8 m) *Phoenix I* at Vergennes in the spring of 1815. This vessel, commanded by Jahaziel Sherman and "fitted in elegant style," commenced a twice-weekly round trip over the length of the lake between St. Johns, Quebec, and Whitehall. Three more Vergennes-built steamers followed, *Champlain, Congress,* and *Phoenix II,* all of which regularly passed their weathering predecessor in the channel below Whitehall. The Lake Champlain Steamboat Company suffered setbacks (*Champlain* burned in 1817, and *Phoenix I* burned in 1819) but nevertheless prospered until the late 1820s, when new steamboat lines began to offer stiff competition. The final owner, Isaiah Townsend of Albany, sold the company's boats and assets to a rival firm in 1833.[19]

Unless they are rigorously maintained, wooden vessels on freshwater tend to have a short lifespan—there is no salt in the water to infuse the timber and deter rot—and as we have seen on the other lakes, the hastily built and hard-used 1812 warships were particularly susceptible to decay. *Ticonderoga* and the other ships at Whitehall required extensive recaulking in 1817, and only two years later, in 1819, all were exhibiting signs of rot. The navy saw no reason to pay for expensive overhauls, and by 1821 *Ticonderoga*'s hull was reported to be "unsound in rotten condition." The schooner was moved with the rest of the squadron into the nearby Poultney River and minimally maintained until 1825, when the warships, by this time hopelessly decayed, were sold to salvagers for the value of the iron fasteners contained in their hulls. Abandoned and unwanted, *Ticonderoga* slipped beneath the murky waters of the river, where it would reside for the next 133 years.[20]

Salvage and Archaeology

Ticonderoga sank to the bottom in shallow water with a heavy list to port, and in the years that followed the exposed starboard side and upperworks disintegrated, probably helped along by the work of salvagers and souvenir hunters. Even after the structure above the river was gone, the location of the navy's sunken ships was not entirely forgotten, and from time to time timbers, shot, and even parts of a hull were recovered from the Poultney River.[21]

The resurrection of *Ticonderoga* in the fall of 1958 was undertaken as part of the celebrations surrounding the two-hundredth anniversary of the founding of Whitehall. In late June, a visiting diving club, the US Dolphins, explored the 1812 wrecks and reported their finds to the town's Bicentennial Committee. At a meeting on June 30, the committee discussed the matter and concluded that one of the hulls would make a fine display in a museum of local history that was to open in downtown Whitehall. According to the *Whitehall Times,* "the opinion . . . was expressed that many farmers with tractors would be glad to cooperate in an effort to retrieve one of the ships." Frank Martucci of the Bicentennial Committee took charge of the operation, while the actual salvage was directed by Steve and John Galick (the salvors of *Linnet* nine years earlier).[22]

The work began on September 17 when Martucci asked local divers Bruce and Carol Manell to find a suitable hull beneath the river.[23] The wreck they selected was *Ticonderoga,* although its identity was not known at the time. A week later, on September 25, Steve Galick rigged a steel cable to the stem and pulled it taut with his bulldozer. The bow rose out of the water, but this initial salvage attempt ended when the stem broke off the wreck. The operation continued the next day, reinforced by an additional bulldozer and the town dump truck, but in each of three attempts to wrench the hull free of the bottom, the cables snapped.

A new approach was needed, and on September 29, after the forwardmost keelson timber was torn from the hull in yet another recovery attempt, the decision was made to cut the wreck in half and take it out in pieces. Chainsaws were used above the water and a crosscut saw below the water, and the next day the salvagers were rewarded with the recovery of a 40-foot (12.2 m) section of the vessel from the stem to just abaft the midship frame. A pump from the town fire company was used to wash out the mud that filled the interior. In this and other parts of the hull, the salvagers found iron bolts and spikes, grapeshot and round shot, a bottle, a spoon, an awl, a patch and scupper of lead, and the King George III–crested leather cartridge pouch flap.

The two-thirds of the wreck still underwater retained part of the port quarter—preserved up to the level of the deck—and the river bottom mud held the entire structure in a firm grip. After another series of pulls yielded only more broken cables (and the supply of steel cables in Whitehall was now about exhausted), the salvagers elected to plant dynamite around the stern to break the suction. This plan was effected on October 3, and it worked, for the stern at last slid free of the mud and across the river. The next day the wreck was maneuvered into shallow water, although the remaining section of port side separated at the turn of the bilge. The hull was cut into more sections and dragged up the river bank. An attempt was also made to recover the detached side section, but it apparently broke up, since the only recognizable element later displayed with the wreck was a length of waterway timber that also served as a shot garland.

By October 10 the salvage of *Ticonderoga* was over (fig. 9.5). The six sections of the hull were loaded onto a heavy-machinery trailer, trucked to the new Skenesborough Museum in Whitehall, and reassembled. The artifacts and shot garland were proof that the vessel was a warship, and since the dimensions of the hull strongly suggested the wreck was *Ticonderoga,* the new exhibit was identified as this vessel. The sections were supported by a framework of railroad ties, and a tin roof was erected over the hull to shelter it from the elements; wire fencing was later added to discourage souvenir seekers and vandals (delinquent juveniles set the stern deadwood afire one evening, but the blaze was extinguished before it could spread). The waterlogged timbers cracked and checked as they dried out, but the spread of rot was somewhat contained by periodic applications of creosote or similar preservative compounds.

Archaeological study of *Ticonderoga* was delayed for twenty-two years until the winter of 1981. During the previous August, the charred wreck of the Lake Champlain Steamboat Company's *Phoenix I* was measured by a Champlain Maritime Society diving team, of which I was a member.[24] While drafting plans of *Phoenix I,* I learned of *Ticonderoga*'s existence in Whitehall and organized a recording project so that we might com-

Figure 9.5. *The salvaged stern section of* Ticonderoga *in 1958. This photograph shows the lower hull prior to its removal to downtown Whitehall, New York. The visitor aboard the newly emerged wreck appears to be holding a nail or small spike in her left hand. (Courtesy of Carol Manell Senecal, Whitehall, NY.)*

pare its construction and form with *Phoenix*. This was the beginning of a two-decade program of archaeological research on the lake's 1812 warships that would eventually include investigation of all the squadron's known survivors: *Ticonderoga, Eagle, Linnet,* and the US Navy row galley *Allen.*

Despite its rough treatment during salvage and the inevitable decay that followed, *Ticonderoga*'s hull was in a reasonable state of preservation, and there was certainly much to be learned from it. We estimated that approximately 35 percent of the original hull still existed. The keel, most of the keelson, and the lower stern assembly were nearly complete, and the base of the stem was represented. On the port side, the floors and first futtocks were largely complete to the turn of the bilge, but on the starboard side the frames were sawn off an average of 4 feet (1.2 m) from the keel (the work of salvagers sometime between 1825 and 1958).

Not much of the ceiling planking remained, but beneath the frames the external planking was in very good condition. The port-side waterway timber was the only surviving element from the upperworks of the schooner.

The recording methodology we employed in 1981 was uncomplicated (fig. 9.6). The dimensions of every accessible timber were measured, each timber's location within the structure was referenced to a centerline tape, and hull sections were taken every tenth frame by the offset method. Numerous black and white and color photographs were taken inside and out. The measurements and sketches were used to prepare plan and profile views of the wreck and detail views of its construction.[25] Since 1981 the hull has been reexamined on several occasions, frame offsets were retaken with an electronic level in 2000, and wood samples were collected for identification.

Figure 9.6. *Recording* Ticonderoga's *lower hull at Whitehall in 1981. This view of the hull, facing aft from the stem, shows the near-flat of the floor timbers and (to the right) the upcurving of the broken-off port-side frame ends, where the first futtocks were cut to fit the hard turn of the bilge. In the left foreground may be seen the combination waterway timber and shot garland that was so helpful for reconstructing* Ticonderoga's *gunports. (Photo by William Noel,* Ticonderoga *project files of Kevin J. Crisman.)*

The Construction of *Ticonderoga*

Although only a shadow of its former self, *Ticonderoga* is still an impressive sight. With its gray, weathered timbers, rot-ridden frames, and splintered scars from the 1958 salvage, the hull conveys a sense of the mystery and pathos inherent in the ruins of a once-beautiful object. By looking beyond the effects of age and hard use, however, you can begin to get a sense of the original vessel. The keel is large and deep, and amidships the frames have so little deadrise that they appear almost flat. The planking on the outside of the hull is thick, and on the starboard side the lower strakes sweep from amidships to the sternpost in a graceful run. The living ship is long gone, but its bones have stories to tell us about early-nineteenth-century steamboats and naval vessels.

For one thing, it is evident on closer inspection that a great quantity of iron went into *Ticonderoga*'s construction. The hull is entirely iron fastened, with long, 1-inch-square (2.54 cm) or 1½-inch-diameter (3.2 cm) bolts in the centerline timbers, square ¾-inch (1.9 cm) bolts securing frame floors to futtocks, and square iron spikes that attach ceiling and planking to the frames. *Ticonderoga* was built in close proximity to the Monkton Iron Works at Vergennes, which meant that bolts and spikes were cheap and plentiful.

The one element in *Ticonderoga*'s hull that is entirely complete is the keel, which extends for a length of 113 feet 9 inches (34.7 m) and is made up of seven individual white oak timbers (fig. 9.7).[26] Perhaps more than any other part of the extant hull, the keel shows evidence of the changes made by Noah Brown to convert the steamer hull into a good sailing warship. I strongly suspect that only the two uppermost keel

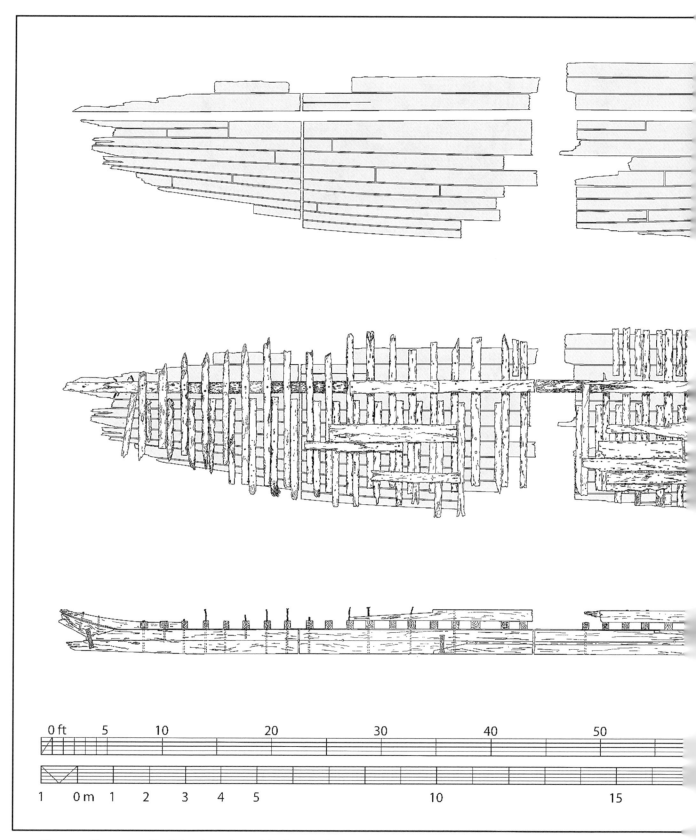

Figure 9.7. *Plan and profile of* Ticonderoga's *surviving lower hull. These views show details of the planking, frame construction, and extent of preservation. Of particular interest are the additional timbers added to the bottom of the keel to increase longitudinal strength and improve* Ticonderoga's *sailing characteristics. (Drawing by Kevin J. Crisman, with planking details by Douglas Inglis.)*

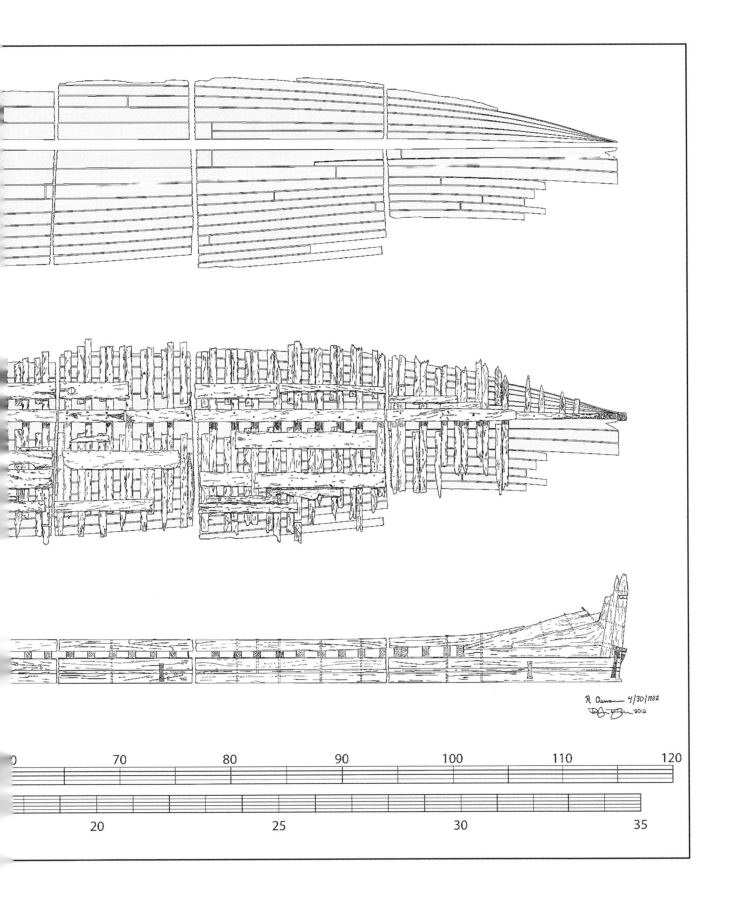

A. Cumm— 4/30/1982
2012

70   80   90   100   110   120

20   25   30   35

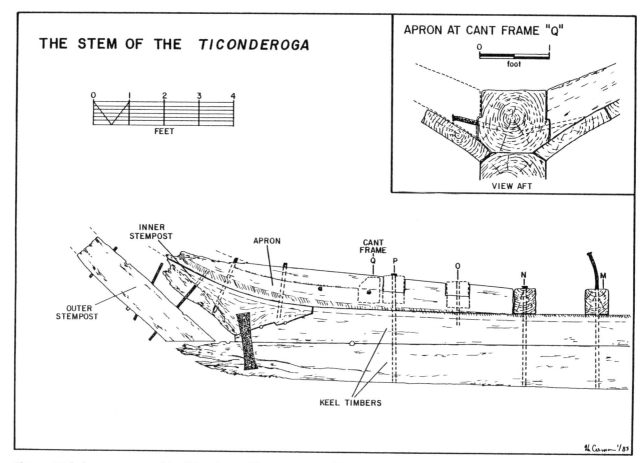

THE STEM OF THE *TICONDEROGA*

FEET

APRON AT CANT FRAME "Q"

foot

VIEW AFT

INNER STEMPOST
APRON
CANT FRAME
Q P O N M

OUTER STEMPOST

KEEL TIMBERS

Figure 9.8. *The lower stem assembly of* Ticonderoga. *The outer stem and lower keel were likely added by Noah Brown when he converted the unfinished steamboat into a schooner. The bow area shows the effects of long-term decay and the overenthusiastic salvage operation in 1958. (Drawing by Kevin J. Crisman.)*

timbers, connected amidships with a long flat scarf, are original to the steamer. These pieces were broad (13 inches [33 cm] sided) but shallow (10 inches [25.4 cm] molded); once the rabbets for the outer planking were cut into the keel at the top of each side, the amount of keel extending below the hull planking was a mere 7 inches (17.8 cm). This modestly exposed keel was entirely appropriate for a steamer, where lateral resistance to winds was not much of a concern and the ability to navigate in shallow waters was a definite advantage.

When Brown took over the unfinished hull, he had to find a way to increase the draft if it were to be a weatherly and stable sailing vessel. His solution was to add five more keel timbers to the underside of the vessel, three large pieces scarfed end to end, and two thinner filler pieces, thereby increasing the depth of the keel by 14 inches (35.6 cm). These extra timbers must have helped to stiffen *Ticonderoga* longitudinally

as well, resisting the hogging that would result from the immense weight of guns on the main deck. Long, round iron bolts were driven through the keelson, frames, and keel timbers to fasten the entire assembly together, and five pairs of wrought-iron dovetail plates, arranged over the length of the keel, also held the additional timbers securely in place. Round wooden pegs called stopwaters were driven across the scarfs and seams between timbers to prevent water from seeping into the hull and to limit shifting of the timbers along the seams. When Brown was finished, *Ticonderoga* had an especially deep, robust keel and, this, perhaps more than any other single modification, must have greatly improved the sailing qualities of the vessel.

Ticonderoga's bow assembly consisted of three elements: an inner stem, an outer stem, and an apron (fig. 9.8). Only the lower portions of these timbers remain, and the outer stem is detached from the rest of the structure. The short surviving length of the outer stem

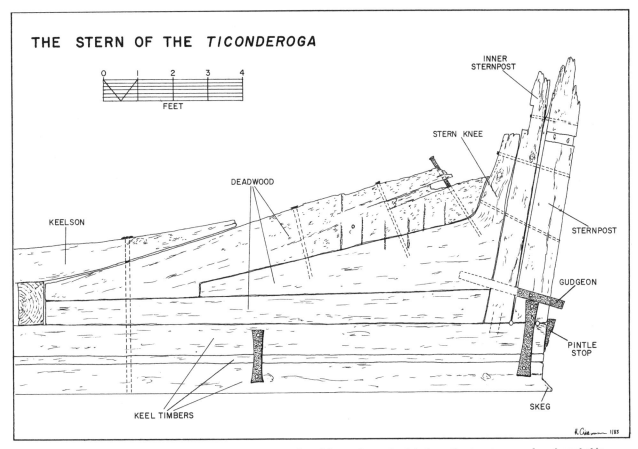

Figure 9.9. *The stern assembly of* Ticonderoga. *With the exception of the two lowest keel timbers, the structure seen here is probably all the work of* Ticonderoga's *original builder John Lacy. Notches in the timbers show the locations of half frames on the deadwood, a transom atop the inner sternpost, and a second gudgeon at the top of the sternpost. (Drawing by Kevin J. Crisman.)*

was sawn or chopped off at the top, damage that likely predates the salvage of the hull (there would have been no reason to cut the timber in 1958). This suggests that *Ticonderoga* sunk with its bow close to the river bank, where the upper stem was accessible to scavengers of iron and timber. The inner stem is severely splintered along its forward edge and port side, probably from the initial salvage attempt on September 25, 1958, when the Galick's bulldozer tugged on the steel cable wrapped around the bow and broke off "six feet of keel" (the outer stem).

The inner stem was fashioned from a naturally curved, somewhat gnarly piece of timber, perhaps from a tree root or the juncture of a tree trunk and branch. It was hook-scarfed to the forward end of the uppermost (original) keel and reinforced by an overlying apron of substantial dimensions. The outer stem, by contrast, is a straight piece of timber, and its heel sits flat atop the forward end of the add-on keel. I be-

lieve that the inner stem was shaped and fitted by John Lacy when he started construction of the steamer and that the outer stem was added by Noah Brown during his alteration of the hull in April 1814. Increasing the size of the forefoot beneath the water would have improved the schooner's ability to maintain a steady heading under sail.

Unlike the stem, the stern assembly is much more complete and includes nearly the entire length of the sternpost (fig. 9.9). The contrasting states of preservation are a sure sign that the after end of *Ticonderoga* settled in deeper water than the bow and was thereby protected from pre-1958 salvagers and the accelerated decay caused by annual wetting and drying of timber. The stern structure contains a sternpost, an inner sternpost, and three deadwood timbers (one of which served as the stern knee). All were fashioned from white oak. Some of the rudder hardware has also survived on the after edge of the sternpost and keel.

The sternpost, broken off 7 feet 5 inches (2.2 m) above the top of the keel, rakes aft at an angle of eight degrees and was fastened to the top of the keel by a 4-inch (10.2 cm) square wooden tenon and a pair of iron dovetail plates. Square rabbets were cut into the forward corners of the post for fitting the hood ends of the planking. The inner post, which has a preserved length of 7 feet (2.1 m), was fastened to the top of the keel by a 3-inch-square (7.6 cm) tenon. This post tapered considerably fore and aft and was the surface to which the ends of the planks were spiked in place. A notch cut into the forward face near the top of the inner post once contained the transom piece that formed the base of *Ticonderoga*'s counter.

The lowest of the three deadwood timbers was 12 feet 6 inches (3.8 m) in length and was seated atop and parallel to the keel. The middle deadwood timber, the stern knee, was fashioned from a tree trunk and branch, increased in its molded dimension as it extended aft, and had the branch seated vertically against the forward face of the inner post. The branch, incidentally, had been debarked but was otherwise nearly round. The uppermost deadwood piece extended diagonally between the aftermost floor and the top of the stern knee; its upper surface was damaged by both rot and fire. The deadwood timbers were fixed to the keel and sternposts with square iron bolts. Shallow notches were cut into each side of the deadwood assembly to fit the heels of the half frames.

The stern construction described above was probably all the work of John Lacy prior to the hull's acquisition by the navy. The rudder-related hardware and features, however, were most likely added by Noah Brown and his shipwrights. *Ticonderoga*'s rudder swung on two iron gudgeons bolted to the sternposts and deadwood; the lower gudgeon is still fastened in place, while a notch and two bolt holes indicate the location of the upper gudgeon. An iron wedge or "dumb brace" was fixed by two spikes to the keel and sternpost below the lower gudgeon to support the weight of the rudder.[27] The after lower corner of the keel had a short projection, the skeg, to protect the rudder in the event of grounding.

The after face of the sternpost was hollowed above the upper gudgeon to fit a plug stock rudder, a design coming into general use in the early nineteenth century. The earlier rule joint–style rudder swung in an arc like a door and required a substantial opening in the transom and deck. Because the plug stock was offset slightly ahead of the rudder's forward edge, with its center directly over the axis of the gudgeons and pintles, it revolved rather than swung and so required only a small circular opening in the transom.[28] The presence of the hollow for the stock is a good indication that nearly the full length of the sternpost is preserved.

Ticonderoga's hull was assembled with a total of fifty square frames, six pairs of half frames at the stern, and at least three pairs of cant frames in the bow. John Lacy may have carved a wooden half model of the steamboat's hull prior to beginning construction to work out details of the design with Jahaziel Sherman and the steamboat company directors and to provide a template with sections that could be scaled up in a mold loft to frame the full-sized ship. After the keel, stem, and stern assemblies were completed, Lacy and his assistants began framing the vessel by first lofting and constructing the midship frame, which defined the maximum breadth of the hull. They then lofted, shaped, and assembled every fourth square frame, fastening the floors and futtocks together with ¾-inch (1.9 cm) square iron bolts. Frames preassembled in this manner include D, H, L, and P forward of midships and 1, 5, 9, 13, 17, 21, 25, 29, and 33 abaft the midship frame (frame 30, with two floor timbers, was also preassembled).

Once the molded frames were bolted to the top of the keel, Lacy and his crew shaped the remaining thirty-five floor timbers, bolted them to the keel, and began planking. As planking strakes extended out from the keel, futtocks were fitted to the port and starboard sides of each frame, held in place solely by the spikes that fastened them to the planks. The technique of preassembling every third or fourth frame and adding the remaining frame timbers piecemeal saved time and effort in both lofting and bolting the individual frame elements together. This practice dates to the seventeenth century and has been identified in the wrecks of other North American vessels, including the Royal Navy schooner *Nancy* (described in chapter 3 of this book) and the 16-gun sloop *Boscawen*, built on Lake Champlain by colonial shipwrights in 1759.[29]

The twenty-three frame floors and futtocks sampled for wood identification purposes all proved to be of white oak, suggesting that this particular species of tree was sought by Lacy for the steamboat's frames.

The floor timbers were bolted to the keel on 2-foot (61 cm) centers and averaged 8 inches (20.3 cm) molded and 7 inches (17.8 cm) sided. The floors increased in molded dimensions near the stern, allowing the keelson to rise and lap over the deadwood. The port-side arms of the floors are preserved for their full lengths, about 9 feet to 9 feet 6 inches (2.7 to 2.9 m) from the keel centerline to the floor headline. Each floor between frames M and 30 had a pair of limber holes cut into its base to facilitate the drainage of bilge water into the pump well. The first futtocks are about the same molded and sided dimensions as the floors, and their heels are located an average of 12 inches (30.5 cm) from the side of the keel. The floors terminate at the turn of the bilge, and the first futtocks are all broken at this location. The stumps of four second futtocks were still attached to frames on the port side.

Not much was left of the port frames above the floor head line, but enough survived to show that the bottom had a sharp turn of the bilge, giving *Ticonderoga* a boxy shape in its central section. This hull form is capacious, but hard bilges constitute a weak point in the sides of a wooden vessel. The potential weakness was exacerbated by the manner in which John Lacy achieved the required futtock shapes. Instead of seeking out timber crooks with sharp, near-ninety-degree curves that matched the turn of the bilge, Lacy instead simply cut pieces of timber across the grain to get the shape he wanted for the first futtocks. This is not a recommended way to build strong, durable vessels, for straight-grained timber cut to a curve lacks the strength of grown timber and in this case surely added to the weakness already inherent in the hard-bilged design.

There were other places where Lacy chose to cut the shapes he needed from straight-grained timber. In the bow, the floors and futtocks of frames I through P were mainly fashioned in this manner. Besides leaving the timber weaker and more likely to split, cutting across the grain exposes more of the end grain to invasion by moisture and rot. These bow frames are certainly in very poor condition today. What was the rationale behind this seemingly careless practice? Very likely because it was fast, cheap, and adequate. The Lake Champlain Steamboat Company's new boat would be operating seasonally on a semiprotected lake, never out of sight of land, and usually close to sheltered anchorages. These were nothing like North Atlantic

conditions and did not require North Atlantic–grade shipbuilding. As well, steam technology was evolving rapidly, and Lacy and Sherman may have calculated that the boat would be obsolete and due for replacement before weakness and rot in the frames became a problem. Finally, it was widely recognized that wooden ships on freshwater tended to decay quickly, so what was the point of meticulous workmanship? Shortcuts could be taken under these circumstances.

The keelson of *Ticonderoga* was originally composed of three timbers, each molded and sided 12½ inches (31.8 cm), flat scarfed end to end, and extending from the apron to the deadwood. The forwardmost keelson timber is gone, and a section is missing from the central timber, a result of the 1958 salvage. The two surviving keelson timbers are of white oak; the rings on the central piece indicate that it was at least 240 years old at the time it was cut in 1814. The keelson was probably installed by Brown and his carpenters, for the 1¼-inch-diameter (3.2 cm) bolts that fasten it in place extend to the bottom of the add-on keel.

A wreck's keelson is often a useful source of information about missing features such as deck-supporting stanchions, mast steps, and pumps. *Ticonderoga*'s keelson is in rough shape, however, and relatively few features can be discerned. Evidence for the foremast step disappeared when the forward-most keelson timber was torn from the hull, but the location of the mainmast, over frames 14 to 16, is defined by a pattern of bolt holes and ¾-inch (1.9 cm) square iron bolts that once held some type of step in place.

It is unfortunate that the section of upper port side still attached to the hull in 1958 was lost during the salvage of *Ticonderoga*; this structure could have told us much about the schooner's hull form and appearance. The one bit of evidence left to us is a 27-foot, 8-inch (8.4 m) length of waterway that was originally attached to the insides of the frames above the main deck's beams (fig. 9.10). The timber was squared at its after end and broken off forward. If only one timber from the upperworks could be preserved, this is a good one, because it contains so many informative features.

The waterway, fashioned from white oak, measured 6 inches (15.2 cm) molded and 11 inches (27.9 cm) sided and has thirty-two bowl-shaped indentations chiseled into its top surface, each 4½ inches (11.4 cm) in diameter and 1½ inches (3.8 cm) deep. Each indentation has a small hole drilled in its bottom, sloping

Figure 9.10. *A combination waterway and shot garland from the port side of* Ticonderoga's *main deck. The piece has a diagonally sloping scupper cut through its side to drain water from the deck, as well as a series of carved circular depressions for holding round shot in proximity to the guns. The two gaps between the shot garlands are the locations of gunports. This piece provided vital information for reconstructing* Ticonderoga's *upper structure. (Drawing by Kevin J. Crisman and Douglas Inglis.)*

down and inboard, to drain water onto the deck. These circular features—shot garlands—were designed to hold round shot in close proximity to the guns and are spaced, from forward to aft, in three groups of six, twelve, and fourteen. The two 38-inch (96.5 cm) spaces between the shot garlands mark the locations of gunports. A distance of 9 feet 2 inches (2.8 m) separates the centers of the two positions, indicating the spacing of gunports along the vessel's sides. The size of the gunport openings appears to closely match that of the Brown-built brig *Eagle,* which had ports 37 inches (94 cm) square (*Eagle*'s gunports were on 10-foot [3.04 m] centers).

Each of the two gun positions on *Ticonderoga*'s waterway has a large, vertical hole in its center that closely resembles the holes for carronade pivot bolts in some of *Eagle*'s gunport sills. The shot garland was cut to fit 12-pounder shot, however, not shot for 32-pounder carronades. *Eagle*'s waterway, which also doubled as a shot garland, had nine indentations 7 inches (17.8 cm) in diameter between the 32-pounder carronade ports and eleven indentations 5 inches (12.7 cm) in diameter between the ports for 18-pounder long guns. The garlands on *Ticonderoga*'s waterway suggest that the two positions were for 12-pounder long guns but that holes for pivot bolts were drilled in case it was necessary to mount 32-pounder carronades in these ports.

The waterway was fastened to the deck beams by ¾-inch (1.9 cm) square iron bolts; the spacing of the bolts suggests that *Ticonderoga*'s beams were centered about every 3 feet (91.4 cm). The waterway was also secured to the frame top timbers by 1-inch-diameter (2.54 cm) iron bolts pounded through from the inside. The timber's function as a waterway along the edge of the deck is demonstrated by a sloping, 3-inch-diameter (7.6 cm) scupper beneath the forward gun position. The similarities between the waterways on *Ticonder-*

oga and *Eagle* suggests that using these timbers as a shot garland was a distinguishing characteristic of warships built by the Brown brothers.

The planking attached to the undersides of *Ticonderoga*'s lower frames was mostly intact. The white oak planks averaged 2½ inches (6.4 cm) thick and ranged in width from 18 inches (45.7 cm) at the garboard to 9 inches (22.9 cm) at the turn of the bilge. The planks were fastened to the frames with ⅜-inch (.95 cm) square iron spikes, four per plank per frame. Plank butts were reinforced at the frames forward and abaft the butt by the addition of one ¾-inch-diameter (1.9 cm) iron bolt. The bolts were driven from the outside, and their interior ends were then headed over an iron ring. This is an exceptionally solid method of securing plank butts, and it is little wonder that most of *Ticonderoga*'s surviving planking is still tightly fastened to the frames.

Photographs taken of *Ticonderoga* during the salvage in 1958 show that much of the ceiling planking was intact on the interior surfaces of the frames. Time and decay have taken their toll, and only twenty-four white pine ceiling planks or parts of planks were still fastened to the hull during the 1981 recording. The planks ranged between 12 and 18 inches (30.5 and 45.7 cm) wide and 1½ to 2 inches (3.8 to 5.1 cm) thick. They were fastened to the frames with the same type of ⅜-inch (.95 cm) square wrought-iron spikes that were used to fasten the external planking.

Steamboat to Schooner

Historical sources tell us that *Ticonderoga* underwent a transformation from a steamer to a schooner during its construction, but these sources have little to say about the nature of that transformation. It is only through archaeological study that we can begin to see the steamboat that John Lacy framed and learn how

Noah Brown subsequently modified and completed the hull for naval service. Evidence of both men's work was visible in the wreck, and while we can wish that more of it was recovered during the 1958 salvage, there is nevertheless enough information in the surviving structure to draw conclusions about both the steamboat and the schooner (fig. 9.11).

Steamship design was redefined in 1813 when Elihu Bunker built his *Fulton* on Long Island Sound, and it is apparent that *Ticonderoga,* begun one year later, closely followed the new model. This is no surprise since Jahaziel Sherman, who supervised Lacy's work at Vergennes, was a former steamboat captain for Bunker and may even have suggested some of the design changes that went into *Fulton. Ticonderoga*'s hull, like *Fulton*'s, dispensed with the flat floors and hard chine of many earlier steamers and instead incorporated frames with modest deadrise and a rounded rather than angled turn of the bilge. *Ticonderoga* also seems to have been built with slightly heavier scantlings than some of the earlier-style steamers.[30]

Ticonderoga also featured the more moderate length-to-breadth ratio introduced by Bunker's *Fulton.* Measuring approximately 120 feet (36.57 m) in length on deck and 24 feet (7.3 m) in beam, the Lake Champlain Steamboat Company's hull had a length-to-breadth ratio of about 5:1. *Fulton,* at 133 by 29 feet (40.54 by 8.84 m), had a ratio of 4.58:1. These can be contrasted to Robert Fulton's *North River,* which at about 150 by 16 feet (42.67 by 4.87 m) had a ratio of 9.37:1. The Lake Champlain steamer *Vermont* was more moderate than *North River* at 125 by 20 feet (36.57 by 6.09 m), but its length-to-beam ratio of 6.25:1 still exceeded *Ticonderoga*'s by a substantial margin. The vessel framed by Lacy and Sherman at Vergennes was on the cutting edge of steamer design, with a hull that was stronger, more seaworthy, and probably more stable than many steamships built between 1807 and 1813.

If Lacy and Sherman had stuck to the earlier model of steamboat, it is doubtful whether the resulting hull would have been of much use to Macdonough. As it was, he and Brown must have found the relatively narrow, lightly built craft difficult to convert to their purposes. The hard-bilged form and cut-to-a-curve futtocks were inherently weak, but it would have required too much expense, effort, and time to reframe the hull, so Brown made changes elsewhere. The most obvious of these on the present-day wreck is the greatly enlarged keel, an addition that added longitudinal strength and improved the stability of the vessel. It appears that he also increased the size of the forefoot by the addition of an outer stem.

If completed as a steamer, *Ticonderoga* would have carried its boilers and engines amidships, bolted to longitudinal bed timbers in the hold, but as a warship, the greatest concentration of weight, the iron cannon, was placed high in the hull on the main deck and was spread out over the length of that deck from stem to stern. We can say with certainty that this adversely affected the strength and stability of the vessel. Brown no doubt made a number of modifications to the upperworks to compensate for deficiencies in strength. These likely included adding additional deck-supporting stanchions atop the keelson; adding more or larger deck beams, ledges, carlings, clamps, and wales; and fitting more knees to reinforce the join of the deck and sides. Since steamer decks were typically enclosed with an open rail, we can be sure that part of Brown's conversion included the construction of solid timber bulwarks between gun positions.

Two curious features of the completed vessel hint that strength and stability were a concern for Brown, Macdonough, and Stephen Cassin. By early-nineteenth-century standards, this was a large warship to be sailing with a schooner rig, for most vessels of this length were square rigged as two-masted brigs or three-masted ships. A square rig on a narrow and top-heavy hull like *Ticonderoga,* however, might have been too great a weight of masts and spars and too much sail area. A fore-and-aft rig also permitted *Ticonderoga* to steer a little closer to the wind than would have been possible with a square rig, which, considering the narrowness of the lake and the schooner's shallow and near-flat-bottomed design, was probably a good thing.

According to a British intelligence report, *Ticonderoga* had eleven gunports on a side, about what we could expect for a warship 120 feet (36.57 m) in length.[31] Even if the forwardmost ports did not mount guns (and they were customarily left open), there were still ports for twenty cannon, yet *Ticonderoga* never carried more than seventeen. Why did the schooner sail with empty ports? Every cannon was essential for Macdonough in the summer of 1814, and it is hard to believe that he could not have obtained three more of them if there were places to mount them on one of his vessels. We can only conclude that the weight of the seventeen

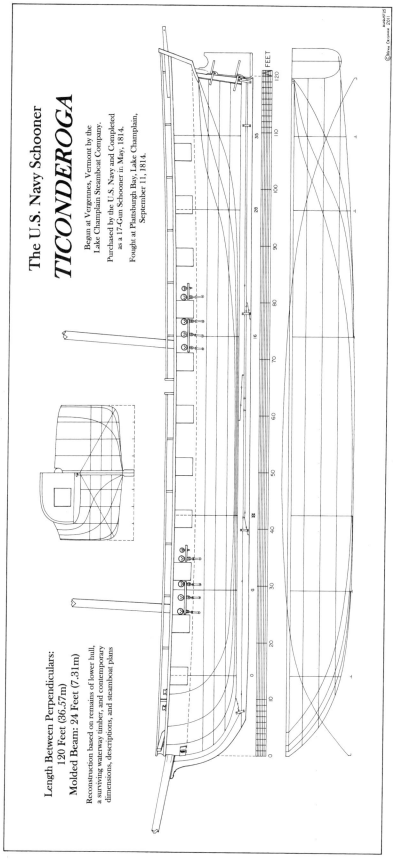

The U.S. Navy Schooner
TICONDEROGA

Begun at Vergennes, Vermont by the
Lake Champlain Steamboat Company.

Purchased by the U.S. Navy and Completed
as a 17-Gun Schooner in May, 1814.

Fought at Plattsburgh Bay, Lake Champlain,
September 11, 1814.

Length Between Perpendiculars:
120 Feet (36.57m)
Molded Beam: 24 Feet (7.31m)

Reconstruction based on remains of lower hull,
a surviving waterway timber, and contemporary
dimensions, descriptions, and steamboat plans

FEET

Figure 9.11. Reconstructed lines of the US Navy schooner Ticonderoga. These plans are based on measurements of the surviving lower hull and on contemporary dimensions and descriptions. The vessel's steamboat origins are evident in the boxy shape of the hull amidships, although the entrance and run are surprisingly fine. A British intelligence report from 1814 noted eleven gunports on each side, and the spacing of those ports was indicated by the surviving waterway timber that was recorded in 1981. These two sources, when combined with the overall length of the vessel, suggest there were no ports at the forward and after ends of the deck, perhaps because the deck was too narrow or because Noah Brown was concerned that the lightly framed hull would hog if too much weight was placed at either end. (Reconstruction by Kevin J. Crisman.)

guns—estimated to be 35 tons—was already testing the limits of the hull's strength and stability. Any additional weight on the deck might have been too much.

Every ship design represents a compromise, since hull characteristics that improve a vessel in one of its aspects (seaworthiness, weatherliness, speed, stability, strength, and capacity) often diminish other desirable features. *Ticonderoga* represents an extreme example of this principal at work, for the characteristics that made for a good steamboat hull did not match what the navy needed for a good sailing warship. Necessity overcame any reservations that Macdonough might have had concerning the steamer hull, however, and with a few crucial modifications Noah Brown was able to launch a 17-gun schooner that, whatever its design defects, effectively served the cause of the United States on Lake Champlain in 1814.

NOTES

1. Doris Morton, Town Historian, Whitehall, NY, personal communication with the author, February 1981.

2. Andrea Sutcliffe, *Steam: The Untold Story of America's First Great Invention* (New York: Palgrave Macmillan, 2004), pp. 179–200.

3. Rebecca Davison, ed., *The Phoenix Project* (Burlington, VT: Champlain Maritime Society, 1981).

4. Jean Baptiste Marestier, *Memoir on Steamboats of the United States of America* (Mystic, CT: The Marine Historical Association, 1957), pp. 7–8, 17–18, 48; David J. Blow, "*Vermont I*: Lake Champlain's First Steamboat," *Vermont History* 34, no. 2 (April, 1966), pp. 117, 119; Barney Fowler, *Adirondack Album* (Schenectady, NY: Outdoor Associates, 1974), pp. 33–34; A. Peter Barranco, "Dimensions of Str. *Vermont* raised from the Richelieu River in 1953," notes and plans of wreck of *Vermont I* recorded by A. Peter Barranco in 1963 (copy on file with K. Crisman). *Vermont's* floors had no deadrise, but unlike *North River* the hull had rounded bilges rather than a chine (see the photographs on pp. 33–34 of Fowler's *Adirondack Album*).

5. Jones to Macdonough, February 22, 1814, entry 149, record group 45 (RG 45), National Archives and Records Administration (NARA); Macdonough to Jones, March 7, 1814, entry 147, RG 45, NARA.

6. Daniel D. Tompkins, *Public Papers of Daniel D. Tompkins, Governor of New York 1807–1817*, vol. 3 (Albany: State of New York, 1902), pp. 457–59.

7. Macdonough to Jones, April 30, 1814, entry 147, RG 45, NARA.

8. Macdonough to Jones, May 13, 1814, entry 147, RG 45, NARA.

9. Macdonough to Jones, April 30, 1814, entry 147, RG 45, NARA; "A Report on the State and Condition of the Naval Force

. . . under the Command of Thomas Macdonough, Esquire on the 31st day of August 1814," manuscript document, Lake Champlain Maritime Museum, Vergennes, VT. Courtesy of Arthur B. Cohn. The estimated weight of *Ticonderoga's* cannon, carriages, and gun equipment was derived through the following calculations:

Cannon	Carriage	Combined	Total on Ticonderoga
32-pdr carronad 2000 lbs	500 lbs	2500 lbs	× 5 12,500 lbs
12-pdr long gun 3800 lbs	600 lbs	4400 lbs	× 8 35,200 lbs
18-pdr long gun 4700 lbs	700 lbs	5400 lbs	× 4 21,600 lbs
Gun tools and tackle		1200 lbs	1200 lbs
		TOTAL:	70,500 lbs (35.25 tons)

Individual cannon weights are from Spencer Tucker, *Arming the Fleet, U.S. Navy Ordnance in the Muzzle-Loading Era* (Annapolis: Naval Institute Press, 1989), p. 125. Some of Macdonough's ships carried 18-pounder columbiads, which were a shorter, lighter version of the long gun, but the August 31 inventory and other sources indicate that *Ticonderoga* carried the standard, heavier 18 pounders.

10. Macdonough to Jones, March 7 and April 30, 1814, entry 147, RG 45, NARA.

11. Christopher McKee, *A Gentlemanly and Honorable Profession: The Creation of the U.S. Naval Officer Corps, 1794–1815* (Annapolis: Naval Institute Press, 1991), pp. 335–36; Thomas Macdonough to John Rodgers, May 6, 1815, Subject File NI, RG 45, NARA.

12. Abstracts of Service Records, US Navy, Microcopy 330, RG 45, NARA; McKee, *Gentlemanly and Honorable Profession,* pp. 309–25; Macdonough to Rodgers, May 6, 1815, Subject File NI, RG 45, NARA; Thomas Macdonough, "Roll of Commissioned & Warrant Officers Late under Command of Thomas Macdonough," May 6, 1815, Subject Files, Box 224, Folio 1, RG 45, NARA. Paulding rose to the rank of rear admiral and played a prominent role in the US Navy before and during the Civil War. See Cmdr. R. W. Meade, USN, "Admiral Hiram Paulding," *Harper's New Monthly Magazine* (February 1879), pp. 358–64, and Rebecca Paulding Meade, *Life of Hiram Paulding, Rear-Admiral, U.S.N.* (New York: The Baker and Taylor Company, 1910).

13. Macdonough to Jones, May 29, 1814, entry 147, RG 45, NARA.

14. Macdonough to Jones, May 21, 1814, entry 147, RG 45, NARA.

15. Jahaziel Sherman to William Jones, June 20 and July 20, 1814, entry 124, RG 45, NARA; Jones to John Bullus, July 1, 1814, entry 441, RG 45, NARA.

16. William Wood, ed., *Select British Documents of the Canadian War of 1812,* vol. 3, pt. 1 (Toronto: The Champlain Society,

1926), pp. 400–98. The descriptions of the British gunboats during the battle are taken entirely from the Royal Navy court martial transcripts contained in *Select British Documents,* principally pages 429–36.

17. Benson Lossing, *The Pictorial Fieldbook of the War of 1812* (New York: Harper & Brothers, 1868, facsimile reprint by the New Hampshire Publishing Company, 1976), pp. 868–70; Meade, "Admiral Hiram Paulding," p. 359; Kevin Crisman, *The History and Construction of the United States Schooner* Ticonderoga (Alexandria, VA: Eyrie Publications, 1983), pp. 19–25. Lt. John Stansbury's remains were recovered two days after the battle and, along with the other dead officers from both squadrons, he was buried in the Plattsburgh Cemetery rather than in the mass graves of the common sailors on Crab Island.

18. B. N. Clark, ed., "Accounts of the Battle of Plattsburgh, September 11, 1814: From Contemporaneous Sources," *Vermont Antiquarian* 1, no. 3 (1903), pp. 82, 87; Cassin ordered to *Spitfire,* National Archives Microfilm Publication, roll 5, pt. 3, no. 92, entry 147, RG 45, NARA; "Stephen Cassin," roll 3, entry 330, RG 45, NARA. Cassin was awarded $4552.25 in prize money for the captured British squadron, the equivalent of over seven years of his pay as a lieutenant, see roll 12, pt. 12, no. 133, entry 149, RG 45, NARA.

19. Ogden Ross, *The Steamboats of Lake Champlain, 1809 to 1930* (Champlain Transportation Company, 1930; facsimile reprint, Vermont Heritage Press, 1997), pp. 29–41, 55–56. The *Phoenix* has undergone archaeological study and was found to be similar in design and construction to *Ticonderoga.* See Davidson, ed., *The Phoenix Project;* George Robert Schwarz, "The Passenger Steamboat *Phoenix*: An Archaeological Study of Early Steam Propulsion in North America" (PhD diss., Texas A&M University, 2013).

20. Crisman, *The United States Schooner* Ticonderoga; Kevin Crisman, *The* Eagle*: An American Brig on Lake Champlain During the War of 1812* (Shelburne, VT: The New England Press; Annapolis: Naval Institute Press, 1987). Both of these publications summarize the decade-long history of the US Navy's establishment at Whitehall, New York.

21. Four photographs in the Whitehall Historical Society, Whitehall, NY, show a diver wearing a homemade helmet recovering round shot from a narrow, murky body of water, unquestionably the Poultney River. The pictures appear to date from the 1930s or 1940s. The brig *Linnet* was dragged out of the river and partly salvaged in 1949 (see chapter 11).

22. *The Whitehall* (NY) *Times,* July 3, 1958 and March 12, 1959.

23. A detailed account of the salvage of *Ticonderoga* was recorded by Carol Manell Senecal of Whitehall, NY. The Senecal diary is now in the collections of the Skenesborough Museum in Whitehall, NY.

24. The Champlain Maritime Society was a nonprofit coalition of historians, divers, and archaeologists dedicated to studying the lake's maritime past; it subsequently merged with the Lake Champlain Maritime Museum at Basin Harbor, VT.

25. Crisman, *The United States Schooner* Ticonderoga. Details of the archaeological study may be found in this publication.

26. Identification of wood species used in the construction of *Ticonderoga* was made by Dr. Roy Whitmore, professor emeritus, University of Vermont Department of Forestry, July 2000.

27. E. W. Petrejus, *Modelling the Brig of War* Irene*: A Handbook for the Building of Historical Ship Models* (Hengelo: Uitgeversmaatschappij "De Esch," 1970), pp. 91–92; William Hutchinson, *A Treatise on Naval Architecture Founded upon Philosophical and Rational Principles* (Liverpool: T. Billinge, 1774; facsimile reprint, London: Conway Maritime Press, 1970).

28. Howard I. Chapelle, *The History of the American Sailing Navy* (New York: W. W. Norton, 1949), pp. 169–70.

29. Kevin J. Crisman, "Struggle for a Continent: Naval Battles of the French and Indian Wars," in *Ships and Shipwrecks of the Americas,* ed. George F. Bass (London: Thames and Hudson, 1988), p. 146; early eighteenth-century descriptions of this framing practice can be found in William Sutherland, *The Ship-Builders Assistant* (London: R. Mount, 1711, facsimile reprint, East Sussex: Jean Boudriot Publications, 1989), p. 26, and in David H. Roberts, ed., *18th Century Shipbuilding: Remarks on the Navies of the English & the Dutch from Observations Made at their Dockyards in 1737 by Blaise Ollivier* (East Sussex: Jean Boudriot Publications, 1992), p. 357.

30. Fowler, *Adirondack Album,* pp. 33–34; Barranco, "Dimensions of Str. *Vermont.*" Photographs and recorded dimensions suggest that *Vermont*'s timbers were generally of modest dimensions.

31. Capt. Daniel Pring to Lt. Col. Williams, May 14, 1814, vol. 683, series C (I), record group 8, Library and Archives Canada.

10 "A PERFECT WILLINGNESS TO SEE THE ENEMY ON FAIR TERMS"

The US Navy Row Galley *Allen*

ERIC EMERY

Introduction

Sailing Master William M. Robbins surveyed his battered passengers through the pouring rain on the morning of September 16, 1814. Almost a week had passed since the Battle of Plattsburgh Bay, and still its aftershocks consumed his daily activities. Standing on the deck of the US Navy row galley *Allen,* he counted sixty wounded British sailors and marines. Attendants John Pearson and Augustus Barbes had carefully stowed them in sitting positions to make room for the galley's crew. The injured bore expressions of pain carved deeply into their faces, but there was one consolation to ease their suffering—they were going home.[1]

The previous day, Robbins and his galleymen left the US naval squadron at anchor off Plattsburgh, New York, on an official mission into British Canada. Their orders were to transport wounded prisoners of war to the Royal Navy Yard at Isle aux Noix inside the Richelieu River. "Owing to my hospital establishment being small and having such few surgeons," lamented Comm. Thomas Macdonough, "I thought it not improper to place these persons (being badly wounded) on Isle aux Noix where they could receive the medical attention so much needed." He felt assured that the US Navy Department would assent to a courtesy intended to express "feelings of humanity and liberality to a brave enemy."[2]

The cold, stiff-fingered oarsmen pulled vigorously in time as *Allen* scudded down the Richelieu. Light, variable winds pinwheeled spray over the galley's bow gun, leaving the crew shivering beneath sodden uniforms.[3] As the outline of Isle aux Noix drew closer, Robbins may have reminisced about his enlistment in the US Navy, just days after the official declaration of hostilities, or the moment that he first assumed command of *Allen* at Vergennes, Vermont. The most vivid recollection, however, had to be the "highly honorable" conduct that distinguished his galley division in the previous week's battle.[4] The US victory lifted the young republic from its darkest hour and altered the course of the War of 1812. Yet in the wave of relief and patriotic celebration that followed, the original mission of *Allen* and the Lake Champlain galley flotilla soon became forgotten. This is their story.

"One Great Object of the War in Vision"

Allen and the other vessels of the Lake Champlain galley flotilla emerged piecemeal during the War of 1812 against a background of waffling strategic plans, disjointed military campaigns, and financial insolvency. Well before the start of the conflict, President James Madison and his advisors made invasion of British Canada a principal objective of the war. This lightly defended territory could be a useful bargaining chip or perhaps even be annexed outright by the United States. The key to US success was Montreal, the crossroads of communication, transportation, and trade between Upper and Lower Canada. The city's capture would cleave the vital St. Lawrence River lifeline that sustained Canadian defenses. All of the plans made in 1812 and 1813 to secure this decisive position had a serious tactical omission, however. The United States failed to create a flotilla of oared warships capable of operating on the Richelieu River (also known as the "Sorrell") that straddled the border and emptied into the St. Lawrence a short distance below Montreal.

The events that led to the construction of *Allen* began on November 23, 1813, when Thomas Macdonough submitted a plan to the US Navy Department for invading Canada via the Lake Champlain–Richelieu River corridor. His proposal hinged on the use of row galleys to control the river. "We should be prepared," wrote Macdonough, "to go down the Sorrell River pass the Chamblee Rapids (of six miles) and enter the St. Lawrence, there to cooperate with the Army." The Richelieu contained open water, shoals, and rapids, conditions that called for long, shallow-draft vessels able to navigate under sails and oars and rugged enough to endure a pounding without falling apart. In addition, they had to be sufficiently armed to challenge the fortifications at Isle aux Noix and St. John that guarded the river's passage into Lower Canada.[5]

Oared warcraft were hardly a novelty in this region of North America in 1813. The Great War for Empire (1756–63) and the American Revolution (1775–83) had demonstrated the usefulness of these vessels for block-

ades, shore bombardment, raids, and troop transport in confined waterways. Gunboats boasted a number of unique advantages. The simplicity of their designs meant that the same set of plans could be used to mass-produce a flotilla in a short period of time. Compared to larger warships, they were inexpensive to build and outfit. Their shallow draft allowed them to go almost anywhere on lakes, rivers, bays, and inlets without the risk of grounding, and the use of oars as well as sails enabled them to move regardless of the winds and currents. The large number of oarsmen needed to row one of these vessels provided a numerical advantage in the event of a boarding action. Finally, their narrow breadth and low freeboard made them difficult targets to hit when they directly engaged an enemy. There were drawbacks, of course: gunboats required large numbers of sailors to row them, oarsmen felt exposed with their backs to the enemy and sometimes avoided close action, and on open waters they were vulnerable to both rough weather and larger warships.[6]

In confined waters, however, gunboats could be highly effective against bigger ships. This was demonstrated in the Richelieu on June 3, 1813, when Lt. Sidney Smith and Sailing Master Jairus Loomis sailed the US sloops *Growler* and *Eagle* into the narrow river channel to engage three British row galleys a short distance above Isle aux Noix. The two sloops quickly found themselves trapped in the narrow channel by adverse winds and the strong current and were harassed by the more maneuverable oared gunboats that swarmed like stinging insects. After enduring more than three hours of cannon and musket volleys, *Growler* and *Eagle* struck their colors.[7]

The Richelieu River fiasco awakened the US Navy to the importance of augmenting its force on Lake Champlain with smaller, more versatile warships. In its aftermath, Secretary of the Navy William Jones gave Macdonough a free hand to rebuild his squadron in a manner that would ensure his control of not only the broad lake, but the surrounding river systems as well. "You are to understand," wrote the Secretary, "that upon no account are you to suffer the enemy to gain the ascendancy on Lake Champlain." Specifically, Macdonough's orders gave him permission to add "4 or 5 barges, of 50 or 60 feet long, to carry a 12 or 18 pound carronade."[8]

The "barges" of which Secretary Jones spoke are interchangeably referred to as "galleys" in his correspondence with Macdonough. However, they were a smaller, lighter-built version of the 2-gun row galleys that came into service on Lake Champlain the following year. William Doughty, Chief Naval Constructor at the Washington, DC, Navy Yard, completed the first design for this new class of gunboat in June 1813. His drawings showed a shallow, open, double-ended vessel with no living quarters; it measured 50 feet (15.24 m) in length and 12 feet (3.65 m) in beam, with a depth of 3 feet 6 inches (1.06 m) and a displacement of 19 tons. Doughty never specified a particular type of sail rig, but his design included stations for up to twenty-eight oars. Each barge's armament consisted of a single gun mounted on the bow. When fitted for sail, they stepped a single mast and the rig varied from a triangular lateen to a quadrilateral lug sail depending on the user's preference.[9] Doughty's barge was intended for use on inland and coastal waterways, where maneuverability was essential.

The Lake Champlain squadron already possessed two gunboats, *No. 169* and *No. 170*. The oldest of Macdonough's warships, they were originally built to catch smugglers and enforce the Embargo Act of 1808, but the repeal of the embargo prompted their retirement in 1809.[10] At the beginning of the war, Macdonough found *No. 169* and *No. 170* lying derelict near Basin Harbor, Vermont, their timbers badly deteriorated and plank seams "so open as to admit the hand."[11] The gunboats were refurbished and armed with a single gun each but spent most of 1813 out of service due to a shortage of sailors.[12] After the loss of his two sloops in early 1813, Macdonough worked diligently at Burlington, Vermont, to reassemble a squadron. This included arming three merchant sloops and constructing two barge-type gunboats, *Alwyn* and *Ballard*.[13] In late July 1813, before the new US Navy vessels were ready, the British commenced a raid on Lake Champlain. Commanded by Lt. Col. John Murray of the British Army, the expedition left Isle aux Noix with the sloops *Broke* and *Shannon* (formerly *Growler* and *Eagle*), three gunboats, and forty bateaux. Eight merchant sloops were captured or destroyed on the lake and government buildings at Plattsburgh, New York, and Swanton, Vermont, were burned. On August 2 the raiders approached Burlington and exchanged long-range fire with a 10-gun battery on shore, as well as four of Macdonough's gunboats. Failing to lure the US ships out from under the shore battery, the British withdrew and two days later returned to Canada.[14]

On September 6, 1813, Macdonough's refurbished squadron left Burlington Bay. He apparently chose to lay up at least two of his galleys, as these vessels did not offer any real advantage for patrols on the open lake. In fact, the commodore was learning that they demanded a disproportionate number of sailors for the number of guns they could bring to bear. He hesitated to take them permanently out of service, however, should he need them for maneuvers along the northern reaches of the lake.[15] He had no intention of venturing into Canada at such a late point in the season, for Secretary Jones's instructions had been to stay on the defensive and keep all enemy ships confined within the Richelieu River until the onset of winter.

The War Department had different plans for the Lake Champlain squadron. Secretary John Armstrong had long championed an assault on the St. Lawrence River Valley via Lake Champlain and the Richelieu River. However, many of his colleagues considered it too well defended and US strategy in early 1813 instead focused on the Great Lakes region to the west.[16] In the late summer, Armstrong finally initiated a two-pronged assault on Montreal by way of the Upper St. Lawrence River and the Champlain-Richelieu corridor. The twin attacks were intended to split British forces and thereby weaken the defenses. Armstrong entrusted this complex operation to two profoundly incompetent generals: James Wilkinson, who was massing troops at Sackets Harbor, Lake Ontario, and Wade Hampton, commander of the army in the Champlain Valley. From the outset Wilkinson and Hampton procrastinated, bickered, and mismanaged logistics. Separated by less than 150 miles (241 km), they nevertheless ignored one another and stubbornly insisted on conducting their own ill-conceived offensives.[17] Macdonough remained uninformed about the operation until days before its intended departure date.

General Hampton and the War Department presumed that the US Navy could navigate as easily on the Richelieu River as it did on Lake Champlain. This simply was not true, for as *Growler* and *Eagle* had demonstrated in June, Macdonough's cumbersome sloops could not safely enter the river. *Alwyn, Ballard, No. 169,* and *No. 170* were suited for river service, but the four gunboats each mounted only a single cannon and together carried less than 150 sailors and soldiers. Their numbers were not sufficient to the task, and consequently, when Hampton finally consulted the commodore on September 7 about using the squadron against British positions on the Richelieu, Macdonough flatly rejected the plan.[18]

Seeing little hope of success on the Richelieu without naval support, Hampton chose instead to cross the border to the west, down the Chateauguay River that emptied into the St. Lawrence a few miles above Montreal. French-Canadian regulars and militia turned back this invasion at the Battle of Chateauguay, in Quebec. By November, Hampton had abandoned the plan to rendezvous with Wilkinson's army and retreated to winter quarters at Plattsburgh.[19]

Macdonough's refusal to assist the army caused immediate controversy in Washington, where Armstrong—scrambling to deflect blame—insinuated that mismanagement of the squadron had undermined his offensive. "It is much to be regretted," carped the secretary, "that our naval means on Lake Champlain should have fallen so far short of their object." In Armstrong's opinion, the squadron should have been ready to enter the Richelieu, and because it failed to do so, the army had to "pass up the enemy in their fortresses."[20] Macdonough's actions hardly deserved such reproach. The Navy Department had made it plain that command of Lake Champlain was the top priority in 1813, and to risk losing it for the second time in one year was reckless. Nevertheless, Macdonough felt compelled to assure the navy secretary that he had always kept the "one great object of the war in vision (the conquest of Canada)" and that he "manifested a perfect willingness to see the enemy on fair terms."[21]

The British made several brief forays out of the Richelieu River in November and December.[22] Spies reported that these attacks were likely to get worse in 1814, for the British were bringing up additional row galleys from the St. Lawrence River. The galleys, it was said, each mounted a long 24 pounder in the bow fixed in line with the keel and a traversing 32-pounder cannonade in the stern. It was in this deteriorating situation that Macdonough wrote to the Navy Department on November 23, proposing that twenty to twenty-five row galleys be added to his squadron during the upcoming winter. These vessels would counterbalance the British and strengthen the US blockade of the northern reaches of Lake Champlain. But more importantly, an expanded flotilla of row galleys would enable Macdonough to effectively cooperate with the army in the next invasion of Canada.[23]

Building the Mosquito Fleet

On December 7, 1813, Secretary Jones instructed Macdonough to build fifteen galleys, "for which plans and draughts will be immediately forwarded to you, similar to those now constructing at Baltimore for the flotilla of the Chesapeake." The galley plans sent to Lake Champlain, recently prepared by William Doughty, were for a larger, more heavily armed version of *Alwyn* and *Ballard* (fig. 10.1). The hull was to measure 75 feet (22.86 m) in length and 15 feet (4.57 m) in breadth and draw no more than 22 inches (55 cm) of water when fully loaded. The recommended armament was substantial: a 42-pounder carronade in the bow and a long 24 pounder in the stern.[24]

Secretary Jones's approval of this and other gunboat projects must have come as a surprise to some in Washington in light of his known dislike of oared warships. Earlier in the war he warned that these vessels offered few advantages and that the hard labor at the sweeps and lack of onboard accommodations would scare off recruits. In a letter to Lloyd Jones, his brother, the secretary complained that the navy's gunboats were "scattered about in every creek and corner as receptacles of idleness and objects of waste and extravagance without utility."[25] His view changed, however, as the fighting continued and the government slipped deeper into debt. Gunboats could be cheaply mass-produced in remote areas using local resources and in many cases were the navy's only means of responding to British depredations.

The builder of the new gunboats arrived on Lake Champlain in the last week of February 1814. Noah Brown came highly recommended by the Navy Department for his construction of Oliver Hazard Perry's fleet on Lake Erie the previous year.[26] He had a reputation for keeping the job simple and employing as many shortcuts as possible but never sacrificing structural integrity. Once, when an employee on Lake Erie complained of being rushed, Brown reminded him "plain work is all that is required; they will only be wanted for one battle; if we win, that is all that is wanted of them; if the enemy are victorious, the work is good enough to be captured."[27] Brown brought with him hundreds of carpenters, joiners, caulkers, and other laborers; in exchange for coming to the lake, they could count on at least two months of steady work, lodging, and pay.[28]

Brown's arrival in Vermont coincided with new intelligence from Canada that profoundly altered Mac-

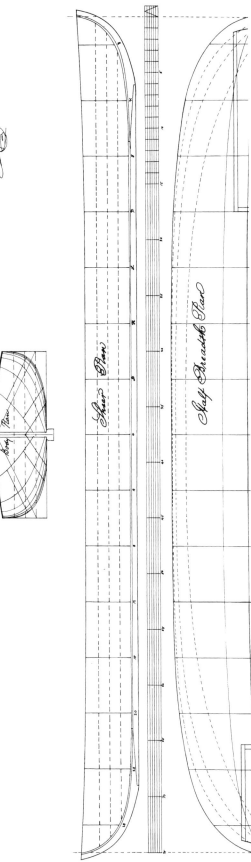

Figure 10.1. The design for a "first class" 75-foot-long, 2-gun row galley. Approved by Chief Naval Constructor William Doughty on October 11, 1813, this became the blueprint for US Navy galleys built for service on Chesapeake Bay, Lake Champlain, and Lake Ontario. (Traced from the original by E. B. Emery, ship plan 80-7-23, Record Group 19, National Archives and Records Administration.)

donough's plans. Spies reported intensive building at Isle aux Noix, with every indication that the British were preparing a large warship capable of overpowering a galley flotilla on the open lake. The commodore had very little choice: the new threat had to be met with a ship of equal or greater size. Brown was ordered to cut timber for a ship of 26 guns, and the number of galleys slated for construction was reduced from fifteen to six.[29] This change in the squadron's composition marked the beginning of a shift from an offensive to a defensive strategy in 1814.

Vergennes, Vermont, the site selected for Noah Brown's temporary shipyard, must have seemed a great improvement over the previous winter's yard on Lake Erie. The town contained a sawmill that could easily cut thousands of feet of planks, the furnaces and forges of the nearby Monkton Iron Works could produce iron fittings, and the surrounding forests held an abundance of white and red oak, pine, ash, hard maple, and beech. The building area was located 7 miles (11.3 km) up the Otter Creek from the lake, providing a measure of protection from raiding parties. Within days of Brown's arrival, the tiny community resounded with the noise of axes, adzes, hammers, and saws transforming raw timber into a new naval squadron.[30]

Brown and his assistants began their work on the six galleys by laying down the keel, stem, and sternpost for each hull (fig. 10.2). These components defined the overall length of the hull and the rake, or angle, of the ends. On *Allen* the white oak keel measured 69 feet 4 inches (21.13 m) in length and probably consisted of two pieces scarfed together amidships (Brown would have been hard-pressed to find a single straight piece of oak this long). The keel averaged 6 inches (15 cm) molded and 10 inches (25 cm) sided and tapered in its sided dimensions at either end. The shallow depth of the keel was a good indicator that keeping the draft to a minimum was more important than making the galley a weatherly sailor; clearly these vessels were designed principally for navigating shoal waters under oars.

Allen's stem included two pieces, a main stem of American elm fitted to the forward end of the keel with a flat scarf and an apron of white ash. Two stopwaters extended across the scarf between the stem and keel to keep water from seeping into the hull. The stem followed the Doughty plan, but Brown made a significant alteration to the stern. The original design called for a double-ended hull with curved posts at both ends.

Brown built *Allen* with no transom aft but opted for a straight sternpost instead of a curved post, probably because it is easier to hang a rudder on a straight post and because more gudgeons can be used (it is impossible to align more than two gudgeons on a curved post). The white oak sternpost was fitted to the keel, reinforced with a knee of American elm, an outer post of red oak was fastened to the after side of the main post, and iron eyebolts were driven into the after post to serve as gudgeons.

One of the more time-consuming tasks facing Brown and his shipwrights was framing the six galleys. *Allen* alone contained forty-five square frames, including two that notched down over the apron forward and one that notched down over the stern knee aft. Every square frame consisted of five overlapping pieces: a single floor timber, a pair of first futtocks, and a pair of second futtocks. Altogether the galleys required well over one thousand two hundred floor timbers and futtocks, each of which had to be cut and shaped by hand and then fastened to the other frame timbers with either iron bolts or treenails. Brown used white oak for most of these timbers, but the occasional piece of American beech, red oak, and white ash also found its way into the assembly.

Construction of the frames was functional but rough and irregular, which was about what could be expected for gunboats assembled from green timber in a matter of weeks. Floors were fastened atop the keel on centers that varied between 2 and 2½ feet (60 to 76 cm). Molded dimensions of individual timbers ranged from 3½ to 5½ inches (8.9 to 13.9 cm), and sided dimensions fell between 5 and 7½ inches (12.7 to 19 cm). To save time, the shipwrights did not cut limber holes in the undersides of the floors. Framing of *Allen* and the five other galleys began with the placement of six more-or-less identical frames amidships; referred to as the "dead flat," these frames constituted the widest part of the hull. Frames forward of the center of the keel had the first futtocks located abaft the floor timber; those aft of the center point had the futtocks forward of the floor. Frame K, forward of amidships, had its first futtock attached to the wrong side of the floor timber, an oversight no doubt considered of little consequence by the builders but perhaps indicative of some carpenter's haste.

Once the frames were up, the shipwrights bolted the keelson atop the floors and keel. *Allen*'s keelson con-

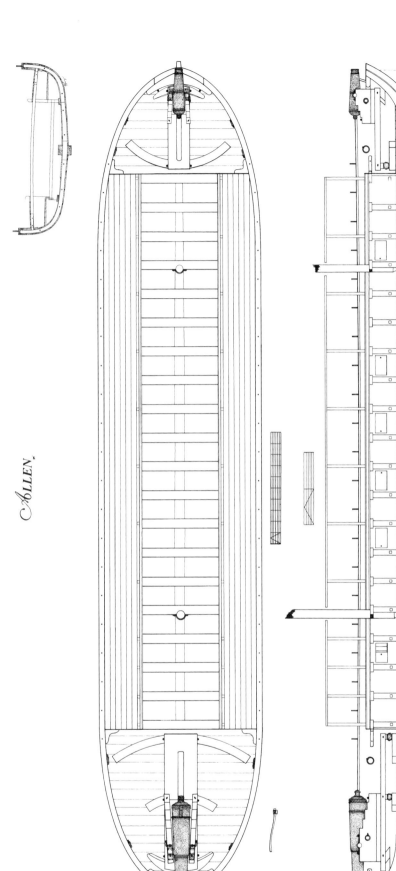

*A*LLEN.

Figure 10.2. Reconstructed interior profile and deck plan of Allen. The assembly details shown here are based on historical evidence and archaeological studies of the wreck in 1982 and 1995. Reconstruction of the upper hull and interior details relied heavily on Joseph Heatly Dulles's eyewitness description of the flotilla off Plattsburgh Bay and row galley specifications provided in William Parsons's contract of July 1813. The plan and profile views do not show the awning system in its entirety, to avoid obscuring other important construction features. (Reconstruction by E. B. Emery.)

sisted of two pieces of white oak flat scarfed together about one-third of the vessel's length abaft the stem. The overall length was 67 feet 3 inches (20.49 m), with a cross-section that averaged 4 inches (10 cm) molded and 7 inches (18 cm) sided. Two rectangular mortises were cut into the top of *Allen*'s keelson for the mast steps: the foremast step over frame M and the main-mast step over frame 9 were nearly identical in dimensions, about 10 inches (25 cm) long, 5 inches (12.7 cm) wide, and 4 inches (10 cm) deep. A third, smaller mortise was cut into the after end of the keelson, possibly to fit a stanchion that supported the after gun deck.

White oak planking 1 inch (2.5 cm) thick was fastened to the outsides of the frames with iron spikes; the widths of these planks varied from 15 to 6 inches (38 to 15 cm), with the wider pieces on the bottom and the narrower pieces at the turn of the bilge to accommodate the curve of the frames. The garboard strakes averaged 11 inches (27.9 cm) wide and were beveled on their inside edges to fit into the keel rabbets. By cutting the rabbets slightly below the top corners of the keel, the shipwrights created narrow ¼- to ½-inch (6 to 12 mm) gaps between the undersides of the floors and the garboards, spaces that served in lieu of limber holes for draining bilge water.

The interior was planked with white pine ceiling that averaged 1 inch (2.5 cm) thick and from 7 to 15 inches (17.7 to 38 cm) wide. The ceiling was fastened down with iron nails that had a distinctive "T" head to increase their holding ability on the relatively thin planks. The upper works were completed with clamps, deck beams, a gun platform at each end, partial decks or gangways up each side, rowing stations, and a low toe rail around the top of each side. Lockers were installed in the narrow spaces below the deck. Caulkers sealed external plank seams with oakum and pitch to make them watertight. Within about forty days of the laying of their keels, the galleys were ready for launching.[31]

The six new galleys, named *Allen, Borer, Burrows, Centipede, Nettle,* and *Viper,* slid from their ways into the Otter Creek on April 17, 1814. Sleek and fast looking, *Allen* and the other galleys differed from Doughty's plan by showing more pronounced frame deadrise. The Chesapeake Bay galleys, built with the near-flat bottom shown on the original design, had problems with lateral slippage during sail trials earlier that year.[32] Brown must have been aware of this, or perhaps he intuitively saw the problem in the plan, and therefore attempted to improve the lateral resistance of the galleys by increasing their deadrise.

All six of the galleys stepped two lateen-rigged masts (fig. 10.3). In addition, each held twenty wooden benches for seating up to forty men. Oarsmen sat less than three feet above the galleys' ceiling and presumably braced their heels against foot-stretchers for leverage. *Allen* and the other galleys lacked accommodations for the crews—there was simply no room to sling a hammock or stow much personal gear. The small, cupboard-like lockers on either side of the hull provided for stowage of shot, gunpowder, and equipment. Macdonough assigned sloops to the galley divisions to carry provisions and spare equipment and to provide living quarters. Galley crews also camped on shore when operating within their own territory.

The long, narrow, lightly built galleys would have been prone to hogging, the drooping of the ends due to greater buoyancy amidships. Mounting guns at opposite ends of a galley's keel made the situation even worse, for they applied immense downward pressure and encouraged upward bowing in the keel's midsection. The two guns—an 18-pounder columbiad and a long 24 pounder—together weighed around 8000 pounds (3629.7 kg), exclusive of their wooden mounts.[33] Doughty's design compensated for some of this weight with its relatively full bow and stern, which not only provided extra buoyancy below the waterline but had the added benefit of widening the gun platforms above.

Brown mounted the galleys' guns on slides, which did a better job of absorbing recoil than wheeled carriages. The guns were not fixed on the centerline (which was the case with some gunboats) but pivoted on a bolt at the forward end of the mount, while the after end traversed on trucks that ran atop a one-eighth-of-a-circle track on the deck. The arrangement allowed the guns a forty-five-degree arc of fire (twenty-two and a half degrees off the centerline to starboard and to port).

Although Macdonough's six new galleys mounted heavy guns, individually they were not much of a challenge to larger warships. Their advantage always lay in the ability to maneuver, to swarm and pester rather than slug it out at close range. Macdonough hinted as much by naming four of them *Borer, Centipede, Nettle,* and *Viper.* The names of the other two honored US Navy

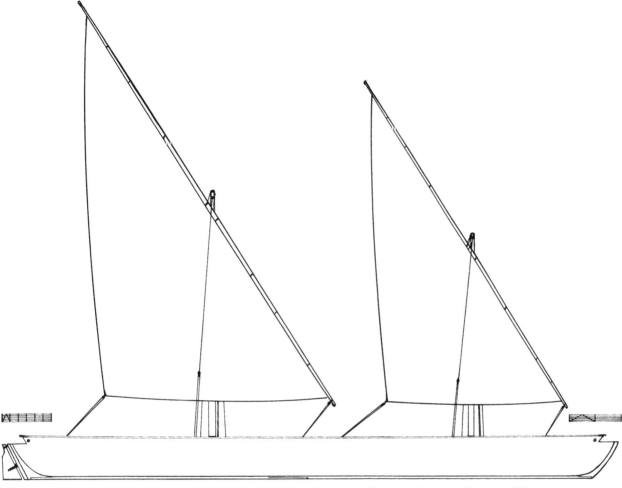

Figure 10.3. *A hypothetical mast, yard, and sail plan for* Allen. *Historical and archaeological sources tell us very little about the rigs of the US Navy's Lake Champlain galleys. The locations of* Allen's *two masts are known from the steps on the keelson, but the dimensions of the masts and lateen yards can only be estimated. This sail plan would not have been compatible with the galley's awning system; it is likely that the awnings were mainly used when the crewmen were at their rowing stations or when the vessel was at anchor. (Reconstruction by E. B. Emery.)*

captains killed in action the previous year, Lt. William Henry Allen of the brig-sloop *Argus* and Lt. William Burrows of the brig *Enterprise*.[34]

"Unquestionably the Best Description of Vessels"
By the time the new galleys were completed, the US Navy's mission on Lake Champlain had changed dramatically from what had been envisioned just a few months earlier. In April 1814, the French dictator Napoleon Bonaparte abdicated and was sent into exile. For the first time since 1803, peace was at hand in Europe. The British government could now give its full attention to the US war. In the Champlain Valley, the Royal Navy was increasing the size of its squadron, and Canada's Gov. Gen. Sir George Prevost was prom-

ised veteran troops straight from the Duke of Wellington's ranks for invading the United States. US hopes of conquering Canada in 1814 waned, and Macdonough's earlier plan to lead his galleys into the Richelieu River was shelved before the campaigning season even started.[35]

The Champlain Valley got a taste of the new British offensive strategy on May 9 when the British squadron (the new 16-gun brig *Linnet*, the sloops *Chub*, *Finch*, *Canada*, and *Icicle*, and seven row galleys) entered the lake. This expedition was a pre-emptive strike against the unfinished US ships, intended either to burn them or bottle them up in the Otter Creek by sinking captured sloops in the river. Macdonough dispatched Lt. Stephen Cassin to the mouth of the Otter Creek to erect an earthwork battery of 12 pounders, and the six new galleys were sent to support the battery (fig. 10.4). The enemy squadron appeared on May 14 and commenced a two-hour bombardment, but Fort Cassin and the gunboats replied with such vigor that the British abandoned the idea of landing and withdrew.[36]

Macdonough's chronic lack of sailors and officers in 1814 particularly bedeviled his galley flotilla. "Gallies are unquestionably the best description of vessels for the northern parts of this lake," he wrote, "but the number of men they require is a very serious objection to them."[37] When his recruiters failed to produce enough sailors for the squadron, Macdonough turned to the US Army to fill out the crews of the gunboats. It was not an ideal arrangement ("soldiers are miserable creatures on shipboard," the commodore observed), but he could not afford to leave any part of his fleet unmanned.[38] General George Izard loaned the soldiers with the understanding that they would be replaced by sailors as soon as possible, but many remained in the galleys throughout the summer and fall. The six galleys were each manned by forty oarsmen and ten men to work the guns, but even with the soldiers it appears that they rarely had full complements.

All accounts agree: service aboard a gunboat was the least desirable assignment on the lakes. Living conditions were rudimentary and crowded, even by warship standards, and crews were exposed to every kind of weather. It was little wonder that pneumonia and dysentery were common ailments among the squadron's sailors.[39] One of the sick, Gunner Thomas Butler of *Allen*, wished to stay in Macdonough's squadron, "provided he does not remain in a galley, which his health makes it bad."[40] Finally, there was the matter of reliability. Sailors who ended up on gunboats were often not provided with the training and discipline that were part of the routine on larger warships. Secretary Jones recognized the problem, complaining that "the temptations to insubordination and vice are much greater in this scattered and amphibious kind of force."[41]

Naval officers also found much to dislike about gunboats, for assignment to these vessels could retard one's promotion up the chain of command. The Navy Department, for example, considered time on gunboats as "a service in which those who are to form the officers for the ships of war ought not to be engaged."[42] Lieutenants and midshipmen commanded them when

necessary, but the position was considered best suited to sailing masters, a dead-end rank as far as promotion was concerned. Macdonough's gunboats brought out the best and the worst in his officers: they were a proving ground for leadership and bravery but also served as a dump for the inept.

Perhaps the most successful appointment to the gunboats was twenty-seven-year-old Sailing Master Eli A. F. Vallette; he commanded *Burrows* during the summer and then was promoted to "acting lieutenant" and transferred to the flagship *Saratoga.* Macdonough considered Vallette "an excellent young Man, a good seaman, sober, steady—studious & brave." Lt. Francis Mitchell of *Viper,* on the other hand, was described by Macdonough as "the most profane man in the service," who did the navy "more disgrace than honor." Sailing Master William M. Robbins of *Allen* fell somewhere in the middle of the spectrum. "Old & infirm, subject to intoxication occasionally [and] not to be trusted with much," was the commodore's assessment of Robbins, yet he was "careful of public property" and always kept his vessel "neat in arrangement."[43] Robbins was serving on the inactive sloop of war *Alert* at New York in August 1813 when he requested a transfer to Lake Champlain. The transfer was approved, and in the spring of 1814 he was assigned to *Allen,* his first command of a government vessel.[44]

On May 26, the galleys left Otter Creek and in company with the rest of the US Navy squadron sailed north to Plattsburgh. The six new row galleys, described by Macdonough as "remarkably fine vessels," were divided among two of three smaller flotillas.[45] Division No. 1 under Lt. Francis Mitchell consisted of *Borer, Nettle,* and *Viper,* while Division No. 2 under Sailing Master William M. Robbins included *Allen, Burrows,* and *Centipede.* The four older gunboats, *Ludlow, Wilmer* (formerly *No. 169* and *No. 170*), *Alwyn,* and *Ballard,* were temporarily taken out of service in order to provide guns for the schooner *Ticonderoga* but rejoined the fleet in June as Division No. 3, commanded by Sailing Master Daniel Stellwagen.[46]

Allen and the other galleys cruised the northern lake during the summer of 1814, gathering intelligence and patrolling for British raiders and American smugglers. The smuggling of contraband into British Canada was a constant source of friction between the navy and the many residents of the Champlain Valley who depended on this trade for their livelihood. Most distressing from

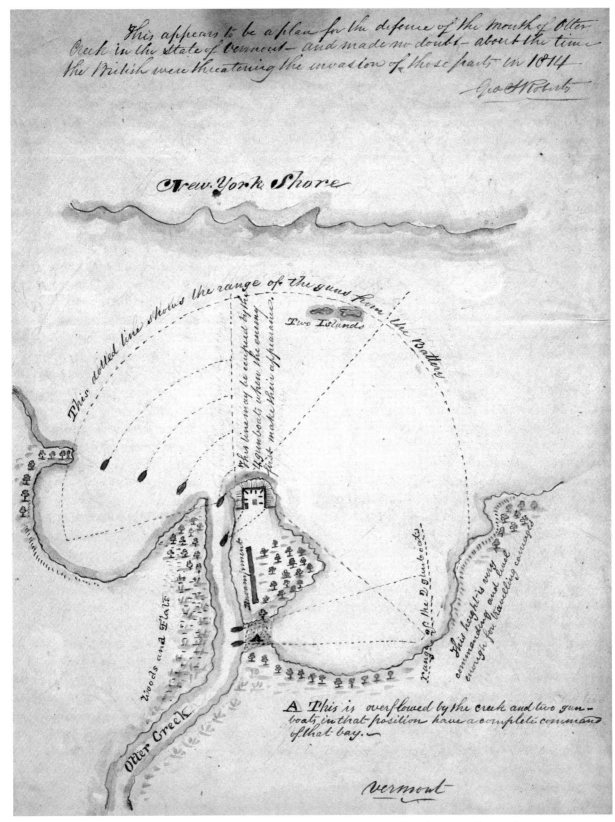

This appears to be a plan for the defence of the mouth of Otter Creek in the State of Vermont — and made no doubt — about the time the British were threatening the invasion of those parts in 1814 —

Geo H Roberts

New York Shore

This dotted line shows the range of the guns from the Battery

Two Islands

This line may be occupied by the 4 gunboats when the enemy first make their appearance.

Range of the 2 Gunboats

This height is very commanding and level enough for travelling carriages

Woods and Flats

Otter Creek

A This is overflowed by the creek and two gunboats in that position have a complete command of that bay. —

Vermont

Figure 10.4. *A contemporary map of the US defenses at Otter Creek, May 1814. The earthwork-protected battery known as Fort Cassin was prepared at the mouth of Otter Creek and protected on its flanks by the US squadron's galleys. (Manuscripts and Special Collections, New York State Library, Albany, NY.)*

the navy's point of view was the traffic in naval stores, including spars, ship timber, and tar, which found its way into the hands of British shipbuilders at Isle aux Noix. Galleys patrolled both day and night but only snared a fraction of these shipments.[47]

Robbins' division of galleys proved particularly adept at capturing smugglers as they emerged from their hiding places, and during the months of June and July seized over $6000 worth of illegal goods. On June 29 Sailing Master Eli Vallette of *Burrows* intercepted four local men attempting to float spars into the Richelieu River. On July 23 he captured a raft carrying 13,000 feet of plank, oak ship timbers, and tar through "a narrow and unfrequented passage." Vallette also captured the raft's crew, but the Navy Department had no policy for dealing with smugglers. Macdonough requested instructions from Secretary Jones concerning the detainees, adding, "the supplying of the enemy by many citizens of Vermont is in daily practice."[48]

Macdonough's intelligence network provided ample evidence that the British were organizing a major offensive on Lake Champlain. His spies reported that a large army of veteran troops under General Prevost was prepared to advance up the New York shore of the lake and only awaited the completion of a frigate at Isle aux Noix to commence its march south. On September 1 the land offensive began, forcing Macdonough to withdraw from his exposed position near the Canadian frontier to await the British squadron at Plattsburgh. During the passage south, the galleys were briefly employed as towboats when the larger warships of the US squadron were immobilized by a lack of wind.[49]

In Plattsburgh Bay, the galley flotilla took an active role against the British army on September 6 when Macdonough directed galley divisions No. 1 and No. 2 to a near-shore position where they could harass the enemy's advancing columns. Division commanders Robbins and Mitchell formed a line abreast facing Dead Creek Road along the northern shore of the bay. British troops marching down the road were spotted through an opening in the trees and scattered when fired on by the galleys. The tables soon turned, however, when a stiff wind arose, churning the lake and making it impossible for the galleys to aim their guns with any accuracy. British artillerymen screened by the woods opened a bombardment on the galleys, killing one seaman and wounding three marines.[50]

Yet another injury occurred during this action when Macdonough sent Acting Lieutenant Silas Duncan in a gig to recall the galleys from their perilous situation. While relaying the commodore's orders aboard *Allen,* Duncan was struck in the shoulder by an enemy shot, a wound that was first judged mortal. The ball passed between his scapula and upper arm, destroying the muscles but fortunately not severing the brachial artery. Macdonough shipped Duncan to Burlington's military hospital, where Dr. James Mann prepared to amputate the arm. The lieutenant firmly refused to submit to the operation, claiming that he would rather die than live with one arm. Acceding to his patient's wishes, Mann removed the ragged pieces of bone, muscle, and the head of the humerus and then sutured up the wound. Duncan survived but for the rest of his life had a pronounced slope to one shoulder and a useless arm, a vivid reminder of how hazardous flying shot could be in the tight quarters of a row galley.[51]

Five days after the skirmish off Dead Creek Road, the Royal Navy squadron rounded Cumberland Head and sailed into Plattsburgh Bay to confront the US Navy. Macdonough had prepared for this action by anchoring his largest warships in a "line ahead" formation across the mouth of the bay, a static defense that may have been influenced by the low numbers and inexperience of his ships' crews. The gunboats carried minimal complements of soldiers at the sweeps and sailors at the guns and were hardly in a state for fighting. Probably for this reason, Macdonough assigned them a minor part in the battle. Separated into their three divisions, the gunboats were situated on the disengaged side of *Saratoga, Eagle,* and *Ticonderoga.* Their commanding officers were instructed to keep between the large warships and to "fire when you get a chance," hardly an aggressive role in the action.[52]

During the battle, the galleys followed Macdonough's instructions, using their sweeps to hover behind the larger warships, showing themselves just long enough to fire and then retreating behind cover. As a result, they did not suffer the death and destruction that swept the rest of the US squadron. Nevertheless, casualties occurred. *Borer,* commanded by Midshipman Thomas Conover, advanced to the bow of *Ticonderoga* and received a direct hit that killed a purser's steward, a boy, and a marine and badly wounded a marine corporal. *Centipede* and *Wilmer* each had one sailor injured, but seven of the galleys escaped with no casualties at all.[53]

Figure 10.5. *A contemporary watercolor showing the US Navy galleys on Lake Champlain, fall 1814. In the aftermath of the battle at Plattsburgh Bay most of the US squadron retired to Whitehall, New York, while* Eagle *and the ten row galleys kept watch on the Canadian frontier. In this painting the galleys lie at anchor in a small inlet, while* Eagle *and the squadron's sloops (kept for galley-crew quarters) are anchored farther out in the lake. (Courtesy of the Shelburne Museum, Shelburne, VT.)*

The galleys may not have been at the forefront of the battle, but they proved immensely useful in its aftermath. Their crews manned the pumps on the riddled warships, transported the wounded to hospitals ashore, and recovered shot and stores dumped in the lake by the retreating British.[54] The galley *Allen,* sailing under a flag of truce, returned more than sixty paroled British officers and sailors to Canada on September 16 and 17. When the battle damage was repaired, Macdonough sent the larger ships south to Whitehall, retaining only the brig *Eagle* and the ten galleys to protect against incursions by the British gunboat flotilla (fig. 10.5). The sloops were also kept on the lake to accommodate the galley crews, a vital necessity as cold weather descended upon the Champlain Valley. There was no further fighting, and in late November *Eagle* and its galley consorts sailed south to winter quarters.

It was the end of the galley flotilla's service on Lake Champlain. On Christmas Eve 1814, the Treaty of Ghent brought the war to a close. When news of the peace arrived a month later, newly appointed Navy Secretary Benjamin Crowninshield ordered Macdonough to dismantle the squadron.[55] The five large ships were emptied of equipment and moored in the channel, and the five sloops were sold at auction along with the four older galleys *Ludlow, Wilmer, Alwyn,* and *Ballard.*[56] The

six Brown-built galleys were also offered for sale, but bidding was so low that they were instead kept by the navy and sunk for preservation. One of the six, *Allen,* returned to service in the spring of 1817 under the provisions of the Rush-Bagot Agreement that allowed the United States and Great Britain to maintain one vessel of less than 100 tons on Lake Champlain and the Richelieu River.[57] Armed with a single 12-pounder cannon, *Allen* thereafter patrolled the lake intermittently.

The US Navy's presence on Lake Champlain dissipated as the naval squadron deteriorated. In 1820, the ships were moved into the Poultney River to ensure that they would not impede commercial shipping. At least one row galley accompanied the larger vessels, but it is not clear if the other five were raised and moved at this time or left where they were originally sunk on the side of the main channel. According to an 1821 inventory of the squadron, the six gunboats were still in good condition, even if the larger warships were falling apart.[58] When the navy disposed of its ships in 1825, all six galleys went on the auction block as well.[59] At least one galley was left sunk in the Poultney River; the other five may have been left on the bottom as well, or they may have been raised to be broken up or converted into commercial carriers.

The Archaeology of the US Navy Row Galley *Allen*
The story of the US Navy's galley flotilla on Lake Champlain was all but forgotten until 1981, when an archaeological survey of the Poultney River turned up three wrecks. One of them, a battered hull with a surviving length of 71 feet 2 inches (21.69 m) and a breadth of 12 feet (3.65 m), fit the general dimensions and appearance of the larger galley design prepared by William Doughty. The scantlings were relatively small for a vessel of this length, a further clue that the hull was one of the six galleys built by Noah Brown in 1814. The wreck lay close beside the river bank in shallow water, upright with a slight list to port. Although much of the galley's port side was broken or badly eroded, its starboard side was covered by the slumping river bank. An estimated 50 percent of the hull survived, including the keel, the keelson, the lower ends of the stem and stern assemblies, and much of the starboard frames and planking. Enough of the vessel was left to provide insights into gunboat design, construction, and outfitting practices.

Preliminary study of the wreck took place in 1982,

at the same time as the brig *Eagle* investigation.[60] Measurements of the exposed timbers, limited test excavations, and recovery of a small collection of artifacts confirmed the earlier identification of the wreck as a US Navy gunboat. Two rectangular mast steps cut into the top of the keelson corresponded with the placement of masts on the Doughty plans, iron grapeshot were found between the frames, and a brass-plated uniform button from the US Army's 13th Infantry Regiment was discovered between the keel and keelson. Macdonough employed scores of soldiers to man his galley squadron, and since the 13th Infantry was present in this district in 1814, the discovery of an army button on a naval ship was not too surprising.

Which of the six galleys—*Allen, Borer, Burrows, Centipede, Nettle, Viper*—was this particular wreck? Two lines of evidence, one historical and the other archaeological, suggested the vessel was *Allen*. The historical evidence is in the correspondence between the Whitehall Naval Station and the Navy Department. This tells us that the six galleys were sunk for preservation in 1815 and that *Allen* was raised and placed back into service in 1817. *Allen* was presumably laid up in the Poultney River when the other ships of the squadron were moved there in 1820. The fate of the six galleys is not mentioned in the navy records that have been examined.

The archaeological clue to the wreck's identity, a collection of cast-iron ballast stacked in the stern, provided a second convincing piece to the puzzle. Ballast was typically placed on either side and along most of the length of a vessel's keelson to adjust trim and give it added stability. When *Allen* patrolled the lake after the war, it mounted only a single 12 pounder at the bow; because the weight of this gun was not counterbalanced by a second gun at the other end of the hull, a load of ballast would have been necessary in the stern to float the galley on an even keel.

The significance of this warship wreck was undeniable. It represented the only example of a War of 1812 row galley ever found in Lake Champlain and was one of the vessels that participated in the pivotal Battle of Plattsburgh Bay.[61] It was likely to contain insights into naval life, especially life on the unpopular galleys, during the early years of the nineteenth century. *Allen* was the work of New York City shipwright Noah Brown and could tell us more about this skilled craftsman and

the ways he experimented within his trade. Finally, the hull was part of an early US Navy effort at mass-producing vessels from a single set of plans. Row galleys of this type were built not only on Lake Champlain but on Lake Ontario and the Chesapeake Bay as well. How closely did Brown and other shipwrights follow Doughty's plan?

Necessity sometimes forced shipwrights like Noah Brown to deviate from the intentions of designers and contractors. Ship plans and other forms of historical records may thus be incomplete, divulging little information on the assembly techniques that were actually employed during construction. Put simply, the designer and the shipwright often worked in two different arenas; one dealt with the theoretical problems of naval architecture on paper and the other translated these abstract concepts into three-dimensional reality based on the tools, labor, materials, time, and talent available. *Allen* offered an exceptional research scenario, for by combining historical records with an archaeological analysis of a hull, a better understanding of this largely overlooked form of warship was possible. The 1982 survey was only a start, and much more study of the galley was obviously needed.

Three important considerations defined the renewed study of *Allen*: time, funding, and the availability of a conservation facility. Nautical archaeologists in recent years have promoted the investigation of submerged sites in situ to avoid inflating costs and to minimize disturbance and destabilization. The Poultney River had already witnessed two traumatic shipwreck recoveries in the mid-twentieth century, the operation that nearly destroyed *Linnet* in 1949 and the salvage of *Ticonderoga* in 1958. In light of these earlier efforts, raising *Allen*'s hull was not an option.

The excavation of *Allen* was jointly sponsored as an archaeological field school by Texas A&M University, the University of Vermont, the Institute of Nautical Archaeology, and the Lake Champlain Maritime Museum, with assistance from the Naval Historical Center (now known as the Naval History & Heritage Command).[62] Researchers defined five objectives for the July 1995 project: (1) to gather sufficient information to develop a complete site plan; (2) to complete the documentation of the keel, keelson, and stem and stern assemblies; (3) to record as many frame sections as possible; (4) to conduct an intensive study of the vessel's starboard side, including its surviving ceiling planking and decking; and (5) to recover the vessel's ballast and other artifacts for conservation and analysis.

The procedures and equipment employed in the field project were kept as simple as possible (fig. 10.6). In places where the hull structure was exposed, the timbers served as the main reference grid for recording construction details and artifact positions. A steel grid was placed over the starboard side for better horizontal and vertical control when excavating in areas where the hull was buried. A water-powered dredge system was employed to systematically remove sediments from the site. All items removed from the hull were measured, catalogued, photographed, and drawn to scale before being conserved at the Lake Champlain Maritime Museum or, in the case of timbers and planks found within the hull, being reburied on the site.

As the hull was exposed by the excavators, other crew members followed close behind to record all visible components and assembly details. *Allen*'s condition and construction soon took shape in our minds and in our notes. The features and locations of the keel, stem, sternpost, frames, and keelson were measured relative to a centerline tape, and their molded and sided dimensions were recorded, along with fastener locations and tool marks (fig. 10.7). Excavators fully exposed the galley's stem (fig. 10.8a) and sternpost (fig. 10.8b) assemblies, neither of which showed signs of extraordinary craftsmanship, but instead seemed to exemplify Noah Brown's strong, simple, "no extras" approach to wartime shipbuilding.

Artifacts recovered from the excavation units or by sifting dredge spoil included iron spikes and nails, glass and ceramic tableware fragments, gun flints, iron grapeshot, and lead musket balls and buckshot. Divers uncovered clusters of copper tacks in the after part of the hull between frames 3 and 5 and frames 7 and 10. One tack still had a piece of sheet lead attached at its head. The tacks and bit of lead might have come from scuppers along the galley's gangway, may have been part of the pump assembly, or possibly were evidence of a lead-lined storage area for gunpowder or other perishable stores.

There were, as well, two curious finds that we classified as personal effects. The first was a brass uniform button bearing the crest of the British Army's 100th Regiment. Members of this regiment served as

Figure 10.6. *Preparing the wreck of* Allen *for excavation, July 1995. Eric Emery and Scott Padeni lower an excavation grid to waiting divers, assisted by Steve Bilicki. The grid provided divers with a reference while excavating and measuring the galley wreck in the limited visibility of the Poultney River. (Photo by Steven Butler,* Allen *project files of E. B. Emery.)*

crewmen on the gunboats that captured the US Navy sloops in the Richelieu River and raided Lake Champlain in 1813, but throughout most of 1814, the 100th was involved in the intense fighting around the Niagara Peninsula.[63] The button's discovery on a US Navy galley on Lake Champlain, therefore, raises some questions: by what combination of circumstances did it end up in the Champlain Valley in 1814, and was it brought aboard the galley as a souvenir by one of the crew, or did it fall off the uniform of a prisoner? The second personal item found in the bilges was a nearly intact clay tobacco pipe with the finely molded effigy of a bearded, turbaned head and the words "United States of America" in raised letters around the rim. Effigy pipes were a popular style among smokers in the first half of the nineteenth century, but for US sailors, a pipe like this may also have been symbolic of the navy's victories over the Barbary corsairs of North Africa (plate 9a).[64]

One important objective of the field study was to map and recover the plank-and-ballast feature in the stern. The team started with the transverse planks that extended across the keelson, covering the ballast and providing an even surface upon which *Allen*'s crew

~ALLEN

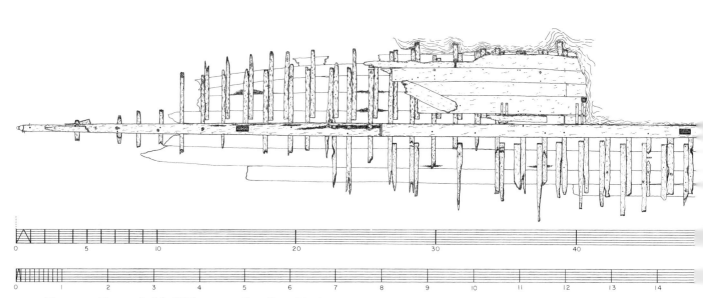

Figure 10.7. *The wreck of the US Navy row galley* Allen. *This plan and profile view was prepared from measurements and sketches of the hull's timbers and assembly features in 1995. The vessel's wide, shallow keel and keelson are evident here, as are the preserved ceiling planking on the starboard side of the hull and the cast-iron ballast pieces stacked alongside the keelson at the stern. The two rectangular mortises in the top of the keelson are mast steps. (Drawing by E. B. Emery.)*

could walk. Each plank was recorded, tagged, and carefully removed. Once on shore, they were photographed and drawn to scale before being reburied on the site. A total of thirty cast-iron ballast pieces were found neatly stacked in the stern (fig. 10.9). They shared a half-moon shape in cross-section and ranged in size from 6½ inches (16.51 cm) long by 3½ inches (8.89 cm) wide to one 2 feet 2 inches (66.04 cm) long by 6¼ inches (15.87 cm) wide with a 9¼-inch (23.49 cm) flare at one end. The irregular dimensions and rough external appearance of the ballast showed that it was cast in open sand molds (probably by the Monkton Iron Works in Vergennes). As noted earlier, the ballast's location in the stern points to its use as a counterweight for a

gun mounted in the bow. While not definitive, this evidence certainly suggests that the wreck was of the one galley armed after the war with a single 12 pounder— namely, *Allen.*

Ceiling planking taken from different hull locations appeared to be softwood, probably white pine. Despite 175 years under the river, some of the strakes floated to the surface upon being released from their fasteners, which is not unusual for pine timbers removed from freshwater wrecks. Features associated with the ceiling planks were also removed and documented. Of particular interest were two pairs of wooden strips nailed to the ceiling at a right angle to the keelson. Each pair was nailed side by side, leaving a small channel be-

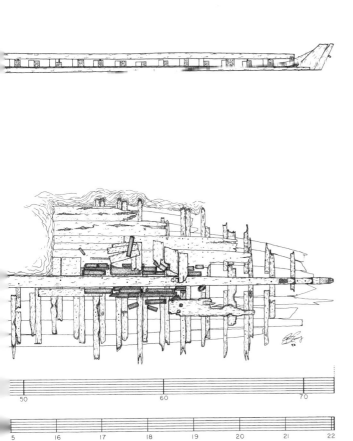

(fig. 10.10). The tools came primarily from an area between frames 17 and 19, while the crew-related items were mostly between frames 13 and 16.

The significance of copper tacks and sheet copper fragments found in the bow and stern initially escaped our notice, but study of 1812-era Chesapeake Bay galley contracts showed a compartment abaft the bow gun mount for what was likely a magazine.[65] Shipwrights often lined warship magazines with copper sheets to prevent any iron-on-iron sparks from touching off an explosion. The locations of the flattened copper fragments suggested that the galley may have had a magazine at either end, certainly a more efficient arrangement than a single magazine. The galley's rowing stations restricted fore-and-aft movement amidships to narrow gangways running inside of each rail. In battle, these passages would have been impeded by moving oars. A small fragment of thick blue-green glass found on the wreck looked as if it may have been from a deck light similar to those recovered from *Jefferson* and *Tecumseth*. It may have been used to illuminate one of the magazines.

Capturing *Allen*'s hull shape was perhaps the most important task of the 1995 project (fig. 10.11). A digital goniometer was used to document frame curvatures at eighteen different locations, or stations. In general, *Allen*'s starboard side had the most complete frames, and we focused our efforts on this half of the hull. When the frame recording was complete, timbers removed for study were returned to the site and the wreck was reburied with river-bottom sand to protect it from further erosion and decay.

Conclusions

During the colonial wars of the eighteenth century, oar-propelled gunboats were widely used on the inland waters of North America. It was no wonder: their construction was inexpensive and relatively uncomplicated, their maneuverability and light draft allowed them to navigate shallow or narrow passages with ease, and they provided vital support for waterborne armies. The requirements of inland naval warfare had not changed when war again broke out in 1812, and both the American and the British navies on Lake Champlain once more relied on these craft. The squadron cobbled together by Thomas Macdonough during the first year of the war included a pair of small gunboats, but two events in 1813 highlighted their in-

tween them. The pieces probably served as battens to secure vertical partitions used for storage compartments.

The discovery of crew possessions and other remnants of shipboard living shed some light on the layout of *Allen*'s internal spaces. The galley's after end yielded the highest density of these types of artifacts. Tools, tableware, and personal items included a brass straight pin, a well-worn caulking iron bearing the name "Maxfield," a folding knife blade, fragments of green and clear bottle glass, ceramic shards, plain buttons of copper alloy and bone, a domino and two disk-shaped gaming pieces (one with an X carved into a side), and a broken but nearly complete salt-glazed stoneware jug

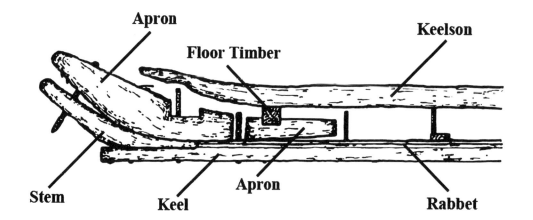

Apron

Floor Timber

Keelson

Stem

Keel

Apron

Rabbet

Feet

0   1   2   3

A

Meters

0   1

Main Sternpost

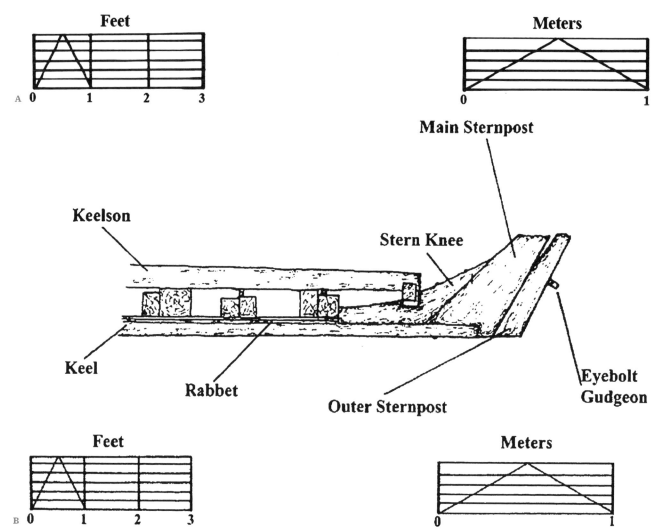

Keelson

Stern Knee

Keel

Rabbet

Outer Sternpost

Eyebolt
Gudgeon

Feet

0   1   2   3

B

Meters

0   1

Figure 10.8. *Interior profile views of Allen's stem: (a) and stern (b) assemblies (as recorded in 1995). While well crafted, both ends of the galley are relatively uncomplicated in their design and assembly. Note the straight sternposts, Noah Brown's modification of the curved-sternpost design in William Doughty's original galley plans. (Drawings by E. B. Emery.)*

Figure 10.9. *The collection of cast-iron ballast pigs found in the stern of* Allen. *Shown here shortly after their recovery from the stern of* Allen, *the thirty ballast pigs were cast in semicircular sand molds and varied considerably in their length and breadth. Altogether they added up to 330 pounds (149.6 kg) that helped to counter-balance the 12-pounder long gun that* Allen *mounted in its bow during the postwar years. (Photo by Nathan Power, courtesy of the Lake Champlain Maritime Museum.)*

Figure 10.10. *A salt-glazed stoneware jug found in the stern of* Allen. *Alcohol provided a daily comfort for many early-nineteenth-century naval officers and sailors but also resulted in sickness, accidents, and breaches of discipline. Abuse of alcohol was a chronic problem for the US Navy. Commodore Macdonough reported to the Navy Department that* Allen's *wartime commander, Sailing Master William M. Robbins, had a reputation as a drunkard. (Photo courtesy of the Lake Champlain Maritime Museum.)*

adequacy. The capture of the sloops *Growler* and *Eagle* in June and the inability of the squadron to assist the offensive of Gen. Wade Hampton in September made it clear that if Macdonough intended to resist incursions by British gunboats, fight inside the Richelieu, or spearhead an offensive into Canada, he was going to need not only more but more heavily armed gunboats.

Macdonough's proposal to greatly expand his galley flotilla met with the blessing of the navy secretary, and during the winter of 1814 he set up a shipyard at Vergennes. The Royal Navy's decision to build the 16-gun brig *Linnet* forced a change in the commodore's strategy, however, and the number of galleys to be built was cut back from fifteen to six. Shipwright Noah Brown worked from a plan provided by the navy to mass-produce the six, but he altered the shape of

the sternposts to strengthen the rudder mountings and slightly increased the frame deadrise to improve their sailing qualities. The construction was fast and rough yet substantial enough to win battles, characteristics that earned Brown-built ships such acclaim during the war.

When the strategy of the US Naval squadron shifted to defensive in the spring of 1814, it deprived the row galleys of their intended offensive role. They instead became support vessels for the larger warships, patrolling, chasing smugglers, providing a tow when the winds died, and carrying communications. The hard work of rowing, the constant outdoor living, the overcrowded conditions, and the general lack of amenities

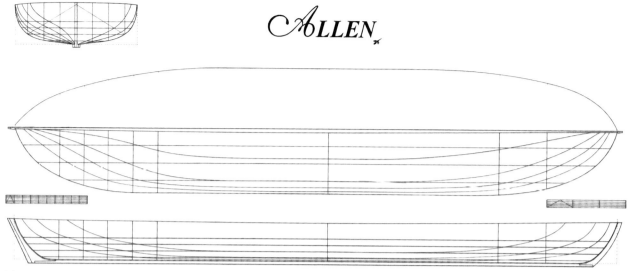

ALLEN

Figure 10.11. *Reconstructed lines of the US Navy row galley* Allen. *These plans are based principally upon the archaeological measurements and offsets taken from the surviving lower hull of the galley. The shallow draft and light construction of* Allen *and the other galleys in the US Navy's Lake Champlain squadron was well suited to the vital task of patrolling near-shore areas and restricted waterways such as rivers. (Reconstruction by E. B. Emery.)*

made the galleys an unpopular and unhealthy assignment for officers and sailors alike. Due to the lack of protection for their crews in action and their generally undermanned state, Macdonough assigned them a supporting role in the Battle of Plattsburgh Bay. In light of the dismal failure of the British gunboats to board the schooner *Ticonderoga,* this was probably a judicious use of the US flotilla. It was in the aftermath of the battle that the galleys proved most useful, for their crews were at the forefront of the repair and recovery efforts.

In the aftermath of the war, the six Brown-built galleys showed scant promise as commercial carriers, for they failed to achieve minimum bids at an auction. Sunk for long-term preservation instead, they disappeared from sight both literally and figuratively, for with one exception we do not know the fate of the row galleys after 1825. Fortunately for us, the Poultney River still holds one example of these largely forgotten warships, and *Allen* survives as a reminder of a gifted craftsman, a plan that failed, and a struggle that was won.

NOTES

1. "List of Paroled Wounded Men Sent to Isle aux Noix, US Galley *Allen,* September 16, 1814," Subject Files, Box 575, Folder 2, record group 45 (RG 45), National Archives and Records Administration (NARA).

2. Thomas Macdonough to William Jones, September 17, 1814, entry 125, RG 45, NARA.

3. "The Log Book Kept on Board the United States Sloop of War Surprise of Twenty Guns. Robert Henley Esqre Commander. Kept by Daniel Records, Acting Sailing Master," transcribed in Kevin J. Crisman, *The* Eagle*: An American Brig on Lake Champlain during the War of 1812* (Shelburne, VT: The New England Press; Annapolis: Naval Institute Press, 1987), pp. 226–28.

4. William M. Robbins to Macdonough, September 13, 1814, entry 125, RG 45, NARA.

5. Macdonough to Jones, November 23, 1814, entry 147, RG 45, NARA.

6. For additional information on the role of oared naval craft in nineteenth century US history, see Gene A. Smith, *For the Purposes of Defense: The Politics of the Jeffersonian Gunboat Program* (Newark: University of Delaware Press, 1995); Spencer C. Tucker, *The Jeffersonian Gunboat Navy* (Columbia: University of South Carolina Press, 1993). See Howard I. Chapelle, *The History of the American Sailing Navy* (New York: Bonanza Books, 1949) for gunboat design and construction details.

7. Macdonough to Jones, June 4, 1813, entry 148, RG 45, NARA; for contemporary accounts of the Richelieu River engagement, see William S. Dudley, ed., *The Naval War of 1812: A Documentary History,* vol. 2 (Washington, DC: Naval Historical Center, 1992), pp. 488–92; Rodney Macdonough, *Life of Commodore Thomas Macdonough, U.S. Navy* (Boston: Fort Hill Press, 1909), pp. 26–28, 113–21.

8. Jones to Macdonough, June 17, 1813, entry 149, RG 45, NARA. On July 5, 1813, the US Congress appropriated $250,000 for their construction. See Tucker, *Jeffersonian Gunboat Navy,* pp. 105–107; Spencer C. Tucker, "The Jeffersonian Gunboats in

Service, 1804–1825," *American Neptune* 55, no. 2 (Spring 1995), p. 100.

9. A copy of William Doughty's barge design of 1813 (the predecessor of the larger 75-foot row galley class) can be found in the NARA, Cartographic Section in College Park, MD. See also Chapelle, *American Sailing Navy,* pp. 276–78; Donald Shomette, personal communication, Corpus Christi, TX, January 4, 1997. A contemporary description of Doughty's barges can be found in Charles W. Dulles, *Extracts from the Diary of Joseph Heatly Dulles* (Philadelphia: J. B. Lippincott, 1911), p. 5.

10. "A Proclamation by the President of the United States, April 1808," *Records of the Governor and Council of the State of Vermont,* vol. 5 (Montpelier: Steam Press of J. & J. M. Pland, 1877), pp. 473–74; Secretary of the Navy Robert Smith to Lt. Melancthon Taylor Woolsey, July 2, 1808, entry 173, RG 45, NARA; "Proposal of John Winans for Building Two Gunboats on Lake Champlain," in John Rodgers to Robert Smith, July 16, 1808, John Winans to US Navy Department, entry 125, RG 45, NARA; Woolsey to Smith, July 19, 1808, entry 148, RG 45, NARA; "Articles of Agreement Entered into Concluded and Agreed Upon By & Between John Winans, Shipcarpenter of Poughkeepsie in the State of New York on the One Part and M.T. Woolsey, Lieutenant of the United States Navy on the Other Part," July 22, 1808, no. 352, entry 235, vol. 1, RG 45, NARA; John Montresor Haswell to Woolsey, December 4, 1808, entry 273, RG 45, NARA. Gunboats *No. 169* and *No. 170* were launched at Burlington, VT, in the late fall of 1808. Rodgers to Smith, July 7, 1808, entry 125, RG 45, NARA; "Proposal of Henry Eckford and Christian Bergh for Building Two Gunboats on Lake Champlain," in John Rodgers to Robert Smith, July 13, 1808, entry 125, RG 45, NARA. Not much is known about *No. 169* and *No. 170,* for the contract only specified that the vessels "not exceed twenty tons each" and that they be "sufficiently large to carry one long twelve pounder."

11. R. Macdonough, *Life of Commodore Macdonough,* p. 108; Sidney Smith to Secretary of the Navy Paul Hamilton, June 16, and Daniel D. Tompkins to John Bullus, Navy Agent of New York City, July 13, 1812, in *The Naval War of 1812: A Documentary History,* vol. 1, ed. William Dudley (Washington, DC: Naval Historical Center, 1985), pp. 275, 282–83.

12. Macdonough to Jones, January 22, May 1, and July 11, 1813, entry 148, RG 45, NARA; "The Deposition of Gamaliel Bradford Sawyer, February 8, 1856," H. B. Sawyer Papers, Fol. 1, Special Collections, Bailey Howe Library, University of Vermont.

13. Macdonough to Jones, July 11, 1813, entry 148, RG 45, NARA; Thomas Everard to Gov. Gen. Sir George Prevost, August 3, 1813, in Dudley, ed., *Naval War of 1812,* vol. 2, p. 519. While at Burlington, Macdonough also built two flat-bottomed, 1-gun scows to serve as floating batteries.

14. Everard to Prevost, August 3, 1813, in Dudley, ed., *The Naval War of 1812,* vol. 2, p. 519; Russell P. Bellico, *Sails and Steam in the Mountains: A Maritime and Military History of Lake George and Lake Champlain* (Fleischmanns, NY: Purple Mountain Press,

1992), pp. 208–10; Allen S. Everest, *The War of 1812 in the Champlain Valley* (Syracuse, NY: Syracuse University Press, 1976).

15. Macdonough to Jones, September 9, 1813, entry 147, RG 45, NARA.

16. John Armstrong to William Eustis, January 2, 1812, in E. Cruikshank, ed., *The Documentary History of the Campaign Upon the Niagara Frontier,* vol. 1 (Welland, ON: Tribune Office, 1898–1908), p. 33; David C. Skaggs and Gerard T. Altoff, *A Signal Victory: The Lake Erie Campaign 1812–1813* (Annapolis: Naval Institute Press, 1997), p. 9.

17. Wade Hampton to John Armstrong, August 23, 1813, in Robert S. Quimby, *The U.S. Army in the War of 1812: An Operational and Command Study* (East Lansing: Michigan State University Press, 1997), pp. 308–309; E. Cruikshank, *Niagara Frontier,* vol. 7, pp. 54–55; *Vermont Centinel* (Burlington, VT), October 15, 1813; Karen Campbell, "Propaganda, Pestilence, and Prosperity: Burlington's Camptown Days During the War of 1812," *Vermont History* 64, no. 3 (Summer 1996), p. 150.

18. Bellico, *Sails and Steam,* p. 211; Dudley, ed., *The Naval War of 1812,* vol. 2, p. 583; R. Macdonough, *Life of Commodore Macdonough,* pp. 128–29; Quimby, *The U.S. Army in the War of 1812,* pp. 324–25; Dennis M. Lewis, *British Naval Activity on Lake Champlain During the War of 1812* (Plattsburgh, NY: Clinton County Historical Association, 1994), pp. 2–30. Lewis counts the number of British row galleys at Isle aux Noix around five in September and six in November. See also Macdonough to Jones, November 23, 1813, entry 147, RG 45, NARA.

19. Donald R. Hickey, *The War of 1812: A Forgotten Conflict* (Chicago: University of Illinois Press, 1989), Chapter 6; Quimby, *The U.S. Army in the War of 1812,* pp. 346–47.

20. Armstrong to Hampton, September 11, 1813, in R. Macdonough, *Life of Commodore Thomas Macdonough,* p. 128; Armstrong to President James Madison, September 21, 1813, James Madison Papers, in Dudley, ed., *Naval War of 1812,* p. 583. See also Hickey, *The War of 1812,* p. 144; Quimby, *The U.S. Army in the War of 1812,* p. 325.

21. Macdonough to Jones, December 18, 1813, entry 147, RG 45, NARA.

22. Daniel Pring to Prevost, November 3, 1813, vol. 731, series C (I), record group 8, Library and Archives Canada; Lewis, *British Naval Activity,* p. 17; *The Plattsburgh* (NY) *Republican,* November 20, 1813, p. 3 gives details of another British raid on November 17, 1813.

23. Macdonough to Jones, November 23, 1813, entry 147, RG 45, NARA.

24. Jones to Macdonough, December 7, 1813, entry 149, RG 45, NARA; Macdonough to Jones, January 17, February 6, February 7, and February 22, 1814, entry 147, RG 45, NARA; Jones to Macdonough, January 28, 1814, and Jones to John Bullus, February 10, 1814, in K. J. Bauer, ed., *The New American State Papers: Naval Affairs,* vol. 4 (Wilmington: Scholarly Resources, 1981), pp. 330–31, 333. A copy of William Doughty's plan for the 75-foot

class of row galley may be found in the NARA, Cartographic Section, College Park, MD.

25. Jones to Lloyd Jones, February 27, 1813, William Jones Papers, Uselma Clark Smith Collection, Historical Society of Pennsylvania, quoted in Tucker, *Jeffersonian Gunboat Navy*, pp. 104–107. See also Dudley, ed., *Naval War of 1812*, vol. 2, p. 52.

26. Noah Brown, "The Remarkable Statement of Noah Brown," *Journal of American History* 8, no. 1 (January 1914), pp. 5–9; Chapelle, *American Sailing Navy*, pp. 260–62.

27. Oliver H. Perry to Isaac Chauncey, April 18, 1813, Perry Papers, William L. Clements Library, University of Michigan; Skaggs and Altoff, *Signal Victory*, p. 72; W. W. Dobbins, *History of the Battle of Lake Erie* (Erie, PA: Ashby Printing, 1913), pp. 31–32.

28. Macdonough to Jones, February 22, 1814, entry 147, RG 45, NARA.

29. Jones to Macdonough, February 22, 1814, entry 149, RG 45, NARA; Macdonough to Jones, March 7, 1814, entry 147, RG 45, NARA.

30. Vergennes during the winter of 1813–14 has been thoroughly illustrated in Crisman, *The* Eagle, pp. 16–18, and Bellico, *Sail and Steam*, pp. 211–12.

31. A useful source of information on galley construction that complements archaeological data from *Allen* may be found in the Chesapeake Bay row galley contracts from the War of 1812. Each contract for a Doughty-designed boat included a detailed "Dimensions and Description" section. See "Articles of Agreement Entered into Upon this Twenty Third Day of July Eighteen Hundred and Thirteen Between Thomas Hall and Benjamin White, Both of Baltimore, Shipwrights, and James Beatty Navy Agent of the United States of America at Baltimore One Row Galley Conformable to a Draught to be Furnished by the Proper Offices of the Navy Department," entry 235, vol. 2, pp. 232–73, RG 45, NARA.

32. Dudley, ed., *Naval War of 1812*, vol. 2, pp. 373–401.

33. The guns and types of mounts on each galley are listed in the "Report of the State and Condition of the Naval Force Employed in the Defense of the Harbors & Waters of the United States Under the Command of Thomas Macdonough, on the 31st Day of August, 1814," manuscript document, Lake Champlain Maritime Museum, Vergennes, VT; gun weights are from Spencer Tucker, *Arming the Fleet: U.S. Navy Ordnance in the Muzzle-Loading Era* (Annapolis: Naval Institute Press, 1989), p. 125. An experimental gun designed to fire solid shot or shells, the columbiad combined characteristics of the carronade, long gun, and howitzer. The Lake Champlain squadron seems to have been one of the few instances where they were used during the War of 1812. They must have used solid shot exclusively, since there is no mention of shells being used by the squadron. The average weight of an 18-pounder columbiad is unknown but was likely around 2200 pounds (1000 kg). See Tucker, *Arming the Fleet*, pp. 182–84.

34. Theodore Roosevelt, *The Naval War of 1812* (Annapolis: Naval Institute Press, 1987), pp. 198–200, 206–208; Ira Dye, *The Fatal Cruise of the* Argus*: Two Captains in the War of 1812* (Annapolis: Naval Institute Press, 1994).

35. J. MacKay Hitsman, *The Incredible War of 1812* (Toronto: University of Toronto Press, 1965) provides an overview of the British counteroffensive strategy for 1814. See also Hickey, *The War of 1812*, Chapter 8.

36. Macdonough to Jones, May 14, 1814, entry 147, RG 45, NARA.

37. Macdonough to Jones, June 11, 1814, entry 147, RG 45, NARA.

38. Macdonough to Jones, January 22, 1813, entry 148, RG 45, NARA.

39. Evidence of galley crews remaining at their oar stations overnight or camping on shore is illustrated in the "*Eagle* Logbook" reprinted in Crisman, *The* Eagle. The effects of such duties on the human body can be seen in James Mann, *Medical Sketches of the Campaigns of 1812, 1813, and 1814* (Dedham, MA: H. Mann, 1816), pp. 60–79.

40. Macdonough to William M. Robbins, August 9, 1814 (manuscript no. 41.83, Macdonough Collection, Shelburne Museum, Shelburne, VT).

41. Bauer ed., *Naval Affairs,* vol. 1, p. 307. See also Tucker, *Jeffersonian Gunboat Navy.* The lack of discipline introduced an added element of risk, for weapons of any kind in unskilled hands are bound to result in disaster. Lt. George Evans of the Wilmington, NC, station provided a gruesome illustration of this problem when he reported on August 23, 1814 that gunboat *No. 146* "was within the last hour blown up" after one of its crewmen attempted "to draw or get a ball out of a musket by striking it with the muzzle on the deck over the magazine when unfortunately the musket went off." George Evans to Jones, August 23, 1814, entry 148, RG 45, NARA.

42. Bauer ed., *Naval Affairs,* vol. 1, p. 307.

43. Macdonough to the Board of Naval Commissioners, May 6, 1815, and "Roll of Commissioned & Warrant Officers Late under Command of Capt. Th. Macdonough to May 6th, 1815," Subject File NA, Box 224, Fol. 1, RG 45, NARA.

44. "Abstracts of Service Records, United States Navy," microcopy 330, RG 45, NARA.

45. Macdonough to Jones, May 29, 1814, entry 147, RG 45, NARA.

46. The galley divisions are listed in Daniel S. Stellwagen, "Signal Book and Orders of the Third Division of Gallies," Library of Congress, Washington, DC. In addition, galley division Commanders Mitchell, Robbins, and Stellwagen submitted reports following the Battle of Plattsburgh Bay. Mitchell to Macdonough, Robbins to Macdonough, Stellwagen to Macdonough, September 13, 1814, entry 125, RG 45, NARA.

47. H. N. Muller, "A Traitorous and Diabolical Traffic: The Commerce of the Champlain-Richelieu Corridor During the War of 1812," *Vermont History* 44 (1976), pp. 78–96; Macdonough to Jones, July 23, 1814, entry 147, RG 45, NARA.

48. Macdonough to Jones, July 23, 1814, entry 147, RG 45, NARA; Bellico, *Sails and Steam,* pp. 218–19.

49. Crisman, *The* Eagle, "*Eagle* Logbook."

50. Macdonough to Jones, September 7, 1814, entry 147, RG 45, NARA.

51. Mann, *Medical Sketches,* pp. 206–208.

52. The commanders of the gunboats at the time of the battle were Lt. Francis J. Mitchell (*Viper*), Midshipman Thomas A. Conover (*Borer*), Midshipman Samuel L. Breese (*Nettle*), Sailing Master William M. Robbins (*Allen*), Sailing Master Samuel Keteltas (*Burrows*), Sailing Master Daniel Hazard (*Centipede*), Midshipman James M. Freeman (*Ludlow*), Sailing Master Daniel S. Stellwagen (*Wilmer*), Acting Sailing Master Henry Bancroft (*Alwyn*), and Master's Mate Stephen Holland (*Ballard*). Stellwagen, "Signal Book"; R. Macdonough, *Life of Commodore Macdonough,* p. 162.

53. US Senate, "Report of the Naval Committee, Expressive of the Gallant Conduct of Captain Macdonough, the Officers, Seamen, Marines, &c. in the Capturing of the British Squadron on Lake Champlain, on the 11th September, 1814" (Washington, DC: Roger C. Weightman, 1814). A copy of this report can be found in the Macdonough Collection (manuscript no. 41.108, Shelburne Museum, VT). For a list of the killed and wounded on the gunboats, see B. N. Clark, "Accounts of the Battle of Plattsburgh, September 11, 1814: From Contemporaneous Sources," *Vermont Antiquarian* 1, no. 3 (1903), p. 91.

54. Macdonough to Jones, September 14, 1814, entry 124, RG 45, NARA; Macdonough to Jones, September 17 and November 6, 1814, RG 45, entry 125, NARA.

55. Board of Navy Commissioners to Navy Commandants, Circular, February 1815, entry 216, RG 45, NARA.

56. Benjamin Crowninshield to Purser George Beale, May 20, 1815, entry 149, RG 45, NARA; "Register of US Naval Vessels, 1797–1814," entry 169, RG 45, NARA. The quality and condition of the four older gunboats may be judged by the low sale price of their hulls; the two prewar boats *Ludlow* and *Wilmer* sold for $75 and $90, respectively, while the two barges built in 1813, *Ballard* and *Alwyn,* sold for $52.50 and $42, respectively.

57. James T. Leonard to John Rodgers, May 20, 1817, entry 220, RG 45, NARA; Leonard to Crowninshield, January 1, 1818, entry 125, RG 45, NARA.

58. US Department of State, *A Register of Officers and Agents Civil, Military, and Naval in the Service of the United States on the 30th of September, 1821; Together with the Names, Force, and Condition of all the Ships and Vessels Belonging to the United States and When and Where Built* (Washington, DC: Davis and Force, 1822); Crisman, *The Eagle,* Chapter 7; Kevin Crisman, "Coffins of the Brave: A Return to Lake Champlain's War of 1812 Ship Grave-

yard," *Institute of Nautical Archaeology Quarterly* 22, no. 1 (Spring 1995), pp. 4–8.

59. *National Gazette and Literary Register* (Philadelphia), June 11, 1825.

60. In 1982, Elizabeth Warren, Jay Heaton, Mike Janson, and Dave Phinney logged more than sixty hours of dive time recording the vessel's remains. The work was directed by Kevin Crisman and Arthur Cohn and sponsored by the Champlain Maritime Society and the Vermont Division for Historic Preservation. See Elizabeth J. Warren, "Gunboat #1: Results of the 1982 Lake Champlain Shipwreck Survey," in *A Report on the Nautical Archaeology of Lake Champlain,* ed. Arthur B. Cohn (Burlington, VT: Champlain Maritime Society, 1982).

61. The gunboat flotilla of the Chesapeake Bay, scuttled in the Patuxent River in August 1814, has been located and test excavations have been carried out on selected wrecks. A number of the boats in this flotilla were row galleys built to the 75-foot Doughty plan.

62. The New York State Education Department and Vermont Division of Historic Preservation provided additional support to the 1995 study of the wrecks in the Poultney River. The project was directed by Kevin Crisman and Arthur B. Cohn and carried out by ten field-school students and volunteer divers. The results of the fieldwork are reported in detail in: Eric B. Emery, "The Last of Mr. Brown's Mosquito Fleet: The History and Archaeology of the American Row Galley *Allen* on Lake Champlain, 1814–1825" (PhD diss., Texas A&M University, 2003).

63. Maj. George Taylor to Maj. Gen. Richard Stovin, June 3, 1813, in Dudley, ed., *Naval War of 1812,* vol. 2, pp. 488–89, 516–17; William Wood, ed., *Select British Documents of the Canadian War of 1812,* vol. 3, pt. 1 (Toronto: The Champlain Society, 1926), pp. 166, 178, 191, 223.

64. A pipe identical to the one found in *Allen* can be seen in Lee H. Hanson Jr., "Pipes from Rome, New York," *Historical Archaeology* 5, no. 1 (1971), pp. 92–99. The Rome pipe is from a feature dated 1839 to c.1860, whereas the *Allen* pipe was deposited between 1814 and 1825, suggesting that this style was produced for well over a decade. Similar but not identical pipes have been recovered from a mid-nineteenth-century site in Sacramento; see Richard V. Humphrey, "Clay Pipes from Old Sacramento," *Historical Archaeology* 3, no. 1 (1969), pp. 12–33. Turban-and-beard effigy pipes are sold in Turkey today.

65. "Articles of Agreement Entered into Upon this Twenty Third Day of July Eighteen Hundred and Thirteen Between Thomas Hall and Benjamin White, Both of Baltimore, Shipwrights, and James Beatty Navy Agent of the United States of America at Baltimore One Row Galley," entry 235, RG 45, NARA.

"A REMARKABLY FINE LOOKING VESSEL"

The Royal Navy Brig *Linnet*

ERIKA WASHBURN

Introduction

In the fall of 1949, Ray Stevens stood on the muddy river bank that bordered his New York farm and studied the mysterious shipwreck before him. Protruding from the brownish water just a few feet away were water-worn timbers, the remains of a vessel about 80 feet (24.4 m) in length, whose origins and history were as murky as the river that covered them. Many people in White-hall, New York, knew about the sunken ships in East Bay (the local name for the lower Poultney River), but no one knew precisely how old they were. According to some of Stevens's neighbors, the wrecks dated to the Revolutionary War or perhaps as far back as the French and Indian War. Others said they were from the third conflict that swept the Champlain Valley, the War of 1812. This particular hull was said to be filled with war relics such as cannon and cannonballs, but salvage had never been attempted. Unable to resist the mystery and the possibility of unusual finds, Stevens decided to recover the wreck. He enlisted the help of three Vermonters whose farm occupied the opposite bank of the river: Tony, John, and Steve Galick.

On an October evening, the Galick brothers joined Ray Stevens with three tractors, several draft horses, and lengths of steel cable to begin their salvage effort. They started by wrapping cables around the heavier timbers, hooked them up, and tugged the hull across the narrow river from the New York to the Vermont bank (fig. 11.1). During this process, the forward one-third of the wreck broke off and floated away.[1] The remainder of the hull spun around, leaving the bow facing downriver.

The work of Stevens and the Galicks attracted an audience, many of them also curious to know more about the ship pulled from the river. The *Whitehall Times* conducted its own research and reported to its readers on October 20 that the salvaged wreck was a 75-foot-long (22.9 m) "battleship" of French construc-

Figure 11.1. *The stern of* Linnet *in 1949. The ends of the hull were extensively damaged during the salvage of the vessel. The photograph was taken from the starboard side of the stern, looking forward. The notched upper surface of the stern deadwood is visible in the lower left, along with several disarticulated floor timbers from the aftermost frames. The rectangular mainmast step can be seen midway up the keelson; the second block atop the keelson (with the round hole in the center) may have seated the lower end of the capstan barrel. (Photo from Collection Series 17672, Department of Public Works, New York State Archives, Albany, NY.)*

tion, dating to the Revolutionary War.[2] The *Times,* alas, had neither the correct war nor the correct ship: the salvaged vessel was actually the War of 1812 ex–Royal Navy brig *Linnet.* The identity would not be conclusively determined, however, until forty-six years later, when nautical archaeologists began an intensive study of the wreck.

Over the course of several weeks in the fall of 1949, more than three hundred people visited the Galick farm to look at the wreck and remove artifacts and hull timbers. Hundreds of cast-iron shot—round shot, bar shot, and hollow bomb shells—were discovered; according to the Galicks, the spaces between the frames were packed with cannonballs that Ray Stevens sold to visitors for "two dollars a pop."[3] One noteworthy artifact discovered in the hull was a copper coin, located in or near the mainmast step, that bore the date 1812 and the inscriptions "Trade and Navigation" on one side and "half penny token" on the other. The American Numismatic Society of New York identified the coin as an 1812 half-penny from Canada.[4]

Among the other recovered artifacts were four cast-iron artillery pieces: two 8-foot-long (2.4 m) 9-pounder cannon without trunnions, a split mortar, and a 6-foot-6-inch-long (2 m) cannon weighing 1200 pounds (544.3 kg). All were broken or worn out and were serving as ballast aboard *Linnet.* The two 9 pounders and the split mortar were sold to Fort Ticonderoga for display on the parade grounds; the third cannon was first sold to the Mount Hope Society of Ticonderoga, New York, and later acquired by Fort Ticonderoga.[5]

Although many of *Linnet*'s top timbers had deteriorated before 1949 as a result of exposure and rot, the damage to the hull and loss of timbers as a result of the salvage was profound. After the bow broke off and floated away, only a 58-foot (17.7 m) length of the hull remained, consisting of the keel, floor timbers, and first futtocks, some planking and ceiling, the stern deadwood assembly, and the keelson with the mainmast step. The ceiling and most of the stern timbers were removed or dismantled during or shortly after the salvage. Some of these timbers were collected and sold to an antique and relics dealer in Rutland, Vermont.[6] Others, including a piece that is probably a section of keelson, were displayed in a shed at Fort Mount Hope in Ticonderoga under a sign stating that the ship was likely one of Benedict Arnold's ships from the 1776 Battle of Valcour Island.

Late in the fall of 1949, New York State authorities investigated the salvaged hull, which legally belonged to the state because it was found in New York waters. During the investigation, photographs were taken of *Linnet* and the other ships in the river (fig. 11.2). Now in the New York State Archives, these photographs were later helpful in identifying some of *Linnet*'s timbers during the archaeological excavation, as well as in determining which end of the wreck was the bow.

The state authorities placed "No Trespassing" signs on the remainder of the hulls in the river, but for *Linnet* this action came too late. The degree of damage to the wreck and the extent of the artifact removal are readily apparent when the 1949 photographs are compared with what archaeologists found in the 1990s. The salvage obliterated part of *Linnet*'s story, but the wreck has nevertheless contributed to our understanding of the war and naval construction on the lakes.

"To Maintain an Ascendancy on the Lakes": The Career of *Linnet*

The story of the brig *Linnet* begins at the island of Isle aux Noix, in the province of Lower Canada, in the year 1813 (fig. 11.3). Located in the middle of the Richelieu

Figure 11.2. *New York State officials examine the battered hull of* Linnet *in 1949. By this time the cast-iron cannon and shot in the bilges had been taken up by the salvers and sold to relic collectors. The state officials nailed "No Trespassing" signs to the exposed timbers of other wrecks still under the river, but this did not prevent the salvage of* Ticonderoga *nine years later.* Linnet's *considerably diminished hull was relocated at this place in 1981 and underwent detailed archaeological study in 1995. (Photo from Collection Series 17672, Department of Public Works, New York State Archives, Albany, NY.)*

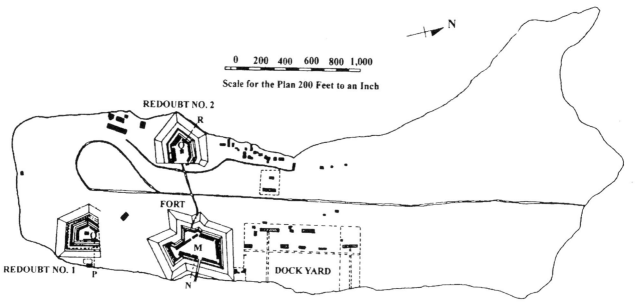

Figure 11.3. *Plan of the shipyard and defenses of Isle aux Noix, Lower Canada. This diagram of the island was prepared shortly after the War of 1812. The fortifications were strengthened to resist US attacks and the ship-building facilities were greatly expanded during the final year of the war to accommodate the construction of the brig* Linnet, *the frigate* Confiance, *and several gunboats. (Traced for clarity by Erika Washburn from "Plan of Isle aux Noix," April 27, 1816, No. 4, MR 643, Public Record Office.)*

River 12 miles (19.3 km) north of the United States–Canada border, the island served as the Royal Navy's shipyard and base on Lake Champlain during the War of 1812. Defensive preparations at Isle aux Noix got off to a slow start in the summer of 1812: the fortifications were in disrepair and the British naval force on the lake—under the direction of the Provincial Marine—consisted of the rotted hulk of an elderly, 1794-vintage ship, three gunboats, and several bateaux armed with small cannon.[7] Luckily for the British, the US naval force under Lt. Thomas Macdonough—three armed merchant sloops and two old gunboats—was not much

of a threat.[8] No encounters took place on Lake Champlain before the close of the 1812 navigation season.

The year 1813 was marked by the arrival at Isle aux Noix of Lt. Daniel Pring, a key participant in *Linnet*'s career. Pring was part of the Royal Navy contingent under Sir James Lucas Yeo sent to the lakes in early 1813, when the Admiralty took over all operations on the inland waters of North America. A native of Hamilton, Devonshire, Pring entered the navy at a young age and served as a midshipman at the Jamaica station. He was aboard H.M.S. *Russell* at the Battle of Copenhagen in 1801 and received both his lieutenant's commission and command of the schooner *Paz* at the Halifax station on May 12, 1808. Captain Pring initially commanded the sloop of war *Wolfe* on Lake Ontario in 1813, but in July Canada's Governor General Sir George Prevost and Yeo agreed to give Pring command of the naval forces on Lake Champlain.[9] By the middle of this month, Pring was recruiting or impressing additional seamen at Montreal and Quebec for his flotilla at Isle aux Noix.

Daniel Pring's official duties included manning and outfitting the existing Lake Champlain vessels, defending Canada, and harassing the US Navy's flotilla. He would need warships to successfully execute his duties, but what he found at Isle aux Noix was not very promising. The Royal Navy's flotilla increased in early June with the capture of the US sloops *Growler* and *Eagle* of 11 guns each, but these were not sufficient to ensure superiority. The first mention of the construction of a brig is in a report from Gen. Sir Roger Sheaffe to Prevost after his visit to Isle aux Noix on July 29, 1813.[10] Sheaffe stated that Mr. William Simons was certain he could complete a brig of 16 guns in six weeks and that sufficient timber was deposited on the island for him to do so. Simons, a shipwright from Renfrew, Scotland, had been working in the naval yard at Kingston on Lake Ontario when he was called to Isle aux Noix to evaluate the captured *Eagle* and *Growler.*

Shortly after a British mid-summer attack on Lake Champlain, known to history as "Murray's Raid," Royal Navy Capt. Thomas Everard (temporarily serving on the lake) and Pring strongly recommended the immediate construction of a brig and two gunboats.[11] For the brig they proposed a vessel with a length on deck of 110 feet (33.5 m), an extreme breadth of 30½ feet (9.3 m), a draft of water aft of 9½ feet (2.9 m), and a hull measuring between 350 and 390 tons. The ship was to mount fourteen 32-pounder carronades in broadside and two long 24 pounders on centerline pivot mounts. Pring added, "There is now laying at Isle aux Noix, 4 to 5,000 feet oak timber with sufficiency of pine, by collecting all the carpenters to be found in Quebec and here, [the brig] could be launched from 6 to 8 weeks from the laying the keel, might probably cost the hull afloat with spars from 14 Pounds to 15 Pounds per ton. A suit of sails belonging to Mr Dunlop intended for a ship of 300 to 350 tons might be had for 550 Pounds."[12] On August 8, Prevost approved construction of the

two gunboats, each of two guns.[13] He agreed with Pring and Everard that a brig was needed but requested a detailed estimate for its construction. Simons projected the total cost, including the hull, spars, four boats, anchors, cables, hawsers, blocks, pumps, sails, and rigging, at £7738 10s.[14] Lobbying in a not-so-subtle fashion for the new vessel, Pring sent reports detailing the growth of the US naval force, writing Prevost on October 10, "The Enemy having lately increased their force on this Lake to five Sloops, three of which are very superior in size and Weight of metal to either of the two at present under my command, I hope Your Excellency will be pleased to authorize the Building of a Brig of 16 Guns at this Post, or two smaller Vessels, which additional force is absolutely required to enable me to meet the enemy squadron."[15]

Prevost, seeking to avoid the expense of a large warship, suggested building a sloop or schooner. Pring dismissed the idea, writing on October 18 that a vessel of this size would be little better than the armed merchant sloops he currently commanded, which were, he declared, "by far too much crowded with their Guns."[16] Prevost responded the next day, stating that it was not his intention to limit the tonnage of the proposed vessel; he was simply concerned that the dimensions of the proposed brig were too big for the Richelieu River. Military Secretary Noah Freer also had reservations about a naval race on this lake, noting, "It is not within the Compass of His Excellency's expectations that we can cope with the Enemy in the building of Vessels on Lake Champlain, their resources on that Water being so far Superior to those we possess."[17]

Despite his reservations, on November 7 Prevost finally agreed to Pring's request to build a 16-gun brig. The next day a contract was drawn up by William Simons, who requested that supplies and additional artificers be procured as soon as possible.[18] The contract specified that Simons would assemble the vessel (but not the joinery, inboard work, or small boats) for £6 Halifax currency per ton and have it launched and completed by or before May 1, 1814. Spikes, bolts, and ironwork were to be forwarded without delay, the workmen were to be furnished with lodgings and marine rations, and Simons was permitted to employ ten to twenty military craftsmen, including ship carpenters and blacksmiths, at a rate of one shilling and nine pence per day.[19] With the signing of Simons's contract, the British side of the shipbuilding race on Lake Champlain had officially begun.

Work on the brig did not commence immediately after contract approval due to a lack of ironwork, supplies, laborers, and a proper shipyard. In early December, Pring (newly promoted to the rank of commander) wrote Prevost to report that the Engineers Department had failed to procure the necessary materials and that he feared he would not be able to collect them himself.[20] This may indicate that Simons was forced to use local supplies rather than material sent from Great Britain, which the original contract had specified. Whatever the source, supplies and men trickled in, and a dockyard, some storehouses, a hospital, naval barracks, and a forge were built.[21]

Construction on the brig continued throughout the winter, hastened by reports of US shipbuilding activity at Vergennes, Vermont.[22] Initially named *Niagara,* the vessel's name changed when the Admiralty placed the North American lake warships on the Royal Navy List. The Admiralty recommended the name *Linnet.*[23] A January 1814 statement of the naval force on the lake listed *Linnet* as 85 feet (25.9 m) in length and 26½ feet (8.1 m) in breadth.[24] The brig was completed and launched in April and thereafter became Pring's flagship (fig. 11.4).

Historical sources disagree on *Linnet*'s armament. The January 1814 statement listed proposed broadsides of two long 18 pounders and fourteen 32-pounder carronades, while a contemporary source lists 18 guns.[25] Modern historians agree on sixteen guns, all long 12 pounders, because this was the weaponry listed in the court martial records.[26] *Linnet* was nearly battle ready by May, lacking only a galley or camboose, which Pring intended to purchase from a merchant vessel.[27] Simons's work impressed Pring so much that on April 27 he recommended that the shipwright be appointed master builder at Isle aux Noix, and on May 6 Simons received his appointment and a pay raise.[28]

Linnet first saw action in a May 1814 raid up Lake Champlain. Ordered by Yeo to destroy the enemy's vessels or at least prevent them from entering the lake, Pring set out for Otter Creek and the US shipyard at Vergennes, several miles above the mouth of the river. The British flotilla consisted of *Linnet,* the sloops *Chub* and *Finch* (ex-*Growler* and ex-*Eagle*), the auxiliary sloop-rigged tender *Canada,* seven gunboats, and two additional transport vessels. Headwinds from the south prevented them from reaching Otter Creek until May 14, giving the US forces plenty of time to prepare. At dawn the gunboats engaged the recently constructed earthwork battery Fort Cassin at the mouth of Otter Creek, and *Linnet* later sailed within range of the battery. The British bombardment had little effect, however, and Pring called off the assault against what he perceived to be a well-prepared and decidedly superior defensive force.[29]

The enlarged US Navy squadron entered the lake not long after Pring's return to Canada, and for the remainder of the late spring and summer *Linnet* and its consorts were bottled up in the Richelieu River. The naval base at Isle aux Noix was a beehive of activity as William Simons and a crew of builders assembled a frigate that promised to give the Royal Navy parity with, if not superiority over, the US ships. In late June, Pring was superseded by Capt. Peter Fisher as the commanding officer at Isle aux Noix, although Pring retained command of *Linnet.*[30] Late that summer, on August 25, Capt. George Downie, a more experienced officer than Pring or Fisher, was given command of the Lake Champlain squadron.[31] When Downie arrived at Isle aux Noix, the lack of manpower was still a problem. Throughout the summer, Pring and Fisher had asked for men, but their requests were consistently turned down by Yeo, who insisted that sailors were more urgently needed on Lake Ontario.[32] Eventually, the Admiralty ordered the 1st Battalion Royal Marines to Isle aux Noix and Prevost was promised 190 seamen from ships in the St. Lawrence River.[33]

By late August, a force of ten thousand seasoned British troops, personally commanded by Sir George Prevost, was poised on Lower Canada's border with New York, ready to commence the long-anticipated offensive in the Champlain Valley. Prevost was reluctant to begin, however, until his left flank, the western shore of Lake Champlain, was protected by a naval squadron. The Royal Navy was far from ready, for despite Simons's best efforts, the new frigate *Confiance* was not launched until August 25. Interior work, ballasting, arming, rigging, and manning required additional time, time that Prevost did not have if he hoped to complete his conquest of the Champlain Valley before the onset of winter. In addition to the 37-gun *Confiance* and the 16-gun *Linnet,* the British squadron consisted of the 11-gun sloops *Chub* and *Finch,* twelve gunboats, the small tenders *Canada* and *Icicle,* and a

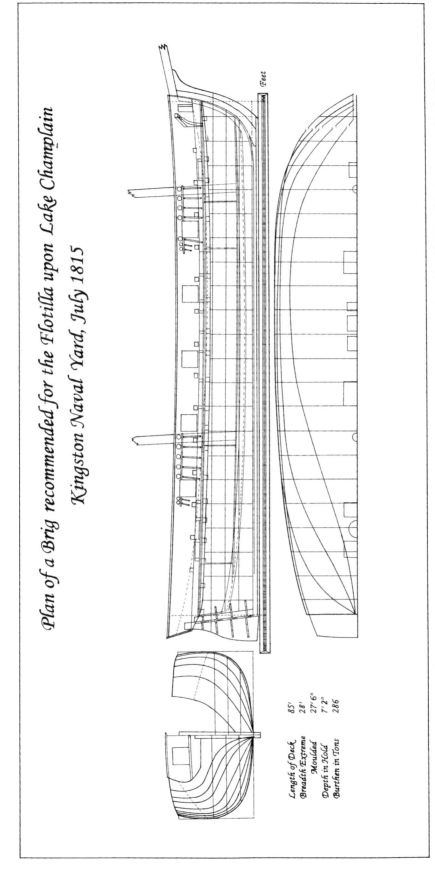

Plan of a Brig recommended for the Flotilla upon Lake Champlain

Kingston Naval Yard, July 1815

Feet

Length of Deck	85'
Breadth Extreme	28'
Moulded	27' 6"
Depth in Hold	7' 2"
Burthen in Tons	286

Figure 11.4. Plan of a brig recommended for the flotilla on Lake Champlain, 1815. No contemporary plans of Linnet have been identified, but this plan, proposed for building new brigs in 1815, closely matches the known dimensions of Linnet. The 1815 plan may well have been derived from the lines of the earlier brig, a vessel admired by friend and foe alike. The 1815 brigs, which were never built, were intended to carry 10 long 24-pounder guns and thus had only six ports on each side; Linnet, with 16 long 12-pounders, probably had nine ports per side. (Traced and faired from the original plan by Erika Washburn, from "Three Brigs," Box 56, Reg. No. 6411A, National Maritime Museum.)

small barge.[34] Altogether the squadron mounted 92 guns capable of firing 1804 pounds (818 kg) of iron in a broadside and was manned by 917 officers, sailors, and marines.[35] The US squadron, in comparison, carried 86 guns with a broadside weight of 2224 pounds (1009 kg) and was manned by 820 crew members.[36]

On September 1, Prevost felt he could not wait any longer, and his army poured across the border and marched on the US Army cantonment at Plattsburgh. The British troops brushed aside the scant opposition they met and by September 5 had captured Plattsburgh and moved into position along the river that fronted the thinly manned US earthworks south of town. Still uneasy about the US naval force on his flanks, Prevost postponed his attack until the US ships anchored in Plattsburgh Bay were captured or sunk. On September 9 he prodded Commodore Downie, "I need not dwell with you on the Evils resulting to both services from delay."[37] Downie, struggling to complete *Confiance,* responded to an earlier summons: "I am advancing with Squadron as fast as the wind and weather will allow. I stated to you that this Ship was not ready. She is not ready now, and, until she is ready, it is my duty not to hazard the Squadron before an Enemy who will be Superior in Force."[38]

Delayed by last-minute carpentry work and then by headwinds, *Confiance, Linnet,* and the smaller vessels did not reach the entrance to Plattsburgh Bay until dawn on September 11. Downie reconnoitered his foe's line of anchored ships from a gig, and then he returned to his flagship to issue a plan of attack. *Linnet* and *Chub* were to engage the brig *Eagle* at the van of the American line, *Confiance* was to attack the ship *Saratoga* in the center, and *Finch* and the twelve gunboats were to attack the schooner *Ticonderoga* and the sloop *Preble* at the rear.[39] Downie ordered the scaling of *Confiance*'s guns as a prearranged signal to the land forces that the attack was under way, and the British fleet sailed into the bay at 9:00 a.m. As *Linnet* passed the US flagship *Saratoga,* Pring ordered a broadside fired, although it seems to have done little damage.[40]

By 9:40 a.m. the battle was fully joined. Pring sailed *Linnet* to the northernmost position in the line of battle and, together with *Chub,* commenced firing upon *Eagle* (fig. 11.5). *Linnet*'s guns were well-served, for Capt. Robert Henley of *Eagle* later described the Royal Navy brig's fire as "raking and most destructive."[41] After

Figure 11.5. Linnet *engages the US squadron at the Battle of Lake Champlain. This detail from Thomas Birch's watercolor of the battle on September 11, 1814 shows the brig at anchor at the northern end of the British line, where it delivered "a raking and most destructive fire" on the US brig* Eagle. *(Courtesy of the New York Historical Society, New York.)*

more than an hour of punishment from *Linnet,* Henley cut *Eagle*'s bower anchor cable and sailed past the US flagship *Saratoga* to a new position out of reach of *Linnet*'s guns. Pring shifted his fire to *Saratoga.* Aboard the British brig the action was going according to plan, but that was about the only part of Commodore Downie's plan that did work for the Royal Navy that day.

Confiance met headwinds and raking fire from *Saratoga* while attempting to sail into position, and Downie was forced to anchor the frigate prematurely, before gaining its intended position across the US flagship's bow. *Confiance* became the primary target of the enemy vessels and sustained tremendous damage. The sloop *Chub* entered the fray near *Linnet* but under intense fire from *Eagle* soon lost its cables, sweeps, bowsprit, and main boom and in a few short minutes became the first British vessel to surrender. The US vessels *Preble* and *Ticonderoga* poured fire into the sloop *Finch,* which lost steerage when trying to tack and ran aground off Crab Island. Eight of the twelve British gunboats stayed out of the battle altogether.[42]

Confiance was plagued with ill luck from the beginning: Commodore Downie was mortally wounded 15 minutes after the battle commenced, the crew suffered horrific casualties from shot and splinters, most of the guns on the engaged port side were disabled, the ship was fast taking on water, and American fire did not diminish appreciably. Unable to fight on and unable to escape, Lt. James Robertson hauled down *Confiance*'s flag shortly after 11 a.m.[43] By this time, *Linnet* was also badly damaged and unable to withdraw, but Pring kept up the fight for a few more minutes in the hope that the gunboats would come to his assistance. No help was forthcoming, and by 11:20 a.m. *Linnet* had over 1 foot (0.3 m) of water above the lower deck. Pring had no choice but to strike his colors.[44] His Majesty's brig *Linnet* was the last warship to surrender on Lake Champlain, then or ever since.

The Battle of Plattsburgh Bay lasted 2 hours and 20 minutes, with a heavy human toll on both sides. *Linnet*'s casualty list numbered twenty-four: eight seamen and marines killed and thirty wounded; casualties among the officers included two killed, Lt. William Paul and Boatswain Charles Jackson, and one wounded, Midshipman John Sinclair. In his after-action report to Commodore Yeo, Pring commended several officers and men aboard the vessel: Lt. William Drew, Purser Giles, Gunner Muckle, and Surgeon Mitchell, who performed amputations during the action and tended to his patients even as water rose above the lower deck.[45] The builder of *Linnet* and *Confiance,* William Simons, remained aboard the latter vessel as it sailed into action and was seriously wounded; he recovered and in 1818 returned to his native Scotland, where he would prosper as the owner of a large ship-building firm.[46]

The Treaty of Ghent ended the war between the United States and Great Britain on December 24, 1814, but the Royal Navy's investigation of the debacle at Plattsburgh Bay had just begun. The answers to the government's inquiries were recorded at the court martial of Daniel Pring and other officers of the Lake Champlain squadron, held aboard H.M.S. *Gladiator* in Portsmouth Harbor between August 18 and 21, 1815. The navy needed a scapegoat for the defeat and easily

found one—Sir George Prevost. Pring pointed the finger of guilt the day after the battle in his first official report, wherein he asserted that the fleet had been rushed into the engagement in order to cooperate with Prevost's land forces. Pring's superior Commodore Yeo concurred: "It appears to me, and I have good reason to believe that Captain Downie was urged, and his ship hurried into Action before she was in a fit state to meet the Enemy."[47]

When Pring took the stand at his trial, the court asked him directly, "To what cause do you attribute the failure of the Engagement?" He replied: "To the want of the promised Co-operation of the Land Forces, I conceive that we should otherwise have been successful in our Attack."[48] This theme appears again and again in the officers' testimony during the proceedings. Not surprisingly, the court agreed, stating in its verdict that the capture of *Confiance, Linnet,* and the two sloops was due to Prevost goading Downie into battle before *Confiance* was ready and to Prevost's failure to carry out the joint attack at the agreed-upon time. With the exceptions of *Chub*'s commander James McGhie, who did not attend the court martial, and gunboat commander Lt. Raynham, who deserted in Canada, all of the surviving officers were honorably acquitted and Daniel Pring was promoted to captain within a month.[49]

The spoils of battle taken by the United States at Plattsburgh Bay were heavily damaged: *Confiance* was in total shambles and *Linnet* was in a similar condition. The brig was holed between thirty and fifty times, and its masts, sails, rigging, and yards were completely shot to pieces.[50] The captured vessels were well stocked with the tools of war. *Linnet* alone yielded sixteen long 12-pounder cannon and carriages, 1102 powder cylinders for the 12 pounders, four kegs of priming powder, 1394 round shot, seventy-three 32-pounder shot, 161 canister shot, 122 stands of grapeshot, six boxes of hand grenades, thirty-five muskets, four pairs of pistols, fifteen swords, thirty cartridge boxes, thirty-five boarding pikes, and twelve rammers and sponges.[51] The total value of *Linnet*'s hull, equipment, and stores was estimated at $55,000 and the cost of repairs about $2500.[52]

In early October 1814, *Linnet* sailed south to Whitehall, New York, to be moored with the rest of the squadron in the narrow lake channel below town. The ships were still there in February 1815 when news of peace ended the struggle for the lake. On February 28, 1815, Macdonough ordered the ships dismantled, with the guns, sails, ballast, powder, shot, and stores removed to shore for storage. The empty hulls were then white-washed inside and out and roofed over.[53] While clearing *Linnet*'s hull of its contents, the US sailors uncovered a cache of cast-iron cannon and munitions in the bilges, much of it probably damaged or condemned material loaded as ballast. The haul included two long 18 pounders, eleven long 12 pounders, fifteen heavy swivel guns, 1224 round shot for 6-, 12-, and 32-pound cannon, and three thousand grapeshot.[54]

In a relatively short time the naval presence on the lake dissipated, and much of the US Navy's equipment was either auctioned off to help pay the war debt or placed in permanent storage. The empty warship hulls were left in a line by the side of the lake, where they were maintained in a half-hearted manner. In March 1817, Capt. James T. Leonard, commander of the naval station at Whitehall, reported that the ships would "require caulking from the waterline to the bends, their seams are very much open."[55] Decay was inevitable. In January 1820, Leonard reported, "*Saratoga, Eagle, Linnet* and *Ticonderoga* are free of leaks, their timbers upon inspection appear yet to be good but each lately exhibits considerable spots of dry rot along the water line and . . . on the outside planking."[56]

By the summer of 1820, shipping activity had increased in Whitehall, and *Linnet* and its ragtag consorts, moored alongside the main channel, threatened to block the passage of commercial vessels. The squadron was moved into the mouth of the nearby Poultney River and left to rot for a few more years. The navy attempted to sell the ships at auction in 1825, but there were no takers. The ships, including *Linnet,* eventually sank at anchor along the New York bank of the river. *Linnet* would remain relatively undisturbed for the next 124 years, until that fateful October evening in 1949 when Ray Stevens and the Galick brothers decided to salvage the old shipwreck and its contents.

Archaeological Study of *Linnet*

Linnet was rediscovered by Kevin Crisman and Arthur Cohn during an archaeological survey of the lower Poultney River on July 23, 1981. Finding the wreck was merely a matter of standing on the river bank and looking into the water, since the starboard frame tops were just beneath the surface. Sometime after the 1949 sal-

Figure 11.6. *Rediscovering* Linnet's *lower hull. In 1995 the wreck of* Linnet *underwent a long-overdue recording of its worn and damaged timbers. Here Erika Washburn advises Erich Heinold on procedures for measuring the after end of the keel. (Photo by Kevin J. Crisman,* Linnet *project files of Erika Washburn.)*

vage, *Linnet* had slipped (or was pushed) back into the river, with a list to port and a pronounced longitudinal twist; this resubmergence was fortunate, for if the wreck had remained high and dry it would not have lasted for long. A few preliminary measurements were taken from the hull in 1981 and 1982, enough for the wreck to be tentatively identified as *Linnet*. This identification was based principally on timber dimensions and a simple process of elimination: the wrecks of *Eagle* and *Ticonderoga* had already been found and the scantlings were far too small to be part of *Saratoga* or *Confiance*; ergo, this formerly ordnance- and munitions-laden wreck, sunk in the middle of the US Navy's boneyard for the five large War of 1812 ships, was almost certainly *Linnet*.

After the preliminary recording in 1981–82, no further study of *Linnet* took place until July 1995, when I directed the re-excavation and recording of the wreck as part of a nautical archaeology field school jointly sponsored by the Lake Champlain Maritime Museum, the Institute of Nautical Archaeology, and Texas A&M University (fig. 11.6). When the other team members and I first walked the muddy Vermont bank of the river and examined *Linnet*'s remains, it was obvious that not much was left of this once-formidable warship. A total of 58 feet (17.7 m) of the original 85-foot-long (25.9 m) vessel still existed; the missing 27 feet (8.2 m) included a short section of the stern and most of the bow. Many of the frames at the stern were missing, and only three first futtocks were still attached to the starboard arms

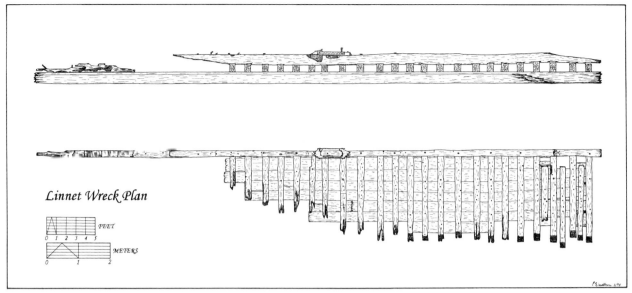

Figure 11.7. *Plan and profile of* Linnet*'s surviving lower hull. Photographic and documentary evidence show that* Linnet*'s lower hull and its load of cast iron ballast survived in relatively good condition until October 1949. The brutal treatment of the hull during its initial salvage and the continued depredations of souvenir-hunters since that time have greatly reduced the structure. Enough has survived, however, to give us some clues to the materials and techniques used by shipwright William Simons to build* Linnet. *The port-side frames were not excavated in 1995 and thus are not shown on this plan. (Drawing by Erika Washburn.)*

of the floor timbers. We later searched for the missing bow and stern sections in the river but found no other remains.

Our goal in 1995 was to record hull form and timber dimensions and arrangements and to use the data to prepare a plan of the wreck. With this we could attempt a limited reconstruction and analysis. To this end, four to five divers worked on *Linnet* for four weeks, with the keel, keelson, frames, futtocks, and mast step serving as the focal points of our study. Overall, this was a shallow excavation, for parts of the wreck were nearly exposed during low water (plate 9b). Visibility in the river was quite poor, rarely exceeding 2 feet (0.6 m).

The wreck was recorded in imperial units (feet and inches) rather than metric because *Linnet* was built using this system of measurement and any patterns in construction would appear in feet and inches. The thorough salvage job in 1949 made it unlikely that many small finds remained except between the frames or atop the keel, and so we used *Linnet*'s exposed frames and keelson as a reference system during excavation to record the provenience of features and artifacts. For this purpose, the starboard frame floors were numbered, from the stern forward, 1 through 23. The sediment between every other starboard frame section was excavated with a water dredge, and the timber di-

mensions and curvatures were then recorded in detail. The port side of the wreck was deeply buried under the coarse sand river bottom, and only limited excavation was attempted on this side of the hull.

The surviving section of the keel appeared to be composed of a single white oak (*Quercus alba*) timber (fig. 11.7). The forward end was broken off somewhere under frame 19 during the 1949 salvage, while the after end appeared to have been sawn off by a misguided souvenir hunter. The total preserved length was 58 feet (17.7 m), but only the keel's aftermost 8 feet (2.4 m) and forwardmost 6 feet (1.8 m) were recorded in detail because the rest was deeply buried. The timber was consistently molded 13½ inches (34.3 cm) and had a maximum sided dimension of 8¼ inches (20.96 cm). The original keel was probably composed of two timbers scarfed together amidships.

The midship frame was not identified during the excavation and indeed may have been part of the forward section lost during the 1949 salvage. There were no significant differences in the dimensions and placement of any of the frames, which were spaced along the keel on 18- to 24-inch (45.7 to 61 cm) centers. All appear to be fashioned from compass timber and were shaped along the grain. The futtocks were bolted to the after sides of the floor timbers with their heels approxi-

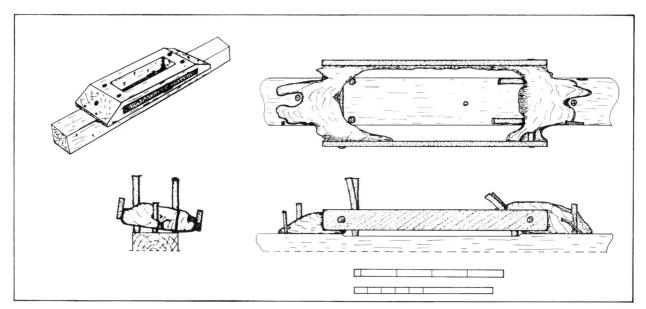

Figure 11.8. *The mainmast step of* Linnet. *The drawing shows three views of the step as it appeared in 1995, while the perspective view in the upper left shows a reconstruction of the step's original appearance.* Linnet's *step differs from the saddle-type steps seen on the earlier* General Hunter *and* Nancy *and from the steps seen on the contemporary Royal Navy frigates at Kingston. (Drawing by Scott Padeni.)*

mately 1 foot (30.5 cm) from the side of the keelson. Wood samples from floor timbers and futtocks were all identified as white oak. Limber holes were not always present in the floors; frames 3 and 15 had none, and several others were not cut square.

Some of the planking was still attached to the starboard side of the frames, although the ceiling was missing. The planks were consistently 2 inches (5.1 cm) thick but varied between 10 and 20 inches (25 to 56 cm) in width. Seven strakes were identified between the keel and the starboard turn of the bilge. Planks were fastened to the floors and futtocks exclusively with iron spikes, a number of which were driven into the open spaces between the frames and thus contributed nothing to the fastening of the hull.

The surviving keelson section was 44 feet (13.4 m) long and consisted of a single piece of white oak that averaged 12 inches (30.5 cm) molded and 6 to 8½ inches (15.2 to 21.6 cm) sided. Like the keel, the complete keelson was probably made from two timbers. The piece was generally well preserved, except for a deteriorated area under the mast step. Shallow notches were roughly cut in the bottom of the keelson to fit over the floors; these varied in depth and were not consistently present (there were no notches for frames 5 through 8, directly under the mast step). Notching the underside of the keelson appears to be a British

shipbuilding practice because these notches are not evident on US lake warships from the 1812 era (*Eagle, Ticonderoga, Allen,* and *Jefferson*) but are present on the British-built *Tecumseth, Newash, Nancy,* and Brown's Bay Vessel.[57] When *Linnet* was assembled, the two keelson timbers were flat scarfed to one another slightly forward of amidships; the after end of the surviving keelson timber is tapered to lap over the stern deadwood assembly. Iron bolts fastened the keelson to the floor timbers and keel at every other frame down the centerline of the keelson.

The mast step was a separate timber fastened to the top of the keelson with six ⅞-inch-diameter (2.2 cm) iron bolts and four spikes, with three bolts and two spikes at each end (fig. 11.8). It was a block of oak with a rectangular mortise in the center for the mast, reinforced by an iron bar on each side. It was the mainmast step, located about one-third of the vessel's length forward of the stern of the ship. The step was in extremely poor condition and had loosened from its bolts. It measured 3 feet, 8½ inches (1.13 m) long by 1 foot (30.5 cm) wide.

A second, step-like feature can be seen in some of the 1949 photographs, bolted to the top of the keelson 8 feet (2.4 m) abaft the mainmast step. It was missing from the wreck when *Linnet* was relocated in 1981, although four bolt holes were evident in the top of the keelson. This object, a block of wood with a large circular opening in the center, may have seated the base of *Linnet*'s capstan.

In 1995, team members recorded the only surviving timber from the deadwood, the lowest section. Sadly, this piece of white pine was deteriorated, making the original shape difficult to discern. It measured 9½ feet (2.9 m) in length and was attached to the keel by three iron bolts, from which it had worked loose and was easily lifted off and recorded. The use of white pine for a deadwood timber is curious, for one would expect to see stronger oak timbers in this critical assembly. It hints that Simons had difficulty finding good shipbuilding timber for *Linnet* in 1814.

After the field excavation in the Poultney River was completed, several team members volunteered to record *Linnet*-related timbers and artifacts at Ticonderoga, New York. At Fort Ticonderoga, we found the two trunnionless cannon and split mortar carried as ballast in 1814 and sold to the fort after the 1949 salvage. The mortar was found on the parade grounds within the fort, and the cannon were located among a group of guns just outside the fort's entrance. At Mount Hope, many of *Linnet*'s missing stern frames were found under a rustic shelter and in extremely poor condition, having been subjected to the extremes of upstate New York's climate for forty-six years. We recorded a total of three floor timbers, eight futtocks, and fourteen miscellaneous timbers and planks. When we were through, the pieces were placed out of the weather in a nearby storage facility.

The archaeological data, even when combined with historical information, only allow for a very limited reconstruction of *Linnet*. As we have seen, the damage caused by the 1949 salvage and later timber scavenging was extensive. In addition, our examination of the wreck's port side in 1995 was limited by the great depth of sand over the timbers. Thus, the hard data available for reconstruction are based on the 58-foot (17.7 m) starboard-side floor timbers and futtocks; the keel, keelson, and mast step; the deadwood; and two timbers from Mount Hope that were found to match the curvatures of two in situ frames.

Original builder's plans or lines have never been found for *Linnet* and may not exist. There is a half-hull model in Glasgow, Scotland, that was cited in an 1896 newspaper article as the brig *Linnet* that William Simons "built for the British Government in 1810."[58]

This model is still on display in the Museum of Transport in Glasgow, alongside a fully rigged frigate model said to be *Confiance*. The proportions evident in the so-called *Linnet* model are inconsistent with both historical and archaeological data and appear to represent a deeper-draft, ocean-going vessel. Therefore, the Glasgow model is either an inaccurate rendition of the 1813–14 Lake Champlain *Linnet* or represents an entirely different ship.[59]

We know *Linnet*'s principal dimensions from two contemporary sources: a statement sent to the Royal Navy Board in 1814 and measurements taken of the hull by the US Navy after it acquired the brig as a prize.[60] The Royal Navy statement lists *Linnet*'s dimensions as 85 feet (25.9 m) in length and 26½ feet (8.1 m) in breadth. The US Navy surveyors recorded dimensions of 82½ feet (25.1 m) on deck, 27 feet (8.2 m) in beam, and 6 feet 8 inches (2.0 m) in the depth of hold, very close to the Royal Navy's measurements. Howard Chapelle suggested that the lines of *Linnet*'s hull would have been similar to those shown in an Admiralty draft for 24-pounder brigs to be built on Lake Champlain in 1815 (these brigs were never constructed—see fig. 11.4).[61] The brig shown in the Admiralty draft has a length on deck of 85 feet (25.9 m), a breadth of 28 feet (8.5 m), and a depth of hold of 7 feet 3 inches (2.2 m).[62] The close similarities between *Linnet*'s dimensions and the 1815 lines suggest that the latter may have been based on now-missing plans of the former.

By comparing the body shape indicated by the archaeological data to that in the 1815 Admiralty draft, it is possible to determine something of *Linnet*'s hull form and how closely the postwar design resembled it. As it turned out, the archaeological data suggest fuller body sections, making the vessel flatter floored than the Admiralty draft. In building *Linnet,* William Simons was clearly trying to balance the size and armament requirements for a brig of war with the need to pass through shallow parts of the Richelieu River and Lake Champlain. Even with the different frame deadrise, the archaeologically recorded shape and historical information imply that *Linnet*'s hull is close enough to the 1815 plan to use the latter as a guide for the general configuration of the brig. The reconstructed lines, therefore, show a combination of the archaeological data melded with the 1815 Admiralty draft (fig. 11.9).

Because of the lack of data beyond the recorded remains, the conjectural lines sketch is quite simple.

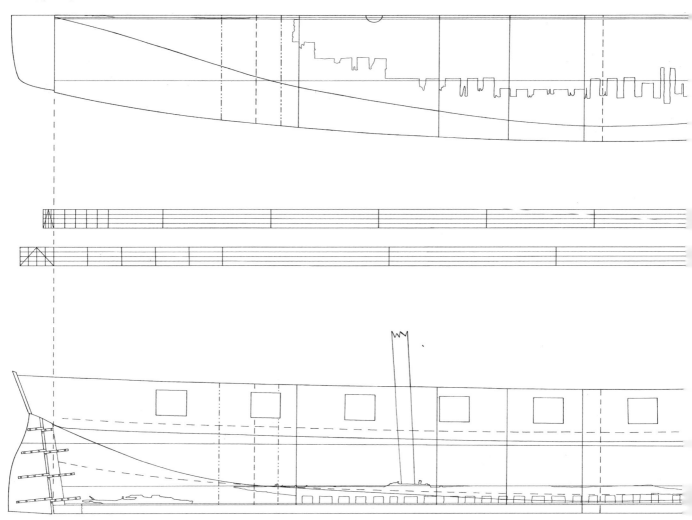

Figure 11.9. *A conjectural lines sketch of the Royal Navy brig* Linnet. *The limited remains of the lower hull aligned with some of the design and construction features seen on the 1815 brig plans (see Figure 11.4) and provided the basis for this limited reconstruction of the brig's form and appearance. The surviving hull and several partial frame sections are shown in the three views. (Reconstruction by Erika Washburn.)*

Within the profile and half-breadth views, the excavated and recorded remains of *Linnet*'s starboard side have been shaded. Since the data do not extend above the keelson or more than 10 feet (3.1 m) outboard of the keel, everything above and beyond these points is conjectural and based on the 1815 draft. In addition, as indicated in the body plan, the floor timbers on the wreck do not extend past the turn of the bilge. The single buttock and waterline represent the hull remains as much as possible but are primarily based on the general shapes in the Admiralty draft.

The shape of the hull seen in the body plan is the most useful result of the proposed lines. To obtain the body shape, the turn of the bilge must be preserved, but on *Linnet* none of the surviving hull extended to the

turn of the bilge. Fortunately, four detached timbers from Mount Hope (MH), consisting of floor timbers and first futtocks, were more informative. Timbers MH 1 and 2 and MH 3 and 4 worked as a frame set—with the floor timber and first futtock—thereby providing information on two curves that extend above the turn of the bilge to approximately 5 feet 9 inches (1.75 m) above the baseline of the hypothetical lines drawing. MH 1 and 2 and MH 3 and 4 have curvatures that place them more or less adjacent to the Admiralty draft's section 16. With this information, it was possible to determine their approximate locations on the centerline and fit them into the hull, which gave an indication of the hull shape. Compared to the US brig *Eagle*, the lines proposed for *Linnet* suggest a vessel with a

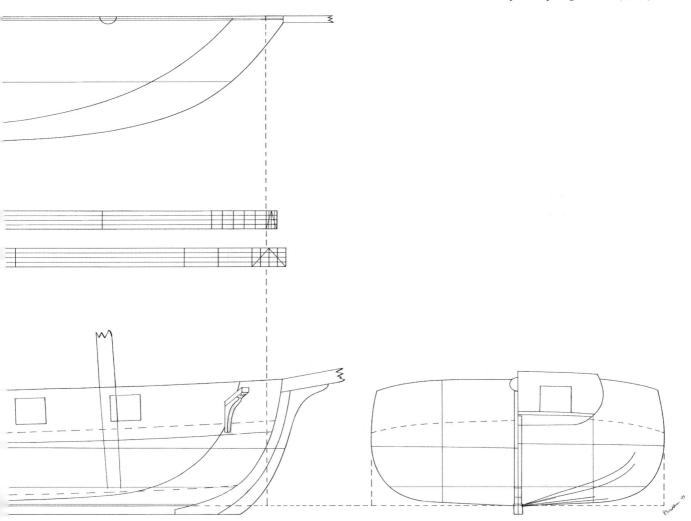

much fuller run. *Linnet*'s reconstructed lines also show a vessel that is relatively flat floored with little deadrise and a length-to-beam ratio of 3:1.

Everything we have seen suggests that *Linnet* was a solid ship. Most of the timbers were fashioned from oak, including the surviving lengths of keel and keelson. All wood samples were identified as either red oak (*Quercus rubra*) or white oak (*Quercus alba*), with the exception of one plank and the deadwood, which were fashioned from white pine (*Pinus strobus*). All the in situ floor timbers and many floors and futtocks at Mount Hope were made from compass timber. The floor timber notches in the underside of the keelson suggest a certain level of craftsmanship in the assembly of the brig. It also suggests a labor-intensive approach to shipbuilding and fits with Surveyor Gen. Joseph Bouchette's observation, quoted in Chapter 7, that British and Canadian shipwrights were often more meticulous than their American counterparts. In sum, *Linnet*'s construction indicates a well-built although lightly timbered vessel. As for the brig's general appearance, we can do no better than to quote Thomas Macdonough, who commented upon seeing *Linnet* for the first time that it was "a remarkably fine looking vessel."[63]

The wreck of *Linnet* was the principal artifact we examined in 1995, but the excavation also yielded a few small finds overlooked by salvers in 1949. These totaled 105 objects and included fasteners, munitions, and items associated with dress (fig. 11.10a, b). Most

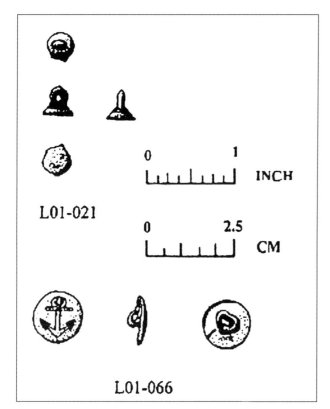

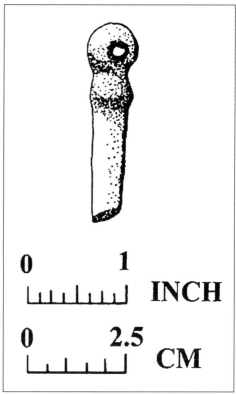

Figure 11.10. *Overlooked in 1949: artifacts found on* Linnet *in 1995. The hull of* Linnet *was thoroughly picked over in 1949, but some smaller items lying between the frames escaped the notice of relic hunters. The cockscrew or vise screw secured a flint between the jaws of a musket cock; the style of the screw suggests it was possibly from a pre-1809 India-pattern or similar musket. The button with the anchor design is probably from a naval officer's uniform, although whether British or American has not been determined. (Drawings by Erick Tichonuk.)*

were found between the floors and atop the keel and garboards. The majority of the artifacts were metal fasteners such as spikes, nails, and bolts, and many were poorly preserved. The twenty-eight spikes or spike fragments were manufactured in T-head and rosehead styles and were, with one copper-alloy exception, all made of iron. Spikes were used to fasten planking to the frames, the mast step to the keelson, and the ceiling to the frames. Of the twenty-nine nails recovered, all but one were made of iron (the exception was made from a copper alloy). The nails were likely used for light internal joinery such as ladders or bulkheads. Only one loose bolt was found, although many were in situ. Bolts seen in the hull were used to connect the keelson to the frames, frames to the keel, and mast step to the keelson and in the deadwood construction.

Other finds included four lead balls, three iron grapeshot, one iron canister shot, a gunflint, and the cockscrew from a musket. The lead shot measured 0.3 to 0.6 inches (.76 to 1.3 cm) in diameter and was intended for small arms such as pistols or muskets. The Galick family donated one grapeshot and a 1-inch-diameter (2.5 cm) canister shot to the Lake Champlain Maritime Museum. According to Bill Galick, at least one stand of grape was recovered from *Linnet* in 1949 with the shot still stacked around the iron spindle.

The cockscrew from a musket lock might have been a highly diagnostic item if it were in better condition. Fortunately, it is still possible to narrow down the musket patterns from which it may have originated, based on its nonreinforced throat and pierced but not slotted head. The cockscrew could represent one of three possible musket types: the old Short Land; New Pattern Musket (type 3 or 4), often called the "Second Model Brown Bess"; or a pre-1809 India Pattern Musket. By 1814 all of these were outdated weapons, but as the most-recent issue, the pre-1809 India Pattern seems the most likely source for the *Linnet* cockscrew.[64]

Also found on *Linnet* was a small (½ inch or 1.3 cm diameter) copper button with an anchor design in the center, similar to the types worn on British naval uniforms of the early nineteenth century. It lacks the crown and oval that were standard on many Royal Navy buttons, however, and has no maker's mark or name to indicate its origin. There is, unfortunately, a great deal of uncertainty surrounding early naval buttons, especially those worn by lower-ranking officers. The design on this button does not match any found in the reference works consulted, and the possibility exists that it was a Provincial Marine or US Navy pattern. Since *Linnet* was in active service much longer as a British warship than as a US warship, there seems a greater likelihood of it being from a Royal Navy or Marine uniform.

The artifacts recovered during the 1995 archaeological excavation add little to the story of the brig *Linnet*. Items like the button and cockscrew provide only tantalizing hints about crew uniforms and weapons they carried. The lead and iron shot represent typical munitions of the period. The variety of cast-iron shot carried as ballast, as well as the split mortar and the trunnionless cannon, together suggest that for the Royal Navy on Lake Champlain, ballast consisted of whatever scrap iron lay at hand.

Conclusions

Despite *Linnet*'s reduction by decay, salvage, and artifact removal, the combined archaeological and historical study of the wreck has yielded insights into the naval war on Lake Champlain in 1814. First, it is noteworthy that while Pring originally pushed for a 110-foot (33.5 m) vessel mounting heavy 24- and 32-pounder guns, *Linnet* was only 85 feet (25.9 m) in length and mounted long 12 pounders. Why was the brig reduced in size? Timber was available (if not always of the best quality), so that was probably not a limiting factor. The reduction may reflect a cost-saving measure on the part of a government that was already pouring vast sums into the naval race on Lake Ontario. Or perhaps Simons and Pring just concluded that this was a better size of vessel to build, man, and outfit under the circumstances. When the brig's contract was prepared in November of 1813, the US Navy's plans for shipbuilding that winter were unknown to the British. If Macdonough had chosen not to match the Royal Navy's construction efforts, then *Linnet*'s 85-foot hull and sixteen 12-pounder cannon would have easily ruled the lake in 1814.

The vessel's shape provides some new information about Royal Navy shipbuilding on the lakes. The hypothetical lines, based on a combination of archaeological data and the 1815 Admiralty draft, suggest a shallow, beamy vessel, with nearly flat floors amidships. The limitations imposed by the constricted, sometimes shallow navigational conditions on the Richelieu River and Lake Champlain are plainly evident in the design. Macdonough's favorable comment about the brig and *Linnet*'s ability to reach its assigned position in the Battle of Plattsburgh Bay (when other British warships failed to do so) indicate that the vessel handled reasonably well under sail and otherwise had what naval officers looked for in a ship.

The similarity in dimensions between *Linnet* and the 1815 Admiralty plan for Lake Champlain brigs suggests that the ship designer may have used information about the former to prepare the lines of the latter, although the 1815 draft was intended to produce a vessel slightly beamier and with more deadrise in the floors. The fact that the Royal Navy planned to build more warships of this type on Lake Champlain also tells us that *Linnet* must have met the expectations of its builders and combined good sailing qualities, cheap and easy construction, and a draft shallow enough to allow navigation on much of the lake. The 1815 design, incidentally, was intended to mount ten 24 pounders instead of the sixteen 12 pounders *Linnet* carried, since the larger guns packed a bigger punch in terms of broadside weight. The naval race on the inland lakes had made 12-pounder cannon inadequate as armament on larger warships by 1814.

The abandoned ships in the Poultney fascinated the people of Whitehall and surrounding communities, generating folklore about the origins of the wrecks and inspiring efforts to retrieve relics of the lake's past. The botched salvage effort of 1949, misguided and unethical by today's standards, brought *Linnet*'s story into the mid-twentieth century. Even at that time, not everyone thought that the salvage was a good idea, and at least one reporter complained of the "casual attitude towards these priceless boats."[65] Time moves on, attitudes and methods change, and as archaeologists and historians of the early twenty-first century, we have been given the challenge—and the opportunity—of trying to reassemble the pieces of a damaged and scattered puzzle as best we can. The evidence and the tools at hand allow us only a glimpse of the British brig, distant and unfocused, as it took shape on the stocks at Isle aux Noix and sailed into action at Plattsburgh Bay. Our archaeological quest for answers has answered some questions and generated new ones, as archaeological quests are prone to do.

NOTES

1. Tony Galick, interview with author, August 1995.

2. "Many Visitors Attracted Here by 1777 Relics," *Whitehall* (NY) *Times,* October 20, 1949, p. 1. Copies of this newspaper may be found in the Whitehall Public Library, Whitehall, NY.

3. Russell P. Bellico, *Sails and Steam in the Mountains: A Maritime and Military History of Lake George and Lake Champlain* (Fleischmanns, NY: Purple Mountain Press, 1992), p. 234.

4. "First US Fleet—in Conflict 177 Years Later," *Whitehall* (NY) *Times,* September 24, 1953.

5. "Recent Accessions," *The Bulletin of the Fort Ticonderoga Museum* 8, no. 7 (1951), p. 327; the mortar has an interesting story. Evidence suggests that it was left at Fort Ticonderoga after the French and Indian War, taken to Boston by Henry Knox, Washington's commander of artillery during the American Revolution, and then returned to the fort in the spring of 1776. The mortar split during test firing in 1776 and was placed in an American gunboat as ballast. The gunboat was subsequently captured by the British, who kept the mortar until it was used again as ballast aboard *Linnet.* See "An Historic Mortar," *The Bulletin of the Fort Ticonderoga Museum* 10, no. 4 (February 1960), pp. 299–303.

6. "Many Visitors Attracted Here," *Whitehall* (NY) *Times,* October 20, 1949; William Galick, interview with author, August 1995.

7. E. A. Cruikshank, "From Isle-aux-Noix to Chateauguay: A Study of the Military Operations on the Frontiers of Lower Canada in 1812 and 1813" in *Transactions of the Royal Society of Canada,* series 3, vol. 7 (Ottawa: Royal Society of Canada, 1913), p. 147; quoted in Thomas Hooper, "The Royal Navy Station at Isle aux Noix (1812–1839)" in *Miscellaneous Historical Reports (1965– 70)* (manuscript record no. 167, Ottawa: Parks Canada, 1967), p. 51; Dennis M. Lewis, *British Naval Activity on Lake Champlain During the War of 1812* (Plattsburgh, NY: Clinton County Historical Association, 1994), p. 2.

8. Macdonough to Secretary of the Navy Hamilton, October 26, 1812, in William S. Dudley, ed., *The Naval War of 1812: A Documentary History,* vol. 1 (Washington, DC: Naval Historical Center, 1985), pp. 325–27.

9. Sir John Warren to Sir George Prevost, May 5, 1813, vol. 1222, p. 326, record group 8 (RG 8), Library and Archives Canada (LAC). Prevost requested that Pring be given his captain's epaulets, but on November 13, 1813, the Admiralty promoted him to

the lesser rank of commander. Pring is referred to as "captain" in most sources and throughout this chapter, although he did not receive his captain's commission until 1815. Prevost to Bathurst, July 18, 1813, Colonial Office and Predecessors: CO 42/151, pp. 69–72, The National Archives of the UK (TNA): Public Record Office (PRO); David Syrett and R. L. Dinardo, ed., *The Commissioned Sea Officers of the Royal Navy, 1660–1815* (Aldershot: Scolar Press and Naval Records Society, 1994), p. 367.

10. Sheaffe to Prevost, July 29, 1813, vol. 1221, p. 111, RG 8, LAC.

11. Sheaffe to Prevost, August 5, 1813, vol. 679, pt. 1, p. 339, RG 8, LAC.

12. Sheaffe to Freer, August 8, 1813, vol. 679, pt. 1, pp. 360–62, RG 8, LAC.

13. Freer to Sheaffe, August 8, 1813, vol. 1221, pp. 32–33, RG 8, LAC.

14. Sheaffe to Freer, August 17, 1813, vol. 679, pt. 1, p. 466, RG 8, LAC.

15. Pring to Prevost, October 10, 1813, vol. 731, p. 12, RG 8, LAC.

16. Pring to Freer, October 18, 1813, vol. 731, p. 52, RG 8, LAC.

17. Freer to Pring, October 19, 1813, vol. 1221, p. 200, RG 8, LAC.

18. Pring to Freer, November 8, 1813, vol. 731, p. 109, RG 8, LAC.

19. Simons to Pring, November 7, 1813, vol. 731, p. 110, RG 8, LAC.

20. Pring to Freer, December 1, 1813, vol. 731, p. 155, RG 8, LAC.

21. Hooper, *Royal Navy Station,* p. 62.

22. Lewis, "British Naval Activity," pp. 17–18.

23. Admiralty to the Earl of Mulgrave, January 22, 1814, Ordnance Office and War Office Correspondence: WO 44/250, pp. 55–56, TNA: PRO.

24. Richard O'Conor, Acting Commissioner, "A Statement of His Majesty's Naval Force on Lake Champlain," January 26, 1814, CO 42/156, p. 99, TNA: PRO.

25. Richard O'Conor, Acting Commissioner, "A Statement of His Majesty's Naval Force on Lake Champlain," January 26, 1814, CO 42/156, p. 99, TNA: PRO; Prevost to Bathurst, September 11, 1814, CO 42/157, pp. 187–89, TNA: PRO.

26. William Wood, ed., *Select British Documents of the Canadian War of 1812,* vol. 3, pt. 1 (Toronto: The Champlain Society, 1926), p. 476; Lewis, "British Naval Activity," p. 18; Oscar Bredenberg, *The Battle of Plattsburgh Bay; The British Navy's View* (Plattsburgh, NY: Clinton County Historical Association, 1978), p. 21.

27. Pring to Freer, April 27, 1814, vol. 732, pp. 156–57, RG 8, LAC.

28. Baynes to Rowan, May 6, 1814, vol. 1171, p. 264, RG 8, LAC.

29. Pring to Yeo, May 14, 1814, vol. 683, pp. 160–63, RG 8, LAC; Lewis, "British Naval Activity," pp. 20–21.

30. Hooper, *Royal Navy Station,* p. 66; Syrett and Dinardo, *Commissioned Sea Officers,* p. 156. Frigates had to be commanded

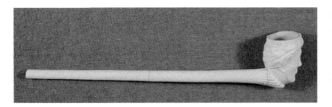

A clay smoking pipe found in the bilges of Allen. The bowl of the pipe was molded in the shape of a bearded man with a turban on his head. The rim around the top of the pipe bowl has raised letters reading "United States of America," indicating that the pipe was probably of domestic manufacture. The pipe appeared to be practically unused but was recovered in three pieces. (Photo courtesy of the Lake Champlain Maritime Museum.)

Amphibious archaeology: three divers working on Linnet in 1995. Sometime after the salvage of the hull in 1949, Linnet slipped back under the river with a pronounced list to its port side. During periods of low water the broken-off ends of its starboard floor timbers were visible at or above the surface of the water. Here Erich Heinold (background), Kevin J. Crisman, and Rob Wilczynski (foreground) excavate and record in the zone halfway between air and water. The visibility was poor, especially when the dredge was running, but the shallow water permitted very lengthy dives. (Photo by Pierre Larocque, Linnet project files of Erika Washburn.)

Eagle under sail. Eagle's logbook tells us that on Sunday, September 4 at 1:30 p.m., the crew weighed anchor and got underway "to try the brig's sailing." Despite deteriorating weather that was "squally with some rain," Eagle did not return to anchor until 5:30 p.m. In this conjectural painting by Peter Rindlisbacher, Eagle sails east into the open lake. The anchored US squadron can be seen in the distance on the right: the sloop Preble, the schooner Ticonderoga, and the flagship Saratoga. The Battle of Lake Champlain will take place at this location in one week. (Courtesy of the artist and Kevin J. Crisman.)

Macdonough's Victory on Lake Champlain. First issued in 1816, this popular depiction was engraved by Benjamin Tanner, who based his work on a painting by Hugh Reinagle. The relative positions of the five large ships are correct, but the artists followed the standard convention of showing the vessels farther inside the bay and in closer proximity than they were during the battle. The US gunboats, shown in a column here, were actually arrayed in a line abreast behind the US ships. Tanner's engraving and others like it reminded Americans of the triumphs attained by their small, inexperienced navy. (Courtesy of the New York Historical Society, image 1925.135.)

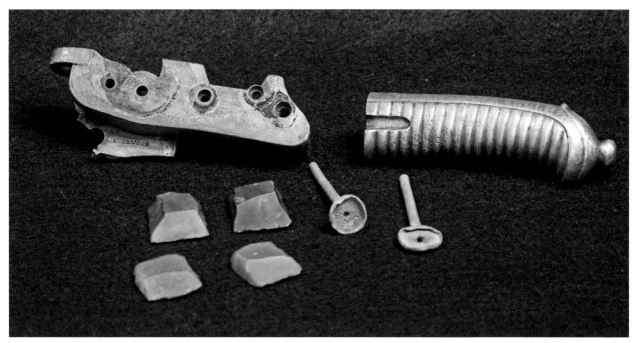

Battle debris from Plattsburgh Bay: weaponry-related finds. This sample of ordnance and weapon-related artifacts found by William Leege and the LCAA includes a brass cannon lock made by "Sherwood," a brass sword or dagger grip, two lead cannon primers, and four gunflints. (Photo by Thomas Larsen, courtesy of the Lake Champlain Maritime Museum.)

Battle debris from Plattsburgh Bay: glass and ceramic containers. This small representative sample of containers for storing and consuming food and beverages includes two intact bottles, a wine goblet, a salt or pepper shaker, a hand-painted bowl, and a small undecorated pitcher. The great quantities of glass and ceramics recovered by William Leege and the LCAA indicate that crew quarters suffered widespread shot damage. In contrast to deep-drafted seagoing warships, the below-deck spaces on the shallow lake vessels offered scant protection to people or objects during the fighting. (Photo by Thomas Larsen, courtesy of the Lake Champlain Maritime Museum.)

Plattsburgh Bay Anchor No. 2 during its recovery from the lake in September 1998. The overall excellent condition of the anchor after 184 years on the bottom can be seen in this photograph. Portions of the anchor that were buried beneath the silt appeared nearly unchanged from the day it was lost in the lake. (Photo courtesy of the Lake Champlain Maritime Museum.)

by a post captain, hence the Royal Navy sent Fisher to replace Pring as the senior officer at Isle aux Noix. Fisher received his captain's commission on February 19, 1814.

31. Lewis, "British Naval Activity," p. 29. Fisher left the Lake Champlain station after Capt. George Downie assumed overall command.

32. Hooper, *Royal Navy Station,* p. 65.

33. Prevost to Bathurst, August 15, 1814, CO 42/157, p. 142, TNA: PRO; Prevost to Yeo, August 19, 1814, vol. 1225, pp. 21–22, RG 8, LAC.

34. Hooper, *Royal Navy Station,* pp. 64–65; Lewis, "British Naval Activity," p. 29.

35. Allan S. Everest, *The War of 1812 in the Champlain Valley* (Syracuse, NY: Syracuse University Press, 1981), p. 205; Wood, ed., *Select British Documents,* vol. 3, pt. 1, p. 476.

36. Everest, *War of 1812,* p. 205. This source erroneously lists the broadside in tons.

37. Wood, ed., *Select British Documents,* vol. 3, pt. 1, p. 381.

38. Downie to Prevost, September 8, 1814, CO 42/158, p. 204, TNA: PRO.

39. Wood, ed., *Select British Documents,* vol. 3, pt. 1, pp. 368–73, 412–13.

40. Kevin J. Crisman, *The Eagle: An American Brig on Lake Champlain During the War of 1812* (Shelburne, VT: New England Press; Annapolis: Naval Institute Press, 1987), p. 70. There is a time discrepancy of one hour between British and American accounts of the battle, with British reports being one hour earlier. For consistency, the times in this chapter are based on the American battle reports.

41. Crisman, *The* Eagle, p. 70.

42. Wood, ed., *Select British Documents,* vol. 3, pt. 1, pp. 429–32.

43. Pring to Yeo, September 12, 1814, CO 42/157, pp. 214–22, TNA: PRO; Robertson to Pring, September 15, 1814, CO 42/157, pp. 223–27, TNA: PRO.

44. Everest, *War of 1812,* p. 184; Crisman, *The* Eagle, p. 77.

45. Pring to Yeo, September 12, 1814, CO 42/158, pp. 214–22, TNA: PRO.

46. "The Renfrew Exhibits," Glasgow International Exhibition, 1896, vol. 733, p. 35a, RG 8, LAC; L. A. Ritchie, ed., *The Shipbuilding Industry: A Guide to Historical Records* (Manchester: Manchester University Press, 1992), p. 142; "Relics of the Confiance: Valuable Collection in Private Hands," *The New York Times,* June 26, 1887.

47. Wood, ed., *Select British Documents,* vol. 3, pt. 1, pp. 458–59.

48. Wood, ed., *Select British Documents,* vol. 3, pt. 1, p. 437.

49. George Prevost, of course, blamed the navy's defeat for the failure of the land offensive. He died shortly before the commencement of an inquiry into his conduct. Yeo to Prevost, November 26, 1814, CO 42/157, p. 416, TNA: PRO; Wood, ed., *Select British Documents,* vol. 3, pt. 1, pp. 458–59.

50. Pring to Yeo, September 12, 1814, CO 42/158, pp. 214–22, TNA: PRO.

51. Sailing Master P. Brum, "Inventory of the Armament and Stores of the Prize Brig *Linnet* captured on the 11th September 1814," November 21, 1814, entry 110, Naval Records Collection of the Office of Naval Records and Library, record group 45 (RG), National Archives and Records Administration (NARA). Courtesy of Dennis M. Lewis.

52. "The valuation of vessels & armament," April 8, 1815, entry 110, RG 45, NARA. Courtesy of Dennis M. Lewis.

53. Roll 43, no. 38, entry 125, RG 45, NARA.

54. Roll 43, no. 42, RG 45, NARA. Some of these cannon and shot loaded as ballast were apparently left in *Linnet* and were part of the materials salvaged and sold in 1949.

55. Entry 220, vol. 1, RG 45, NARA.

56. Roll 64, no. 170, entry 125, RG 45, NARA.

57. Crisman, *The* Eagle, pp. 146–47; Kevin Crisman, *The History and Construction of the United States Schooner* Ticonderoga (Alexandria, VA: Eyrie Publications, 1983), pp. 55–56; Eric B. Emery, interview with author, August 1995; Kevin Crisman, "The *Jefferson*: The History and Archaeology of an American Brig from the War of 1812" (PhD diss., University of Pennsylvania, 1989), pp. 288–89; Erich M. Heinold, interview with author, September 1997; Crisman, interview with author, March 1998; Christopher Sabick, interview with author, September 1997.

58. "The Renfrew Exhibits," Glasgow International Exhibition, 1896, vol. 733, p. 35a, RG 8, LAC; Alastair Smith (Curator, Museum of Transport, Glasgow, Scotland), interview with author, March 5, 1997.

59. J. J. Colledge, *Ships of the Royal Navy: The Complete Record of All Fighting Ships of the Royal Navy from the Fifteenth Century to the Present* (Annapolis: Naval Institute Press, 1987), p. 202; David Lyon, *The Sailing List: All the Ships of the Royal Navy—Built, Purchased, and Captured, 1688–1860* (London: Conway Maritime Press, 1993), pp. 182, 298. Although Colledge lists nine other *Linnets* in addition to the 1814 brig, none of these are possibilities for the model because they either postdate it or have the wrong dimensions. Colledge also describes *Linnet* as ex-*Growler,* but as Lyons states, this is most likely a different vessel in service in 1830. The model identified as *Confiance* in the Glasgow Museum of Transport is also too deep to be an accurate representation of the Lake Champlain frigate.

60. Register of US Naval Vessels 1797–1814, entry 169, RG 45, NARA; Richard O'Conor, Acting Commissioner, "A Statement of His Majesty's Naval Force on Lake Champlain," January 26, 1814, CO 42/156, p. 99, TNA: PRO.

61. Howard I. Chapelle, *The History of the American Sailing Navy* (New York: W. W. Norton, 1949), pp. 270–72.

62. June 24, 1815. ADM 106/1997, TNA: PRO.

63. Crisman, *The* Eagle, p. 216.

64. Anthony D. Darling, *Red Coat and Brown Bess* (Ottawa: Museum Restoration Service, 1971), p. 40.

65. Barnett Fowler, "Benedict Arnold's Warships Rot in Champlain," *The Pictorial Review* (January 25, 1953).

12 "IT HAS AGAIN BECOME NECESSARY TO ADD TO OUR FORCE ON LAKE CHAMPLAIN"

The US Navy Brig *Eagle*

KEVIN J. CRISMAN

Introduction

This story starts with my first dive on a large, unidentified wreck sunk in the Poultney River near Whitehall, New York, in the summer of 1981. Seen from up close in the brownish murk—and up close was the only way to see anything—the mysterious hull was a confusing obstacle course of eroded frames, jutting plank ends, and rusty spike points. Beavers living in a nearby lodge had stuffed scores of ready-to-eat branches under the keelson, and these poked out at all angles, ready to spear the unwary diver. The fine silt that covered the timbers swirled up with the slightest movement, turning turbid water opaque. Our goal on this dive was to figure out what ship we had found, and so, starting at the sternpost and moving forward, we extended a measuring tape along the centerline of the ship. When the reel reached the curving timbers of the stem, the tape read 115 feet (35.05 m). It was one of those "ah hah," light-bulb-above-your-head moments that occasionally happen in archaeology: a wreck of this length, in this location, with a row of gunports along its top side, could only be the long-lost US Navy brig *Eagle.*

It was a far greater find than we knew at the time, for of the many warships built on the North American lakes during the War of 1812, *Eagle* has what may be the most dramatic and peculiar story of all. Its building and service were surrounded by high anxiety and national peril, controversy, presidential intervention, superhuman efforts in the shipyard, heroism under fire, and charges of incompetent leadership. Completed and outfitted just in time to fight in one of the great naval battles of US history, the brig's cannon were manned by an odd mix of man-of-war sailors, convicts from a chain gang, and band musicians. And *Eagle*'s story has its poignant moments: in the midst of the battle, the young wife of a US Army band musician rushed gunpowder to the cannon only to discover, along the way, that she had become a widow.

The vessel's archaeological story would prove as interesting as its history. A product of the famed Brown brothers of New York, the hull would demonstrate the creative approaches to building that allowed the lake warships to be completed in a matter of weeks. Of the War of 1812's many shipbuilding races, *Eagle*'s construction takes the prize for brevity: only nineteen days elapsed between the laying of the keel and the launching of the ship.

Eagle's history and the secrets of its construction were largely unknown to us on the July afternoon in 1981 when we first identified the wreck in the Poultney River. My colleague Arthur Cohn and I nevertheless knew that we had made an extraordinary find. Much of the hull was preserved, perhaps as much as half of the ship, and we knew that with persistence we could recover architectural details from beneath the muddy river and historical details from libraries and archives. Miraculously spared from the salvage efforts that damaged so many 1812-era shipwrecks, *Eagle* survived to tell us the story of shipwrights and sailors who came to their country's aid during a crucial hour in North American history.

"Engage Mr. Brown to Proceed Instantly to the Lake"

On May 26, 1814, the newly completed US Navy warships of Comm. Thomas Macdonough emerged from Otter Creek onto the waters of Lake Champlain, unfurled their sails, and turned northward. Together they comprised a far-stronger squadron than the ill-assorted flotilla of armed merchant sloops and gunboats that had entered the creek six months earlier. Thanks to the efforts of shipwright Noah Brown and his carpenters, Macdonough now commanded the 26-gun flagship *Saratoga*, the 17-gun schooner *Ticonderoga*, and six new row galleys, making a more formidable force than the squadron the Royal Navy had managed to assemble over the winter of 1814. Macdonough was confident of his ability to repel any British attack, informing Secretary of the Navy William Jones on May 29, "There is now a free communication between all parts of the lake—and at present there is no doubt of this communication being interrupted by the enemy."[1] US superiority on Lake Champlain was ensured by a fast and well-executed, albeit expensive, program of naval construction.

Secretary Jones had good reason to be pleased with the state of affairs on Lake Champlain in the spring of 1814, for it was one of the few bright spots in the otherwise dismal situation that beset the US Navy. With Napoleon defeated on the European continent, the British were now free to bring their immense military and naval strength to bear on the US war. The consequences of their new resources and resolve were being felt on the high seas, along the Eastern Seaboard of the United States, and on the Canadian border. Noah Brown's work at Vergennes, Vermont, had been costly, but Jones had the satisfaction of reporting to President James Madison, "I do not anticipate anything to disturb our complete control on Lake Champlain . . . indeed there is good reason to believe the enemy will not venture on the lake."[2]

As it turned out, William Jones' prediction was premature. Far from remaining a relatively quiet backwater of the conflict, Lake Champlain was about to experience the greatest British offensive of the war. The first intimations of the coming storm reached Macdonough in early June when his network of spies brought word that "the enemy are again building with dispatch and determination to have the ascendancy on the lake."[3] The earliest reports were vague, but confirmation came on June 11 when four deserting British sailors told of a 32-gun frigate under construction at Isle aux Noix, as well as the transfer of gunboats from the St. Lawrence River flotilla to the lake. Macdonough saw three options for dealing with this unexpected threat: fortify the outlet of the lake with batteries of heavy cannon, build more row galleys, or build one schooner or brig of 18 guns. Whichever choice the navy made, Macdonough warned Jones, "I am sure that [the enemy] intends risquing nothing, but will endeavor to out build us, and there is no knowing where his building may stop, for . . . there is a probability of his not meeting us unless he is pretty confident of being successful."[4]

This was the worst possible news for hard-pressed Secretary Jones. The US Navy had already committed itself to an enormously expensive shipbuilding race on Lake Ontario—Isaac Chauncey was then launching his second large frigate—and the government was simply running out of money and credit to pay for new ships. There was no system of forced conscription, and manning ships was becoming increasingly difficult. Perhaps worst of all, the American seaboard and its cities were now being subjected to frequent and destructive British raids that the US Navy was nearly powerless to resist.

William Jones was beginning to believe that matching the British ship for ship on the lakes was a strategic mistake. "Have we adequate object in that quarter for all this hazard and expenditure of blood & treasure?" he queried Madison. "Is one fourth of our naval force employed for the defense of a wilderness, while our Atlantic frontier, our flourishing cities, towns, and villages, cultivated farms, rising manufactories, public works & edifices are deprived of the services and protection of this valuable body of men?"[5] The shipbuilding mania on the northern frontier had to stop somewhere, and William Jones saw this as the time and the place to put his foot down. In mid-June he gave Secretary of War John Armstrong "an explicit declaration that he would not add to the naval means on Lake Champlain."[6] Thomas Macdonough would have to fight the British with his existing squadron, whatever the consequences.

President Madison was all too aware of the scarcity of money, men, and equipment that plagued his government's efforts to fight this war. However, he also foresaw disastrous results, both military and political, if US defenses on Lake Champlain folded up before a British attack. Too much had already been invested in building up Macdonough's squadron to now leave it at the mercy of a superior foe. Madison stepped in, for the first and apparently only time during the War of 1812, to reverse one of William Jones's policy decisions: the brig that Macdonough requested would be built, and as soon as possible.[7]

Jones was unenthusiastic about the president's decree (he later wrote Madison, "I almost regret commencing the new ship at Vergennes—God knows where the money is to come from!"), but he dutifully issued instructions for building and outfitting this addition to the Champlain squadron.[8] To John Bullus, the navy's agent in New York, he wrote on July 5:

> It has again become necessary to add to our force on Lake Champlain a brig of 18 guns for which purpose you will engage Mr Brown to proceed instantly to the lake and after consulting with Captain Macdonough commence and complete the work with the celerity which has heretofore acquired him so much reputation.[9]

At the same time Jones sent instructions directly to Adam and Noah Brown and to Macdonough, informing them that they were to proceed with construction at the Vergennes shipyard.

If his correspondence is any indication, Macdonough was close to despair by the middle of July. Despite his many letters to the Navy Department requesting permission to build, there had been no orders to proceed with the work and time was rapidly running out.[10] With each passing day, the possibility of assembling, outfitting, and manning an additional vessel seemed increasingly doubtful.

Macdonough was still awaiting word from Washington on July 18 when a boat pulled alongside *Saratoga* and Noah Brown's younger brother Adam climbed aboard, announcing that he was there to build the Lake Champlain squadron a new brig. We can be certain that he was a welcome sight. The Browns knew just how little time Adam had to complete the job, and within twenty-four hours of receiving Secretary Jones' orders at their New York City shipyard, they enlisted 200 shipwrights and laborers, collected all necessary tools, and embarked the entire contingent on a Hudson River steamboat bound for Albany. During their brief meeting on *Saratoga* the shipwright and the commodore settled on the dimensions and armament of the brig, and Adam Brown then departed for Vergennes.[11]

Brown and his carpenters spent four days gathering materials (the navy still had timber stored at Vergennes from the earlier building effort), contracting for nails, spikes, bolts, and other hardware from the nearby Monkton Iron Works and preparing a set of ways to support the hull as it took shape on the bank of the Otter Creek. On July 23, they scarfed three timbers end to end to form the brig's keel. Oaken posts were bolted to either end, defining the overall length of the hull, and the shipwrights then began the laborious job of shaping and assembling the square and half frames that constituted the sides of the vessel. They worked fast, employing shortcuts in materials and assembly techniques wherever possible.

As Adam Brown and his shipwrights worked to complete the hull at Vergennes, other individuals—navy agents, sailors, sailmakers, gunsmiths, and shippers—labored to manufacture or purchase, pack, and ship the mass of equipment needed to sail and fight a wooden warship. The weightiest of these were the cannon. Macdonough first proposed arming the vessel with eighteen long 18 pounders, guns that he felt would be effective for engaging the British gunboats at a distance. There was a limited number of long 18 pounders in New York, however, so the armament sent north was a mix of eight long 18 pounders and twelve 32-pounder carronades, a total of twenty guns.[12] These guns could discharge 264 pounds (119.75 kg) of iron shot in a single broadside, a respectable weight of iron for a brig of this class.

Other items shipped to the lake included anchors and cables, coils of rigging and barrels of cordage and blocks, boxes of ironwork for the gun carriages, and a case of brass gunlocks recently manufactured by New York gunsmith Enoch Hidden. The iron cook stove or camboose on the captured British sloop of war *Alert* was removed for use on the new brig. Navy Agent Bullus received a list of spar dimensions from the Brown brothers, and sailmakers were soon at work cutting and stitching canvas into a suit of sails. By the beginning of August, most of this equipment was on its way northward in the holds of sloops and steamboats.[13]

The brig also needed a crew, which proved far more difficult to obtain on short notice than cannon, sails, or a camboose. Macdonough was already short of hands in his squadron and had no illusions about the problems he faced manning the new warship. He immediately dispatched an officer to Newport, Rhode Island, to open a "rendezvous" for enlisting sailors, while his recruiters at New York and Boston were instructed to start signing up men for this ship as well. Macdonough was also desperately short of officers and begged William Jones to send five more: a master commandant to command the new warship, two lieutenants, a sailing master, and a surgeon. The choice of commanders was critical, since much of the outfitting would take place at Vergennes, far from the commodore's oversight. The brig's captain was also expected to turn newly enlisted sailors into an effective crew within a matter of days, a daunting task. Macdonough specifically asked for John Orde Creighton, an experienced acquaintance, but Jones instead sent him Robert Henley (fig. 12.1).[14]

The 32-year-old Henley would prove to be, in Macdonough's eyes, a singularly poor choice. Henley's start in the service had been promising: a midshipman's

ROBERT HENLEY.

Figure 12.1. *Mstr. Cmdt. Robert Henley, commander of the US brig* Eagle. *It is abundantly clear from official reports and correspondence that the independently minded Henley and Commodore Macdonough were never on good terms. Henley would remain on Lake Champlain for only one month in the late summer and early fall of 1814. (From Charles J. Peterson, The American Navy, p. 476.)*

warrant in 1799 at the age of sixteen and six years of service with distinction in the Quasi-War and Tripolitan conflict, where he earned the praise of his commanding officers. He was promoted to lieutenant in early 1807 and ordered to the naval station at Norfolk, Virginia. Here he entered a seven-year period of relative inactivity. "My health & *constitution* were seriously impaired," he later claimed, infirmities that apparently kept him from sea duty. The commanding officer at Norfolk, Capt. John Cassin, hinted that Henley's problem was something other than poor health, informing the navy secretary in 1812, "Mr. H. perhaps would suit better elsewhere. I would prefer a more active officer." Predictably, when William Jones selected fifteen senior lieutenants for promotion to the highly coveted rank of master commandant in July of 1813, Henley's name was not on the list and several officers of lesser seniority were promoted above him.[15]

Henley saw this, correctly, as a reflection of how the Navy Department perceived his merits as an officer and complained to Jones of "the painfulness and delicacy of my situation . . . laboring under the implication that I was unworthy of the rank which I held." Jones was willing to listen, and at a meeting between the two in early 1814, he agreed to reconsider a promotion. Jones also offered the 13-gun schooner *Nonsuch* as a sop to the lieutenant's wounded pride, but Henley turned it down, insisting that he was "deserving of a better command." He subsequently enlisted two powerful allies, Capt. Oliver Hazard Perry and Capt. David Porter, to speak to the secretary on his behalf. Pestered by Henley and his influential friends, William Jones finally promoted Henley to master commandant on August 12 and ordered him north to take command of a warship the secretary had never wanted to build in the first place.[16]

Henley proceeded directly to Lake Champlain, arriving at Vergennes on August 19, where he found the new vessel already in the water and men at work on the masts, spars, and rigging. Adam Brown had launched the hull on August 11, four days ahead of his own schedule and only nineteen days after laying down the keel; it was, as Henley reported to Jones, an "astonishingly short period" for building a warship. A total of fifty-two sailors were at Vergennes, and only the sails were needed for the vessel to depart for the northern end of the lake. Inspired by Brown's fast work, Henley suggested to the secretary that the brig be named *Surprise*.[17]

Henley's August 19 letter to William Jones displayed a notable lack of perception—or was it unwillingness to accept a subordinate role? *Surprise* and its crew were not sailing independently; they were part of a naval squadron commanded by Thomas Macdonough, and once he joined the ship, Henley's correspondence should have been directed to the commodore rather than the Navy Department. Furthermore, *Surprise* was built at the behest of Macdonough, the senior officer on Lake Champlain, and the prerogative of selecting a name belonged to him. In fact, the commodore had long since sent his choice of names to Washington for Jones's endorsement: he wanted the brig to be called *Eagle*. Macdonough expected deference on the part of his subordinates, and thus he and Henley were set on a collision course even before *Surprise-Eagle* entered the lake.

The brig *was* a remarkable achievement. The construction may have been fast, but it was nevertheless substantial, with frames and planking of ample thickness. There were eleven ports on a side for the twenty cannon, an armament that classed the brig as a "sloop of war." With its masts rigged and cannon mounted on their new carriages, *Surprise-Eagle* was nearly ready to quit the Otter Creek. The crew took in iron ore to serve as ballast on August 24, received the new sails and *Alert*'s camboose the next day, and on August 26 bent on the sails and stood down the lake for the Canadian border. Adam Brown and his weary carpenters, their part in the naval race completed, gathered their tools and started back to New York.

"They Continued Undaunted and Unshaken"

Surprise-Eagle joined the US squadron early on August 27. Macdonough was surely relieved to see his new brig, but it was far from ready to meet the British. The fifty-two sailors taken on at Vergennes were less than one-half of the number needed to effectively work the guns in action. More men were expected from the coast, but when they would arrive was anybody's guess. Besides Henley, no other commissioned officers had been sent to serve on the brig, and it was necessary to transfer officers from other ships or temporarily promote warrant officers to fill vacant positions. And then there was the minor but irritating question of the vessel's name. Was it *Surprise* or *Eagle*? Macdonough temporarily side-stepped the issue while he took the measure of Henley, reporting to Jones only that "the US Brig lately built at Vergennes" had arrived.[18]

Henley desperately needed lieutenants, and Macdonough provided him with two: Joseph Smith, *Saratoga*'s second lieutenant, and William Augustus Spencer, a midshipman serving as "acting lieutenant." Smith, twenty-four years of age, was assigned to Lake Champlain in 1812 and promoted to lieutenant in 1813; he knew how to outfit a ship and train its crew, and his services would prove indispensable on the brig. Twenty-one-year-old Spencer joined the squadron in the spring of 1814 but had failed to meet the commodore's high standards; Macdonough thought him "not much of a seaman" and noted—derisively—that Spencer's handsome appearance was probably his best attribute as a naval officer. The brig's other officers included Daniel Records, who was appointed acting sailing master at Vergennes, and Isaac Stoddard, an army doctor loaned to the Lake Champlain squadron in June. Three inexperienced midshipmen were assigned to the brig: William McChesney's warrant was dated 1811, while Henry Tardy and William Chamberlain had only joined the service the previous November. Chamberlain was debilitated and bedridden by the early stages of consumption.[19]

According to Lieutenant Smith, the new brig required a good deal of preparation: "I worked hard, fitting rigging and sails, working early and late—frequently with palm and needle myself—until she was tolerably well fitted out." At Smith's urging, Macdonough transferred forty of *Saratoga*'s sailors to the brig, twenty of them chosen by Smith (who selected the best) and twenty by *Saratoga*'s first lieutenant (who culled out the worst). "Still," Smith lamented, "there were not enough to work the guns properly."[20] Time was running out—the British Army crossed the border into New York on August 31, and the Royal Navy would not be far behind.

Surprise-Eagle had been with the squadron only four days when Macdonough withdrew his warships from the border to a position 20 miles (32 km) to the south, in Plattsburgh Bay, New York (plate 10a). The brig lost a sailor on the passage south when seaman James Willis fell from the main topsail yard, struck the deck, and died three hours later; five other sailors suffering from various illnesses were sent ashore to the hospital. These losses were made good with a draft of five convalescents from the hospital, with sixteen sailors from the armed sloop *Montgomery* and twenty-one US Army soldiers commanded by Lt. Joseph Morrison of the 33rd Infantry Regiment. Still more sailors were found for the shorthanded brig when Lieutenant Smith requisitioned forty convicts from an army chain gang: "They were all at work with ball and chain, digging trenches . . . I told them I had come to take them to the *Eagle* to fight. The prisoners were delighted at the prospect. I stationed them at the guns and drilled them morning and night until the fight came off." Slightly later, on the eve of the battle, the brig received its final reinforcements: six US Army band musicians, one of whom, Pvt. James M. Hale, brought his 22-year-old wife Abigail on board with him.[21]

Robert Henley's lack of recent sea service showed in this period of outfitting. Macdonough later wrote, "I look upon him to be very deficient in seamanship and in the equipment of a vessel of war he is a stranger."

Macdonough acted at this time to quash Henley's independent streak; we do not know exactly how he went about it, but the results are apparent in the historical record. Henley's direct correspondence with the Navy Department stopped abruptly after September 1, and on September 6 the name of the brig changed in the log book from *Surprise* to Macdonough's original choice of *Eagle*.[22]

On the morning of September 11, exactly one month after its launch and two weeks after joining the squadron, *Eagle* was anchored with springs on its cable at the head of a line of US ships inside Plattsburgh Bay. Astern of *Eagle* was *Saratoga,* then *Ticonderoga,* and finally the little sloop *Preble*; the ten US gunboats were arrayed on the landward side of these vessels. According to *Eagle*'s log, the imminent arrival of the British squadron was signaled by a picket boat at 7 a.m.; Henley ordered the crew to beat to quarters and the guns were loaded and run out.

Fights between sailing warships were slow-motion affairs, and there was often a long wait between the first sighting of the enemy and the beginning of the shooting. In this case two hours elapsed while the British commodore reconnoitered the US line in a small boat and issued instructions to his commanders. At 9 a.m. the Royal Navy ships finally rounded the point of Cumberland Head. As they slowly approached, Henley ordered *Eagle*'s long 18 pounders to open fire, the first US guns to do so. Once again, the inexperience showed: the range was too great, and the shot merely threw up sprays of water well short of their intended targets.

By 9:40 a.m. the British ships had closed the distance and were within range, the 16-gun brig *Linnet* and the 11-gun sloop *Chub* off *Eagle*'s starboard bow and the 37-gun frigate *Confiance* off the starboard quarter. Henley directed his two forwardmost 18 pounders to fire on the two smaller vessels, while he concentrated the remaining two 18s and six 32-pounder carronades on the frigate. The action at this point became an endurance match, a test to see which side could deal out more destruction and withstand the pummeling inflicted in return. The lake was calm, the range was only 300 or 400 hundred yards (274 or 366 m) and experienced gunners could hardly miss (fig.12.2).[23]

Despite their limited training, *Eagle*'s mixed crew seems to have performed well, ramming home powder and shot, priming the guns and running them out

Figure 12.2. Eagle *at the Battle of Lake Champlain. This detail from an 1816 engraving shows all five of the large warships that took part in the fight on September 11, 1814. They are, from left to right,* Linnet, Eagle, Saratoga, Confiance, *and* Ticonderoga. *The US gunboats are in the foreground. Midway through the action* Eagle's *captain Robert Henley elected to shift his brig from the location shown here to a new position between* Saratoga *and* Ticonderoga, *a move that made the former vessel the principal target of both British warships. Commodore Macdonough was not pleased. (From Barber Badger,* The Naval Temple, *"Plate Sixth," p. 179.)*

the ports, aiming and firing, repeating the process again and again. Henley later boasted, "During the severest shock of the action they continued undaunted and unshaken, nothing could suppress their coolness and deliberate firing."[24] Most members of *Eagle*'s crew were probably getting their first experience of a naval battle with its unrelenting clamor, chaos, and horror. With every deafening blast the long guns and carronades leaped back, spewing clouds of powder smoke over tightly packed men on the deck, stinging eyes and choking lungs. Officers shouted orders above the din, while young men and boys raced to supply the guns with powder cartridges and shot from the magazine and shot lockers below deck. The ship continually shivered from the recoil of its guns and the impact of British shot, the latter accompanied by a hollow slamming sound and often a spray of splinters and debris. Blocks and bits of rigging dropped from above. Loud metallic ringing signaled shot striking a gun or metal fittings, while a rattle like giant hailstones on the brig's

wooden sides told of hits by grapeshot or canister shot. Sailors abruptly dropped or were knocked across the deck, their bodies torn by shot or splinters; thirteen were killed outright and about as many badly injured, a casualty rate of one of every five men on *Eagle*.

Lieutenant Smith ordered Private Hale's wife, Abigail, to remain below, near the magazine, where she was less likely to be injured; however, when one of the powder bearers was killed, she took his place, braving shot and splinters to supply cartridges to the gun crews. While crossing the deck she had to step over several casualties, among whom she recognized the lifeless body of her husband James. Unlike the Revolutionary War's Molly Pitcher, Abigail Hale's courageous and tragic story never made the history books.[25]

The officers of *Eagle* had several close calls. Lt. Joseph Smith was directing the placement of a kedge anchor when a near miss threw him headfirst onto the deck; carried below unconscious, he eventually recovered his wits and returned to the action. Acting Lt.

William Spencer suffered a facial wound and was also taken below but later resumed his duties. Consumptive midshipman William Chamberlain left his berth to assist his comrades, despite his weakened condition.[26] Even with their various injuries, the officers of *Eagle* were extraordinarily lucky: of the five large American and British warships at Plattsburgh Bay, theirs was the only one that did not have at least one officer killed in the action.

The first vessel to surrender in the battle fell victim to *Eagle*'s gunfire. Shortly before 10 a.m., the armed sloop *Chub* attempted to take a raking position under *Eagle*'s stern but was met by concentrated broadsides from the US brig. The sloop's frail sides were pierced by thirty-four round shot, the rig was shot to pieces, and over half of the crew fell dead or wounded, including the captain. *Chub* withstood only a few minutes of this treatment before the surviving crew sought shelter below deck and the new commander, a midshipman, lowered the Union Jack.[27]

At 10:30 a.m. *Eagle*'s starboard spring line was shot away, and the vessel swung on its cable until the guns would no longer bear. Several of the engaged starboard guns were disabled, and Henley decided to bring the port-side battery into action. The cable at the bow was cut and the light north wind turned *Eagle* about in a half-circle until a fresh row of guns faced the enemy. Instead of reanchoring at this location, Henley ordered the remaining spring line cut and the topsails sheeted home. The brig sailed down the unengaged side of the American line and anchored in a new position south of *Saratoga*, where the crew opened a raking fire on *Confiance*'s stern. Neither *Linnet* nor *Confiance* could easily hit *Eagle* in this new position, and much to Macdonough's dismay they now concentrated all of their fire on *Saratoga*.

By 11 a.m. both flagships had been pounded into wrecks, with most of the guns on their engaged sides dismounted or unworkable. Macdonough ordered *Saratoga*'s crew to wind the ship on its spring lines until the port-side guns could be brought into action; *Confiance*'s crew attempted the same maneuver, but when this proved impossible most deserted their guns and fled below deck. *Confiance* surrendered a little after 11 a.m., and *Linnet* gave up twenty minutes later. The British gunboat flotilla escaped in the aftermath of the battle, but Plattsburgh Bay was otherwise as complete a victory as the US Navy could have wished.

In the battle's aftermath the sailors of the US Navy squadron cleaned up the wreckage, tended to the wounded and prisoners, and buried the dead. For senior officers, this was a time to prepare reports, accounts that were sure to be widely published by a grateful government and the press. Macdonough was in a quandary. He was not inclined to forgive the extra casualties that *Saratoga* suffered as a result of *Eagle*'s withdrawal from the head of the American line, yet clearly he wished to avoid an unseemly public squabble with his second in command. His report was critical but in a circumspect way. After pointing out that Stephen Cassin's *Ticonderoga* "gallantly sustained her full share of the action," he described Henley's repositioning and noted that while *Eagle* subsequently "very much annoyed the enemy," the move left *Saratoga* "exposed to the galling fire of the enemy brig."[28]

If Henley felt any remorse over leaving *Saratoga* in the lurch, it was not evident in his after-action report: its adjective-heavy enthusiasm and gushing wholesale praise had nothing in common with the commodore's own professional and understated style. Macdonough, evidently disgusted by Henley's prose, "lost" this document and never forwarded it to Washington. He also took the unusual step of paring down *Eagle*'s casualty list. Henley claimed twenty-seven wounded ("most of them severely"), but Macdonough accepted only twenty, observing that some were "so scratched or slightly hurt as not to merit the name of wounded." The commodore was not alone in this assessment: one of the squadron's surgeons inspected *Eagle*'s casualties and reported that only twelve of the twenty-seven had truly serious injuries.[29]

Unfortunate rumors also circulated through the squadron about the conduct of *Eagle*'s handsome second lieutenant. Henley's report stated that "gallant Acting Lieutenant Wm. A. Spencer received a severe wound in the head, and was . . . carried below," but a naval surgeon later dismissed the injury as "a slight wound of the cheek." "A bit of skin by some means torn off his face" was the commodore's blunt assessment. Spencer was said to have used this wound as a pretext to skulk below during the action, "to preserve his pretty face from scarification." Macdonough was inclined to believe the rumors and told the Navy Department: "I am sorry that it is out of my power compatible with candor & impartiality to give a good character of this young Man, he did not from all accounts behave well on the 11th Septr. and I regret that I believe there is too Much cause for those accounts to be true."[30]

Henley was fully aware of the scant and unfavorable mention of *Eagle* in Macdonough's official report, the trimming of his casualty list, and the omission of his battle report from the documents sent to the Navy Department. He countered by composing a narrative that he submitted directly to the navy secretary on September 16. By this immodest account, *Eagle* defeated the British almost singlehandedly after enduring the full force of the frigate *Confiance*'s broadsides "for a great length of time after the action commenced." Henley also sent Jones a copy of his missing after-action report. When Macdonough learned of the September 16 letter and its slanted description of the battle, he remarked, "I am very much surprised at the conduct of Lt. [*sic*] Henley. His statement is unquestionably very erroneous and will, I fear, ultimately be injurious to himself. I consider Lt. Henley a brave man . . . yet he did not fight the whole of the battle."[31]

Claiming that ill health required his immediate departure from the lake, Robert Henley left *Eagle* on September 18, exactly one month after assuming command at Vergennes. He proceeded directly to Washington to obtain a new command (and probably to lodge more protests with the navy secretary). Jones quickly reassigned him to the gunboat flotilla at Wilmington, North Carolina. Unlike the acrimonious and highly public debate over Jesse Elliott's lack of assistance to Commodore Perry at the Battle of Lake Erie, Henley's conduct at Plattsburgh Bay aroused little interest after the war. Henley family tradition would maintain that he was the real genius behind the victory, while Macdonough never wavered in his low opinion of *Eagle*'s commander. "He behaved like a brave man on the 11th Sept.," Macdonough later wrote, "though his vessel was badly managed. His disposition I take to be Malicious and base."[32]

The decisive victory allowed Macdonough to lay up most of his ships and transfer crews to other stations. *Eagle*'s first lieutenant Joseph Smith was sent to Lake Ontario on September 30 with 250 sailors for Commodore Chauncey's squadron. *Confiance, Saratoga, Ticonderoga,* and *Linnet* were patched up and sent to Whitehall at the southern end of the lake, the gunboats and sloops were retained to patrol the northern lake, and Macdonough employed *Eagle* as his flagship for the remainder of 1814 (fig. 12.3). The threat to the Champlain

Figure 12.3. *Late autumn, 1814: Eagle at the northern end of Lake Champlain. This rare contemporary watercolor by an unknown artist shows the brig when it was serving as Macdonough's flagship. Eagle is accompanied by the galley flotilla and the squadron's sloops, the latter serving as living quarters for the galley crews. (Courtesy of the Shelburne Museum, Shelburne, VT.)*

Valley was over: the British gunboats stayed within the Richelieu River and the border remained quiet. By the middle of November, ice was forming on the rim of the lake and it was time to prepare the squadron for winter. *Eagle*'s passage to Whitehall was the last time that the brig would ever sail Champlain's waters.

Over the winter of 1814–15, the squadron lay at anchor below Whitehall, anchored in a single line parallel with the run of the channel and protected by a gun battery and a blockhouse situated on surrounding heights of land. According to the reports of a British spy, *Eagle* continued to serve as the flagship and was moored in a protective position across the channel below the other ships, its guns loaded and ready to sweep the ice clear of any raiders who might attempt an incendiary attack on the squadron.[33]

The ships of the Lake Champlain squadron were placed in ordinary at Whitehall when the war ended in early 1815. Emptied of crews and stripped of guns, topmasts, rigging, and bulkheads, they were whitewashed inside and out and their main decks were covered by roofs. Not much changed over the next five years, except that rot, the inevitable scourge of wooden ships, worked its way into the hulls. Despite its hasty construction, *Eagle* held up as well as any of the other ships, although by 1820 all were showing signs of extensive rot along the waterline. The decaying warships were moved into the nearby Poultney River, where, one by one, they settled to the bottom. All were sold by the navy to salvagers in 1825, but the scrap value of their iron or copper fittings did not justify the expense of recovering the sunken hulks. *Eagle* sank from sight, and as the decades passed and its builders and sailors grew old and died, the story of the brig and its short, eventful career passed from living memory as well. By the twentieth century there were only written records scattered in various archives and a shipwreck lying at the bottom of the Poultney River.

The Miraculous Survival of Eagle

Of the five large ships sunk near Whitehall, only *Eagle* would escape the harsh attention of ship breakers, dredgers, and salvers. The two largest ships of the squadron, *Confiance* and *Saratoga,* sank near the main shipping channel and in time became obstructions to navigation or to dredging operations. According to a government topographical map dated 1839, *Confiance* was sunk next to a small shipyard on the New York shore, near the sharp turn in the lake channel known as the Fiddler's Elbow.[34] The frigate's situation remained unchanged until 1873, when a spring flood lifted the hull and deposited it in front of the shipyard's ways. The owner of this establishment hired explosives expert "Nitroglycerin Jack" Holden to get rid of the wreck. Holden filled the hull with a nitroglycerin charge equivalent to twenty-four kegs of gunpowder and on August 10 blew it to pieces. Souvenir hunters swarmed over the debris, finding cannon shot and 300 pounds (136 kg) of copper fittings that included one of *Confiance*'s rudder gudgeons. The owner of the yard turned some of the timbers into souvenir canes, which he sold for $1 each.[35] One local newspaper observed, "The Yanks handled her without gloves at Plattsburgh, and now they place a can of powder under her stern, and give her a shock that makes the splinters fly, and the boys like the fun as well as they did sixty years ago."[36]

The fate of Macdonough's flagship *Saratoga* is less certain. This vessel was allowed to sink to the bottom near the mouth of the Poultney River in 1821 and was left there by the navy after the naval station shut down in 1825. The lake near Whitehall was periodically dredged in the nineteenth century, and around 1915 an entirely new channel was cut north of Whitehall to allow vessels to bypass the Fiddler's Elbow. These operations and later dredging scoured the lake bottom

clean and likely destroyed whatever was left of *Saratoga*. The area has been surveyed by sonars and divers, but no trace of the US flagship has yet been found.[37]

As we saw in the previous chapter, the brig *Linnet* was partially dragged from the Poultney River in 1949, when its forward end was broken off and lost. Nine years later the schooner *Ticonderoga* was sawn into pieces and the lower hull was lifted from the river to serve as a display in downtown Whitehall. The existence of *Eagle* and the gunboat *Allen* was known to many local residents and the wrecks were occasionally visited by divers, but luckily no full-scale salvage efforts were made after 1958.

During the archaeological study of *Ticonderoga*'s hull in 1981, Whitehall historian Doris Morton told us of other 1812-era wrecks in a river north of town, and Carol Manell Senecal, one of the divers who located *Ticonderoga* in 1958, volunteered to show us where they were sunk. A diver survey on July 23, 1981 easily relocated the battered *Linnet* and, just across the river, a large hull that had fallen over on its side. This wreck's starboard side was missing, but the port side was complete up to the waterway and the bottom of the gunports; all of the keel, most of the lower stem and sternpost, and the entire keelson were also preserved (fig. 12.4). The gunports and a 12-pounder round shot found under the keelson provided convincing proof that this was a warship and not an abandoned steamboat. *Eagle*'s dimensions have never been found in historical records, but the wreck measured 115 feet (35.05 m) from stern to stem, about what we could expect for a US Navy 20-gun sloop of war from the 1812 period. We had no doubt that the hull was Adam Brown's nineteen-day wonder *Eagle.*

The wreck was too interesting from a historical and architectural point of view to ignore, and Arthur Cohn and I set about recording it in situ, a process that required two seasons of study by a team of ten divers.[38] We began in July of 1982 (fig. 12.5). The first priority was to record the dimensions and arrangements of the principal timbers: the stem, the stern, the keelson, and the port-side clamp and waterway timbers that supported the main deck. The room and space of all frames were also measured at this time. Finally, details of the gunports and bulwarks were examined. Working conditions in the Poultney River were bearable but not ideal. The wreck lay under no more than 12 feet (3.66 m) of water, but visibility was poor, rarely exceed-

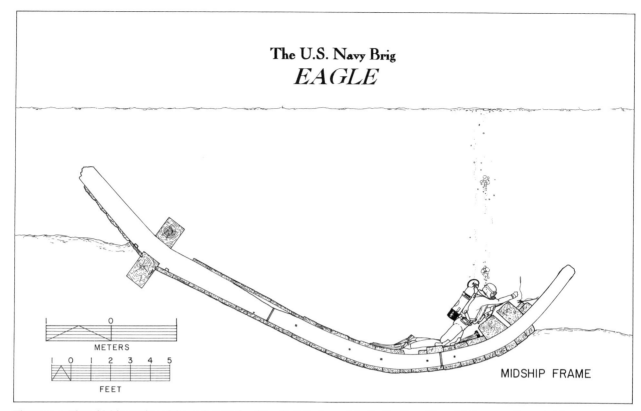

The U.S. Navy Brig
EAGLE

MIDSHIP FRAME

METERS

FEET

Figure 12.4. *The midship section of the sunken* Eagle, *view aft. As* Eagle *sank in the Poultney River it fell over on its port side, which resulted in the preservation of that half of the vessel up to the level of the main deck and gunports. The diver is shown measuring the extra-heavy clamp and waterway timbers that secured the main deck beams (the deck was missing from the wreck). (Drawing by Kevin J. Crisman.)*

ing 1 foot (30.5 cm). We secured baseline tapes to the keelson and clamp to provide reference points for the divers and then measured and sketched the structure piece by piece. Progress was slow, but with each diver spending four to six hours a day in the warm, shallow river, we managed to fill a large notebook with measurements and drawings by the end of the first three-week season.

During the second season, a two-week endeavor in July of 1983, the buried forward ends of *Eagle*'s clamp and waterway were excavated with the aid of a water dredge and then measured. We also dug out the forward end of the keel to obtain dimensions, scarf locations, and wood samples. Ceiling planking was removed at frames H, Ⓧ, and 22 on the port side to record the sections necessary for reconstructing *Eagle*'s lines. Other sections were taken with less effort at frames 32 and M, where the ceiling was missing. Finally, we recorded damaged areas at the ends of the hull, ceiling and external planking, and chainplates and other hull fittings and rechecked some of the measurements re-

corded the previous year. By the conclusion of the 1983 season of study, we had accumulated a two-year total of over one thousand hours of diving time on the wreck and had amassed many pages of data on the timbers.[39]

The Construction of *Eagle*

How do you build a 20-gun warship in nineteen days? This question was uppermost in our minds during the weeks we spent hovering over the wreck with tapes and clipboards and during the months spent reconstructing *Eagle* at a drafting table. The answers did not come all at once, but as our observations accumulated and the reconstruction process advanced we began to recognize Adam Brown's shortcuts. Some were achieved by lowering standards for the materials used in the construction and others by shaping and assembling the timbers in the simplest manner possible. Still other timesaving approaches departed radically from wooden shipbuilding practices of the day and were tailored for the conditions under which *Eagle* sailed and fought.

Figure 12.5. *Diving on the wreck of* Eagle. *Working in the Poultney River had certain advantages: the nearby bank provided a good platform for staging dives and the shallow depth of water allowed crew members to record the wreck for up to four hours each day. The visibility, however, was murky, seldom exceeding one foot (30 cm) on good days. Here volunteer Ken Cameron prepares to don his fins. The white buoy on the right is attached to* Eagle'*s stem. (Photo by Kevin J. Crisman,* Eagle *Project files of Kevin J. Crisman.)*

inches (45.72 cm) molded and 12 inches (30.48 cm) sided amidships; the keel narrowed to 10 inches (25.4 cm) sided at its forward end and 8 inches (20.32 cm) at its after end. The aftermost 24 feet 8 inches (7.52 m) of the keel's top was cut down 6 inches (15.24 cm) to fit the deadwood assembly.

The surviving elements of *Eagle's* bow included the lower stem, the gripe (or forefoot), and the lower apron (fig. 12.7). All were of white oak. The lower stem was flat scarfed to the forward end of the keel and secured with bolts and a pair of dovetail plates. A stopwater at each corner of the scarf prevented water from flowing along the seam and into the hull. The top of the lower stem was cut for a flat scarf that attached the (now missing) upper stem. The gripe, attached to the forward face of the stem, was secured with bolts and by a pair of dovetail plates at its lower end. The lower apron spanned the scarf between the stem and keel. This piece was notched on its after half to fit the floors of frames N, O, and P; the sides of the apron forward of frame P were given angled surfaces to fit the heels of two pairs of cant frames. The corners of the stem and apron were chamfered along the seam, where they met to form rabbets. Bolt heads in the after side of the stem once secured the upper apron timber.

The stern of *Eagle* maintained the theme of simplicity and robustness seen elsewhere in the brig's spine (fig. 12.8). There was only one sternpost, for *Eagle* was built without the inner post seen on other large ships of the period (Henry Eckford's *Jefferson,* for example). *Eagle's* post, of white oak, survived to a height of 6 feet 10 inches (2.08 m), was molded 20 inches (50.8 cm) at the base, tapered to 14 inches (35.56 cm) at the top, and was sided 8 inches (20.32 cm). The post was secured to the keel by a pair of iron dovetail plates and presumably by a tenon as well. Two iron gudgeons were spiked to the sides of the post; there was almost certainly a third gudgeon, but it was no longer on the wreck.

Elementary in its design, the deadwood at *Eagle's* stern consisted of four timbers, two of them large pieces that paralleled the keel and the other two diagonally slanting timbers that formed a triangular wedge at the top. Long iron through bolts fastened the deadwood to the keel and sternpost. Similar in many respects to the deadwood on Eckford's *Jefferson,* this one contained no curved timbers such as a sternson or stern knee; straight pieces of timber made for easy

This examination of the brig's construction will start where Adam Brown began, at the keel (fig. 12.6). *Eagle* had a basic, "no frills" keel that measured 106 feet 5 inches (32.44 m) in length and was composed of three timbers flat scarfed end to end and secured at the scarfs with iron dovetail plates (all fasteners in the hull were of iron). The scarf between the second and third keel pieces was never directly examined during our study (a buried tree trunk was wedged against this part of the hull), but wood samples conclusively proved that the scarf existed: the first two keel timbers were fashioned from maple and the aftermost from white oak. In section, the keel was of substantial dimensions, 18

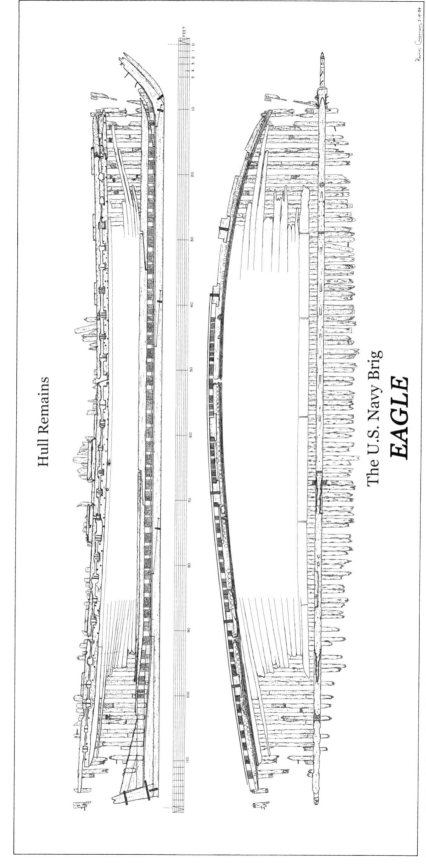

Hull Remains

The U.S. Navy Brig
EAGLE

Figure 12.6. *Wreck plan and profile of the US Navy brig* Eagle, *as recorded in 1981–83. Most of the starboard side, transom, and main deck were missing from the hull, but surviving elements provided many clues to the missing parts. (Drawing by Kevin J. Crisman.)*

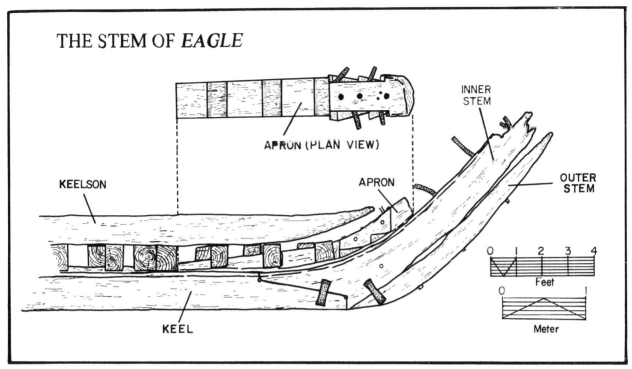

Figure 12.7. *The stem of* Eagle. *The brig's stem was an uncomplicated arrangement of stem, outer stem, and apron. The shipwrights carefully angled the sides of the apron to fit the heels of the first two pairs of cant frames. (Drawing by Kevin J. Crisman.)*

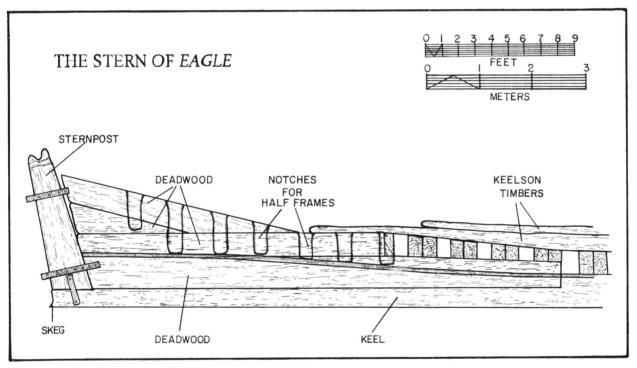

Figure 12.8. *The stern of* Eagle. Eagle's *stern featured an exceedingly simple arrangement with a single sternpost and four deadwood timbers but no stern knee. This uncomplicated approach to building allowed Adam Brown and his carpenters to assemble the brig in record time. (Drawing by Kevin J. Crisman.)*

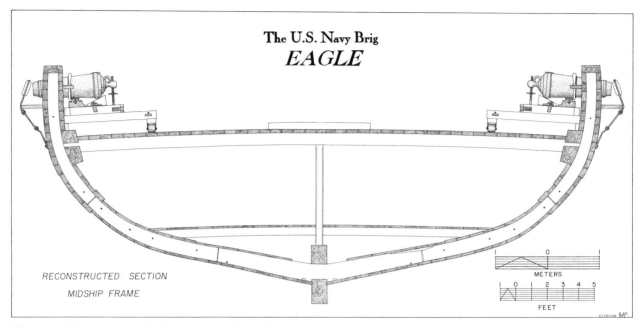

Figure 12.9. *The reconstructed midship section of* Eagle. *The section shows* Eagle's *shallow, slack-bilged shape at the widest frame on the hull (this is the same frame shown in Figure 12.4). The design was well suited for conditions on Lake Champlain, where there was no need to stow water or a large store of provisions in the hold. (Drawing by Kevin J. Crisman.)*

assembly. The sides of the deadwood were notched for the heels of the half frames at the stern. The rabbets extended up the sides of the lowest deadwood timber and along the seam between the first and second deadwoods, and the hood ends of the planks fit into shallow rabbets cut into the forward edges of the sternpost.

A total of fifty-five frames were recorded during the archaeological study: two pairs of cant frames at the apron, forty-four square frames, and nine half frames at the stern (fig. 12.9). There were probably two to four more pairs of cants in the bow, bringing the original total to between fifty-seven and fifty-nine frames. Each square frame consisted of a floor and eight futtocks, doubled and fastened to one another with iron bolts. The individual timbers were of substantial dimensions: floors and futtocks were molded 11 inches (27.94 cm) between the keel and keelson, 12 inches (30.48 cm) at the rabbet, and tapered to 9 inches (22.86 cm) molded at the top timbers. They maintained sided dimensions of 8 to 10 inches (20.32 to 25.4 cm) from the keel to the cap rail. Square frames A through P (forward of the midship frame) were assembled with their first futtocks abaft the floor, while frames 1 through 27 (abaft the midship frame) had their futtocks forward of the floors. Unlike the first futtocks of *Ticonderoga, Lin-*

net, and *Allen,* those of *Eagle* butted over the centerline of the keel. The square frames had a room and space of 2 feet (60.96 cm) along the top of the keel, and each was fastened in place with a single bolt offset from the keel's centerline to make room for the keelson bolts.

Adam Brown and his shipwrights had to locate, cut, haul, shape, and assemble about five hundred individual timbers to create *Eagle*'s frames, surely the single most time-consuming part of the entire construction process. Instead of seeking out well-formed timbers of the preferred white oak, they saved themselves time by cutting floors and futtocks from any tree that had the desired shape. Identified species included white oak, red oak, American elm, white ash, American chestnut, white pine, and spruce. Some floors and lower futtocks were of pine and spruce, weak woods that would have been unacceptable in a seagoing naval vessel. Although the frames were of ample dimensions and well fastened, the finishing was rough, with original log surfaces evident on some timbers; in other places we encountered timbers of inadequate molded dimensions that were leveled with softwood filler pieces. In a ship built under less-pressing circumstances this might be regarded as shoddy workmanship, but in *Eagle*'s case it demonstrates the practical mindset of the shipwrights: better a roughly finished ship ready for battle than a finely finished ship sitting on the stocks.

Eagle's keelson extended from the apron to the uppermost deadwood timber and was made up of four lengths of white oak, fastened end to end by two flat scarfs and bolted through the floors to the keel at every other frame. The two forwardmost keelson timbers measured 14 inches (35.56 cm) molded and 12 inches (30.5 cm) sided, while the other two were stacked and measured 10 and 4 inches (25.4 and 10.16 cm) molded. In addition to its vital function of providing longitudinal strength to the hull, the keelson supported an array of now-missing features. Patterns of bolt holes showed where the steps of the foremast and mainmast were located (each step was fastened by two pairs of bolts); nine shallow rectangular notches amidships once held deck-supporting stanchions, while a pair of notches abaft the mainmast step may have seated the capstan.

Elements that composed *Eagle*'s main deck, namely the clamp, deck beams, and waterway, survived near the top of the brig's port side and reveal much about Adam Brown's approach to building the brig (fig. 12.10). Like his colleague Henry Eckford on Lake Ontario, Brown elected to reduce construction time by the radical step of building this heavily armed ship without any kind of reinforcing knees. The lack of knees was partially offset by making the white oak clamps unusually large, 12 inches (30.5 cm) molded and sided, and by fastening them to the tops of the frames with numerous ¾-inch (1.9 cm) square iron bolts. The heads of these bolts were clenched over iron rings to ensure that the clamps were securely attached to the sides. The top surfaces of the clamps were notched to fit the ends of the deck beams. The carpenters cut a shallow groove around the corners of each notch, apparently to allow the beams a slight degree of motion and thereby prevent the clamps from cracking.

Thirty beam notches were counted in the portside clamp, and there were probably one to two more beams at the ends of the hull (where the clamp was missing), giving the main deck a total of thirty-three beams. The stub ends of twenty-two beams survived between the clamp and waterway. Their spacing and dimensions varied considerably. The beams were on centers that averaged about 3 feet 6 inches (1.07 m). With the exception of the two forwardmost gunports

on each side of the bow, every port was centered over a large beam. The beams were 6 to 10 inches (15.24 to 25.4 cm) molded, and most were 11 inches (27.94 cm) sided. Two 7-inch (17.78 cm) square intermediate beams known as ledges were noted amidships and seemed to correspond to the locations of hatches. All beam ends extended across the top of the clamp and were secured by a pair of ¾-inch (1.9 cm) square bolts. Samples taken from two of the beams were identified as white oak and spruce.

The white oak waterway averaged 10 inches (25.4 cm) molded and 12 inches (30.5 cm) sided and was notched on its underside to fit over the beam ends. The waterway was secured by square bolts, with one bolt driven down through the end of each deck beam and into the clamp; other bolts were driven into the frame tops. A space of 2 to 3 inches (5.08 to 7.6 cm) was left between the clamp and waterway, perhaps to permit circulation of air and inhibit rot.

Brown modified the top surface of the waterway between the gunports by having his carpenters carve out circular hollows to serve as shot garlands. The hollows averaged 2 inches (5.08 cm) deep and were 7 inches (17.78 cm) in diameter for 32-pounder shot and 5 inches (12.7 cm) in diameter for 18-pounder shot. A small, sloping hole was drilled from the inside of each hollow to the inside face of the waterway to allow water in the garlands to drain into the scuppers. Garlands between carronade ports held nine shot, while those adjacent to the long 18 pounders held eleven shot. The use of the waterway as a shot garland, also noted on Noah Brown's steamer-turned-schooner *Ticonderoga*, kept a ready supply of ammunition near the guns and is one of those small details of shipbuilding that rarely gets written down.

Eagle had eleven gunports on each side for its battery of twenty cannon and no doubt had two additional ports in the stern. Most of the bulwarks and all of the cap rail were missing from the wreck, but we nevertheless identified ten of the port side's eleven ports. There were slight variations in size and spacing, but the openings averaged 3 feet 1 inch (93.98 cm) square and were spaced along the side on 10-foot (3.05 m) centers. The bulwarks between the gunports were 7 feet (2.13 m) in length and 3 feet 6 inches (1.06 m) in height from the top of the waterway to the underside of the rail. Of the ten gunports on the wreck, seven still had their white

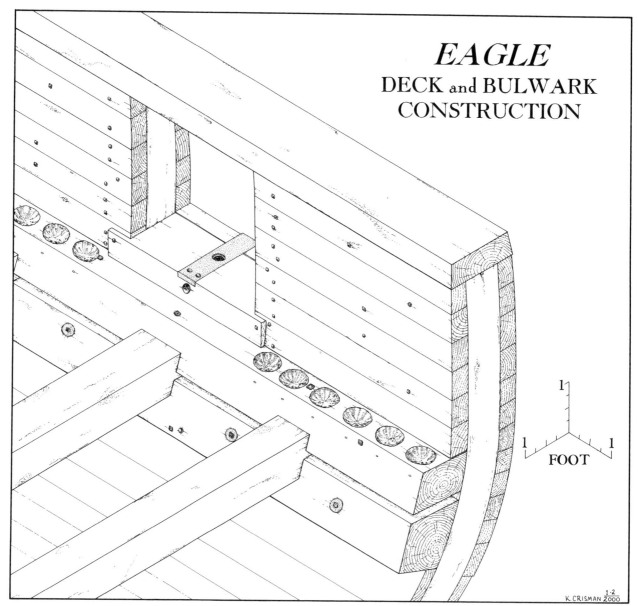

EAGLE
DECK and BULWARK
CONSTRUCTION

K. CRISMAN 2000
1·2

Figure 12.10. Eagle's deck and bulwark construction. Archaeologists recording Eagle's hull in 1982–83 discovered yet another secret to the brig's extraordinarily fast construction: Adam Brown built it without any knees to reinforce the join of the deck to the sides. The extra-large, heavily bolted clamp and waterway timbers partially compensated for the lack of knees. Note also the carved shot garlands in the top of the waterway timber. (Drawing by Kevin J. Crisman.)

oak sills. The sills were 5-inch-thick (12.7 cm) slabs of wood seated atop the waterway and spiked to the top timbers that framed the sides of every port. At each carronade position, a ¾-inch-thick (1.9 cm) iron plate hooked over the outside planking and was fastened to the sill by two bolts; a hole in the center of the plate fit the pivot pin for the carronade slide.

The garboard strakes that fit into the rabbets in *Eagle*'s keel were 13 to 15 inches (33 to 38.1 cm) wide

and 2 inches (5.08 cm) thick. Planking on the underside of the hull, from the garboard to the turn of the bilge, averaged 9 to 11 inches (22.86 to 27.94 cm) wide and 2 inches (5.08 cm) thick. Above the turn of the bilge, planking decreased to 5 to 6 inches (12.7 to 15.24 cm) wide but increased in thickness to 4 inches (10.16 cm) at the wales directly beneath the gunport openings. Planks were attached to the frames with iron spikes. Of the six wood samples taken from planks, five were white oak and the sixth, from the wale, was of American chestnut. Eight iron rigging elements were still attached to the outside planking, including seven chainplates for the mainmast's shrouds and an eyebolt that secured the sheet for the foresail.

The first five to six strakes of ceiling planking outboard of the keelson were wide, relatively thin pieces (1½ inches [3.81 cm] thick) of white pine and spruce. Above these was a series of five to seven strakes of slightly thicker (2 to 3 inches [5.08 to 7.6 cm] thick) white oak that strengthened the hull at the turn of the bilge. Finally, the three ceiling strakes directly below the clamp were long white oak and spruce planks of moderate thickness (2 to 4 inches [5.08 to 10.16 cm]). All ceiling was fastened with iron spikes in a pattern of four spikes per plank per frame. Amidships, the first ceiling plank beneath the clamp had a hole that extended through the underlying frame and planking and that once contained a lead scupper for draining water from the deck. It was the only scupper on the port side, and the pipe was probably no more than 4½ inches (11.43 cm) in diameter, which tells us that Adam Brown was not concerned about excess water accumulation on the main deck.

Reconstructing *Eagle*

Historical evidence of *Eagle*'s design and appearance has been elusive: a lengthy search has never turned up builder's plans or contracts, half models, or even the principal dimensions of the brig. Before 1981 all that could be said of *Eagle* was that it probably resembled the Noah Brown–built 20-gun brig *Niagara* on Lake Erie, a vessel that underwent two massive and largely conjectural reconstructions after its recovery in 1913. The discovery of *Eagle*'s hull changed all of this by providing the bottom and most of the port side of the actual vessel to study. Even elements missing from the wreck could be partially or wholly reconstructed from evidence contained in the surviving timbers. This section examines how the brig was rebuilt on paper, the evidence that aided the work, and what is now known about the original ship.

Eagle's rebuilding began with the drafting of a set of lines, a three-dimensional framework that established the form of the hull (fig. 12.11). Measurements of the wreck provided the length and dimensions of the keel and lower stem and sternpost, the rake of the stern-

post, and curve of the stem, all of which were vital for determining the length and profile of *Eagle*. The stem-to-stern contours of the brig's port side were determined from the sections taken at frames M, H, ⚏, 22, and 32.

Certain features shown in the reconstructed lines drawings were based on evidence from similar wrecks or were simply essential to the ship's operation. The Lake Ontario brig *Jefferson* and the seagoing sloop of war *Peacock* had cap rails that were 6 inches (15.24 cm) thick, and *Eagle* was given a rail of this dimension, too.[40] Warships of the period invariably had rails or irons atop their bulwarks for stowing hammocks where they could provide some protection for the crew during battles. We can be sure that *Eagle* had catheads at the bow to lift the anchors clear of the hull and timberheads to secure the anchors to the top of the rail. We know from archaeological evidence that Noah Brown gave *Ticonderoga* a plug stock rudder, and Adam Brown likely fitted *Eagle* with one as well.

Other aspects of the reconstruction are more debatable. Did *Eagle* have the cutwater and headrails common to most large sailing craft of the time, or did it have a plain, undecorated stem? The one set of contemporary lines we have for a Brown-built lake warship show Macdonough's *Saratoga* with a severely plain stem that lacks even a gammoning knee (see part III-Introduction). The *Saratoga* plan, the very tight construction deadlines on the lakes, and the fact that a cutwater and headrails are not absolutely essential for a sailing vessel led Naval Historian Howard Chapelle to conclude that Perry's *Niagara* and *Lawrence* likely had nothing more than a gammoning knee at the tops of their stems.[41]

Pictorial evidence that was likely unknown to Chapelle suggests otherwise. The 1813 painting of the Lake Erie warships by Lt. Robert Irvine unambiguously depicts *Lawrence* with a knee of the head, rails, and cheeks (see plate 2b). Two excellent contemporary views of US Navy ships on Lake Ontario, one of the 20-gun brig *Jones* by Royal Navy Purser E. E. Vidal and the other of the 26-gun *General Pike* by sailmaker Charles Ware, show each with the same sort of head as *Lawrence* (see fig. 6.6 and fig. II.8). Nor does the absence of a cutwater and headrails on the *Saratoga* lines necessarily mean much: the drawing conveys few details other than the hull's form, and the draftsman may have considered

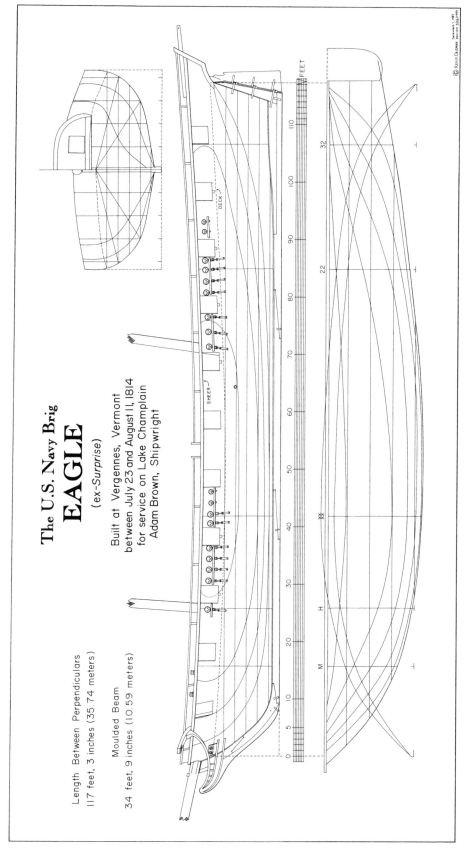

The U.S. Navy Brig
EAGLE
(ex-*Surprise*)

Built at Vergennes, Vermont
between July 23 and August 11, 1814
for service on Lake Champlain
Adam Brown, Shipwright

Length Between Perpendiculars
117 feet, 3 inches (35.74 meters)

Moulded Beam
34 feet, 9 inches (10.59 meters)

Figure 12.11. *Reconstructed lines of the US Navy brig Eagle. Until the identification of the wreck in 1981 and its subsequent recording in 1982–83, nothing was known of the brig's design or appearance (even its dimensions have never been found in contemporary records). Eagle's remarkably short construction time—nineteen days from laying the keel to launching—and the vital edge it provided to the US squadron in the Battle of Lake Champlain make it one of the most noteworthy lake warships of the War of 1812. (Reconstruction by Kevin J. Crisman.)*

the appearance of the completed head unimportant. The combined evidence suggests that Adam Brown built *Eagle* with a cutwater and headrails and the reconstructed vessel is shown with the simple arrangement seen on other small warships of the period.

Eagle, as reconstructed, measured 117 feet 3 inches (35.74 m) in length on deck and had a molded beam of 34 feet 9 inches (10.59 m), giving the hull a length-to-breadth ratio of 3.37:1. The brig was extremely shallow, with a rabbet-to-sheer height of 12 feet 6 inches (3.81 m) at the midship frame and a depth of hold of 7 feet 3 inches (2.2 m). The hull had minimal deadrise and slack bilges amidships (required for extremely shallow draft), giving *Eagle* a full, almost bowl-shaped midship section. The entrance was quite sharp, however, with a steeply raking stem, and the run abaft was long and finely tapered. The brig was designed to be a good sailer, despite the limitations imposed by the lake. The topside of *Eagle* was defined by a gracefully curving sheer that gave the vessel a lively appearance, curiously different from the near flat of the sheer shown on the plans of Noah Brown's *Saratoga*.

The reconstruction of *Eagle*'s interior profile and main deck involved little conjecture, thanks to the well-preserved top surface of the keelson and mostly complete clamp, waterway, gunport sills, and lower bulwarks at the top of the port side (fig. 12.12). From these timbers we knew the location and dimensions of nearly all of the deck beams, as well as the stanchions that supported the beams amidships. Gaps in the stanchions or irregular spacing of the deck beams pointed to probable hatch and companionway locations. Notches in the first futtocks at frame 13 revealed that two pumps were placed alongside the keelson forward of the mainmast. Frame K, just forward of the foremast, had a pair of notches cut into its after corners to seat the posts for the riding bitts. Notches in the keelson abaft the mainmast may have held the ship's capstan. Pivot plates in the gunport sills and the different sizes of shot garlands showed the placement of the long 18-pounder cannon and 32-pounder carronades.

Some elements of *Eagle* disappeared and left no clues to guide the reconstruction. We could find no evidence of the bitts that held the heel of the bowsprit. Not enough of the deck survived to tell us where (or even if) carlings were fitted between the deck beams. Nor do we know how *Eagle* was steered. Oceangoing US Navy sloops of war such as *Peacock* were fitted with a wheel to control the tiller, but *Eagle* probably got by with just the tiller.[42] The freshwater brig was considerably shallower (and presumably required less effort to steer) than its deep-water counterparts, and sailing on Lake Champlain was limited to short passages.[43]

The lower or berth deck on *Eagle* must have been rudimentary, for we could find no trace of it on the wreck. The lack of evidence is not surprising, for this deck was not an integral part of the hull but was only required to support the crew, light internal partitioning, and ship's stores. Its beams must have been small and its planks relatively thin in comparison to the main deck. Divisions of living and working space probably followed the standard arrangement of the period: the captain's cabin at the stern; a wardroom and surrounding cabins for the commissioned officers; a cramped steerage compartment for the midshipmen at the base of the mainmast; quarters for the seamen between the mainmast and foremast; and storerooms for the gunner, sailmaker, boatswain, and carpenter forward of the foremast. The ship's camboose was doubtless located in the customary spot, beneath the hatch that was directly abaft the foremast.

Eagle had little hold space beneath the berth deck for storing anything other than the iron-ore ballast that kept the vessel upright. The powder magazine, shot locker, and cable tier must have been squeezed into the already-tight crew quarters on the berth deck. Provisions were probably stowed on the berth deck as well, and it is unlikely that the brig could have carried more than a one- or two-week's supply of food. It was, of course, unnecessary to carry water.

Evidence for the sailing rig is sketchy. Bolt holes in *Eagle*'s keelson show where the two masts were stepped, and the angle of rake for each mast can be inferred from the locations of the main deck beams above the steps. Chainplates amidships tell us precisely where the shrouds of the mainmast were placed. *Eagle*'s log mentions topsails and topgallant sails, but the configuration, lengths, and diameters of the masts and yards are otherwise a mystery. *Eagle* may have been shallow and heavily gunned, but the hull's full section amidships probably gave it a reasonable amount of stability, at least when compared with the narrow, heavily gunned *Ticonderoga*.[44] I believe the vessel could have supported a lofty rig with a large sail area.

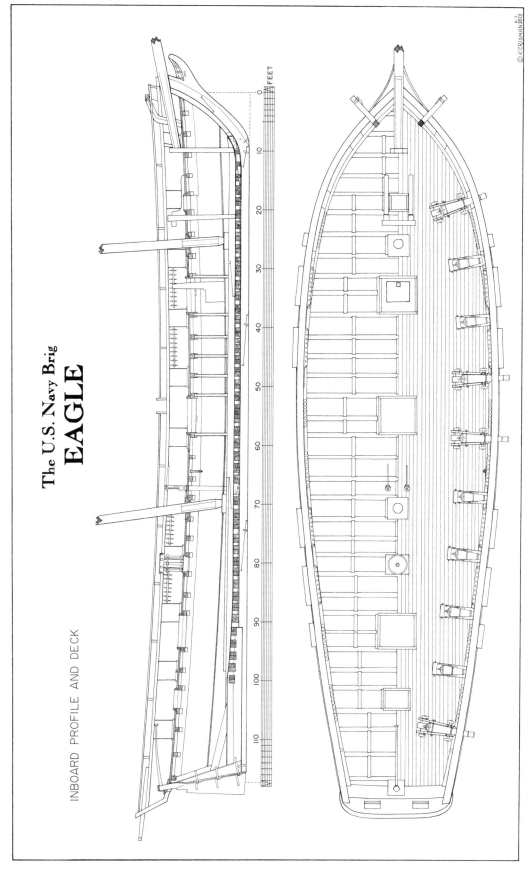

The U.S. Navy Brig
EAGLE

INBOARD PROFILE AND DECK

FEET

0 10 20 30 40 50 60 70 80 90 100 110

© K.CRISMAN 2013

Figure 12.12. Reconstructed deck plan and interior profile of the US Navy brig Eagle. The wreck itself provided most of the information needed to prepare these plans. The shape of the upper stern and the placement of the hatches and companionways forward and aft of the masts are based on plans of similar (but seagoing) US Navy sloops of war. The distribution of long guns and carronades in Eagle's broadsides was reliably indicated by the presence of iron pivot plates for carronades at certain gunports. (Reconstruction by Kevin J. Crisman.)

The wreck of *Eagle* survives as a monument to the work of the Brown brothers during the War of 1812. When the call came in July of 1814 to hurry to Lake Champlain and build another warship, Adam Brown had the conflicting objectives of building a good ship and building it fast. The nineteen-day period between the laying of the keel and the launch tells us that he made fast construction his top priority, but the archaeological study of *Eagle* tells us he also made every effort to build a solid hull. Shortcuts were taken—less than optimal woods were used and knees were omitted—but considering the circumstances the quality of construction was surprisingly high. The assembly was simplified to every extent, yet Brown used timbers of large dimensions and saw that everything was fastened together adequately. The overall design of the hull, with its full section amidships yet sharp ends, suggests a good compromise between shoal draft, stability, and speed.

Eagle presents one of the great "what if" scenarios of the War of 1812. But for the persistence of Macdonough and the intervention of President James Madison, construction might never have been authorized, and without the dedication and skill of Adam Brown and his carpenters, the brig might never have been completed within the required time. In the end, *Eagle* achieved what Macdonough so fervently desired. Delivered to the squadron just two weeks before the climactic confrontation with the British, the brig gave the US squadron the narrow margin of superiority needed to win the Battle of Plattsburgh Bay. The outcome of the fight on Lake Champlain profoundly affected the ongoing US-British negotiations to end the war. News of the Royal Navy's defeat convinced the British government to abandon its demand for punitive concessions from the United States and instead settle for a swift end to hostilities and a return to prewar borders. "If we had either burnt Baltimore or held Plattsburgh," said one of the British negotiators at Ghent, "I believe we should have had peace on [our] terms."[45]

NOTES

1. Macdonough to Jones, May 29, 1814, entry 147, Naval Records Collection of the Office of Naval Records and Library, record group 45 (RG 45), National Archives and Records Administration (NARA).

2. Jones to Madison, May 6, 1814, James Madison Papers (JMP), Library of Congress.

3. Macdonough to Jones, June 8, 1814, entry 147, RG 45, NARA.

4. Macdonough to Jones, June 11, 1814, entry 147, RG 45, NARA.

5. Jones to Madison, May 25, 1814, William Jones Papers, Uselma Clark Smith Collection, Historical Society of Pennsylvania.

6. Edward K. Eckert, *The Navy Department in the War of 1812* (Gainesville: University of Florida Press, 1973), p. 34.

7. Irving Brant, *James Madison, Commander in Chief,* vol. 6 (Indianapolis: Bobbs-Merrill Company, 1961), p. 273.

8. Jones to Madison, July 30, 1814, JMP.

9. Jones to Bullus, July 5, 1814, entry 441, RG 45, NARA.

10. Macdonough to Jones, June 19, June 26, July 9, July 13, 1814, entry 147, RG 45, NARA.

11. Macdonough to Jones, July 18, 1814, entry 147, RG 45, NARA; Noah Brown, "The Remarkable Statement of Noah Brown," *Journal of American History* 8 (January 1914), p. 107.

12. Macdonough to Jones, June 11, July 18, 1814, entry 147, RG 45, NARA; "A Report on the State and Condition of the Naval Force . . . under the Command of Thomas Macdonough, Esquire on the 31st day of August 1814," manuscript document, Lake Champlain Maritime Museum, Vergennes, VT. Courtesy of Arthur B. Cohn.

13. Kevin J. Crisman, *The* Eagle: *An American Brig on Lake Champlain During the War of 1812* (Shelburne, VT: The New England Press, and Annapolis: Naval Institute Press, 1987), pp. 38–40; "The Log Book Kept on Board the United States Sloop of War Surprise of Twenty Guns" (manuscript logbook kept by Daniel Records, RG 45, NARA).

14. Macdonough to Jones, July 18, July 23, August 9, 1814, entry 147, RG 45, NARA; Macdonough to Jones, August 12, 1814, entry 125, RG 45, NARA.

15. Charles J. Peterson, *The American Navy* (Philadelphia: Jas. Smith, 1857), pp. 476–81; Henley to Jones, March 4, 1814, entry 148, RG 45, NARA; Christopher McKee, *A Gentlemanly and Honorable Profession: The Creation of the U.S. Naval Officer Corps, 1794–1815* (Annapolis: Naval Institute Press, 1991), pp. 294–95.

16. Henley to Jones, March 4, 1814, entry 148, RG 45, NARA; Henley to Capt. David Porter, August 17, 1814, Simon Gratz Collection, cs. 5, box 32, Historical Society of Pennsylvania, Philadelphia. Henley wrote Porter, "I have long had reason to believe that some *insidious foe* had impressed the Hon[orable] Sec[retar]y unfavorably towards me," the "insidious foe" presumably being Henley's former commander Capt. John Cassin. By coincidence, one of Henley's comrades on Lake Champlain would be Cassin's son Lt. Stephen Cassin, who commanded *Ticonderoga.*

17. Henley to Jones, August 19, 1814, entry 147, RG 45, NARA.

18. Macdonough to Jones, August 27, 1814, entry 147, RG 45, NARA.

19. Macdonough to the Board of Navy Commissioners, May 6, 1815, Subject File NI, RG 45, NARA; Abstracts of Service Records, microcopy 330, RG 45, NARA; William Chamberlain to Jones, September 15, 1814, entry 148, RG 45, NARA.

20. A. S. Barker, "Naval Reminiscences IX, an Incident from the War of 1812," *The Navy* (February 1914), pp. 66–67.

21. Barker, "Naval Reminiscences," p. 67; "Log Book Kept on Board the United States Sloop of War Surprise," RG 45, NARA; B. N. Clark, "Accounts of the Battle of Plattsburgh, September 11, 1814: From Contemporaneous Sources," *Vermont Antiquarian*, vol. 1 (1903), p. 93.

22. Macdonough to the Board of Navy Commissioners, May 6, 1815, Subject File NI, RG 45, NARA; "Log Book Kept on Board the United States Sloop of War Surprise," RG 45, NARA.

23. Henley to Jones, September 16, 1814, entry 147, RG 45, NARA; John Williams, *Lives and Confessions of John Williams, Francis Frederick, John P. Rog and Peter Peterson* (Boston: J. T. Buckingham, 1819), p. 13.

24. Henley to Macdonough, September 12, 1814, entry 147, RG 45, NARA.

25. Abigail Hale's story was related by *Eagle*'s first lieutenant Joseph Smith, although Smith could not remember her name. See Barker, "Naval Reminiscences," p. 67. Abigail Woodruff and James M. Hale (a shoemaker) married in Spencer, NY, in 1810 (she was eighteen). James enlisted in the US Army in 1812 and was apparently joined in the field by Abigail after their two young children died in 1813. After James's death on *Eagle* Abigail collected the pay and prize money due her deceased husband, and three months later, in December 1814, she married Daniel Tingley at Plattsburgh, NY. She lived out her life in Crawford County, PA, where she filed for, and in 1856 began receiving, a $4 per month war widow's pension. Curiously, the pension application says nothing about Abigail being aboard *Eagle* during the battle and her active contribution to the US Navy's victory. Abigail Tingley, file no. 10022, Pension Application Files, War of 1812, NARA. Courtesy of Erika Washburn.

26. Barker, "Naval Reminiscences," p. 67; Henley to Macdonough, September 12, 1814, entry 147, RG 45, NARA; William Chamberlain to Jones, September 15, 1814, entry 148, RG 45, NARA.

27. William Wood, ed., *Select British Documents of the Canadian War of 1812*, vol. 3, pt. 1 (Toronto: The Champlain Society, 1926), pp. 422–29; Henley to Jones, September 16, 1814, entry 147, RG 45, NARA.

28. Macdonough to Jones, September 13, 1814, entry 125, RG 45, NARA.

29. Henley to Macdonough, September 12, 1814, entry 147, RG 45, NARA; Rodney Macdonough, *Life of Commodore Thomas Macdonough, U.S. Navy* (Boston: The Fort Hill Press, 1909), pp. 191–92.

30. Plattsburgh Centenary Commission, *Dedication of the Thomas Macdonough Memorial* (Plattsburgh, NY: Centenary Commission, 1926), pp. 71–72; *Burlington* (VT) *Daily Free Press and Times,* October 17, 1853; Macdonough to the Board of Navy Commissioners, May 6, 1815, Subject File NI, RG 45, NARA.

31. Henley to Jones, September 16, 1814, entry 147, RG 45,

NARA; Macdonough, *Life of Commodore Thomas Macdonough,* p. 192.

32. Crisman, *The* Eagle, p. 88; David Curtis Skaggs, *Thomas Macdonough: Master of Command in the Early U.S. Navy* (Annapolis: Naval Institute Press, 2003), pp. 142–44; Macdonough to the Board of Navy Commissioners, May 6, 1815, Subject File NI, RG 45, NARA. The transcription of Macdonough's victory report in J. Russell Jr.'s *The History of the War, between the United States and Great Britain* (Hartford, CT: B. & J. Russell, 1815) omits the reference to *Eagle* leaving *Saratoga* exposed to enemy fire, an omission that may reflect the American public's desire to celebrate its new naval heroes rather than investigate their shortcomings.

33. Intelligence report on, and a proposed attack upon, the US Navy ships at Whitehall, NY, n.d. (circa late December 1814 to early January 1815), Sir Thomas Makdougall Brisbane Papers, Clements Library, University of Michigan.

34. "Map of the Head of Lake Champlain, Surveyed under the Direction of Maj. J.D. Graham, Corps of Top. Engs. By A.A. Humphreys, Lieut T. E., September, 1839," Civil Works Map File, D 112, record group 77, NARA.

35. *Whitehall* (NY) *Times,* August 13, 1873.

36. *Burlington* (VT) *Daily Free Press and Times,* August 11, 1873.

37. *Whitehall* (NY) *Times,* August 13, 1873; *Essex County* (NY) *Republican,* October 28, 1938; Arthur B. Cohn, ed., *A Report on the Nautical Archaeology of Lake Champlain, Results of the 1982 Field Season of the Champlain Maritime Society* (Burlington, VT: The Champlain Maritime Society, 1984), pp. 73–77.

38. The project was sponsored by the nonprofit Champlain Maritime Society and by the Vermont Division for Historic Preservation, funded by grants from the Vermont Historical Society and the Cecil Howard Charitable Trust, and funded by federal survey and planning grants administered by the Vermont Division for Historic Preservation.

39. A historical and archaeological report on *Eagle* was completed by Kevin Crisman as a master's thesis in nautical archaeology (anthropology) at Texas A&M University in 1984. The thesis was subsequently published as *The* Eagle: *An American Brig on Lake Champlain During the War of 1812.*

40. Howard I. Chapelle, *The History of American Sailing Ships* (New York: W. W. Norton, 1935), p. 373.

41. Howard I. Chapelle, *The History of the American Sailing Navy* (New York: W. W. Norton, 1949), pp. 270–71.

42. Stephen W. H. Duffy, *Captain Blakeley and the* Wasp (Annapolis: Naval Institute Press, 2001), plan and profile views of the *Frolic*'s tiller, pp. 150–51; interior profile and deck arrangements of *Peacock*-class sloops of war, by William Spotswood and William Doughty, July 27, 1813, plan CR41-5-6-G, record group 19, NARA.

43. Since its launch in 1988, the replica 20-gun brig *Niagara* has sailed with only a tiller; relieving tackle is rigged when conditions demand additional purchase on the tiller and rudder.

44. The estimated weight of armament on *Eagle* was 74,400 pounds (33,747 kg) or 37.2 tons, derived from the following calculations:

Cannon	Carriage	Combined	Total on Eagle
32-pdr carronade			
2000 lbs	500 lbs	2500 lbs	× 12 = 30,000 lbs
18-pdr long gun			
4700 lbs	700 lbs	5400 lbs	× 8 = 43,200 lbs
Gun tools and			
tackle		1200 lbs	1200 lbs
		TOTAL:	74,400 lbs (37.2 tons)

Individual cannon weights are from Spencer C. Tucker, *Arming the Fleet, U.S. Navy Ordnance in the Muzzle-Loading Era* (Annapolis: Naval Institute Press, 1989), p. 125; the carriage, tool and tackle weights are based on estimates by Capt. Walter Rybka in Chapter 1 of this book.

45. Donald R. Hickey, *The War of 1812: A Forgotten Conflict* (Urbana: University of Illinois Press, 1989), pp. 285, 295.

13 "I NEVER SEE ANYTHING IN THIS WORLD LIKE IT!"

The Archaeological Legacy of a Naval Battle

ARTHUR B. COHN AND KEVIN J. CRISMAN

Introduction

Most naval battles of the War of 1812 were private affairs, fought in open waters far from the sight of land and experienced only by the participants. Plattsburgh Bay was different. The British attack had been anticipated for many weeks, and the slow progress of the Royal Navy squadron up Lake Champlain was closely watched by residents on the New York and Vermont shores. By the time the first cannon boomed on Sunday morning, September 11, a large audience had gathered to see the battle.

Among the spectators was a fourteen-year-old Vermont boy, Benajah Phelps, who had helped his mother and two sisters into a wagon at dawn and driven them 2 miles (3.2 km) to obtain a commanding view from atop Sawyer's Hill on South Hero Island. From this vantage point, about 3 miles (4.83 km) from the fight, they felt the concussion of the guns, a sensation that Phelps considered more powerful than any thunder he ever experienced. They marveled at the way cannonballs skipped across the water. At times the sheets of flames that issued from fast-firing guns convinced onlookers that the US ships were ablaze (plate 10b). After two and a half hours of smoke, noise, and uncertainty, the British warships *Confiance* and *Linnet* hauled down their colors. The Phelps family and other Vermonters lining the shore let out a cheer of relief and joy.

The temptation to see the US Navy's new trophies was too strong for young Phelps to resist, so he hitched a ride in a four-oared boat that was departing to examine the scene of the action. This impromptu post-battle tour gave the boat's occupants more of an eyeful than they could possibly have anticipated and a grim lesson in the price of naval glory. The sight of the battered, shot-ridden ships and their grisly human wreckage would be etched into Phelps's memory throughout his long life.

Eighty-seven years later, the recollections of 101-year-old Benajah Phelps were shared in the November 2, 1901 edition of *The Outlook* magazine:

> Well, [the surrender] was about twelve o'clock . . . I was bound to go on board the ships. . . . and we rowed out to the big British ship [*Confiance*]. She was a fine ship, I tell ye. The plankin' was white oak six inches thick. The small balls did not go through those planks. They were just stuck solid full of balls. It seemed as if you couldn't git any more balls in. The grape-shot and rifle-balls pooty nearly covered the plankin' all over. The riggin' was cut all to pieces. There wasn't any of it left. The decks was the most awful sight I ever saw. It was—it was awful!

At this point in his narrative, according to *The Outlook,* "The old gentleman shut his eyes and shuddered, as if, even after the lapse of eighty-seven years, the scene of carnage was as vivid as on that September day of long ago."

> Blood, blood was everywhere! The decks was covered with arms and legs and heads, and pieces of hands and bodies all torn to pieces! I never see anything in this world like it! Seemed as if everybody had been killed. They must have fought terribly before they hauled down the flag. It 'most made me sick![1]

Phelps was not the only postbattle tourist to be appalled by the state of *Confiance.* J. C. Hubbell, a lawyer from Chazy, New York, watched the fight from nearby Cumberland Head and canoed out to the ships when the shooting stopped. He first boarded *Saratoga,* where he shook hands with Macdonough and congratulated him on survival and victory. On the US flagship, Hubbell noted, "The dead were all packed up in order here, and the decks were cleaned up, but the seams full of blood, and the torn hull, masts and spars told the story of the fearful struggle." Hubbell then boarded the British flagship, which he described as "a horrible sight. The vessel was absolutely torn to pieces; the decks were strewed with mutilated bodies lying in all directions, and everything was covered with blood. It was the most fearful sight I ever beheld or ever expect to, and one I shall never forget."[2]

Phelps and Hubbell were among the few civilians in their day to see exactly what happened when thou-

sands of cast-iron shot were fired at point-blank range into wooden ships and living men. The casualty reports tell us that they were not exaggerating the extent of the carnage. On board the US ships 52 crew members were dead and 58 listed as wounded, while on the British ships 54 were killed and 116 wounded. *Confiance* had taken the worst of it, for of the 270 sailors, marines, and supernumeraries on the frigate at the start of the battle, 123 people, nearly half of the crew, were dead or injured. Plattsburgh Bay was unquestionably the most lethal of all naval encounters on the lakes during the War of 1812.[3]

What the casualty numbers do not convey is the random nature of survival, injury, and death for the officers and sailors who fought on the ships. The commodores of the rival squadrons at Plattsburgh Bay provide a case in point. British Comm. George Downie was supremely unlucky that day, for he was killed early in the engagement when one of *Confiance*'s cannon, violently thrown off its carriage by a round shot strike, crushed him to death. US Comm. Thomas Macdonough, on the other hand, escaped being fatally struck by shot or splinters, although he was twice knocked flat by flying debris and on another occasion a 24-pound shot whirled through the precise spot where he had been standing only a moment before (fig. 13.1).[4] Many other men around him on the deck of *Saratoga* did not survive the action. The deeply religious Macdonough surely meant it when he wrote his superiors in Washington, "The Almighty has been pleased to grant us a signal victory on Lake Champlain."[5] Under the circumstances, his own survival must have seemed divinely ordained.

Symbols and Souvenirs of a Naval Battle

In the days that followed September 11, the human remains and material wreckage were cleared away. The dead were gathered and buried on shore, the rank-and-file sailors of both squadrons intermingling in one long trench on Crab Island while the US and British officers were ceremoniously placed in individual graves in a Plattsburgh cemetery.[6] Debris-strewn decks were shoveled, swept, and washed clean, and sailors in small boats dragged the bay for anchors lost during the fight. Damaged spars and rigging were replaced, hulls were patched up, and the ships were sent to a protected location at Whitehall, New York.

Even as the battle debris was cleaned up, the news

Figure 13.1. *Macdonough at the Battle of Lake Champlain, September 11, 1814. This later-nineteenth-century engraving imaginatively depicts the deck of* Saratoga *at the height of the action. While certain details are questionable—Macdonough probably was not wearing his best dress uniform, the cannon are too small, and the wounds are all bloodless—the image does capture the chaos and destruction on* Saratoga *and the other large ships during the point-blank cannonading. (Collection of Kevin J. Crisman.)*

of Lake Champlain spread and generated a new material record of the battle: symbols and souvenirs that celebrated the success or commemorated the bravery and sacrifice of its participants. A grateful nation heaped praise and gifts upon Macdonough and his sailors. Many of the squadron's officers received promotions, commemorative gold and silver medals were struck, and presentation swords were engraved.[7] Mementoes were also created for public consumption: accounts of the fight were published, paintings were commissioned, poems and songs were written, and popular prints of the battle were produced on paper and china (fig. 13.2).[8]

The Royal Navy ships were impressive captures, but their value to the US Navy as trophies was limited by geography and durability. Landlocked and doomed by their rushed construction to a short lifespan, they would deteriorate in relative isolation. In 1815, *Confiance, Linnet,* and their three erstwhile opponents were reduced to empty hulks and moored in an inaccessible location alongside a swamp (fig. 13.3). Over the next ten years the line of decaying ships inspired a few writers and artists who passed through Whitehall (Professor Benjamin Silliman wrote his eloquent passage about the "sad monuments" in 1819), but their abandonment in 1825 generated little public interest or concern.[9]

The flags of the British warships *Confiance, Linnet,* and *Chub,* perhaps the most symbolic trophies of the US victory after the ships themselves, were carried to Washington immediately after the battle by Lt. Stephen Cassin of *Ticonderoga.* Thirty-five years later, in 1849, President James K. Polk directed that the Navy's col-

Figure 13.2. Naval Heroes of the United States. *The success of the US Navy during the War of 1812 would remain an enduring source of pride for US citizens throughout the nineteenth century. In this print the hero of Lake Champlain Thomas Macdonough appears above an image of the battle that is borrowed from the Tanner engraving, surrounded by some of the war's other naval heroes. Stars, cannon, flags, and anchors complete this patriotic celebration of their achievements. (Lithograph by N. Currier, 1846, from common domain.)*

lection of captured flags be turned over to the US Naval Academy at Annapolis, Maryland. The largest of the three, the ensign of *Confiance,* measured a whopping 23 feet 8 inches (7.21 m) in length by 13 feet 10 inches (4.21 m) in height. This flag was white and divided by a cross into four quadrants, with the union jack in the upper left quadrant; the ensign of *Linnet* was blue and that of *Chub* red. The faded, somewhat-tattered flags of *Confiance* and *Linnet* are displayed in the Academy's Mahan Hall, while the flag of *Chub* can be seen in the Academy's Museum.[10]

Another battle memento that ended up at Annapolis was an iron cannon cast at the Carron Foundry in 1812 and said to be the gun that fatally crushed *Confiance*'s captain George Downie in the opening minutes of the action (fig. 13.4a, b). The piece is a Blomefield-pattern

24 pounder, a short 6½-foot-long (1.98 m) design first introduced in 1805; the Blomefield pattern was intended to combine the lighter weight and heavier shot of the carronade with the greater range of the long gun. By 1814 Blomefield short guns had seen extensive use on British vessels and were found to be effective for their size; the Royal Navy particularly appreciated their ability to safely fire double-shotted charges at point-blank range. The cannon at Annapolis bears the deep gouge of a shot strike on the upper left face of its muzzle, a feature that lends credence to the claim that it is the same piece that caused the death of Commodore Downie.[11]

The quest for relics and mementoes of "Macdonough's Victory" never really ended. In the years and decades that followed 1814, the US government,

Figure 13.3. *The US naval squadron moored below Whitehall, 1816. After the war officially ended in 1815, the three US Navy ships and the ex–Royal Navy* Confiance *and* Linnet *were stripped of rigging and cannon, covered with roofs, and left to quietly deteriorate in the narrow lake channel below Whitehall, New York. The Battle of Lake Champlain was widely celebrated in the US, but there was no interest in preserving the ships that fought in the action. (Contemporary watercolor by an unknown artist, courtesy of the Lake Champlain Maritime Museum.)*

Figure 13.4. *A Blomefield-pattern 24-pounder cannon from* Confiance. *The crater left by a shot strike is evident on the muzzle (inset). This was an unlucky hit for Commodore Downie of the British squadron, who was fatally crushed when the gun was dismounted from its carriage. The piece is now displayed outside Macdonough Hall at the US Naval Academy in Annapolis, Maryland. (Photos courtesy of Dr. Richard Ruth, Department of History, US Naval Academy.)*

private institutions, souvenir collectors, historians, patriots, antiquarians, archaeologists, and the just plain curious all sought a tangible connection to the momentous encounter on Lake Champlain. Artifacts and commemorative objects were sought, bought, collected, and displayed in museums, historical societies, and homes. During the 1914 centennial, elaborate celebrations took place around the lake and monuments were erected in memory of the event and of those who perished on the ships.[12]

One source of souvenirs remained untapped for almost 150 years. This was the battle debris strewn across the bottom of Plattsburgh Bay, which until the middle of the twentieth century was beyond the reach of souvenir seekers and largely forgotten. This situation drastically changed with the invention of self-contained underwater breathing apparatus (or scuba) in the 1940s and its rapid spread throughout the United States in the 1950s. Simple, inexpensive scuba technology suddenly made it possible for nearly anyone to easily explore the lake. For the intrepid divers of scuba's early years, Plattsburgh Bay was an artifact bonanza. The vast scatter of untouched original relics generated wonder, excitement, and the age-old desire to salvage. Naturally, divers scooped up their finds to bring back home and show to family and friends.

In 1960 the site of Macdonough's victory in Plattsburgh Bay was designated a National Historic Landmark, the nation's highest form of recognition for significant places in our history. It is ironic that at the same time this submerged battle site became recognized for its special contribution to US history, it was being picked apart and forever altered by well-intentioned divers. Indeed, divers in this part of Lake Champlain had an extra bonus, for not far from Plattsburgh was the site of the Revolutionary War's Battle of Valcour Island. The heretofore-undisturbed submerged record of these two naval engagements would never be the same.[13]

The Leege Collection

One of the earliest divers in the Plattsburgh, New York, area was William Leege (fig. 13.5). Leege grew up in the 1940s and 1950s, at a time when the lake's last steamboat *Ticonderoga* still made regular passages, and he developed a strong appreciation for the history of the lake and its surrounding shores. In 1957, at the age of fifteen, he bought his first scuba equipment and shortly thereafter his own compressor. He soon discovered that only 30 feet (9 m) below the surface of Plattsburgh Bay, the lake bottom was composed of hard sand that was perfect for finding naval artifacts lost almost a century and a half earlier.

After many years of on-and-off collecting, Leege decided to carry out a systematic artifact recovery project in Plattsburgh Bay. He invested in a boat and banded with local divers Gary Allen, Dennis Lewis, and Matthew Booth. Calling their group the Lake Champlain Archaeological Association (LCAA), they incorporated with the State of New York. In 1977 alone, Leege logged sixty dives at the naval battle site and recovered ninety-five artifacts. He and his colleagues catalogued their finds, stored them together, and arranged for the exhibition of selected objects at local museums and historical societies.

As the diving continued, the LCAA collection grew in size and variety. Cast-iron shot made up a large percentage of the finds and included round shot, grapeshot, and canister shot, as well as an intact stand of grapeshot, still wrapped in its original canvas covering. The bay yielded many other artifacts: a brass cannon lock stamped with the maker's name (Sherwood), lead cannon primers, gunflints, and pieces of ordnance-related equipment (plate 11a); a cast bronze sword hilt (probably an officer's sword) as well as cheaper wooden-handled naval cutlasses intended for general use; musket parts and fragments of bayonets; iron tools; rigging elements; eating utensils; plain and transfer-printed ceramic plates and bowls and a salt cellar (plate 11b); glass alcohol and medicine bottles, tumblers, stemware, and a crystal decanter; personal effects such as buttons, buckles, and clasps (fig. 13.6).; and unidentified bone fragments.

Figure 13.5. *William Leege. In the 1970s, a group of avocational archaeologists, one of them Leege, formed the Lake Champlain Archaeological Association (LCAA) to locate and preserve artifacts from the lake's naval battles. Here he holds the upper shank and ring of Plattsburgh Bay Anchor No. 1. (Photo courtesy of William Leege.)*

The locations and types of materials revealed previously unknown details of the battle and its aftermath. For example, Leege and his colleagues were able to determine the location of at least one ship during the battle by finding a cluster of lead primers that were ejected out of cannon vent holes upon firing and then dropped into the lake alongside the vessel. By following debris trails, LCAA divers were able to track the postbattle movements of ships from the open bay to a sheltered location where they underwent cleaning and repair. The sailors clearing away the wreckage on the ships were not deliberate in their efforts: they shoveled everything into wooden buckets and then threw the *buckets* overboard rather than simply dumping their contents over the sides. When recovered, the buckets contained a revealing blend of ship's equipment, but-

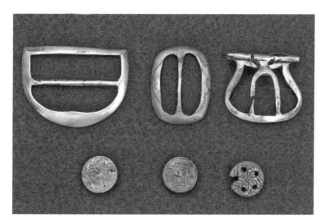

Figure 13.6. *Battle debris from Plattsburgh Bay: buttons and buckles. This is only a small selection of the numerous metal clothing or equipment-related items dropped in Plattsburgh Bay during and immediately after the battle. (Photo by Thomas Larsen, courtesy of the Lake Champlain Maritime Museum.)*

Figure 13.7. *Battle debris from Plattsburgh Bay: a selection of British finds. These include a crossbelt buckle and a uniform button with the fouled anchor symbol of the Royal Navy and a clasp decorated with a lion's head. The two "39" buttons are from the uniforms of soldiers in the British Army's 39th Regiment, ten of whom served on the British frigate* Confiance. *(Photo by Thomas Larsen, courtesy of the Lake Champlain Maritime Museum.)*

tons and parts of uniforms, fragments of high-quality ceramics and glass bottles, as well as assorted bits of wood and bone debris. Some items in the buckets were intact and seemingly still useful, suggesting that the cleanup crews had neither the time nor interest to pick through the mess left on the decks.[14]

Royal Navy equipment could often be identified by broad arrow stamps that signified British government property or by other distinguishing marks. Such items included buttons (including one with a "39" for the British Army's 39th Regiment, ten of whose members served on *Confiance*), a small clasp in the shape of a lion's head, and a cast copper-alloy crossbelt badge and hook with an anchor design (fig. 13.7).[15] One of the more evocative finds was a thick rectangular sheet of copper alloy that had been bent in a half circle around some unknown object and fastened in place by ten tacks. An obsessive government employee or sailor stamped over a dozen broad arrows into the collar's surface to discourage theft. During the battle on Lake Champlain the piece was squarely struck, probably by a US Navy grapeshot, and left torn and bent; its twisted form appears to freeze a violent, destructive moment in time (fig. 13.8).

Two unexpected finds were large, sheet-copper roman numerals, VIII and XX, intended to serve as draft indicators on stem or sternposts (fig. 13.9). They were almost certainly part of the equipment sent from Britain to outfit warships on the lakes. *Confiance* could have used the VIII, since it drew 8½ feet (2.59 m) aft

Figure 13.8. *Battle debris from Plattsburgh Bay: a collar showing the effects of a shot strike. This copper or copper-alloy piece bore multiple broad arrow stamps on one surface to mark it as government property. The iron shot in the photograph was not found with the collar. (Photo by Thomas Larsen, courtesy of the Lake Champlain Maritime Museum.)*

when fully laden, and the XX might have been cut in half to provide 10-foot (3.04 m) draft marks on the frigate's stem and stern. The lack of tack holes tells us they were never used, however, probably because the crew did not have time to attach draft indicators before their unfinished ship entered the battle.[16]

One of the more spectacular naval artifacts to come out of the bay during the era of the LCAA was a large, wrought-iron anchor (fig. 13.10). Referred to here as Plattsburgh Bay No. 1, the anchor was recovered in two pieces by two separate groups of divers. The LCAA found and retrieved a 2-foot (60.9 cm) length of the upper shank and attached ring (which retained some of its protective canvas wrap or "parceling"); the rest of the anchor was discovered and recovered by divers from Vermont.[17] When the two parts were later reassembled (on paper, from measurements), the anchor measured 12 feet 1 inch (3.68 m) from its crown to the head of the shank and 7 feet 1¼ inch (2.16 m) between the tips of the flukes and the ring had an outside diameter of 24 inches (60.9 cm). Which ship lost this anchor is not certain. The log of the US Navy brig *Eagle* tells us that on September 8, 1814, "the small anchor broke off the shank," setting the vessel adrift until another anchor could be dropped.[18] During the battle on September 11, *Eagle* left one or more anchors on the bottom when the crew cut its cables and shifted position and the British flagship *Confiance* had two anchors cut away by shot and lost. After the battle the bay was swept by the US Navy and some of these anchors may have been recovered, although at least two were not.[19]

Leege and other members of the LCAA provide an

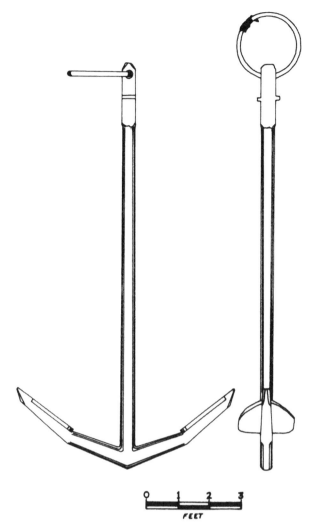

FEET

Figure 13.10. *Plattsburgh Bay Anchor No. 1. Broken in half not far below the ring while it was in service, this anchor was recovered from separate areas of Plattsburgh Bay by different teams of divers. This could be one of the two anchors shot from the British frigate* Confiance *during the opening stages of the battle, but there is a possibility that it is from one of the other warships that fought on September 11, 1814. The top section of the anchor can also be seen with William Leege in Figure 13.5. (Drawing by Kevin J. Crisman.)*

example of divers trying to adopt a responsible approach to artifact collecting, but in the early decades of scuba such an approach was rare. Uncontrolled casual collecting by sport divers and more destructive excavation for profit by professional looters were common in many historic maritime areas around the world. Advancing underwater technologies in the later decades of the twentieth century allowed ever-deeper exploration and enabled a new breed of deep-water wreck seekers to strip mine previously untouched wrecks. Treasure discoveries inspired magazine articles and television programs that glamorized the hunt for underwater riches as a swashbuckling adventure. As entertaining as all this might have been, over time the consequences were also becoming apparent as unique archaeological sites were demolished one by one. Many questioned the wisdom of allowing a few to profit by digging up and selling the world's shared maritime heritage.

The debate escalated and in the United States eventually led to the Federal Government passing the landmark Abandoned Shipwreck Act (ASA) of 1987. This legislation transferred title and management responsibility for National Register–eligible shipwrecks or other types of underwater sites to the states with jurisdiction over lakes, rivers, and coastal waters. The ASA empowered each state to decide the methods by which it administered submerged cultural resources. What the Abandoned Shipwreck Act did not address, however, was the status of archaeological materials recovered prior to 1987. These collections would remain in quasi-judicial limbo as state and federal authorities attempted to define jurisdiction and options under the ASA or state law.

The question of pre-existing collections had relevance for the materials gathered by the Lake Champlain Archaeological Association. As time moved on, the Association's activities tapered off, the group began to lose cohesion, and care of the collection fell entirely to Bill Leege. In 1986, when the Lake Champlain Maritime Museum (LCMM) at Basin Harbor, Vermont, prepared to open its premier exhibit on lake archaeology and history, Leege agreed to loan some of the objects recovered from battle sites. This was the beginning of a lengthy conversation about the ultimate disposition of the artifacts. Leege's sense of responsibility for the collection proved stronger than his need to possess it, and in 1992 he transferred more than four thousand objects recovered from the battle site at Plattsburgh Bay to the Lake Champlain Maritime Museum for cataloguing, study, and public exhibition.

Plattsburgh Bay Anchor No. 2

Even with all of the collecting activity between the 1950s and 1980s, Plattsburgh Bay was not done yielding evidence of the War of 1812 battle. In 1996, the depth sounder on Capt. William Curry's tugboat recorded a curious blip in the bay, an anomaly that Curry passed along to divers William and Ken Van Stockum. Their subsequent survey of this area revealed a wrought-iron anchor lying with both flukes buried in the bottom and one end of its wooden stock jutting above the lakebed. The Van Stockums told veteran diver Frank Pabst of the find, and with his assistance they recovered the anchor and brought it to shore.[20]

It was an impressive artifact, with a 13-foot-long (3.96 m) shank, a distance of 7 feet 9 inches (2.36 m) between the tips of its flukes, and a ring diameter of 23½ inches (60 cm); together with its 14-foot (4.26 m) wooden stock, the anchor weighed around 3000 pounds (1361 kg). The size and obvious historical association of the anchor quickly generated attention from the public and press. Unsure what to do next, the finders called the Lake Champlain Maritime Museum for advice, and the museum immediately sent an artifact conservator to evaluate the anchor and its condition. This preliminary examination revealed that the wood and iron were in excellent condition and that the anchor held a trove of information. There were many words, numbers, and symbols inscribed into the surfaces of the anchor and stock that indicated both its origin and connection to the Plattsburgh battle. These included the broad arrow mark of British government property, the doubly inscribed date 1813 on the anchor's crown (fig. 13.11a), and the word "Quebec" stenciled in white paint on one of the flukes (fig. 13.11b). It was evident that the anchor would not stay in excellent condition for long without preservation treatment, however, since the wood and iron were beginning to react with the air and deteriorate. The New York State Museum in Albany was consulted, and a consensus was quickly reached by the finders, conservators, and state officials that the best course of action was to temporarily return the anchor to the lake bottom while plans were made for preservation and exhibition and funding was secured to pay for it all.

The Van Stockums, the Clinton County (New York) Historical Association (CCHA), and New York State officials asked the LCMM to draft a proposal for the anchor's conservation while they looked for an institution to protect and display the anchor. The necessary elements were soon in place: New York State officials assured local residents of their support for keeping the anchor in Plattsburgh, the CCHA was designated the local permit holder for the project, Plattsburgh City

A

B

Figure 13.11. *Identifying marks on the crown (a) and one fluke (b) of Plattsburgh Bay Anchor No. 2. Engraved inscriptions on one side of the crown include a large British government broad arrow, the name of the maker (Hawks), and the year 1813 (inscribed twice, presumably once by the maker and once by the Royal Navy); one of the flukes features the stenciled word "Quebec" applied with white paint. (Photo courtesy of the Lake Champlain Maritime Museum.)*

Hall was selected to be the long-term repository for the anchor, and State Senator Ronald Stafford arranged for a state appropriation to pay for conservation expenses. Finally, the LCMM contracted to treat the anchor at its Basin Harbor laboratory.

The legal status of the anchor was also evolving at this time. The Abandoned Shipwreck Act transferred title and responsibility for submerged archaeological materials to individual states, but one significant class of site—warships and associated naval or military artifacts—was omitted from the ASA's charge. By international agreement, these remain, in perpetuity, the property of the nation that owned them when they sank to the bottom. The 1813 manufacturing date and the British government's broad arrow together sug-

gested that Plattsburgh Bay Anchor No. 2 was carried into the engagement by a Royal Navy ship. It was therefore determined that the US Navy, not New York State, was the owner by virtue of its capture of the four largest British ships at Plattsburgh. The Naval Historical Center in Washington, DC (now the Naval History and Heritage Command) was supportive of the anchor recovery and preservation project, and by August 1998 the CCHA was ready for a second recovery of the anchor, an event that would coincide with the Battle of Plattsburgh celebration scheduled for September 11 of that year.

With permits, a conservation program, and permanent exhibition in place, all that was needed was for the US Navy to formally sign off on the project. An unexpected legal complication appeared at the eleventh hour, however, and threatened to halt the recovery project: Navy lawyers now determined that the British government still owned the anchor. No one questioned the fact that the four British ships became US property at the conclusion of the battle, but a detailed analysis of historical records indicated that the anchor was probably shot off a vessel *before* the British squadron struck its colors and therefore remained British property.

This opinion was issued ten days before the scheduled raising, an event that had become the focal point of a major weekend celebration in Plattsburgh. The Naval Historical Center enlisted the help of the State Department and authorities in the British government to resolve the problem. It began to look as if the anchor project would have to be postponed until some future date, but, happily, the day before the scheduled recovery the Navy announced that the British Defense Forces had formally endorsed the plan. The British Admiralty transferred its ownership to New York so the anchor could be managed by the state and raised, conserved, and exhibited by the local community.

The rest, as they say, is history. Capt. Frank Pabst and the Van Stockums reraised the anchor and after a short public viewing at Plattsburgh transferred the anchor by barge to the Lake Champlain Maritime Museum. Conservation of the anchor took two years and involved evaluating, cleaning, disassembling, drawing, photographing, and researching anchors in general and this artifact in particular. LCMM researchers hoped to determine if the anchor was from *Confiance* by tracing its history and correlating the location where

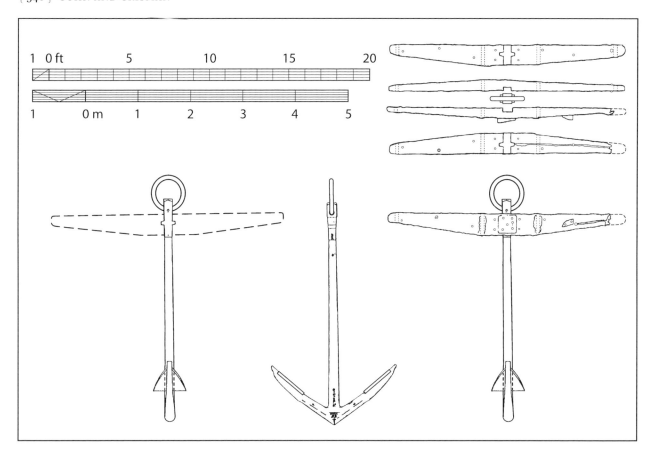

Figure 13.12. *Scale views of Plattsburgh Bay Anchor No. 2. Elements shown here include the forged iron anchor itself and the two halves of the wooden stock. Lake Champlain Maritime Museum researchers determined that this was a Richard Pering–pattern, old-style Admiralty Longshank anchor, a type commonly in use during the War of 1812. (Drawing courtesy of the Lake Champlain Maritime Museum, with modifications by Douglas Inglis.)*

the anchor was found with the movement of the British vessels before and during the battle (see plate 12).

The Archaeology of an Anchor

To casual viewers, Plattsburgh Bay Anchor No. 2 may look like nothing more than an ordinary, old-fashioned anchor. For the archaeologists and historians who labored over it day after day, however, the anchor was a complex, encoded story that could be read by studying the materials, dimensions, construction techniques, many markings visible on its wood and metal surfaces, and evidence of use and damage during its short service life (fig. 13.12). Some clues were easy to read, while others took time and much research to decipher. When it came to determining the year of the anchor's manufacture and for whom it was made, the doubly inscribed date on the crown and the British government's broad arrows were unequivocal: it was made in 1813 for use by Royal Navy ships. The dimensions and general form matched those of a Richard Pering–pattern, old-style Admiralty Longshank anchor, a type widely used throughout the eighteenth and into the second decade of the nineteenth centuries (it would be superseded by an improved pattern after 1815).[21]

Ships' cannon of this era were cast by pouring molten iron into a hollow mold, but cast iron was far too brittle a material to be used for anchors. A very different process was used to manufacture these items. The iron for anchors started as cast metal but was repeatedly heated, hammered, and pressed between rollers until the impurities were driven out and the metal was transformed into much tougher wrought iron. Anchors were assembled by bundling wrought-iron bars together, heating them to a white-hot temperature, and then forge-welding them into a single piece with the blows of an enormous hammer.[22] It was a complex undertaking that required good-quality iron, plenty of fuel for the furnace, a well-equipped forge, much labor, and above all a comprehensive knowledge of the forging process. The materials and craftsmanship that went into making each anchor mattered, for the safety of a ship, its cargo, and its crew depended on the strength of the final product.

The word "HAWKS" inscribed in three places on the Plattsburgh Bay anchor's crown and shank allowed LCMM archaeologists to identify the manufacturer as Hawks Iron Works. This firm was founded by William Hawks in the 1740s at Gateshead, a town located across the Tyne River from Newcastle in far northeastern England. Although it was initially a small and not-very-prosperous operation, Hawks's eldest son William Jr. gradually built it into a profitable concern that was, by the 1790s, producing steel, anchors, heavy chains, and steam-engine parts. It was a major supplier of anchors to the Royal Navy over the two decades of near-continuous war that Britain experienced between 1793 and 1815.[23]

LCMM conservators tested the quality of the workmanship and materials at Hawks Iron Works by coring a small sample from the anchor's shank for analysis at the laboratories of the BF Goodrich Company. The structure and purity of the metal was determined by X-ray fluorescence in conjunction with scanning electron microscopy and standard microscopic inspection. The results showed that the anchor was composed of remarkably pure, highly processed mild steel. The properties of the metal suggested that the anchor was forged at a uniform temperature and allowed to cool slowly, a practice that allowed for a more uniform crystal structure in the metal and yielded a higher level of tensile strength. According to Matthew Kurtz of BF Goodrich, the anchor founders at Hawks "possessed a superior working knowledge of iron's physical properties, and . . . were able to manufacture a highly refined product."[24]

Besides the manufacturer's name, the year of its forging, and the government's ownership stamps, the finished anchor acquired other inscriptions and markings. Some of these have remained enigmas, for example the "H·T·1242" on the shank, which may have been a production or inventory number. The numbers "20–3–8" inscribed into the shank and one arm and painted in white on one of the anchor's flukes indicated the anchor's weight in the avoirdupois system of measurement then employed by the Royal Navy. In this system, a single hundredweight amounts to 112 pounds

(50.8 kg); quarters are one-fourth of a hundredweight or 28 pounds (12.7 kg). Thus, the numbers 20–3–8 indicate 20 hundredweight, 3 quarters, and 8 pounds, which adds up to a weight (not including the wooden stock) of 2332 pounds (1057 kg).[25]

Royal Navy tables of anchor weights and dimensions dating from 1763 to 1830 were consulted to determine the Plattsburgh Bay anchor's possible classification (bower, stream, or kedge) and the size of the warship that would carry an anchor of this weight. Only two large Royal Navy vessels participated in the Plattsburgh Bay action, the 16-gun brig *Linnet* and the 37-gun frigate *Confiance,* and the size of the anchor already had researchers convinced that it was from the latter warship. According to the tables, however, the Plattsburgh Bay anchor was too heavy to be used as a stream or kedge anchor for either *Linnet* or *Confiance* and was the correct size for a bower anchor on a sloop of war of 300 to 400 tons. A seagoing frigate mounting an armament comparable to that of *Confiance* was supposed to carry a bower of 40 to 44 hundredweight, twice the weight of the Plattsburgh Bay anchor.[26]

Does this mean that the anchor actually belonged to *Linnet* and not *Confiance*? Possibly, but not necessarily, since neither of the large British vessels on Lake Champlain in 1814 could be considered typical warships of the era. Above the waterline they may have resembled seagoing ships of their class, but unusually shallow hulls meant their displacements were far less than those of equivalent saltwater brigs or frigates.[27] Furthermore, Lake Champlain has neither massive waves nor strong tidal currents, conditions that demanded extra-heavy ground tackle for ships anchoring in coastal waters. *Linnet* and *Confiance* could get by with smaller, easier-to-handle anchors, a fact that must have been obvious to the administrators, officers, and artificers preparing the two ships at Isle aux Noix.

The word "Quebec" elegantly stenciled in white paint on one fluke gave LCMM researchers a reference point in their attempt to document the route this anchor followed from the Hawks Iron Works to Lake Champlain in 1813–14. "Quebec" was almost certainly the equivalent of an address label, indicating the anchor's destination when it shipped out of Britain. Given the time necessary to assemble and finish the anchor at the iron works, transfer it from the manufacturer to a Royal Navy yard or storehouse, and then transport it to Canada, it seems unlikely that this one could have arrived at Quebec before the fall of 1813. Arrival in 1814 seems more plausible.

The Royal Navy took command of Britain's lake squadrons in the spring of 1813, and its campaign to build overwhelmingly superior naval forces on Lakes Ontario and Champlain was in full swing by that fall. At the end of October 1813, a convoy of ships arrived at Quebec from Great Britain carrying a large contingent of Royal Navy officers and sailors, as well as much-needed equipment and stores.[28] The demand for materials to build and outfit the lake ships was ceaseless, however, and over the winter of 1813–14 the Admiralty prepared another large convoy at Portsmouth, England, to sail for Canada in April.

It was during the organization of this effort that the Admiralty Office in London issued a list on January 26, 1814, entitled "An Account of Stores to be provided at Portsmouth for Quebec." Among the many items of equipment destined for North America were thirty anchors; of these, fourteen appear to have been large-ship bowers that ranged in size from 35 to 20 hundredweight (3920 lbs [1778 kg] to 2240 lbs [1016 kg]) and sixteen were stream- or kedge-sized anchors that ranged from 8½ to 3½ hundredweight (952 lbs [432 kg] to 392 lbs [178 kg]).[29] The list specified that six anchors of 20 hundredweight were to be sent to Quebec, and it is very possible that the anchor found in Plattsburgh Bay was among them.

The same Admiralty document indicated that the anchors were to be shipped in *Abundance,* a 24-gun armed naval transport built in 1799 at Southampton. The anchor-laden *Abundance* was one of 27 ships that departed from Portsmouth in early April 1814 under the protection of the 74-gun third-rate *Spencer* and a handful of frigates. They crossed the Atlantic as part of a much larger convoy of 120 ships, and once they reached the western side, ten ships (including *Abundance*) separated and made their way to Quebec, where they arrived on June 2.[30] Some of the vessels unloaded here, while others of shallower draft were instructed to proceed up the St. Lawrence River to discharge their cargoes at Montreal. The much-needed naval stores and equipment—including the anchors—were loaded into smaller transport boats and forwarded up the St. Lawrence to Kingston on Lake Ontario or sent up the Richelieu River to the naval yard at Isle aux Noix, where work was getting underway in early June on the frigate that would be launched on August 25 as *Confiance.*

A second possible source for the Plattsburgh Bay anchor must be considered, and that was the transports and warships laid up at Quebec. Because the war against France was wrapping up at this time, the Royal Navy found itself with extra ships that could serve as a source of men and materials for the freshwater squadrons. This began late in 1813 when the ship *Æolus,* after delivering sailors and stores at Quebec, was stripped of every useful item for the new frigates building on Lake Ontario and left an empty hulk. During the spring and summer of 1814 the third rates *Ajax, Centaur,* and *Warspite* were also laid up at Quebec and picked clean of equipment needed for the lakes.[31] Any one of these ships could have provided the Plattsburgh Bay anchor, but two lines of evidence suggest that this was not the case. First, according to the Royal Navy's tables, the anchor is far too small to be a bower anchor and slightly too large to be a stream anchor from an oceangoing 74-gun ship. Second, the "Quebec" freshly painted on the Plattsburgh Bay anchor's fluke strongly hints that it was sent to Canada as cargo, rather than as equipment belonging to an active-service ship.

The archival collections consulted by LCMM researchers did not yield any documents specifically mentioning the Plattsburgh Bay anchor. Given the Royal Navy's ability to generate records, however, it is possible that such a document exists and may yet be found. What is certain is that by the late summer of 1814, the anchor was at Isle aux Noix and had been readied for service on Lake Champlain.

Preparation of the anchor included attaching a wooden stock to the upper end of the shank so that it was perpendicular to the arms and flukes at the anchor's base. The stock ensured that a ship was held firmly in place after the anchor was dropped to the sea (or lake) bottom: the first strong pull on the cable tipped the stock over to a horizontal position and raised the arms upright, forcing the lower fluke to dig in. The stock was fashioned from a single, 14-foot-long (4.2 m) piece of white oak that was sawn in half lengthwise. A mortise carved in the center of each half fit the square upper shank and its two protruding nuts. In addition, the interior surfaces of the two halves were planed or shaved from the ends to within 1 foot (30.5 cm) of the center on each side; the resulting gaps allowed for dynamic tensioning when two wrought-iron hoops were fit over each end of the reassembled stock and driven toward the center. Small iron nails helped lock the hoops in place. The halves were further secured with four iron bolts through the center of the stock and three wooden treenails through each end. The tension created by pinching the two halves of the stock together was maintained over 184 years, for when conservators removed the hoops and cut the fasteners, the two pieces sprang apart with considerable force.[32] The letters "HMS" and a Roman numeral (now unreadable) were found carved into one end of the anchor's stock after it was recovered from Plattsburgh Bay, and the hoops were stamped with the broad arrow.

In order to protect valuable cables from excessive chafing on the anchor's iron ring, sailors puddened the ring. They started by winding strips of tar-soaked fabric—parceling—around the metal and then covered this with a continuous tight wrap of quarter-inch (6.35 mm) line.[33] When the anchor was found by divers in 1996 the puddening appeared well-preserved, but the subsequent lifting and lowering of the anchor by its ring and the alternate water-air-water exposure caused this fragile iron-infused organic material to disintegrate. Only the impression of the fabric and rope was left in the surface of the ring at the start of conservation.

Which warship, *Linnet* or *Confiance,* lost Plattsburgh Bay Anchor No. 2 during the battle on September 11, 1814? We cannot be absolutely certain, but the battle reports and court martial transcripts of the surviving Royal Navy officers and the location where the anchor was found together strongly suggest it was the frigate *Confiance.* In both his after-action report and his court martial testimony, Capt. Daniel Pring of *Linnet* listed in detail the setbacks, casualties, and mounting damage that ultimately forced the surrender of his brig. He said nothing, however, about *Linnet* losing anchors or experiencing difficulty in holding its position during the battle.[34]

Anchors featured prominently in the battle report and testimony of Lt. James Robertson, who became the senior officer on *Confiance* after the death of Capt. George Downie. According to Robertson, *Confiance* sailed into Plattsburgh Bay with three anchors bent on cables and ready for use: the small bower and best bower prepared for deployment from the bow and the sheet anchor bent onto a stream cable that led through one of the stern ports. Anchors had an important part in Captain Downie's battle plan: *Confiance* was to enter the bay, sail alongside the brig *Eagle* at the van of the

American line and deliver a double-shotted broadside from the starboard guns, and then turn and cross the bow of the US flagship *Saratoga.* Here the British frigate would drop two or even all three anchors to hold its position and then commence a raking fire on *Saratoga* with the port broadside.

Downie's plan fell apart as *Confiance* approached the US Navy squadron. The American gunfire proved unexpectedly heavy, and one of the anchors, described as the small bower in Robertson's action report and the sheet in his court martial testimony, was "shot from the bows," depriving the ship of one-third of its ground tackle. At the same time, the wind shifted to a head-on direction and fell off, forcing the frigate to let go a second anchor—either the small bower or the sheet—at a distance of ½ mile (804 m) from the American line. Within moments the cable and spring line were cut by shot, and this anchor was lost as well. The last remaining anchor, the best bower, was then dropped, but its spring was soon severed, leaving only the cable intact. *Confiance* fought the rest of the battle on this single-point mooring. Late in the action the crew managed to get a new spring on the best bower's cable, but their attempt to haul the ship around and present a fresh row of guns ended when raking fire killed several of the men working the spring. At this point in the battle, Robertson stated dryly, the surviving members of *Confiance*'s crew "evinced an evident disposition to discontinue the Action" by fleeing below deck.[35]

The location where the anchor was found in Plattsburgh Bay is substantially to the south of the area where many published plans show the battle took place.[36] The distribution of shot and debris observed by William Leege and his associates, however, indicates that these maps are in error and that the fight took place in the entrance to the bay rather than up inside the bay itself.[37] The location of the anchor also agrees with four charts prepared as evidence for the Royal Navy court martial held in 1815 (fig. 13.13).[38] The distances shown on the inquiry charts are not accurate, but bearings and ship positions relative to major landmarks do appear to be correct, and they show *Confiance* moored in the vicinity of where the anchor was recovered.

By itself, the apparent correlation between where the anchor was found in the bay and the position of *Confiance* on the court martial charts is meager evidence. However, when combined with other evidence,

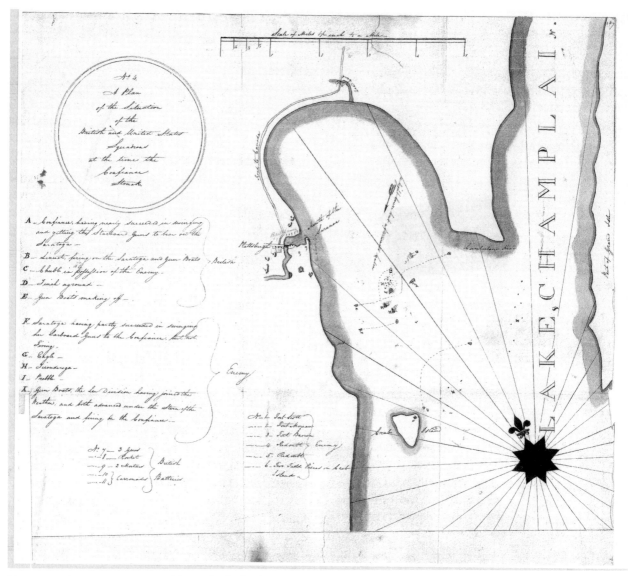

Figure 13.13. *A contemporary map of the Battle of Lake Champlain. Entitled "A Plan of the Situation of the British and United States Squadrons at the Time the Confiance Struck," this is one of four charts prepared for the Royal Navy court martial of the officers who fought at Plattsburgh Bay. It was used at the inquest to establish the relative positions of ships during the battle. The charts were entered as evidence and can be considered reasonably accurate (if not exactly precise) versions of what happened on September 11, 1814. (Admiralty Fonds, ADM 1, Reg. No. 5450, National Archives of the UK, Public Record Office.)*

the case for this being a *Confiance* anchor becomes more compelling. We know that the Plattsburgh Bay anchor was a nearly new piece of Royal Navy equipment in 1814, that the British frigate lost two large anchors to enemy gunfire, and that there is no mention of *Linnet* losing any anchors in the battle. The possibility that one of the US Navy ships on Lake Champlain was carrying a Quebec-tagged, 1813-dated Royal Navy anchor seems remote. Given all of this, it is hard to believe that this anchor could be anything other than one of the two lost by *Confiance.*

Eloquent testimony to the ferocity of the opening broadsides between the two squadrons at Plattsburgh Bay was also engraved into the surface of Anchor No. 2. The historical record tells us that both of *Confiance*'s anchors were lost in the early stages of the battle. Despite its relatively narrow profile and short period of exposure to enemy shot, the anchor did not entirely escape the opening fusillade of the US squadron. When LCMM conservators began to document and clean Plattsburgh Bay Anchor No. 2 in 1998, they discovered a crater-like impact scar from a round shot on top of one arm, not far from the shank. Impact damage from a small shot was also found at one end of the anchor's wooden stock.

Conclusion

The Battle of Plattsburgh Bay was a short, violent encounter that resulted in the strategic Lake Champlain corridor remaining firmly under US control. Macdonough's victory not only frustrated British intent to use this route to invade part of the United States but also contributed to bringing the wider war to a negotiated close on Christmas Eve 1814. For both the winners and losers, the price was steep. The battle resulted in the death of over one hundred sailors and officers, the greatest loss of life in a single action on any of the lakes. Many who survived endured permanent physical injuries, and no doubt many suffered from stress disorders for the rest of their lives. Even those like Benajah Phelps and J. C. Hubbell who watched the battle from a safe distance were thoroughly shaken by what they saw after the shooting was over.

Battles like Plattsburgh Bay represent a great throw of the dice when competing societies summon their human and material resources and risk them in the hope of achieving a desired outcome. Such prodigal and hazardous endeavors invariably leave a trail of historical and archaeological evidence, a record that holds different meanings for people of every era. Plattsburgh Bay was no exception. In the immediate aftermath of the fight, Americans wanted to see evidence of their nation's naval prowess at a time when military, economic, and even political collapse appeared imminent. Following long-established precedent, Macdonough sent tangible symbols of the US Navy's victory, the captured British flags, to Washington, where they could be displayed as trophies. The victory also inspired creation of medals, swords, and similar gifts for the country's new heroes and generated commemorative artwork, music, poetry, prints, ceramics, books, and monuments for the general public. The location and condition of the captured British ships made them disappointing as trophies, but their abandonment in an out-of-the-way river would fortuitously allow parts of *Linnet* to survive for future archaeological study.

Another type of archaeological record was created in the midst of the battle, one that would be inaccessible (and therefore overlooked) for a century and a half. During the battle and in its immediate aftermath, shot, equipment, and assorted materials rained down from the warships and littered the bottom of Plattsburgh Bay. These objects remained unseen and unmolested until the invention of scuba technology unlocked the vault and exposed the submerged battlefield to intense and unregulated collecting. The activities of William Leege and his colleagues in the Lake Champlain Archaeological Association were, in their way, ahead of the times. Driven by their love of history and the excitement of discovery, they salvaged not for personal gain but because of a desire to learn about the lake's past and to share their knowledge with the public. Today their discoveries remain together as a collection for study and education. Still left unresolved and begging a solution is the fate of similar artifact collections from Plattsburgh, Valcour Bay, and other sites that reside in the homes of aging divers, collections that exist in a jurisdictional and management limbo.

Plattsburgh Bay Anchor No. 2 symbolizes an important chapter in American and British naval history as well as a significant success in modern archaeological resource management. The discovery, recovery, conservation, and public exhibition of the anchor provided a new and powerful connection to the naval battle that can be shared by all. It also gives us a case study of how individuals, local organizations, and governments can come together to build a jurisdictional consensus and thereby preserve elements of our shared history for the benefit of future generations.

NOTES

1. Benajah Phelps, "The Battle of Lake Champlain: The Story of an Eye-Witness, Retold by J.E. Tuttle," *The Outlook* 69, no. 9 (New York, November 2, 1901), pp. 573–78.

2. *Plattsburgh* (NY) *Republican,* February 1, 1879; reprinted in New York State Historian, *The Centenary of the Battle of Plattsburgh, September 6–11, 1814–1914* (Albany, NY: The University of the State of New York, 1914), pp. 33–34.

3. B. N. Clark, "Accounts of the Battle of Plattsburgh, September 11, 1814: From Contemporaneous Sources," *Vermont Antiquarian* 1, no. 3 (1903), p. 88. An after-action tally of dead, injured, and damage on *Confiance* may be found in William Wood, ed., *Select British Documents of the Canadian War of 1812,* vol. 3, pt. 1 (Toronto: The Champlain Society, 1926), pp. 468–82. In the action of September 10, 1813 on Lake Erie, the other major freshwater battle of the war, the American squadron suffered twenty-seven dead and ninety-seven wounded, and the British squadron forty-one killed and ninety-three wounded. David Curtis Skaggs and Gerard T. Altoff, *A Signal Victory: The Lake Erie Campaign 1812–1813* (Annapolis: Naval Institute Press, 1997), pp. 151–52.

4. New York State Historian, *Centenary of the Battle of Platts-burgh,* p. 34.

5. Macdonough's report, as well as other British and American accounts of the battle at Plattsburgh Bay, have been reprinted in Michael J. Crawford, ed., *The Naval War of 1812, A Documentary History,* vol. 3 (Washington, DC: Naval Historical Center, 2002), pp. 607–17.

6. Simeon Doty, "Account of Simeon Doty," *The Plattsburgh* (NY) *Republican,* September 22, 1877; Rodney Macdonough, *Life of Commodore Thomas Macdonough, U.S. Navy* (Boston: The Fort Hill Press, 1909), p. 189.

7. Macdonough, *Life of Commodore Thomas Macdonough,* pp. 193–95; David Curtis Skaggs, *Thomas Macdonough: Master of Command in the Early U.S. Navy* (Annapolis: Naval Institute Press, 2003), pp. 147–48.

8. Examples of the songs and verse inspired by the victory can be seen in Ralph Nading Hill, *Lake Champlain: Key to Liberty* (Woodstock, VT: The Countryman Press, 1991), p. 191; Phelps, "Battle of Lake Champlain," p. 578; New York State Historian, *Centenary of the Battle of Plattsburgh,* pp. 39, 43, 52–53, 68–69.

9. Benjamin Silliman, *Remarks Made on a Short Tour Between Hartford and Quebec in 1819* (New Haven, CT: S. Converse, 1820), pp. 180–81; an evocative pencil sketch of the moored fleet by the French naturalist and artist Charles Alexandre Lesueur may be seen in Doris Begor Morton, *Day Before Yesterday* (Whitehall, NY: The Whitehall Times, 1977), p. 15 (the original is in the Lesueur collection at the Musée Bibliothèque at Le Havre, France).

10. Harold Connett Washburn, *Illustrated Case Inscriptions from the Official Catalogue of the Trophy Flags of the United States Navy* (Baltimore: The Lord Baltimore Press, 1913), pp. 16–17, 62–63, 96–97; James W. Cheevers, Associate Director, US Naval Academy Museum, personal communication with Laura White, October 17, 2011.

11. Spencer Tucker, *Arming the Fleet: U.S. Navy Ordnance in the Muzzle-Loading Era* (Annapolis: Naval Institute Press, 1989), p. 138; Adrian B. Caruana, *The History of English Sea Ordnance 1523–1875, Volume II: The Age of the System, 1715–1815* (East Sussex: Jean Boudriot Publications, 1997), pp. 324–28.

12. The 1914 centennial (and subsequent) anniversaries of the battle generated a plethora of commemorative books and pamphlets. See New York State Historian, *Centenary of the Battle of Plattsburgh;* New York State Commission, Plattsburgh Centenary, "A Fitting, Permanent Memorial," Chapter 8 in *The Battle of Plattsburgh: What Historians Say About It* (Albany, NY: J. B. Lyon Company, Printers, 1914); Daughters of the American Revolution, Saranac (NY) Chapter, *Macdonough Day, April 14, 1914* (New York and New Jersey Committees, 1914); Macdonough Commission of Vermont, *Macdonough Centennial, Vergennes, Vermont 1814–1914* (Vermont Publicity Bureau, 1914); Plattsburgh Centenary Commission, *Dedication of the Thomas Macdonough Memorial* (Plattsburgh, NY: Centenary Commission, August 18, 1926).

13. The Revolutionary War site at Valcour Bay has undergone archaeological study in recent years; see: Arthur B. Cohn, Adam I. Kane, Christopher R. Sabick, Edwin R. Scollon, and Justin B. Clement, *Valcour Bay Research Project: 1999–2004 Results from the Archaeological Investigation of a Revolutionary War Battlefield in Lake Champlain, Clinton County, New York* (Basin Harbor, VT: Lake Champlain Maritime Museum, March 2007).

14. William Leege, personal communication with Kevin Crisman, July 1997. The authors wish to thank Anne W. Lessmann for her research and compilation of information on the LCAA surveys in Plattsburgh Bay.

15. Three of the ten soldiers from the 39th Regiment who served on *Confiance* were slightly wounded in the battle. Wood, ed., *Select British Documents,* vol. 3, pt. 1, pp. 375, 479, 481.

16. Wood, ed., *Select British Documents,* vol. 3, pt. 1, p. 422.

17. The portion recovered by Leege's group is now in the collections of the Lake Champlain Maritime Museum. The lower part of the anchor recovered by the Vermont divers was given a coat of paint and displayed at the Shelburne Bay Yacht Club in Shelburne, Vermont, where it was measured by Kevin Crisman and Virginia West in 1985.

18. Kevin J. Crisman, *The* Eagle: *An American Brig on Lake Champlain during the War of 1812* (Shelburne, VT: The New England Press; Annapolis: Naval Institute Press, 1987), p. 225.

19. Crisman, *The Eagle,* pp. 228–29.

20. The story of the anchor's discovery and recovery, as well as the results of the anchor conservation and research, are published in David S. Robinson, Elizabeth R. Baldwin, Arthur B. Cohn, Ian Griffin, Anne W. Lessmann, and Christopher R. Sabick, *Conservation of a War of 1812 Anchor from Plattsburgh Bay, Clinton County, New York* (Basin Harbor, VT: Lake Champlain Maritime Museum, May 2001).

21. Betty Nelson Curryer, *Anchors: An Illustrated History* (Annapolis: Naval Institute Press, 1999), pp. 57, 62, 73–76; Robinson et al., *Conservation of a War of 1812 Anchor,* pp. 113–15.

22. Denis Diderot, *A Diderot Pictorial Encyclopedia of Trades and Industry,* vol. 1 (New York: Dover Publications, 1987), plates 102–107; Curryer, *Anchors,* pp. 62–72.

23. Robinson et al., *Conservation of a War of 1812 Anchor,* pp. 128–39.

24. Robinson et al., *Conservation of a War of 1812 Anchor,* pp. 85–88.

25. Robinson et al., *Conservation of a War of 1812 Anchor,* p. 140.

26. Curryer, *Anchors,* p. 58; Robinson et al., *Conservation of a War of 1812 Anchor,* pp. 140–45.

27. *Confiance* had a depth of hold of only 7 feet (2.13 m) and drew no more than 8 feet 6 inches (2.59 m) of water. Wood, ed., *Select British Documents,* vol. 3, pt. 1, p. 422; Register of US Naval Vessels, 1797–1814, entry 169, record group 45, National Archives and Records Administration.

28. Robert Malcomson, *Lords of the Lake: The Naval War on Lake Ontario 1812–1814* (Toronto: Robin Brass Studio, 1998), p. 232.

29. Film B-1009, 3179: 1–18, Library and Archives Canada; Robinson et al., *Conservation of a War of 1812 Anchor,* p. 147.

30. *Quebec Mercury* (June 2, 1814); Robinson et al., *Conservation of a War of 1812 Anchor,* p. 148.

31. Malcomson, *Lords of the Lake,* pp. 232, 295.

32. Robinson et al., *Conservation of a War of 1812 Anchor,* pp. 79–80.

33. A description and two excellent illustrations (Figs. 360 and 361) of anchor ring puddening may be seen in Darcy Lever, *The Young Sea Officer's Sheet Anchor, or A Key to the Leading of Rigging, and to Practical Seamanship* (Leeds: Printed by Thomas Gill, 1808), p. 68.

34. Wood, ed., *Select British Documents,* vol. 3, pt. 1, pp. 368–73, 460–65.

35. Wood, ed., *Select British Documents,* vol. 3, pt. 1, pp. 373–77, 468–82.

36. The tendency to locate the battle farther inside the bay seems to have been nearly universal; even a very rough sketch of the action by Thomas Macdonough shows the line of ships extending farther to the north than was probably the case. See Macdonough, *Life of Commodore Thomas Macdonough,* plates 1 and 2; Robert Malcomson, *Warships of the Great Lakes 1754–1834* (London: Caxton Editions, 2003), p. 130; Benson J. Lossing, *The Pictorial Fieldbook of the War of 1812* (New York: Harper and Brothers, 1868; facsimile reprint, New Hampshire Publishing Company, 1976), p. 871.

37. William Leege, personal communication with Kevin Crisman, July 1997.

38. "A Plan of the Situation of the British and United States Squadrons," No. 1: "At the time the Confiance and Linnet Anchored," No. 2: "half an hour after the Confiance anchored," No. 3: "about the middle of the Action," and No. 4: "at the time the Confiance Struck," reg. no. 5450, Admiralty Fonds, ADM 1, The National Archives of the UK: Public Record Office. *Confiance*'s Master Robert A. Brydon testified at the court martial that the four charts were correct copies "to the best of his knowledge and belief," Wood, ed., *Select British Documents,* vol. 3, pt. 1, p. 416.

14 CONCLUSIONS

"Coffins of the Brave" — Two Hundred Years Later

KEVIN J. CRISMAN

Two hundred years have passed since the War of 1812 roiled the landscape of North America and the oceans of the world (fig. 14.1). As wars go, this one was brief and did not change the boundary maps. This is hardly surprising: neither the United States nor Great Britain ever committed the forces necessary to conquer and hold large swaths of territory. After two and a half years of fighting, both readily signed a peace treaty that called for a return to prewar borders and trade: status quo ante bellum. Despite its limited scope and seemingly "neutral" outcome, the war's events, particularly the naval battles on the oceans and lakes, have fascinated the public and inspired generations of historians to produce thousands of books and articles. There is no shortage of popular and scholarly reading on the subject.

The bounty of historical publications on the War of 1812 has also served to highlight the gaps in traditional scholarly sources. Significant elements of the story are missing, many of which never made it to the documentary record in the first place. This is particularly true of the shipwrights and sailors who served in the lake campaigns; we know the broad outlines of their travails and accomplishments, but so many details of their work, of the ships they built and sailed, and of their material world and daily experiences have remained tantalizingly out of our reach. Fortunately, as we have seen in the preceding chapters of this book, evidence of the past survives in more places than archives and libraries. A parallel record is available for us to study, a record embedded in shipwrecks and artifacts. In recent decades the field of archaeology has guided a new approach to understanding the events of 1812–15, one that blends the evidence in contemporary documents and images with a wealth of details derived from objects lost, discarded, and otherwise left behind. The synergism to be found in this kind of research is exciting, for material remains often raise questions that

Figure 14.1. *The Brown's Bay Vessel at Fort Wellington, Ontario, in 2012. Scholarly and popular interest in the people, places, events, and archaeological heritage of the War of 1812 remains strong in Canada and the United States two centuries after the conflict. The Brown's Bay Vessel was the centerpiece of this new exhibit on the War of 1812 in the upper St. Lawrence River region. (Photo by Thierry Boyer, courtesy of Parks Canada.)*

we never thought to ask of the historical record and the written sources in turn are crucial for interpreting artifacts and structures. The combination provides a powerful tool for our attempts to understand the past since it generates a narrative whole that is greater than the sum of the parts.

What have we learned? For one thing, it is clear that the War of 1812 was an odd sort of war from start to finish. Historical evidence tells us that there was nothing inevitable about it: with more astute leadership, diplomatic finesse, and faster communications, the two belligerents might have avoided going to the brink and beyond. Like most conflicts, once the shooting started, events moved in directions that were unintended and largely unwelcomed by the war's proponents. "Free trade and sailors' rights" were the maritime casus belli that led the US Congress to declare war in June of 1812, but the fight for control of the oceans—however brilliant and newsworthy—yielded results that were more

symbolic than decisive. The disparity of forces was just too great. Naval construction and naval battles on North America's freshwater lakes ultimately had a greater influence on the outcome of the war.

The shift of focus to the continent's interior was entirely predictable, given the miniscule size of the US Navy's seagoing fleet, the longstanding American designs on its northern neighbor, and the fact that the US-Canadian border was the only place where the two protagonists were in continuous contact throughout the war. The intense naval activity on inland waters also owed much to the challenges of mobility and logistics in a wilderness region; in such a remote location the success of armies hinged on command of the waterways. Three self-contained border arenas, the Upper Lakes, Lake Ontario, and Lake Champlain, together offered the best opportunities for changing the map of North America. Throughout the War of 1812, from its muddled beginning to its sudden end, the lakes would remain the geographical focal point for each side's strategic planning and resources.

The importance of commanding the inland waters was repeatedly demonstrated over the course of the war. During the crucial first summer campaign in 1812, a mere handful of poorly manned Provincial Marine warships on Lakes Ontario, Erie, and Huron made it possible for the numerically inferior British Army and its native allies to capture American strongpoints and soundly defeat the forces that were massing to invade Upper Canada. Whatever advantage of surprise the United States gained by its declaration of war was completely wasted by the failure to prepare naval squadrons on the Great Lakes. The time and momentum lost in 1812 would never be fully recovered by the United States.

Determined shipbuilding efforts over the following winter and spring enabled the US Navy to defeat the Royal Navy on Lake Erie in September 1813. This battle yielded important results for the victors: it ended a year-long series of US Army defeats and setbacks in the Upper Lakes region, reinvigorated the morale of the American public and government, and cleared the way for a successful—if strategically limited—offensive in the far west. The turnaround in US fortunes in the west did not lead to the permanent acquisition of Canadian territory but did have dire consequences for Native Americans living south and west of the Great Lakes. British military and diplomatic support faded away in 1814–15, leaving native populations without allies in their struggle to prevent further loss of their lands.

Lake Ontario was the gateway to the entire Great Lakes region, and its outlet was one of two inland water routes leading to the heart of Lower Canada. Both sides considered Ontario the pivotal theater for freshwater naval operations and carried out awe-inspiring feats of shipbuilding between 1812 and 1815. The enormous efforts and expenditures on this lake prevented defeat but did not yield victory: the inherent caution of the opposing commanders and their determination to match one another ship for ship allowed neither to achieve dominance. The end of the war cut short a campaign of shipbuilding and outfitting that outweighed all previous efforts on the lakes: one ship of the line was already in service and four more were ready to be launched. Would Lake Ontario have experienced a colossal battle in 1815, or just more maneuvering and shipbuilding? We will never know.

The third inland naval theater, Lake Champlain, saw relatively little activity during the first two years of the conflict, a neglect that is surprising when we consider its proximity to Montreal and Quebec City. In the war's third year the naval rivalry on the lake rapidly heated up, although the catalyst was a British incursion from the north rather than an American attack from the south. The defensive victory of the US Navy at Plattsburgh Bay in September 1814 thwarted the largest British counter-invasion of the war and encouraged the British government to settle on a nonpunitive, lasting peace just three months later. Given this fight's intensity and its obvious influence in ending the wider conflict, we must agree with Theodore Roosevelt's assessment of Plattsburgh Bay as "the greatest naval battle of the war."[1]

Even now, two hundred years after the guns have fallen silent and the ships have been broken up or sunk, the War of 1812's freshwater ships and naval campaigns continue to excite our fascination. It is not hard to see why. It was an event with few parallels in history: the navigational conditions, environmental extremes, tactical limitations, logistical demands, and time constraints differed in so many ways from conditions on the high seas. Every naval conflict has its peculiarities, but the War of 1812 on the lakes most assuredly ranks among the most peculiar and dramatic.

One obvious factor that set the 1812–14 campaigns apart from history's other great naval struggles was the remote location and unusual medium on which they were fought. Our world has relatively few large bodies of freshwater and none that match the combined surface area of the Great Lakes and Lake Champlain. These lakes share a common outlet to the sea, but impassable rapids and waterfalls sharply defined the limits of navigation. As we have seen in the previous chapters, it was impossible to bring in battle-ready ships from elsewhere and thus the only way to add new ships to a naval squadron was to build them on the spot.

There was also an unusual naval intelligence factor at play on the lakes. The rapid flow of information across the border—in both directions—made it nearly impossible to conduct secret shipbuilding activity. Commodores were invariably well-apprised of their foe's strength in ships, guns, and sailors, even if they could not always divine the enemy's next move. This element of certainty about opposing forces was unusual for a naval war.

Other anomalies that set the lake war apart were the logistical and environmental conditions under which the inland squadrons were created. Warships are the most expensive and technologically complex mobile fighting machines a nation can build. The "modern" sailing navies of the seventeenth, eighteenth, and nineteenth centuries depended on a vast infrastructure for their construction and maintenance. The War of 1812 lake squadrons were created in an entirely different environment, a rugged near-wilderness with plenty of old-growth timber but not much else in the way of shipbuilding facilities, stores, equipment, and manpower. Everything depended on the speed and resourcefulness of transportation agents and shipwrights tasked with preparing the warships. Some shortfalls were met by adapting locally available materials (the iron-ore ballast found on the US brig *Eagle* is an example of this), but most of the stores that were required had to be imported by river and road from the seaboard. The timely shipment of naval supplies was a constant and very expensive challenge.

The enclosed nature of the lakes might suggest they were safer for navigation than the open seas, but as Captain Rybka observed in his chapter on the brig *Niagara,* this was emphatically not the case in the early nineteenth century. The mid-continent region of North America is subject to frequent and sudden changes in winds and weather, with powerful gales in the spring and fall and fast-moving, highly potent squalls in the summer. There was no reliable means of weather forecasting to warn ships of impending danger, and as we have seen, even experienced mariners could fall victim to hazardous conditions. It was a fast-moving squall that sent the US Navy schooners *Hamilton* and *Scourge* to the bottom in August 1813, while similar sharp blasts of wind dismasted the Royal Navy schooner *Tecumseth* in September 1815.

Slower, longer-lasting storms were no less dangerous. The shores of the lakes, particularly Erie and Ontario, offered few protected harbors, and unlike ships at sea, which might run before a storm for days on end, ships on the lakes encountered a lee shore no matter which direction they turned. In September 1814, early fall storms nearly sank the US brigs *Jefferson* and *Jones* at the western end of Lake Ontario and threatened the US ships under Comm. Arthur Sinclair at the eastern end of Lake Erie.

Every year, winter weather effectively shut down most naval operations on the lakes from late fall to early spring. This annual timeout provided opportunities for repairs and new construction, but the enforced idleness and intense cold were clearly not welcomed by many officers and sailors. Winter on the lakes created an unusual hazard for warships: the threat of incendiary attacks over the ice by saboteurs or sleigh-borne infantry. Historical records tell us that such attacks were frequently planned or anticipated, but the only major success in this line was the British destruction of the US Navy vessels *Ariel, Trippe, Little Belt,* and *Chippewa* on Lake Erie in late December 1813.

Finally, the bathymetric features of the lakes placed restrictions on warship design and naval operations. All of the lakes, especially the Upper Lakes and Lake Champlain, contain shallow harbors, channels, and rivers, while subsurface hazards such as sand bars and rock outcrops abound. These shoal areas imposed strict draft limits on ships and required the employment of pilots with local knowledge.[2]

Prior to the advent of archaeological research, our knowledge of the 1812-era lake warships was quite limited. Plans exist for a few of the Provincial Marine's pre-war Great Lakes schooners, the ship sloop *Royal George,* and the US Navy's brig *Oneida.* After the war the Royal Navy took the lines off its largest Lake Ontario warships, and a plan exists for the Upper Lakes schooners *Newash* and *Tecumseth.* The architectural record of the US Navy's wartime-built lake ships is extremely sparse and consists only of Charles Ware's sail plan of the corvette *General Pike,* rudimentary lines for the corvette *Saratoga,* and a set of row galley lines by William Doughty.[3] The lines and appearance of most ships built during the war were never recorded. Even when lines do exist for a ship, they rarely tell us much about its materials, assembly techniques, and timber scantlings, information that is vital for understanding construction philosophies and practices. It is in the areas of ship design and construction that nautical archaeology has thus far made its greatest contributions to our knowledge of the lake war.

In the preceding chapters we have looked at sixteen

different examples of 1812-era naval and commercial shipbuilding. These include four prewar vessels (the schooners *Nancy, Hamilton,* and *Scourge* and brig *General Hunter*), four 16- or 20-gun brigs (*Niagara, Jefferson, Linnet,* and *Eagle*), three warships of much greater size (the frigates *Prince Regent* and *Princess Charlotte* and ship of the line *St. Lawrence*), a steamboat hull converted into an armed schooner (*Ticonderoga*), two gunboats (the Browns Bay Vessel and *Allen*), and two postwar schooners (*Newash* and *Tecumseth*). Despite their differing degrees of preservation and archaeological study, all have told us something about how their creators sought the best balance of strength, durability, capacity, stability, speed, weatherliness, and seaworthiness. These vessels all differed from one another, reflecting the experience and skills of the shipwrights, factors imposed by sailing conditions on the individual lakes, the availability of time, materials, and funds for construction, and what role each ship was expected to perform during its lifetime.

When we examine the general form of the lake-built schooners, sloops of war, corvettes, frigates, and the line-of-battle ship, it is apparent that most would not have been good open-ocean cruisers, particularly if they carried full complements of guns and sailors. Some were sharp-hulled and others were quite full in section, but all were shallower than high-seas ships of similar length, breadth, and armament. Two key factors determined the form of naval vessels on the lakes. First, if they were to be useful, these ships had to be able to sail to where they were needed; keeping the draft to a minimum allowed them to safely venture into near-shore waters, river channels, and shallow harbors. Second, building warships that drew only a few feet of water fore and aft was operationally practical on the lakes thanks to the unlimited fresh water and short duration of passages. No hold space was required for carrying drinking water, and only a few weeks' supply of provisions had to be carried to feed the crew instead of the several months' supply needed for an ocean cruise.

Comparison of hull forms suggests that ships built for the Upper Lakes and Lake Champlain had much in common despite the very considerable difference in their range of navigable waters. Shallows abounded in the Upper Lakes: in the passages between Lakes Erie and Huron (particularly in the St. Clair River), the upper

Niagara River, the entrance to Grand River, Upper Canada, and the harbor at Erie, Pennsylvania, to name but a few troublesome places. Together they made shallow draft an imperative feature on ships. Similar conditions existed on Lake Champlain. Archaeological and historical evidence shows that the larger ships built on these lakes tended to have a very full form in the central part of the hull, with slight to modest deadrise at the midship frame, slack bilges, and a minimal depth of hold. The brig *Eagle* provides us with an example of a builder striving to improve sailing qualities by combining a full, bowl-like midship section with a sharp entrance at the bow and a relatively long, tapering run at the stern.

Lake Ontario has rocks and shoals, but most of its expanse has deep water and so draft limitations were not as extreme here as they were elsewhere. Not surprisingly, vessel designs on this lake followed a somewhat different course during the war. Plans of *Royal George* and *Oneida* indicate that pre-war vessels bore some resemblance to the minimal-draft, full-bodied form seen on the other lakes, although *Royal George* showed moderate amount of deadrise at the midship frame. The US Brig *Oneida*'s notably shallow hull and full midship section were imposed by the building location on the Oswego River, where the entrance to the lake was impeded by a shallow bar. The subsequent establishment of Sackets Harbor as the US Navy's shipbuilding center on Lake Ontario made it possible to build vessels with deeper-draft hulls than were advisable on Erie, Huron, and Champlain.

As Ontario's naval contest intensified and the rival commodores sought every possible advantage, warship design became more extreme. The lines of *Jefferson, Princess Charlotte, Prince Regent,* and *St. Lawrence* show us that by 1814, if not earlier, builders at Kingston and Sackets Harbor were producing ships with a remarkably high angle of deadrise at the midship frame and, in the case of *Jefferson* at least, considerable drag to the keel. These designs had a lot in common with the fast-sailing clipper schooners used by contemporary American privateers on the oceans, but they were built at a much larger scale, with more guns and sailors packed aboard (fig.14.2).

Ship design is always a balancing act. Modification or improvement of one aspect generally comes at the expense of other desirable characteristics. In the case

Figure 14.2. *Model of Henry Eckford's 20-gun brig* Jefferson. *This vessel, examined in Chapter 6, epitomizes the wartime innovations in design and construction made on the lakes by both belligerents. Sharp-built, shallow, and very heavily armed,* Jefferson *and its sister brig* Jones *had many desirable sailing and fighting characteristics, but stability and seaworthiness were probably not among them. (Photo by C. Wayne Smith,* Jefferson *model by Glenn Grieco, Center for Maritime Archaeology and Conservation, Texas A&M University.)*

of the lake warships, the combination of shallow hulls, low freeboard, and batteries of heavy guns had serious consequences for stability, seaworthiness, and sailing qualities. Stability was surely a central concern for officers and sailors who served on these vessels; Captain Rybka's observation that the original, fully armed and manned *Niagara* "must have had frighteningly small stability margins" probably applies to most other freshwater naval craft of the 1812 era. As we have seen, this problem proved fatal for *Hamilton* and *Scourge* (along with the majority of their crews). There were other incidents of near-capsizing during the war, such as *Jefferson* going over on its beam ends during the gale of September 1814.

Seaworthiness, or the ability to comfortably handle a range of different sea conditions, can be closely related to issues of stability. Here again, the freshwater warships clearly had a narrower range of ideal weather and lake conditions than was usual for their seagoing counterparts. In his reports to the US Navy Department in the autumn of 1814, Lake Erie Comm. Arthur Sinclair complained that his ships were too shallow and unable to carry enough ballast to counteract their guns and spars. Waves from the side caused them to "lurch their whole topside under every roll," and when anchored in heavy seas the vessels pitched uncomfortably, "frequently lifting their rudders nearly above water" and dipping their bows deeply with every swell.[4] Contemporary and reconstructed lines of wartime-built ships nearly all show relatively sharp entrances, a design characteristic that could improve sailing qualities but that also lessened the bow's buoyancy and caused ships to ride into waves rather than over them. This surely explains why the captains of *Jefferson* and *Jones* chose to remove the 18-pounder pivot guns originally mounted on their forecastle decks and to re-step the brigs' mainmasts farther aft.

The shallow draft of the lake warships was a desirable feature when it came to picking up speed and maneuvering in light to moderate airs and low seas. It was disadvantageous, however, when sailing in rougher conditions or when attempting to sail close to the wind. In the latter circumstances it is likely that these ships experienced a considerable degree of lateral drift, the tendency to slide off to leeward due to the minimal grip on the surface of the water. A clear-cut example of a shipwright working to improve lateral

resistance (as well as overall hull strength) can be seen in the extra pieces fitted to the bottom of *Ticonderoga*'s keel when it was converted from a steamer to a sailer.

Archaeological studies of 1812-era hulls have revealed many insights into the construction philosophies and techniques of British, Canadian, and American builders during the War of 1812. This evidence tells us that not only were shipwrights designing their hulls to meet specific sailing conditions on the individual lakes, but that they also employed materials, components, and assembly methods that departed—sometimes radically—from seagoing warship construction. The differing approaches were the result of a number of factors. Time, or the lack thereof, was perhaps the most crucial element influencing wartime construction; the demanding timetables imposed by impending military or naval campaigns forced shipwrights to find ways to assemble ships in the fastest possible manner. As we have seen in the preceding chapters, a range of time-saving shortcuts were devised to meet wartime construction schedules. Other factors influenced freshwater building practices, too, such as the availability of timber and fasteners, the anticipated effects of lake conditions and hard service on both structural integrity and longevity, and the lack of pre-existing shipyards and related infrastructure.

Trees grew along every lakeshore in a profusion that would have dazzled workers at contemporary European yards, but even in this densely forested landscape, finding preferred species and shapes of timber was evidently not easy for shipwrights who were in a rush. The examples of *Nancy* and *General Hunter* show that when time was not an overriding concern it was possible to select timber that would improve a hull's strength and longevity. *Nancy,* in particular, stands out in this regard: the builders sought good-quality oak for the lower hull and rot-resistant red cedar for the top timbers. "The expense to us will be great," wrote the supervisor of construction in 1789, "but there will be the satisfaction of her being strong and very durable."[5] *Nancy*'s twenty-five-year career (which included at least one major rebuilding) proves the accuracy of this prediction.

Timber selection varied between shipwrights and shipyards. In general, the builders of the Royal Navy ships seem to have made every effort to seek out the best woods. Two of William Bell's ships on Lake Erie got high marks from contemporary observers: *Queen Charlotte* (launched in 1810) was said to have been built of the "best seasoned Oak & Cedar," while the wartime-built *Detroit* was reported to contain "green timber, but . . . select."[6] Timber samples taken from the 1814-built *Princess Charlotte, Prince Regent,* and *St. Lawrence* at Kingston suggest that British and Canadian builders at this location made every effort to use the optimal white oak.[7]

Wartime exigencies sometimes forced builders to be less discriminating. Timber selections made by the Royal Navy shipwrights on Lake Champlain were likely constrained by the deforested condition of the Richelieu River valley—the area had been settled since the seventeenth century—and their dependence on wood smuggled in from the United States. The lower hull of the William Simons–built brig *Linnet* was mostly composed of good white oak, but it also incorporated a lower deadwood timber of white pine, a weak and rot-prone wood that was ill-suited to serve as this member.[8] The hull of the British Lake Champlain frigate *Confiance* has not been found, but a contemporary report of it containing "the very worst timber for building ships" suggests that the Royal Navy's builders cut corners when they had no other choice.[9]

The Henry Eckford–built *Jefferson* contained a high proportion of white oak, with occasional pieces of hard maple and elm in the lower floors and futtocks and lightweight white pine, spruce, and hemlock in the top timbers.[10] Despite its construction in only two and a half months, *Jefferson*'s hull gives the impression of a discerning approach to timber selection. The same does not appear to be true of the Adam and Noah Brown–built brigs *Niagara* and *Eagle.* Commodore Sinclair declared that the Lake Erie brigs *Niagara* and *Lawrence* were "composed of various kinds of timber without selection"; this was confirmed by samples taken from the former in 1913, which included oak, poplar, cucumber, and ash in the frames and red cedar and black walnut in the top timbers.[11] *Eagle,* Adam Brown's nineteen-day wonder, also had a varied assortment of woods in its floors, futtocks, and top timbers: white and red oak, American elm, white ash, white pine, spruce, and chestnut. In their rush to complete this brig, Brown and his carpenters paid scant attention to the species of trees they were shaping and assembling. The inclusion of white pine and spruce in

the floor timbers and first futtocks was particularly telling, since neither was appropriate for use in lower frames. *Eagle*'s centerline timbers were more carefully selected, with the keel of hard maple and white oak and all other elements (the stem and sternposts, deadwood, apron, and keelson) of oak.[12]

The density of the forests around the lakes likely influenced the design and assembly of the 1812 warships. When Researcher Glenn Grieco of Texas A&M University constructed his 1:36 scale model of the US Brig *Jefferson,* he determined that the hull's form allowed nearly all components to be shaped from straight-grained pieces of timber. A similar pattern can be discerned in the lines and composite framing of the three Royal Navy wrecks at Kingston. This suggests that shipwrights were trying to avoid complex hull shapes that required naturally curved compass timbers, perhaps because the dense, old-growth forests around the lakes mostly produced tall, straight-grained trees. Broad, low-growing trees yield the kinds of compass timber sought by shipwrights, but such trees may have been hard to find in the forests of northeastern North America.

Time constraints and a dearth of tightly curving trunks, crotches, and branches likely explain one of the most significant departures from standard construction practices seen in lake warships, the omission of knees at the juncture of the deck beams and frames. Grown knees serve as vital reinforcing elements in a wooden ship, locking decks and sides together and preventing the hull from flexing excessively. Their use was especially desirable on warships due to the weighty batteries of guns that stressed hulls and hastened the drooping or hogging of the bow and stern. The practice of building without knees was clearly seen on the wrecks of Henry Eckford's *Jefferson* and Adam Brown's *Eagle*; Commodore Sinclair's complaint about the "temporary manner" in which *Niagara* and *Lawrence* were built, "without a knee in them," tells us that Noah Brown also left them out when building on Lake Erie in 1813.[13]

In the American version of kneeless deck construction, compensation for the missing knees was provided by greatly enlarging the clamps and waterways; these were notched to fit around the beam ends, locking the beams tightly in place. Eckford hedged his bets in *Jefferson* by adding diagonal riders between the keelson and the undersides of the clamps, elements that not only supported the clamps but also stiffened the hull. The midship section of the Royal Navy's line-of-battle ship *St. Lawrence* shows a somewhat similar arrangement, with straight-grained filler pieces, "deck shelves," triangular chocks, and numerous bolts compensating for the scant numbers of grown knees installed in the deck assemblies. The schooners *Newash* and *Tecumseth,* built in a hurry immediately after the war by shipwright Robert Moore, provide another example of Canadian-British kneeless deck construction with their longitudinal "deck shelf" and clamp arrangement that resembled one long, continuous hanging knee. Omitting grown knees saved time, effort, and topside weight, but it was a fair-weather expedient that carried potential risks. The separation of *Jefferson*'s waterway in the storm of September 1814 was probably a direct result of this shortcut. Vessels built in this manner may also have suffered from hogging sooner than if knees had been fitted.

Two of the wartime-built US brigs, *Jefferson* and *Eagle,* also lacked a stern knee in their deadwoods. A standard feature in contemporary wooden ship construction, the stern knee was bolted to the top of the deadwood to reinforce the join of the horizontal deadwood timbers and the vertical posts. *Jefferson*'s deadwood was simply a stack of six horizontal timbers that incorporated the aftermost pieces of the keelson, while *Eagle*'s deadwood was rudimentary in the extreme, with two horizontal bottom timbers and two diagonally slanting timbers on top.

Two additional departures from contemporary construction practices were found in the 1812-era lake wrecks. The first was in the selection of fastenings. Contracts for seagoing ships commonly specified that planks be fastened to frames with treenails, but evidence of treenail use on the lakes was only seen in the prewar-era *Nancy* and *General Hunter.*[14] Treenails were strong and durable but took extra time and labor to fit. The wartime-built lake ship hulls examined in this book all employed iron fasteners—bolts, spikes, and nails—throughout their assemblies. This was not especially surprising: iron fasteners required less time and effort to install, were cheap, plentiful, and strong, and in freshwater did not have corrosion problems.

By the end of the eighteenth century both the Royal Navy and the US Navy were copper sheathing the bottoms of their seagoing ships to improve sailing speed, resist fouling, and prevent infestation by wood-boring teredos. No evidence of sheathing was found on any of the lake wrecks, nor was there any compelling need for it: the lakes are free of shipworms, metallic sheathing was expensive, and placing copper plates in close proximity to iron spikes and bolts results in an electrolytic reaction that quickly degrades iron. For this reason copper-sheathed ships must have either treenails or expensive copper spikes and bolts below the waterline to avoid fastener disintegration. Documentary evidence tells us that the Royal Navy did send unnecessary copper fittings to the lakes, some of which may have ended up in the partially copper-fastened Browns Bay Vessel and in the frigate *Confiance* (which yielded 300 lbs [136 kg] of copper fittings, including a rudder gudgeon, when it was demolished in 1873).[15]

Comparison of the materials and assembly techniques seen in the lake wrecks suggests that American and British or Canadian shipwrights approached their work with different philosophies on how ships should be constructed. Our sample of wartime-built ships is admittedly small, but the three Royal Navy wrecks at Kingston, and *Linnet, Newash,* and *Tecumseth,* all exhibited certain labor-intensive assembly methods. Individual elements in hulls were often composed of more pieces than their US counterparts, timber scarfs on keels, stems, and sterns were relatively elaborate (as were the complex lower frame assemblies in *Prince Regent* and *Princess Charlotte*), and keels and some keelsons were notched to fit frame floors. The complexity of construction seen in the centerline timbers of *Newash* and *Tecumseth,* with the boxing scarf at the join of the stem and keel, the rising deadwood atop the keel, and the many individual pieces, is frankly surprising given the small size and short period of construction of these vessels. Overall, the Royal Navy wrecks give the impression of craftsmanship, hinting that despite wartime demand for fast construction, care and precision were still expected in the shaping and fitting of individual pieces.

Our archaeological and photographic sample of US Navy hulls built from the keel up to be warships, *Niagara, Jefferson, Allen,* and *Eagle,* suggests a different approach to shipbuilding was practiced south of the border. Timber choices were more random, the timber scarfs and butts were less elaborate, knees were left entirely out of decks and deadwoods, and the shaping, fitting, and fastening of the hull members were all uncomplicated. The final products appear to have been sturdy enough, but the attention to detail seen in the Canadian and British work was lacking.

This archaeological impression is backed up by the observations of contemporary naval officers and shipwrights. We have already noted Commodore Sinclair's disappointment with the "temporary manner" of building evident in *Niagara* and *Lawrence*. Even more trenchant are the comments of three British officials who recognized the differences in building philosophies and techniques and judged their relative merits. The first of these individuals, the Kingston yard's Foreman of Shipwrights John Aldersley, inspected American ship carpentry during a tour of the mothballed squadron at Sackets Harbor in February 1816. He was appalled by what he saw:

> I was not in the least impressed at their Building or rather making Ships in so short a time when I came to examine into the workmanship—the first thing which caught my attention was the frames. I never could have believed if I had not seen it: the most abominable, neglectful, slovenly work ever performed, no regard for heads, heels or scarphs of Timbers, nor even the Ports—The Timbers are in many instances thrown in one upon the other, without even the Bark of the Tree being taken off.[16]

As we read in chapter 7, Comm. Sir Edward Campbell Rich Owen could see positive aspects in the US approach. He concluded that the rough-and-ready work of US shipwrights "kept a greater quantity of timber in their ships, which gives them greater strength, and their people better shelter, whilst it diminishes in some degree the labour of the building."[17] Surveyor General of Lower Canada Joseph Bouchette agreed with this assessment and went on to comment on the work of the Royal Navy's builders:

> The Americans build their ships much faster than we do on our side, and for this reason, strength is the chief object with them, and if that be obtained they care but little about beauty of model or elegance of finishing; in fact, they receive no other polish than what is given them by the axe and the adze. On the other hand, we employ as much

time upon ours as we should in the European dock-yards: they are undoubtedly as strong as the Americans, they are handsomer and much better finished, but they are far more expensive, and will not endure a longer period of service.[18]

This divergence in building techniques and standards is curious, since the shipwrights working on either side of the border shared a common cultural heritage; indeed, Henry Eckford served his apprenticeship in Canada before establishing his own yard in the United States. The difference probably lies in individual and collective prior experience—how builders learned to balance the costs of materials and labor with expectations for strength and longevity. Shipwrights from yards in Great Britain worked in a country where timber was increasingly scarce and expensive but labor was relatively plentiful and cheap. Ship carpenters schooled in this tradition, whether in Britain or in Canada, were practiced in the fine art of methodically shaping and assembling smaller pieces of timber into a strong, long-lasting whole. By 1812 most of Europe had been at war for nearly two decades, and it is likely that a high proportion of the shipwrights at Kingston and the other Canadian lake yards had prior experience building or repairing naval vessels to meet the Royal Navy's high standards. Obviously, for professionals like these, the habits of craftsmanship learned over many years could not be discarded overnight. And, if John Aldersley's horrified reaction to slapdash frame construction is any indication, many were not prepared to lower their standards at all.

The US Navy's principal contractors on the lakes, Henry Eckford and the Brown brothers, were part of a different tradition: they were merchant ship builders with only modest experience in naval construction prior to the war. Eckford learned the shipwright's trade through the usual apprenticeship, but the Browns's entrée into the business was unconventional, to say the least. They started off as house carpenters and only later discovered that they had an aptitude for building ships. The yards of Eckford and the Browns were located in New York City, a place where high-quality timber was readily available at a relatively low cost; they got accustomed to having a generous supply of wood on hand. Most of the ships they built were business ventures, tools of commerce designed to carry cargoes safely and economically. Unlike warships, merchant ships were not overt symbols of national power and prestige; they did not have to be especially beautiful or long-lasting but only sturdy, functional, and inexpensive. Eckford and the Browns were pragmatists through and through, and they brought to the lakes a practical approach to building that is best summed up by Noah Brown's famous admonishment to an overly meticulous carpenter: "plain work is all that is required, they will only be wanted for one battle."[19]

The spectacular feats of fast naval construction performed by the Brown brothers and Henry Eckford on the lakes were widely remarked upon during the war, and as contributing "architects" to the US naval victories on freshwater, their work became a point of national pride. The boasting continued long after the war ended. In May 1831, Englishman James Boardman passed down the length of Lake Champlain on the steamboat *Franklin.* Shortly after crossing into Canada, *Franklin* steamed past the old Royal Navy dockyard at Isle aux Noix, where Boardman was struck by the sight of unfinished gunboats rotting and falling to pieces on the stocks:

> I asked an American passenger, whether it was true that, during the last war, his countrymen had converted growing trees into vessels of war in the short space of a month. The answer was in the affirmative, and that one of these hastily-constructed floating batteries mounted 100 guns. On my remarking that ships so quickly built could not last, my friend replied, with a dry smile, that they lasted long enough: they lasted until they took all yours. Unfortunately for my national credit, this was true to the letter.[20]

Archaeological research has brought us a flood of insights into the design and construction of the War of 1812's lake warships, but the yield of information on the material world of their crews has been more limited. Only three of the sixteen wrecks examined in this book were lost during wartime service. *Nancy* burned to the waterline in 1814, and its artifacts were dug up a century later and scattered into private collections. Today only the hull is left for us to study. *Hamilton* and *Scourge* are another story: sunk without warning in deep water in August 1813, the location and condition of the two schooners remained a mystery until their rediscovery in 1975. Photographic and sonar images of the two wrecks on the bottom of Lake Ontario have told us much about the masts, spars, rigging, armament, ship's equipment, and crew possessions carried on these vessels. The below-deck spaces of the two schooners promise many more revelations if their contents are ever recovered. The archaeological potential of *Hamilton* and *Scourge* remains enormous.

Artifact collections excavated from the wrecked and salvaged *General Hunter* and the abandoned *Jefferson* and *Allen* are modest in size, but they have nevertheless added greatly to our understanding of the vessels and their crews. All three hulls contained random, evocative, surprising details of early-nineteenth-century naval life on the lakes: the swivel gun, stove pieces, and highly varied collection of uniform buttons in *Hunter;* glass deck lights, mustard bottles, a hand-carved snow shovel, and Ordinary Seaman James New's personalized spoon in *Jefferson;* and the stoneware jug and clay smoking pipe with its molded image of a bearded, turbaned man found in *Allen.* The remaining wrecks were partially cleared of materials before abandonment and later heavily picked over by souvenir hunters; artifact finds have consequently been few and yielded limited information.

No ships were sunk at Plattsburgh Bay on September 11, 1814, but archaeological surveys and research can still inform us about the battle and its aftermath. That much was proven by the pioneering efforts of William Leege and his colleagues in the Lake Champlain Archaeological Association. The naval debris they recovered testifies to the intensity of the fighting. Their work also shows us how concentrations and trails of artifacts can reveal the location and movement of ships and how survivors went about cleaning up after the battle. The more recent "Hawks 1813" anchor project demonstrates that even mundane pieces of ship's equipment can be a font of information when properly conserved and studied. The anchor project also shows what can be accomplished for the common good when individuals, private institutions, and governments work together as a team to protect and study our maritime archaeological heritage.

Truth and Consequences

In the end, what did the shipwrights, sailors, naval vessels, and battles described in this book accomplish? More than might be evident from the articles in the Treaty of Ghent. Even short, small wars can have long-term consequences. The War of 1812 ended with status quo ante bellum, but the struggles in North America, particularly the great naval contests on the lakes, clearly shaped the future of the continent. For the Native American peoples of the midcontinent, the war was a disaster: they lost their best chance to stop the westward expansion of the United States (if indeed they ever had much of a chance). A tidal wave of settlers and speculators rolled into the interior after 1815, and within two decades the region's original inhabitants would lose nearly all of their lands east of the Mississippi River.

The effects of the war were far less calamitous for non-native Americans and Canadians; indeed, the war clearly fostered a stronger sense of political and social self-identity for the people of both nations. Neither side exactly won, neither side exactly lost, but for each a point had been made. The 1812-derived national pride and cohesion began to manifest itself as soon as the war ended, and it would prove to be a remarkably durable sentiment on both sides of the border.

We can get a glimpse of the general mood in the United States two years after the war through the eyes of Henry Bradshaw Fearon of London. When he toured the republic in 1817, Fearon encountered a pervasive—and to him perplexing—feature of American society: his hosts would not stop talking about their navy. Like many Britons, Fearon considered the recent Anglo-American conflict a very minor sideshow in the greater struggle against Napoleon and his continental allies. "My knowledge . . . of the late war was extremely limited when I first landed in this country," he admitted. He went on to warn compatriots of the ceaseless tedium and irritation that awaited them on the far side of the Atlantic Ocean:

A short residence here . . . will force upon the attention of all persons an acquaintance with naval history. Every man, woman, and child in America talk about the Guerriere, the Java, the Macedonia, the Frolic, Lake Erie, Lake Champlain, and the "vast inferiority of British sailors and soldiers to the true-blooded Yankees." A knowledge of such events is certainly desirable; but to cause them, as they are here, to be the never-ending theme of conversation, the circle round which everything revolves, is to make the going into society a punishment instead of a pleasure.

As a loyal British citizen, Fearon was particularly rankled by the assertions of innate American superiority in all things naval. Boasting on this subject, he declared, was "so extravagant that it burlesques the object of its praise":

The Americans are deserving of great honour for what they really achieved. School-boys in the art of war, they were yet better prepared for it, and evinced more practical dexterity, than our hoary-headed practitioners. But with this limited degree of praise, they are not content; they are, forsooth, "the Lords of the ocean!" "Neptune's choicest sons!" "Victorious, though the English had great superiority of force!" "the star-spangled banner is the astonishment, the admiration, and the glory of the world!"—with volumes more of such frothy, senseless bombast.[21]

Fearon had stumbled onto a curious postwar phenomenon among citizens of the United States. From the moment that the peace treaty was ratified by the US government on February 17, 1815, Americans started mentally burying all the failures: the acrimony, disunity, and ineptitude before and during the war, the US Army's inability to conquer Canada, the near-collapse of the country's economy and insolvency of the US government, the Royal Navy's blockading and raiding of the coast, the burning of government buildings in Washington, DC in August 1814, and the fact that most of the reasons for declaring war were rendered irrelevant by the collapse of Napoleon's regime. Americans instead collectively chose to celebrate the struggle as a trial by fire, a second war of independence from Britain, wherein the republic proved its mettle in battle.[22] This swift redefinition of the war and its results led one twentieth-century historian to comment, "seldom has a nation so successfully practiced self-induced amnesia!"[23]

The series of unexpected defensive victories in the final months of the war certainly helped to obscure the many setbacks and the bleak nadir at Washington. Indeed, only three weeks after the ratification of the peace treaty, *Niles Weekly Register* joyfully declared, "The last six months is the proudest period in the history of the

ENGRAVED FOR THE NAVAL MONUMENT

Com. Macdonough's Victory on Lake Champlain Sep.r 11th 1814

Figure 14.3. *Commemorating the victories of September 11, 1814. In the decades that followed the War of 1812 the conflict was popularly portrayed as a time of national crisis that miraculously terminated "in a blaze of glory" and as such became a unifying theme for Americans. Along with the repulse of the British at Baltimore and New Orleans, the simultaneous (and successful) defensive battles of the US Army and Navy at Plattsburgh were widely celebrated in songs, stories, and prints. (From Abel Bowen,* The Naval Monument, *p. 145, collection of Kevin J. Crisman.)*

republic. The review presents us with a galaxy of glorious war-deeds, terminating in an honourable peace, happily signed in the very arms of victory." The *Register* continued on in the grand American style that would vex and amuse Britons and Canadians for years hence:

> Success has crowned our arms in a wonderful manner. The eagle banner, sustained by the hand of GOD, through hosts of heroes, triumphantly waved over *Champlain,* at *Plattsburgh,* at *Baltimore,* at *Mobile,* and *New Orleans*; and some signal victories were obtained at sea—so that the war was finished in a blaze of glory, as though the Great Arbiter of all things had decreed that the wisdom and fortitude of our government, and the desperately daring courage, invincible patience and ingenious qualities of our people, should be tried in a short contest, to *secure* future peace and *establish* our mild and benevolent institutions. Hail, holy freedom![24]

Thus it was that this short war of limited scope, high drama, and few long-term negative consequences

would become a powerful unifying symbol for citizens of the United States (fig. 14.3). The momentarily shared danger and the ability of the republic's navy and army to successfully engage a powerful (if distracted) European foe drew the people of a widely separated and culturally fragmented nation together in a common bond. The perceived moral victory over an outside enemy and the newly reinforced sense of common purpose and destiny would help to carry the country whole through the next half-century of astounding growth in territory, population, industry, agriculture, and cultural traditions.[25]

The War of 1812 was a defining moment in Canadian nationhood as well, although in a characteristically less-flamboyant manner. When the war began, citizens of Canada found themselves at a political and social fork in the road: they could be forcibly annexed by the raucous republic to the south or continue as colonial subjects of the world-spanning British Empire. If Canadians were at all ambivalent about this choice in the summer of 1812, two and a half years of war, devastation, and sacrifices decided the question

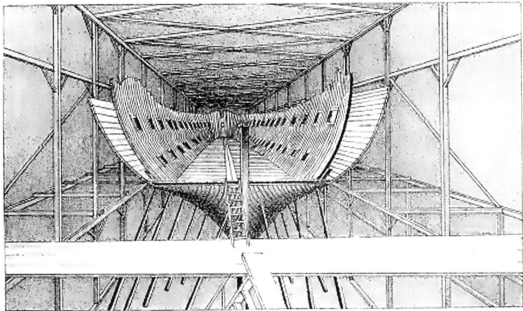

INTERIOR of HULL of LINE-of-BATTLE SHIP "NEW ORLEANS", LOOKING FROM PLATFORM AT STERN.

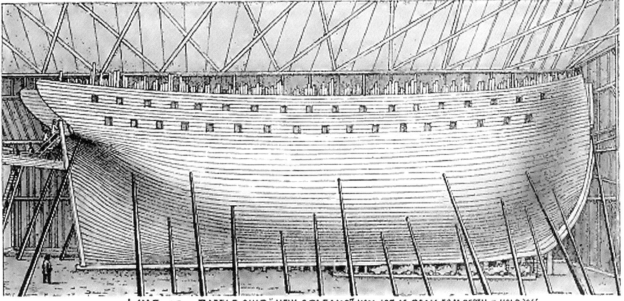

LINE-of-BATTLE SHIP "NEW ORLEANS". KEEL 187 FT. BEAM 58 FT. DEPTH of HOLD 30 FT. MEASUREMENT 3200 TONS, 120 GUNS.

Figure 14.4. *What Capt. Basil Hall saw during his North American tour. This 1878 lithograph provides two inside-the-shiphouse perspectives of the unfinished line-of-battle ship* New Orleans *at Sackets Harbor. This naval behemoth would sit unlaunched on the stocks for seven decades, providing an irresistible attraction for tourists like Hall. (From Samuel W. Durant and Henry B. Peirce,* History of Jefferson County, New York, *p. 411.)*

firmly against union with the United States. The British Army and Navy may have orchestrated the defense of Canada, but native-born soldiers, sailors, and militia also fought on land and on the lakes; Canadian artificers and laborers struggled to deliver supplies and prepare ships and fortifications; and members of the Canadian populace, particularly those living in Upper Canada, endured destructive American invasions and raids. Having fought and suffered under the banner of Great Britain, Canadians would long continue under British rule even as they began to carve out their own identity and independence. The process was slow and deliberate: creation of a self-governing Canadian nation would only get underway a half-century after the conflict.[26]

If the War of 1812 helped to define the United States and Canada, it also marked the beginning of a lasting peace between the former belligerents. Such an outcome seemed unlikely to many in 1815. In the aftermath of the conflict, both sides of the border saw the construction of new fortifications, canal systems, and other defensive infrastructure designed for use in a future war. However, contrary to the dire predictions of alarmists and despite occasional economic or territorial squabbles, that war never came to pass. At least some credit for this happy turn of events is due to the Rush-Bagot Agreement of 1817, the document wherein Great Britain and the United States agreed to reduce their naval forces on the lakes to a token number of schooners and gunboats.[27] The elimination of warship squadrons on the lakes clearly had a calming effect on relations, a fact recognized by many in the decades that followed.

One approving commentator on the disarmament agreement was Capt. Basil Hall of the Royal Navy. In 1827, during the course of a two-year grand tour of North America, Hall visited Sackets Harbor, New York, the scene of the US Navy's greatest shipbuilding effort of the war (fig. 14.4). While he was duly impressed by the sight of Henry Eckford's unfinished ship of the line *New Orleans* sitting housed-over on its ways, Hall could also see just how far the place had fallen from prominence in the twelve years since 1815:

The town of Sacketts has a stand-still look about it, which leads one to suspect that, as its rise was certainly owing to the War, its fall is traceable to the judicious [Rush-Bagot Agreement]. Had

there been no such stipulation, rival fleets would have been maintained on the lakes to beard and plague one another, and keep both nations in perpetual hot-water, while no mortal would have benefitted, except perhaps the worthy inhabitants of Sacketts.[28]

NOTES

1. Theodore Roosevelt, *The Naval War of 1812* (Annapolis: Naval Institute Press, 1987), p. 337.

2. The hazards encountered in navigating the shallows of Lakes Huron and Erie are frequently mentioned in the summer and fall 1814 correspondence of US Navy Capt. Arthur Sinclair. See Michael J. Crawford, ed., *The Naval War of 1812: A Documentary History,* vol. 3 (Washington, DC: Naval Historical Center, 2002), pp. 516–17, 557–58, 564, 572–74, 600–604, 645–46.

3. Copies of existing ship plans may be seen in this volume or in Robert Malcomson, *Warships of the Great Lakes 1754–1834* (Annapolis: Naval Institute Press, 2001).

4. Crawford, ed., *Naval War of 1812,* vol. 3, p. 600; Malcomson, *Warships of the Great Lakes,* p. 98.

5. Christopher R. Sabick, "His Majesty's Hired Transport Schooner *Nancy*" (Master's thesis, Texas A&M University, 2004), p. 21.

6. Crawford, ed., *Naval War of 1812,* vol. 3, p. 694.

7. Daniel R. Walker, "The Identity and Construction of Wreck Baker: A War of 1812 Era Royal Navy Frigate" (Master's thesis, Texas A&M University, 2007), pp. 114–15.

8. Erika L. Washburn, "*Linnet*: The History and Archaeology of a Brig from the War of 1812" (Master's thesis, Texas A&M University, 1998), pp. 60–66.

9. James T. Leonard to the Board of Navy Commissioners, November 19, 1819 and January 10, 1820, entry 220, record group 45, National Archives and Records Administration.

10. Kevin J. Crisman, "The *Jefferson*: The History and Archaeology of an American Brig from the War of 1812" (PhD diss., University of Pennsylvania, 1989), pp. 271–302.

11. Crawford, ed., *Naval War of 1812,* vol. 3, p. 694; Perry Memorial Commission, *Perry's Victory Memorial* (Washington, DC: Government Printing Office, 1921), p. 56; Max Rosenberg, *The Building of Perry's Fleet on Lake Erie, 1812–1813* (Harrisburg, PA: The Pennsylvania Historical and Museum Commission, 1987), p. 37.

12. Kevin J. Crisman, *The Eagle: An American Brig on Lake Champlain During the War of 1812* (Shelburne, VT: The New England Press; Annapolis: Naval Institute Press, 1987), pp. 232–34.

13. Malcomson, *Warships of the Great Lakes,* p. 98. Photographs of the wreck raised from Misery Bay, Erie in 1913 and identified as *Niagara* clearly show dagger knees fitted below the deck beams, suggesting that these were added sometime after the fall of 1814.

14. For one example of early-nineteenth-century seagoing naval ship construction specifications, see the US Navy sloop of

war *Peacock* contract transcribed in Howard I. Chapelle, *The History of American Sailing Ships* (New York: W. W. Norton, 1935), pp. 365–76.

15. *Burlington* (VT) *Daily Free Press and Times,* August 11, 1873 and *Whitehall* (NY) *Times,* August 13, 1873.

16. Aldersley to Owen, February 24, 1816, p. 367, ADM 1/2265, The National Archives of the UK (TNA): Public Record Office (PRO). Courtesy of Gary Gibson, Sackets Harbor, NY.

17. Owen to Croker, October 10, 1815, p. 123b, ADM 1/2263, TNA: PRO.

18. Joseph Bouchette, *A Topographical Description of the Province of Lower Canada with Remarks upon Upper Canada* (London: W. Faden, 1815), pp. 600–601.

19. Noah Brown, "The Remarkable Statement of Noah Brown," *Journal of American History* 8, no. 1 (January 1914), pp. 103–107.

20. James Boardman, *America and the Americans* (London: Longman, Rees, Orme, Brown, Green, and Longman, 1833), pp. 383–84.

21. Henry Bradshaw Fearon, *Sketches of America: A Narrative of a Journey of Five Thousand Miles Through the Eastern and Western States of America* (London: Longman, Hurst, Rees, Orme, and Brown, 1818), pp. 373–76.

22. The War of 1812 as a second fight for independence theme is evident in the title of US histories of the conflict, such as Samuel R. Brown's *An Authentic History of the Second War for Independence* (Auburn, NY: Published by J. G. Hathaway, 1815).

23. Bradford Perkins, *The Creation of a Republican Empire, 1776–1865* (Cambridge: Cambridge University Press, 1993), p. 146.

24. *Niles Weekly Register,* vol. VIII, no. 1, March 4, 1815.

25. Daniel Walker Howe, *What Hath God Wrought: The Transformation of America, 1815–1848* (Oxford: Oxford University Press, 2009).

26. The War of 1812's promotion of Canadian identity and nationhood has been discussed in many publications, including George F. G. Stanley, *The War of 1812: Land Operations* (Toronto: Macmillan of Canada, 1983), Chapter 15, and Pierre Berton, *Flames Across the Border, 1813–1814* (Toronto: McClelland and Stewart, 1981), pp. 423–29.

27. A transcript of the Rush-Bagot Agreement can be found in LeeAnne Gordon, "*Newash* and *Tecumseth*: Analysis of Two Post-War of 1812 Vessels on the Great Lakes" (Master's thesis, Texas A&M University, 2009), Appendix C, pp. 265–67.

28. Capt. Basil Hall, *Travels in North America in the Years 1827 and 1828* (Edinburgh: Cadell, 1829), p. 357.

Appendix A

Principal Dimensions, Armament, and Broadside Weight of the Ships Built at Kingston in 1814

	Kingston ex–*Prince Regent* ex–*Ship No. 1*	*Burlington* ex–*Princess Charlotte* ex–*Vittoria* ex–*Ship No. 2*	*St. Lawrence* ex–*Ship No. 3*
DESIGN, CONSTRUCTION, AND RATING[1]			
Design	Patrick Fleming	George Record	William Bell
Keel laid	July 1813	September 1813	March 1814
Launched	April 14, 1814	April 14, 1814	September 10, 1814
Admiralty rating 1814	28 Gun 6th Rate	24 Gun 6th Rate	98 Gun 2nd Rate
Admiralty rating 1816	44 Gun 5th Rate	24 Gun 6th Rate	98 Gun 2nd Rate
Kingston rating 1816	4th Rate	5th Rate	1st Rate
Admiralty rating 1819	4th Rate	5th Rate	1st Rate
War complement 1814 (as per Kent)	550	330	
War complement 1816 (as per Owen)	491	317	837
PRINCIPAL DIMENSIONS 1815[2]			
Length of gun deck	155′ 1″	121′ 0″	191′ 2″
Length of keel	131′ 1″	100′ 3/8″	157′ 8 5/8″
Extreme breadth	43′ 1″	37′ 8″	52′ 7″
Molded breadth	42′ 6″	37′ 2″	52′ 0″
Depth of hold	9′ 2″	8′ 8½″	18′ 6″
Tonnage	1293-58/94	755-90/94	2304-90/94
Light draught afore	11′ 0″	11′ 0″	12′ 0″
Abaft	13′ 0″	13′ 0″	15′ 0″
Load draught afore	16′ 0″	14′ 4″	19′ 0″
Abaft	17′ 0″	16′ 4″	20′ 0″
Length to beam ratio	3.60:1	3.21:1	3.64:1
Midship deadrise	21°	31°	19°
ARMAMENT 1814–15[3]			
Number of guns × caliber. Carronades denoted by *.			
Gunports (exclusive of stern ports)	56	42	102
APRIL 13, 1814			
Forecastle		6 × 32*	
Quarterdeck		10 × 32*	
Upper deck	2 × 24 8 × 68* 20 × 32*		
Middle deck			
Gun deck	28 × 24	24 × 24	
Total guns	58	40	
Broadside (pounds [percentage])			
Long guns	360 (38%)	288 (53%)	
Carronades	592 (62%)	256 (47%)	
Total broadside	952	544	
OCTOBER 14, 1814			
Forecastle		6 × 32*	
Quarterdeck		2 × 68* 10 × 32*	

	Kingston ex–*Prince Regent* ex–*Ship No. 1*	*Burlington* ex–*Princess Charlotte* ex–*Vittoria* ex–*Ship No. 2*	*St. Lawrence* ex–*Ship No. 3*
OCTOBER 14, 1814 (CONTINUED)			
Upper deck	4 × 68*		2 × 68*
	24 × 32*		34 × 32*
Middle deck			34 × 24
Gun deck	28 × 24	24 × 24	34 × 32
Total guns	56	42	104
Broadside			
Long guns	336 (39%)	288 (47%)	612 (39%)
Carronades	520 (61%)	324 (53%)	952 (61%)
Total broadside	856	612	1564
MARCH 23, 1815			
Forecastle		6 × 32*	
Quarterdeck		2 × 68*	
		10 × 32*	
Upper deck	2 × 24		3 × 68*
	6 × 68*		37 × 32*
	22 × 32*		
Middle deck			36 × 24
Gun deck	30 × 24	24 × 24	27 × 32
			5 × 24
			4 × 32*
Total guns	60	42	112
Broadside			
Long guns	384 (41%)	288 (47%)	924 (55%)
Carronades	556 (59%)	324 (53%)	758 (45%)
Total broadside	940	612	1682

1. Source: PRO, ADM 1, vol. 2262, p. 137, Thomas Strickland, "Statement . . . ," March 23, 1815; AL, *List of the Navy,* 1814, pp. 5, 52, 54, 1816, p. 26; PRO, ADM 106, vol. 1997, Laws, Moore, and Spratt to Navy Board, October 10, 1816, enclosing "War Complement of the Ships and Vessels on Lake Ontario June 1816"; LAC, RG 8, IIIa, vol. 30, Barrie to Laws, May 14, 1819 and March 24, 1820; Malcomson, *Sailors of 1812,* pp. 79–80.

2. Source: NMM, *Prince Regent,* ZAZ1633, Reg. No. 1284, *Princess Charlotte,* ZAZ2293, Reg. No. 6013, *St. Lawrence,* ZAZ0131, Reg. No. 73; light and load draughts from PRO, ADM 1, vol. 2262, p. 137, Thomas Strickland, "Statement . . . ," March 23, 1815. The draught figures for the *Prince Regent* vary slightly from those in Appendix C; length-to-beam ratios and midship deadrise calculated by J. Moore from NMM profiles and body plans, cited above.

3. Source: PRO, ADM 1, vol. 2737, p. 78, Yeo to Prevost, "Statement of the Force of His Majesty's Fleet on Lake Ontario as it will appear in the Spring of 1814," April 13, 1814; PRO, ADM 106, vol. 1997, Richard O'Conor, "Statement of the Naval Force on Lake Ontario," enclosed with O'Conor to Navy Board, October 14, 1814; PRO, ADM 1, vol. 2262, p. 137, Thomas Strickland, "Statement . . . ," March 23, 1815. In these contemporary statements, the lowermost gun carrying deck is referred to as the "Gun Deck." For the *Kingston* and *St. Lawrence,* the spar deck is referred to as the "Upper Deck." For the *Burlington,* the flush spar deck was divided nominally into a "Quarter Deck" and "Forecastle."

Appendix B

Prince Regent *(Kingston) Sailing Qualities Report, 1815*[1]

	A Report of the sailing & other Qualities of His Majesty's
21st Day of June 1815	Ship Prince Regent as found on strict Observation thereof
	between the 1st Day of October 1814 and this Date

		Feet	Inches
		Forward	11	: 0

Her light Draught of water was stated to be — Forward 11 : 0 — Abaft 13 : 0

The Draught of water which was estimated by the Builder to be her best Trim — Forward / Abaft — Not known

The Draught of water found on Trial to be her best sailing Trim — Forward 16 : 4 — Abaft 17 : 0

What should be the Difference between her Draught of water forward & abaft to give her the best possible Trim when from circumstances she happens to be

considerably deeper in the water than her best sailing Draught as above stated

considerably lighter than Do.

I have never known her considerably deeper than when stored for Service but I should think not more than 6 inches

No difference. I think she ought to be on an even keel

		Tons
Quantity of Ballast necessary to bring her to her best Trim	Iron	------
	Shingle	------

			Feet	Inches
When stored for Lake Service	Draught of Water	Forward	16	: 4
		Abaft	17	: 0
	Height of Ports	Foremost	6	: 6
		Midships	5	: 9
		Aftermost	6	: 9
When loaded with provisions &c. for the Army	Draught of Water	Forward	16	: 5
		Abaft	17	: 3
	Height of Ports	Foremost	6	: 5
		Midships	5	: 7
		Aftermost	6	: 6

How arm'd			No.	Pounders
	On the Main Deck	Guns	30	24
		Carronades	---	---
	Spar Deck	Guns	2	24
		Carronades	6	68
			22	32

Character of the ship after a Trial of nearly nine months

How does she stow her provisions?	Three Months under Hatches
Does she ride easy at her Anchors?	Yes
How does she stand under her sails?	Very stiff when in proper Trim
How does she carry her lee ports?	[No Entry]
Does she roll easy or uneasy in the Trough of the sea?	No Trial
Does she pitch easy?	Yes
Is she generally speaking an easy or an uneasy ship?	A very easy ship
How does she in general carry her helm?	Carries a good Helm when in Trim
How does she steer?	Not very well
How does she wear & stay?	She is long in stays but never misses if properly attended

			Knots		fathoms

Is she weatherly or leewardly compared with other ships?
How does she behave lying to?

Compared with other ships on the Lake she is as weatherly as any except the Psyche
No trial

She has run pr. Hour by the Log with as much Wind as she could safely bear

Close haul'd — Under whole or single reef'd Topsails & TopGallt. Sails — 8 : 0
Under double reefd topsails — 7 : 4
Under Courses — No trial

Large under all sail that could with propriety be set — 10 : 0
Before the wind under similar circumstances — 9 : 4

What is her best point of sailing? — Before the wind

Comparative Rate of sailing with other Ships — Equal to the St. Lawrence on all points & superior to every other ship on the Lake before the Wind but inferior to the Psyche by the wind.

Is she generally speaking a well built & strong ship? or does she on the contrary shew any unusual symptoms of weakness — By no means a strong built ship—And I think shews great signs of weakness.

Remarks

The Draught of Water stated to be the ships best sailing Trim was such as far as the Trial went; but I am of Opinion that if she was brought more on an even keel, or nearly quite so, she would sail (on a wind especially) and work infinitely better.

The ship is sufficiently ballasted when every thing is in for Service but I have no means of ascertaining the Quantity as it is great part of it [sic] stone—The Carpenter has eighty two Tons of Iron Ballast on charge and the Gunner eighty five Tons of shot—Perhaps there may [be] about 100 tons of stone, but there is no Memorandum left in the ship to certify the quantity received when she was first commission'd and the Log Book goes no further back than the 9th June.

The ship is long in answering her Helm. I think if the rudder was made something broder [broader] she would steer much better.

H. Davies   Captain

1. Source: PRO, ADM 95, Reports, Estimates, Orders and Other Papers Relating to Ship Building and Repair, vol. 44, no. 160, *Prince Regent*. Reports for the *Princess Charlotte* and *St. Lawrence* were not found in this record group.

Appendix C

Principal Timber Scantlings (in Inches) and Wood Species of the Ships Built at Kingston in 1814[1]

Wreck Name	Timber Name	Sided	Molded	Wood Name	Wood Species
St. Lawrence					
	Half-floor	11	16	Rock elm	*Ulmus thomasii* Sarg.
	First futtock	11	18	White oak	*Quercus* spp.
	Limber strake	10	4½	White oak	*Quercus* spp.
	Ceiling plank	7	2½	White oak	*Quercus* spp.
	Hull planks	12	2–2½	White oak	*Quercus* spp.
	Space	12			
	Room and space	34			
Wreck Able (Kingston, ex–*Prince Regent*)					
	Keelson	11	14½	White oak	*Quercus* spp.
	Rider keelson	11	6	White oak	*Quercus* spp.
	Sternpost	11	18½	White oak	*Quercus* spp.
	Floor	14	35	White oak	*Quercus* spp.
	Floor chocks	11	10	White oak	*Quercus* spp.
	First futtock	12	17	White oak	*Quercus* spp.
	Limber strake	7½–8	4	White oak	*Quercus* spp.
	Ceiling plank	10	2½	White oak	*Quercus* spp.
	Hull plank	10–15	2	White oak	*Quercus* spp.
	Strake for foremast step	6	10	White oak	*Quercus* spp.
	Mainmast bolsters	10	16	White oak	*Quercus* spp.
	Strake for mainmast step	6	12		
	Floor centers	28			
	Space	1–2			
	Room and space	28–30			
Wreck Baker (Burlington, ex–*Princess Charlotte*)					
	Keelson	12	13	White oak	*Quercus* spp.
	Rider keelson	12	5	White oak	*Quercus* spp.
	Keel	12	16	White oak	*Quercus* spp.
	False keel	12	2½	Chestnut	*Castanea* spp.
	Stem	10		White oak	*Quercus* spp.
	Sternpost	10½	9	White oak	*Quercus* spp.
	Inner sternpost	15	14		
	Stern Knee	15±		White oak	*Quercus* spp.
	Half floor	11½–12	12	White oak	*Quercus* spp.
	Half-floor cross-chock	4–7	13½–16	White oak	*Quercus* spp.
	First futtock chock	11	4	White oak	*Quercus* spp.
	First futtock	12	12	White oak	*Quercus* spp.
	Second futtock	11	13		
	Ceiling plank	10	2	White oak	*Quercus* spp.
	Hull plank	12	2	Chestnut	*Castanea* spp.
	Wale	8	4	White oak	*Quercus* spp.
	Half-floor centres	28			
	Room and space	27½–32			
	Space	2–4			

1. Source: Jonathan Moore, "Archaeological and Historical Investigations of Three War of 1812 Wrecks at Kingston, Ontario: HMS *St. Lawrence,* HMS *Kingston* and HMS *Burlington*" (archaeological report, Ottawa, December 2006). Selected comparisons of the scantlings were made against tables in David Steel, *The Elements and Practice of Naval Architecture* (London, 1805). This reveals that the scantlings recorded on the wrecks are in line with design specifications for Royal Navy warships of the period.

Glossary

Abaft. In the direction of the stern, used in relation to another feature on the ship.

Adze. Woodworking tool with its blade attached perpendicular to the axis of the handle, used by shipwrights to shape and smooth timbers.

Aft. Toward the back or stern of a ship.

Amidships. The point on a vessel halfway between the stem and stern.

Anchor. A heavy weight, typically made of wrought iron in the shape of an inverted T, that is connected to a vessel by a cable or a chain and holds it in place by hooking into the sea bottom. Features of an anchor include the following:

Arms. The pair of angled extensions at lower end of the anchor shank.

Crown. The part of the anchor where the arms and shank meet.

Fluke. The pointed or chisel-shaped extension at the end of an anchor arm.

Nut. Small protrusion on the shank of an anchor designed to fit into mortises in a wooden stock to keep the stock from twisting on the shank.

Palm. The broad, flat, triangular face of an anchor's fluke.

Ring. The circular feature at the head of the anchor for attaching a cable or chain.

Shank. The shaft of an anchor.

Stock. The wood or metal crosspiece fitted near the top of an anchor shank, designed to pivot the anchor on the sea bottom so that one fluke catches on the bottom.

Apron. A curved internal timber, attached to the lower end of the stem and the forward end of the keel.

Athwartships. Across the longitudinal axis of a ship.

Axe. Woodworking tool with its blade attached in line with the handle, used by shipwrights for the preliminary cutting and squaring of timbers.

Ballast. Heavy material such as iron, stone, or sand placed in a vessel's hold to lower the center of gravity and increase stability.

Beam. 1) A transverse timber that supports a deck and holds the sides of a ship together; 2) the width of a ship; see Breadth.

Beam Ends. A ship lying over on one side is said to be "on its beam ends."

Belaying Pin. A pin to which ropes are made fast.

Berth Deck. The deck situated immediately below the main deck of a vessel that serves as living quarters for the crew.

Bevel. See Chamfer.

Bilge. The curved portion of a hull beneath the waterline.

Bitts. Upright posts for belaying ropes or anchor cables.

Block. A device for increasing mechanical purchase on a line, used on shipboard for heavy lifting or pulling tasks; they are variously shaped to meet different requirements but consist of a shell, a pin, and one or more wheels called sheaves.

Bobstay. Element in a ship's standing rigging that extends between the cutwater or stem and the outboard end of the bowsprit; the bobstay counters the upward pull of the foremast stays.

Body Lines. See Station Lines.

Bolt. Cylindrical metal fasteners used to fasten a ship's timbers or the chainplates of the standing rigging or for securing tackle, cables, and standing rigging; a variety of types exist; see Clench Bolt, Drift Bolt, Eyebolt, Forelock Bolt, and Ring Bolt.

Boom. Spars used to extend sails, such as the spanker boom that extends the foot of a fore-and-aft sail, the stuns'l boom that extends studdingsails from the outboard ends of yards, or the jibboom that extends the headsails forward of the bowsprit.

Boom Irons. Metal fittings at the ends of yards that secure stuns'l booms and allow them to be easily extended or retracted.

Bow. The forward end of a ship.

Bowsprit. A spar that angles forward of the bow and serves to extend the head sails and to secure the stays of the foremast.

Bowsprit Cap. See Mast Cap.

Boxing Scarf. A complex scarf with an interlocking mortise and tenon, used to join the keel to the stem or keel pieces to one another.

Brails. Lines that extend to the edges of a sail, used to draw the sail up when not in use.

Breadth. The width of a ship; molded breadth is the width at the outside faces of the frames; extreme breadth is the width to the outside of the planking.

Breast Hook. A horizontally oriented knee fitted inside the bow to fasten the stem, apron, and forwardmost frames together and reinforce the entire assembly.

Breechings. Heavy ropes or cables that extend from the bulwarks on either side of a gunport around the back of a cannon, used to arrest the gun's recoil after it fires.

Brig. A square-rigged vessel with two masts.

Broadside. The combined firepower of all guns on one side of a warship.

Bulkhead. An upright partition within a hull.

Bulwarks. Frame ends and planking that extend above the edge of a ship's uppermost deck.

Butt. The end of a plank or timber that is cut perpendicular to the length of the piece.

Butt Joint. The meeting of two ship timbers or planks with their ends cut perpendicularly to their lengths.

Buttock Lines. Geometric lines drawn on the plan of a ship's hull to illustrate the longitudinal shapes of a vessel at selected intervals above and parallel to the keel.

Cable. A strong, thick line composed of multiple smaller ropes, used for attaching an anchor to a ship.

Cable Tier. Compartment within a ship used for storing anchor cables.

Camber. The slight curve of a ship's timber; ship's decks are typically cambered to shed water to the sides.

Camboose. A ship's cook stove, typically made of cast iron on warships of the 1812–15 era.

Canister Shot. A cannon projectile composed of a thin metal casing filled with dozens or hundreds of small-diameter lead or iron shot; when fired from a cannon the casing opens and scatters the shot. Typically used at close range against people, sails, and rigging.

Cant Frames. The frames at each end of a hull that are not perpendicular to the keel. Those at the stem slant forward; those at the stern slant aft.

Cap Rail. A timber attached to the top of a vessel's frames.

Capstan. A vertically mounted winch drum of heavy wooden construction used to lift anchors or other heavy objects. Sometimes called a capstern in ship contracts.

Carling. Short stiffening timbers located between and perpendicular to deck beams.

Carronade. A short, lightweight, wide-bore cannon that fires a heavy shot over short distances. Developed at the Carron Foundry in Scotland in the late eighteenth century, these guns were also known as "ship smashers."

Carvel Planking. A method of planking a vessel wherein the strakes are laid side by side over a ship's frames, with flush edges between planks.

Catfalls. The tackle arrangement at the end of a cathead, used to lift an anchor from the water.

Catheads. Short timber davits projecting from either side of a ship's bow, they contain sheaves that are used to lift anchors from the water and hold them clear of the side of a ship.

Caulking. Filling materials such as oakum, cotton fiber, and tar, driven or poured onto a ship's plank seams, to render the hull and decks watertight.

Ceiling. The internal planking of a ship.

Centerboard. A wood or metal fin, housed in a watertight trunk within a ship, that can be raised or lowered through the bottom of the hull to increase lateral resistance. Centerboards were developed in the early nineteenth century and widely used on North American shallow-draft sailing vessels from the 1820s onward.

Chainplates. Metal fastenings for attaching mast shrouds and backstays to the sides of a ship.

Chamfer. The flat, sloping surface created by cutting the edge off a timber.

Channels. Projections on a vessel's bulwarks resembling thick planks set on edge, designed to extend mast shrouds and stays out from the side of the hull. Sometimes called chain wales.

Cheek. A horizontal reinforcing knee between the side of the bow and the knee of the head.

Chine. The angular join between the bottom and side of a vessel, typically found on flat-bottomed boats.

Chock. A wedge of wood secured across the butt of two frame timbers.

Clamps. Thick internal strakes, generally opposite wales, that reinforce the sides of a vessel. See Shelf Clamp.

Clench Bolt. A metal bolt that is secured in place by hammering one or both ends into a mushroom shape, typically over a metal washer.

Clinker-Built. See Lapstrake.

Coaming. The raised border around a hatch designed to keep water out.

Columbiad. A light, short-barreled, large-bored cannon used by the U.S. Navy in the 1812 period.

Companionway. Stairs between decks, or small deck openings designed for crew access between decks.

Compass Timber. Naturally curved timber used for frames, stems, or other hull elements.

Copper Fastened. A vessel assembled with copper bolts and spikes below the waterline.

Corvette. A flush-decked, ship-rigged warship mounting 24 to 26 guns, an intermediate size between sloops of war and frigates.

Crossbeam. A heavy timber fastened between two bitts, typically used to secure an anchor cable.

Crosstree. Transverse elements in the framework structure fitted around the tops of lower and upper masts; crosstrees notch down into the fore-and-aft trestletrees, and their outboard ends can serve as spreaders for shrouds.

Counter. The portion of a vessel's stern that overhangs and projects aft of the sternpost.

Cutter. A lightly built yet capacious ship's boat intended primarily for transporting men.

Cutwater. The forwardmost part of the stem that forms a curved leading edge that is widest at the top. The cutwater is designed to part the water as the vessel advances.

Dagger Knee. A diagonally oriented, angled reinforcing timber, used to strengthen the join between a deck beam and the side of a hull.

Davits. Short timbers that project from the sides or stern of a vessel, used to lift small boats or anchors from the water.

Deadeye. A circular block with a groove around its circumference and three holes in the center to fit a lanyard; used in pairs to adjust the tension of standing rigging elements such as shrouds and stays.

Deadrise. The angle of the bottom of a hull above the horizontal plane of the keel.

Deadwood. Longitudinally oriented reinforcing timbers bolted to the top of the keel.

Deck Beam. An athwartship timber that supports a deck.

Deck Light. A glass lens or prism installed in a watertight opening in the deck to allow natural light into the between-deck space below.

Depth of Hold. The centerline distance between the top of the floor timbers and the top of the deck beams at the midship frame.

Dolphin Striker. A short spar or bar extending below the Bowsprit Cap to provide a down-angle on the martingale stays; this spar is also called a martingale.

Double Framing. A term used to describe frames composed of two rows of timbers.

Doubling. The overlap of a lower mast and an upper mast, secured by a mast cap, trestletrees and crosstrees, and a fid.

Dovetail Plates. Paired plates of iron or copper alloy that are through-bolted over timber seams, designed to secure the join of major hull elements such as the stem, keel, and sternpost. Also called Fish Plates.

Draft. 1) The depth of water a ship draws; 2) a two-dimensional delineation or plan that shows a ship's design or construction features.

Draft Marks. Lines or numerals carved into or attached to a ship's stem and sternpost to indicate how deeply the vessel is sitting in the water.

Drag. When a vessel is trimmed with the after end of the keel deeper than the forward end.

Drift Bolt. A metal bolt driven into a hole of slightly smaller diameter.

Dumb Brace. A metal support bracket fitted on a sternpost below a gudgeon to support the end of a pintle (and the weight of the rudder).

Entrance. The forwardmost portion of a hull below the waterline.

Eyebolt. A metal bolt with a circular opening at one end.

False Keel. A timber fastened to the bottom of the keel to protect it from damage or increase the vessel's draft. Also called a shoe in some ship contracts.

False Sternpost. An additional sternpost, fastened abaft the main post, designed to protect or reinforce the stern.

Fashion Piece. A frame that defines the shape of a vessel's stern.

Fid. 1) A pointed wood or metal tool used by sailors to loosen knots or splices in a ship's rig; 2) a wood or metal key used to secure the heel of an upper mast between the trestletrees at the overlap of two masts.

Fish Plates. See Dovetail Plates.

Flat Scarf. A diagonal join between two timbers or planks where the ends of each are squared off with a nib.

Floor. The timber of a frame that is fastened across the keel; also called a floor timber.

Floor Head Line. The line along each side of the hull where the floor timbers end.

Fore-and-Aft Rig. A sailing rig with the sails set parallel to the axis of the keel. Common fore-and-aft rigs during the early nineteenth century include sloops and schooners; fore-and-aft sails of this era include gaff, stay, jib, and lateen sails.

Forecastle. The part of a vessel forward of the foremast; also a raised deck at the bow of a ship.

Forefoot. See Gripe (1).

Forelock Bolt. A metal bolt with a slot at one end to fit a metal key or wedge that holds the bolt in place.

Foremast. The forewardmost mast on a ship-, brig-, or schooner-rigged vessel.

Forward. Toward the front or bow of a ship.

Foot Ropes. Ropes suspended below yards to provide footing for sailors who are working on the sails; they consist of short lengths of rope (stirrups) eye-spliced around a yard at intervals and a longer rope (the horse) that extends between the ends of a yard and is rove through thimbles at the lower ends of the stirrups.

Foot Wale. A thick longitudinal ceiling plank located at the floor head line or turn of the bilge.

Frame. The skeletal structure of a vessel mounted perpendicularly to the keel and composed of a floor timber and several futtocks. Sometimes informally referred to as a rib.

Freeboard. The distance between a ship's waterline and the main deck.

Frigate. A moderately sized, square-rigged warship mounting guns on two decks; in the War of 1812 era, frigates carried between 28 and 44 guns, with most falling in the 32- to 38-gun range.

Futtocks. The upper timbers of a frame.

Gaff. A short spar used to extend the head of a fore-and-aft sail from a mast.

Galley. See Gunboat.

Gallows. A heavy wooden support structure used for above-deck stowage of spare spars, sweeps, and small boats.

Gammoning. A heavy lashing of rope between a vessel's stem and bowsprit, designed to hold the latter in place and counter the upward pull of the foremast stays.

Gammoning Knee. A curved timber at the top of a vessel's stem to which the bowsprit is lashed.

Garboard. The external planking strake that is closest to the keel; typically its inboard edge is shaped to fit into a groove or rabbet carved into the top of the keel.

Grapeshot. A cannon projectile composed of a disk-shaped wood or metal base with an upright post in the center; medium-diameter iron shot (generally nine in number) are stacked on the stand and secured with a cover of canvas and twine. When fired from a gun, the shot scatter in a broad pattern. Typically used against small boats, people, or rigging.

Grate. A latticework wooden hatch cover or platform that allows the passage of light and air.

Gripe. 1) A curved stem element that extends from the forward end of the keel up to the knee of the head; 2) the tendency of a vessel to point its bow into the wind when sailing close-hauled.

Ground Tackle. The collective term for the anchors and cables used to hold a ship in place.

Gudgeon. A metal hinge bracket attached to the sternpost on which the rudder is hung by means of a pintle.

Gunboat. The smallest class of warship, typically mounting one cannon at the bow or a cannon at the bow and stern and fitted with a simple sailing rig and sweeps for rowing. Also called Galleys or Row Galleys.

Gun Carriage. The wooden support structure for a cannon or carronade, typically fitted with small wheels (called trucks) to allow movement on the deck.

Gundeck. The deck or decks on a warship that support broadside guns.

Gunlock. A flintlock firing mechanism that is attached above a cannon's vent and triggered by pulling a lanyard.

Gunport. A square or rectangular opening in a ship's side for a cannon.

Gunport Sill. The timber that frames the bottom of a gunport.

Gunwale. The uppermost wale or strake on a vessel's side.

Half Frame. A frame that does not extend across a keel but instead rises up from either side.

Hammock Irons. Metal brackets fitted around the top of a ship's rail through which a series of ropes were rove; the ropes were designed to hold the crew's hammocks when they were not in use.

Hammock Rail. An open wooden framework around the top of a ship's rail designed to hold hammocks when they were not in use.

Hanging Knee. A vertically oriented, angled reinforcing timber, mostly used to strengthen the join between deck beams and the side of the hull.

Hatch. An opening through the deck of a ship.

Hawse Pieces. Internal bow timbers that abut the cant frames at their heels and run parallel to the stem.

Hawse Pipe. An opening at the bow of a vessel, often fitted with a sleeve of lead or other metal, through which an anchor cable passes. Also called a hawse hole.

Head. 1) The forwardmost part of a vessel; 2) the upper end of a frame timber, end post, mast, or bowsprit; 3) a seat of ease or toilet on a ship.

Headed Bolt. See Clench Bolt.

Headrails. Curved rails extending from the bow of a vessel to its cutwater.

Head Sails. Sails set forward of the foremast.

Heart Block. A block of wood grooved around the outside to attach a stay and with a single large hole in the center that is scored at one end to fit a lanyard; these blocks are used in pairs to adjust the tension of stays.

Heel. 1) The lower end of a frame timber, end post, mast, or bowsprit; 2) the leaning of a vessel to one side due to the pressure of wind on the sails, unbalanced loading, or taking in water.

Helm. The tiller or wheel that steers a vessel.

Hog. The tendency for a vessel's ends to droop due to the lack of longitudinal strength, overloading of the ends, or excessive strain in heavy seas.

Hold. The interior space in the bottom of a vessel that contains cargo or supplies.

Hood Ends. The ends of planks that fit into stem or sternpost rabbets.

Hook Scarf. A diagonal scarf between two timbers or planks with a joggle in the middle designed to prevent the pieces from separating.

Horseshoe Plate. A heavy metal plate used to secure the timbers of the stem. See Dovetail Plate.

Inner Sternpost. A sternpost fastened to the keel forward of the main sternpost, often used as a surface to fasten the hood ends of the planking.

Jackstay Batten. A wooden rail used to secure hammocks, attached to deck beams or clamps on the berth deck.

Jib. A triangular fore-and-aft sail bent on the jib stay above the head of the jibboom.

Jibboom. A spar that extends forward of the bowsprit to support the jib sail.

Kedge. The smallest anchor on a ship. Kedging is the process of pulling a vessel through the water by dropping the kedge anchor to the bottom and reeling in the cable.

Keel. The backbone of a ship, to which the stem, sternpost, and frames are attached.

Keelson. An internal longitudinal timber, set atop the frames directly over the keel, that serves to longitudinally reinforce the hull.

Kentledge. Pig-iron ballast used to stabilize a ship.

Knee. An angled timber used to reinforce critical joins in the hull.

Knee of the Head. An inverted knee fastened to the forward face of the stem, designed to serve as a cutwater and to support the headrails and ship's figurehead.

Knightheads. 1) The forwardmost frame timbers in a ship's hull that are fitted parallel to and on either side of the stem; their heads can rise above the deck to form bitts that support the bowsprit; 2) bitt posts used to secure anchor cables or a ship's running rigging.

Lanyard. A length of line used to secure two or more items on a ship or used to adjust the distance between two deadeyes or two heart blocks and thereby adjust the tension of a shroud or stay.

Lapstrake. A method of planking the sides of a vessel by overlapping the planks and fastening their edges with rivets.

Lateen. A fore-and-aft rig common to Mediterranean ships (and widely used on 1812-era North American gunboats) with a large triangular sail spread by a long yard hanging diagonally from a short mast.

Lateral Drift. The tendency of a vessel to move sideways as it advances through the water, generally caused by a combination of winds, waves, and currents.

Launch. A heavily built and capacious boat, intended for transporting anchors, provisions, guns, and other weighty cargoes.

Ledge. A small athwartship beam located between larger deck beams.

Limber Boards. Ceiling planks immediately adjacent to the keelson, generally left unfastened to permit access to the bilges.

Limber Holes. Holes cut in the undersides of the floor timbers and first futtocks, on either side of the keel, that allow bilge water to circulate inside the hull. Also called watercourses.

Lines. The three-dimensional shape of a hull, or a set of plans that delineate its shape.

Linstock. A simple device used to ignite a cannon's priming powder, consisting of a wooden handle for holding a length of smoldering slow match; this item of gunner's equipment was largely replaced by gun locks in the U.S. and Royal Navies by the early nineteenth century.

Lodging Knee. A horizontally oriented, angled reinforcing timber, generally fitted between deck beams to strengthen the join between the beams and the side of a hull.

Magazine. The compartment in a ship used to store gun powder.

Mainmast. The tallest mast on a vessel, usually the central mast on a ship-rigged vessel and the second mast on a brig- or schooner-rigged vessel.

Martingale Stays. Standing rigging located beneath the bowsprit and jibboom, used to counteract the upward pull of the foremast stays. See Dolphin Striker.

Mast. A vertically oriented timber or assembly of timbers, typically made of pine or similar light, strong softwoods, used to support a vessel's spars and sails.

Mast Cap. A rectangular block of wood (later iron) placed over the head of a lower mast to secure the overlap (or "doubling") of two masts; a similar block at the head of the bowsprit was called a Bowsprit Cap.

Mast Partners. Fore-and-aft beams or carlings that support a mast where it passes through a deck; also called mast carlings.

Mast Step. A mortise cut to fit the heel of a mast; the mortise may be cut directly into the keelson or be in a block of wood fastened atop the keelson.

Mast Top. 1) The head of a mast; 2) the platform at the doubling of two masts.

Messenger. A flexible cable looped around a capstan drum and set up as an endless loop around a ship's deck; this is temporarily fastened to an anchor cable with nippers and used to raise an anchor.

Midship Frame. The widest frame on a vessel, indicated by the symbol ⋈.

Mizzen Mast. The third mast on a ship-rigged vessel.

Molded Dimension. The measurement of height or width as seen in the body plan of a vessel; the shapes of timbers derived from the sheer and body plan of a vessel.

Mortise. A recess cut into the surface of one timber to fit the heel or tenon of another timber.

Nibbing. The squaring of deck plank ends where they meet the side of the hull, intended to reduce the likelihood of splitting. A nibbing strake extends along the inside of a vessel's waterways and is notched on its inboard edge to fit the nibbed ends of the deck planks.

Nippers. Short lengths of line used to temporarily attach an anchor cable to the messenger cable when raising an anchor.

Oakum. Caulking composed of old hemp rope fibers soaked in pitch or tar and driven into planking seams to render them watertight.

Orlop. The lowest deck in a ship.

Outboard. Located toward the outside or completely outside of a vessel.

Parceling. The wrapping of strips of old canvas, well tarred, around a rope to protect it from wear and moisture; parceling is also applied to anchor rings to reduce wear on anchor cables.

Partners. Reinforcing timbers set around a deck opening to support deck features such as masts or bitts.

Pay. To cover a vessel's bottom with a protective layer of pitch, tar, or similar substance.

Pinrail. A rack for holding belaying pins, located inside the bulwarks of a vessel.

Pintle. A metal bracket, attached to the forward face and sides of a rudder, that fits into the gudgeon on a sternpost, forming a hinge for the rudder.

Pintle Stop. See Dumb Brace.

Pissdale. A trough fitted to the inside of a ship's bulwark to serve as a urinal.

Planking. The outer lining of a hull.

Planking Strake. A continuous line of planks from stem to stern.

Plug Stock Rudder. A rudder designed to pivot on the axis of its stock.

Port. The left-hand side of a vessel, when one is facing forward. Also referred to as larboard.

Primer. A small charge of fine-grained, easily ignited gunpowder that is inserted into a cannon's vent prior to firing; this is ignited by a slow match or flintlock mechanism to set off the larger propelling charge. A priming charge can be poured from a flask or carried premeasured in either a hollow goose quill or a lead cup with a hollow stem.

Puddening. The wrapping on the ring of an iron anchor, consisting of tar-soaked canvas strips covered by tightly wound small line, added to protect anchor cables from chafing.

Pullover. A post set above the boarding steps on the outside of a ship, designed to hold a rope that assists people ascending or descending the sides.

Pump Well. An opening between or on top of frames where bilge water collects and where a pump for removing the water is located; pump wells are typically found near the base of the mainmast.

Quoin. A wooden wedge placed under a cannon's breech that allows aiming by elevating or depressing the barrel.

Rabbet. A groove cut into each side of the keel, stem, and stern, into which the garboards or plank ends are seated.

Rake. The angle at which the stem slants forward and sternpost slants aft; also used to refer to the aft-slanting angle of a mast.

Rat Lines. Lengths of small rope attached to shrouds at equal distances, which together serve as a ladder for sailors climbing to the mast tops.

Rider. An internal reinforcing timber fastened atop the ceiling planking and frames.

Riding Bitts. Heavy upright posts to which anchor cables are secured.

Ring Bolt. Metal bolt with an eye at one end that holds a separate ring; used for securing gun tackle, as stoppers for an anchor cable, or as attachment points for other rigging elements.

Row Galley. See Gunboat.

Royal Mast. The mast, and its associated yard and sail, located above the topgallant mast.

Rudder. The blade hung on a vessel's sternpost by metal hinges that pivots to one side or the other to control the direction of a ship.

Rudder Stock. The heavy vertical timber in a rudder that extends up into the hull and into which the tiller is fitted.

Rule Joint Rudder. A rudder designed to turn by pivoting its stock from side to side.

Running Rigging. The ropes and blocks in a vessel's sailing rig that are used to adjust spars and sails relative to the wind.

Sag. The rocker formed in a ship's keel and hull when it is overloaded or overstrained.

Scantlings. The principal framing timbers of a vessel, or the dimensions of those timbers.

Scarf. The joint connecting two timbers.

Schooner. A fore-and-aft–rigged vessel with two or more masts.

Scupper. A water drain on a vessel's deck.

Scuttle. 1) A small opening for light and air in the deck or side of a ship; 2) to intentionally sink a ship.

Seam. The longitudinal joint between two timbers or planks.

Seizing. Small cordage used to secure elements in a ship's rig.

Sennit. Braided or plaited rope yarns used in a ship's rig.

Service. Spun-yarn line tightly wrapped around a rope with a serving mallet or wrapped around an anchor ring, intended to protect rope surfaces from excessive wear.

Sheer. The upward curve of a ship's hull or bulwarks as seen from the side.

Sheer Plan. The side view of a vessel's hull seen on a set of plans.

Shelf Clamp. A clamp timber that also supports deck beams along its upper edge.

Ship. Generally, any large seagoing or lake-going vessel; specifically, a three-masted, square-rigged vessel.

Ship of the Line. The most powerful classes of square-rigged warships during the age of sailing navies, so-called for their ability to engage in a fleet battle; the average line of battle ship in the early nineteenth century mounted 74 guns, although the largest mounted over 100 guns.

Shipwright. A builder of ships.

Shoe. See False Keel.

Shot Garland. A row of cannon shot stored in close proximity to the cannon, or a timber structure built to hold shot.

Shot Locker. A compartment where cannon projectiles are stowed.

Shrouds. Paired heavy ropes that laterally support a mast; part of a vessel's standing rigging.

Sided Dimension. The measurement across outer frame faces or tops of longitudinal timbers; the dimensions of nonmolded timber surfaces.

Skeg. A small triangular projection on the after end of the keel, intended to protect the forward edge of the rudder.

Skylight. A framed enclosure on the upper deck fitted with glass panes to allow light into below-deck compartments.

Sloop. A fore-and-aft-rigged vessel with a single mast.

Sloop of War. A brig- or ship-rigged warship mounting 18 to 22 cannon.

Spanker. Fore-and-aft sail set on the aftermost mast of a square-rigged ship.

Spars. The long wooden elements of a sailing rig used to spread the sails.

Square Frame. A frame that is perpendicular to the keel and extends across both sides of the hull. See Frame.

Square Rig. A sailing rig with the sails set perpendicular to the axis of the keel. Common early-nineteenth-century square rigs included the ship and the brig.

Stanchion. An upright supporting post.

Standing Knee. A vertically oriented, angled reinforcing timber, sometimes used to reinforce bitt posts against the pull of anchor cables.

Standing Rigging. Rope, wood, and metal elements in a sailing rig that support the masts against the forces of wind and the motion of the ship.

Starboard. The right-hand side of a vessel when one is facing forward.

Station Lines. Geometric lines drawn on the plan of a ship's hull to illustrate its transverse shape.

Stays. Light or heavy ropes that support masts; part of the standing rigging.

Steerage. The living quarters allocated to a warship's midshipmen and surgeon's mates, typically located alongside the mainmast on a sloop of war.

Steeve. The upward angle of a ship's bowsprit and jibboom.

Stem. The upward-curving timber attached to the forward end of the keel.

Stern. The back of a ship.

Stern Framing. The assembly of timbers that forms the stern, including the sternpost, transoms, fashion pieces, and counter timbers.

Stern Knee. An angled timber that reinforces the join between the keel, stern deadwood, and sternpost.

Sternpost. An upward-angling timber attached to the after end of the keel.

Stocks. A structure used to support a vessel under construction or repair.

Stopper. A length of heavy line used to absorb the strain on the cable of an anchored ship. Stoppers are rove through an eye or ring bolt in the deck and lashed to the cable with several turns of a smaller lanyard. They can be used to temporarily secure a cable or to prevent too great a strain on the anchor bitts.

Stopwater. A wooden dowel driven across the seam between two external timbers (such as the stem and keel) to deflect water traveling along the seams and prevent the timbers from shifting.

Strake. A continuous line of planks extending from the stem to the stern.

Studdingsail or Stunsail. Extensions of square sails that are spread from booms extending beyond the yards; typically used in light or moderate winds to increase sailing speed.

Sweep. A large oar, worked by crewmen standing inboard of the bulwarks or rail who push or pull on the sweep.

Sweep Port. An opening in a ship's bulwark that allows the outboard extension of a sweep.

Tackle. Arrangements of ropes and blocks that provide mechanical leverage for heavy lifting or pulling tasks on board a ship.

Taffrail. The upper part of the stern or the rail extending across the stern of a ship.

Tenon. A projecting element on a timber that fits into a corresponding mortise on another.

Thick Stuff. Thick ceiling strakes that parallel the keelson and longitudinally reinforce the hull.

Tiller. A lever fitted to the top of a ship's rudder, used for turning the rudder from side to side.

Topgallant. The mast, and its associated yard and sail, located above the topmast and below the royal mast.

Top Mast. The mast, and its associated yard and sail, located above the main or lower mast and below the topgallant mast.

Top Timbers. The futtocks located at the top of a frame.

Transoms. Beams or timbers extending across the sternpost of a vessel.

Treenail. A wooden dowel driven into a hole drilled to the same or slightly smaller diameter; used to fasten hull timbers, usually external planking to frames.

Trestletree. The paired fore-and-aft elements in the framework structure fitted around the tops of lower and upper masts; trestletrees were notched on top to fit the transversely oriented crosstrees, and their forward ends supported the heel of the upper mast at the doubling.

Trucks. 1) The wheels of a gun carriage; 2) small, wooden, acorn- or disk-shaped decorative pieces placed over the heads of masts, sometimes containing a sheave for raising signal flags; 3) fist-size wooden beads strung together on a line and used to attach boom or gaff jaws, or lower yards, to masts.

Tumblehome. The incurving of the tops of a vessel's frames above the waterline, designed to reduce a hull's topside weight and improve its stability.

Turn of the Bilge. The area of a hull where the bottom curves toward the side.

Waist. The part of a ship's upper deck located between the forecastle and the quarterdeck.

Wale. A thick planking strake that reinforces the side of a vessel.

Ward Room. A compartment with surrounding cabins occupied by the ship's officers; on a naval vessel this might be occupied by lieutenants, a sailing master, a surgeon, and a purser.

Watch. 1) The division of time and duty aboard a ship,

typically measured in four-hour intervals; 2) the division of the crew for alternating watch periods.

Watercourses. See Limber Holes.

Waterlines. In ship drawings, geometric lines that illustrate the horizontal shapes of the hull at intervals parallel to the baseline; sometimes called level lines.

Waterway. A strake or timber located at the juncture of the deck and bulwark; on some vessels this timber was hollowed to channel water to the scuppers.

Way. The framework structure upon which a ship is built and from which it is launched.

Weather Deck. The uppermost and thus uncovered deck.

Well. See Pump Well.

Wheel. A windlass that provides mechanical leverage for the helmsman of a ship, the wheel turns the rudder by winding or unwinding a pair of ropes or chains attached to the tiller. Wheels were first used on large ships in the early eighteenth century.

Windage. 1) The surface area of a ship above the waterline that is subject to the forces of the wind pressing upon it; 2) the difference in diameter between the bore and the shot of a musket or cannon.

Windlass. A horizontally mounted winch drum fitted to upright posts, used to lift anchors or other heavy objects.

Yard. A spar of pine or similar softwood that tapers at either end; suspended from a ship's mast, the yard spreads the head of a square sail.

Bibliography and Sources

PUBLISHED SOURCES

Allodi, Mary, ed. *Canadian Watercolours and Drawings in the Royal Ontario Museum,* vol. 2. Toronto: The Royal Ontario Museum, 1974.

Altoff, Gerard T. *Deep Water Sailors, Shallow Water Soldiers: Manning the United States Fleet on Lake Erie—1813.* Put-in-Bay, OH: The Perry Group, 1993.

Altoff, Gerard T. *Oliver Hazard Perry and the Battle of Lake Erie.* Put-in-Bay, OH: The Perry Group, 1999.

Anderson, Fred. *Crucible of War: The Seven Years' War and the Fate of Empire in British North America, 1754–1766.* New York: Alfred A. Knopf, 2000.

Ansley, Norman. *Vergennes, Vermont and the War of 1812.* Severna Park, MD: Brooke Keefer Limited Editions, 1999.

Badger, Barber. *The Naval Temple: Containing a Complete History of the Battles Fought by the Navy of the United States, from its Establishment in 1794, to the Present Time.* Boston: Published by Barber Badger, 1816.

Bamford, Don, and Paul Carroll. *Four Years on the Great Lakes, 1813–1816: The Journal of David Wingfield, Royal Navy.* Toronto: Natural Heritage Books, 2009.

Barker, A. S. "Naval Reminiscences IX, an Incident from the War of 1812," *The Navy* (February 1914).

Barkhausen, Henry N. *The Riddle of the Naubinway Sands.* Manitowoc, WI: Association of Great Lakes Maritime History, 1991.

Bauer, K. J., ed. *The New American State Papers: Naval Affairs,* vol. 4. Wilmington: Scholarly Resources, 1981.

Bellico, Russell P. *Sails and Steam in the Mountains: A Maritime and Military History of Lake George and Lake Champlain.* Fleischmanns, NY: Purple Mountain Press, 1992.

Berton, Pierre. *The Invasion of Canada, 1812–1813.* Toronto: McClelland and Stewart, 1980.

Berton, Pierre. *Flames Across the Border, 1813–1814.* Toronto: McClelland and Stewart, 1981.

Binnie, Nancy E. "Overloaded? Mussels, Biofouling, and Material Condition Observations for the *Hamilton* and *Scourge* Shipwreck Site," in *ACUA Underwater Archaeology Proceedings, 2009,* eds. Erika Laanela and Jonathan Moore (Advisory Council on Underwater Archaeology, 2010).

Blow, David J. "*Vermont I*: Lake Champlain's First Steamboat," *Vermont History* 34, no. 2 (1966).

Boardman, James. *America and the Americans.* London: Longman, Rees, Orme, Brown, Green, and Longman, 1833.

Bouchette, Joseph. *A Topographical Description of the Province of Lower Canada with Remarks upon Upper Canada.* London: W. Faden, 1815.

Bowen, Abel. *The Naval Monument, Containing Official and Other Accounts of All the Battles Fought between the Navies of the United States and Great Britain During the Late War.* Boston: George Clark, 1838.

Brant, Irving. *James Madison, Commander in Chief,* vol. 6. Indianapolis: Bobbs-Merrill Company, 1961.

Bratten, John R. *The Gondola* Philadelphia *and the Battle of Lake Champlain.* College Station, TX: Texas A&M University Press, 2002.

Bredenberg, Oscar. *The Battle of Plattsburgh Bay: The British Navy's View.* Plattsburgh, NY: Clinton County Historical Association, 1978.

Brown, Noah. "The Remarkable Statement of Noah Brown," *Journal of American History* 8, no. 1 (January 1914).

Brown, Roger H. *The Republic in Peril: 1812.* New York: W. W. Norton, 1971.

Brown, Samuel R. *An Authentic History of the Second War for Independence.* Auburn, NY: J. G. Hathaway, 1815.

Burt, A. L. *The United States, Great Britain, and British North America: From the Revolution to the Establishment of Peace after the War of 1812.* New York: Russell & Russell, 1961.

Cain, Emily. "Building the *Lord Nelson,*" *Inland Seas* 41, no. 2 (1985).

Cain, Emily. "Customs Collection—and Dutiable Goods: Lake Ontario Ports 1801–1812," *FreshWater* 2, no. 2 (1987).

Cain, Emily. *Ghost Ships* Hamilton and Scourge*: Historical Treasures from the War of 1812.* Toronto: Musson/Beaufort Books, 1983.

Cain, Emily. "Naval Wrecks from the Great Lakes," in *History from the Sea: Shipwrecks and Archaeology, from Homer's Odyssey to the* Titanic, ed. Peter Throckmorton (London: Mitchell Beazley, 1987).

Cain, Emily. "Provisioning Lake Ontario Merchant Schooners, 1809–1812: *Lord Nelson* (*Scourge*), *Diana* (*Hamilton*), *Ontario* and *Niagara,*" *FreshWater* 3, no. 1 (1988).

Campbell, Karen. "Propaganda, Pestilence, and Prosperity: Burlington's Camptown Days During the War of 1812," *Vermont History* 64, no. 3 (1996).

Campbell, Marjorie Wilkins. *The Northwest Company.* Toronto: Macmillan, 1957.

Canney, Donald L. *Sailing Warships of the U.S. Navy.* Annapolis: Naval Institute Press, 2001.

Cantelas, Frank J. "A Portrait of an Early 19th-Century Great Lakes Sailing Vessel," in *Underwater Archaeology Proceedings from the Society for Historical Archaeology Conference, Kansas City, Missouri, 1993,* ed. Sheli O. Smith (Tucson: The Society for Historical Archaeology, 1993).

Caruana, Adrian B. *The History of English Sea Ordnance 1523–1875, Volume II: The Age of the System 1715–1815.* East Sussex: Jean Boudriot Publications, 1997.

Chapelle, Howard I. *The Baltimore Clipper.* Salem, MA: The Marine Research Society, 1930.

Chapelle, Howard I. *The History of American Sailing Ships.* New York: W. W. Norton, 1935.

Chapelle, Howard I. *The History of the American Sailing Navy.* New York: W. W. Norton, 1949.

Chapelle, Howard I. *The History of the American Sailing Navy.* New York: Bonanza Books, 1949.

Chapelle, Howard I. *The Search for Speed Under Sail.* New York: W. W. Norton, 1967.

Clark, B. N., ed. "Accounts of the Battle of Plattsburgh, September 11, 1814: From Contemporaneous Sources," *Vermont Antiquarian* 1, no. 3 (1903).

Cohn, Arthur B., ed. *A Report on the Nautical Archaeology of Lake Champlain, Results of the 1982 Field Season of the Champlain Maritime Society.* Burlington, VT: The Champlain Maritime Society, 1984.

Cohn, Arthur B., Adam I. Kane, Christopher R. Sabick, Edwin R. Scollon, and Justin B. Clement. *Valcour Bay Research Project: 1999–2004 Results from the Archaeological Investigation of a Revolutionary War Battlefield in Lake Champlain, Clinton County, New York.* Basin Harbor, VT: Lake Champlain Maritime Museum, 2007.

Colledge, J. J. *Ships of the Royal Navy: The Complete Record of All Fighting Ships of the Royal Navy from the Fifteenth Century to the Present.* Annapolis, MD: Naval Institute Press, 1987.

Cooper, James Fenimore, ed. *Ned Myers; or, a Life Before the Mast.* 1843; reprint Annapolis: Naval Institute Press, 1989.

Crawford, Michael J., ed. *The Naval War of 1812: A Documentary History,* vol. 3. Washington, DC: Naval Historical Center, 2002.

Crisman, Kevin J. "Coffins of the Brave: A Return to Lake Champlain's War of 1812 Ship Graveyard," *Institute of Nautical Archaeology Quarterly* 22, no. 1 (1995).

Crisman, Kevin J. *The* Eagle*: An American Brig on Lake Champlain During the War of 1812.* Shelburne, VT: The New England Press; Annapolis, MD: The Naval Institute Press, 1987.

Crisman, Kevin J. *The History and Construction of the United States Schooner* Ticonderoga. Alexandria, VA: Eyrie Publications, 1983.

Crisman, Kevin J. "The *Jefferson*: The History and Archaeology of an American Brig from the War of 1812" (PhD diss., University of Pennsylvania, 1989).

Crisman, Kevin J. "Struggle for a Continent: Naval Battles of the French and Indian Wars," in *Ships and Shipwrecks of the Americas,* ed. George F. Bass (London: Thames and Hudson, 1988).

Crisman, Kevin J. "Two Deck Lights from the U.S. Navy Brig *Jefferson* (1814)," *Seaways' Ships in Scale* 3, no. 6 (1992).

Crisman, Kevin J. "Sails on an Inland Sea: The Evolution of Lake Champlain's Sailing Merchant Fleet," in *The Philosophy of Shipbuilding: Conceptual Approaches to the Study of Wooden Ships,* eds. Fredrick M. Hocker and Cheryl Ward (College Station, TX: Texas A&M University Press, 2004).

Cruikshank, Ernest A. "The Contest for the Command of Lake Erie," in *The Defended Border: Upper Canada and the War of 1812,* ed. Morris Zaslow (Toronto: MacMillan Company of Canada, 1964).

Cruikshank, Ernest A., ed. *The Documentary History of the Campaign Upon the Niagara Frontier,* vols. 1, 7. Welland, ON: Tribune Office, 1898–1908.

Cruikshank, Ernest A. "An Episode of the War of 1812: The Story of the Schooner *Nancy,*" *Ontario Historical Society Papers* 9 (1910).

Cruikshank, Ernest A. "From Isle-aux-Noix to Chateauguay: A Study of the Military Operations on the Frontiers of Lower Canada in 1812 and 1813," in *Transactions of the Royal Society of Canada,* series 3, vol. 7 (Ottawa: Royal Society of Canada, 1913).

Curryer, Betty Nelson. *Anchors: An Illustrated History.* Annapolis, MD: Naval Institute Press, 1999.

Curwood, James Oliver. *The Great Lakes.* New York: G. P. Putnam's Sons, 1909.

Cushman, Paul. "Usher Parsons, M.D.," *New York State Journal of Medicine* 71 (1941).

Darling, Anthony D. *Red Coat and Brown Bess.* Ottawa: Museum Restoration Service, 1971.

Daughters of the American Revolution, Saranac (NY) Chapter. *Macdonough Day, April 14, 1914.* New York and New Jersey Committees, 1914.

Davey, Peter, ed. *The Archaeology of the Clay Tobacco Pipe, Vol. 10: Scotland,* BAR British Series, 178 (Oxford: B.A.R., 1987).

Davidson, Gordon Charles. *The North West Company.* New York: Russell and Russell, 1967.

Davis, Paris M. *An Authentic History of the Late War Between the United States and Great Britain.* New York: Ebenezer F. Baker, 1836.

Davison, Rebecca, ed. *The Phoenix Project.* Burlington, VT: Champlain Maritime Society, 1981.

De Roos, Lt. F. F. *Personal Narrative of Travels in the United States and Canada in 1826 — With Remarks on the Present State of the American Navy.* London: W. H. Ainsworth, 1827.

Delafield, Joseph. *The Unfortified Boundary: A Diary of the first survey of the Canadian Boundary Line from St. Regis to the Lake of the Woods by Major Joseph Delafield, American Agent under Article VI and VII of the Treaty of Ghent. From the original manuscript recently discovered.* Eds. Robert McElroy and Thomas Riggs (New York: Privately Printed, 1943).

Diderot, Denis. *A Diderot Pictorial Encyclopedia of Trades and Industry,* vol. 1. New York: Dover Publications, 1987.

Dobbins, W. W. *History of the Battle of Lake Erie.* Erie, PA: Ashby Printing, 1913.

Douglas, W. A. B. *Dictionary of Canadian Biography Online,* s.v. "Barclay, Robert Heriot (Herriot)" (Laval University, 2000, http://www.biographi.ca/009004-119.01-e.php ?&id_nbr=3228).

Duncan, John M. *Travels through Part of the United States and Canada in 1818 and 1819,* vol. 2. New York: W. B. Gilley, 1823.

Dudley, William S., ed. *The Naval War of 1812: A Documentary History,* vol. 1: 1812. Washington, DC: Naval Historical Center, 1985.

Dudley, William S., ed. *The Naval War of 1812: A Documentary History,* vol. 2: 1813. Washington, DC: Naval Historical Center, 1992.

Duffy, Stephen W. H. *Captain Blakeley and the* Wasp*: The Cruise of 1814.* Annapolis: Naval Institute Press, 2001.

Dulles, Charles W. *Extracts from the Diary of Joseph Heatly Dulles.* Philadelphia: J. B. Lippincott, 1911.

Dunlop, William. *Diary of William Dunlop (1766–1839),* vol. 2. New York: The New York Historical Society, 1930.

Dunnigan, Brian L. *The British Army at Mackinac 1812–1815: Reports in Mackinac History and Archaeology,* no. 7. Lansing, MI: Mackinac Island State Park Commission, 1980.

Durant, Samuel W. and Henry B. Peirce. *History of Jefferson County, New York.* Philadelphia: L. H. Everts, 1878.

Dye, Ira. *The Fatal Cruise of the* Argus*: Two Captains in the War of 1812.* Annapolis: Naval Institute Press, 1994.

Eckert, Edward K. *The Navy Department in the War of 1812.* Gainesville: University of Florida Press, 1973.

Eddy, Richard. "'. . . Defended by an Adequate Power': Joshua Humphreys and the 74-Gun Ships of 1799," *The American Neptune* 51, no. 3 (1991).

Emery, Eric B. "The Last of Mr. Brown's Mosquito Fleet: The History and Archaeology of the American Row Galley *Allen* on Lake Champlain, 1814–1825" (PhD diss., Texas A&M University, 2003).

Emori, Eiko. *Shipbuilding at Fort Amherstburg 1796–1813.* Ottawa: Parks Canada, 1978.

Everest, Allen S. *The War of 1812 in the Champlain Valley.* Syracuse, NY: Syracuse University Press, 1981.

Farrington, L. "The Decline of Naval Bases on the Lakes of Canada, 1815–1834." Paper presented for the Barry German Naval History Prize, 1955.

Fearon, Henry Bradshaw. *Sketches of America: A Narrative of a Journey of Five Thousand Miles Through the Eastern and Western States of America.* London: Longman, Hurst, Rees, Orme, and Brown, 1818.

Fincham, John. *A Treatise on Masting Ships and Mast Making.* London: Conway Maritime Press, 1982.

Fontenoy, Paul E. *The Sloops of the Hudson River: A Historical and Design Survey.* Mystic, CT: Mystic Seaport Museum and Hudson River Maritime Museum, 1994.

Foster, John W. *Limitation of Armaments on the Great Lakes,* pamphlet no. 2. Washington, DC: Carnegie Endowment for International Peace, Division of International Law, 1914.

Fort Ticonderoga. "Recent Accessions," *The Bulletin of the Fort Ticonderoga Museum* 8, no. 7 (1951).

Fort Ticonderoga. "An Historic Mortar," *The Bulletin of the Fort Ticonderoga Museum* 10, no. 4 (1960).

Fowler, Barnett. "Benedict Arnold's Warships Rot in Champlain," *The Pictorial Review* (January 25, 1953).

Fowler, Barney. *Adirondack Album.* Schenectady, NY: Outdoor Associates, 1974.

Gardiner, Robert, ed. *The Naval War of 1812.* London: Chatham Publishing, 1998.

Gardiner, Robert. *Warships of the Napoleonic Era.* London: Chatham Publishing, 1999.

Gilpin, Alec R. *The War of 1812 in the Old Northwest.* East Lansing: Michigan State University Press, 1958.

Goldowsky, Seebert J. *Yankee Surgeon: The Life and Times of Usher Parsons (1788–1868).* Boston: The Francis A. Countway Library of Medicine in cooperation with the Rhode Island Publications Society, 1988.

Goodwin, Peter. *The Construction and Fitting of the English Man of War, 1650–1850.* Annapolis: Naval Institute Press, 1987.

Gordon, LeeAnne Elizabeth. "*Newash* and *Tecumseth*: Analysis of Two Post-War of 1812 Vessels on the Great Lakes" (Master's thesis, Texas A&M University, 2009).

Gough, Barry. *Fighting Sail on Lake Huron and Georgian Bay.* Annapolis: Naval Institute Press, 2002.

Gough, Barry. *Through Water, Ice & Fire: The Schooner* Nancy *of the War of 1812.* Toronto: The Dundern Group, 2006.

Graves, Donald E., ed. *Merry Hearts Make Light Days: The War of 1812 Journal of Lieutenant John Le Couteur, 104th Foot.* Ottawa: Carleton University Press, 1994.

Grodzinski, John R. "The Duke of Wellington, the Peninsular War and the War of 1812: Part II: Reinforcements, Views of the War and Command in North America," *The War of 1812 Magazine,* no. 6 (April 2007, http://www.napoleon-series.org/military /Warof1812/2007/Issue6/c_Wellington1.html, accessed July 4, 2008).

Hall, Capt. Basil R. N. *Travels in North America in the Years 1827 and 1828.* Edinburgh: Cadell, 1829.

Hall, Francis. *Travels in Canada and the United States, in*

1816 and 1817. London: Longman, Hurst, Rees, Orme & Brown, 1818.

Halpenny, Francess G. *Dictionary of Canadian Biography,* vol. 6. Toronto: University of Toronto Press, 1987.

Hamil, Fred C. *The Valley of the Thames 1640 to 1850*. Toronto: University of Toronto Press, 1951.

Hanson, Lee H. Jr. "Pipes from Rome, New York," *Historical Archaeology* 5, no. 1 (1971).

Harris, Ryan, Andrew Leyzack, and Brandy M. Lockhart. "Recent Multibeam and Side-Scan Sonar Surveys of the *Hamilton* and *Scourge* Shipwreck Site," in *ACUA Underwater Archaeology Proceedings, 2009,* eds. Erika Laanela and Jonathan Moore (Advisory Council on Underwater Archaeology, 2010).

Hepper, David J. *British Warship Losses in the Age of Sail: 1650–1859*. Rotherfield, East Sussex: Jean Boudriot Publications, 1994.

Herriot, George. *Travels Through the Canadas Containing a Description of the Picturesque Scenery on Some of the Rivers and Lakes*. Rutland, VT: Charles E. Tuttle, 1971.

Hickey, Donald R. *Don't Give Up the Ship! Myths of the War of 1812*. Urbana: University of Illinois Press, 2006.

Hickey, Donald R. *The War of 1812: A Forgotten Conflict*. Urbana: University of Illinois Press, 1989.

Hill, Ralph Nading. *Lake Champlain: Key to Liberty*. Woodstock, VT: The Countryman Press, 1991.

Hitsman, J. Mackay. *The Incredible War of 1812: A Military History*. Toronto: Robin Brass Studio, 1999.

Hitsman, J. Mackay. *Safeguarding Canada, 1763–1871*. Toronto: University of Toronto Press, 1968.

Hooper, Thomas. "The Royal Navy Station at Isle aux Noix (1812–1839)," in *Miscellaneous Historical Reports (1965–70)*, manuscript record no. 167 (Ottawa: Parks Canada, 1967).

Hough, Richard. *Fighting Ships*. London: Michael Joseph, 1969.

Howe, Daniel Walker. *What Hath God Wrought: The Transformation of America, 1815–1848*. Oxford: Oxford University Press, 2009.

Howe, Henry. *Memoirs of the Most Eminent American Mechanics*. New York: Alexander V. Blake, 1841.

Hume, Edgar Erskine. "Letters Written During the War of 1812 by the British Naval Commander in American Waters (Admiral Sir David Milne)," *William and Mary College Quarterly Historical Magazine,* 2nd ser., 10, no. 4 (1930).

Humphrey, Richard V. "Clay Pipes from Old Sacramento," *Historical Archaeology* 3, no. 1 (1969).

Hutchinson, William. *A Treatise on Naval Architecture Founded upon Philosophical and Rational Principles*. Liverpool: T. Billinge, 1774; facsimile reprint, London: Conway Maritime Press, 1970.

Ilisevich, Robert D. *Daniel Dobbins: Frontier Mariner*. Erie, PA: Erie County Historical Society, 1993.

Innis, Harold A. *The Fur Trade*. New Haven: Yale University Press, 1930.

Jackson, John W. *The Pennsylvania Navy, 1775–1781: The Defense of the Delaware*. New Brunswick, NJ: Rutgers University Press, 1974.

James, William. *A Full and Correct Account of the Military Occurrences of the Late War between Great Britain and the United States of America*. London: Printed for the Author, 1818.

James, William. *The Naval History of Great Britain: During the French Revolutionary and Napoleonic Wars, Vol. 5: 1808–1811*. London: Conway Maritime Press, 2002.

James, William. *The Naval History of Great Britain: From the Declaration of War by France in February 1793 to the Accession of George IV in January 1820,* vol. 6. London: Harding, Lepard, 1826.

Johnson, Allen and Dumas Malone, eds. *Dictionary of American Biography,* vol. 4. New York: Charles Scribner's Sons, 1930.

Keyes, Darren, and Jonathan Moore. "The *Hamilton* and *Scourge* Shipwreck Site Condition Survey 2008: Rationale, Organization, and Objectives," In *ACUA Underwater Archaeology Proceedings, 2009,* eds. Erika Laanela and Jonathan Moore (Advisory Council on Underwater Archaeology, 2010).

Kopp, Nadine. "The Navy Bay Wreck: An Unidentified Wreck in Kingston, Ontario," in *ACUA Underwater Archaeology Proceedings, 2009,* eds. Erika Laanela and Jonathan Moore (Advisory Council on Underwater Archaeology, 2010).

Laughton, J. K. *Oxford Dictionary of National Biography,* s.v. "Yeo, James Lucas (1782–1818)," Rev. Michael Duffy (Oxford University Press, 2004, http://www.oxforddnb.com/view/article/30217, accessed November 5, 2009).

Lavery, Brian. *The Ship of the Line, Vol. 2: Design, Construction and Fittings*. Annapolis: Naval Institute Press, 1984.

Lever, Darcy. *The Young Sea Officer's Sheet Anchor, or A Key to the Leading of Rigging, and to Practical Seamanship*. Leeds: Printed by Thomas Gill, 1808.

Lever, Darcy. *The Young Sea Officer's Sheet Anchor, or A Key to the Leading of Rigging and to Practical Seamanship*. London: John Richardson, 1819; facsimile reprint, Mineola, NY: Dover Publications, 1998.

Lewis, Dennis M. *British Naval Activity on Lake Champlain During the War of 1812*. Plattsburgh, NY: Clinton County Historical Association, 1994.

Lockhart, Brandy M., Jonathan Moore, and Robert Clarke. "New Insights into the Nautical Archaeology of the *Hamilton* and *Scourge,*" in *ACUA Underwater Archaeology Proceedings, 2009,* eds. Erika Laanela and Jonathan Moore (Advisory Council on Underwater Archaeology, 2010).

Longridge, C. Nepean. *The Anatomy of Nelson's Ships.* London: Percival Marshall, 1955.

Lossing, Benson. *The Pictorial Fieldbook of the War of 1812.* New York: Harper & Brothers, 1868; facsimile reprint, New Hampshire Publishing Company, 1976.

Lyon, David. *The Sailing List: All the Ships of the Royal Navy—Built, Purchased and Captured, 1688–1860.* London. Conway Maritime Press, 1993.

Macdonough Commission of Vermont. *Macdonough Centennial, Vergennes, Vermont 1814–1914.* Vermont Publicity Bureau, 1914.

Macdonough, Rodney. *Life of Commodore Thomas Macdonough, U.S. Navy.* Boston: The Fort Hill Press, 1909.

Malcomson, Robert. *Capital in Flames: The American Attack on York, 1813.* Montreal: Robin Brass Studio, 2008.

Malcomson, Robert. *Capital in Flames: The American Attack on York, 1813.* Annapolis: Naval Institute Press, 2008.

Malcomson, Robert. *Lords of the Lake, The Naval War on Lake Ontario, 1812–1814.* Toronto: Robin Brass Studio, 1998.

Malcomson, Robert. "HMS *St. Lawrence*: The Freshwater First-Rate," *The Mariner's Mirror* 83, no. 4 (1997).

Malcomson, Robert. *Sailors of 1812: Memoirs and Letters of Naval Officers on Lake Ontario.* Youngstown, NY: Old Fort Niagara Association, 1997.

Malcomson, Robert. *Warships of the Great Lakes 1754–1834.* London: Caxton Editions, 2003.

Malcomson, Robert. *Warships of the Great Lakes 1754–1834.* London: Chatham Publishing, 2001.

Malcomson, Robert. *Warships of the Great Lakes 1754–1834.* Annapolis: Naval Institute Press, 2001.

Mann, James. *Medical Sketches of the Campaigns of 1812, 1813, and 1814.* Dedham, MA: H. Mann, 1816.

Marestier, Jean Baptiste. *Memoir on Steamboats of the United States of America.* Mystic, CT: The Marine Historical Association, 1957.

McAllister, Michael F. "Museum under the Waves: Preserving and Interpreting the *Hamilton* and *Scourge* National Historic Site of Canada," in *ACUA Underwater Archaeology Proceedings, 2009,* eds. Erika Laanela and Jonathan Moore (Advisory Council on Underwater Archaeology, 2010).

McKee, Christopher. *A Gentlemanly and Honorable Profession: The Creation of the U.S. Naval Officer Corps, 1794–1815.* Annapolis: Naval Institute Press, 1991.

Meade, Comm. R. W., U.S.N. "Admiral Hiram Paulding," *Harper's New Monthly Magazine* (February 1879).

Meade, Rebecca Paulding. *Life of Hiram Paulding, Rear-Admiral, U.S.N.* New York: The Baker and Taylor Company, 1910.

Milbert, Jacques. *Picturesque Itinerary of the Hudson River and the Peripheral Parts of North America.* Ridgewood, NJ: Gregg Press, 1968.

Moore, Jonathan. *Archaeological and Historical Investigations of Three War of 1812 Wrecks at Kingston, Ontario: HMS* St. Lawrence, *HMS* Prince Regent *and HMS* Princess Charlotte. Ottawa: Jonathan Moore, 2006.

Moore, Jonathan and Darren Keyes. "Initial Visual Results from the *Hamilton* and *Scourge* Shipwreck Site Condition Survey 2008," in *ACUA Underwater Archaeology Proceedings, 2009,* eds. Erika Laanela and Jonathan Moore (Advisory Council on Underwater Archaeology, 2010).

Morton, Doris Begor. *Day Before Yesterday.* Whitehall, NY: The Whitehall Times, 1977.

Muller, H. N. "A Traitorous and Diabolical Traffic: The Commerce of the Champlain-Richelieu Corridor During the War of 1812," *Vermont History* 44 (1976).

Murphy, Rowley. "Resurrection at Penetanguishene," *Inland Seas* 10 (1954).

Nelson, Dan. "The Sinking of the *Hamilton* and *Scourge*—How Many Men Were Lost?" *FreshWater* 2, no. 1 (1987).

Nelson, Daniel A. "*Hamilton* & *Scourge*: Ghost Ships of the War of 1812," *National Geographic Magazine* 163, no. 3 (1983).

Nelson, Daniel A. "The Hamilton-Scourge Project," *International Journal of Nautical Archaeology and Underwater Exploration* 8, no. 3 (1979).

New York State Commission, Plattsburgh Centenary. "A Fitting, Permanent Memorial," in *The Battle of Plattsburgh: What Historians Say About It* (Albany, NY: J. B. Lyon Company, Printers, 1914).

New York State Historian. *The Centenary of the Battle of Plattsburgh, September 6–11, 1814–1914.* Albany, NY: The University of the State of New York, 1914.

Onions, C. T., ed. *Shorter Oxford English Dictionary on Historical Principles,* 3rd ed., vol. 2. Oxford: Clarendon Press, 1970.

Palmer, Richard F. "The Forwarding Business in Oswego, 1800–1820 (Part I)," *Inland Seas* 41, no. 2 (1985).

Parsons, Usher. "Surgical Account of the Boston Battle on Lake Erie," *New England Journal of Medicine and Surgery* 7 (1818).

Perkins, Bradford. *Prologue to War: England and the United States, 1805–1812.* Berkeley: University of California Press, 1968.

Perkins, Bradford. *The Creation of a Republican Empire, 1776–1865.* Cambridge: Cambridge University Press, 1993.

Perry Memorial Commission. *Perry's Victory Memorial.* Washington, DC: Government Printing Office, 1921.

Peterson, Charles J. *The American Navy.* Philadelphia: Jas. Smith, 1857.

Peterson, Mendel. *History Under the Sea: A Handbook for Underwater Exploration.* Washington, DC: The Smithsonian Institution, 1965.

Petrejus, E. W. *Modeling the Brig of War* Irene: *A Handbook for the Building of Historical Ship Models.* Hengelo: Uitgeversmaatschappij "De Esch," 1970.

Phelps, Benajah. "The Battle of Lake Champlain: The Story of an Eye-Witness, Retold by J. E. Tuttle," *The Outlook* 69, no. 9 (1901).

Plattsburgh Centenary Commission. *Dedication of the Thomas Macdonough Memorial.* Plattsburgh, NY: Centenary Commission, August 18, 1926.

Preston, Richard A. "The Fate of Kingston's Warships," *Ontario History* 44, no. 3 (1952).

Pullen, H. F. *The March of the Seamen.* Halifax, Nova Scotia: Maritime Museum of Canada, 1961.

Quaife, Milo M., ed. *The John Askin Papers,* vol. 2. Detroit: Detroit Library Commission, 1931.

Quimby, Robert S. *The U.S. Army in the War of 1812: An Operational and Command Study.* East Lansing: Michigan State University Press, 1997.

Rankov, Boris. "Fleets of the Early Roman Empire, 31 B.C.–A.D. 324," in *The Age of the Galley: Mediterranean Oared Vessels since Pre-Classical Times,* ed. John Gardiner. (London: Conway Maritime Press, 1995).

Ratliff, Colan D. "Early Running Square Sails Used by the Navy on Schooners and Sloops," *Nautical Research Journal* 30, no. 4 (1984).

Ritchie, L. A., ed. *The Shipbuilding Industry: A Guide to Historical Records.* Manchester: Manchester University Press, 1992.

Ritchie, M. K. and C. Ritchie. "A Laker's Log," *American Neptune* 17 (1957).

Roberts, David H., ed. *18th Century Shipbuilding: Remarks on the Navies of the English & the Dutch from Observations Made at their Dockyards in 1737 by Blaise Ollivier.* East Sussex: Jean Boudriot Publications, 1992.

Robinson, David S., Elizabeth R. Baldwin, Arthur B. Cohn, Ian Griffin, Anne W. Lessmann, and Christopher R. Sabick. *Conservation of a War of 1812 Anchor from Plattsburgh Bay, Clinton County, New York.* Basin Harbor, VT: Lake Champlain Maritime Museum, May 2001.

Roosevelt, Theodore. *The Naval War of 1812.* Annapolis: Naval Institute Press, 1987.

Rosenberg, Max. *The Building of Perry's Fleet on Lake Erie, 1812–1813.* Harrisburg, PA: Pennsylvania Historical and Museum Commission, 1968; reprint 1987.

Ross, Ogden. *The Steamboats of Lake Champlain, 1809 to 1930.* Burlington, VT: Champlain Transportation Company, 1930; facsimile reprint, Quechee, VT: Vermont Heritage Press, 1997.

Royal Military College. "Further Notes on the Early History of the College," *Royal Military College of Canada Review* 8 (1927).

Royal Military College. "The Wreck in Navy Bay," *Royal Military College of Canada Review* 16 (1935).

Russell, J. Jr. *The History of the War, between the United States and Great Britain.* Hartford: B. & J. Russell, 1815.

Sabick, Christopher R. "His Majesty's Hired Transport Schooner *Nancy*" (Master's thesis, Texas A&M University, 2004).

Scarpitti, Allison. "Niagara/Lawrence," *The Journal of Erie Studies* 26, no. 1 (1997).

Schwarz, George Robert. "The Passenger Steamboat *Phoenix*: An Archaeological Study of Early Steam Propulsion in North America" (PhD diss., Texas A&M University, 2013).

Selig, Steven M. *Draughts: The Henry Eckford Story.* Scottsdale, AZ: Agreka History Preserved, 2008.

Seppings, Robert. "On a New Principal of Constructing Ships," *The Repertory of Arts, Manufactures, and Agriculture* 27, 2nd series (1815).

Silliman, Benjamin. *Remarks Made on a Short Tour Between Hartford and Quebec in 1819.* New Haven, CT: S. Converse, 1820.

Silliman, Benjamin. *Remarks Made on a Short Tour Between Hartford and Quebec in 1819.* Second edition. New Haven, CT: S. Converse, 1824.

Simcoe, John Graves. *The Correspondence of Lieutenant Governor John Graves Simcoe,* vol. 2, ed. E. A. Cruikshank. Toronto: Ontario Historical Society, 1923.

Skaggs, David Curtis. *Thomas Macdonough: Master of Command in the Early U.S. Navy.* Annapolis: Naval Institute Press, 2003.

Skaggs, David C. and Gerard T. Altoff. *A Signal Victory: The Lake Erie Campaign 1812–1813.* Annapolis: Naval Institute Press, 1997.

Slosek, Anthony M. *Oswego: Hamlet Days, 1796–1828.* Oswego, NY: Slosek, 1980.

Smith, Gene A. *For the Purposes of Defense: The Politics of the Jeffersonian Gunboat Program.* Newark: University of Delaware Press, 1995.

Snider, C. H. J. *In the Wake of the Eighteen-Twelvers: Fights and Flights of Frigates and Fore 'n' Afters in the War of 1812–1815 on the Great Lakes.* London: John Lane, 1913.

Snider, C. H. J., ed. *Leaves from the War Log of the* Nancy: *Eighteen Hundred and Thirteen.* Toronto: Huronia Historical Development Council, 1967.

Snider, C. H. J. "Recovery of H.M.S. *Tecumseth*," *Ontario History* 46, no. 2 (1954).

Snider, C. H. J. *The Silent St. Lawrence: An Angel of Enduring Peace.* Toronto: Rous & Mann Press, 1948.

Spurr, John W. *Dictionary of Canadian Biography Online,* s.v. "Yeo, Sir James Lucas" (Toronto: University of Toronto Press, 1983, http://www.biographi.ca/009004 -119.01-e.php?&id_nbr=2722, accessed November 5, 2009).

Stacey, C. P. "The Myth of the Unguarded Frontier, 1815–1871," *The American Historical Review* 56, no. 1 (1950).

Stacey, C. P. "The Ships of the British Squadron on Lake Ontario, 1812–14," *Canadian Historical Review* 34 (1953).

Stanley, George F. G. *The War of 1812: Land Operations.* Toronto: Macmillan of Canada, 1983.

Steffy, J. Richard. *Wooden Ship Building and the Interpretation of Shipwrecks.* College Station, TX: Texas A&M University Press, 1994.

Steel, David R. *Steel's Elements of Mastmaking, Sailmaking, and Rigging.* Largo, FL: Edward W. Sweetman, 1982.

Steel, David. *The Elements and Practice of Naval Architecture.* London: Steel, 1805.

Stevens, John R. *The Construction and Embellishment of Old Time Ships.* Toronto: Printed for the Author, 1949.

Stevens, John R. "H.M. Provincial Marine Schooner *General Hunter,* 1805," *Nautical Research Journal* (October 1951).

Stevens, John R. "Naval Dockyards on Lake Ontario in the War of 1812–14," *Nautical Research Guild Secretary's Monthly Letter* 3, no. 2 (1950).

Stevens, John R. "The Story of H.M. Armed Schooner *Tecumseth,*" in *The March of the Seamen,* ed. H. F. Pullen (Halifax, Nova Scotia: Maritime Museum of Canada, 1961).

Strum, Harvey. "Virtually Impossible to Stop: Smuggling in the North Country—1808–1815," *The Quarterly* 27 (1982).

Sutherland, William. *The Ship-Builders Assistant.* London: R. Mount, 1711; facsimile reprint, East Sussex: Jean Boudriot Publications, 1989.

Syrett, David and R. L. Dinardo, eds. *The Commissioned Sea Officers of the Royal Navy, 1660–1815.* Aldershot: Scolar Press and Naval Records Society, 1994.

Toivanan, Pekka. "The Burial Grounds of the Russian Galley Fleet in the Gulf of Bothnia (Finland) from 1714," in *Underwater Archaeology Proceedings from the Society for Historical Archaeology Conference,* ed. John Broadwater (Tucson: Society for Historical Archaeology, 1991).

Tompkins, Daniel D. *Public Papers of Daniel D. Tompkins, Governor of New York 1807–1817,* vol. 3. Albany: State of New York, 1902.

Townsend, Robert B., ed. *Tales from the Great Lakes based on C. H. J. Snider's "Schooner Days."* Toronto: Dundern Press, 1995.

de Tousard, Louis. *American Artillerist's Companion, or Elements of Artillery,* vol. 1. Philadelphia: 1809; reprint, New York: Greenwood Press, 1969.

Tucker, Spencer C. *Arming the Fleet, U.S. Navy Ordnance in the Muzzle-Loading Era.* Annapolis: Naval Institute Press, 1989.

Tucker, Spencer C. *The Jeffersonian Gunboat Navy.* Columbia: University of South Carolina Press, 1993.

Tucker, Spencer C. "The Jeffersonian Gunboats in Service, 1804–1825," *American Neptune* 55, no. 2 (1995).

Tucker, Spencer C. and Frank T. Reuter. *Injured Honor: The Chesapeake-Leopard Affair, June 22, 1807.* Annapolis: Naval Institute Press, 1996.

United States Department of State. *A Register of Officers and Agents Civil, Military, and Naval in the Service of the United States on the 30th of September, 1821; Together with the Names, Force, and Condition of All the Ships and Vessels Belonging to the United States and When and Where Built.* Washington, DC: Davis and Force, 1822.

United States Congress. *American State Papers: Documents, Legislative and Executive, of the Congress of the United States: Class VI, Naval Affairs.* Washington, DC: Gales and Seaton, 1834.

United States Government. *American State Papers, Naval Affairs,* vol. 1. Washington, DC: Gales and Seaton, 1860.

United States Senate. "Report of the Naval Committee, Expressive of the Gallant Conduct of Captain Macdonough, The Officers, Seamen, Marines, & C in the Capturing of the British Squadron on Lake Champlain, on the 11th September, 1814, United States Senate Report." Washington, DC: Roger C. Weightman, 1814.

Vanhorn, Kellie Michelle. "Eighteenth-Century Colonial American Merchant Ship Construction" (Master's thesis, Texas A&M University, 2004).

Van Gemert, Richard C. "Ships of the Great Lakes," in *A History of Seafaring Based on Underwater Archaeology,* ed. George F. Bass (London: Thames and Hudson, 1972).

State of Vermont. *Records of the Governor and Council of the State of Vermont,* vol. 5. Montpelier: Steam Press of J. & J. M. Pland, 1877.

Walker, Daniel Robert. "The Identity and Construction of Wreck Baker: A War of 1812 Era Royal Navy Frigate" (Master's thesis, Texas A&M University, 2007).

Walker, Iain C. *Clay Tobacco-pipes, with Particular Reference to the Bristol Industry.* Canada National Historic Parks and Sites Branch History and Archaeology Series 11 C. Ottawa: Parks Canada, 1977.

Warren, Elizabeth J. "Gunboat #1: Results of the 1982 Lake Champlain Shipwreck Survey," in *A Report on the Nautical Archaeology of Lake Champlain,* ed. Arthur B. Cohn (Burlington, VT: Champlain Maritime Society, 1982).

Washburn, Erika Lea. "*Linnet*: The History and Archaeology of a Brig from the War of 1812" (Master's thesis, Texas A&M University, 1998).

Washburn, Harold Connett. *Illustrated Case Inscriptions from the Official Catalogue of the Trophy Flags of the United States Navy.* Baltimore: The Lord Baltimore Press, 1913.

Watkins, Charles Alan and Mark Matusiak. "Is This the *Real Niagara?*" *Naval History* 15, no. 1 (2001).

Wilder, Patrick A. *The Battle of Sackett's Harbour, 1813.* Baltimore: The Nautical and Aviation Publishing Company of America, 1994.

Williams, John. *Lives and Confessions of John Williams, Francis Frederick, John P. Rog and Peter Peterson.* Boston: J. T. Buckingham, 1819.

Wood, William, ed. *Select British Documents of the Canadian War of 1812,* vol. 1. Toronto: The Champlain Society, 1920.

Wood, William, ed. *Select British Documents of the Canadian War of 1812,* vol. 2. Toronto: The Champlain Society, 1923.

Wood, William, ed. *Select British Documents of the Canadian War of 1812,* vol. 3, pt. 1. Toronto: The Champlain Society, 1926.

Wright, Phillip J. "Armed Schooners from the War of 1812: *Hamilton* and *Scourge,*" in *Excavating Ships of War, International Maritime Archaeology Series 2,* ed. Mensun Bound (Oswestry: Anthony Nelson, 1998).

Zacharchuk, Walter. "The Raising of the Mallorytown Wreck," in *The Conference on Historic Site Archaeology Papers, 1967,* vol. 2, pt. 1, ed. Stanley A. South (Raleigh, NC: Conference on Historical Archaeology, 1968).

Zacharchuk, Walter and John M. Rick. "The Mallorytown Wreck," *Historical Archaeology* 3 (1969).

MANUSCRIPT REPORTS

Ames, John. "Hamilton-Scourge Project Artifact Inventory Second Draft" (manuscript report, Hamilton-Scourge Project, City of Hamilton, September 1987).

Aqua-Probe. "The Remote Survey of Deep Water Archaeological Sites Referencing and Scaling" (manuscript, Hamilton-Scourge Project, City of Hamilton, April 1983).

Aqua-Probe. "The Remote Survey of Deep Water Archaeological Sites Referencing and Scaling: Additional Notes" (manuscript, Hamilton-Scourge Project, City of Hamilton, May 1983).

Bazely, Susan M. "Preserve Our Wrecks (Kingston), Underwater Survey Licence No. 88–42" (manuscript report, Ontario Ministry of Culture, Toronto, 1988).

Beattie, Judith. "Gunboats on the St. Lawrence River (1763–1839)" (manuscript report no. 15, National Historic Sites Service, Ottawa, 1967).

Cain, Emily. "Early Schoonerdays on Lake Ontario: Building Lord Nelson" (manuscript, Hamilton-Scourge Project, City of Hamilton, n.d.).

Cain, Emily. "Merchant Schooners Converted for War: Lake Ontario, 1812" (manuscript, Hamilton-Scourge Project, City of Hamilton, n.d.).

Cassavoy, Kenneth A. "Hamilton/Scourge May, 1982 Survey Preliminary Archaeological Report" (archaeological report, Ontario Ministry of Culture and Recreation, Toronto, October 1982).

Cassavoy, Kenneth A. "Southampton Beach Shipwreck Project: 2004/2005 Excavation & Preliminary Research Report" (archaeological report, Peterborough, ON, December 2005).

Cassavoy, Kenneth A. "The Southampton Beach Shipwreck Project: Recovery, Conservation and Display, Preliminary Study" (archaeological report, Peterborough, ON, 2005).

Crisman, Kevin J. and Arthur Cohn. "The 1985 Underwater Archaeological Survey of the War of 1812 Brig in Sackets Harbor, New York" (excavation report, Bureau of Historic Sites, New York State Office of Parks, Recreation, and Historic Preservation, Waterford, NY, June 1985).

Crisman, Kevin J. and Arthur Cohn. "The 1987 Archaeological Investigation of the U.S. Navy Brig *Jefferson*" (excavation report, Bureau of Historic Sites, New York State Office of Parks, Recreation, and Historic Preservation, Waterford, NY, April 1988).

Hett, Charles E. S. "Report on Visit to Penetanguishene" (letter, *Tecumseth* and *Newash* Archival and Field Record Collection, Texas A&M University, College Station, TX, October 6, 1976).

Howland, Jonathan C., Stephen R. Gegg, and Steven Lerner. "Archaeological Data from the 1990 Jason Project Surveys of the Hamilton and Scourge Using the Jason ROV" (Woods Hole Oceanographic Institution, Woods Hole, MA, October 2001).

Florian, Mary-Lou to Charles E. S. Hett. "Wood Samples from *HMS Tecumseth*" (letter, *Tecumseth* and *Newash* Archival and Field Record Collection, Texas A&M University, College Station, TX, November 5, 1976).

McKennon, A. "The H.M.S. Radcliffe" (manuscript, St. Lawrence Islands National Park, Mallorytown, ON, 1973).

McQuest Marine Sciences Limited. "Report on Hamilton-Scourge Project Side Scan Sonar Survey" (manuscript report, Ontario Ministry of Culture and Recreation, Toronto, September 1983).

Moore, Jonathan. "Archaeological and Historical Investigations of Three War of 1812 Wrecks at Kingston, Ontario: HMS *St. Lawrence,* HMS *Kingston* and HMS *Burlington*" (archaeological report, Ottawa, December 2006).

Moore, Jonathan. "Fort Henry National Historic Site of Canada Submerged Cultural Resource Inventory: 2004, 2006 & 2007 Surveys" (manuscript report, Underwater Archaeology Service, Parks Canada, Ottawa, 2008).

Moore, Jonathan, Brandy Lockhart, Ryan Harris, Nancy E. Binnie, and Darren Keyes. "*Hamilton* and *Scourge* National Historic Site: A Condition Survey of Two War of 1812 Shipwrecks (AhGt-9) in Lake Ontario" (survey report, Underwater Archaeology Service, Ontario Service Centre, Parks Canada, Ottawa, 2011).

Morgan, Ian L. and John H. Ames. "[Notes] . . . Made During an Analysis of Hamilton-Scourge Project Slide and Videotape Records, Fall 1986" (manuscript report, Hamilton-Scourge Project, City of Hamilton, March 23 1987).

Murdock, Lorne D. "Examination and Maintenance Recommendations for Browns Bay Shipwreck on display at St. Lawrence Islands National Park, Mallorytown, Ontario" (manuscript, Conservation Division, Parks Canada, Ottawa, 1985).

Nation, P. T., transcriber. "Contracts, Approved Tenders and Other Documents: The Royal Naval Dockyard, Kingston, Upper Canada, 1813–1824" (document 17, 1992 copy *Tecumseth* and *Newash* Archival and Field Record Collection, Texas A&M University, College Station, TX).

Nelson, Daniel A. "Deep Water Archaeology in Lake Ontario" (paper presented at the First Annual Canadian Ocean Technology Congress, Toronto, March 11–14, 1982. Manuscript, Hamilton-Scourge Project, City of Hamilton).

Nelson, Daniel A. "Homeward Bound—The Hamilton and Scourge Project—A Personal View" (manuscript report, Hamilton-Scourge Project, City of Hamilton: Aqua-Probe, December 1984).

Nelson, Daniel A. "Status Report Hamilton-Scourge Project September, 1978" (manuscript report, Hamilton-Scourge Project, City of Hamilton, 1978).

Nelson, Daniel A. "Report of the Photographic and Videotape Investigation of the Armed Schooners Hamilton and Scourge in Lake Ontario during May, 1982" (manuscript report, Hamilton-Scourge Project, City of Hamilton: Aqua-Probe, May 1982).

Rule, Margaret. "Work on the Hamilton-Scourge Site, Lake Ontario, April-May 1990, Preliminary Report of the Project Archaeologist Margaret Rule" (manuscript report, Hamilton-Scourge Project, City of Hamilton, n.d.).

Sly, Peter G. "Side Scan Sonar Survey and Study of Red and White Targets in Lake Ontario—1978. Report to the Hamilton-Scourge Committee" (Environment Canada, National Water Research Institute, Toronto, February 1982).

Snider, C. H. J. "A Report on the Schooner Nancy, 1789–1925" (manuscript report, Archives of Ontario, Belmont, ON, n.d.).

Zacharchuk, Walter. "Architectural Report on the Browns Bay Gunboat" (manuscript, National Historic Parks and Sites Branch, Parks Canada, Ottawa, 1981).

Zacharchuk, Walter. "One of a Thousand Wrecks" (manuscript, National Historic Parks and Sites Branch, Parks Canada, Ottawa, 1969).

NEWSPAPER ARTICLES

American and Commercial Daily Advertiser (Baltimore). April 8, April 10, 1815.

Buffalo (NY) *Gazette.* August 1, September 19, 1815; May 28, 1816.

Burlington (VT) *Daily Free Press and Times.* October 17, 1853; August 11, 1873.

Canton Ohio Repository. July 4, 1816.

Essex County (NY) *Republican.* October 28, 1938.

Freeman's Advocate (Sackets Harbor, NY). May 31, 1827.

Globe and Mail. February 4, 1938.

Kingston (ON) *Chronicle.* January 21, 1832.

Kingston (ON) *Chronicle and Gazette.* May 7, 1836.

Kingston (ON) *Gazette.* February 8, March 1, June 2, 1814.

Kingston (ON) *Whig-Standard.* February 8, 1938.

Marine Record (Cleveland, OH). June 11, 1885.

Montreal Gazette. January 5, 1833.

National Gazette and Literary Register (Philadelphia, PA). June 11, 1825.

The New York Times. June 26, 1887.

Niagara Journal. October 17, 1815.

Niles Weekly Register (Baltimore). July 31, September 4, 1813; March 4, 1815.

Ottawa Sun. August 17, 2011.

Plattsburgh (NY) *Republican.* November 20, 1813; September 22, 1877; February 1, 1879.

Quebec Mercury. June 2, 1814.

Burlington Vermont Centinel. October 15, 1813.

Toronto Telegram. April 21, 1934; November 16, November 23, December 7, 1935; March 26, 1949.

Watertown (NY) *Daily Times.* April 22, October 19, October 22, 1931.

Whitehall (NY) *Times.* August 13, August 29, 1873; October 20, 1949; September 24, 1953; July 3, 1958; March 12, 1959.

MANUSCRIPT SOURCES

Ballingall, David James. Diary. Queen's University Archives, Kingston, ON.

Bell, William. Papers. Military Group 24. Library and Archives Canada, Ottawa.

Brisbane, Sir Thomas Makdougall. Papers. William L. Clements Library, University of Michigan, Ann Arbor.

Chauncey, Isaac. Letter Books. Vols. 1, 2. New York Historical Society, New York.

Chauncey, Issac. Letter Book. William L. Clements Library, University of Michigan, Ann Arbor.

Chew Family Papers. Clements Library, University of Michigan, Ann Arbor.

Division of Transportation, Records. 1927–1973. Smithsonian Institution Archives, Washington, DC.

Duggan, Thomas. Journal. Clements Library, University of Michigan, Ann Arbor.

Frome, Edward Charles, R. E. *View of Kingston Looking Over the Dockyard from Fort Henry.* Ink drawing, 1833. Agnes Etherington Art Centre, Queen's University, Kingston, ON.

Gratz, Simon. Collection. Historical Society of Pennsylvania, Philadelphia.

Humphreys, Joshua. Papers. Wharton and Humphreys

Notebook, Historical Society of Pennsylvania, Philadelphia.

Jones, William. Papers. Uselma Clark Smith Collection, Historical Society of Pennsylvania, Philadelphia.

List of the Navy, 1833, 1824, 1837, 1839. Admiralty Library, London.

Macdonough Collection, Shelburne Museum, Shelburne, VT.

Macdonough, Thomas. Manuscript. "A Report on the State and Condition of the Naval Force . . . under the command of Thomas Macdonough, Esquire on the 31st day of August 1814." Lake Champlain Maritime Museum, Vergennes, VT.

Madison, James. Papers. Library of Congress, Washington, DC.

Mossington, Thomas. Papers. Archives of Ontario, Toronto.

Owen, Comm. Sir Edward, Letterbook. Queen's University Archives, Kingston, ON.

Patton, Jonathan. Papers. Lake Champlain Maritime Museum, Vergennes, VT.

Perry Papers. William L. Clements Library, University of Michigan, Ann Arbor.

Porter, Augustus. Papers. Buffalo and Erie County Historical Society Library & Archives, Buffalo, NY.

Porter, Peter B. Papers. Buffalo and Erie County Historical Society Library & Archives, Buffalo, NY.

Preston Papers. Royal Military College of Canada Archives, Kingston, ON.

Ridgely, Charles G. "Journal of Charles G. Ridgely, 1815–21, On Board Erie, Independence, and Constellation." Manuscripts Division, Library of Congress, Washington, DC.

Sawyer, H. B. Papers. Special Collections, Bailey Howe Library, University of Vermont, Burlington.

Senecal, Carol Manell. Manuscript diary describing the salvage of the *Ticonderoga,* fall, 1958. Skenesboro Museum, Whitehall, NY.

Snider, C. H. J. Papers. Queen's University Archives, Kingston, ON.

Stellwagen, Daniel S. "Signal Book and Orders of the Third Division of Gallies." Library of Congress, Washington, DC.

Strickland, Thomas. "*St. Lawrence* (May 1815)" ZAZ 0131–ZAZ 0137, reg. nos. 93–78, Admiralty Collection, National Maritime Museum, London.

Taylor, William V. Papers. "Sloop of War *Lawrence* Journal, 31 July–28 September, 1813." Newport Historical Society, Newport, RI.

"*Tecumseth* (1815), *Newash* (1815) Deck." ZAZ 6138, reg. no. 4563. Admiralty Collection, National Maritime Museum, London.

Townsend Papers. New York State Archives, Albany.

"United States Corvete [*sic*] Erie Cap[n] Ch[s] Gamble." Philadelphia Maritime Museum.

Van Cleve, James. "Reminiscences of Early Steam Boats, Propellers and Sailing Vessels." Manuscript, 1877. Buffalo Historical Society Collection, Buffalo, NY.

Woolsey Family Papers. Burton Historical Collection, Detroit Public Library.

Woolsey, Melancthon. "Journal of the U.S. Brig Jones," Detroit Public Library.

BIBLIOTHÈQUE ET ARCHIVES NATIONALES DU QUÉBEC (BANQ), MONTREAL

Contracts, Notary Public W. F. Scott, CN 301, S 253

Contracts, Notary Public J. Bélanger, M173/37

LIBRARY AND ARCHIVES CANADA, OTTAWA (LAC)

Record Group 8: British Military and Naval Records

Series C (I): vols. 0, 370, 679, 683, 727, 729, 730, 731, 732, 733, 736, 737, 738, 1171, 1708, 1709, 1219, 1220, 1221, 1222, 1225, 2737

Series 3 (A): Admiralty Lakes Service Records, vols. 31, 42, 49, 59

Military Group 24

Series A13: Sir Charles Bagot Fonds, vol. 1

National Map Collection

Department of National Defense Fonds, vols. 78903, 81203, 97256

NATIONAL ARCHIVES AND RECORDS ADMINISTRATION (NARA), WASHINGTON, DC, AND COLLEGE PARK, MD

Record Group 19: Records of the Bureau of Ships

Ship Plan Files, Cartographic and Architectural Branch

Record Group 41: Records of the Bureau of Marine Inspection and Navigation

Entry 119, Certificates of Enrolments 1815–1866 (*Charles & Ann, Hunter, Fair American*)

Record Group 45: Naval Records Collection of the Office of Naval Records and Library

Entry 124: Miscellaneous Letters Received by the Secretary of the Navy

Entry 125: Letters Received by the Secretary of the Navy from Captains

Entry 147: Letters Received by the Secretary of the Navy from Commanders

Entry 148: Letters Received by the Secretary of the Navy from Officers Below the Rank of Master Commandant

Entry 149: Letters Sent by the Secretary of the Navy to Officers

Entry 169: Register of U.S. Naval Vessels, 1797–1814

Entry 173: Letters Sent by the Secretary of the Navy Relating to Gunboats, 1803–1808

Entry 209: Miscellaneous Letters Sent by the Secretary of the Navy

Entry 216: Board of Navy Commissioners to Navy
    Commandants
Entry 220: Commanders Letters from Sackets Harbor,
    Whitehall, and Erie Naval Yards, 1815–1833 to the
    Board of Navy Commissioners
Entry 224: Roll of Commissioned & Warrant Officers
Entry 235: Contracts of the U.S. Navy
Entry 273: Records of the General Courts Martial and
    Courts of Inquiry of the Navy Department
Entry 330: Abstracts of Service Records, U.S. Navy
Entry 441: Letters Sent by the Secretary of the Navy to
    Commandants and Agents
Entry M625: Area File of the Naval Records Collection,
    1775–1910
Entry T829: Miscellaneous Records of the U.S. Navy,
    1789–1925
Subject File NI, Macdonough to the Board of Navy
    Commissioners
Box 110. "Inventory of the Armament and Stores of the
    Prize Brig *Linnet* Captured on the 11th September,
    1814."
Box 224, "Roll of Commissioned & Warrant Officers
    Late Under Command of Thomas Macdonough"
Box 575, List of Paroled Wounded Men Sent to Isle aux
    Noix, U.S. Galley *Allen*
Record Group 77, Civil Works Map Files
D 112, "Map of the Head of Lake Champlain"
Record Group 98: Records of United States Army
    Commands, 1784–1821
    General Orders, 5th Military District
Record Group 107: Records of the Secretary of War
    Entry 18: Letters Received 1801–1889
Record Group 217: Records of the Accounting Officers of the
    Department of the Treasury
    Fourth Auditor Settled Accounts

THE NATIONAL ARCHIVES OF SCOTLAND,
EDINBURGH (NAS)
Papers of the Dundas Family of Melville, Viscounts Melville
    (Melville Castle Papers) GD 51/2: Letters and Papers on
    Admiralty and Naval Affairs

THE NATIONAL ARCHIVES OF THE UK: PUBLIC RECORD
OFFICE (TNA: PRO), KEW, RICHMOND, SURREY
Records of the Admiralty, Naval Forces, Royal Marines,
    Coastguard, and Related Bodies
Records of the Navy Board and the Board of Admiralty
ADM 1: Admiralty, and Ministry of Defense, Navy
    Department: Correspondence and Papers, vols. 2002,
    2262, 2263, 2264, 2563, 2737, 5450
ADM 3: Admiralty: Minutes, vol. 181
ADM 106: Navy Board: Records, Letters, vols. 1997, 1999,
    2002
Records of Accounting and Pay Departments
ADM 42: Navy Board and Admiralty: Yard Pay Books, vol.
    2167
Records of H.M. Ships
ADM 51: Captains' Logs, vol. 2072 (Log of the *Tecumseth*),
    vol. 2607 (*Newash*), vol. 2641 (*Prince Regent*); vol. 2700
    (*Princess Charlotte*)
ADM 52: Masters' Logs, vol. 189 (*Montreal*), vol. 3928
    (*Princess Charlotte*), vols. 3933 (Log of the *Tecumseth*),
    4548 (Log of the *Newash*)
Records of the Navy Board and the Board of Admiralty
ADM 106: Navy Board: Records, Letters, vols. 1997, 1999,
    2002
Records of Service
ADM 196: Admiralty: Officers' Service Records (series 3),
    vols. 3, 5
Records of the Colonial Office
Correspondence with the Colonies, Entry Books and
    Registers of Correspondence
CO 42: Colonial Office and Predecessors: Canada, Formerly
    British North America, Original Correspondence, vols.
    151, 156, 157, 158
Records Created or Inherited by the War Office
Records of the Ordnance Office and its Successors at the
    War Office
WO 44: Ordnance Office and War Office Correspondence,
    vol. 250
National Maritime Museum, Greenwich (NMM)
Admiralty Ship Plan collection

General Index

*There are two indexes: General Index and Index of Ships.
*Abbreviations: a (or b) = left or right column; t = table; n (or nn) = note(s); fig = any illustration (photo, drawing, painting, etc.); pl. = color plate; RAr = Royal Army; PM = Provincial Marine; RN = Royal Navy; USAr = United States Army; USN = Untied States Navy

A bandoned Shipwreck Act (ASA), 344, 345
Additional Regulations and Instructions 1813 (ship captain's reports), 196a
Albany Steamboat Co., 249
Aldersley, Foreman of Shipwrights John, 363
Allen, Gary, 341
Allen, USN Lt. William Henry, 279
Amer, Christopher, 220, 235n28
American Lake Erie squadron, 21fig1 (painting)
American Numismatic Society of New York, 295
Ames, John, 133, 151n70
Amherstburg, ON, 73, 74; British situation at, 13–14, 15, 64; commercial shipping at, 89b; disputed territorial boundary, 90; shipbuilding at, 13, 65, 191; US takeover of, 74b
anchors. See Plattsburgh Bay Anchor No. 1; Plattsburgh Bay Anchor No. 2
Angus, USN Lt. Samuel, 11
Appling, USAr Major, 121n49
armament:, 126t, 371t; and bursting, 49–50n27; burden on vessels, 30, 38, 177; carronade, p1.6b (photo), 22fig2A (drawing), 31fig11 (photo), 43fig18 (photo), 50n27, 44; columbiad, 269n9, 278, 292n33; and comparisons of US and British firepower, 162, 197, 245n11; dangers of, 292n41; and displacement, 44, 49n25; and gunboats (barges), 220, 222, 273; limited by Rush-Bagot Agreement of 1817, 55; long gun, p1.7a (photo), 21–22, 22fig2B (drawing), 43–44, 116b, 128; on pivot mounts, 145, 252; and seaworthiness, 182; weights of, 49n25. See also Appendix A; also armament *under individual ships in* Index of Ships
Armstrong, US Secretary of War John, 273, 274; and Jones, 314a
artifacts and souvenirs: search for, 339–43. See also hulks: as curiosities and sources of souvenirs
ASA. See Abandoned Shipwreck Act (ASA)
Ashdown, Dana, 235n36

ASI Group Ltd., 136
Askin, John, 55, 64, 69n17; "Askin Papers," 69n17

Baker, William Avery, 27
Ballingall, RM Capt. David James, 201
Bancroft, USN Acting Sailing Mstr. Henry, 293n52
Barbary States (North Africa), 111, 238, 253; naval victory over, 285
Barbes, Augustus, 271
Barclay, RN Cmdr. Robert Herriot, 13, 13fig4 (portrait); and appeals for guns, stores, and sailors, 13–14, 20, 115; at the Battle of Lake Erie, 14, 23, 64; and the need for shoal-draft warships, 221
Barrie, RN Comm. Robert, 91, 199, 201, 233
Basin Harbor, VT, 273, 345
Battle at Sandy Creek, 117, 121n49, 222
Battle of Chippewa, 118
Battle of Copenhagen (1801), 296
Battle of Crysler's Farm, 222
Battle of Lake Champlain: 255fig4 (engraving), 366fig3 (print); map of battle, 350fig13; map of lake, 237fig1. See also Battle of Plattsburgh Bay
Battle of Lake Erie, 19–24, 32, p1.1b (painting); and Bell-built ships in action, 65; casualties in, 22, 24, 44, 351n3; compared to Battle of Lake Champlain, 243; decisive role of, 64b; and Elliot controversy, 20–22, 37, 320 (see also Elliot, Lt. Jesse Duncan); 150th anniversary (1962), 27; 175th anniversary (1988), 28; Perry Centennial (1913), 24–25; US ship losses after, 15; US victory, 243. See also Index of Ships: *General Hunter; Nancy; Niagara*
Battle of Lundy's Lane, 118
Battle of Plattsburgh Bay, 243–44, 254–56, 271–72, 282–83, 283fig5 (watercolor), 301, 351; after-action report, 319–20; and *Allen*, 244, 284; artifacts of, 7, 340 (see also Plattsburgh Bay Anchor No. 2); casualties in, 271, 282, 301, 318–19, 337, 283a; debris from (photos), p1.11a, p1.11b, 342–43figs6–

9; and *Eagle*, 244, 333; and *Linnet*, 244, 309; location of, 349b, 353n36; and the Royal Navy, 282b, 298, 300, 301; strategic importance of, 243, 290, 351, 356; and *Ticonderoga*, (USN schooner, Lake Champlain), 244; US victory, 333, 338. See also Battle of Lake Champlain; Index of Ships *for individual ships by name*
Battle of Sackets Harbor (NY), 11, 116; effect on offensive military action, 117–18; and lake gales, 127b. See also Sackets Harbor, NY
Battle of the Thames (ON), 13, 24, 234n3
Battle of Valcour Island, 221, 295, 341
Bell, RN Lt. Christopher, 256
Bell, Mstr. Shipwright William, 52, 360b, 212: draft plans and designs by, 65–66, 70n40, 105n3, 191, 198, 371t; William Bell Papers, 66. See also Index of Ships: *Detroit; Queen Charlotte*
BF Goodrich Co., 347
Bignell, RN Lt. George, 64, 69n28
Bilicki, Steve, 285fig6 (photo)
Birch, Thomas: his *Battle of Lake Champlain* (watercolor), 244figs5, 300figs5 (detail of *Linnet*); his *Battle of Lake Erie*, p1.1b (painting)
Black Rock, NY, 11, 12, 14, 124
Board of Naval Commissioners, 163b
Boardman, James, 364
Boden, USN Midn. William, 254
Bogardus, USN Mstr.'s Mate Peter, 130
Bois Blanc Island dispute, 90
Booth, Matthew, 341
Bouchette, Surveyor Gen. Joseph, 195–96, 307, 363
Bourchier, RN Capt. William, 87, 90, 104b
Breese, USN Midn. Samuel L., 293n52
Brevoort, Henry B., 70n33
British Admiralty, 345, 348
British Army: and border crossing into New York, 317; line of supply and communication, 221; preparedness of, 10; Quartermaster General's Department, 10; on Richelieu River, 320; and transport/supply vessels needed, 87; in the Upper Lakes, 11. *For units by name see*

British Army (*cont.*)
under British military units. *See also* Royal Navy

British Defense Forces, 345

British military units: 5th Infantry Regiment, 73; 10th Royal Veterans Battalion, 62; 37th Regiment, 62; 39th Regiment, 342, 352n15; 41st Regiment, 62, 64, 66, 74; 49th Regiment of Foot, 73; 100th Regiment, 285; 104th Regiment, 194; Royal New Foundland Regiment, 66, 74; Royal Newfoundland Fencibles, 62, 64

Brock, RAr Maj. Gen. Isaac, 64, 74

Brockville, ON, 223

Brown brothers (shipbuilders), 7, 12, 155, 315, 333, 363; recommended by Secretary Jones, 154, 314; shipbuilding background, 363–64; ships built by, 48n6, 118, 119, 313 (*see also under* Index of Ships: *Allen, Chippewa, Eagle, Niagara, Prince de Neufchatel*); shot garland design, 266 (*see also under main entry*); and Eckford, 154, 165, 327. *See also* Brown, Shipwright Adam; Brown, Shipwright Noah

Brown, Shipwright Adam, 7, 12, 118, 154; construction features and techniques used by, 49n23, 322, 323, 326–27, 329, 331; and *Eagle,* 243, 314, 316, 325*fig*8, 328*fig*10; skill of, 333. *See also* Brown brothers

Brown, USAr Maj. Gen. Jacob, 118, 187

Brown, Shipwright Noah, 7, 49n23, 313, 314; advice on "plain work," 24, 274, 363; and *Allen,* 283; armament requirements, 43; as builder of galleys/gunboats, 251, 274, 283, 289; commendation of, 154, 274; lines/plans of, 26*fig*6, 28, 37*a,* 268*fig*11; and price of steamship hull, 252, 254; and *Saratoga,* 239, 252, 313; and shipbuilding on Lake Erie, 13, 19, 36, 118; and steamship conversion, 252, 313, 327 (see also *Ticonderoga* [USN schooner, Lake Champlain]); timber choices of, 361; and the use of sweeps, 37

Browns Bay (ON), 219, 223, 234

Browns Bay Vessel. *See* Index of Ships: Browns Bay Vessel

Bruce County Museum and Cultural Centre (Southampton, ON), 63, 65*fig*13, 70n57

Bryant, Lemuel, 130*a*

Brydon, RN Mstr. Robert A., 353n38. *See also* Pring, Capt. Daniel: court martial of

Bull, John, 129*a*

Bullus, USN Agent John, 314*a,* 315

Bunker, Elihu, 249, 251, 267*a*

Burlington Bay, 273*b*

Burlington, VT: British raid on, 239, 273; Macdonough's shipbuilding at, 273, 291n13; military hospital, 282*b*

Burrows, USN Lt. William, 279

Bushby, RN Lt. Thomas, 87, 89, 101*b;* logbook of, 106n41; rigging warrant of, 97*fig*12, 98, 101, 102, 106nn36, 56, and 57

Butler, USN Gunner Thomas, 280*a*

Cain, Emily, "Early Schoonerdays": on *Lord Nelson*'s spar dimensions, 152n90; *Ghost Ships* Hamilton *and* Scourge, 132; 151n82, 152n96; "Merchant Schooners": on Chauncey's schooners, 150n52

Calhoun, John C., 2

Calypso (French research vessel), 131. See also *Soucoupe*

Canada Centre for Inland Waters (CCIW), 131, 132, 150n56

Canadian Conservation Institute (CCI), 62, 69n12, 224

Canadian Department of Indian Affairs and Northern Development, 220. *See also* Parks Canada

Canadian Freeman (newspaper), 91

Canadian Navy, 202

Canton Ohio Repository (newspaper), 70n56

Carron Foundry (Scotland), 339

Cassavoy, Kenneth, 51, 132, 150n58; and flag of *General Hunter,* 65*fig*13; and *Hamilton*'s beakhead, 151n88

Cassin, USN Capt. John, 315, 333n16

Cassin, USN Lt. Stephen: after-action trip to Washington, 256, 338; command of *Ticonderoga,* 253, 255–56, 267*b,* 319; defense of Otter Creek, 279; and Henley, 315, 333n16; and Macdonough, 253*fig*3, 255*fig*4, 256; personal history of, 253; portrait of, 253*fig*3; prize money awarded for capture of British, 270n18; and Secretary Jones, 251, 254

Cataraqui River (ON), 188, 188*fig*1 (map)

CCHA (Clinton County [NY] Historical Association), 344, 345

CCI (Canadian Conservation Institute, Ottawa), 62, 69n12

Chamberlain, USN Midn. William, 317, 319

Chambly, QC, 238

Champlain Maritime Society, 257*b,* 270n24, 293n60, 334n38. *See also* Lake Champlain Maritime Museum

Champlain Valley, 243, 280, 294; British offensive in, 298; conditions in 1814, 252, 279

Chantry Island, ON, 53*fig*2 (photo); its Imperial Lighthouse, 53*fig*2, 68n3

Chapelle, Howard I., 28; and hull design, 186n62, 305*b;* and *Niagara,* 27, 329*b;* and rigging proportions, 98, 104*a,* 106n39

Chateauguay, NY, 274

Chateauguay River, 274*a*

Chatham (Eng.), 191, 195, 198

Chauncey, USN Comm. Isaac: 16n12, 112*fig*4 (painting), 158*fig*3, 190; after-action report, 147; and the army offensive at Battle of Chippewa, 118; appointment and instructions, 10, 12, 111, 112; and armament of *Hamilton* and *Scourge,* 127, 149n21; and ballast needs, 49n19; 155; and blockade of Kingston, 162, 194; and caution in engaging battle, 117, 119, 127–28, 194; and chase of *Royal George,* 112, 125, 149n23; on construction of *Superior, Jefferson, Jones,* and *Mohawk,* 166, 121n45; end of the war, 187, 195; illness of, 118, 159; and the merchant schooners (*Conquest, Hamilton, Julia, Growler*), 125, 128–30, 149n37; and mothballing of shipyards and squadron, 119, 163; and the need for crewmen, 14, 156, 157, 159, 320; offensive action plan of, 114–15; and *Oneida,* 112; personal history of, 111; and Ridgely, 157, 163, 183n14; at Sackets Harbor, 114, 116, 125 (*see also* Battle of Sackets Harbor); and the shipbuilding/outfitting race with British, 12, 19, 117–18, 155, 190, 195, 197, 238, 313; and shipwright Dobbins, 16n9, 19–20; and shipwright Eckford, 112, 114, 118, 154–55, 180; and shipwright Noah Brown, 12, 19–20, 42–43, 118, 154; and *Sylph*'s building time, 183n5; warning Secretary Jones of British buildup, 154

Chesapeake Bay: blockade, 156; gunboat flotilla, 293n62; row galleys (*see* row galleys: Chesapeake Bay row galleys)

Chew, USN Midn. John, 159–60

Child, James: logbook of, 98

City of Hamilton (ON), 131, 132, 136

clinker-style construction, 225*a,* 227–31, 235n34. *See also under* Index of Ships; Browns Bay Vessel: construction features of; lapstrake construction

Clinton County (NY) Historical Association (CCHA), 344, 345

Clydesdale Wreck, 68n4

Cocke, USN Midn. Harrison, 162*b*

Cohn, Arthur B., 165, 166; and *Boscawen,* 16n4; and *Eagle,* 313, 321*b*; and *Jefferson,* 167*fig*12, 168*fig*14; and *Linnet,* 302; and Poultney River wrecks, 293n62. *See also individual ships by name in* Index of Ships

Colledge, J. J., *Ships of the Royal Navy:* and identification of *Linnet,* 311n59

Collinson and Son (Southwark, Eng.), 202*b*

Conboy, F. J., 76, 76*fig*3, 82

Conover, USN Midn. Thomas, 282, 293n52

Cook, RN Capt. James, 42

Cooper, James Fenimore, 125*b*; *Ned Myers* (published story), 125*b*; and *Scourge,* 149n21

Cousteau, Jacques, 131, 151n86

Crab Island, NY, 255*fig*4 (engraving), 256*a,* 301; burial site of casualties, 270n17, 337

Crawford, US Secretary of War William, 66

Creighton, USN Mstr. Cmdt. John Orde, 315

Crisman, Kevin, 132, 165, 334n39; and Anchor No. 1, 352n17 (*see also* Plattsburgh Bay Anchor No. 1); and *Boscawen,* 16, 16n4; and *Eagle,* 312–13, 321*b*; and *Hamilton*'s beakhead, 151n88; and *Jefferson,* 168*fig*14, 180; and *Linnet,* 302; and *Phoenix I* dive, 257*b*–58; and Poultney River wrecks, 293n62; and wreck of *Linnet* (photo), p1.9*b*

Croghan, USAr Lt. Col. George, 75, 85n33

Crooks, James, 124–25, 138

Crooks, William, 124*b,* 138

Crowninshield, US Secretary of the Navy Benjamin, 163*a,* 283

Currie, Leslie, 68n1

Curry, Capt. William, 344

Cusson, Chris, 31*fig*12 (photo)

Daniel Dobbins Papers, 37*b. See also* Dobbins, Daniel

Darwin, Charles, 42

Davidson, Flora, p1.8*b* (photo)

Davies, RN Capt. Henry Thomas, 196

Davis, USN Rear Adm. Charles H., 48n8

Davis, John, 67

Dead Creek Road (NY), 282

Deadman Bay, ON (earlier, Hamilton Cove), 201–205; archaeological look at, 205–208; artifacts found at, 202; identification of shipwrecks at, 202–204; and salvaged wrecks, 203*fig*8 (photo); wrecks compared to the Strickland

plans, 204, 211–12. *See also under* Wreck Able; Wreck Baker; Wreck Charlie

Dearborn, USAr Gen. Henry, 237, 239

Deer, USN Boatswain William, 129*b*

deck lights, 287, 90*fig*3 (photo), 171*fig*15 (drawing). *See also* Index of Ships: *Allen; Jefferson; Tecumseth*

Deiss, Jonathan Webb, 66, 70n51

Delafield, Joseph, 153–54, 154*fig*1

"Derelict Site," 68n4

Dempsey, William, 7*fig*4 (photo)

Detroit (city), 55; and border dispute with Amherstburg, 90; retaken by the US, 14, 24, 74*b*; Gen. Prevost ordered to occupy, 240; shipbuilding at, 72; supplies at, 81; occupied by the British, 9–11, 64, 67, 74, 110

Detroit River, 10, 13, 52, 64; blockade of, 20; shipyards on, 72

diagonal riders. *See* riders (angled, diagonal, transverse). *See also* Index of Ships, *Franklin* (USN): and use of diagonal riders

Dickson, John, 64

disarmament. *See* Rush-Bagot Agreement of 1817

Discovery Harbor (Havre de la Découverte, ON), 91, 93

Dobbins, Shipwright Daniel, 11–12, 16n9, 19–20; Daniel Dobbins Papers, 37

Dominion of Canada, 202

Doughty, Chief US Naval Constructor William: design features of, 276, 278; and mast placement, 284; row galley lines, plans of, 273, 274*b,* 275*fig*1, 283*b,* 357*b*

Downie, RN Comm. George, 311n31, 339, 340*fig*4; at battle at Plattsburgh Bay, 254, 300, 349; as commander of Lake Champlain squadron, 298; death of, 301*a,* 337, 339, 349; defended by Yeo, 301*b*; and difficulties preparing for battle, 300; and orders to fight, 243; and use of anchors during action, 349

Drew, RN Lt. William, 301

Drummond, RAr Lt. Gen. Gordon, 118

Drummond, Robert, 199; brewery of, 200, 202, 210

Drummond Island (MI), 90

Drury, RN Capt. Augustus Vere, 190, 207

Duff, James, 165

Duffy, Ebenezer (ship's cook), 130

Duggen, Thomas, 73

Duncan, USN Acting Lt. Silas, 282*b*

Eagle, Henry, 124, 125; and craftsmanship of beakhead, 142

Eckford, Mstr. Shipwright Henry, 7, 181*fig*23, 194; his approach to ship building, 180, 182, 327, 361, 363–64; commended by Chauncey, 154, 180, 194; and 1814 shipbuilding project, 154–55, 170; personal history of, 114, 120n21, 183, 363; portrait of, 114*fig*7; as shipbuilder and designer, 114*b,* 118, 124, 154, 183, 186n62, 364; work compared to that of Brown brothers, 165, 327

Elliot, USN Lt. Jesse Duncan, 16n12; actions at the Battle of Lake Erie, 20–22, 37*b,* 320; at Black Rock, 11; and capture of *Caledonia,* 12; and *Diana,* 149n19

Embargo Act of 1808, 124*a,* 273*a*; reinstated in 1812, 124*b*

Emery, Eric, 285*fig*6

Erie County Historical Society, 37*b*

Erie Maritime Museum: and *Niagara*'s bell, 32; live fire gunnery video, 45–47

Erie, PA (*formerly* Presque Isle): British plan to attack, 13, 15, 20, 86 (*see also* Battle of Lake Erie); harbor at, 11, 15, 35, 358; Perry's transfer of ships to, 14*a,* 15; as Presque Isle, 11, 20, 64.; US shipbuilding at, 11–14, 15, 19. *See also* Lake Erie; Index of Ships: *Niagara*

Evans, USN Lt. George, 292n41

Everard, RN Capt. Thomas, 297

Fearon, Henry Bradshaw, 365

"Fig Channel Site," 68n4

Fincham, John, 98; and schooner rigging, 100*a,* 104*a,* 106n39

Fisher, RN Capt. Peter, 298, 311n31; promotion to captain, 311n30

Fitzgerald, USN Purser Edward, 130

Flagship Niagara League (nonprofit), 28

Fleming, Patrick, 189, 190, 212, 371t

Folkes, Patrick, 64, 68n1, 70n41

Fontenoy, Paul E.: *The Sloops of the Hudson River:* on size of Hudson River sloops, 148n9

Forsyth Richardson and Co., 72, 73

Fort Cassin (VT), 280, 281*fig*4 (map), 298. *See also* Cassin, USN Lt. Stephen; Otter Creek (VT)

Fort Erie (ON), 32, 73; supplying and reinforcing, 74, 89

Fort Frontenac (Kingston, ON), 202*b*

Fort George (ON), 125; attack on, 127

Fort Henry (ON), p1.8*a* (aquatint)

Fort Henry Museum, 202*b*

Fort Indiantown Gap (PA), 45

Fort Mackinac (MI). *See* Mackinac Island

Fort Malden (Amherstburg, ON), 14, 52, 70n56; as base for boarding and inspecting vessels, 68; blockade of, 20; shipbuilding at, 52, 65. *See also* Amherstburg, ON

Fort Meigs (OH), 64, 74

Fort Michilimackinac (MI). *See* Mackinac Island

Fort Mount Hope (NY), 295. *See also* Mount Hope Society of Ticonderoga

Fort Niagara (NY), p1.5b

Fort Oswego (NY), 222*fig*3, p1.5a (print), p1.7b (print)

Fort Stephenson (OH), 74

Fort Ticonderoga (NY), 295, 305, 310n5

Fort Wellington (Prescott, ON), 355*fig*1, p1.8b

40-Mile Creek (ON), 222

"Free Trade and Sailors' Rights," 2, 355

Freeman, USN Midn. James, 254, 293n52

Freer, Noah (British Military Secretary), 297

French and Indian War, 10, 109, 247, 310n5; use of gunboats during, 221

Fuller, Ken (diver): and *St. Lawrence,* 214*fig*19 (photo)

Fulton, Robert: and Livingston monopoly, 248–49, 252. *See also* Index of Ships: *North River Steamboat*

Galick family, 263, 295, 302, 308

Galick, Bill, 308

Galick, John, 257*a*, 294

Galick, Steve, 257*a*, 294

Galick, Tony, 294

galleys. *See* row galleys

Galveston Historical Foundation (TX), 41

Gananoque, ON, 221, 223

Gardiner, Robert, 196*b*

George III (England), 247; and King George III-crested cartridge pouch artifact, 257

Georgian Bay (ON), 71, 75, 76, 87

Gibson, Gary, 148n5

Giles, (RN Purser on *Linnet*), 301

Gillman's Club, 166*fig*11

Glasgow, Scotland, 223, 305

Goldsmith, Tom, 129*b*, 130*a*

Gordon, LeeAnne Elizabeth, 98, 105n10

Goudie, John, 189*b*, 190*b*, 195, 214n8, 251n16

Grand Portage (Lake Superior), 72

Grand River (MI), 89, 90, 358

Grant, PM Comm. Alexander, 10, 68n2

Grant, RN Maj. L. F., 202*b*

Gray, PM Capt. Andrew, 74

Gray, James, p1.8a

Great Lakes: difficulties of sailing on,

34*b*, 77, 89, 102, 162; private/commercial navigation on, 72, 124; and Provincial Marine transport fleet, 4, 52; strategic importance of, 3, 84, 221. *See also individual lakes by name*

Great War for Empire (1756–63), 272. *See also* French and Indian War

Grieco, Glenn, 185n49, 186nn59, 61, 359*fig*2, 360*b*

Griffiths, John, 183

Guenter's Wreck, 217n98

gunboat(s), 219, 235n34, 272, 318*fig*2; archeological study of, 283*a*, 293n61; commanders of, 293n52; construction for use on the Great Lakes, 221–22, 287, 297; decommissioned (RN), 223; deterioration and demise of, 293n56, 364; illnesses aboard, 280*a;* "List of His Majesty's Gun Boats," 221–22; new class design, 273; and patrol duty, 320; role of, 282*b;* status of officers serving on, 280*a;* underside and deck reconstruction, 232*fig*10; uses of, 220–21, 289. *See also by name in* Index of Ships; row galleys (oar warcraft/gunboats); schooners

Hale, Abigail Woodruff, 317, 318; marriages, 334n25

Hale, USAr Pvt. James M., 317, 318, 334n25

Halifax, NS, 189, 297

Hall, RN Capt. Basil, 367, 368*fig*4

Hall, RN Commissioner Robert, 87, 191, 194, 195, 199*a*

Hamilton and Scourge Foundation Inc., 132

Hamilton, RN Capt. Thomas: and clinker-hulled gunboats, 235n34

Hamilton Cove (ON), 187, 188*fig*1 (map), 201. *See also* Deadman Bay

Hamilton, US Secretary of the Navy Paul, 10, 12, 111, 125

Hampton, USAr Gen. Wade, 237, 273–74, 289

Harris, USN Seaman John, 159–60

Harrison, USAr Gen. William Henry, 14–15, 20; and congratulatory message from Perry, 24

"Hawks 1813" anchor project. *See under* Lake Champlain Maritime Museum (LCMM): anchor project

Hawks Iron Works, 345*fig*11, 347

Hawks, William, 347

Hawks, William Jr., 347

Hazard, USN Sailing Mstr. Daniel, 293n52

Heaton, Jay (diver), 293n60

Heersen, Wesley, 31*fig*12 (photo)

Heinold, Erich (archeologist): and wreck of *Linnet* (photo), p1.9b; and wreck of *Newash* (photo), 94*fig*8

Henley, USN Mstr. Cmdt. Robert, 300, 315*fig*1, 320; after-action report of, 319–20; commendations for the crew of *Eagle,* 318; departure from Lake Champlain, 320; and *Eagle* in battle, 318*fig*2; and Macdonough's after-action report, 319–20; at Plattsburgh Bay, 317–19; portrait of, 315*fig*1; at Vergennes, 315–16

Hett, Charles, 93

Hidden, Enoch, 315

Holland, USN Mstr.'s Mate Stephen, 293n52

Hookey, William, 106n34

Hubbell, J. C., 337, 351

Hudson River: as shipping route toward the Great Lakes, 111, 158, 237, 314; commercial shipping on, 248; and the Hudson River sloops, 124, 148n9, 248, 249

Hugunin, Daniel, 124

Hugunin, Peter, 124

Hugunin, Robert, 124, 163

hulks (hulls): as "coffins of the brave," 2; as curiosities and sources of souvenirs, 5, 7, 166*fig*11, 220, 223, 257, 303, 303*fig*7, 321, 364. *See also under individual ships by name in* Index of Ships

Hull, USAr Gen. William, 64

Humphreys, Joshua, 177

Humphreys, Samuel, 185n54

Hunter, Peter, 69n20

impressment, 2, 9, 297*a*

in ordinary: 1*fig*1 (defined), 4, 320; *Jefferson,* 163; at Kingston, ON, 187, 199; at Sackets Harbor, 164*fig*7; *Tecumseth* and *Newash,* 90; *Ticonderoga,* 256; at Whitehall, NY, 320

Institute of Nautical Archaeology, 284*b*, 302*b*

Irvine, Hugh, 201*fig*7

Irvine, RN Lt. Robert, p1.2b, 49n13, 329

Irwin, RAr Capt. J. B., 234n6

Isle aux Noix (QC), 238*b*, 273; arrival of Downie at, 298; and British buildup, 276, 282*a*, 291n18, 297–98, 313*b;* and commander Pring, 239, 297, 298, 311n30; fortifications, 272*a*, 296; hospital, 271; plan of shipyard and defenses, 296*fig*3; and Plattsburgh Anchor No. 2, 344–48 (*see also* Plattsburgh Bay Anchor No. 2); shipbuilding at, 240*b*, 243, 252, 297, 347–48 (*see also* Index of

Ships: *Linnet*); Royal Navy Yard at, 271, 295–96, 310, 364
Izard, USAr Gen. George, 280*a*

Jackson, USAr Gen. Andrew, 2
Jackson, RN Boatswain Charles, 301
James, William (naval historian), 179
Janson, Mike (diver), 293n60
Janusas, Scarlett, 68n1
Jason Foundation for Education, 133
Jarvis, John Wesley, 12*fig*3
Jenks, Jackson, 166*fig*11 (photo)
Jones, Lloyd, 274*b*
Jones, US Secretary of the Navy William: administrative skills of, 12, 156; after-action reports to, 84, 163, 320; and assessment of the British, 313; authorization of shipbuilding by, 19, 114, 154–55, 272, 274, 314; and cost of shipbuilding, 118*b*, 243, 313–14; and need for defensive action, 723; and lack cooperation with the army, 118*a*; requests for armament, 252; requests for officers, 315–16; and smugglers, 282; and the steamboat at Vergennes, VT, 251–52, 254; and the training of sailors, 280*a*
Jury, Wilfred, 91

Kent, RN Lt. Henry, 87, 194, 251n33
Keteltas, USN Sailing Mstr. Samuel, 293n52
Kingston Gazette (ON), 199*b*, 215n28
Kingston, ON, p1.8a (aquatint), 109; blockade of, 162; and close watch by US navy, 118*b*; and commercial shipping, 109, 124; map of harbor, 188*fig*1; and need for defense of shipping, 221; remoteness of, 189, 212; wreck sites near, 204*fig*9 (map). *See also* Royal Navy shipyard (at Kingston, ON)
Kristof, Emory, 150n58
Kurtz, Matthew, 347*a*

Lacy, Shipwright John: and the Bunker design, 267; and construction of *Ticonderoga*, 263, 263*fig*9, 264, 265; and the steamboat at Vergennes, VT, 249, 251, 252, 254, 264, 266
Lake Champlain Archaeological Association (LCAA) 341–43, 344, 351, 352n14; and battle debris, pl.lla; contribution of, 364. *See also* Leege, William
Lake Champlain Maritime Museum (LCMM), 270n24, 352n17; anchor project, 341*fig*5, 344*b*, 345, 347, 348, 350; and contributions of William (Bill) Leege, 344*a*; and excavation of *Allen*, 284–85; and excavation of *Linnet*,

302; munitions donated by the Galicks to, 308. *See also* Champlain Maritime Society
Lake Champlain Steamboat Co., 256*b*; investors, 249; and Bunker's design modifications, 251; replacement steamship *Phoenix I,* 256, 257, 265, 267; sale of steamship hull to the navy, 251, 254
Lake Champlain: navigational conditions, 238, 305, 331, 347, 356–57, 358; pathway for invasion, 3–4, 272–73, 351; strategic location of, 237, 238, 355, 356
Lake Erie: and availability of shipbuilding materials, 33, 72; harbors, 11, 358*b*; *Lake Erie Patrol 1812* (painting), 11*fig*2; navigational hazards, 10, 360*a*, 367n2; and Provincial Marine, 4 (*see also* Provincial Marine); weather hazards on, 15, 89, 90. *See also* Battle of Lake Erie
Lake Huron: and availability of shipbuilding materials, 72; Georgian Bay (*see under main entry*); and navigational hazards, 90, 367n2, 358; Penetanguishene shipyard on, 15, 87; shoreline of, 238; strategic location of, 356*a*; weather hazards on, 16, 52, 65, 67, 74; wreck locations, 67, 69n21, 86 (*see also* Index of Ships: *Newash; Tecumseth*)
Lake Michigan, 10; commercial shipping, 73; and the fall of Fort Mackinac, 9; Millecoquins River wreck, 151n74
Lake Ontario: and archaeological legacy of the war, 119; battle on the lake (*see* Battle of Sackets Harbor; Kingston, ON); commercial shipping on (schooners), 72, 123; and cost of naval ship race, 309, 313; and disposal of RN fleet, 223; loss of personnel on, 222; muster roll of USN squadron on (1814), 184n21; naval action on, p1.6a (watercolor); navigational concerns on, 153, 162, 188–89, 358; and paradoxical role in War of 1812, 119; and Provincial Marine, 4; and shipbuilding efforts of both navies, 119, 154–55, 180, 187–88, 212, 238, 313*b*; ships built on, 81–82, 114, 155, 284; ships designed for, 180, 183, 188–89, 329, 358; strategic importance of, 7, 10–14, 16, 109, 117, 118, 162, 355, 356; and US balance of power, 112, 116, 163; and US interdiction of British supplies, 116; as US military goal, 111; wreck locations on, 219, 231, 364
Lake St. Clair, 73
Lake Superior, 9, 10, 72, 74
Lane, David, 164, 165*fig*10, 185n51
Lansing, Abraham, 249

lapstrake construction, 37; and Browns Bay Vessel, 119, 227, 229*fig*8, 232. *See also* clinker-style construction
Laroche, Daniel, 172*fig*16
Laws, Edward, 216n42
LCAA. *See* Lake Champlain Archaeological Association (LCAA)
Leege, William (Bill), p1.11a, p1.11b, 341, 341*fig*5 (photo); contribution of, 343, 351, 352n17, 364; and LCMM, 344; on location of the battle of Plattsburgh Bay, 349. *See also* Lake Champlain Archaeological Association (LCAA)
Leonard, USN Capt. James T., 302
Lessmann, Anne W., 342n14
Lesueur, Charles Alexandre, 352n9
Lever, Darcy: *The Young Sea Officer's Sheet Anchor*, 98, 106n58
Lewis, Dennis M., 341: *British Naval Activity on Lake Champlain,* 291n18
Lewis, USN Seaman Leonard, 129*b*, 130*a*
Lindsay, USN Sailing Mstr. Joseph, 253–54, 256
List of the Navy. See Royal Navy: *List of the Navy* (ships) (RN)
live-fire (armament) test results, 46*fig*19 (photo), 47*fig*20 (photo), 50nn28 and 29
Livingston, Robert, 248; Fulton-Livingston monopoly, 249, 252
Long Island Sound steamers, 249, 267*a*
Loomis, USN Sailing Mstr. Jarius, 272
Lossing, Benson, 164
Lower Canada, 272*a*; defense of, 14, 221, 240; and importance of Lake Ontario, 356; and importance of Montreal, 272; as invasion objective, 109, 237, 272; as leverage for peace negotiations, 240; as staging area for the Champlain Valley campaign, 298
Lyon, David: *The Sailing Navy List:* on frigate armaments, 215n33. *See also* armament

Mackinac Island: and alternate names, 70n34; attack on, 75, 110; fort at, 9, 15, 19; commercial shipping service to, 65, 76; difficulties of supplying British troops at, 86, 87
Mackinac, 70n34
Macdonough Hall at the US Naval Academy. *See* US Naval Academy: Macdonough Hall
Macdonough, USN Comm. Thomas, 338; and *Allen, 272a* (*see also* Index of Ships: *Allen*); on arming and armament of ships, 239, 252, 267*b*, 269, 278, 315; and abortive US army attack

Macdonough, USN Comm. Thomas (*cont.*)
on Montreal, 273–74; and assessment of British strategy in 1814, 276,
282*a,* 245n11, 313; at Burlington, VT,
273, 291n13; on capture and treatment of smugglers, 282; and Cassin,
253*fig*3, 255*fig*4; command on Lake
Champlain, 239, 256, 287, 313*a;* commendation of, 243*b;* correspondence
with US Navy Department, 254*b;* and
crews (availability, composition, numbers needed, recruitment), 253–54,
280, 284*a,* 315; and dismantling of
ships after declaration of peace, 256,
283, 302; during Battle of Lake Champlain (engraving), 338*fig*1; flagships
Eagle, 320, 333 and *Saratoga,* 239–40,
320, 337; and Henley, 315*fig*1, 318*fig*2;
and lake patrol, 273*b;* and *Linnet,* 307,
309, 245n11; *Macdonough's Victory on
Lake Champlain* (engraving), pl.10b;
and naming of *Surprise-Eagle,* 315–17;
in *Naval Heroes of the United States*
(print), 339*fig*2; and 1-gun scows,
201n13; personal history of, 238*b;* portrait of, 239*fig*2; and refurbishing of
vessels, 273*a;* requests permission to
build more ships, 243*a,* 251, 272, 274,
289, 313–14; and shallow-draft vessels,
272, 278, 280, 287, 289; and the situation in 1812, 296; and the steamboat
hull, 251, 252, 254, 267, 269; and *Ticonderoga,* 252, 253, 256*a;* on transfer of
wounded to Isle aux Noix, 271; at Vergennes, VT, 239, 251, 276; and victory
at Plattsburgh Bay, 243, 320, 340, 351
(*see also* Battle of Plattsburgh Bay)
Macomb, USAr Brig. Gen. Alexander, 66,
243
MacPherson, USN Lt. Joseph, 127
Madison, US President James: British
objective to destroy credibility of,
240*b;* and invasion of British Canada,
272; and Jones's hesitancy to fund
the Lake Champlain squadron, 118,
243, 314*a,* 333; and Jones's premature
report of naval superiority on Lake
Champlain, 313*b*
Maguaga (Battle of), 64*b*
Malcomson, Robert, 196*b,* 197*a; Lords of
the Lake,* 120nn3 and 27; *Warships of
the Great Lakes,* 104n3
Mallet, Jack, 147*b*
Mallorytown Landing, ON, 220, 223,
235nn36, 42
Manell, Bruce, 257*a*
Manell, Carol, 257*a*
Mann, Dr. James, 282*b*

Marine Record, 64, 66; on wreck of *Gen-
eral Hunter,* 69n21
Maritime Museum of Canada (Halifax,
NS), 203
Marks, RN Purser John, 201
Martucci, Frank, 257*a*
Maumee River (OH), 74
McCallum, Duncan, 51–52, 52*fig*1 (photo)
McChesney, USN Midn. William, 317
McClellan, Stan, 60, 68n1
McDouall, RAr Lt. Col. Robert, 75
McGhie, RN Lt. James, 301
McKay, Donald, 183
McNair, Matthew, 124*a,* 125*a*
Mepkin Abbey Wreck, 68n4
Michilimackinac Island (MI). *See* Macki-
nac Island (MI)
Michilimakinac (MI). *See* Mackinac
Island (MI)
Milbert, Jacques, 154*fig*1
Millecoquins/Naubinway Sands Wreck,
68n4
Milne, RN Adm. David, 240*a*
Misery Bay, 5*fig*3, 24, 24*fig*4, 367n13. *See
also* Index of Ships: *Niagara* (USN brig-
rigged sloop of war, Upper Lakes)
Mitchell (surgeon on *Linnet*), 301
Mitchell, USN Lt. Francis, 280*b,* 282*a,*
292n46, 298n52
Monkton Iron Works, 238*a,* 249*b,* 259,
276, 286, 314*b*
Montgomerie, Hugh, 240*a*
Montreal: abortive attack on, 117; and
the Plattsburgh Bay anchor, 348, 356;
and Quebec-Montreal supply line, 109,
189; and restrictions on commercial
shipping, 72; and RN gunboat convoys, 221, 222; source of British naval
supplies, 10, 119, 238, 348; source of
shipwrights and artificers, 297; strategic importance to the British, 237, 240,
272–73
Moore, Jonathan, 150n63
Moore, Shipwright Robert, 191*b;* and design features of *St. Lawrence,* 198; and
kneeless deck construction, 362; and
schooner lines/plans, 98–99, 104*a;*
and supply transports, 87, 96
Morgan, Ian, 132, 133; 151nn70, 80; and
Scourge's sail plan, 152n96
Morrison, USAr Lt. Joseph, 317, 215–
16n40
Morrison, USN Capt, William L., 25, 48n8
Morton, Doris, 321
Mossington, Shipwright Thomas, 199*b*
Mount Hope (NY) Society of Ticonder-
oga, 295, 305, 306
Moy Hall (ON), 73*fig*2 (painting)

Muckle, (RN Gunner on *Linnet*), 301
Murray, RAr Lt. Col. John, 273*a*
Murray's Raid, 297*a*
Museum of Transport (Glasgow, Scotland), 305*b*
Myers, USN Seaman Edward (Ned):
assigned to *Scourge,* 125; and British
raiding duties, 127; and Chauncey,
127; comparisons of Ned's account
with the archeological finds, 137–38,
140–43, 144–47; eye witness account of
the sinking of *Scourge,* 129–30; leap-
ing from sinking *Scourge* (painting),
131*fig*2; and the sinking of the *Scourge,*
129–30, 138, 140, 144; sweeping (rowing) duty, 129; and troop transport
duties, 125–26, 127

Nancy Island Historic Site (ON), 71, 76,
77. *See also* Index of Ships: *Nancy*
Napoleon Bonaparte: abdication of, 279;
defeat's impact on the war with the US,
15, 117, 313; importance of the defeat
of, 240, 365
National Archives of Canada, 77
National Geographic (magazine), 132
National Geographic Society, 132
National Historic Landmark (US), 340
National Historic Site of Canada: *Hamilton* and *Scourge,* 131
National Historic Sites Service (NHSS),
220, 223. *See also* Parks Canada
Native American(s): -British alliance, 9,
10, 15*b,* 73, 74*b,* 75, 86, 356; and effect
of the war, 356, 365; Oneida Indians,
117, 222; resistance to US territorial
expansion, 3, 15*a;* and US transcontinental expansion, 2; tribute to, 87*b.
See also* Tecumseth (Native American
leader)
nautical archaeology: defined, 5–7; lessons from lake-built ships, 104, 354–
55, 357–58, 360–67; and remote survey
techniques, 131–37; and value of pub-
lic/private cooperative efforts, 364*b*
Naval Historical Center, 284*b,* 345. *See
also* Naval History and Heritage Command
Naval History & Heritage Command,
284*b,* 345
Navy Bay (ON), 191; abandoned ships/
wrecks at, 199, 201, 202, 203; archeological surveying at, 203–204; deep
draft launch depth, 188*b;* location,
188*a;* maps and paintings of, 188*fig*1
(map), 201, 202
Neilson, Rick, 216n82
Nelson, Daniel A., 131, 132, 147, 151n80;

and *Hamilton's* beakhead, 151n88; and *Hamilton-Scourge* site plan, 150n61; "Homeward Bound": on gun dimensions, 152n101; on *Scourge's* gun crew, 152n109; and *Scourge's* sail plan, 152n96

Nelson, RN Adm. Horatio, p1.1a, 21, 142

Neuschel, Fred, 70n31

New, USN Seaman James, 170b, 384

New France, 109, 221, 237

New Naval Instructions of 1806 (RN), 196b

New York (state): jurisdictional dispute over artifact ownership, 295, 344–45; Legislature, 249; steamship prize, 248

New York Bureau of Historic Sites, 172

New York Park Commission, 165

New York State Archives, 295

New York State Education Department, 293n62

New York State Museum (Albany), 344

New York State Naval Militia, 164

Newport, Rhode Island, 12, 315

NHSS. *See* National Historic Sites Service

Niagara Peninsula, 15, 195, 285; attacked by US forces, 16n19

Niagara River, 11; anchorage, 12, 15; and attacks on Fort George, 125, 127; blockade of 1814, 118b; and navigational hazards, 87, 358; and US offensives, 115, 118, 160, 162

Niles Weekly Register (Baltimore), 14, 154, 183n5, 365–66

North West Co., 72, 74

Nottawasaga River (ON), 15, 84; location of *Nancy*, 71, 75–77; US attack on, 75

O'Conor, RN Cmdr. Richard, 215n28; acting commissioner at Kingston, 189; and the Admiralty rating, 197a; and contractual shipbuilding, 190, 191; and workforce issues, 190b

oared warcraft, 219, 272, 274. *See also* row galley(s); gunboat(s)

Ontario Marine Heritage Committee (OMHC), 51, 68n1

Orders in Council (British trade restrictions), 2b

Osgood, USN Sailing Mstr. Joseph, 146, 147; commander of *Scourge,* 127; at the sinking of *Scourge,* 129–30, 140

Oswego River (NY), 111, 358b

Oswego, NY, 110, 112, 163; British raid on, 117, 194, 222; shipbuilding at, 123–24, 125, 258; shipping center, 124b, 143

Otter Creek (VT): battle map of, 281fig4; British advance on, 240, 279, 298; Cassin earthworks at, 279 (*see also* Fort Cassin); shipbuilding materials at, 238,

249; shipbuilding on, 251, 276, 278, 280, 314, 316; US squadron at, 313

Outlook (magazine) 337

Owen, RN Comm. Edward Campbell Rich: appointment of, 87; assigned to *Royal Sovereign,* 199a; comments on US shipbuilding techniques, 363; on honor, 89; observations on the lake fleet, 195–97; reports to England, 195; and the schooners, 90

Owen, RN Comm. Sir, E.W.C.R., K.C.B., 216n54

Owen, RN Capt. William Fitz William, 199a, 216n54

Pabst, Capt. Frank (diver), 344, 345

Padeni, Scott, 285fig6 (photo)

Parks Canada, 136, 220, 224; Fort Wellington National Historic Site, 235n42; Underwater Archaeology Service survey, 203. *See also* National Historic Sites Service

Parson, USN Surgeon's Mate Usher, 32

Patterson (smuggler), 219

Patuxent River (MD): gunboat flotilla locations, 293n61

Paul, RN Lt. William, 301

Paulding, USN Midn. Hiram, 254, 255; career, 269n12

Pearson, John, 271

Peasley (Boston manufacturer), 170b

Penetanguishene Harbour, ON, 91fig4 (watercolor)

Penetanguishene Public Library, 98

Penetanguishene, ON, 88fig1, 104; auction of naval ships at, 91; British shipbuilding at, 15, 76, 87; ships stationed at, 90; wrecks found at, 86, 91

Pennsylvania Historical and Museum Commission (PHMC), 27–28

Pennsylvania National Guard, 45

Penny, Burke, 68n1

Perry Centennial, 24. *See also* Perry, USN Mstr. Cmdt. Oliver Hazard

Perry, USN Mstr. Cmdt. Oliver Hazard: after-action recovery, 15a; and his Brown-built fleet, 239, 274, 329; and the effective use of armament, 17n22, 127b; and Elliott actions, 20–22, 37b, 320 (*see also* Elliot, USN Lt. Jesse Duncan); and extraction of the Black Rock merchant vessels, 14, 115; intercession on behalf Henley, 316; at the Lake Erie battle, 14b, 20–24; outfitting ships under his command, 14, 20, 32, 34; personal history, 12–13; portrait of, 12fig3; as role model, 156, 238; taking command of *Niagara,* 22b and transfer

from *Lawrence* to *Niagara* p1.1b, 23fig3 (engraving); and victory, 15b, 86; and victory Centennial celebrations, 5fig3, 27fig8 (photo)

Phelps, Benajah, 336–37, 351

Philips, Joseph (diver), 129b

Phinney, Dave (diver), 293n60

PHMC. *See* Pennsylvania Historical and Museum Commission (PHMC)

Plattsburgh Bay Anchor No. 1, 341fig5 (photo); 343fig10 (drawing)

Plattsburgh Bay Anchor No. 2, p1.12 (photo), 344–49, 346fig12 (drawing); battle scars on, 350–51; identifying marks, 345fig11 (photo). *See also* Lake Champlain Maritime Museum (LCMM): anchor project

Plattsburgh Bay. *See* Battle of Plattsburgh Bay

Plattsburgh, NY, 239, 273a, 280b; British capture of, 300; City Hall location for Plattsburgh Anchor No. 2, 344–45. *See also* Battle of Plattsburgh Bay; Plattsburgh Bay Anchor No. 2

Point Frederick (Kingston, ON), 188, 201, 202; plan of, 200fig6

Point Henry (Kingston, ON), 188, 188fig1 (map)

Polk, US President James K., 338

Porter Barton & Co., 124a

Porter, Augustus, 124a, 143a

Porter, USN Capt. David, 316, 333n16

Portsmouth (Eng.), 195, 248a, 348

Portsmouth Harbor (Eng.), 301

Poultney River, (NY), 294; artifacts recovered in, 257, 270n21; and the Brown-built galleys, 283; Fiddlers Elbow, 321; naval ships moored in, 256, 283, 302a, 320; and wreck *Allen*, 283–84, 285fig6; 290; and wreck *Eagle*, 312–13, 320–21; and wreck *Linnet*, 284, 302, 305, 309; and raising wreck *Ticonderoga*, 247, 257, 284; wrecks of, 293n62

Poyntz, RN Lt. Newdigate, 75

Prescott, ON, 124–25, 221

Preserve Our Wrecks (org.), 203

Presque Isle, PA, 11, 20, 64. *See also* Erie, PA

Preston, Richard: "The Fate of Kingston's Warships," 203–204

Prevost, British Gov. Gen. George, 191; and additional troops from the European war, 279; and attack on Sackets Harbor, 116; authorization of Pring's command, 297, 310, 310n9; and capture of US *Hamilton* and *Scourge*, 130; and court martial of Pring, 301; and defeat at Plattsburgh, 301, 311n49;

Prevost, British Gov. Gen. George (*cont.*)
instructions to, 240, 243; orders to Barclay, 14; at Plattsburgh Bay, 243, 282*a,*
298; and preparations for battle, 298–
99, 300; removed as Yeo's superior,
191; and shipbuilding projects, 188–90,
297–98

Pring, RN Capt. Daniel: after-action
report, 301, 349; and attack on Otter
Creek, 240, 298; command at Isle
aux Noix, 298, 311n30; command of
naval forces on Lake Champlain, 297;
court martial of, 301, 349; and Fisher,
311n30; and flagship *Linnet,* 298, 309;
personal history, 296–97; at Plattsburgh Bay, 300–301; and Prevost, 297–
98; and promotion, 310n9; and shipbuilding at Isle aux Noix, 239, 296–98

Proctor, RAr Maj. Gen. Henry: defeat of,
14–15, 86; and lack of troops, 13; and
siege of Fort Meigs (OH), 64, 74; and
Thames River wreck, 234n3

Provincial Marine (PM), 4: as adminis-
trator of British lake vessels, 10*a*, 187,
296; as army-managed transportation
service, 4; attack on *Royal George,* 112,
125*b;* blockade at Ogdensburg, NY, 110;
command turned over to RN, 13, 112,
188, 221; fleet, 7, 13, 52, 64, 67, 81, 109;
lack of preparedness, 110, 188, 221,
356; prospects for acquisition of merchant ships, 74; and resignation of officers, 115; retirement of Comm. Grant,
10; shipbuilding, 195–96, 357; shipyard
at Kingston, ON, 188; squadron, 11*fig*2
(painting)

Public Record Office (London), 77

Put-in-Bay, OH, 21*fig*1 (painting), 28;
naval battle, 74 (*see also* Battle of
Lake Erie); as Perry's forward base,
20

Quasi-War (US/French conflict), 315

Quebec (Quebec City), 64; and the Plattsburgh Bay Anchor No. 2, 348, 356;
Quebec-Montreal supply line, 109,
189; source of British naval supplies,
10, 117, 119, 191, 194, 238, 348; source
of shipwrights and artificers, 189, 190,
194, 216n42, 287, 297

Raynham, RN Lt., 254–55, 301

reconstruction (conjectural): archeological tools used in, 136; and mosaic mapping, 57, 136, 152n88

Record, George, 189*b;* George Record-
designed ships, 109, 212, 371t; leaving
Kingston, ON, 198

Records, USN Acting Sailing Mstr.
Daniel, 316

Reinagle, Hugh (artist), p1.10b

Revolutionary War (American Revolution): effect on Canada, 72; Battle of
Valcour Island, 341; and attempt to
conquer Canada, 2, 272*a;* use of gunboats during, 221, 272

Richardson, John, 72. *See also* Forsyth
Richardson & Co.

Richelieu River (*also known as* Sorrell), 7;
British forays out of, 274; capture of US
sloops on, 239, 272*b,* 285; navigational
hazards, 273*b,* 305, 309*b;* strategic
location on Lake Champlain, 237, 238,
272–73, 279; US defensive positions at,
273*b,* 298. *See also* Isle aux Noix

riders (angled, diagonal, transverse),
177, 177*fig*20, 186n61, 212; on *Franklin,*
185n54; on *Jefferson,* 165*fig*10, 180,
182–83, 185n51, 361–62; on *St. Lawrence,* 197*b*

Ridgely, USN Mstr. Cmdt. Charles Goodwin: and Chauncey, 183n14; command
of *Erie,* 156–57, 163*a,* 185n58; and the
discipline of Midn. Chew, 160; and
Jefferson, 158–59, 160*fig*5, 176, 177, 183,
184n18; personal history of, 156–57;
portrait of, 159*fig*4; and promotion,
163*a;* at Sackets Harbor, 162–63

Rigby, John, 52*fig*1 (photo)

rigging: cringles and bridles, 106n6; of
brig *Niagara,* 38–42; conjectural for
Tecumseth and *Newash,* 98–104; reconstructed of *Allen,* 279*fig*3; reconstructed of *Jefferson,* 182*fig*24; sail rigging, 106n7n63, 107n67; stay rigging,
106n44; "triatic stay," 106n40; tables
of dimensions of, 106n62

Rindlisbacher, Peter (artist): *Eagle* under
sail (painting), p1.10a; *General Hunter*
(paintings), p1.3b, p1.4b; *Harbour at
Niagara* (painting), p1.5b; *Lake Erie
Patrol* (painting), 11*fig*2; *Nancy* under
sail (painting), 73*fig*2; *Niagara* in
Battle of Lake Erie (painting), p1.2a;
Prelude to Battle (painting), 21*fig*1;
"skirmish," 221*fig*2 (sketch)

River Rouge (MI), 72

Robbins, USN Sailing Mstr. William M.,
289*fig*10; after-action report, 292n46;
assessment by Macdonough, 280;
command of *Allen,* 280*b,* 293n52; lake
patrol duties, 282; at Plattsburgh Bay
battle, 282; and transport of wounded,
271

Robertson, RN Lt. James, 301; after-
action report, 349

Rolette, PM Lt. Frederic, 64

ROM (Royal Ontario Museum), 131

Roosevelt, US President Theodore: *Naval
War of 1812,* 44; and importance of
Plattsburgh Bay, 243, 356

Rothenberg, Ken, 52*fig*1 (photo), 68n1

Rousseau, USN Lt. Lawrence, 162, 163

row galleys (oar warcraft/gunboats),
255*fig*4 (engraving), 273; in action at
Plattsburgh Bay, 282–83, 290; archeological study of (*see* Index of ships:
Allen); and battle of Otter Creek,
281*fig*4; of the British fleet, 272*b,* 274,
279, 291n18; Brown-built, 251*a,* 276,
278; Chesapeake Bay galleys, 284,
278, 292n31; construction of, 292n31,
293n61; defensive role of, 289; design
for (drawing), 275*fig*1; 279*fig*3; Doughty
lines/plans for, 273*a,* 274*b,* 276, 278,
283–84, 293n61, 357; important role
of, 290; on Lake Champlain (watercolor), 283*fig*5; Macdonough's need
for, 272, 274, 289, 313; offered at auction, 283*b,* 290; and sailing qualities,
278; and the US squadron, 239, 280,
283*fig*5

Royal Artillery, 74

Royal Marines: 1st Battalion, 298

Royal Military College of Canada, 202

Royal Navy (RN): buildup in Canada
after the end of war in Europe, 15,
240, 348; blockade of Sackets Harbor (1814), 117–18; comparisons of RN
and US ships, 195–96, 360–64 (*see also*
under US naval squadron); defensive
priorities on Lake Erie, 14; difficulty
manning and outfitting ships, 117;
losses at the Battle of Lake Erie, 24; at
Plattsburgh Bay, 317; raids on the Eastern seaboard, 313–14; shipbuilding
on the Lakes, 238, 348, 360*b;* tables of
anchor weights, 347*b,* 348*b*

Royal Navy Board (*also* Navy Board), 199,
305

Royal Navy *List of the Navy* (ships): of
1814, 196*b,* 199*b,* 298; of 1833, 199, 203,
204; vessels no longer listed in, 201*a*

Royal Navy shipyard (at Kingston, ON),
188; acquisition of armament and
equipment, 189; buildup of British
forces at, 115, 201, 212; deterioration
and closing, 119, 187, 199, 201, 202*a,*
223; dockyard at, 201*fig*7 (painting);
and Bell, 65; ship construction at, 6,
112, 117, 119, 154, 155, 162, 188–90,
196; ships based at, 109, 112, 118, 221;
workers, 189–90, 194; wrecks at, 362–
63; and US plan to attack, 114–15, 117.

See also York, ON: British shipbuilding at

Royal Ontario Museum (ROM), 131

Rush-Bagot Agreement of 1817 (disarmament): allowance of one vessel (*Allen*), 283; effects of, 367; limits on naval armament, 55; limits on naval vessels, 68n5, 86, 90, 104, 163, 199

Russell, J. Jr., *The History of the War:* and Macdonough's report on *Eagle,* 334n32

Rutland, VT, 295

Rybka, Walter: and lake-weather gales, 357a; and vessel stability, 360

Sackets Harbor Historic Site, 172

Sackets Harbor, NY, 113fig5 (etching), 128fig1 (painting); after-war use of, 70n55, 164; arrival of Ridgely, 156 (*see also* Ridgely, Mstr. Cmdt. Charles Goodwin); attack on, 110, 222; blockades of, 117–18a, 159, 162, 194a, 212; condition of the naval yard in 1817–18; 153, 154fig1 (print); mothballing the shipyards, 163a, 165fig8 (lithograph), 187, 363, 367 (*see also under* in ordinary); and news of peace, 119a; and preparations for war, 112, 116, 125, 273; and shipbuilding for US Navy, 114, 117b, 139, 145, 154–55, 187, 358; wrecks found at, 164–65

Sandom, RN Capt. Williams, 201: and *Netley/Niagara,* 217n91; and the wrecks at Kingston, 201–202, 204

Sandy Creek (NY). *See* Battle at Sandy Creek

Schlecht, Richard, 132; and *Scourge,* 152n99, 152n96

schooners, 358; conversion from commercial to fighting ships, 4, 7, 110, 123–25; impact on the Rush-Bagot Agreement, 104, 367; reconstructed lines of, 82fig10; sailing qualities of, 116, 125; transport duty (troops and supplies). *See by name under* Index of Ships

Soucoupe (French research submarine), 131, 151n86

Selig, Steven M.: *Draughts,* 120n21

Senecal, Carol Manell, 270n23, 321

Seppings, Surveyor of the Navy Robert, 117, 233b

Seven Years War, 221. *See also* French and Indian War

Sheaffe, Gen. Roger, 297

Shelburne Bay Yacht Club (Shelburne, VT): and Anchor No. 1, 352n17. *See also* Plattsburgh Bay Anchor No. 1

Sherman, Capt. Jahaziel, 249b, 251; and the design of *Ticonderoga,* 264, 265,

267a; and *Phoenix,* 256; sale of a hull to the US Navy, 254

Silliman, Benjamin, 4, 338; and hulks at Whitehall, 1–2, 1fig1 (watercolor)

Simons, Shipwright William: contract of, 297; and *Confiance,* 298b, 301a; and *Linnet,* 298, 303fig7, 305, 361a; and Pring, 309a

Sinclair, USN Mstr. Cmdt. Arthur: afteraction report, 84, 85n33, 147; comments on US shipbuilding techniques, 363, 363; complaints of seaworthiness of ships, 360a; and *General Pike,* 128, 148; on gunboats, 130b; and lake hazards, 357, 367n2; and *Hunter,* 67; and attempted recapture of Fort Michilimackinac, 15, 75; report on the loss of *Hamilton* and *Scourge,* 147, 148

Sinclair, RN Midn. John, 301

Skenesborough Museum (Whitehall, NY), 247, 257, 270n23

sloop of war: general description, 156fig2. *See also under* Index of Ships

Sly, Peter, 132

Smith, USN Lt. Joseph, 316, 317–18, 320, 334n25

Smith, Melbourne, 28

Smith, USN Lt. Sidney, 272b

smugglers/smuggling, 219; and *Allen,* 280; by the British, 238, 361; and use of galleys, 273, 282, 289; and *Lord Nelson,* 123, 125; navy policy for treatment of, 282a. *See also* Embargo Act of 1808

Snider, Charles Henry Jeremiah; and discovery of a hull, 76; *In the Wake of the Eighteen-Twelvers,* 8n12; and exploration of 1812 wrecks, 8n14; 202; and *Nancy,* 82; and *Netley,* 202; and *St. Lawrence,* 202

Southampton Beach (ON), 52fig1 (photo), 53fig2 (photo)

Southampton Beach Wreck, p1.4a (photo); breast hook of, 56; buttons found on (photo), 62fig10; frame sections (drawings), 61fig9, 69n9–10; keelson, 69n11; photomosaic of, 57fig6; plan view of, 58–59fig7; profile of (drawing), 60–61fig8; saddle mast step of (drawing), 55fig4; site plan, 54fig3; swivel cannon: 56fig5 (photo), 63fig11 (drawing), 69n14 (bore of). *See also* Index of Ships: *General Hunter/Hunter; Weazell*

Southampton Harbour of Refuge, 54, 68n3

Southampton Marine Heritage Society, 51, 52fig1, 68n1

Southampton, ON, 51; shipbuilding at,

348; ship wrecks, 52, 55, 64, 66–68, 69n21. *See also* Bruce County Museum and Cultural Centre; Index of Ships: *General Hunter/Hunter*

Spanish half Real (artifact), 62

Spears, Michael, 69–70n31

Spencer, USN Acting Lt. William Augustus, 316, 319

Spicer, USN Acting Midn. Peter, 144

Spratt, Mstr. Attendant Michael, 191b, 202b, 210

St. Clair River: controlled by the US, 74; rapids, 67; and the storm of 1813, 74–75; shallowness of, 10, 358

St. George, RAr Lt. Col. Thomas, 74

St. Ignace Republican (newspaper): on wrecking of *General Hunter,* 69n21

St. John (QC), 272

St. Lawrence Islands National Park (Mallorytown, ON), p1.8b, 224

St. Lawrence River, 224; and Browns Bay, 219; and the Canadian invasion plan, 272–73; and gunboats, 223, 313; and row galleys, 110, 274; and shallow-draft vessels, 188, 221, 231, 233; as strategic supply and transport route, 109, 114, 119, 189, 194, 272, 384; theater of action, 7

Stacey, Charles P., 198

Stafford, Ronald (state senator of NY), 345

Stannard, Asa, 124; and Stannard & Clark, 124a

Stansbury, USN Lt. John, 253, 255, 270n17

steam powered vessels, 199, 202; conversions to war vessels, 7, 81, 247–48, 251, 254, 259, 266–67, 269, 321, 358, 360 (*see also* Index of Ships: *Ticonderoga:* conversion); design of, 249, 251, 252, 259, 267, 269; on Lake Champlain, 248–49, 256, 314, 315, 341; 248, 249; steamboat company sale to US Navy, 251–52, 254. *See also* Index of Ships: *Fulton; Hope; North River Steamboat; Perseverance; Vermont; Wolverine. See also* Lake Champlain Steamboat Co.

Steel, David R., 98

steerage: defined, 49n16

Steffy, J. Richard, 70n44

Stellwagon, USN Sailing Mstr. Daniel, 280b; after-action report, 292n46; as commander of galley *Wilmer,* 293n52

Sterling, Michael, 52fig1 (photo), 68n1

Stevens, John R.: and *General Hunter,* 70n40; and *Nancy,* 80; and *Tecumseth,* 98; and Wreck Able, 203

Stevens, Ray, 249–95, 302

Stewart, USN Midn. David R., 162b

Stoddard, USAr Surgeon Isaac, 316
Streets Creek (ON), 87, 89, 89*fig*2 (watercolor)
Straits of Mackinac, 73
Strickland, Mstr. Shipwright Thomas, 191*b;* and design/construction features of *St. Lawrence,* 197, 198, 211–12; lines/plans of, 204; and *Prince Regent,* 192*fig*2; and *Princess Charlotte,* 193*fig*3, 215n16; and *St. Lawrence,* 195*fig*4, 198*fig*5; and survey of the fleet, 196, 199. *See also* ships by name in Index of Ships
Swanton, VT, 273*a*

Tanner, Benjamin (engraver), p1.10b
Tardy, USN Midn. Henry, 317
Taylor, USN Sailing Mstr. William: and *Lawrence* log entries, 36, 37
Tecumseth (Native American leader), 86. *See also* Native Americans
Texas A&M University: and *Allen,* 284; and *Jefferson,* 361; and *Linnet,* 302; and *Newash,* 93; and *Tecumseth,* 93; and Wreck Baker, 203; Nautical Archaeology Program, 77
Thames River, ON, 14, 234n3
Thomas Ashton (manufacturer), 76
Tingley, Daniel, 334n25. *See also* Hale, Abigail Woodruff
Tompkins, Daniel (NY governor), 251, 252
Toronto Telegram (newspaper), "Schooner Days" (column), 202*a*
Tousard, Louis de: *American Artillerist's Companion,* 147*b*
Townsend, Isaiah, 249, 256
Trafalgar, 13, 21
Trant, USN Sailing Mstr. James, 130
Treaty of Ghent, 301; consequences of, 283; delay in receiving news of, 195; peace terms, 90, 240, 243, 333, 365
Tripoli conflict, 111, 315
Tucker, Spencer: *Arming the Fleet,* 152n101
Turkey Point (Lake Ontario), 15, 87–89
Turnblatt, George, 129

University of Vermont: and *Allen,* 284
Upper Canada, 272*a;* British campaign of 1813, 74, 112; British defenses of, 115; invasion of, 64, 118, 356; region of war, 9*fig*1 (map); shortage of shipwrights and artificers in, 189, 367 (*see also* Royal Navy shipyard [at Kingston, ON]); supply lines for, 109, 221, 223
Upper Canada Rebellion (1837), 201
US Army, 45: and attack on York, 115; 125; attacked by Native Americans, 2–3; band musicians, 317; and Canadian invasion attempts, 3, 9–10, 14, 20, 118, 365; and Canadian supply convoys, 222; defeat of, 15, 19, 110, 116–18; and defense of Sackets Harbor, 117; 1st artillery Regiment artifact, 62; and goal to recapture Detroit, 24, 64; infantry button artifacts, 66, 284; on Lake Erie, 356; source for ship crews, 280, 317; success at Sandy Creek, 222; 13th Infantry Regiment artifact, 284; 33rd Infantry Regiment, 317; and troop transport *Hunter,* 65, 67, 68. *See also individual battles*
US Congress: appropriations for shipbuilding, 290n8; lake service pay for seamen, 157; declaration of war, 2, 9, 355; and Embargo Act of 1808 (*see under main entry*)
US Dolphins (diving club), 257
US Marshal, 125
US National Archives, 66*b*
US Naval Academy (Annapolis, MD), 339; and flag of *General Hunter,* 65*fig*13; Macdonough Hall, 340*fig*4
US naval squadron: broadside strength of, 216n57; comparisons of RN and US ships, 195–96 (*see also under* Royal Navy: comparisons of RN and US ships); in ordinary at Sackets Harbor, NY (sketch), 164*fig*7; at Otter Creek, 313; at Whitehall, NY, (watercolors): 1*fig*1, 340*fig*3
US Navy Department: Canadian invasion plan, 272, 274; and care for enemy combatants, 271; and gunboat duty, 280; lack of guidance and material support, 110–11; and postwar disposition of ships, 284; reports, 19, 163, 254, 316, 319, 320, 360; and requests to build ships, 314; sale of hulls, 163; and smugglers, 282 (*see also* smugglers/smuggling); reports by Sinclair, 360, 361. *See also* Jones, Secretary of the Navy William
US War Department, 273
US-Canadian border region, 3, 3*fig*2 (map)

Valcour Bay (NY), 351, 352n13
Vallette, USN Sailing Mstr. Eli A. F., 280, 282
Van Stockum, Ken, 344, 345
Van Stockum, William, 344, 345
Vergennes, VT: commercial shipbuilding at, 249, 251, 256; Henley at, 316, 320 (*see also* Henley, USN Mstr. Cmdt. Robert); ironworks, 4, 284 (*see also* Monkton Iron Works); Noah Brown at, 276, 313 (*see also* Brown, Mstr. Shipwright Noah; Brown, Adam); and the steamboat, 251 (*see also* Index of Ships: *Ticonderoga*); timber at, 4; US naval shipyard at, 238, 252, 289, 314–15
Vermont Division for Historic Preservation, 293n60, 293n62, 334n38
Vidal, RN Purser Emerich Essex (artist): and *Jones,* 161*fig*6, 185n56, 329*b*
Vikings, 225*a*
voyageurs (canoe men), 84n2

War of 1812: causes of, 2, 7n2, 355; consequences of, 364*a*–66; decay and disposal of hulks following, 4*b* (*see also* hulks: as curiosities and sources of souvenirs); and decommissioning of naval squadrons, 4; as defining moment for Canada, 367; exhibit in 2012, 70n57; history of, 2–4, 355–356; Lake Ontario region of, 109*fig*1 (map); and Native American involvement, 3, 356*a*, 365*a*; and nautical archeology, 354–55, 357*b*, 364*b*; ship-building race of, 4*a*, 356–57, 360*b*, 361, 363–64; and sources for American and British warships, 4
Ware, Charles, 182*fig*24, 329, 357
Warren, Elizabeth (diver), 293n60
Wasaga Beach (ON), 71; and *Nancy* display, 84
Washington, DC, 365
Way, Ronald, 202
Webb, Isaac, 183
Webb, John, 66
Webb, William, 183
West, Virginia, 172*fig*16 (photo); and Anchor No. 1, 352n17
Whitehall (NY) Bicentennial Committee, 247, 257
Whitehall (NY) Historical Society, 247, 270n21
Whitehall Naval Station (NY), 283, 284, 337
Whitehall Times (newspaper), 257, 294–95
Whitehall, NY, 1, 237, 283, 337; centennial celebrations, 247, 257; and commercial shipping, 256; and *Linnet,* 301–302; and the raising of *Ticonderoga,* 256, 321; refitting of ships at, 239; and ships in ordinary, 320, 338; US Navy history at, 270n20; wrecks, 4, 8n11, 294, 309, 312, 321
Whitmore, Dr. Roy, 270n26
Wilczynski Robert: and wreck of *Linnet* (photo), p1.9b

Wilkinson, USAr Gen. James, 237, 273*b*, 274

William Bell Papers, 66. *See also* Bell, Mstr. Shipwright William

Willis, USN Seaman James, 317

Willson, Lt. Cmdr. W. H., 202–203

Wilmington, NC, 320

Winne, Julius Jr., 249

Winter, USN Lt. Walter, 127

Woods Hole Oceanographic Institution, 133

Woolsey, USN Mstr. Cmdt. Melancthon T., 112: command of *Oneida,* 110, 124; command at Sackets Harbor, 163*b,* 164; ordered to enforce the US embargo, 124 (*see also* Embargo Act of 1808); and the refitting of *Lord Nelson,* 125; and risk taking, 184n27

Works Progress Administration, 27

Worsley, RN Lt. Miller, 75, 85n33

Wreck Able: descriptions of the the wreck and site, 205, 212; identified as *Kingston,* 203, 217n95 (*see also under* ships: *Kingston*); location of, 202*b,* 205

Wreck Baker: location of, 202*b;* identity, 203, 205, 217nn94, 95 (*see also under* ships: *Burlington;* survey of, 203)

Wreck Charlie, 202*b,* 203

wrecks: as curiosities and sources of souvenirs, 4b–5, 7; RN *Linnet,* 5; RN *Nancy,* 5; RN *Tecumseth,* 5; USN *Lawrence,* 5; USN *Niagara,* 5; USN *Ticonderoga,* 5; and efforts to preserve, 5–7. *See also ships by name under* Index of Ships

XY Co., 74

Yeo, RN Comm. James Lucas: attack on or blockade of Sackets Harbor, 116, 118, 127–30, 190, 194–95 (*see also* Battle of Sackets Harbor); command on Lake Ontario, 112, 115, 188, 212, 296: on losses at battle of Sandy Creek, 121n49; and news of peace, 119*a,* 195; personal history of, 112; portrait of, 113*fig*6; and Prevost, 188*b,* 189*b,* 190*a;* and *Princess Charlotte,* 215n16; and Pring, 297–98, 301; refusal to fight the US squadron, 117–19, 162, 194*a;* shipbuilding projects of, 117, 188–91, 196*b,* 221–22; on ship-type preference, 159, 197, 215nn31, 33; and *St. Lawrence,* 162, 197; on strategic importance of Lake Ontario, 13, 14

York, ON: assessment of location, 112, 114; attacks on, 16n19, 115, 125–26, 127, 143; British shipbuilding at, 112; and burning of *Sir Isaac Brock,* 188; as part of overland supply route, 75. *See also* Royal Navy shipyard (at Kingston, ON)

Index of Ships

*Abbreviations: *a* (or *b*) = left or right column; t = table; n (or nn) = note(s); *fig* = any illustration (photo, drawing, painting, etc.); pl. = color plate; RAr =Royal Army; PM = Provincial Marine; RN = Royal Navy; USAr = United States Army; USN = Untied States Navy

Abundance (RN armed transport), 348*a*

Adams (US brig, later PM *Detroit,* Upper Lakes): captured at Detroit, 10, 11; salting of frames, 81; renamed *Detroit* by the British, 10

Æolus (RN frigate), 191*a,* 348*b*

Ajax (RN third-rate), 348*b*

Alert (USN sloop of war), 280, 315

Allen (USN gunboat, Lake Champlain), 7, 271, 280, 293n52, 304; archeological study of, 258, 283, 284–85; armament, 278*b*; artifacts from, 284*a*, 285, 287, 364; clay smoking pipe, p1.9*a* (photo), 293n64; deck lights, 90*fig*3 (photo); jug, 289*fig*10 (photo); commander of: Robbins, 293n52; assigned to carry provisions and spare equipment, 278; ballast of, 285–86; ballast pigs from, 289*fig*9 (photo); compared to the brig *Eagle,* 326; construction of, 276–77; excavation of, 285*fig*6 (photo); lessons learned through examination of, 358; mast, yard, and sail plan of (conjectural), 279*fig*3; at Plattsburgh Bay, 282*b*, 284*a*; and patrol duties, 280*b*; profile views of stem and stern of (drawing), 288*fig*8; reconstructed lines of, 290*fig*11; reburied for preservation after study, 287; reconstructed profile and deck plan of, 277*fig*2; returned to service in 1817, 283*b*, 284*a*; survived into the twenty-first century, 244, 321; wreck plan of, 286–87*fig*7

Alvin Clark (schooner), 68n4

Alwyn (USN gunboat, Lake Champlain), 274, 293n52; armament loaned to *Ticonderoga,* 280*b*; commander of: Bancroft; construction of, 273*a*; sold at auction, 283*a*, 293n56

Amelia: (USN schooner, Upper Lakes), 14; as *General Wilkinson,* 70n49

Argus (USN brig), 279

Ariel (USN schooner, Upper Lakes): at the Battle of Lake Erie, 21; burning of, 15, 85, 357; Dobbins-and-Brown built, 14

Asp (USN schooner, Lake Ontario): tonnage, armament, and crew composition, 126t1

Ballard (USN gunboat, Lake Champlain); 273*a*, 274, 293n52; armament loaned to *Ticonderoga,* 280*b*; commander of: Holland, 293n52; offered at auction, 283*a*; sale price of hull, 293n56

Beagle (RN barque), 42

Beckwith (RN transport brig, later RN *Charwell,* Lake Ontario), 201

Beresford. See also *Index of Ships: Lord Beresford*

Black Snake (RN gunboat, Lake Ontario and Upper St. Lawrence River), 222

Blucher (RN gunboat, Lake Champlain), 256

Bolivar (Eckford-built corvette), 183

Borer (USN gunboat, Lake Champlain), 278, 284*a*; at the Battle of Plattsburgh Bay, 282*b*; commander of: Conover, 293n52; patrol duties on the lake, 280*b*

Boscawen (British Army sloop, Lake Champlain), 16n4, 81, 264; and saddle mast step, 68n4

Brock (RN schooner, Lake Ontario), 201. See also Index of Ships: *Sir Isaac Brock*

Broke (RN sloop, ex-USN *Growler,* later RN *Chub,* Lake Champlain), 239, 273*a*

Browns Bay Vessel (poss. RN gunboat *Radcliffe,* Lake Ontario and Upper St. Lawrence River), p1.8*b* (photo), 7, 81, 223; artifacts of, 223*b*; bow timbers, 227*fig*6 (photo); and British design features, 220, 230*b*–31, 233*b*, 304; construction features of, 119*b*, 225, 227–30, 233–34; copper-fastened, 362; on display at Fort Wellington National Historic Site, 235n42, 355*fig*1 (photo); frame sections of, 229*fig*8 (drawings); lessons learned through examination of, 358; moisture contents of hull timbers, 235n17; plan and profile of wreck, 226*fig*5; possible postwar RN navy gunboat *Radcliffe,* 231; profile of stern, 228*fig*7 (drawing); reconstructed lines of, 231*fig*9; recovery and preservation of, 223–25*a*; refitted for use as a merchant vessel, 220, 231–33

Bullfrog (RN schooner, Lake Ontario), 201

Burlington (RN frigate, ex-RN *Ship No. 2,*

ex-RN *Vittoria,* ex-RN *Princess Charlotte,* Lake Ontario), p1.8*a* (aquatint), 212; Admiralty rating, 196*b*; archeological look at, 208–10, 212–13; armament, 197*a*; commission status, 199*a*; compared to US vessels, 197; deterioration and demise, 199, 201; principal dimensions, 371–72t; profile, 210*fig*15 (drawing); renaming of, 196; and saddle mast step, 68n4; timber scantlings and wood species of, 375t; as Wreck Baker: at Deadman Bay, 203, 204–205; frame assembly, 211*fig*16 (drawing); view from stern, 209*fig*14 (drawing)

Burrows (USN galley/gunboat, Lake Champlain), 278, 284*a*; commander of: Keteltas, 293n52; patrol duties on the lake, 280*b*, 282*a*

Caledonia (RN ship of the line), 197

Caledonia (North West Company schooner, later PM brig, later USN brig, Upper Lakes): at the Battle of Lake Erie, 21; as *General Wayne,* 70n49; grounded and burned, 15; military action in the War of 1812, 75; as part of Lake Erie squadron; 14; suitability as a warship, 74; US capture of, 12

Calypso (French research vessel), 131

Canada (RN ship of the line, ex-RN *New Ship No. 2,* Lake Ontario), 119, 198; deterioration and demise, 201

Canada (RN sloop, Lake Champlain); at Otter Creek battle, 279, 298

Centaur (RN ship of the line), 194, 348*b*

Centipede (USN gunboat, Lake Champlain), 278, 284*a*; at the Battle of Plattsburgh Bay, 282*b*; commander of: Hazard, 293n52; patrol duties on the lake, 280*b*

Champlain (US steamboat, Lake Champlain), 256

Charles and Ann (US schooner, Lake Ontario), 124*b*

Charwell (RN transport brig, ex-RN *Beckwith,* Lake Ontario): gun-deck length, 218n99

Chippewa (merchant schooner, later PM, later RN, later USN, Upper Lakes), 13; burning of, 15, 87, 357

Chippewa (USN ship of the line, 1814): unfinished, 119, 164

Chub (RN sloop, ex-USN *Growler,* ex-RN *Broke,* Lake Champlain); in Battle of Lake Champlain (water color), 244*fig*5; the flag/ensign of, 338, 339; at Otter Creek battle, 279, 298; at Plattsburgh Bay, 298, 300; surrender of, 319, 338

Collector (US schooner), 152n90

Cockburn (RN schooner, Lake Ontario), 201

Confiance (RN frigate, later USN, Lake Champlain): artifacts from anchors, 343, 343*fig*10, 347; battle debris, 342*figs*6 and 8, 343*fig*9; buttons, 342*fig*7; Blomfield canon, 340*fig*4; copper roman numerals, 343*fig*9; in Battle of Lake Champlain, 244*fig*5 (water color), 255*fig*4 (engraving), 318*fig*2 (engraving); in battle at Plattsburgh Bay, 254*b*, 256, 300, 301, 317, 319, 320, 352n15; building of, 240, 243, 296*fig*3; copper-fittings in, 362; delays in, 298, 300; and depth of hold, 352n27; and poor materials for construction, 243, 245n19, 261; capture of, 300-301; carnage and casualties on, 337; deterioration and demise, 320-21, 338, 361; the flag/ensign, 338, 339; as misidentified Scotland model, 305*b;* and Plattsburgh Anchor No.2, 345-46, 347*b,* 348-50; reconstruction of (conjectural), 242*fig*4; and souvenir hunters, 8n14, 321; surrender of, 319, 336

Confiance (RN schooner, ex-USN *Julia,* Lake Ontario), 130

Confiance (RN schooner, ex-US Navy *Scorpion,* Penetanguishene), 90, 91

Congress (US steamboat, Lake Champlain), 1, 256

Conquest (USN schooner, Lake Ontario), 125*b;* tonnage, armament, and crew composition, 126t1

Constitution (USN frigate), 177; displacement of, 49n25

Cuyahoga (US packet schooner, Upper Lakes), 64

Detroit (PM brig, ex-US *Adams,* Upper Lakes): captured at Detroit, 10; run aground and burned, 12. *See also* Index of Ships: *Adams*

Detroit: (RN ship-rigged sloop of war, later USN, Upper Lakes), p1.1b (painting), p1.2a (painting), p1.2b (water-

color); armament, 21; as Barclay's flagship, 20; at the Battle of Lake Erie, 20-24, 64, 65*fig*12, 65; British loss of, 12, 65; construction, 13, 361; short on armament and stores, 13-14

Diana (US schooner): archeological study of, 137, 139, 141, 143; armament, 149n19; commercial trade history, 123-24; and control of smuggling, 123; hull design, 151n74; refitted for military use, 125, 126t1; renamed *Hamilton,* 125. *See also* Index of Ships: *Hamilton*

Dover (British troopship), 190

Duke of Gloucester (PM schooner, later USN *York,* Lake Ontario), 109

Eagle (USN brig-rigged sloop of war, ex-USN *Surprise,* Lake Champlain), 7, 48n6; anchors, 343; archeological study of, 165, 258, 284*a,* 322-23, 326; armament, 266, 315, 332*fig*12; armament weights, 335n44; ballast, 357; casualties and chaos of battle, 318-19; compared to *Niagara,* 329; construction, 313*a,* 314, 316, 323, 326-29 (*see also* Brown, Adam); deterioration and demise, 320-21; dimensions and measurements, 321, 323, 326, 329, 331; discovery of wreck, 312, 321; gunports, 327; hull design, 361, 362; on Lake Champlain: p1.10a (painting), 318*fig*2 (engraving), 244*fig*5 and 283*fig*5 (watercolor), 320*fig*3 (watercolor); launch, 243*a,* 316; lessons learned through examination of, 358; missing elements for the reconstruction, 331; naming (*Surprise-Eagle*), 316, 317*b;* officers and crew, 315, 316-17, 320; outfitting of, 314-15, 317; at Plattsburgh Bay, 254, 300, 317-19, 349; permission to build, 313-14; reconstructed deck and bulwark construction (drawing), 328*fig*10; reconstructed deck plan and profile, 332*fig*12; reconstructed lines of, 330*fig*11; reconstructed midship section (drawing), 326*fig*9; reconstruction, 322, 329; recording in situ (1982/83), 321*b*-22; stem of wreck (drawing), 325*fig*7; stern of wreck (drawing), 325*fig*8; sunken midship section (drawing), 322*fig*4; survival into the twenty-first century, 244; wreck of (photo), 323*fig*5; wreck plan and profile of, 324*fig*6

Eagle (USN sloop, later RN *Shannon,* later RN *Finch,* Lake Champlain), outfitting, 239; surrender and capture of, 272*b,* 273, 289, 297, 298

Earl of Moira (PM ship, later RN brig *Charwell,* Lake Ontario), 81-82, 109, 115; on the Lake, 127*b,* 188

Elissa (iron barque), 41, 42

Endeavour (RN barque), 42

Enterprise (USN brig), 279

Erie (USN ship-rigged sloop of war), 158*fig*3 (painting); 183n17; compared to *Jefferson,* 158; failure to run the British blockade, 156; provisions on, 185n58; under the command of Ridgely, 157

Erie (PM sloop, later RN, Upper Lakes), 13, 16n18

Experiment (US schooner, later USN *Growler,* Lake Ontario), 124*b,* 126t1, 152n90

Fair American (US schooner, later USN, Lake Ontario), 124*b;* tonnage, armament, and crew composition, 126t1

Finch (RN sloop, ex-USN *Eagle,* ex-RN *Shannon,* Lake Champlain); in Battle of Lake Champlain, 255*fig*4 (engraving); at Plattsburgh Bay, 254, 256, 300, 301; at Otter Creek battle, 279, 298

Fox (US privateer sloop, Upper St. Lawrence River), 222

Franklin (US steamboat, Lake Champlain), 364

Franklin (USN ship of the line): and use of diagonal riders, 185n54

Frolic (USN ship-rigged sloop of war), 33

Fulton (US steamboat): design features, 249*b,* 251, 267; profile, deck plan, and midship section (drawing), 250*fig*2

General Hunter/Hunter, p1.3b (painting), p1.4b (painting), 7, 65*fig*12 (painting), 304*fig*8, 10, 13, 16; armament, 69n15; artifacts, 62-64, 66, 364; building of, 65-66; British loss of, 69n21; captured by the US Navy, 64 (see *Hunter*); construction features, 81; discovery of the wreck, 51-52; documentation of loss and location, 66-67; early history of, 68n2; exhibit, 70n57; flag of, 65*fig*13 (photo); flag/ensign, 65*fig*13; hull design, 360*a;* hull's interior excavation (2004), 56-60, 62; identification process, 64, 66-67; keelson excavation (2002), 54-55; lessons learned through examination of, 358; military action in the War of 1812, 16, 64, 66, 75; private ownership, 64*b*-65; rigged as schooner for troop transport, 64*a;* salvage of 1816, 66*b*-67; test excavations (2001 and 2002), 52-53; under sail (painting), 11*fig*2; US Army *Hunter,* reposession of, 52, 64–65, 66; use of GPR information, 53. *See also* Index of Ships: *Hunter*

General Pike (USN corvette, Lake Ontario): armament, 159, 189; Eckford-built, 114, 154 (*see also* Ekford, Henry); difficulties outfitting, 127*b;* and the rig of *Jefferson,* 182*fig*24; launched, 188; and Mstr. Cmdt. Sinclair, 128, 148; in ordinary, 164*fig*7 (sketch); at Sackets Harbor battle, 116, 160; Ware's sail plan of, 115*fig*8, 329, 357

Gladiator (RN ship), 301*a*

Glenmore (RN frigate), 177

Governor Simcoe (PM schooner, later RN *Sir Sidney Smith,* later RN *Magnet,* Lake Ontario), 115, 188; chasing of, p1.6a (watercolor), 125*b,* 143

Governor Tompkins (USN schooner, Lake Ontario), 125*b,* 130; armament load, 148; and the chase of *Royal George,* 149n23; contemporary watercolor of, 143, p1.6a; tonnage, armament, and crew composition, 126t1

Grampus (USN schooner), 183, 185n56

Growler (USN schooner, later RN *Hamilton,* Lake Ontario) 116, 125*b;* capture of, 130*b;* and chase of *Governor Simcoe,* p1.6a (watercolor); ordnance load, 148; pre-war name *Experiment,* 126t1

Growler (USN sloop, later RN *Broke,* later RN *Chub,* Lake Champlain): surrender and capture of, 239, 272*b,* 289, 297

Hamilton (RN schooner, ex-USN *Growler,* Lake Ontario), 130

Hamilton (USN schooner, ex-US *Diana,* Lake Ontario), 82, 84, 116, 119*b;* anchor (photo), 141*fig*16; archaeological significance, 364; armament, 127*b,* 132, 138*fig*10 (video frame capture), 139*fig*11 (photo), 144*fig*19 (photo), 145–46; armament as *Diana,* 149n19; beakhead, 151n88; bow figurehead (photo), 142*fig*17; cabin features, 151n74; carronade, p1.6b (photo); causes of the sinking, 147*b*–48, 357; contemporary watercolor of, 143, 144; crew of, 130, 146*b*–47; and *Governor Simcoe,* p1.6a (watercolor); lessons learned through examination of, 358; Lake Ontario, 127*b;* repair and maintenance records, 137; role of weather, 357; ROV inspections of, 136, 147; sinking of, 130, 364; site location (map), 132*fig*3; site plan and profile, 134*fig*5; stability, 360*a;* sonar image of, 136*fig*7; video record

of the wreck's interior, 137; weight-to-tonnage ratio, 147 (*see also* Index of Ships: *Scourge:* weight-to-tonnage ratio); wreck designated a historic site, 131; tonnage, armament, and crew composition, 126t1; wreck survey and analysis, 131–33, 136–45*a*

Hercules (ex-*Bolivar,* corvette), 185n56

Hibernia (RN ship of the line), 197*a*

Hope (PM schooner), 65–66, 70nn40, 41

Hope (US steamboat), 249

Hunter (USN brig, ex-PM and RN *General Hunter,* Upper Lakes): boarded by British in 1816, 70n56; dimensions, armaments, and cost of, 69n30; purchase for private ownership, 69n31; repurchase by US government, 70n33. *See also* Index of Ships: *General Hunter/Hunter*

Hunter (US schooner, Lake Ontario), 124, 148n8

Icicle (RN sloop, Lake Champlain): at the Battle of Plattsburgh Bay, 298*b;* at Otter Creek, 279

Indian (RN sloop of war), 191

Jefferson (USN brig-rigged sloop of war, Lake Ontario), 7, 117, 119*b,* 158*fig*3, 164*fig*7 (sketch), 304; Baltimore Clipper design, 180; deck lights (photo), 90*fig*3; action on western Lake Ontario, 162*a;* archeological excavation and study of, 166, 170; armament, 158–59, 162*b,* 178–79, 183; armament weights, 183–84n18; artifacts found on, 170, 287; bow of, 165*fig*9 (photo), 165*fig*10 (photo), 185n51; built by Eckford, 154, 159; bulwarks and cannons (photo of reconstruction), 179*fig*22; chamfered waterways, 185n49; compared to vessels, 158 (*Erie*), 197 (*Burlington*), 323, 329 (*Eagle*); crew, 156, 157; deterioration and decay of, 153–54, 163*b*–65; dimensions of, 185n57; equipment discovered on (drawings), 171*fig*15; excavations of (drawings), 168*fig*14; gale of 1814, 162, 176, 182, 357; Greico's model of, 177*fig*20, 186n59, 186n61, 359*fig*2 (photo); hull design, 323, 361, 362; interior profile of (drawing), 160–61*fig*5; and *Jones,* 359*fig*2; launch, 155*b;* lessons learned through examination of, 358; lines/plans of, 156–57*fig*2, 358*b;* mainmast, 178*fig*21; mainmast steps (isometric view), 178*fig*21; modifications by Ridgely, 159, 177; personal posses-

sions found on, 173*fig*17 (drawings); reconstructed lines of, 181*fig*23; reconstructed rigging profile of, 182*fig*24; reconstructed section, 176*fig*19; reconstruction plans of, 172, 175–80, 182, 185n57; scale model of, 361*b;* section of (drawing), 167*fig*13; sold, 163*b;* setting sail with squadron in 1814, 160, 194; souvenirs from (photo), 166*fig*11; stability of, 360*a;* stern assembly (drawing), 174*fig*18; timbers of (photos), 167*fig*12, 172*fig*16; in Vidal's watercolor of Sackets Harbor, 185n56

Jones (USN brig-rigged sloop of war, Lake Ontario), 117, 161*fig*6 (tracing), 164*fig*7 (sketch), 166; action on western Lake Ontario, 160, 162*a;* built by Eckford, 159; compared to RN *Burlington,* 197; contemporary depiction (watercolor), 180, 185n56; dimensions of, 185n57; in the gale of Sept. 1814, 162; and *Jefferson,* 181*fig*23; launch, 155*b;* outfitting of, 159; and *Peacock,* 156*fig*2; stability, 360*a;* storm sailing performance of, 184n27; unaccounted for, 163*b*

Julia (USN schooner, later RN *Confiance,* Lake Ontario), 116, 125*b,* 144; armament, 147, 149n37, 152n101; capture of, 130*b;* and chase of *Governor Simcoe,* p1.6a (watercolor), 143; crew of, 147; renamed *Confiance,* 130; and survivors of the *Hamilton* and *Scourage,* 130; tonnage, armament, and crew composition, 126t1

Kingston (RN frigate, ex-RN *Ship No. 1,* ex-RN *Prince Regent,* Lake Ontario), 7, 212; Admiralty rating, 196*b*–97; archeological look at, 205–208, 212–13; in attack on Fort Oswego (print), p1.7b; commission status, 199*a;* compared to USN *Superior,* 196*b;* deterioration and demise of, 199, 201; identified as Wreck Able, 202*b*–203, 205, 217n95; plan of, 192*fig*2; principal dimensions of, 371–72; sailing qualities of (as *Prince Regent*), 373–74; scantlings and wood species of, 375; stern of, 206*fig*11 (photo). As Wreck Able: mainmast step and bolsters of, 6*fig*4 (photo), 208*fig*13 (photo); midship frame of, 207*fig*12 (drawing); perspective view of, 205*fig*10 (drawing)

Lady of the Lake (USN schooner, Lake Ontario), 114, 163, 164*fig*7 (sketch), 187; built by Ekford, 154 (*see also* Ekford, Mstr. Shipwright Henry); as post-war

Lady of the Lake (*cont.*)
merchant vessel, 163*b;* spying activities of, 114; tonnage, armament, and crew composition, 126t1

Lady Prevost: (PM schooner, later RN, later USN, Upper Lakes), 10, 11*fig*2 (painting), 13, 65; troop transport duty, 74

Lawrence (USN brig-rigged sloop of war, Upper Lakes); in Battle of Lake Erie, p1.1*b* (painting), p1.2*b* (watercolor), 20–22, 24, 36; Brown-built, 14, 20, 329; casualties and chaos of battle, 44*b;* contemporary depiction of, 329*b;* knee-less construction, 329, 361*b;* log of, 36, 37; military action in the War of 1812, 75; and *Niagara,* 12*fig*3; and rigging, 39; sick list, 48n4; and spare masts, 49n15; timber usage, 361*a*

Leander (RN frigate), 196*b*

Linnet (RN brig, later USN, Lake Champlain), p1.9*b* (photo), 7, 239, 289, 351; archeological study of, 258, 284*b,* 302–10; armament, 245n11, 298, 301, 309*b;* artifacts found on, 295, 307–308, 308*fig*10 (drawings); button, 309; split mortar found on (history of), 310n5; battered hull of (photo), 296*fig*2; in Battle of Lake Champlain: 244*fig*5 and 300*fig*5 (watercolor), 318*fig*2 (engraving); capture of, 300–301; compared to the brig *Eagle,* 306, 326; construction of, 81, 296*fig*3, 297–98; deterioration and demise of, 295, 302, 320–21, 338; dimensions of, 298, 302*b*–304, 305, 309*a;* and 1815 Admiralty draft, 305, 306, 309*b;* flag/ensign, 338, 339; history of, 295–96; hull design, 361*a;* hull plan and profile, 303*fig*7; labor-intensive assembly techniques, 362; lessons learned through examination of, 358; mainmast step of (drawing), 304*fig*8; model of, 305*b;* naming of, 298; at Otter Creek, 279; plan of brig similar to, 299*fig*4; and Plattsburgh Anchor No.2, 347*b,* 349, 350; at Plattsburgh Bay, 254*b,* 298*b,* 300, 301, 317, 319; postwar at Whitehall, 320, 340*fig*3 (watercolor); reconstruction (conjectural), 305–307, 306*fig*9, 309*b;* recording the wreck (1981–82), 302, 304 (1994–95), 302–304; salvage of, 257*a,* 270n21, 295, 302, 303, 305, 307, 309*b,* 321; salvage of lower hull (photo), 302*fig*6; salvage of stern (photo), 295*fig*1; surrender of, 319, 336, 338; survival into the twenty-first century, 244

Little Belt (PM sloop, later RN, later USN, Upper Lakes), 13; burning of, 15, 85, 357

Lord Beresford (RN schooner, ex-PM *Prince Regent,* later RN *Netley,* Lake Ontario), 115, 128

Lord Melville (RN brig, later RN *Star,* Lake Ontario), 115, 127*b*–28; outfitting of, 189; unfinished, 188

Lord Nelson (Canadian schooner, later USN *Scourge,* Lake Ontario), p1.5a, 194; capture and refitting for military use, 124*b*–125; commercial trade history, 123–24, 141, 142–43; supplies purchased for, 138, 142. *See also* Index of Ships: *Scourge*

Ludlow (USN gunboat, ex-USN *No. 169,* Lake Champlain), 243; commander of: Freeman, 293n52; offered at auction, 283*a;* patrol duties on the lake, 280*b;* sale price of hull, 293n56

Madison (USN corvette, Lake Ontario), 164*fig*7 (sketch), 166; armament, 159; built by Eckford, 154 (*see also* Eckford, Mstr. Shipwright Henry); launch, 112, 125*b;* on Lake Ontario, 127*b;* as postwar merchant vessel, 163*b;* with squadron at Sackets Harbor, 160

Magnet (RN schooner, ex-PM *Governor Simcoe,* ex-RN *Sir Sidney Smith,* Lake Ontario), 118*a;* destruction of, 162

Michigan (USN steamship, later Pennsylvania Naval Militia sidewheeler *Wolverine*), 27

Mink (US schooner, Upper Lakes), 89

Mohawk (USN frigate, Lake Ontario)), 117, 118, 164*fig*7 (sketch); compared to *Burlington,* 197; launch, 159; with squadron in 1814, 160; unaccounted for, 163*b*

Montgomery (USN sloop, Lake Champlain), 317

Montreal (RN ship-rigged sloop of war, ex-RN *Wolfe,* Lake Ontario), p1.8a (aquatint); as candidate for Guenter's Wreck, 217–18n98; as candidate for wreck at Deadman Bay, 203, 205; deterioration and demise, 199, 201; gun deck length, 218n99; in painting of Kingston dockyard, 201*fig*7

Murray (RN gunboat, Lake Champlain), 256

Nancy: (Northwest Company schooner, later PM, later RN, Upper Lakes), 10, 15, 304*fig*8; archaeological measurements of, 77–81; armament, 75; arti-

facts found on, 76, 364; Capt. Mackintosh's logs, 85n39; captured by British, 87; construction features and analysis, 77–84, 264; deck plan, 83*fig*11; defeat and destruction of, 16, 71, 75, 85n33, 364; excavation of (photo), 76*fig*3; hull design, 360*b;* hull display (photo), 72*fig*1; hull plan, 78*fig*6, 79*fig*7; hull preservation (*see* Nancy Island Historic Site); lessons learned through examination of, 84, 358; lines of, 82*fig*10; as oldest documented vessel, 84; and peacetime voyages, 71–73; plan of salvaged molded frames and midship section, 79*fig*8; as prewar commercial vessel, 7; and reconstructed *Nancy* plans, 82–84; saddle mast step (drawing), 68n4, 80*fig*9; salvage and display of, 16, 77*fig*5; under sail (painting), 73*fig*2; wartime history of, 74–75

Nelson (RN ship of the line), 197*a*

Neptune (US privateer sloop, Upper St. Lawrence River), 222

Netley (RN schooner, ex-RN *Prince Regent,* ex-RN *Lord Beresford,* Lake Ontario); deterioration and demise, 199, 201; as misidentified wreck, 202*b*

Nettle (USN gunboat, Lake Champlain), 278, 284*a;* commander of: Breese, 293n52; patrol duties on the lake, 280*b*

New Orleans (USN ship of the line, Lake Ontario), 119*a,* 164, 163*fig*7 (sketch), 165*fig*8 (lithograph), 368*fig*4 (lithograph) 367

New Ship No. 1 (RN ship of the line, later RN *Wolfe,* Lake Ontario), 195

New Ship No. 2 (RN ship of the line, later RN *Canada,* Lake Ontario), 195

Newash (RN schooner, Upper Lakes), 7, 304; abandonment of, 90; archeological study of, 93–94, 96, 98; carlings, 151n75; completion of, 15, 87; construction features, 81, 87, 89, 98; decommissioned, 9, 91*fig*40; hull of (watercolor), 91*fig*4; kneeless construction, 362; labor-intensive assembly techniques, 362; launch (water color), 89*fig*2; lessons learned through examination of, 358; lines of, 88*fig*1, 357; postwar deterioration and demise, 16; re-rigged for winter 1815–16, 90; rig reconstruction, 98–102; sail plan (hypothetical), 103*fig*13, 103–104; wreck plan, 95*fig*9

Newcastle (RN frigate), 196*b*

Niagara (USN brig-rigged sloop of war, Upper Lakes), 49n23; construction by Noah Brown, 13, 19–20; during Battle

of Lake Erie, p1.1b (painting), p1.2a
(painting), p1.2b (watercolor), 14, 16,
20–23; and the Battle of the Thames,
24; compared to *Eagle,* 329; construction features, 81, 329; construction
materials for, 48n10; contemporary
British comments about US shipbuilding techniques, 363; and dagger
knee and knee-less construction, 361,
367n13; deterioration and demise, 199,
201; displacement of, 49n25; fasteners
used for, 48n9; hull design, 361; identification of, 48n6; lapstrake boats of,
49n22; lessons learned through examination of, 358; and Perry's shifting of
command (painting), 12*fig*3; rebuildings of, 7; reconstructions of, 26*fig*6;
restoration for the Perry Centennial
(1912–13), 5*fig*3 (photo), 16, 24–28;
restoration for the 150th celebration
(1920–1962), 27; restoration for the
175th celebration (1986–88), 27–28; salvaged hull photos, 24*fig*4, 25*fig*5, 27*fig*7
Niagara, (1988 rebuild of USN brig, Upper
Lakes): appearance (present-day),
p1.3a (photo), 7, 29–31, 27*fig*8 (photo),
30*fig*10 (photo), 39*fig*16 (photo); armament, 30, 43–44; authenticity of, 34*a;*
in battle reenactment, 31*fig*11 (photo);
capstan, 35*fig*13 (photo); certifica-
tion (present-day), 33; crew duties and
quarters, 31, 32–34, 41; as "Flagship
of the Commonwealth" (1990), 28;
ground tackle, 34–35; launch, 29*fig*9
(photo); performance under sail, 42,
47; responsibility of the PHMC, 27; rigging and sails, 39–42, 41*fig*17 (photo);
sailing conditions, 334n43; sailing program, 48–49n12; ship's boats, 35–37,
36*fig*14 (photo), 49n22; stability, 38*b*–
39, 360; and the sweeps (oars), 37–38,
38*fig*15 (photo)
Niagara (RN ship, ex-PM and RN *Royal
George,* Lake Ontario), 199, 201
No. 169 (USN gunboat, later USN *Ludlow,*
Lake Champlain), 273*a;* contract for
and launching of, 291n10
No. 170 (USN gunboat, later USN *Wilmer,*
Lake Champlain), 273*a;* contract for
and launching of, 291n10
Nonsuch (USN schooner), 316
North River Steamboat (US steamboat),
248; design features, 249*b,* 267*a;* hull
construction of, 269n4

Ohio (USN schooner, later RN *Sauk,*
Upper Lakes), 14, 185n56; captured
by British, 15, 87

"Old British Gunboat," 234n3
Oneida (USN brig, Lake Ontario), 109–
110, 111*fig*3 (drawing), 164*fig*7 (sketch);
in action on western Lake Ontario,
127*b,* 162*a;* attacked by British, 110*b;*
attacks on British ships, 112, 124*b;*
building of, 114, 124*a;* construction
plans for, 357; hull form, 358*b;* as postwar merchant vessel, 163*b;* and transport of troops to York, 125–26; with
squadron at Sackets Harbor, 160
Ontario (US schooner, later USN, Lake
Ontario), 124; tonnage, armament,
and crew composition, 126t1

Paz (RN schooner), 297
Peacock (USN ship-rigged sloop of war)
33; class, 179; compared to *Eagle,* 329,
331*b;* contract for, 369n14; in contrast
to the Ekford-built brigs, 155, 180;
through-bulwark breechings, 185n55
Perseverance (US steamboat), 249
Pert (USN schooner, Lake Ontario), 125*b;*
and chase of *Royal George,* 149n23; ordnance load, 148; tonnage, armament,
and crew composition, 126t1
Phoenix I (US steamboat, Lake Champlain), burning of, 256*b;* study of
wreck, 257; comparison to *Ticonderoga,* 258, 270n19
Phoenix II (US steamboat, Lake Champlain), 256*b*
Porcupine: (USN schooner, Upper Lakes),
14
Preble (USN sloop, Lake Champlain),
p1.10a (engraving), 255*fig*4 (engraving); at Plattsburgh Bay, 254, 255, 300,
301, 317
President (USN sloop, Lake Champlain),
239
Prince de Neufchatel (US privateer
schooner), 49n23
Prince Regent (PM schooner, later RN
Lord Beresford, later RN *Netley,* Lake
Ontario), 109, 115, 188
Prince Regent (RN frigate, ex-RN *Ship
No. 1,* later RN *Kingston,* Lake Ontario),
7, 212; Admiralty rating, 196*b*–97;
archeological look at, 205–208, 212–13;
armament, 65, 117; in attack on Fort
Oswego (print), p1.7*b;* blockading
Sackets Harbor, 159; change of name,
196; commission status, 199*a;* com-
pared to US *Superior,* 196*b;* construc-
tion of, 190–91, 194, 212; designed by
Patrick Fleming, 189; deterioration
and demise of, 199, 201; identified as
Wreck Able, 202*b*–203, 205, 217n95;

and frame assembly, 119, 362; plan of,
192*fig*2, 358; principal dimensions of,
371–72; sailing qualities of (as *Prince
Regent*), 373–74; scantlings and wood
species of, 361, 375; stern of, 206*fig*11
(photo). As Wreck Able: mainmast step
and bolsters of, 6*fig*4 (photo), 208*fig*13
(photo); midship frame of, 207*fig*12
(drawing); perspective view of, 205*fig*10
(drawing); size of, 119, 187, 358; as
Yeo's flagship, 191*b.* See also Index of
Ships: *Kingston*
Princess Charlotte (RN frigate, ex-RN *Ship
No. 2,* ex-RN *Vittoria,* later RN *Burlington,* Lake Ontario), 7, 194; armament,
194*a;* in attack on Fort Oswego, p1.7*b*
(print); blockading Sackets Harbor,
159; construction of, 117, 189*b*–91; construction features of, 119*b;* designed by
Bell, 65; hull design, 361, 362; launch,
191*b;* lessons learned through examination of, 358; lines/plans, 193*fig*3,
215n16, 358*b;* renamed *Burlington,*
196*b;* repairs needed in 1815, 196
Psyche (RN frigate, Lake Ontario), 119,
195; as candidate for Wreck Baker,
217n95; deterioration and demise,
199, 201

Queen Charlotte (PM ship, later RN, later
USN, Upper Lakes), 10, 11*fig*2 (painting), 13, 32; in Battle of Lake Erie,
p1.1b (painting), p1.2a (painting),
p1.2b (watercolor), 20, 22–23, 24, 64;
British loss of, 65; selection of hull
timbers, 361*a*

Radcliffe (RN gunboat, Lake Ontario and
Upper St. Lawrence River), 223, 231;
possible identity of Browns Bay Vessel,
235n36. *See also* Browns Bay Vessel
Raven (USN schooner): tonnage, armament, and crew composition, 126t1
Rideau (Canadian side-wheeler steamboat, Lake Ontario), 199*b*
Royal George, (PM ship, later RN *Niagara,*
Lake Ontario) 109, 115, 116; chased
by US squadron, 112, 125*b;* construction plans of, 357; deserters from, 114;
drawing of, 110*fig*2; hull form, 358*b;* on
Lake Ontario, 127*b,* 188
Russell (RN ship of the line), 296

Saratoga (USN corvette, Lake Champlain), 280*b,* 302, 313, 314; armament,
240; in Battle of Lake Champlain:
244*fig*5 (watercolor), 318*fig*2 (engraving); construction of, 239–40, 329;

Saratoga (cont.)
deterioration and demise, 320–21; flat of sheer, 331; officers and crew, 317; plans of, 241*fig*3, 357; at Plattsburgh Bay, 254, 282*b,* 300, 317, 319, 349; and witness report of carnage, 337

Sauk (RN schooner, ex-USN *Ohio,* Upper Lakes). See *Ohio*

Scorpion (USN schooner, later RN *Surprise,* Upper Lakes), 14; at the Battle of Lake Erie, 21; captured by British, 15, 75, 91

Scourge (USN schooner, ex-Canadian *Lord Nelson,* Lake Ontario), 82, 84, 116, 119*b;* archaeological value, 364; armament, 127b, 132, 139*fig*12 (photo), 145–46, 147, 149n21; attack at York, 126–27*a;* in battle, 128; bottom of Lake Ontario (painting), 133*fig*4; bow figurehead (photo), 142*fig*18; cabin features, 151n74; cabin window (photo), 141*fig*14; capture of Fort George, 127; construction accounts for, 137; crew of, 130, 146*b*–47; on Lake Ontario, 127b; lessons learned through examination of, 358; long gun from, p1.7a (photo), 139*fig*12 (photo); military transport, 7; prewar commercial vessel, 82*fig*10; pump tubes (photo), 141*fig*15; refitting of, 125; role of weather in the sinking, 357; ROV inspections of, 136, 147; sinking of, 130, 364; site location (map), 132*fig*3; site plan and profile, 134*fig*5; small boat (photo), 140*fig*13; small-boat oar, 151n80; sonar images of, 137*figs*8, 9; stability, 360a; tonnage, armament, and crew composition, 126t1; weight-to-tonnage ratio, 147 (see also *Hamilton:* weight-to-tonnage ratio); stern windows, 14*fig*14 (photo), 151n82; wreck designated a historic site, 131; wreck deterioration, 136; wreck survey and analysis, 131–33, 136–45*a*

Shannon (RN sloop, ex-USN *Eagle,* later RN *Finch,* Lake Champlain), 239, 273*a*

Ship No. 1 (RN frigate, later RN *Prince Regent,* later RN *Kingston,* Lake Ontario), 189*b*–90

Ship No. 2 (RN frigate, later RN *Vittoria,* later RN *Princess Charlotte,* later RN *Burlington,* Lake Ontario), 189*b*–90

Ship No. 3 (RN ship of the line, later RN *St. Lawrence,* Lake Ontario), 191; building of, 194

Simcoe. See ships *Governor Simcoe; Sir Sidney Smith; Magnet*

Sir Isaac Brock (RN sloop of war, Lake Ontario), 188. See also Index of Ships: *Brock*

Sir Sidney Smith (RN schooner, ex-PM *Governor Simcoe,* later RN *Magnet,* Lake Ontario), 115, 128

Somers (USN schooner, later RN *Huron,* Upper Lakes), 14; captured by British, 15, 85

Southampton (RN frigate), 112

Spencer (RN ship of the line), 348

Spitfire (RN gunboat, Lake Ontario and Upper St. Lawrence River), 222

Spitfire (USN schooner), 256*a*

St. Lawrence (RN ship of the line, Lake Ontario), 7, p1.8a (aquatint), 119*b;* Admiralty rating, 196*b;* archeological look at, 210–13; armament, 194*b,* 195, 196*b,* 197*b;* built at Kingston, ON, 117, 162, 212; commission status, 199*a;* compared to first rates *Ville de Paris* and *Hibernia,* 197*a;* construction features, 197–99; deterioration and demise, 199, 201, 202; frame assembly of (drawing), 213*fig*18; hull design, 361*a,* 362; launch, p1.1a (watercolor), 194*b;* lessons learned through examination of, 358; lines/plans, 195*fig*4, 358*b;* outfitting, 162*b,* 195; perspective view of wreck (drawing), 212*fig*17; photo of wreck, 214*fig*19; principal dimensions, 371–72; repairs needed in 1815, 196; scantlings and wood species of, 375; section of (drawing), 198*fig*5; superintended by Bell, 65

Star (RN brig, ex-RN *Lord Melville,* Lake Ontario), 199, 201

Superior (USN frigate, Lake Ontario), 117, 164*fig*7 (sketch), 194*b;* compared to RN *Kingston,* 196*b*–97; flagship of squadron in 1814, 160; launch, 159; and officers' peace grand ball, 119; unaccounted for, 163*b*

Surprise (RN schooner, ex-USN *Scorpion,* Upper Lakes), 90, 91

Surprise (US privateer schooner), 163, 170

Surprise (USN brig-rigged sloop of war, later USN *Eagle,* Lake Champlain), 316–17. See *Eagle* (USN brig-rigged sloop of war, Lake Champlain)

Sylph (USN schooner, later brig, Lake Ontario), 114, 160, 166; in action on western Lake Ontario, 162*a;* building time required, 183n5; built by Eckford, 154 (see also Eckford, Mstr. Shipwright Henry); deterioration and decay, 163*b;* as post-war merchant vessel, 163*b*

Tecumseth: (RN schooner, Upper Lakes), 7, 304; abandonment of, 90; archeological study of, 93–94, 96, 98; artifacts of, 90, 287; deck lights (photo) 90*fig*3; carlings, 151n75; completion of, 15; construction features, 81, 87, 89, 98; damaged bow of (photo), 92*fig*5; decommissioned, 90, 91fig4 (watercolor); dismasted by gale, 357; kedging, 89; kneeless construction, 362; labor-intensive assembly techniques, 362; launch (watercolor), 89*fig*2; lessons learned through examination of, 358; lines of, 88*fig*1, 357; postwar lay up and decay, 16, 90; re-rigged in winter 1815–16, 90, 99*a;* reconstructed mast, spar, and rigging plan, 97*fig*12; reconstructed midship section, 97*fig*11; reconstructed rig, 98–104; reconstructed sail plan, 103*fig*13, 103–104; salvage of, 91, 93; salvaged bow assembly (photo), 96*fig*10; salvaged hull (photo), 92*fig*5; wreck plan, 93*fig*7

Thunder (RN gunboat, Lake Ontario and Upper St. Lawrence River), 222

Ticonderoga (20th-century steamboat), 341

Ticonderoga (USN schooner, Lake Champlain), 81, 177, 302, 304, 313; addition of outer stem, 263; archaeological study of, 257*b;* armament weights, 269n9; armament, 252–53, 267*b,* 269n9, 280*b;* artifacts, 247, 257; Battle of Lake Champlain: 244*fig*5 (watercolor), 255*fig*4 (engraving); compared to *Eagle,* 326, 329, 331*b;* construction features, 239, 259, 262–66 (see also General Index: Lacy, Shipwright John); converted steamboat, 7, 252, 262, 266*b*–67, 327, 360 (see also Brown, Mstr. Shipwright Noah); crew, 253; design by Elihu Bunker, 267; deterioration and demise, 256*b,* 320–21; hull of (photos), 248*fig*1, 259*fig*6; hull plan and profile of, 260–61*fig*7; hull's stern section (photo), 258*fig*5; hull's waterway and shot garland (drawing), 266*fig*10; improvements in strength and stability, 254; keel, 259; lessons learned through examination of, 358; lines of (reconstructed), 268*fig*11; modifications by Noah Brown, 267, 269; Plattsburgh Bay, 254–56, 282*b,* 290, 300, 301, 317; rigging and weight, 267*b;* rudder-related hardware, 264, 329; salvage of (1958), 247, 256*b*–57, 266*b,* 270n23, 284*b,* 321*b;* stability and strength of, 267*b;* stem assembly (drawing), 262*fig*8; stern assembly (drawing), 263*fig*9; survival into the twenty-first century, 244

Tigress US (USN schooner, later RN *Confiance,* Upper Lakes), 14; captured by British, 15, 75

Trippe (USN sloop, Upper Lakes), 14; burning of, 15, 357

Troy (Lake Champlain canal schooner), pivoting centerboard keel, 235n38

United States (Eckford-built corvette), 183

United States (USN frigate), 177

Vengence, (British privateer, 1789), 72

Vermont (US steamboat, Lake Champlain), 249, 267*a;* hull construction, 269n4; timbers of, 270n30

Victory (RN ship of the line), 40

Ville de Paris (RN ship of the line), 197*a*

Viper (USN gunboat, Lake Champlain), 278, 284*a;* commander of: Mitchell, 293n52; patrol duties on the lake, 280*b*

Warspite (RN ship of the line), 348*b*

Wasp (USN ship-rigged sloop of war), 33

Weazell (British schooner, Upper Lakes), 55–56, 64

Wilmer (USN gunboat, ex-USN *No. 170,* Lake Champlain), 244; at the Battle of Plattsburgh Bay, 282*b;* commander of: Stellwagen, 293n52; offered at auction, 283*a;* patrol duties, 280*b;* sale price of hull, 293n56

Wolfe (RN ship-rigged sloop of war, later RN *Montreal,* Lake Ontario), 188–89; battle at Sackets Harbor, 112, 115, 116; candidate for Guenter's Wreck, 217n98; and Captain Pring, 297; deterioration and demise, 199, 201; on Lake Ontario, 127*b;* log entry from, 131

Wolfe (RN ship of the line, ex-RN *New Ship No. 1,* Lake Ontario), p1.8a (aquatint); construction of, 195, 198, 201; left unfinished on the stocks, 119

Wolverine (USN sidewheel steamer), 27. *See also* Index of Ships: *Michigan*